A History of Art History

A History of Art History

Christopher S. Wood

A History
of Art
History

Princeton University Press
Princeton and Oxford

Copyright © 2019 by Princeton University Press

Requests for permission to reproduce material from this work
should be sent to Permissions, Princeton University Press

Published by Princeton University Press,
41 William Street, Princeton, New Jersey 08540
In the United Kingdom: Princeton University Press,
6 Oxford Street, Woodstock, Oxfordshire OX20 1TR

press.princeton.edu

Cover: Spinello Aretino (?), *Scenes of the Martyrdom of St. Potitus* (?)
(c. 1400) (detail). Pen drawing, 27.2 × 19.2 cm. Paris, École des Beaux-Arts.
Beaux-Arts de Paris—Dist. RMN-Grand Palais / Art Resource, NY

First paperback printing, 2021
Paperback ISBN: 978-0-691-20476-5
Cloth ISBN: 978-0-691-15652-1

LCCN: 2018957591

British Library Cataloging-in-Publication Data is available

The author is grateful to his former and present editors at
Princeton University Press, Alison MacKeen and Michelle Komie,
as well as to the designer, Julie Fry.

This book has been composed in Albertina

Printed in the United States of America

CONTENTS

A History of Art History

The abbey church of Doberan, in Mecklenburg in the far north of Germany, not far from the Baltic sea, is one of the best preserved of all Cistercian churches, a brick pile in the Gothic style, still furnished with its original fourteenth-century altars, tombs, choir stalls, chalice-cabinet, and astronomical clock. The Crucifixion Altar is a retable, an altarpiece adorned with narrative images carved in relief and coated with gold leaf and bright paint and crowned by a carved wooden Crucifix. The retable divides the choir from the nave; there are images on both sides. Readily enough you identify a scene among the stacked panels on the side of the altar facing west, towards the nave and the lay worshippers: Christ with his sleeping disciples at Gethsemane on the Mount of Olives. Christ is kneeling; he directs his prayers to a chalice on the mountain. But the scene next to it is a puzzle. Here, too, there is a praying figure on a mountain accompanied by three smaller figures. You cannot identify the subject.

If an art historian were standing at your side, you would soon learn that the panel on the right depicts an episode from the Old Testament, the ascent of Mount Carmel by the messianic prophet Elijah (1 Kings 18:42). Elijah was seeking guidance from the Lord, a sign of support in his contest with King Ahab and the false god Baal. A treatise composed probably by an English Cistercian around 1200, the *Pictor in carmine*—a text doubtless known to the monks at Doberan—had identified this episode as a type or prefiguration of Christ's colloquy with God on the Mount of Olives. The art historian would explain that such typological pairings, the infrastructure of salvational history, a symmetry evincing the preexistence of history in God's plan, were transferred from manuals such as the *Pictor in carmine* into illustrated manuscripts, stained-glass windows, mural paintings, and altarpieces like the Crucifixion Altar at Doberan. The altar is composed of such pairings, interrupting but explicating the pictorial narratives of the lives of Christ and Mary. The typological schema legitimated the work's sensuous allure, traditionally held in suspicion by Cistercian clerics. The altar was created around 1368 by artists from Hamburg, perhaps from the workshop of Master Bertram. It is one of the earliest scenic altarpieces in Germany. The scenes are hemmed in above by intricate baldachin-like carvings and below by perforated grill-like panels. These micro-architectural frames reminded the beholders of the time that the proper function of an altar was to store relics—in the cavities concealed by the grills, for example—and that the proper and traditional occupants of the spaces above were not scenic compositions but statues of saints, housed in niches whose remnants are the flat wooden baldachins.

This is often all that is asked of an art historian: knowledge about the art of the past. The art historian is summoned to decode the symbolic messages and account for forms, formats, and functions peculiar to the world that produced the work. The art historian clears it all away, clears away all the unfamiliar conventions, and gives you an unobstructed view.

An unobstructed view onto what? That is just the question. Some might say a view onto Christian doctrine. Others might say a view onto the mentalities and forms of life of clerics and churchgoers in northern Germany in the fourteenth century, in the realm of the Hanseatic League, the trading confederation, or onto the tension between the lay patrons' desire for extravagant liturgical furniture and the religious order's ideal of simplicity, or onto the roles of buildings and altarpieces and ceremonies in creating new publics. Yet another will look to scholarship to track the real experiences of historical worshippers, their movements in sacred space, or to track the movements across land and sea of supplies of pigment and gold, or itinerant artisans. I will tell you, however, that the art historian is the one who makes you see the carved relief again as a work of art.

The artist wedged the necessary figures into the narrow spaces. Christ's form is straight and tall, undaunted. The heads of his sleepy disciples bob in comic rhythm. Unable to draw on ready-made formulas for the Old Testament scene, the artist devised a visual rhyme with

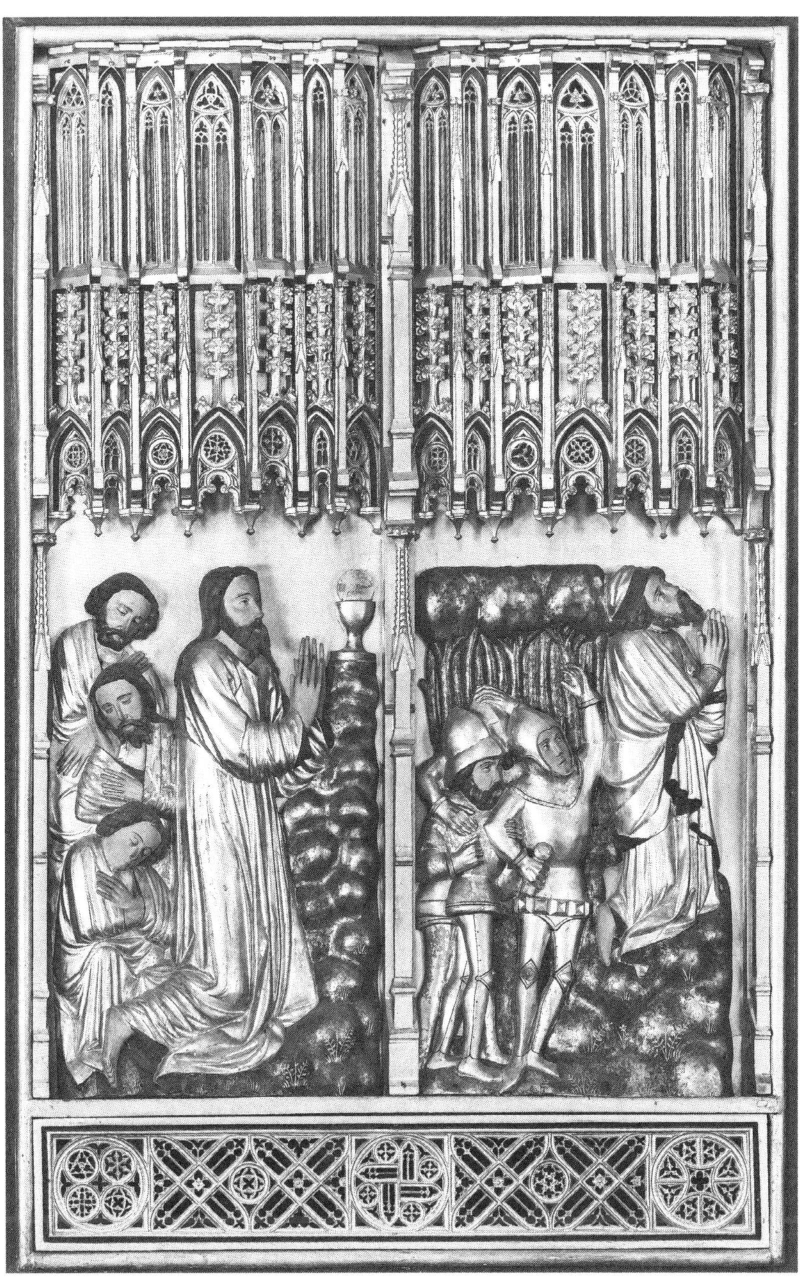

Christ in the Garden of Gethsemane and *Elijah on Mount Carmel,* from the Crucifixion or Cross Altar in the abbey church of Doberan, Mecklenburg (c. 1368). Polychromed wood sculpture. The micro-architecture frames a pair of Biblical scenes: an event from the life of Christ on the left, and its "type" or foreshadowing event from the Old Testament on the right.

the New Testament scene. He gives us three soldiers or servants, a number not specified in the text. Elijah, head cocked back, peers out for a sign. Whereas Christ's all-too-human disciples retreated into sleep, the familiars of the prophet sense the nearness of chaos. The gesticulating servants cling to one another in dread and confusion. Elijah and Christ on their diminutive precipices—sculptural shorthand for mountains—glimpse territories beyond knowledge. The artwork itself is such a precipice, perhaps. The Cistercians hired an artist because an artist can recreate with forms the dread, the aspiration to metaphysics, the narcosis of prophecy, the conviction of an underlying pattern. They ran a risk because an artwork will overrun any liturgical or didactic function it is assigned. An altarpiece is neither a lesson nor an instrument; its mode is neither history nor theology, but poetry; its matter not local but universal. The scholar brings all this out, paradoxically, by relocating the Crucifixion altarpiece in its historical matrix, closing the gap between the present and the past.

And then the cicerone, or loquacious tour guide, makes it vivid; so too does the knowledgeable sacristan who describes altarpieces to churchgoers, as well as the college professor who comments on a sequence of images projected in a dark lecture hall. But in the end the cicerone or the scholar is expected to stand aside. Once translated into the present, it is believed, the artwork will speak for itself. Self-evidence and mute beauty are qualities often demanded of a work of art. The painting or relief, unlike a treatise, just shows you, without telling; and unlike many a sermon, it offers pleasure.

Impressed by the obviousness of the image, the philologist Ernst Robert Curtius in his treatise *European Literature and the Latin Middle Ages* (1948) formed a low opinion of the art historian. A painting, he said, unlike a work of literature, is available to intuition, a direct insight into its essence. There is no need for learned commentary or mastery of dead languages. "So-called *Kunstwissenschaft* [meaning something like "the systematic study of art"] has an easier time [than philology]. To understand Pindar's poems requires severe mental effort—to understand the Parthenon frieze does not." If only Curtius had stopped to tell us what the Parthenon frieze so evidently means.

Curtius forgot that a work of art is never just an image, for it never shows anything clearly, and moreover it is never merely beautiful. The artwork reframes and reshapes reality, sometimes to the limits of recognizability, covering any tracks that might lead us back to that reality. Art feeds back into its own determinations: art is worked up into spectacle; art supplements liturgy or prayer; art not only projects but also provokes desire. The work of art emerges at once out of a collectivity and out of an individual consciousness. The art historian Henri Focillon, writing in 1934, described the artwork as "the translation of a free and superior reverie." And yet in that same work "the energies of civilizations converge." Art reorients the familiar to the unheard-of; art registers an adjustment of living consciousness to dead things. Ernst Robert Curtius also believed that whereas works of art are stuck in place, "for literature, all the past is present, or can become so." "With the literature of all times and peoples I can have a direct, intimate, and engrossing vital relationship, with art not." Book-bound, Curtius was unable to see that the painting or sculpture that arrives from a remote time and place is doubly mysterious, first for its compliance with obsolete conventions of art, and second for being a work of art at all. The art historian dispels one layer of mystery—the historical difference—only to reveal a second and more intractable mystery. This is just the appeal of historical art: any interpretation is staggered, dilated. The historical decoding prepares an aesthetic decoding which, in the event, is never completed.

So art history at the very least brings you to the threshold of the work. But the art historian who is not also asked to provide some orientation to the work's *promesse du bonheur*, its beauty (Stendhal), is underemployed. The pleasure in art that figures felicity in life is not a crass one-dimensional sort of pleasure but an ambiguous appeal involving recognition and misrecognition, questioning and disappointment, prompts and restagings of desire. Enswirled in this pleasure you swim upstream and enter into the interplay of the collective and the individual, into the conditions of life, now repeated and intensified. The artwork forces you to adjust to the alterities thrown up by history. The engagement with the painting or drawing as art, and not just as supplement to scripture or as display of wealth, recapitulates original but long-lost dispositions of body and mind to things made and natural, the dispositions of the historical artists and beholders.

Art history tries to do all that, and yet still comply with the conventions of scholarship, to provide that learned commentary that Curtius thought artworks did not require. Art history as a scholarly discipline is a modern discipline. And yet it is not so very young—older in fact than several other academic disciplines that speak to specially modern concerns, such as economics, sociology, anthropology, and psychology. In 1920, for example, there were already eighteen *Ordinarien* or full professors of art history in the German universities, but only one full professor of psychology. To win space in the university, art history had to commit itself to the empirical method of historical study. This meant building accessible archives of documents connected to the making of art; establishing a hierarchy of primary sources (direct witnesses of historical episodes) and secondary sources (subsequent commentaries on these witnesses as well as on other commentaries); and enforcing an ethics of disinterest and honor in the matter of acknowledging the ideas and discoveries of previous scholars. Scholarship may be defined simply as an ongoing accumulation of knowledge that at every step discloses the sources of its own authority. Empiricism was the basis of the pact between scholarship and society.

Society's expectation that the scholar deliver explanations creates a predicament for the art historian, because a work of art is not the effect of any cause, and is not easily lodged in a linear history. A causal art history would be a reverse alchemy, converting gold back into base earth. And yet the historian, if she is not to be reduced to pointing to features of artworks, will want to tell a story, and so pens the biography of form itself. That life-story has a plot, very often the movement from order to disorder. Theodor W. Adorno, in his *Aesthetic Theory* (1970), when he asserted that formal harmony will always produce its opposite, formal dissonance, was translating a common art-historical fable into philosophical language:

> The more deeply artworks immerse themselves in the idea of harmony, of the appearing essence, the less they can be satisfied with that idea.... Dissonance is the truth about harmony. If the ideal of harmony is taken strictly, it proves to be unreachable according to its own concept.

Why is harmony unattainable? Because for Adorno, art expresses suffering, that is, reality, through formal disorder: "Dissonance is effectively expression; the consonant and harmonious want to soften and eliminate it." Harmony or formal plenitude is a false immanence, that is, a contrivance of order that does not dwell in the work: "expression is the element immanent to art through which, as one of its constituents, art defends itself against the immanence that it develops by its law of form." The ongoing exposure of the lie of harmony is the very logic of the modern history of art since the nineteenth century, or arguably since the sixteenth century. The rejection of the formal equilibrium of the classic style in favor of a changeful, unballasted Baroque style was the theme of Heinrich Wölfflin's *Principles of Art History* (1915), the most widely read art-historical book of the twentieth century. Adorno, like Wölfflin, did not believe that the movement from the High Renaissance or classic style to the Baroque style could be explained by shifts in "historical temperament," or as an arbitrary change in fashion. The repudiation of the classical ideal, Adorno said, is rather

> the result of the coefficient of friction in harmony itself, which in corporeal form presents what is not reconciled as reconciled and thereby transgresses the very postulate of the appearing essence at which the ideal of harmony aims.

The struggle between order and disorder has its own career which moves through historical time but is not of it. This is a story that art history can tell. And yet such stories are destined to lose their focus, to lose their particular object, because those stories always take the same shape: the movement from integrity of image to confusion, from continuity to discontinuity. Classic form is image-like, stilled, exempt from time. Baroque form is plunged back into time. To become more art-like the image must become less image-like and more difficult to distinguish from the rest of turbulent, discontinuous reality. Such fables about form are built on top of the more responsible and fact-based stories that empirical research supports.

The improbable biographies of form won the most intense admiration from readers outside the field of art history. Wölfflin was invoked for example by José Ortega y Gasset, Boris Eikhenbaum, Sergei Eisenstein, Walter Benjamin, Marshall McLuhan, Gilles Deleuze, Richard Wollheim, and many others, including the literary scholars Walther Rehm, Marcel Raymond, Jean Rousset, René Wellek, Joseph Frank, Renato Poggioli, and Fredric Jameson. Meanwhile the Viennese art historian Alois Riegl, like Wölfflin a formalist, was invoked by Georg Lukács, Mikhail Bakhtin, Oswald Spengler, Karl Mannheim, Ernst Bloch, Otto Rank, Benjamin again, Eisenstein again, Béla Balázs, Walter Gropius, Henri Maldiney, Adorno, again Deleuze, again Wollheim, and Paul Feyerabend.

The art historians treated form as if it were a dynamic reality, a third term intervening between the myth of active man and the myth of passive nature (Focillon), a counterpart to life, which is itself a form (in the phrase of the metaphysician Henri Bergson, whose thought had an impact on Focillon). They treated form as if it were only temporarily attached to content. For many non-art historians of the twentieth century, struck by the simplicity of this model, the life-story of form *was* art history.

For some, Riegl and Wölfflin provided support for the thesis of the irreducibility of art to knowledge, technology, aesthetics, or culture. For others, unexpectedly, formal analysis cleared the way to a deeper coordination of art with history. Take for example Benjamin's essay "Eduard Fuchs, Collector and Historian" (1937). The problem of cultural history, according to Benjamin, was spelled out already by Friedrich Engels, who criticized in a letter of 1893 the tendency of historians to tell edifying stories of the evolution of the arts, generating the illusion that each cultural form followed its own independent laws. According to Engels, cultural history holds up for our contemplation fixed, "epic" images of the past. Benjamin agreed with Engels about the shortcomings of conventional cultural history, and was prepared to join the dialectical-materialist project of "blasting" art out of its reified epochs. But he turned to Fuchs to muster unexpected support for his own conviction that an historical account is "marred" unless it grasps the work of art *as* a work of art, even including the nature of its "success" as art. Fuchs, in developing his own study of "mass" or popular art, including caricature and pornography, "had to come to deal with formalism," and above all Wölfflin. In Wölfflin he found the proposition that historical artistic styles did not evolve according to shifts in an "idea of beauty." Fuchs and Benjamin understood this to mean that art responds to "more elementary processes." Wölfflin, for example, had observed that sixteenth-century Italian painting had a strong feeling for the relation of individual and interior space: the new art, wrote Wölfflin, could "scarcely imagine an existence that is not architecturally framed and founded." Because the art historian saw, according to Benjamin, that paintings "were increasingly devoted to people as inhabitants of dwellings (rather than people as worshipers)," he grasped "the role played by Renaissance painting in prefiguring the new architecture" and the new secularism.

———

Intimacy with art is a prerequisite of good art history. Yet modern university- or college-based art historians often mistrust critics, collectors, dealers, and museum curators because their scholarship is too directly involved in the assignation of value, even the setting of prices. The proximity of art history to the art market and to museums, the entanglements with entertainment, haute couture, tourism, and the consumption of heritage, is felt by many scholars as a curse on the discipline, a burden that scholars of literature, for example, do not share. But the intellectual costs of professional alienation from art are steep. If the campus-bound scholar will not listen to the partisans and familiars of art, his writing will be dry and flavorless. An empirical art-historical scholarship that loses sight of its object—art—will not hold the interest of readers from beyond the discipline, who look to art history to reveal something new about art, not about history. Ideally the artist, the art historian, and the poet will be "of imagination all compact."

The balance between intuitive intimacy and impersonal rigor is perhaps what readers prized in the "philosophical" art historians, as Richard Wollheim called Riegl, Wölfflin, and Focillon, the art historians "who have sensed most clearly the essentially transformational character of art."

This book is not only a history and prehistory of the academic discipline of art history but also more generally a history of historical thinking about art. The art-historical mentality long predates its enshrinement in the university. Societies have represented the histories of art in the fabric of their cities, in the juxtapositions of one building to another; in rituals and dances that preserve handed-down patterns; in costumes; in myths and legends about the origins of art; in anecdotes about artists; and in the descriptions of places and local cults. People in many times and places have given art a history in gathering, rearranging, and displaying artworks. In ancient and medieval Europe inscribed or carved stones from old buildings, or buildings belonging to conquered societies, were inserted into new buildings, mounted as "spoils," the perceptible stylistic difference between container and contained symbolizing the superiority of here to there, now to then.

Among all the possible histories, it is the one written down that has the strongest grip on the future. Writing stores, publicizes, permits comparison. Words written and, even more so, words published take on unearned authority. Grammar and syntax create a semblance of continuity even when there was none. Already in the first century AD the

Roman encyclopedist Pliny wrote histories of Greek painting and sculpture. Pliny, a practical man, was not intimate with art. He was interested in the arts as applied chemistry, as engineering, and as the manipulation of materials and tools, the "know-how" that the Romans called *ars* and the Greeks *techne*. But Pliny spoke with Roman aristocrats who collected art, and he read texts by older Greek writers who knew that an artwork's value could not be equated with its technical accomplishment.

In the present book the main story runs from the European Middle Ages to the mid-twentieth century; Pliny remains in the deep background. But the art-historical mentality is hardly a European monopoly. It is shared by all societies that have collected art as art: China, Japan, and Korea; ancient Greece and Rome; Persian, Ottoman, and Mughal court cultures; and Europe and its colonies and ex-colonies since the early Renaissance; as well as courts and religious communities of Africa, South Asia, and ancient Mesoamerica. A limitation of this book is its linguistic horizon: the author reads only some European languages and is unable to offer more than superficial comments on the non-European historiographies of art. Historical judgment not grounded in long familiarity and study is always venturesome. Some examples from the Chinese and Safavid traditions, drawn from translated texts, are summoned because they add dimensions to the argument of the book.

Relativism

The most basic way of evaluating a work of art is to hold it up to a fixed measuring stick: Is it well-crafted, are the materials rare and expensive, is it graceful, refined, marvelous, imposing, realistic? All works, no matter when or where fabricated, are held up to the same standard. If a work is ugly or unintelligible, so much the worse for it. No one will make any effort to compensate for deficiency by holding up an alternative yardstick (a "canon," in Greek and Latin). Art history in this impassive evaluative mode winnows the good from the less good.

In modernity the widened horizon of knowledge has revealed that each society has its own idea of the proper yardstick. One cannot justly hold up one culture's yardstick to another culture's art. Relativism, or the recognition of not just one but many different concepts of art, is the basis of the modern discipline of art history. The relativist assesses each work not by a fixed measure outside of time but only in relation to its own time. The artwork is as beautiful, well-crafted, or realistic as one may expect a work made in Rome in the first century, China in the ninth century, Persia in the fourteenth century, or Spain in the eighteenth century to be. The relativist considers artistic value nothing more than a ratio of ends to available means. The roots of this mentality lie in the collector's capacity—learned from artists, presumably—to discern quality in spite of the stylistic difference between one artist and another. Cicero, a quick learner, commented: "Sculpture is a single art, in which Myron, Polycletus, and Lysippus excelled; all of whom differed one from another, but so that you would not wish any one of them to be unlike himself. The art and science of painting is one, yet Zeuxis, Aglaophon, and Apelles are quite unlike one another in themselves, though to none of them does anything seem wanting in his peculiar style." The next step was to extend this hospitality to the divergent styles of art past and distant. Since 1800 the expert on art does this routinely, explaining away the gap between the Middle Ages and modernity, between South Asia and Europe, and so expanding the corpus of valued artworks. And that is the modern paradigm of art history: intercontinental, ecumenical, nonpartisan. Relativism expanded the canon, revealing that great art has been made in all times and places. It may look different, but it isn't. For a long time, to prefer or even grudgingly admire the art of little-understood cultures, such as India or Africa, was for the European (as for the Chinese, for that matter) unthinkable. But those obstacles fell away, and relativism of historical form—though not relativism of artistic value itself—became the principle of the Musée du Louvre and the Metropolitan Museum of Art.

Under the modern, relativist paradigm of art history, artworks of lesser quality are not discarded. But they are segregated. The Kunsthaus in Zurich, an art museum founded in 1910, displays several painted retables or altarpieces of the late fifteenth and early sixteenth centuries. Down the hill, in the Schweizerisches Landesmuseum, a historical museum founded in 1898, stocked with folk art, pottery, textiles, and didactic displays about the history of Switzerland, you will find several more such altarpieces, similar but less beautiful. The altarpieces were acquired by the historical museum because, like costumes and firearms, they too testify to a worldview, to a lifeworld. The only difference between the altarpieces in the Kunsthaus and those in the Landesmuseum is their artistic quality. An art historian or amateur of art focused on the finer works will still wish to visit the history museum because lesser works contribute not only to knowledge of the past generally but also to appreciation of the greater works. And vice versa, because the finer paintings up the hill are also a kind of historical evidence. A different kind of evidence than the paintings in the historical museum? That is a hard question.

Relativism, its invention and its detractors, its use and misuse, is a main theme of this book. The relativistic attitude to art, or to anything, was rare in premodern times. Some contemporaries of Leonardo da Vinci or Michelangelo, including the art historian Giorgio Vasari, while convinced that these artists had surpassed the artists of prior centuries, did charitably praise older painters—the artists of the Middle Ages—making allowances for the times they lived in. In China relativism was by the sixteenth century a mental habit of long standing. Already the ninth-century art historian Zhang Yanyuan, writing about painters of the Qin dynasty (third century BC), said: "To explain the significance of the ancients, one should focus upon demonstrating their strengths, and not concentrate on popular changes [in taste and style]."

To make allowances was one thing. Another was to prefer the older, simpler art. Such preferences were frequently expressed by the Chinese cognoscenti. Zhao Mengfu (1254–1322), for example, a landscape painter born in the Song period who went on to work for the Mongol court under Kublai Khan, wrote:

> The important thing in a painting is the antique spirit. A painting may be very well done, and yet be worthless if the antique spirit is lacking. People today only think of delicate lines and fresh colours and call themselves competent artists.... My paintings seem to be simple and crude, but those who understand know that they are akin to the antique way, and therefore good.

By "antique spirit" Zhao Mengfu meant simplicity, austerity, sparseness. No one in Europe, not before the late eighteenth century, was ready to express a preference for art that was "simple and crude."

Not until the nineteenth century did any European writer find language to express admiration for the architecture, sculpture, and painting of the eleventh and twelfth centuries, a period now given the style-label Romanesque. In 1834 the author and scholar Prosper Mérimée was appointed by the French state as inspector general of historic monuments. Mérimée commissioned from the architect Eugène Viollet-le-Duc the restorations of the church of the Madeleine at Vézélay, the walled city of Carcassonne, and other medieval structures. Alerted by the writer George Sand, Mérimée classed as an historical monument the mysterious Lady and the Unicorn tapestries, created around 1500 and then hanging in a chateau in central France. Mérimée brought them to Paris and had them restored. But it was easy to admire the charm of the tapestries with their tall slender figures and hundreds of animals, birds, and flowers scattered on a red ground. More challenging were the dour old religious paintings Mérimée came across on his tours. In a report on the abbey church at Saint-Savin in the Poitou, published in 1845, Mérimée defends the faulty drawing of the murals in the church's nave depicting scenes of the Old Testament (c. 1100). Mérimée notes the "hieroglyphs" that the painters employed to describe clouds, trees, and buildings and concedes that a modern observer, accustomed to the high degree of technical proficiency of modern painting, must wonder how the public of the Middle Ages could ever have been satisfied with such crude expediencies. But there is nothing easier, Mérimée contends, than the production of illusion. He points out that in the theater, simple shorthand indications of setting have always sufficed to conjure up a world.

The medieval painter, supported by his illusion-generating shorthand, was free to focus on the figures and the heads, endowing them with a nobility and regularity learned from the best ancient models. Mérimée praises a scene in the nave that he identifies as possibly *The Prayer of Enos and the Vocation of Noah*. The figure on the left is "very beautifully drawn, and the draperies are adjusted with a rare elegance. Note the graceful ornament of the hem of the robe; it is completely hellenic." Romanesque painting, according to Mérimée, chastises a decadent bourgeois realism:

> On first sighting the paintings of Saint-Savin, one is struck by the incorrectness of the drawing, the coarseness of the execution, in short the ignorance and clumsiness of the artist. A more attentive examination brings recognition of a certain grand character completely foreign to works of a more recent date. Compare one of the compositions of the nave with a picture by Jan van Eyck, for example: the van Eyck is undoubtedly much more correct, much more exact, much closer to nature, but its style is low, and *bourgeois*, to use an expression from the painter's studio.

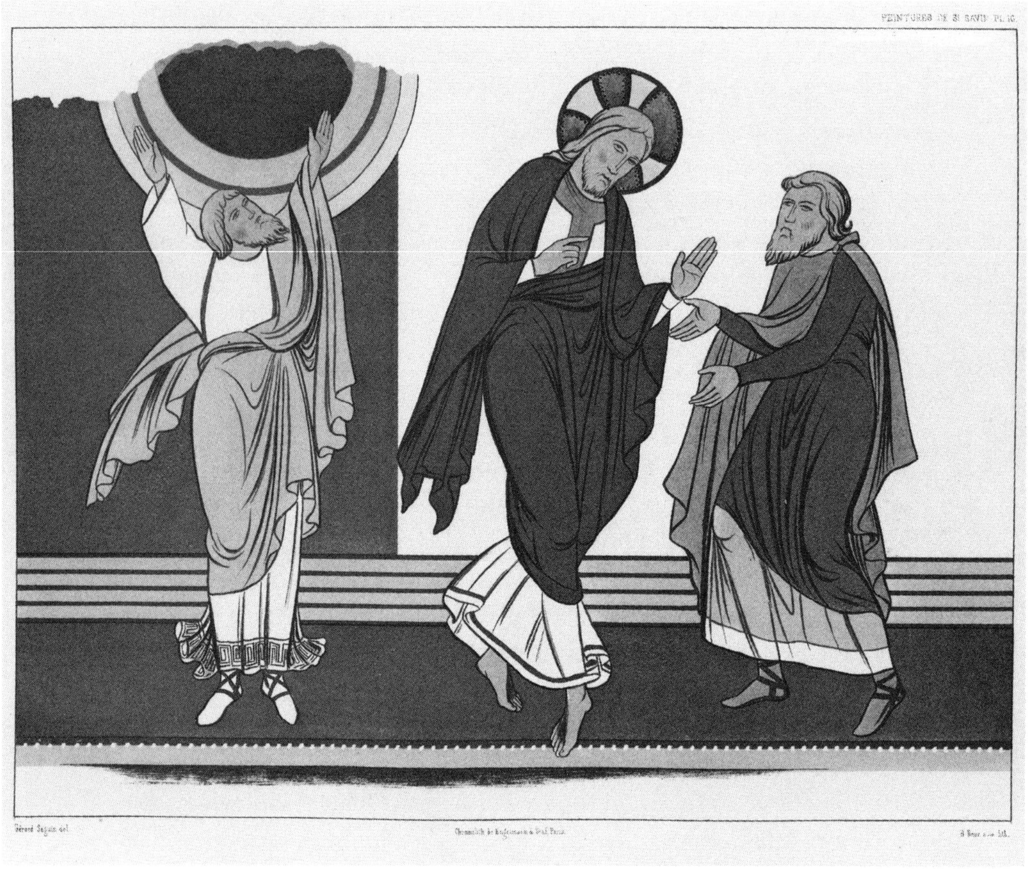

The Prayer of Enos (?) and the Vocation of Noah (c. 1100). Fresco in the nave of the abbey church of Saint-Savin-sur-Gartempe, Poitou. Chromolithograph in Prosper Mérimée, *Notice sur les peintures de l'église de Saint-Savin* (Paris, 1845), plate 10, reproducing a watercolor by Gérard-Seguin based on tracings made from the wall painting.

He prefers Saint-Savin to the works of the great fifteenth-century Flemish painter Jan van Eyck because van Eyck's technical proficiency delivers nothing more uplifting than an exact picture of the world around him. Van Eyck, he is saying, was in effect already a photographer. In defending Saint-Savin, Mérimée defends the art of painting in general against the threat of the new technology unveiled in Paris only a few years before. Photography, he is saying, has relieved painting—modern and medieval alike—of the burden of verisimilitude.

Did Mérimée favor Romanesque because he favored the old religion over modern secularism? By no means. He looks through the intended significance and import of the pictorialized Bible on the walls at Saint-Savin, looks through the content to artistic form. That form in turn gives him access to what he considers a truer, more enduring content: something like gravitas or spiritual nobility, preferable to mere realism. The old art survives on the basis of its form.

To arrive at even a low level of susceptibility to artistic form one needs to factor out content. The mark of a sophisticated culture of collecting was always indifference to subject matter. Cicero, whose eloquence every cicerone emulates, wrote in a letter in the 60s BC to his friend Marcus Fadius Gallus about recent purchases and non-purchases:

> But Bacchae! What place is there in my house for them? But, you will say, they are pretty…. The sort of statues that I am accustomed to buy are such as may adorn a place in a palaestra after the fashion of gymnasia. What, again, have I, the promoter of peace, to do with a statue of Mars? I am glad there was not a statue of Saturn also: for I should have thought these two statues had brought me debt! I should have preferred some representation of Mercury: I might then, I suppose, have made a more favourable bargain with Arrianus.

Cicero is pretending to speak like a philistine who does not grasp that the most meaningful referent of a statue of Mercury is not Mercury but Praxiteles. His remarks signal that he knows perfectly well that he is not inviting the gods into his home. His home is not a temple. Cicero is collecting sculpted representations of the Greek gods. He has no intention of reintroducing such artifacts into the force field of worship, any more than we feel addressed by Mars or Mercury today. The focus on form comes easily when the content is familiar and yet no longer active.

If the content is alien or offensive, however, even the most sophisticated ancient collector will be less charitable to splendor and craft. Content reasserts itself as the resistance of reality, in the sense developed by Northrop Frye, following the poet Wallace Stevens: if form is a shaping power mysterious even to the artist, then content is "the sense of otherness, the resistance to the material, the feeling that there is something to be overcome." Alterity on the level of content—content too assertive to be "looked through"—can pose hurdles to the evaluation of historical art. Esteem for older art flourishes in stable successions of societies, when continuity of content can bridge even discontinuities of language, geography, or mentality: Romans collecting Greek art, Song or Ming connoisseurs collecting Tang art. Familiarity of content neutralizes content, allowing form to occupy the foreground.

In 1845 the capacity to admire Jan van Eyck was itself still relatively new, hardly predating the French Revolution. Only a generation after van Eyck was elevated, he was already cast down, by Mérimée. Every style can now be challenged by a more humble style.

Mérimée's embrace of the humble is a pastoral fable, reversing the hierarchy of more civilized and less civilized. He holds dear the relics of art's innocence; the child is father of the man. The childhood of art is regarded as a state of low competence and low self-consciousness but heightened receptivity. Mérimée approves of the cultic sincerity of the Romanesque frescoes but not because he is sincere about what the painters at Saint-Savin were sincere about. Mérimée simply prizes sincerity as such. He envies the childlike and guileless state of mindfulness they evince, a state of imaginative credulity.

Eventually art historians took the last step and asked whether not only forms and contents but also the ends of art, the idea of art itself, might be relative. If each society were to have its own idea of art, then assessments of the value of the artwork, it would seem, or even what counts as art, can only ever be local. Any fabricated, shaped thing is a valid object of study, so long as you look at it from the right point of view. An art historian might well decline to evaluate altogether, choosing instead to grasp the work of art as an index of its time, a material relic of the past like any other, and an effect waiting to be assigned a cause. Such an art historian would simply be an historian who accepts as evidence not only paintings and sculptures but also furniture, costumes, tableware, and other artifacts that cannot be considered artworks at all. There are no limits to this line of thinking, unless it is checked by the desire to possess the artwork, or to ponder it. If the artworks are not seen any longer to be resisting their instrumentalization as evidence, then you might as well cart all the old paintings from the Kunsthaus down the hill to the Landesmuseum, and fill the Kunsthaus to its last corner with modern and contemporary art, so that apples can finally be compared to apples, no relativizing adjustments necessary.

A Cast of the Dice

Already in the nineteenth century the relativist approach to art, relocating each work in its original bed of functions and values, threatened to deliver an excessively pragmatic account of art. This was staved off by the reification of artistic form in the writings of the form-oriented historians of the last decades of that century and the first decades of the twentieth century. Their approach recovered a premodern and decorous concept of the artwork as integrated, even while allowing that modern works tended to slide toward a redemptive disintegration. The biographies of form had the merit of calling into question the basic aim of the discipline of art history as established in the nineteenth century, namely, the coordination of art with the *saeculum*, with experienced, sublunary time. Henri Focillon, protesting the persistence of the myth of secular time into the twentieth century, asserted that "a work of art is non-temporal, its proper activity, its debate, occur primarily in space." The work "measures space." But the work "is only apparently immobile. It expresses a wish of fixity, it is arrested, but like a moment in the past. In reality it is born of one change and prepares another." The work "bursts roughly in on the moment"; it is "a structure, a defining of time," an "event" without being an historical event. The artwork opposes the harshness of determinism by introducing cleavage and discord. Formalism revealed that the attempt to coordinate artworks with measurable time depended upon a misrecognition of art as symbolic expression, as technology or technique, or as instrument of worldly power. The form-oriented approach opened old dossiers, pre- and nonrelativist, also non-European and non-elite. This challenge to rational timekeeping remains unanswered, surviving the demise not only of idealist art but also of "formal" art, art preoccupied with form.

Focillon's declarations on art are metaphors, images. They will persuade few who are not already persuaded. He circles around art, patrols its frontiers, as all do who try to define art. This periphrastic discourse serves to keep historical thinking at bay.

Attempts to attribute timelessness to art, even when unsuccessful, nevertheless point to some quality of art that is felt intuitively but cannot yet be named. If art were neither in nor out of time, then both a soft relativism (great art can be found in many different forms) and a hard relativism ("art" means something different to everyone, and therefore means nothing) would be foiled. Such challenges to historical thinking may seem unreal and unlikely. Yet the possibility of a poor fit between art and time has shadowed all art history, and this book must therefore be more than a genealogy of art-historical relativism. For if art is insecurely lodged in time, and the distance between the artwork and the beholder can never be measured, then there is no hope of finding a standpoint offering a new, clarifying perspective. Art demands partisanship—a collapse of perspective.

In Mexico, since the eighteenth century or even earlier, people who pray for and receive relief from illness or injury offer thanks to the Virgin Mary in the form of small painted panels. These paintings, known as ex votos because they fulfill a vow, depict the sufferer in the state of dire need, in prison, in a foundering ship, or in bed. In the picture reproduced on the next page the Virgin Mary appears as Our Lady of Loreto, one of her titles, inside a wreath of clouds. The inscription explains that in 1867 Maria Chagolla was suffering from a gangrenous leg. "Her daughter Manuela Ybarra entrusted her to the miraculous (*milagrosa*) image of Our Lady of Loreto of the chapel of this parish who freed her from the danger in which she was and in a few days she was cured and in testimony of this wonder (*marbilla*) she dedicates this little picture (*retablito*) in perpetual memory." On the left Manuela points to the leg extending from under the sheets of her mother's bed. On the right Manuela raises a candle to the image of the Virgin floating above a landscape. Each miracle is personal. And yet in Anita Brenner's account, in her book *Idols Behind Altars* (1929), "a miracle is a thing without chronology." No matter that the facts of the case—a date, sometimes a name or a place—are inscribed on the painting itself. Even these data, she says, are not "a sequence." The name, the date, and the place "are stated as factors, in words, like a formula of the composition." There is no chronology of miracles because all

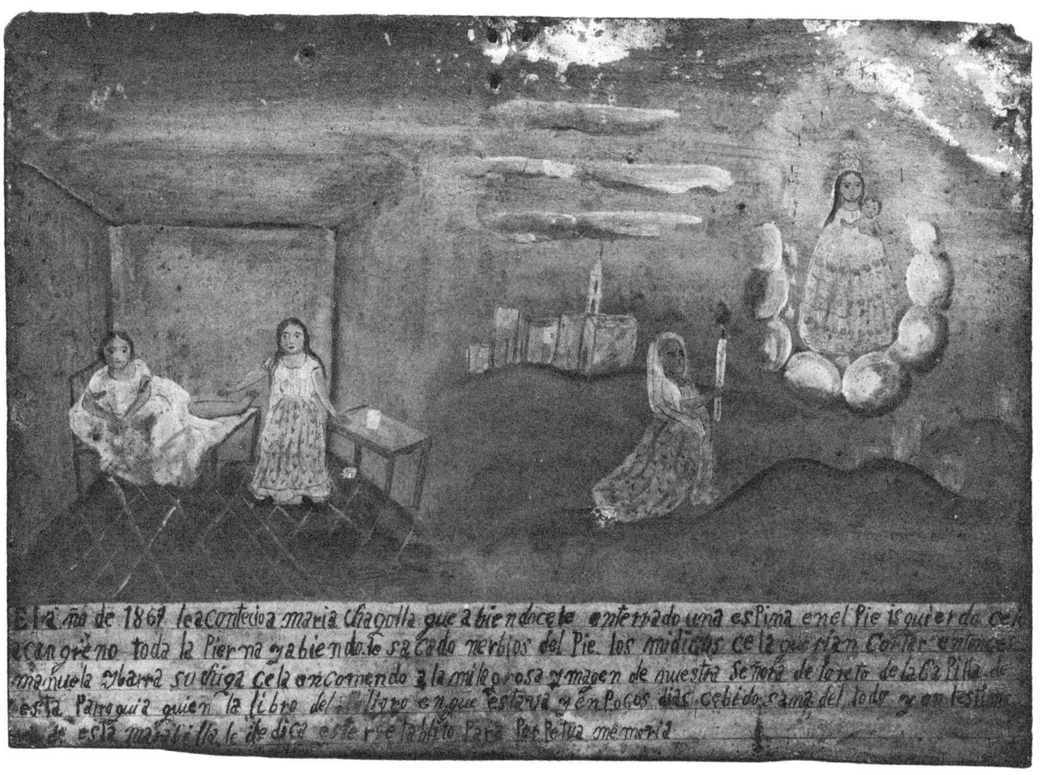

Ex voto of Manuela Ybarra dedicated to Our Lady of Loreto, Mexico (1867). Paint on metal, 17.8 × 25.4 cm. Private collection. The inscription describes the illness, the prayer for relief, and the miraculous cure. Note the nailholes along the top.

miracles are the same miracle. When you see a painted ex voto, you see every miracle. In Mexico the panel itself is called a *milagro*. The miracle and its depiction relocate the mechanisms of cause and effect to a plane beyond common experience. Meaningless misfortune, a cast of the dice, intervenes in the sequence of days; the extramundane saint contravenes the intervention and restores the ordinary. The subject matter of the ex voto is the transformation of the time of emergency back into everyday time, permitting a recoordination of the time of your life with the only really stable time frame, the history of salvation. The miracle restructures your life, but it does not restructure history.

The little paintings function like photographs. They document a moment in a life, freeze appearance at that moment. Such capturings were once rare, in anyone's life. The ex votos of the eighteenth century captured the misfortunes of people who would never be portrayed by a painted portrait. Later, photography democratized portraiture. The formats and styles of painted ex votos are highly conventional, but so were those of early photographic portraits.

The painting is not only a report on the episode but also plays a role within the miracle. The panel testifies to the supplicant's honorable fulfillment of his vow, publishing the miracle and so priming the community for more miracles. Two, sometimes three time frames are represented in the picture: the grievous dislocation of daily rhythms, the attentive Mary or other saint who is outside of time, and the restored time of health and safety. The latter is the state of unawareness of time, the sustaining illusion that we are invulnerable to time and aging, that things will just go on as they always have. The miracle itself—the readjustment of time—cannot be depicted. Nevertheless Brenner says that because a miracle has no chronology, "a picture is closer to its nature than a story." Stories rise and sink on the tide of discourse, talk, blending with all the other stories, whereas paintings are exceptions, parentheses. A painting is an artificial stilling of the flux, an imposition on time symbolized by its frame. A painting adds something to the world, and it lasts a while.

The stability of the ex voto across time paralyzes the art historian. Any attempt to coordinate the ex votos with histories of Baroque and modern painting in Europe and in the New World, which followed their own internal logics, increasingly disengaged from the religious cult and from the lives of ordinary people, seems forced. From the Spanish conquest of the New World to the twentieth century, the ex voto persists. Unable to discern or impose pattern, the historian of the ex voto is susceptible to the Christian view of history, namely, that Mexicans were marooned in pagan error until the Spanish arrived. According to this view, there is only one meaningful caesura in history: the introduction of the Christian cult into Mexico.

Brenner contests this view by arguing that the conquest of Mexico by the Spanish in the sixteenth century was not real. The thesis of her book is that the underlying beliefs and habits of the people, shaped over millennia by the landscape—which "seems unfinished and at the same time forever fixed"—and by the Maya and Aztec cosmologies, persist in Europeanized and Christianized Mexico. The Spanish friars tapped into the long-standing customs with subtle substitutions. They replaced the teocallis, or pyramid-temples, with churches, and the ceremonial rites with miracle plays. The Black Christ of Chalma filled a gap left when the friars destroyed a cylindrical idol associated with Oxtoteotl, a cave god. Brenner shifts attention away from the pagan-Christian rupture and instead onto the rupture marked by the votive panel. Each *milagro* starts history all over again and at the same time leaves everything in place. Brenner disables art history by not even attempting to coordinate form with history. In disengaging the ex voto from art history, she is treating it like an artwork, recognizing that the form-poor pictures, even if they do not appear to resemble art, keep their own time. Art history comes closer to art when it opens itself to non-art.

Anita Brenner (1905–1974) was born in Mexico, the daughter of immigrants from Latvia, and later lived for a number of years in the United States. In the late 1920s, while she was writing and publishing *Idols Behind Altars*, she studied ethnology and anthropology at Columbia University. Under the guidance of Franz Boas she wrote a dissertation on designs found on Aztec potsherds, and yet she never adopted the academic mentality. Brenner invented a new way of writing about Mexican art so as not to miss the point of the ex voto.

The Origin of Art History

The successes and failures of the form-oriented approach to art history allow us to imagine art history's eventual endpoint. But what was its origin? The first art histories were told by artifacts themselves. The work that tries to overrule fortune—cast the dice back at life—is the monument. The monument imposes order on the landscape or the city, just as an artwork imposes order on a room. A domineering artifact that preempts and preshapes the work of a future art historian, the monument signals the authority of the state over resources and skills as well as over time itself. In the twenty-sixth century BC the Egyptian king Khufu (later Hellenized as Cheops) built the Great Pyramid at Giza, a tomb, as a monument to himself. The construction of the causeway, the underground chambers, and the pyramid itself took thirty years. The Greek historian Herodotus described it more than two thousand years later: "Each of its sides, which form a square, is eight plethra long and the pyramid is eight plethra high as well. It is made of polished blocks of stone, fitted together perfectly; none of the blocks is less than thirty feet long." This is "cosmic" art: it reorders the world (the Greek *kosmos* means order).

To write a history of such monuments would not seem much of a challenge. But a history of art must peer beyond the works' own horizons. Herodotus noted the displacement of energy the construction of the pyramid required. Cheops reduced the country "to a completely awful condition. He closed down all the sanctuaries, stopped people performing sacrifices, and also commanded all the Egyptians to work for him…. They worked in gangs of 100,000 men for three months at a time." A pyramid remonstrates against entropy and oblivion. But Cheops had to induce disorder in order to create the pyramidal order. According to Herodotus, the king dared, in an inscription, to give a glimpse of the suffering behind the monument:

> There is a notice in Egyptian script on the pyramid about how much was spent on radishes, onions, and garlic for the labourers, and if my memory serves me well, the translator reading the notice to me said that the total cost was sixteen hundred talents of silver.

The inscription reveals that there is a multiplicity of actors behind every monument. The colossal dimensions of the pyramid cannot conceal the fact that art is not just an object but an event. The king claims authorship, letting the monument point to him alone, but then undermines this ambition with his own inscription. Herodotus, in relating all this, relativizes the self-testimony of the pyramids. The principle is the same applied by Prosper Mérimée to the frescoes at Saint-Savin: the works are evaluated on the basis of the ratio of ends to means, except that Herodotus's intent was not to upgrade but to downgrade. The Greek historian did not take the monument at face value. Instead he located the work's other—disorder—lurking just outside the work, so correcting and historicizing its message.

Herodotus relates a story in which the king's daughter found a way herself to build an ironic countermonument concretizing the relation between suffering and creation:

> Cheops was such a bad man that when he was short of money he installed his own daughter in a room with instructions to charge a certain amount of money (I was not told exactly how much) for her favours. She did what her father had told her to do, but she also had the idea of leaving behind her own personal memorial, so she asked each of the men who came into her to give her a single block of stone in the work-site. I was told that the middle pyramid of the group of three was built from these blocks of stone.

The king's brother Chephren, meanwhile, built his own pyramid. From the two kings' point of view, the pyramids stave off oblivion. The art historian will only be necessary when the pyramids crumble; in other words, not yet.

Annalistic History

Once there are art historians, they will adopt one of three modes of historical writing: annals, typology, and fables.

Annals are the roll call of great artists, often managed by artists themselves. Artists are no more eager than kings are to embrace relativism. In 1557 the town council of Salò, on the shores of Lake Garda in Lombardy, commissioned from the local painter Antonio Maria Mazzoleni a pair of organ shutters for the cathedral. The town agreed to pay the artist fourteen lire. When the paintings were complete, but before handing over the money, the councilors summoned an older painter from Brescia, the provincial capital, to assess the quality of the work. This was Girolamo Romani, known as Romanino (c. 1484–c. 1566), a native of Brescia, whose works were widely distributed in the palaces and churches of northern Italy, including works in the cathedral of Salò as well as the organ shutters of the cathedral of Brescia. Romanino judged the younger artist's organ shutters severely and recommended that the council withhold payment. Mazzoleni was incensed and wrote a letter of protest. Why should the councillors trust the old painter? he demanded. Mazzoleni conceded that Romanino, whom he guessed to be over eighty years of age, had made many worthy works. But he also pointed out that Romanino's name did not appear in the *Supplementum chronicarum* of Jacopo Filippo Foresti, a list of notable events first published in 1483 and frequently updated, which named Giotto and Gentile Bellini; nor in the treatise on architecture of Sebastiano Serlio, which mentioned a number of modern artists including Raphael, Bramante, and Baldassare Peruzzi as well as several artists still living: Giulio Romano, Giovanni da Udine, and Giovanni Francesco Caroto; nor in the thirty-fifth canto, praising several famous painters, of Ludovico Ariosto's *Orlando Furioso*, whose third edition had appeared in 1532; nor in the dialogues of Sperone Speroni, published in 1542; nor in the *Ternali to the Glory of Pope Julius III and the Most Christian Queen* by Pietro Aretino, a poem of 1551 that mentions more than two dozen illustrious artists; nor in any of the "many other celebrated writers who make mention of the worthy painters beginning from ancient times right up to the ones living today." This last phrase seems to echo the title of the *Lives of the Most Excellent Italian Architects, Painters, and Sculptors, from Cimabue to our own Times* (Le vite de' più eccellenti pittori, scultori ed architettori), published in Florence in 1550 by the painter Giorgio Vasari, suggesting that Mazzoleni was well aware of this great book, as nearly all Italian artists must have been. Mazzoleni could not mock Romanino for being ignored by Vasari, however, because the first edition of the *Lives* offered biographies of only two living artists: Michelangelo Buonarroti, Vasari's idol and the paragon of modern art, the standard against which all others were measured, and the Tuscan sculptor Benedetto da Rovezzano, whose career had been cut short by blindness. (In fact, Vasari did mention Romanino, with a sentence of praise, in the life of Vittorio Carpaccio.) Only in the second edition of 1568 would Vasari open the gates to living artists (here, too, Romanino gets a short mention though no independent biography).

Mazzoleni was indignant because the council members, in his view, knew nothing about modern art. They had turned for guidance, he complained, to an arbiter who had not achieved the degree of fame that would entitle him to deliver career-hampering judgments on other painters.

Artists mistrust the judgments of non-artists, even if they are glad to win their admiration. Artists prefer to talk about art with other artists, even if they rarely agree. In sixteenth-century Italy such conversations were amplified for the first time by the printed book. A provincial painter was able to overhear opinions about art first expressed in Florence, Venice, and Ferrara; opinions held both by artists (Vasari, Serlio) and non-artists (Foresti, Speroni) as well as poets (Aretino, Ariosto). The medium of the printed book implied that these assessments transcended local tastes and complied instead with universal standards of craftsmanship and beauty.

The younger painter's outrage was stoked by his fear that he himself would never be inscribed in the annals. And he was right to fret, because Antonio Maria Mazzoleni left no further trace, not a single work and not a single mention in any document published or unpublished, apart from his angry letter (though one historian believes that some of his work on the organ shutters survives). Mazzoleni's complaint provides us with the simplest definition of art history: it is the story that every artist wants to be written into.

In many societies the performative arts are the most prestigious because they are direct, unique gifts to the senses, in real time. But their histories are as written on water. There was no Vasari of the arts of dance, music, or cookery. The performances of dancers and musicians left no relics, and the notation systems that might have captured the forms were crude or not yet existent. Buildings, sculptures, and paintings, however, made of stone, metal, wood, or egg- or oil-based pigment, persist for centuries. Yet even the nonperformative arts, if they are to have a history, depend on writing. Although paintings, like books, are often signed by their authors, many works—most works—are destroyed, altered, or replaced, and unless written down the names of their makers are forgotten. In his *Remedies for Fortune Fair and Foul* (1360), a series of dialogues between Joy and Reason, Petrarch pointed out that

> statues were highly appreciated long ago. How much these objects were favored and desired by the most eminent men in Antiquity is demonstrated by the elaborate searches of Augustus and Vespasian, and other emperors and kings, and some of the illustrious of the second order...—their care for the statues once they had been found, their concern to keep them safe, their dedicating them. Here belongs also the great fame of the artists, based not on the babble of the crowd or on the silent works themselves, but loudly proclaimed and celebrated in the works of established authors—a fame so great that it cannot possibly have an insignificant root.

Vasari, in turn, commenting on the art of ancient times, said that "of the works that are the life (*vita*) and glory (*fama*) of the craftsmen, the first, and eventually the second and the third, too, were lost, consumed by time that consumes all things, and since for lack of writers they could not even by that means become known to posterity, their craftsmen were forgotten." The annalist need not give the history of art a shape, tell where it is heading or what it all amounts to. The roster of great artists is simply a selection based on some criterion of excellence invulnerable to time. If Mazzoleni reads the annals well, he will adjust his art to match their selection criteria. The microhistories of painting assembled by Foresti, Ariosto, and Aretino, skeletal as they are, mere lists of names, give him something to aim at.

Any work by any artist draws on techniques and forms developed by earlier artists. For the traditional artist the past is summed up in the person and the precepts of the teacher. The artist knows there is a past that stretches back before the teacher, but does not need to think about it. You know you have distant ancestors even if you don't know their names. The relation to the tradition is complicated when tradition, no longer simply personified by the painter's teacher, is made real by relics and by inscription, that is, by surviving works and by a published narrative. Now the tradition has names and faces. Printed books and printed images—engravings that published and archived the best forms and compositions—were a living, compounding accumulation of commentary that invited self-correction. Later, collections and public museums extended the self-archiving of the visual arts that distinguishes them from performance. Print initiated a feedback loop between the historiography of art and the making of art.

When artists read an account of art's history, and feel invited to readjust their own relation to that account, they interfere, as it were in live time, with the very flow of tradition that is sustaining them. European artists since 1550 have been making art under a heavy awareness of the history of art. Vasari was no longer offering simple lists, but a shaped narrative about the ancient greatness of art, the fall of art, and the restoration of the highest standards in recent times. Artists entered into a call-and-response relation to such writing, or to the collections of paintings that illustrated its narrative principles. The annalist or historian set out to describe the past but ended up steering the present.

Art history managed by artists keeps art in the foreground. Not every discursive host of historical art does this. The discipline of anthropology treats works of art as if they were elements within a system of symbol exchanges. Archeology treats works of art as if they were traces of a vanished way of life. Modern artists, almost without exception, suspect academic art history and art historians of similar crimes. They believe that the art historian is too eager to anchor the work of art in the world that produced it, too quick to lace it into a series of causes and effects, too ready to force art to make a point about the history of technology or diplomacy or commerce or religion. Artists themselves tend not to want their works to be explained so much as esteemed. Vasari also had much to say about potentates and donors, the state and the Church, as sponsors of art. But as an artist Vasari was interested in the whole scene of art-making, the workshop, the personalities, the processes. He collected artists' drawings but was interested in creativity even when it left no permanent traces: he does not omit to mention the snowman carved by Michelangelo for Piero de' Medici.

The attitude of any artist to tradition, whether it has been chronicled or not, is ambivalent. On the one hand, you seek to append yourself to a worthy sequence of works and artists. On the other hand, you seek to innovate and so diverge from that tradition. The artist manages this paradox with psychological tricks. Every artist, even the artist who is expected by society to produce faithful copies of a revered cult image, hopes to contribute something rarefied to the process, some singular quality of vision or refinement. No artist sees himself as a copyist who performs over and over again the same approved tasks. This is true not only in societies that have cultivated the private appreciation of art beyond ritual function. Franz Boas, Anita Brenner's teacher, recounted a story about a painter from Vancouver Island whom he met probably around 1900, a story that may serve as a parable about artistic originality. The painter "was suffering of a lingering malady that confined him to his bed. He had been a good painter but his productions did not differ stylistically in any way from those of his tribe. During his long illness he would sit on his bed, holding his brush between his lips, silent and apparently oblivious of his surroundings. He could hardly be induced to speak, but when he spoke he dilated upon his visions of designs that he could no longer execute." Artists in this tradition, according to Boas, do not copy, although they may appear to be doing so from the outside. They are confined by the expectation that they obey a tradition and a style. But they do not work from patterns; rather, they work out the design in their head and then try to realize it, inevitably encountering practical obstacles that force them to alter their plan. The artists of Vancouver Island, insisting on their own creativity, "claim that the new pattern actually appeared to them in a dream." From the outside, the tradition seems closed. The premium is on continuity, not innovation. Yet the artists themselves are inspired. They do not simply copy but rather see patterns in visions and dreams. To the artist it feels like creativity, just as it must have to European medieval artists (most—some really were creative).

Such enabling fictions depend on limited knowledge of the art of the past. When there is too much knowledge, the artist feels oppressed. The thickening of the annals bore upon European and American artists in the eighteenth and nineteenth centuries. The piling up of historical knowledge must be finally the main cause of modernism in art. Some artists tried to redefine artistic achievement as total independence from art history, declining any longer to force their inventive powers into alignment with the tradition. This is completely different from Mazzoleni's attitude. The most restless artists of the nineteenth century either wanted to scrap the canon and build an entirely new one, or proceed without looking backwards at all. Some artists broke with the state-sponsored art academies, arbiters of good form since Vasari's time.

Artists feel but resist pressure to participate in a narrative defined and chronicled by historians, critics, and curators of modern art. They do not wish to hear that their works rhyme with patterns of collective production, nor do they wish to think that one day their work will be judged only in relation to the standards of their own time. Therefore they do not like to hear this said about artists of the past. For an artist, the art of the past is either alive, in the sense that it requires no apologies and no translation by a scholar, or it simply no longer exists as art.

The attitude of the architect Frank Gehry (b. 1929) is typical. Gehry professes great interest in the history of art. This is an aspect of his claim to have defied, as an architect, the formal principles established by the International Style, a movement dominant throughout the middle of the twentieth century that asserted its independence from the entire previous history of architecture. Gehry defines his whole achievement as a break with an architectural style that defined itself as amnesiac. But when the anamnesiac Gehry says he is interested in history, he is not saying that he spends hours in the library reading scholarly books, nor is he saying that he endeavors to enter imaginatively into the past in order to understand artists in their own historical settings. What he means is that he looks to artists of the past whom he admires and tries to imitate whatever it is that makes them timeless. For example, Gehry says that "if you look at a Rembrandt painting, it feels like he just painted it, and I was looking for that immediacy in architecture." In other words, what distinguishes the "great" historical artist like Rembrandt is, for Gehry, the fact that his paintings don't look historical at all.

Gehry is not intimidated by art-historical scholarship. He feels free to identify his peers among historical artists by his own lights, without any advice from historians. He does not credit art historians with creating or framing Rembrandt, except in the practical sense that they help sustain the institutions of collecting and conservation that have protected the canvases all these years.

Gehry meets the historical work of art in the present tense. Some mid-twentieth-century thinkers offered support to such an approach. The French philosopher Gaston Bachelard, for example, wrote in 1957, about poetry, that

> a philosopher who had formed all his thought by adhering to the fundamental themes of the philosophy of science, who followed, as closely as he could, the active axis of rationalism, the axis of rationalism emerging out of contemporary science, must forget his learning, break with all his habits of philosophical inquiry, if he wishes to study the problems posed by the poetic imagination. Here, the cultural past does not count; the long labor of connections and constructions of thoughts, day in and day out, is ineffectual.

And this is simply what many artists believe. The past of art like the past of thought is "ineffectual." The image is no more dependent on the past than is a cast of the dice. The image appears out-of-state, displaced, an "ecstasy" in Bachelard's phrase: "You have to be present, present to the image in the instant of the image: if there is a philosophy of poetry, this philosophy must be born and reborn on the occasion of a dominant verse, in the total adherence to an isolated image, precisely in the ecstasy of the image's novelty."

The artist rolls the dice and starts art history over again, every time. The sculptor Eva Hesse (1936–1970), in an interview near the end of her life, put it in plain terms:

> I don't know if I am completely out of the tradition. I know art history and I know what I believe in. I know where I come from and who I am related to or the work that I have looked at and that I am really personally moved by and felt close to or am connected or attached to. But I feel so strongly that the only art is the art of the artist personally and found out as much as possible [sic] for himself and by himself. So I am aware of connectiveness — it is impossible to be isolated completely — but my interest is solely in finding my own way.… Critics, art historians, museums, and galleries do like to make a movement for their own aims and for art history and to make people understand, but I wonder about that.

Hesse was not interested in the progressive narrative of art history, but she was also not interested in an ironic, primitivist counternarrative either. In this interview — in which she spoke of the "fantastic chaos," inexplicable in its day, of the paintings of Vincent van Gogh, who died young but not as young as Hesse would — she expressed ambivalence about duration itself:

> CN: But you are concerned with the idea of lasting?
>
> EH: Well, I am confused about that as I am about life.… Life doesn't last; art doesn't last. It doesn't matter…I feel that if I make something, I'd like a photograph of it and then I could keep it or give it away or sell it, but I would like some record.

Hesse brings art-historical consciousness down to the level of the absolutely personal. She says she simply wants a photo of her work as a supplement to her own memory. She trusts no written narrative and is not interested in being inscribed into someone else's annals. The symbiosis between the writing of art history and the making of art, initiated in the mid-sixteenth century, is arrested.

Gehry and Hesse's indifference to scholarship, even disrespect for writing, repersonalizes memory. According to Plutarch and Pausanias, Mneme, or memory, was one of the three original muses. She supported the performance of music and poetry. Later, there were nine muses and Clio, History, was one of them. In these myths memory and history are differentiated. Learning from experience is not the same as studying a history which lies beyond your experience. Eva Hesse was not poring over books, but she was also not performing the same act over and over. She was learning from experience, but it was her own experience, and so she had no need for history.

The weight of historical knowledge is rather greater today than it was for Antonio Maria Mazzoleni. Vasari planted a tree where there is now a forest. The facts amassed between 1550 and 1950 obscure narrative lines and expose causality and continuity as fictions. Artists, in these centuries, oriented themselves by art history. But empirical historical scholarship, in fulfilling itself, also neutralized itself. The twentieth-century artist lost interest in history. Pace Hesse, however, most artists remain attached to the promise of the annals, which do not assess their work relatively but absolutely. The aspiration to fame is a constant that overrides the break in style represented by modernism.

Typological History

The annals give shape to history by preferring some works over others on the basis of supposedly nonlocal criteria. Another form of historical selection, one that uses different criteria, we will call *typology.*

According to Michel de Certeau, a Western society seeks to dominate its pasts in order to clear out space for an autonomous present. Beyond the West, by contrast, "the past is a treasure placed in the *midst* of society." "In India, for example, 'new forms never drive the old ones away.' Rather, there exists a 'stratified stockpiling.'" The West converts the past into a blank page in hopes of writing its own narrative of linear progress on it. The Western approach must fail, for Certeau, because the past will survive, recur, haunt, seep back in around the edges.

The contrasting of linear and nonlinear concepts of time is a standard way of differentiating the West from everyone else. But the temporal stratification and recursivity that Certeau describes are also aspects of the European experience of form. A Christian basilical church remembers the Biblical prescription of a temple's proportions and so is linked to the Jewish synagogue. It also remembers the profane Roman structure, a royal hall, from which it takes its name. In the course of the Middle Ages and especially in the Renaissance, the builders of churches added references to the sacred architecture of the Romans and Greeks, the forms of the temple. Architecture itself became a mnemotechnics through mimicking old ways of building, incorporating real fragments of old structures into the new, and proposing forms as symbols of complicity with the past. Typology is the construal of the overlap between old and new forms as the correlative of an invisible homology between past and present. Typology, as long as it works, encourages an inference of community across time based on a hypothesis of meaningful—that is, not merely expedient or technologically determined—conformity to a remote or lost original.

The aim or effect of typology is to preempt or disable writing. Typology is a way of letting artifacts themselves write history. Authority is located not in the present, but elsewhere.

Typology is vulnerable to empirical scholarship, which is chronologically realist and attempts to identify origin points in close proximity to events and artifacts. The second-century Greek writer Pausanias wrote a detailed description of the notable sights of his country, especially sanctuaries, temples, and tombs. He describes a cave at Mount Elaius, near Phigalia in Arcadia, where Demeter, angry and grieving over the death of Persephone, once hid herself away, ruining the local harvest. A conversation with the Fates, sent by Zeus, softened her heart. "For these reasons, the Phigalians say, they concluded that this cavern was sacred to Demeter and set up in it a wooden image." The people no longer remember, Pausanias says, who made this image, nor how it caught fire. Pausanias reports, however, that they know in some detail what it looked like: Demeter was depicted seated on a rock; she had the head of a horse with images of serpents and beasts coming out of it; her black tunic of mourning reached to her feet. They know this because all cult images of the Black Demeter look alike: "Why they had the image made after this fashion is plain to any intelligent man who is learned in traditions." The image of the Black Demeter has no history, because the tradition provides a template. Every Black Demeter complies with a type, the statue erected at Mount Elaius.

A type is a score, or set of instructions, prefiguring the future production of artifacts, just as the ascent of Mount Carmel by Elijah prefigured the scene in the Garden of Gesthemane. The score yields a class of objects, spread across time, united by their compliance with the score. Tokens of the same type are for all practical purposes equivalent, interchangeable. When the archetype survives, compliance or noncompliance of the tokens can be directly measured. If not, the score or instructions—the list of constitutive and not merely contingent attributes of the arche-type—can only be respected if they have been translated into an archiving medium. The list of attributes of the Black Demeter is such a score, abstracted, supposedly, from a real, once-existing type.

Pausanias found no cult image at all at Mount Elaius. He learned from the locals that after the destruction of the original image, agriculture suffered again, and that the Phigalians were advised by the oracle at Delphi to reestablish the cult of Demeter in the cave. "They persuaded Onatas of Aegina, son of Micon, to make them an image of Demeter at a price." The artist's name permits Pausanias to assign a date to the image: about two generations after the Persian invasion of Greece, i.e., the fifth century BC. He interrupts his description of the site to provide the evidence for this art-historical discovery. He reproduces two inscriptions at Olympia that connect Onatas to a sculpture memorializing a certain Heiron, despot of Syracuse in the time of Xerxes. This is chronological realism, achieved by a collation of different time scales to produce one master time scale that is real, not constructed, and that can serve as a fixed measure.

Pausanias also mentions that Onatas made the statue "for a price," reminding the reader that art is also a commodity and so demystifying the chain of cult images. His research introduces the possibility of a leveling of the sacred and the profane to a common descriptive denominator. Pausanias reveals that he came to Phigalia "mainly to see this Demeter." But he himself did not offer a sacrifice to the goddess, "that being a custom of the natives." He is ready to believe that Onatas made a reliable copy in bronze of the original wooden Demeter, but his explanation of the artist's ability to recover the appearance of that lost, archaic cult image, so protecting the legitimacy of the typological chain, differs from the explanation offered by the locals. Onatas was "guided partly by a picture or copy of the ancient wooden image which he discovered, but mostly (so goes the story) by a vision that he saw in dreams." Pausanias has come up against a system of mental habits that fabricates continuity. The local dream story mystifies the chain of copies and "covers for" the inevitable drift from the aspect of the original. It is also a way of designating the mysteriousness of artistic creation, which can never be reduced entirely to compliance with typology—just as the Mexican miracle-paintings remind us that every painting, no matter how seemingly conventional, springs from an experience of disengagement with everyday time. Pausanias hypothesizes, instead, that the artist was working from a copy.

"Most of the Phigalians," Pausanias reports, "were ignorant that [the cult image] had ever existed at all." And yet someone must have told him about Onatas and the substitution of the wooden image by the bronze image. "The oldest…of the inhabitants I met," meanwhile, told him that "three generations before his time some stones had fallen on the image out of the roof; these crushed the image, destroying it utterly. Indeed, in the roof I could still discern plainly where the stones had broken away." "Three generations" is a formula one often meets with in oral history: someone remembers a tale told to him by his mother, who in turn had heard it from her father. Pausanias is careful to record his verification of the story through autopsy. He inspects the roof.

Unmentioned by Pausanias is the fact that the modern inhabitants of Phigalia had learned to live without any image of Demeter at all, and all the while tending her shrine. They had accepted a break in the tradition comparable to the past ones he has learned about. It is not clear from the account whether the Phigalians had any interest in mending the tradition. Perhaps the Phigalians felt that the bronze image by the celebrated artist Onatas could not so easily be replaced as the old wooden image had been, and their conception of the image as a host for Demeter—as a ritual instrument—no longer outweighed their conception of the image as an artwork. It is possible to imagine a cult without an image. The question is whether an image can survive its disengagement from a cult. Already within Pausanias's account we glimpse the basic superfluity of art that will interfere with art history's struggle for space in the modern university.

Typology allows communities to use art in order to produce a picture of continuity, beyond art, where this is seen to be wanting. Whereas the annals were a pattern imposed on the production of art based on value judgments, typology is the perception of a pattern in historical life beyond art, a pattern that is supposedly really there, even if the elements composing the pattern can be switched in and out. The typological mentality does not recognize an independent history of art. The works of art themselves knit history together. The works are chosen on the basis of their likelihood to support the hypothesis of continuity. Typological accounts exploit qualities of images (to appear as relics, survivals; to act as hosts for deities; to kindle the imagination) in order to sustain that hypothesis.

If buildings, sculptures, and paintings are ever going to provide anything beyond shelter and distraction; if they are to function as symbols; if a society wishes to entrust such artifacts with its stories and its values;

then there will have to be a typological system. If symbolic meaning is to be broadcast beyond local audiences, such artifacts will need to be copied. Typology is an economy: if everything were preserved, and if everything preserved were understood on its own terms, that is, non-typologically, there would be a paralyzing superabundance of meaning. That paralysis is an imaginable destination of modern scholarship and preservationism.

Typology does not recognize a history of art, but it also does not recognize a history of religions. It suppresses plurality in favor of teleology. Typology works backward from a standpoint of confidence in the truth in the present. It creates a genealogy of the present belief system, so marginalizing all the competitors. Not even Pausanias, and certainly not his hosts, were interested in the traces of archaic cults of Phigalia, except insofar as they were the prehistory of the familiar modern cult. Any prehistoric religion that did not fit within a typology was erased. This violence is present also within the examples Certeau gives, although the violence is masked by the function they serve within Western discourse, namely, to relativize or critique the West.

A relic, or real material sample of the past, can either ratify or undermine a typology. Typological links between past and present are sustained by the axiom that all tokens of a given type are mutually interchangeable. The relic has the power to diminish the authority of the tokens, unless the relic is taken to *be* the very type that organizes the tokens. The relic stands to the typological token as the spolium, or real fragment of architecture, stands to the mere citation or repetition of architectural form. The relic evinces a reality that is either suppressed by typology, or is that reality that the typology was designed to assert. The body of the saint, for example, is a focus of devotional attention that has not been authorized by earlier saints, or by scripture. The relic is nonsubstitutable; it is not linked by resemblance to anything else.

The lives of the Christian saints are recorded by hagiography. But their physical remains are also preserved, and the distinction is marked by the attribution of healing powers to the body parts. Typology may be the attempt to do without both writing and relics, but the history of art in Christian Europe is not only sustained by copying (typology, substitution) and by the written annals but is also displayed in churches and museums. Copies and relics are displayed side by side and supplement the writings with what Claude Lévi-Strauss called "diachronic flavor." The nonsubstitutable artwork makes the argument that art is not just a carrier of information and that something is lost in a typological system. The cooperation of relics and writing ensures the very interpenetration of present and past described by Certeau as the marker, supposedly, of the non-Western society.

Artists will see typology as a normative system that diminishes the role of innovative creativity. Typology levels works on the basis of content and on the basis of a link to an origin that is not an artist. The tension between the two ways of thinking about art is clear in the Demeter story recounted by Pausanias. A history of images of Demeter as works of art, such as a modern art historian might produce, is no longer dedicated to maintaining continuity between each work and Demeter herself. Already Pausanias in the second century inserts Black Demeter into a history of art, with dates.

Since typology is a defense against chronological realism, artists may at times choose to ally themselves with typology, depending on whom they perceive to be their enemy. They may feel that typology captures a quality of art that historical thinking overlooks, namely its unstable anchoring in time. For this reason typological thinking has not been limited to premodern or non-European societies. Still, the basic trend in Europe since the century of Vasari is away from typology. The desire for artistic freedom came to outweigh the need to profit from typology's chronological instability.

In European modernity, architecture is where the typological mode is likely to persist. Architecture was slower than painting to extricate itself from typological systems because the meaning of architectural form was less specific and therefore did not interfere so readily with new functions and belief systems. Typology is another way to understand the so-called historicism of nineteenth- and twentieth-century architecture, that is, the programmatic citation and adaptation of historical styles. The Cathedral of Speyer, a mighty basilica of the Romanesque period—the round-arched style of Mérimée's Saint-Savin, the style that preceded Gothic—was heavily damaged by French soldiers in 1689. Nearly a century later the architect Franz Ignaz Neumann rebuilt the westwork or monumental porch in a contemporary, that is to say, Louis XVI style. Some decades later the Bavarian King Ludwig I commissioned a cycle of mural paintings in the interior by painters working in the Nazarene or neo-medieval tradition. Finally the architect Heinrich Hübsch undertook a pioneering and subtle restoration in the spirit of the original imperial church of the eleventh century.

Between 1854 and 1858 Hübsch reversed Neumann's intervention and rebuilt the westwork in the Romanesque manner, now—only a decade after Mérimée's report on Saint-Savin—a style in vogue. Hübsch reconstructed the octagonal tower over the crossing and the west towers. Hübsch was well-versed in medieval architecture, and yet he permitted himself many liberties, not only departing from the reality of the old cathedral, whose appearance was attested in old engravings, but also violating the principles of Romanesque architecture. On the façade he added a pointed gable, flat pilasters, and plenty of colorful brick ornament. He borrowed the form of the windows of the westwork from the south transept. He opened a rose window in the façade. Over the central portal he mounted five statues representing cities. Hübsch valued pastness itself, and so declined to rebuild the church in the style of his own time, whatever that might have been. He revisited the past, and then dominated it.

Hübsch did not want his additions to read as authored, nor do they. Only a small proportion of modern visitors to Speyer notice that many features of the church date to the nineteenth century. In fact, his modifications have fed into the collectively held image of Romanesque architecture, for Speyer is an iconic building, the burial site of eight Holy Roman emperors and German kings, a building much admired and much photographed. Hübsch wanted to participate in the historical building that had been entrusted to him. He took advantage of the typological hypothesis to use the building as something like a painter's canvas.

This is monumental art history in the manner of Cheops, now informed by art historical scholarship.

In 1828, several decades earlier, Hübsch had published a treatise, entitled *In What Style Should We Build?*, on the predicament of modern architects who no longer felt bound by an academic orthodoxy and instead faced an array of historical styles—Egyptian, Greek, Roman, Byzantine, Romanesque, Gothic—laid out for them by the first illustrated art historical publications. Hübsch recommended choosing a historical style, then stripping it of later "reminiscences" or self-conscious emulations of ancient, supposedly authoritative forms. His generation was already tired of the fashion for Gothic form, so he chose Romanesque,

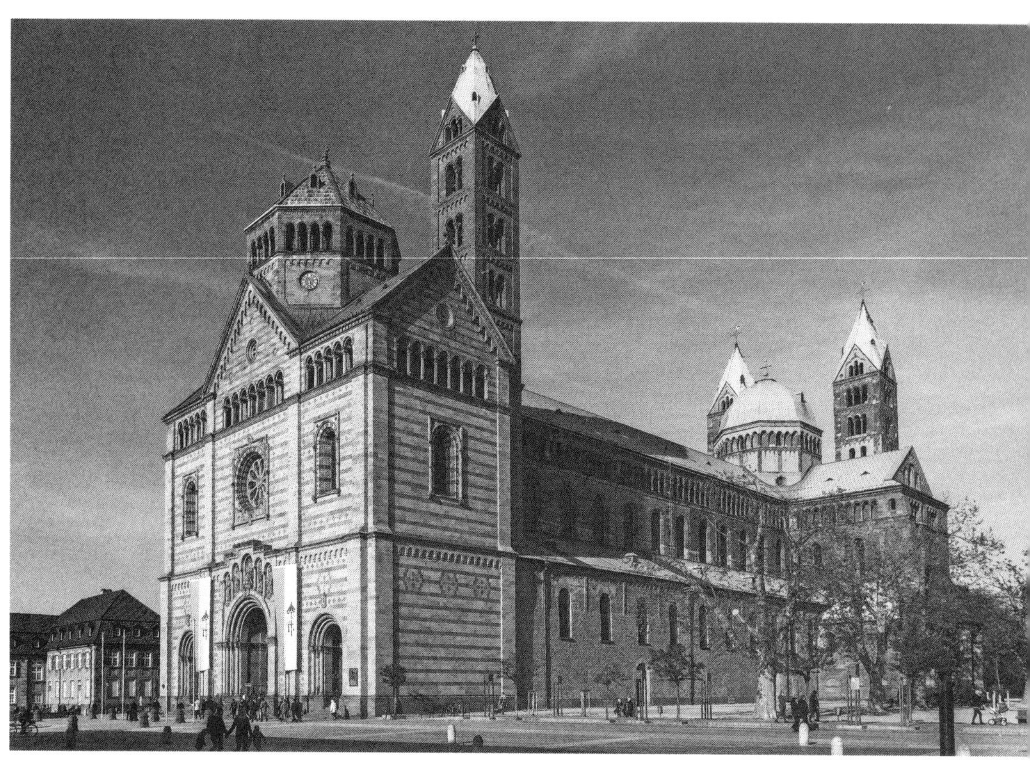

Cathedral of Speyer (eleventh, eighteenth, and nineteenth centuries). The pointed gable on the façade, the rose window, and the five statues above the main portal are inventions by the nineteenth-century architect Heinrich Hübsch.

a style that seemed to have explored the basic principles of building in stone. By analysis Hübsch arrives at what he calls the "objective skeleton" of Romanesque, which can then serve as the basis for a new style, admitting the inventions of the modern artist. This was exactly his procedure at Speyer. This new style was to resemble what the Romanesque would have become if the builders of the Middle Ages had simply gone on building, responding to local and functional conditions, without ever looking back to compare their buildings to ancient Roman forms. Hübsch's fallacy is his assumption that medieval builders were perceiving form purely as form and not instead as the carrier of symbolic and historical meaning, binding their hopeful new constructions to distant authority. When he adapted an historical formal vocabulary to create a modern Romanesque at Speyer, Hübsch appeared to be extending the typological principle deep into post-Enlightenment territory. His own treatise, however, reveals that he was in fact unaware that premodern builders were unable to select freely from a menu of historical forms as Hübsch himself felt entitled to do; rather they were under constant pressure from the past and could not imagine their own freedom.

Fabulous History

An art-historical fable is a story that relativizes a conventional criterion of value by redistributing praise and blame—raising the low and humbling the mighty, for example. This is the mode of irony, the third mode available to the modern art historian.

A fable may expose an incomplete match between art and power. Such a story is often heard in proximity to cosmic art, the art that sustains worldly hierarchy by asserting its homology with the structure of the universe. Herodotus learned that the sovereign Cheops and his brother, after building the pyramids on the backs of the people, had closed the temples for 106 years. The hatred of the people for those kings was so great that they were unwilling to pronounce their names. "Instead, they say the pyramids belonged to a shepherd called Philitis, who at this time used to graze his flocks on the same land." The fable is pastoral because, like the pastoral poetry of Renaissance Italy and England, which transposed criticism of the social order into the coarse speech of shepherds, it ironically prefers the low to the high. The shepherd, who does not participate in agriculture or city building, exposes art as an ornament imposed on lives. That shepherd would not have pitied the people of Phigalia who, in Pausanias's account, became nomads, eating wild fruit, taking up pasturing again, after the failure of agriculture that followed upon the loss of the image of Demeter and the neglect of her cult.

The Egyptian people tried to cancel the sovereign's monument by renaming it. They failed, of course. Herodotus, inclusive, transcribed the pastoral fable but at the same time overwrote it with his own report on the technical achievement of the pyramids. A fable is a protest not only against Cheops's self-assertion through monuments but also against the totalizing explanations produced by the retrospective shaping of history through annals or typologies.

A sophisticated art-historical chronicle will be shot through with such ironic readjustments of value. The Chinese annalist of the ninth century, Zhang Yanyuan, balanced admiration for the technical prowess of recent painters against reverence for the painters of antiquity. He found ways to apologize for the deficiencies of the ancients:

> The paintings of high antiquity were simple in technique and modest
> in conception, yet had an elegant propriety. Such was the school of
> Ku K'ai-chih and Lu T'an-wei [later fourth and fifth centuries].

Implicitly Zhang is identifying a deficiency of modern painters, a shortfall of "elegant propriety." His reverse partisanship questions realism as a goal:

> The painters of antiquity were sometimes able to transmit formal
> likeness while endowing it with a noble vitality (*ku-ch'i*). They sought
> for what was beyond formal likeness in their painting. This is very
> difficult to discuss with vulgar people. As for today's painters, even
> if they attain formal likeness, they do not generate spirit resonance
> (*ch'i-yün*).

Zhang invites his non-vulgar readers into a counternarrative whereby even clumsiness might yield a kind of realism:

> Wang Wei [eighth century] was skilled in painting landscapes whose
> style embraced the present and the past. Those in people's collections
> were mostly done under his direct supervision by artisans. Spreading colors for the primeval wilderness and densely forming distant
> trees, they erred in the direction of clumsiness. Yet if they reverted to
> detailed artfulness, they only missed reality all the more.

Giorgio Vasari, writing in Florence seven centuries later, was incapable of such refined judgments on old artists. He awards even Giotto only half-hearted praise:

> Anyone can grasp, amidst the poverty of art and the poverty of the times, the quality of his judgment in his narrative scenes, his observance of the expressions, and his easy obedience to a natural manner, because it is also clear that his figures do what they are meant to do. Thus it is evident that Giotto had very good judgment, if not perfect.

Vasari's apology for the incorrect drawing of the thirteenth- and fourteenth-century painters was limited:

> I do not wish for anyone to think that I am so crude or so lacking in judgment that I am unaware that the works by Giotto and Andrea Pisano and Nino [Pisano] and all the rest, ... if you compare them to those who came after, do not merit extraordinary nor even middling praise. I was aware of this when I praised them [in the first part of the *Lives*].

He musters two arguments in their favor, however: he says that early Tuscan artists must be judged in relation to their own times, and he notes that aspects of their art point forward to the praiseworthy Florentine art of his own time:

> Anyone who considers the quality of those times, the scarcity of artisans, and the difficulty of finding good assistants, will hold them to be not only beautiful, as I said, but miraculous, and will take infinite pleasure in seeing those first principles and those sparks of quality that began to revive in painting and sculpture.

The old art that Vasari really admires is pagan art, the statuary of ancient Greece and Rome, whose excellence compels him to abandon any pretense of disapproval of the false religion, the compunction that had muted admiration for pagan art throughout the Middle Ages. Vasari's hospitality to the foreign gods permits him to concede that pagan art overpowers Christian art with its sensuality and animation. Vasari and the Florentine academy sponsored a new art that cloaked Christian subjects in forms borrowed from pagan art. This art exposed itself to an ironic challenge from Christians who might have felt that correct content was more important than beautiful style. The praise of the humble and homely is basic to Christian thought and might have prompted calls for the restoration of a simpler, less luxurious devotional art. Cicero had identified three levels of rhetorical or literary style, determined by subject matter: the high, middle, and low styles. The low discourse or *sermo humilis* was colloquial, realist, dialogic, vigorous. Augustine accepted this hierarchy, but deemed the low style appropriate for any subject, even weighty and tragic subjects.

Such irony was not unknown in Vasari's time, even if rarely applied to the arts. In his *Adages* the philologist and theologian Desiderius Erasmus traced the idea of the low style back to pagan thought, recalling the character Alcibiades in Plato's *Symposium*, who speaks of the Silenus statues whose ugly exteriors open to reveal a beautiful youth in the interior, a metaphor for the noncoordination of body and soul. And in fact many reform-minded clerics of Erasmus's day, Protestants and Catholics alike, urged stylistic temperance in the name of a more seemly devotional art. A homely Christian painting, they argued, is a Silenus concealing a worthy message. But the pagan-modern ideal style was irresistible; the gratifying Christian art of Raphael and Michelangelo sealed the new covenant; and a counternarrative to Vasari was slow in coming.

Until the eighteenth century medieval paintings were treated with disrespect. The altarpieces and icons displaced by modern art were relegated to dark corners or storage cupboards, or simply discarded. In the eighteenth century for the first time Italian collectors, clerics, patricians, and antiquaries began to salvage old panel paintings. Some painters copied and restored old panels. This was the zero hour of modern art history: neither Vasari's stinting admiration for the first masters of the Florentine school of painting, nor the celebratory narration of the rise and fall of ancient Greek art of the historian Johann Joachim Winckelmann, but the unexpected assignation of value by a few eccentric collectors and artists to fourteenth- and early fifteenth-century paintings that seemed to match no one's idea of artistic beauty. Modern art history is basically a cycle of fables and counterfables that redistribute artistic value and finally tend toward a total relativity of judgment. European art history over the course of the nineteenth and twentieth centuries will include ever more and censure ever less, learning to praise not only the Italian gold-ground paintings but also the world of forms beyond Europe, long scorned. Against the academic obsession with the idealized human body as depicted in ancient Greek or Italian Renaissance art, art history learned to esteem the unpracticed and abstinent art of the Christian Middle Ages; the apparently unrefined and awkward art of the Bronze Age; the form-worlds of Asia and Africa, so long invisible to European eyes.

Admittedly, the eighteenth-century collecting of Italian and, before long, Netherlandish panel paintings was an art-historical fable that had not yet found its moral, or message. The early collectors did not articulate, or at least did not put into writing, the basis of their reverse partisanship. No doubt, some were simply drawn to the rare and the curious. Not until the very end of the century, inspired by old Netherlandish panel paintings, did some German writers spell out the upending of the history of European art. In 1802 the German critic Friedrich Schlegel visited the Musée du Louvre in Paris where he saw, and described without condescension, the altarpiece of the Adoration of the Lamb by Jan van Eyck, dated 1432, which had been stolen from the church of St. Bavo in Ghent by Napoleon. Of the three life-sized images of the Madonna, God the Father, and John the Baptist, Schlegel wrote:

> The Egyptian sublimity and constraint of these erect, severe divine figures, as if from a gray antiquity, command earnest reverence, and for all that forbidding sobriety attract us like the inscrutable monument of a greater and more austere prehistory.

By the 1820s admiration for Gothic churches and late medieval painting, in direct conflict with the conventional admiration for the high-flown achievements of neoclassical architecture and the modern schools of painting descending not from van Eyck but from Raphael and Michelangelo, was well established. And yet, as we have seen, a further fabulous reversal of value loomed.

Heinrich Hübsch and Prosper Mérimée developed concepts of art sufficiently abstract to bridge the gulf between the twelfth and the nineteenth centuries. A still more thorough relativist, who sees art itself in historical perspective, who considers art an accompaniment to life that evolves in rhythm with social change, would hesitate to pronounce any aesthetic judgment at all. Historical research refers every artistic phenomenon back to a deeper layer of reality, such that all is explicable. Ralph Waldo Emerson, in his essay "History" of 1841, rejects the very concept of pastness: "All inquiry into antiquity,—all curiosity respecting the Pyramids, the excavated cities, Stonehenge, the Ohio Circles,

Mexico, Memphis,—is the desire to do away with this wild, savage, and preposterous There or Then, and introduce in its place the Here and the Now." We are baffled by a Gothic cathedral, which surely "was by man, but we find it not in our man." So we study the history of its making; and we study the history of architecture, back to the very origins of building; and we study the history of the Catholic Church and its art; and in the end "we have, as it were, been the man that made the minster." "I can find … the genius and creative principle of each and of all eras in my own mind." Friedrich Nietzsche quoted a passage from Emerson's essay as the epigraph of his *Gay Science* (1881) (the book's title, too, echoes Emerson): "To the poet, to the philosopher, to the saint, all things are friendly and sacred, all events profitable, all days holy, all men divine." This is a joyous relativism. Not only every artwork but every world and every worldview is equally innocent, equally precious, equally acquainted with the real. The judgment of taste, solidly grounded in the present, comes to seem provincial. The present itself comes to seem provincial. *Tout comprendre, c'est tout pardonner.* To forgive means to hold no one accountable for misrecognizing a norm that stands outside history; to identify no Archimedean point of judgment, no platform even from which to launch an ironic fable. Absolute relativism is an ethical position, tolerant and apologetic. Disharmony or ugliness is "suffered." And as such it is a position not so easily abandoned. The American philosopher Cornel West described the adoption of the historical attitude in the nineteenth century as "a crossing of the Rubicon." West's pragmatist hero John Dewey wrote in the 1930s of a "thorough relativity of technique to form in art":

> While there is not continuation or repetition in any esthetic art, neither is there, of necessity, advance…. What happens in the movement of art is emergence of new materials of experience demanding expression, and therefore involving in their expression new forms and techniques. Manet went back in time to achieve his brush-work, but his return involved no mere copying of an old technique.

Relativism has become second nature to modern historians. It is hard to recover the nonrelativist mentalities that once prevailed and were never questioned: the preference for the local and familiar; the worship of ancestors; the admiration for the precious, the rare, the well crafted, the monumental, the beautiful.

Empirical Scholarship

Art history as an academic subject had to win space within the so-called philosophical faculty, descendant of the faculty of arts, which in the medieval university had provided the propaedeutic course to the faculties of theology, jurisprudence, and medicine. One might be surprised to learn how successful art history was. Between 1850 and 1869, in all the universities in Germany, six individuals received the *Habilitierung* as art historians, the second advanced degree that brings the right to teach at the professorial level. This represented 3 per cent of the total of such degrees awarded in all the *Geisteswissenschaften* or humanistic disciplines. Between 1890 and 1909, 44 *Habilitation* degrees in art history were awarded, 8.7 per cent of the total. In other words, art history between 1869 and 1909 expanded nearly three times faster than did the humanities as a whole. The 44 *Habilitierte* in art history between 1890 and 1909 hold their own alongside the 52 in medieval and modern history, 48 in classical philology, and 44 in German philology.

The academization of art history in nineteenth- and early twentieth-century Europe coincides with the self-emancipation of art from the academies of art. The artists had entered the academy in order to win freedom from market pressures. The art academy had been a free zone for experimentation under the overall umbrella of the state, an extension of the privileges of the court artist to a wider population of artists. Beginning, more or less, with the abandonment in 1810 of the Academy of Fine Arts in Vienna by a group of painters calling themselves the Nazarenes, and culminating in the formation in 1897 of the Wiener Secession by a group of artists who had resigned from the artists' association known as the Künstlerhaus, more and more artists fled the state-sponsored academies, or regrouped in counteracademies. The enshrinement of art history in the university at the very moment when artists turn their backs definitively on the academies symbolizes the modern estrangement of scholarship on historical art from the production of new art.

It is in the nature of a method to be reused (the word means "after-road," a path to be pursued). A method is meant to be impersonal, a road open to all. The German-speaking universities created a model that was already exported to America and Japan in the late nineteenth century, and everywhere else in the twentieth century. Whether empirical method was imposed or invited, and to what extent this method was altered and took on local variations, is hard to say.

The skeptical, empirical attitude was not invented in nineteenth-century Europe. Already Herodotus tested local legends against his own observation, mistrusting what the priests told him and so offering himself as a kind of anti-priest, as does the modern university professor. In exchange for the promise of neutrality and transparency, society has given scholars a high degree of freedom in choosing their own research topics. Empirical method is seen as a liberation from the authorities of the state, Church, custom, and property. Empirical method aims at, and sometimes achieves, a high degree of disengagement from chauvinism, prejudice, and self-interest. The scholar dislocates herself and so multiplies her reality. She can travel from one world to another, or enfold one world in another. This mentality works against the pyramid of Cheops, and against all monuments, which try to impose worlds. The art historian's reluctance to evaluate and so participate in his own objects of study brings with it a certain distanced sympathy for alterity. Instead of asking: how am I involved? the scholar tries to see things from the point of view of the stranger.

The empirical method's pretense to disinterest is total: it dismisses all other written accounts of the past as mere legends, or mere ideology. It depreciates the accounts of the past offered by works of art as unreliable and overly patterned. Empiricism broke the bond between art and the state, but at the cost of a misrecognition of the anarchic, centrifugal nature of art, the very force that the state (and the Church) had once tried to harness.

800–1400

Typological art history creates histories of truth, or religion, by triage: some contents are kept, others are substituted, and still others are obliterated. The sign that something is amiss, that the typological economy is imperfect, is *superstition*, literally a "standing-over." A superstition is an illegitimate survival of a belief into a new age, threatening to reveal that history has been shaped by mere beliefs and not by truth. In medieval Europe, the persistence of ancient Mediterranean or Germanic religious practices into the Christian era was described as such a standing-over, an overstaying. This is the exact opposite of a typological substitution, or legitimating survival. In his *History of the Bishops of Hamburg*, the eleventh-century chronicler Adam von Bremen offers "a few words about the superstitions of the Swedes." He reports that the Swedes have

> a very famous temple called Uppsala, situated not far from the city of Sigtuna and Björkö. In this temple, entirely decked out in gold, the people worship the statues of three gods in such wise that the mightiest of them, Thor, occupies a throne in the middle of the chamber; Wotan and Frikko have places on either side.

Adam's account concedes the failure of the bishops either to extirpate pagan practices from northern Europe or to overlay on the old ways an accommodating adaptation of the Christian cult. He then identifies the statues. Iconography, or: who is represented? is the basic art-historical question.

The significance of these gods is as follows: Thor, they say, presides over the air, which governs the thunder and lightning, the winds and rains, fair weather and crops. The other, Wotan—that is, the Furious—carries on war and imparts to man strength against his enemies. The third is Frikko, who bestows peace and pleasure on mortals. His likeness, too, they fashion with an immense phallus.

Adam diminishes the pagan cult by noting a parallel between the Norse gods and the gods of ancient Greece and Rome:

But Wotan they chisel armed, as our people are wont to represent Mars (*sicut nostri Martem solent*). Thor with his scepter apparently resembles Jove.

Adam von Bremen's comment is based on a confidence that "we," his Christian readers, know the iconography of the pagan gods—presumably from manuscript illuminations—and yet are in no danger of developing a secret admiration for the Norse cult on the basis of the parallel he observes, let alone drifting back into pagan worship. Adam is saying that the pagan and Norse peoples share a conventional system of writing with images—literally an "iconography"—that encourages them to denote a martial god with similar sets of attributes. He does not say whether he believes that Mars and Wotan really exist as irrelevant demons, or that they are pure inventions. The point is that their depictions are conventional and Christians can safely study them. Adam depreciates the Swedish gods as mere imitations of the Mediterranean gods, in fact no more than translations or substitutes. The depictions of the Christian holy personages—Christ, Mary, the saints—are by contrast not the mere products of an image-writing system but are enforced by the real, historical appearances of those individuals, carried down to us by chains of copies of authoritative images. This is typology.

In his comment on the pagan cult of heroes, Adam also suggests that the Swedes practice euhemerism:

The people also worship heroes made gods, whom they endow with immortality because of their remarkable exploits, as one reads in the Vita of Saint Ansgar they did in the case of King Eric.

In other words, they are unable to distinguish between saints and mere heroes and kings. Adam is unwilling to see in the Swedish practices any rapprochement with the Christian cult, which over the course of the eleventh century was still establishing itself in the region. He sees typology operating between two pagan cults, but not crossing the pagan-Christian divide. He is not prepared to see Christianity itself as a mere substitute for Greek and Roman paganism, allowing typology to carry content over from one belief system to another. The distinction between Christian and non-Christian was too decisive. It was identity itself, for there was no concept of Europe at this point, only Christendom. The contrast with Anita Brenner's syncretism is clear; Brenner did not really believe in any gods, only people. An art history like Adam von Bremen's, written from within a total orientation to a single god, is half blind. The typological approach to Christian monuments is too risky; when it develops later, it will signify acceptance of an independent history of building or image-making more real even than cosmology.

Adam von Bremen, secure in his own perch in Bremen—more secure than the missionaries in Mecklenburg, where not until a century later was the path clear to found the Cistercian abbey at Doberan—was sure of the breach between pagan and Christian. Things were not so simple in Italy, where Christianity's origins were commingled with pagan cults.

St. Francis (1181/82–1226) was praying before a painted crucifix in the church of San Damiano near Assisi when the Lord addressed him: "Francis, go and repair my house, which as you see, is falling into ruin." This happened in 1205; a century later the event was depicted on the walls of the basilical church dedicated to St. Francis at Assisi.

According to his biographer Bonaventura, Francis sold his possessions, including his horse, and gave the money to the priest at San Damiano. But nothing was done, and so Francis returned and labored over a period of several years, begging for money and even lugging stones. Francis also repaired the nearby church of St. Peter and the oratory known as the Porziuncola. Still later, Francis understood that God had been asking him to restore the Christian Church as a whole, or even to repair the covenant between God and man, and not literally to shore up crumbling walls. For Francis and his biographer, a church was no more than a structure marked by its form as a place where Christians met. Of course such a building must be in good repair. There is no need, Francis surely believed, for a church to represent by its form its own age. A church might well represent the longevity of the institution of the Church, however, not by the marks of age, but by compliance with the basic formal type of a Christian church: nave and transept forming a cross, the ground plan established in Italy by the Roman basilicas of the fourth century. This was the typological approach to building.

The church of San Damiano depicted by Giotto or his workshop at Assisi bears no resemblance to the actual single-aisled, barrel-vaulted structure. Instead we see the shell of a nave with ruined side aisles and a wooden and tiled roof, half intact. We have a clear view onto Francis and onto the green calotte of the apse and the painted Crucifix above the altar. San Damiano is forced by the painter to stand for all churches.

In 1228, two years after Francis's death, his followers began constructing the basilica on the edge of the hill at Assisi. The Lower Church was a squat crypt bored into the mountainside. A taller, more luminous church was constructed on top of it, and both were consecrated in 1253. The builders interpreted the archetypal form, the basilical hall, below as a reliquary for the remains of Francis, and above as a space for collective worship. Paintings on the walls narrated the Christian and Franciscan myths.

The basilica at Assisi was straightforward and functional, with few windows, a space designed for preaching. Still, the builders overlaid elegant grace notes learned from the cathedrals of France, the latest fashion in architecture: pilasters composed of bundles of colonettes, a rose window, four-part vaults, so introducing a stylistic reference point that would have little interested Francis himself. They ignored a possible third reference point, the point closest at hand but in time most remote: the Roman Temple of Minerva on the main street of the town of Assisi, just up the hill. The builders of the Franciscan basilica did not copy the pagan temple's ten-meter-tall fluted columns or its lavish acanthus-leaved capitals. They ignored the temple, a relic of the first century BC, because it honored the wrong god. The temple at Assisi is one of the best preserved pagan temples in Italy, but it enjoyed no prestige in a Christianized Europe, or only just enough prestige to avoid destruction.

The binarism of right and wrong worship structured the history of Christian art. History was understood as divided in two by the incarnation of God as Christ. The Christian consciousness of an irreversible transformation of life on earth interfered with recognition of the achievements of pre-Christians and non-Christians. Christian church architecture had in fact emerged out of Roman and Greek and other building practices in the eastern Mediterranean. Islamic architecture had in turn developed out of pagan Roman and Christian Roman architecture

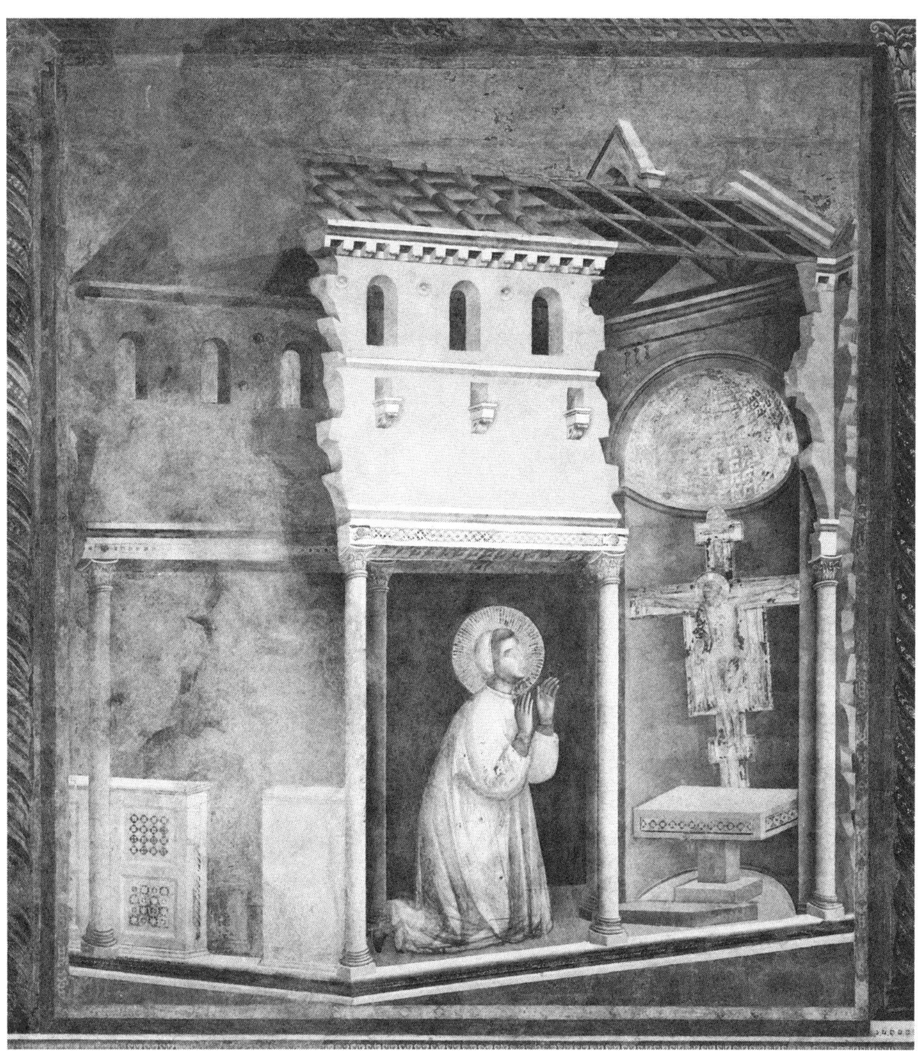

Giotto and workshop, *The Prayer in San Damiano, or The Miracle of the Crucifix* (c. 1300). Fresco in the Upper Church of the Basilica of St. Francis, Assisi, 270 × 230 cm. St. Francis addresses his prayer to a painted Crucifix, and a voice from the painting gives instructions.

as well as many other building traditions in the east. Maintenance of the strict distinction between Christian and non-Christian blocked the perception of difference inside the other-coded class. The twelfth-century Chanson de Roland, an epic poem about Charlemagne's conflict with the Muslims in Spain, described the emir carrying the "standard of Tervagant and Mohammed, and a statue of vile Apollo"—a double error, since the eighth-century Muslim warrior was as unlikely to be bearing an image of Mohammed as an image of an Olympian god. The fourteenth-century traveler's account attributed to John Mandeville described the statue of Jupiter in the Pantheon in Rome as "hir god that was their maumette": their "Mohammed," a generic term for an idol, based on the assumption that Muslims must be idol-worshippers, here transferred to the pagan sphere. European Christians purchased a continuous tradition at the price of the simplification of other peoples' histories.

The Temple of Minerva in Assisi was depicted in one of the wall paintings of the Upper Basilica at Assisi, another scene from the life of St. Francis: a simple man throws his cloak in homage before St. Francis. The portrait of the temple identified the location of the events in Francis's life. In the fresco, as in reality, the temple is neighbor to the Communal Palace with its campanile. But the temple's portrait is distorted. The artist—Giotto or one of his assistants, perhaps—shrank the building to human scale and reduced the number of columns from six to five. The painted columns are slender, in tune with the new French style rehearsed in the basilica housing the mural. The artist has added a cosmatesque frieze to the architrave and a rose window and two angel-like figures in the pediment. The variety of types of building and building styles are on display in the main street of Assisi. The pilgrim may have averted his gaze from this stone picture of art history, but once it has been represented a second time, in a beautiful painting, bent by the lens of the artist's imagination, the temple is harder to forget. Giotto set in motion an alternative history of forms, unlinked to ritual. His fictions of buildings gave buildings and styles a secondary fame, a luster of their own independent of their illustrations of the gods.

Some centuries after Giotto, when the strictly bipartite Christian historical schema and the Christian ritual itself were beginning to lose their grip, people learned for the first time to see the Roman temple as pure form. Johann Wolfgang von Goethe arrived in Assisi on October 26, 1786, and, so he says, hurried past the basilica: "The monstrous substructures of the Babylonian churches piled one on top of the other, where St. Francis rests, I left in my wake, with repulsion, for I thought that the minds one would find there were of the same stamp as that of my captain [a papal officer with whom Goethe had been traveling since Bologna, a man of simple and credulous views concerning religion]." Instead he climbed the hill to see the temple, which had been transformed in 1539 into a Marian church. This was the first complete ancient building Goethe had ever seen: "A modest temple, befitting such a small city, and yet so perfect, so beautifully conceived, that it would shine anywhere." A secular pilgrim, Goethe misprized the basilica for failing to attend to the lessons in good style offered by the temple. Goethe had been primed by his readings in the treatise on architecture by Andrea Palladio and a recent three-volume handbook for German travelers in Italy. The latter reassured him that the columns were in "good taste"; the former convinced him that there was only one good style, that the Greeks and Romans had achieved it, and that we would do well to imitate it. Goethe avers: "I couldn't get enough of the façade, of the artist's inspired logic, here, too." He describes the temple, correcting the exaggerations of Palladio's engraving ("he cannot have seen the temple himself"), which departs from reality, though far less drastically than Giotto's painting had. "What developed in me through looking at this work cannot be expressed, and will forever bring forth fruit."

In the Middle Ages admiration for the ancient forms had been rare and stinting, unless expressed well beyond the semantic reach of the Church. An Italian cleric, Restoro d'Arezzo, wrote a cosmological treatise in 1282, the *Composizione del Mondo*. He describes the excavation of vases near Arezzo, "more than a thousand years old," presumably Etruscan. They were decorated with plants and animals. Restoro reports that the experts, *il conoscitori*—one would like to know who they were—were delighted. Some artists wondered whether the vases were *cose santuarie*, liturgical implements. Others believed they were of divine origin. All marveled at the "human subtlety and artifice" of the objects. Once the questions of function and meaning were set aside, the fact remained: the pots were well made. The Etruscan artisans had understood the properties of their materials and the capacities of their tools. They knew how to match form to function, achieving a quality of rightness that brings a pleasure everyone has known and that transcends time and place. Restoro d'Arezzo could admire the Etruscan

pots because they lacked religious content. Whereas gods created ratios
of proximity and distance, plants and animals belonged to everyone.
The content of the images on the vases was life itself. The excellence of
ancient Etruscan art overrode the discontinuity between pagan and
Christian times mandated by the history of salvation. The criterion of
excellence created a class of well-made things independent of histories.

The historiography of art in thirteenth-century China was far more
developed than in Europe. The basis had been provided by the ninth-
century annalist Zhang Yanyuan, who was himself quoting and relaying still earlier texts. Interpolations to Zhang's text were made in the
Song period (960–1279); the compilation was edited five times in the
Ming period (1368–1644). Zhang's biographical approach is characteristic of courts, where rosters of venerated priests were preserved. Courts
and regimes, aiming to transcend their origins in force and match some
wider pattern of meaning, archive legitimating pasts. Zhang, who came
from a family of officials who were calligraphers and collectors, says that
painting began as a kind of writing. The relation of painting to writing is
remembered by the Chinese logographic and Mayan mixed logographic
and logosyllabic writing systems. But the idea of the painter as a scribe
also holds in cultures where writing is alphabetic, for example, as we will
see, Persian. The scribal basis of the art of painting is reinforced by origin myths. The earliest scribes, according to a text by a seventh-century
court official quoted by Zhang, "had the work of embodying entities so
as to illuminate the distant and reveal the obscure, matching and ordering the multitude of images. Ever since heaven and earth's earliest beginnings, pictures have defined and regularized those things which have
form and can be understood, as well as what remains of the activities of
former worthies." Zhang himself says that "maps and pictures contain
the greatest treasures of the empire, the strands and leading ropes which
can regulate disorder." This legitimates art as a kind of knowledge and
downplays mere beauty.

Connoisseurship, or the informed appreciation of works of fine art,
was highly developed in Song, Yuan, and Ming China. The handbook
entitled *Ko Ku Yao Lun*, a compilation of earlier material, was published
in 1388, more than half a century before printing was even invented in
Europe. The *Ko Ku Yao Lun* comments on the materials, workman-

ship, and styles of bronzes, paintings, calligraphy, tablets and rubbings, ink-stones, jades, and porcelain. The book was continually revised in further editions.

Art history was little developed in medieval Europe because painters were not scholars. Many book illuminators were clerics, but they did not write about their art. In the time of Francis of Assisi and Restoro d'Arezzo, the late twelfth and thirteenth centuries, the main mode of writing practiced by artists was the signature. Many medieval artists signed their works with names, dates, brief statements of pride. A recent compendium collects 820 artists' signatures in Italy alone, and more than 400 from beyond Italy, dating from the seventh to the mid-fourteenth centuries, and not even including paintings. This was not unprecedented: ancient Greek sculptors and painters had signed their works; so had ancient Chinese painters, and the scribes of the classic Maya period (AD 250–900) also included their names in inscriptions on stone stelae and painted pots. The artist who signs and dates a work, not content to disappear into a flow of anonymous copies, tries to punctuate history with his name. When there is no annalist at hand, the works themselves will have to write the history of art. Thus it is no surprise that medieval Italian artists were more likely to sign their works than Renaissance artists.

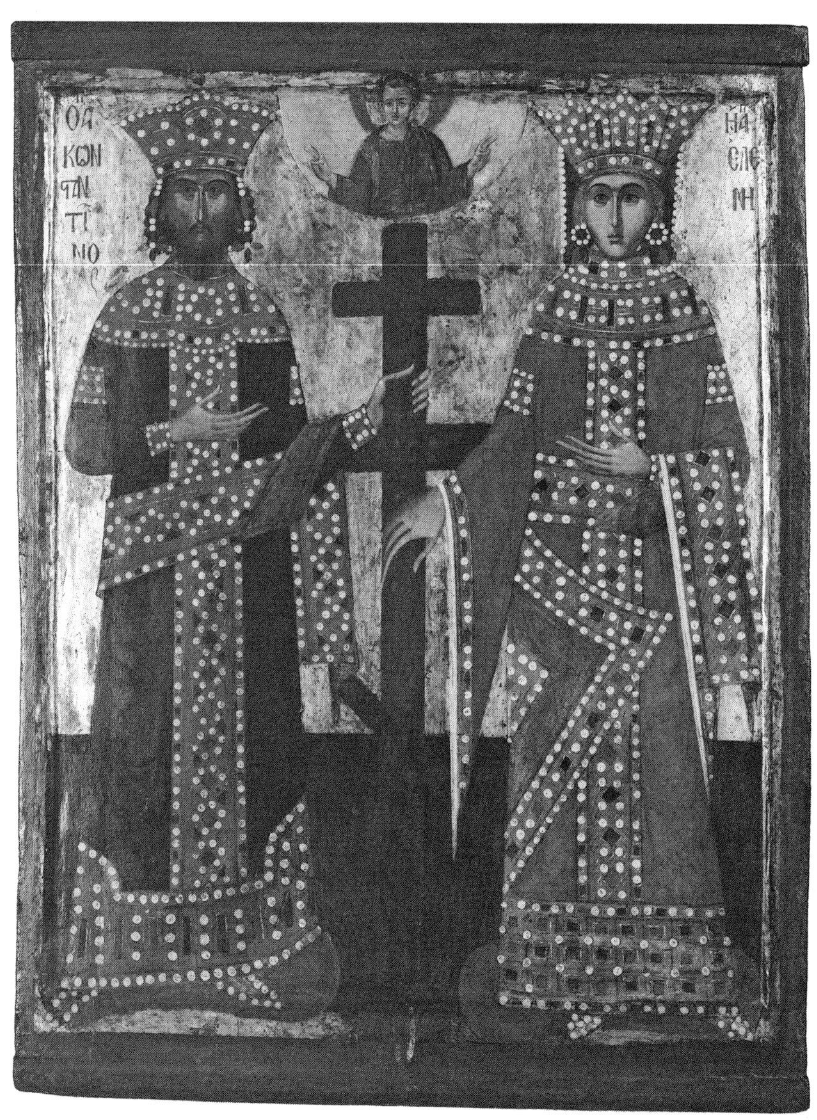

Eastern Mediterranean, *Emperor Constantine and Empress Helena with the True Cross* (early fifteenth century). Painted panel, 102 × 77 cm. Nuremberg, Germanisches Nationalmuseum. According to a story recorded in an eighteenth-century inscription, the panel was rescued from the Turks by Venetian troops in 1436. The Nuremberg merchant Hans Tucher purchased the panel in Venice during his Jerusalem pilgrimage of 1479–80.

1400–1500

The portrait, especially the image of a ruler or a holy figure, retrieved the past by encouraging beholders' confidence in its typological fidelity to an authoritative model. An example is the double portrait of the Emperor Constantine and his mother Helena that arrived in Nuremberg probably in 1480, a souvenir of the merchant Hans Tucher's Jerusalem pilgrimage.

Constantine and Helena gesture to the Cross they grip, reminder of the latter's discovery of the True Cross in Jerusalem in 320. According to an eighteenth-century inscription, now lost, the painting was seized at Mytilene by Venetian troops victorious over the Turks in 1436. The picture faced further attacks from the Turks en route to Venice but remained unharmed. Evidently this was the story that Tucher heard from whoever sold him the icon. The one-meter-tall panel with its forbidding surface of flat jewelled robes and the subjects' implacable gazes was probably painted in the first half of the fifteenth century. Nevertheless Hans Tucher and other Nurembergers considered the icon a precious relic of early Christian times, or at the very least a faithful copy of an original of the fourth century. In 1518 the Nuremberg sculptor Veit Stoss made a carved, winged frame for the painting. The record of the payment to Stoss in the Tucher account book refers to the "old painting from Venice which portrays Emperor Constantine and Saint Helena from life (*in irem leben abcontrafett*)." The Nuremberg icon may well have copied old icons that in turn copied still older icons. The double portrait linked Nuremberg with the two august personages. Buildings and images in many times and places have been understood this way, as tokens, mutually substitutable, fastened one to another in long chains, disciplined by a missing but prestigious type.

Such tokens were not always enough. To allay doubts about the copy, some sought an original, an archetype: the portrait that all the others copied. Clerics assigned dates and authors to paintings, promoting them to originality, if they felt the antiquity of the work would accrue to the prestige of a monastery or church or its founder. To allay doubts about the hypothesis of originality, they conducted research. A cleric in Hildesheim, sorting out the holdings of the church treasury, added a helpful inscription to an ivory plaquette depicting the Descent from the Cross. The inscription, written in ink along one of the edges, reads, "I, Bernward, bishop of Hildesheim, had this made (*explicui*) in the year 1006," crediting with the commission of the work the famous founder of the Benedictine monastery of St. Michael. In fact, the ivory is probably Italian work of the twelfth century, and the hopeful inscription dates from the fifteenth century or even later. The inscription is neither uninformed nor implausible, since the plaquette was indeed imitating or even copying an older Byzantine work. The fifteenth-century connoisseur could see that the ivory was old, even if he lacked the experience and comparanda that would permit a more precise dating. Unblinded by, very likely indifferent to, the work's artistic qualities—its workmanship and poetry—he saw the plaquette as an historical relic with documentary value.

In medieval Europe building materials were scarce and no one scrupled to shift stones from a ruin to a construction site. When people remembered the source of an appropriated stone, preventing it from disappearing entirely into the new building, then it functioned as a relic, or spoil. In 1451 Pope Nicholas V had two or four giant columns found near S. Maria sopra Minerva brought to St. Peter's, the massive basilica built by Constantine himself. At that point no one knew exactly which structure they came from. We know now that the columns had belonged to the Baths of Agrippa, but at the time it would have been assumed that they had supported a pagan temple. At 1.8 meters in diameter and 13.6 meters long they were larger than the columns of the Pantheon porch, which are the largest surviving monolithic columns. The meaning of the translation of these massive trophies to the principal church of Christianity spoke for itself. In order to participate in the logic of triumphal spoliation as established by the Romans, the church risked presenting itself as the mere successor to a pagan temple. The transportation of the columns was described by the German traveler Jakob Muffel. Documents suggest that only two columns actually made it across town and were destined to be, and possibly were, installed in the basilica's triumphal arch. Francesco Albertini, the author of a guide to the wonders of Rome (1510), mentioned two columns in St. Peter's described by Pope Paul II as "worth more than all Venice." The great church, whose link to Constantine was real, not merely typological, was nevertheless destroyed in the sixteenth century, the columns broken down or lost, to make way for the present St. Peter's.

The first Italian artist to take up a pen and seize partial control of the historiography of art was the Florentine Cennino Cennini, court artist in Padua, who wrote a treatise on painting in the first years of the fifteenth century. Cennini offers only the most compact account of the history of the art, framed as self-presentation: he says that his teacher was Agnolo Gaddi, who had been trained by his father Taddeo, who had for twenty-four years worked as a "disciple" of Giotto. Giotto had "changed the profession of painting from Greek back into Latin, and brought it up to date; and he had more finished craftsmanship than anyone has had since." Thus Giotto appears both as pioneer and as unsurpassed paragon. In the rest of the book, Cennini shares his knowledge of materials and techniques. Already the chronicler Filippo Villani, who shared Cennini's nostalgia for the early fourteenth century, the generation of Dante and Giotto, had narrated in his *De origine civitatis Florentiae* (1381–1382) brief lives of notable Florentines, including a chapter on painters, a decision he justified with reference to his ancient predecessor Pliny. Villani named Cimabue as the precursor and then praised Giotto, "superior to the classical painters in art and genius," as the one who "restored painting." He mentioned Giotto's pupils Maso di Banco, Taddeo Gaddi, and the spectral Stefano Fiorentino.

Some decades later the polymath Leon Battista Alberti (1404–1472), scholar, poet, architect, wrote theoretical treatises on architecture, painting, and sculpture, the first rivaling the first-century-BC treatise on architecture by Vitruvius, the latter two lacking any (surviving) model in antiquity. Alberti thought little of medieval art but was impressed by the Florentine artists of his own day. In the dedication of *On Painting* (1435) to the architect Filippo Brunelleschi, he says that he used to regret the wholesale loss of the art of antiquity, but that he now recognizes the great merits of the sculptors Donatello, Lorenzo Ghiberti, and Luca della Robbia and the painter Masaccio. Although there is evidence that

Alberti had a high opinion of Gothic architecture, he says nothing at all in his treatises about painting or sculpture before 1400. In his book on architecture, *De re aedificatoria*, he takes up but then evades the problem of the restoration of old buildings. Mainly he is interested in preventing decay; if you cannot repair the building, he says, then demolish it.

The first really informative history of modern Tuscan art was written by one of the artists admired by Alberti: the bronze-caster, goldsmith, and sculptor Lorenzo Ghiberti (1378–1455). Over a number of years, Ghiberti made notes and composed texts towards a treatise on art. His work was to have three parts: a history of ancient art; a history of modern art comprising comments on a dozen Florentine and Sienese painters and sculptors, beginning with Giotto and culminating in his own autobiography; and a brief treatise on optics, anatomy, and human proportion. When he died the third part or book was still incomplete. Ghiberti's treatise survives in only a single manuscript, dated to the mid-fifteenth century.

For his history of ancient art, and as a general model of how to write art history, Ghiberti relied mostly on Pliny's *Natural History*. Gaius Plinius Secundus (AD 23/24–79) was a soldier and politician, a counsellor to the emperors Vespasian and Titus. His *Natural History* was an encyclopedia in thirty-seven books covering the full range of knowledge about the skies and the earth, plants and animals, medicine and manufacturing. The last five books deal with various telluric materials: gold and silver; copper and bronze; other minerals; marble, mosaic, and glass; and gems. Under these headings Pliny reviews the techniques and histories of the various arts. Like Zhang Yanyuan, Pliny organizes his account whenever he can around famous artists. He gives dates and relays anecdotes that reveal the characters of the artists; he names more than 350 artists and many notable works; he describes the sculptors' and painters' techniques and the different kinds of metals, stones, bricks, and pigments. Pliny is well aware that works have a lifespan:

> There survive even to-day in the temples at Ardea [a town south of Rome] paintings that are older than the city of Rome, which to me at all events are incomparably remarkable, surviving for so long a period as though freshly painted, although unprotected by a roof.

But Pliny offers few critical comments of any interest about works of art. A moralist, he believed that the art of his own time had declined into crass materialism and luxury. Ancient Roman poetic and epistolary texts give us glimpses of more refined opinions about art. But Pliny is the only continuous history of ancient art we have. His pages echo patrician conversations about art and art-oriented tourism as well as ekphrastic poetry. He noted his sources, principal among them the prolific scholar Varro, though he was also dependent on several Greek writers of the third century BC and even earlier, including the artists Apelles and Parrhasius. Pliny's *Natural History* was read throughout the Middle Ages. Already Filippo Villani and Cennino Cennini, before Ghiberti, were well aware of Pliny. The sections dealing with art, however, received comparatively little attention. Those pages were emended and glossed by the fourteenth-century scholar and poet Petrarch, who owned a nearly complete copy of the *Natural History*. Petrarch lent that manuscript to Giovanni Boccaccio, who added his own marginal comments.

To a misreading by Petrarch of a passage in Pliny we owe the first modern biography of a female artist. Pliny had listed several successful women painters, taking special note of Iaia of Cyzicus, whose superiority as a portraitist had been attested by Varro:

> Iaia of Cyzicus, who always remained single, painted at Rome, in the youth of M. Varro, both with the brush, and with the graver, upon ivory, her subjects being female portraits mostly. At Naples, there is a large picture by her, the portrait of an Old Woman; as also a portrait of herself, taken by the aid of a mirror. There was no painter superior to her for expedition; while at the same time her artistic skill was such, that her works sold at much higher prices than those of the most celebrated portrait-painters of her day.

Petrarch misread Iaia's name as Martia and believed her to be Varro's daughter. Boccaccio worked up the spare facts into a biography in his *De mulieribus claris* (On Famous Women) of 1361–1362, adding the observation that Martia depicted mostly women and that, because in antiquity figures were often shown nude or semi-nude, this was a sign of her purity and modesty.

What is the shape of Pliny's history? For moral reasons he admires ancient works in simple materials. From Varro he learned that the Etruscan sculptor Vulca had made cult statues not in marble or bronze but in clay, including a Jupiter commissioned by the Roman king Tarquinius Priscus: "These were the most splendid images of gods at that time; and we are not ashamed of those ancestors for making images of gods in clay." Later, sculptors and painters were asked to make portraits of notable people. Varro supposedly wrote a treatise reproducing 700 portraits of famous men, each accompanied by a eulogy. Realism became the main criterion of artistic achievement. Pliny names the first painter to have distinguished males from females, the first painter to show three-quarter views of heads as well as veins and drapery folds, the first painter to paint open mouths and teeth and expressions, the first painter to depict objects realistically. Realism transforms painting into a source of knowledge, inviting Pliny to lament that painting, "an art that was formerly illustrious," has been "at the present time entirely ousted by marbles, and indeed finally also by gold." This is Pliny's indirect way of saying that the value of an artwork transcends the value of its materials. He perceives links between shifts in taste and historical events:

> It was this victory of Pompey over Mithridates that made fashion veer to pearls and gemstones. The victories of Lucius Scipio and of Cnaeus Manlius had done the same for chased silver, garments of cloth of gold and dining couches inlaid with bronze; and that of Mummius for Corinthian bronzes and fine paintings.

Pliny deplores the association of art with power. In his account taste naturally tends to luxury, a weakness of taste itself. Pliny's contempt for expensive materials leads him to recognize not only that painting offers something that the luxury arts cannot but also that painting delivers some precious surplus not present in the objects it depicts, even if he struggles to name that surplus. According to Pliny, Apelles, the great painter of the fourth century BC, used to say that the works of his rivals "lacked the glamour (*venerem*) that his works possessed, the quality denoted by the Greek word *charis*." If Apelles's works have grace, the works of Protogenes derive from "the impulse of his mind and a certain artistic capriciousness (*quaedam artis libido*)." Protogenes leaves a margin beyond realism for "things that cannot be represented." Aristides of Thebes "was the first of all painters who depicted the mind and expressed the feelings of a human being." These are qualities that would dictate a nonconvergent history of art, since it is impossible to imagine an absolute charm or capriciousness, or an end to the inquiry into human emotions.

Lorenzo Ghiberti encountered in Pliny the names of many artists whose works had perished, encouragement enough to make a record of the art of his own time. Ghiberti began his own treatise with a condensed history of ancient art based on Pliny. His second book opens with the statement that art ceased, and then started again: "The temples remained bare six hundred years or so. The Greeks began the art of painting in a very weak way, and produced very rough work." Ghiberti had found the topos of a disappointing initial revival in Pliny. The ancient writer named several sculptors who had flourished in the 121st Olympiad (295–292 BC). "After that," Pliny continued, "the art languished, and it revived (*ars … revixit*) again in the 156th Olympiad (156–153 BC)." But the new crop of artists was "far inferior to those mentioned above."

Here Ghiberti departed from Pliny by identifying a second, more successful revival. He relates the story of the painter Cimabue discovering the child Giotto drawing a sheep on a flat stone. Soon the Tuscan painters surpassed the Greeks. Ghiberti's schema matched the metaphor of the "dark ages" introduced by Petrarch in his epic poem *Africa* (1339): "After the darkness has been dispelled (*discussis forte tenebris*), our grandsons will be able to walk back into the pure radiance of the past." One of the characters in Boccaccio's *Decameron* (1349–1353) said that Giotto "brought back to light that art which had been buried for many ages (*secoli*) under the error of those who painted rather to please the eyes of the ignorant than the intellect of the wise."

So already there is some shape, some meaning to history. It is not just a sequence of illustrious artists who are always being eclipsed by younger artists, as in Dante, *Purgatorio* 11:

> "Oh," I cried out, "are you not Oderisi,
> glory of Gubbio, glory of that art
> they call illumination now in Paris?"

> "Brother," he said, "the pages painted by
> the brush of Franco Bolognese smile
> more brightly: all the glory now is his;
> mine, but a part.…

> O empty glory of the powers of humans!
> How briefly green endures upon the peak—
> unless an age of dullness follows it.

> In painting Cimabue thought he held
> the field, and now it's Giotto they acclaim—
> the former only keeps a shadowed fame."

["Oh!," diss' io lui, "non se' tu Oderisi,
   l'onor d'Agobbio e l'onor di quell' arte
   ch'alluminar chiamata è in Parisi?"

"Frate," diss' elli, "più ridon le carte
   che pennelleggia Franco Bolognese;
   l'onore è tutto or suo, e mio in parte. (79–84)

. . . . . .

Oh vana gloria de l'umane posse!
   com' poco verde in su la cima dura,
   se non è giunta da l'etati grosse!

Credette Cimabue ne la pittura
   tener lo campo, e ora ha Giotto il grido,
   sì che la fama di colui è scura." (91–96)]

Dante was still thinking about painting—though perhaps not about poetry—in annalistic terms. The poet saw his contemporary Giotto simply as the latest in a series of excellent painters.

A century later, in the early fifteenth century, the fame of Giotto had taken on a new meaning. He was now seen as a precursor to the outstanding masters of the present day. Ghiberti may have been convinced by his reading of Dante—or Petrarch: remember the passage about the dependence of fame on writing, quoted earlier—not to entrust the legacy of Giotto and the other modern artists to the word of the people but rather to reinforce their fame with his own authority. Giotto is now the subject of research. Ghiberti says he saw "preparatory designs" (*provedimenti*), probably drawings, by Giotto for the reliefs on the Campanile or bell tower of the Duomo (in fact Giotto did not design the reliefs, but never mind), revealing that such relics of the production process had been preserved—by artists, by the cathedral workshop. Were they preserved because they were thought to be relics of Giotto? Ghiberti lists and briefly comments on Giotto's disciples up to Andrea Orcagna, "a noble master," then turns to the Sienese painters, whom he praises unstintingly, transcending local patriotism. He describes compositions by Ambrogio Lorenzetti and Simone Martini. Ghiberti has little to say about the artists' personalities, suppressing anecdotes as if to stress the impersonal, technical nature of art. He closes by presenting his own life and works. Ghiberti's vocabulary is limited and repetitive. His modifiers are all much the same: diligent, marvelous, perfect, excellent, refined, unusual, singular, superb, elegant, thorough, delicately finished, noble; and the words are distributed evenly among the good artists. Cavallini and Duccio, he asserts, are excellent and noble even though they kept to the Greek style. Just as in Cennini, it is unclear how Giotto can be both the reviver of art and already perfect. This riddle, which is no riddle to the relativist who does not equate art with technical achievement, is not solved by Ghiberti.

Ghiberti had a judgmental eye, but he reveals his verdicts mainly by inclusion or exclusion. He mentions for example that some artists do not deserve to be mentioned. He omits the whole roster of Florentine artists after Orcagna (d. 1368), even such now-admired masters as Lorenzo Monaco and Masaccio, saying that they do not belong with those others. He does not speak of progress or decline across the entire period from Giotto to the present. Unlike Pliny or Zhang Yanyuan, Ghiberti expresses no admiration for the rudiments of art on ethical grounds and does not chastise the decadent present. Although nearly all the works he describes are sacred, he does not speak of their piety or theological content. Ghiberti's only criterion is artistic excellence.

Ghiberti is not telling an ironic fable: he does not praise lowly art. He respects the split that Franciscanism introduced between the history of art and the history of the soul. Francis praised the humble, renounced his possessions, and made poverty a virtue. But neither Giotto nor Ghiberti considered poverty in art to be a virtue.

Ghiberti interrupts his account of Italian sculpture to tell a story about a mysterious goldsmith, a cautionary parable about art's relation to power. This artist of Cologne is not named by Ghiberti, but a chronicler of the 1540s, the so-called Anonimo Magliabechiano, who used Ghiberti's manuscripts, called him Gusmin. Gusmin or Goswin worked for the Duke of Anjou in the fourteenth century. Ghiberti says that "he was perfect in his works, he was equal to the ancient Greek sculptors…. He had a very refined style (*gentilissima aria nell'opere sue*), he was very learned." But Ghiberti himself only knew "figures cast from" Gusmin's works. He cannot have known the originals because they had all been melted down for military purposes. Gusmin "saw the work he had made with such love and artistry destroyed for the Duke's public requirements; he saw that his labor had been in vain, and cast himself to the ground on his knees, raising his eyes and hands to heaven, saying, 'O Lord, who rules heaven and earth and who made all things, let me not be so ignorant as to follow any but you, have mercy on me.'" Shattered, the artist retreated to a hermitage. Younger artists used to come to him for counsel, and "he received them most humbly, giving them learned lessons and showing them many measurements, and giving them many examples." The warning to artists is that potentates are fickle and in the end do not value art as highly as we do. In signalling the risk of coupling art to power, Ghiberti recovers some of Pliny's moralism. The arts are diminished by the reality of war. Technical knowledge is exposed as an ignorance of God. This reassociates art with spirit and yet acknowledges that for all one's spiritualism, in the end the works are our true legacy, that even fame only partly compensates for death. Fame is hollow if no works survive. Gusmin, grief-stricken, accepts reality's verdict on art and yet goes on giving advice to young artists.

Historically-minded scholars were alert to the documentary value of art. In a letter to the Byzantine emperor John VIII Paleologue, the philologist Manuel Chrysoloras, visiting Rome in 1411, described the Arch of Constantine (315) and its sculpted reliefs depicting battles: "It is possible to see clearly what arms and what costumes people used in ancient times, what insignia magistrates had, how an army was arrayed, a battle fought, a city besieged, or a camp laid out; what ornaments and garments people used," and so forth. "Herodotus and some other writers of history," he continues, "are thought to have done something of great value when they describe these things; but in these sculptures one can see all that existed in those days among the different races, so that it is a complete and accurate history—or rather not a history so much as an exhibition." Presumably Ernst Robert Curtius was thinking along these lines when he said that it was easy to interpret the Parthenon frieze.

Other fifteenth-century Italian artists wrote, but none was as dedicated to the history of art as Ghiberti. The painter Piero della Francesca, an original mathematical thinker, wrote a treatise on perspective but offered no comments on the history of painting. Leonardo da Vinci compiled voluminous notes for a treatise on the art of painting but spared only a few lines for the history of painting. He mentioned for example the painters who succeeded the ancient Romans as painters "who only imitate one another; and so the art declines in quality." Piero and

Leonardo were concerned mostly to tell their readers what good painting is and how it is made. Among nonpainters in Florence who did contribute to the annals of art history, carrying information over the threshold from unedited to edited, from anecdote to history, were the architect and mathematician Antonio Manetti, who wrote a biography of Brunelleschi, and the merchant Antonio Billi, who made notes on artists and works.

The impact on historiography of the printing press, invented in the second quarter of the fifteenth century and established in Italy in the 1460s and '70s, was mixed. Pliny's *Natural History* was one of the first ancient texts to be printed, already in 1469, in Venice. An Italian translation of Pliny was published in 1476. Many seem to have understood movable type mainly as a way of multiplying editions of the classics. Modern authors and readers did not always grasp that print would broadcast the new ideas of their own age to unenvisioned audiences. Ghiberti's treatise was not published until 1823, and then only Book 2, the history of modern Italian art; the other two books did not see the light of day until 1912. Although Alberti's *De re aedificatoria* had been printed in 1485, thirteen years after his death, his more original treatise on painting appeared only in 1540. Giovanni Santi (d. 1494), court painter at Urbino and the father of the painter Raphael, wrote a chronicle in *terza rima* praising his patron in which he lists and praises twenty-seven modern painters, nearly half of them Florentines. Santi's chronicle was not published until modern times. Eventually print would liberate the historian from court service. But for now, none of these authors had much reach.

All the early historians shared the conviction that in the not-too-distant past the history of painting had started over again. Giovanni Santi called the "high and cunning science" of perspective "a new invention of our age." A theory of art keyed to realism invites chronological provincialism and neglectful condescension to the art of the centuries following the fall of Rome.

No European writer up to this point was able to move beyond a simple narrative of progress, or decline and revival succeeded by progress. No one expressed a partiality for an archaic or austere style. If the European writers had studied more closely the first-century treatise on oratory by Quintilian, a text rediscovered by an Italian scholar in 1416 in the monastery of St. Gall in Switzerland (and sent to the printing press already in 1470), they would have learned that some ancient Roman connoisseurs not only admired the simple style, but could also be suspected, when they asserted this preference, of snobbish posing:

> The first great painters whose works are worth looking at for other reasons than their antiquity are said to have been Polygnotus and Aglaophon. Their simple colour (*simplex color*) still has its admirers, enthusiastic enough to prefer these rude objects (*illa prope rudia*), the beginnings, as it were, of the future art, to the greatest of the later masters. I take this to be a pretentious claim to superior understanding.

In other words, ancient collectors saw a social advantage in cultivating a penchant for the simple style.

1500–1550

The first moderns to express a preference for simplicity were religious reformers distressed by the vain extravagances of recent sacred painting. Martin Luther, the German monk who rent European Christendom, no admirer of the city of Rome, which he visited in 1511, was nevertheless well aware that in modern times the arts had been reborn. In a sermon published in 1522 he said, "If you read in all the chronicles, you will find in all the years since the birth of Christ nothing comparable to what you find in the last hundred years." "Building and cultivating, fancy foods and clothes, wit and learning and inventions like the printing press, all brought to new heights. All the arts have ascended and are still ascending, painting, embroidery, carving; there has been nothing like it since the birth of Christ." Admittedly, Luther read modern progress as a sign that the Last Judgment was imminent, and in his sermon he went on to compare the worldly advances to the rise of corruption and iniquity in the Church. Luther's response was to inaugurate his own parallel renaissance, a rebirth not of pagan civilization but of the primitive church. Still, he saw a way to harness the pictorial arts to his mission. Together with the local artist Lucas Cranach he reasserted a traditional conception of Christian art as a means of didactic communication. Guided by Luther, Cranach produced paintings, prints, and illustrated books delivering straightforward narrations of a few episodes of sacred history and unmistakable diagrams of doctrinal truth. In his Protestant works Cranach simplified his style. Luther's opinion on style was captured and published by his disciple Johannes Aurifaber:

"

Doctor Luther once said that Albrecht Dürer, the famous painter of Nuremberg, used to say: "I don't like pictures painted with too many colors, but rather those that are painted as simply as possible, nice and plain (*fein schlecht*)." And so he said that he, too, "liked sermons that were nice and simple, so anyone can understand what you are preaching."

The practice of caring for old pictures, repairing or retouching instead of replacing them, first developed around prestigious icons associated with miracles. But even ordinary Trecento paintings were often reframed by new carpentry and new painting, especially in Tuscany. A polyptych in the church of S. Martino a Mensola near Florence, dated 1391, was restored nearly a century later by the descendants of the work's original patron. The old panels were reinstalled in a modern, neoclassical frame and supplemented by four prophets, wedged in the spandrels, by the fashionable painter Cosimo Rosselli. One could also encounter a relic of sacred painting in a private home, extracted from its ecclesiastical setting: the Venetian patrician Marcantonio Michiel, in his notes on the collection of Alessandro Capella in Padua, mentions a head of St. John attributed to Cimabue, in fresco, that had been rescued from a fire in the Carmelite church and mounted in a wooden frame. Soon Giotto's works, too, were treated as relics, as the traces of another kind of miracle, just because they were by Giotto. In 1543 the destruction of a wall of Old St. Peter's in Rome revealed a fragment of a fresco by Giotto. The fresco was removed and remounted elsewhere in the church by the painter Perino del Vaga and his friend Niccolò Acciaiuoli. The rescuers admired Cimabue and Giotto because they were pioneers.

An Italian artist or patron who identifies simplicity as such as the content of older art is discerning a "second" content below the patent Christian content. Luther and other Protestant reformers compare an older and better Christian content, with a simple style to match it, to a newer. Relativism is possible because the comparisons are drawn within the Christian sphere. So far, there is no affront from an alien content. The test of relativism—and the ancient Romans, syncretists that they were, never really faced this test—was the encounter with someone else's sacred art. Over the course of the fourteenth, fifteenth, and sixteenth centuries, Christians learned to admire the sacred art of the ancient Greeks and Romans, admire it as art. They judged the pagan cult sufficiently extinct to risk engagement with its beautiful instruments. The once deplored or ignored antiquities were elevated to positions of honor in European collections.

In the sixteenth century and in the two following centuries, we hear many assertions that the best ancient Roman art, its pagan content not-withstanding, is agreeable to look at. We also hear many assertions that non-European art, even if well made, is disagreeable to look at because its content is offensive and its forms unfamiliar. When a traveler encountered artifacts associated with non-Christian and nonextinct worship, the reflex was to reject. Mistaken or false reference was an obstacle. In his narration of his travels in the Middle East and south Asia, published in 1510, the Bolognese traveler Ludovico de Varthema attributed to the people of Calicut on the Malabar Coast unholy submission to a demon, the *deumo*, possibly a version of the goddess Durga, or of Deva, a category of divinity. Varthema reports that the *deumo* had been assigned to the people of Calicut by the devil, whom they worship. The king keeps the *deumo* in his chapel in the form of a metal image seated on a metal throne. The artist Jörg Breu designed woodcut images to accompany the German translation of Varthema's book, *Die ritterlich und lobwirdig Rayss* (The chivalrous and praiseworthy journey) (Augsburg, 1515). He illustrates, for example, Varthema's account of a Hindu ritual at a colonnaded temple, "not dissimilar to the Lateran Baptistry in Rome," in the middle of a pool of water, adorned all around with lamps hung on trees. The throngs of pilgrims who come at festival time seeking "grace and indulgence"—again Varthema compares the unknown to the known—worship "an overlifesize devil" on a sacrificial altar in the center of the temples. Breu depicted a robed, barefoot supplicant kneeling before a seated figure with bird's legs and horns, arm outstretched. The worshipper, but for his unbared head, resembles any Christian devout kneeling before an altar. But Breu takes advantage of his medium to depict a grotesque enthroned figure who cannot be said to be either statue or demon, image or reality. The outstretched arm suggests he is real. But it is impossible to say. This wasn't the question—it was understood that the pagan religion would represent its demons accurately. The question was whether this was a proper target of worship, and the animal-like features and horns say "no."

Varthema and Breu were like medieval Christians looking at pagan art, still anxious about the possibility that the demons depicted were real.

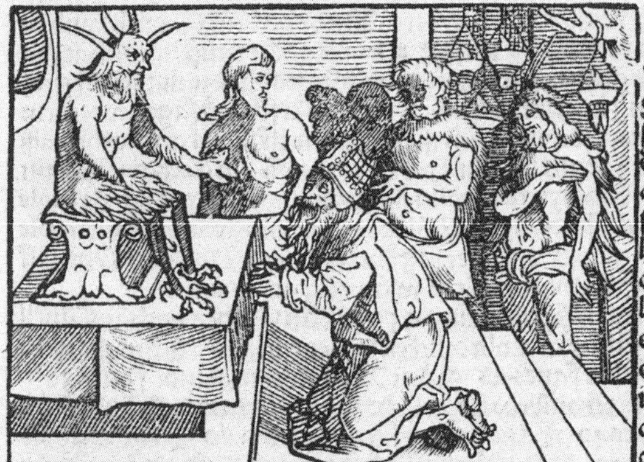

Und ge
rings
vmb an dem
gestat des wa
ser teychs stõ
dē gar vil põ
alle ainer ge-
stalt/Daran
hencken sy lye
chter in amp
len in sollich-
er mämg das
es nit zů zelen
ist/ des geley-
chen auch rin
gs weys vmb
disen tempel so vil angezynter amplen vnd lyechter vngelaüblich zů
sagen/Auf den fünf vñ zwaintzigisten tag im december so hält man
dises vest Also das alles das volck biß in fünffzechen meyl wegs dar-
üb gelegen pfaffen edel vñ paurs leyt kumen gemaingklich zů diser
opfrüg/zům ersten ee mal sy eingond zů volbringen das opfer so wã
schen sy sich all in dem gedachten teych/darnach die fyrnemsten prie-
ster des künigs steygēt als reytent auf die gemelten schiflein darinen
das öl ist/ vñ nach mals alles das volck get zů den pfaffen/wölche ai
nem yeden das haupt salben von dem selben öll/ Darnach thond sy
das opfer auff dem altar darzů geordnet/vnd auff dem mittel des al
tars stat ain über grosser teyfel zů wölchem sy gond so vil ir dar kü-
en knyend fyr in nider vnd betten in an/Nach dem so kert sich ain ye
der wider darhin von dannen er kumen ist vñ ain yeder hab übel tat
auff im was er wölle so hat er die selben zeyt sicherhayt vñ gelayt da
selbst/Vnd in warhayt so hab ich nye mer volck bey ainander gesech
en/Als an disem ort/Vnd da ich zů mecha gewesen bin.

Capitel von der mintz von dem gewicht vnd von der
handlung was zů Calicut verkaufft wirt.

So ir nun vernomen habt gelegenhayt der land vnd stöt vnd vil
ander wunderparlich sachen besunder was ich gehört vñ gesech
en hab zů calicut/ Bedunckt mich nit vnbequem sein auch zer klöten
m

Jörg Breu, *Worship at a Hindu Temple*. Woodcut, 6.9 × 9.6 cm. In Ludovico de Varthema, *Die ritterlich und lobwirdig Rayss* (Augsburg, 1515), fol. Q3r. Munich, Bayerische Staatsbibliothek. The text on this page describes the scene of worship: "In truth I have never before seen so many people together in one place. And I have been to Mecca."

It was much easier when the alien art was secular. Early sixteenth-century European artists and travelers who encountered finely made artifacts recognized, like Restoro d'Arezzo, skill and imagination. In August 1520 the German artist Albrecht Dürer (1471–1528) was shown the gifts given by Moctezuma, ruler of Tenochtitlan, to the Spanish general Hernan Cortés and sent by Cortés to the Habsburg emperor Charles V in Brussels. In his diary of his journey to the Netherlands, Dürer described "a sun made all of gold, a good six feet across, likewise a moon of pure silver, of the same size, also two rooms full of those natives' armour, all manner of their weapons, military gear and missilery, amazing shields, curious costumes, bed coverings, and every kind of spectacular things for all possible uses, more worth seeing than the usual prodigies." (By "prodigies" or *Wunderding* he presumably meant natural curiosities and rarities like ostrich eggs or coconuts.) Dürer marvels not because the Aztec artifacts are unfamiliar or bizarre, but because they are made by human beings. "I have never in my life seen anything that gave my heart such delight as these things, for I saw amongst them marvellously skilful objects and was amazed at the subtle ingeniousness of people in foreign lands. I cannot find words to describe all those things I found there." As in Arezzo in the thirteenth century, workmanship and beauty overcome distance. Dürer could not make sense of all the artifacts. Even today the descriptions remain obscure (what were the "bed coverings"?). The Mexican artifacts did not seem to Dürer to be involved with ritual communication with false deities, but rather to serve basic functions like defense, offense, decoration, signalling of power and authority. Without the obstacle of false belief, one artist could communicate through the artifact with another, and this is the basis of the "delight" Dürer speaks of. This communication is all that poor Mazzoleni was hoping for from the adjudicator Romanino.

A more programmatic relativist than Dürer was the Dominican friar Bartolomé de las Casas (1484–1566), who compiled over many years information about the Mexican people and religion. Las Casas had lived in the Iberian Americas since 1502, initially as a colonist, taking orders in 1510. In his *Apologética historia de las Indias* (1552–1559), an offshoot of a longer *Historia de las Indias*, Las Casas defends the integrity and accomplishments of the indigenous culture, including the craftsmanship already admired by Dürer in 1520. He does this in two ways: first, he compares Mexican customs to ancient Roman and Greek customs; and second, he asserts the absolute mastery of the Mexican artisans. In other words, he says that if modern Europeans admire the ancient pagan world, with its idolatries, sacrifices, and alien marriage customs, then there is no basis for the commonplace deprecation of Mexican practices, and that anyway the Mexicans measure up to the Europeans by the fixed standard of technical accomplishment:

> But what appears without doubt to exceed all human genius…is the art which those Mexican peoples have so perfectly mastered, of making from natural feathers, fixed in position with their own natural colors, anything that they or any other first-class painters can paint with brushes.… And granted that before we Christians entered there they made perfect and wonderful things by this art, such as a tree, a rose, grass, a flower, an animal, a man, a bird, a dainty butterfly, a forest and a stone or rock, so skillfully that the object appeared alive or natural.

Las Casas's long experience among the indigenous people had made him sympathetic. To rescue the honor of the Mexicans and introduce a relativistic appreciation of their work, he avoids discussing the sacred content of their art. He also avoids also discussing artistic form, attributing the beauty of their works either to the objects depicted (birds, flowers, trees) or to technique. He goes on to say that the Mexican artists were also quick learners, adaptable:

> yet after the Spaniards went there and they saw our statues and other things, they had, beyond comparison, abundant material and an excellent opportunity to show the liveliness of their intellects, the integrity and disengagement of their powers [neatness and deliberateness of their faculties] or interior or exterior senses [inner and outer consciousness], and their great talent. For since our statues and altarpieces are large and painted in divers colors, they had occasion to branch out, to practice, and to distinguish themselves in that new and delicate art of theirs, seeking to imitate our objects.

Technical accomplishment is unanswerable.

Europeans in this period did not often attempt to read the literary or sacred texts produced by remote societies. The texts that survived from Greek and Roman antiquity already posed enough interpretive challenges. Fifteenth-century Italian readers of the ancient texts—"philologists," as they called themselves—learned to read those texts nonjudgmentally, without Christian prejudice. To read a text philologically meant to understand the text as a form of rhetoric, that is, as the residue of a speech-act, an attempt to communicate within a local and social context. It meant to understand that an old text was not addressed to you but to its original readers. To read the text well, and to understand a historical literary style as a ratio of ends to available means, you had to meet it halfway, that is, try to reimagine the world that produced it. This perspective could easily be reversed and trained on the style of the present day, that is, to recognize that our own style is merely *our* style, just as Cicero's supposedly exemplary Latin style was merely the style of his own day. This was the position of the so-called anti-Ciceronians, the philologists of the early sixteenth century who rebelled against Cicero's normative status.

Ciceronianism at its worst meant blind allegiance to an ancient model simply because it was ancient: trust in the ancients as if they really were our ancestors. Already Petrarch in a letter of 1363 had said that exclusive reliance on the example of the ancients is foolish because after all they themselves were just people who had invented something.

In the realm of art, the equivalent to the literary quarrel was the conversation about whether to imitate the relics of ancient sculpture or to continue in the paths developed in Italy in the last centuries. The anti-Ciceronian Pico della Mirandola, in a letter of 1512 addressed to the scholar and poet Pietro Bembo—in effect a short treatise on the topic of style—complained that ancient statues are often admired just because they are ancient, even if moderns can make better ones. Unfortunately the conversations of the modern artists themselves on this topic are not recorded. They must have resented the fact that some philologists seemed to doubt that art could even have a style, so dependent was it on its models in the real world. Bembo, a Ciceronian, lamented in his reply to Pico that literary exemplarity was not as simple as it is in the visual arts. Bembo compares allegiance to Cicero, the best model, to the artist's allegiance to Alexander's face when he wants to represent Alexander. This is an opinion worthy of Ernst Robert Curtius. Bembo and Curtius would have done well to read a passage on portraits in the treatise on architecture by the fifteenth-century Florentine architect Antonio di Pietro Averlino, known as Filarete. Many painted portraits of Federico Sforza, according to Filarete, resemble their subject, and yet they are all different, for every painter like every writer has his own style (*stile de ciascheduno*). That is, even a portrait has a style, as if the artist were competing with the sitter. This freedom both from exemplary Cicero-like models as well as from nature permitted art to have its own history. The history of art was the history of imaginative artists. In his response to Bembo—the sequence of three letters was published in Pico della Mirandola's collected works c. 1515—the anti-Ciceronian Pico said as much, quoting remarks by Cicero himself, from *Orator*, 2.9–10, about an ancient artist: "After discussing the skillfully made images of Phidias, Cicero affirmed that the sculptor had produced them not from a living model or from sculpted representations, but 'in his own mind.'"

The anti-Ciceronian position, which prevailed, was extended to more recent literary paragons, for example the fourteenth-century Tuscans, who had created the modern Florentine literary language. In his post-humously published dialogue *In difesa della lingua fiorentina* (1556), the academician Carlo Lenzoni has the Ciceronian character ask: "Do you believe that some words used by Boccaccio are not good?" The reply is: "Though they were very good in Boccaccio's time, they are no longer good now." We cannot but notice that this was the basic view of Giotto, Boccaccio's near contemporary, who enjoyed a comparable status as a pioneer but whose art could only be admired in proportion to its time. Lenzoni has his Ciceronian point this out: "Would you not esteem my judgment as poor if I, desiring to be a painter, imitated Giotto more than Raphael? Even though Giotto is so strangely praised by your Vasari?" Even his interlocutor, who represents Lenzoni's own relativist position, would not go so far. The awkward questions reveal that the judgment of art in this time was keyed to some quality that Giotto absolutely lacked: realism, suavity, or complexity, whereas Raphael absolutely possessed the good qualities and so had achieved a timeless exemplarity.

The Lenzoni dialogue suggests that by the mid-sixteenth century painters were being considered alongside poets. The exchange also shows us that even for painters, and not only for poets, imitation of exemplary models was the basis of pedagogy. Florentine painters used simply to learn by doing, by working side by side with their teacher and by emulating available models in local churches and collections. Relativism in the sixteenth century was limited, never exceeding the recognition that the best style in one epoch looks different from the best style of another epoch. It was taken for granted that not every age attains a good style, and that plenty of centuries produced no admirable painting or writing at all. Even the most relativistic philologists expressed no admiration for medieval Latin; they derided it as rude.

And yet there was the New Testament. Here was a text in a simple, vernacular style that had special prestige because of its proximity to Christ. One could not dismiss it on account of its style. Erasmus, the most eloquent of the anti-Ciceronians, warned that the reader must not approach the New Testament "in the spirit in which perhaps he takes up the *Attic Nights* of Aulus Gellius or the *Miscellanies* of Angelo Poliziano, that is, as if to test against a touchstone the force of its wit, its eloquence, its hidden erudition. We are working with sacred material here, which has been commended to the world above all by its simplicity and purity." Erasmus was saying that the New Testament cannot be measured by the same standards that other texts are judged by. There are two ways to read the gospels, according to Erasmus. Either the gospels are read in context, yielding the insight that their style is simple because the evangelists were simple men, because they were trying to reach broad publics, or because Christ himself spoke simply if obscurely and they were imitating him. Or the gospels are read beyond all context, for this text of texts, unlike Cicero or Boccaccio, was not social and rhetorical. Christ, divinity itself, is speaking through it, directly to you. One could extend the charity of relativism to any text from any time; the privilege of sacrality is shared by few texts.

Some Christian thinkers in the first decades of the sixteenth century defied the new unapologetic generosity toward ancient paganism and the confidence in the modern sciences and arts. We already overheard Luther's doubts about modern progress. The Protestant polemicist Sebastian Franck in his *Paradoxa* (1534) advanced a series of proverb-like assertions of skepticism: "Foolishness alone is wise, ignorance knows all." "The more learned, the more perverse." "Faith fall under no art." "We should unlearn everything, become fools, and spit out all the art that we ate from the Tree of Knowledge." Such reactivations of a traditional Christian *contemptus mundi*, or pessimistic conviction of the fallenness of the world, are on a collision course with the new European self-regard and admiration for technical achievement. Franck's irony, striking Biblical and Socratic notes, will be secularized not many years later in Michel de Montaigne's essay "On Cannibals" (1580), a reflection on reports of the practices of the Tupinambá in Brazil and a check on the automatic European preference for civilization:

They are even savage, as we call those fruits wilde which nature of her selfe and of her ordinarie progresse hath produced: whereas indeed, they are those which our selves have altered by our artificiall devices, and diverted from their common order, we should rather terme savage.

Virtuous and savory are the simple foods produced by the uncultivated earth:

In those are the true and most profitable vertues, and naturall properties most lively and vigorous, which in these we have bastardized, applying them to the pleasure of our corrupted taste. And if notwithstanding, in divers fruits of those countries that were never tilled, we shall finde that in respect of ours they are most excellent, and as delicate unto our taste; there is no reason, art should gaine the point of honour of our great and puissant mother Nature.

Our sophisticated arts have only spoiled what nature gave us:

We have so much by our inventions surcharged the beauties and riches of her workes, that we have altogether overchoaked her: yet where ever her puritie shineth, she makes our vaine and frivolous enterprises wonderfully ashamed.

Montaigne's powerful inversion, elevating the wild over the tame, sent underground cables far forward into European modernity, guiding for example Jean-Jacques Rousseau's *Discourse on the Arts and Sciences* (1750), the manifesto of modern civilization's self-doubt and a blueprint of the histories of art of the future:

One cannot reflect on morals without recalling with pleasure the image of the simplicity of the earliest times.

The loss of our intimacy with the gods, Rousseau says, which has tempted us to transfer the splendor of the temples to the private dwelling, is irreversible:

When innocent and virtuous men loved to have the gods as witnesses of their actions, they dwelt together in the same huts. When they became evil, they grew tired of these inconvenient onlookers and relegated them to magnificent temples. In the end they expelled their deities even from these, in order to dwell there themselves; or in any event the temples of the gods could no longer be distinguished from the homes of the citizens. This was the height of depravity; nor was vice ever carried to greater lengths than when one saw it upheld, as it were, at the portals of the palaces of the great on columns of marble, and carved on Corinthian capitals.

In the sixteenth century there is still no writer on art, no one writing from inside the sphere of art, who transcends the simple narrative of rebirth and constant modern progress.

The conflict between past and present intensified when artists began to record their impressions and were not so dependent on their memories. After the introduction of affordable paper in the early fifteenth century, artists could make drawings of the works they saw. Dürer's diary of his trip to the Netherlands in 1520–1521 registers routines of artistic pilgrimage not unfamiliar to moderns. In the town hall in Brussels, Dürer sees four painted cloths by Rogier van der Weyden; in the chapel in the house of the Count of Nassau he sees a "good painting" by Hugo van der Goes; in Cologne he spends two pennies to gain access to the Three Kings altarpiece of "maister Steffan," Stefan Lochner; in a church in Bruges, he sees the marble Madonna by Michelangelo. Dürer collected drawings by Martin Schongauer and other older German artists, identifying them with brief notations. This was common workshop practice. A drawing of Christ as Salvator Mundi, now associated with Wilhelm Pleydenwurff, or perhaps Dürer's teacher Michael Wolgemut, was inscribed in an old hand—not Dürer's—*uralt hebt auff*: "very old, keep it!"

Over the course of the fifteenth century, Europeans learned to reproduce images mechanically, first as woodcuts and later as engravings. Prints disseminated forms and compositions. From printed reproductions of antiquities and modern Italian paintings artists learned, like the philologists, to see the ancient Greek and Roman style as an available option and not worry about the paganism, less menacing when translated from the three-dimensional statue to the sheet of paper marked with black lines. Beginning in the 1510s, artists all over Europe tried their hand at the new Italian style, called *antico*.

With the embrace of the prestigious "ancient" style, the meaning of the local, customary styles—confusingly, called *moderno*—changed. This happened not only in Italy but also in the Netherlands. The paintings of Jan van Eyck and Rogier van der Weyden, their authority binding for decades, suddenly came to look archaic, and since the old painting manner was no longer automatically sustained by virtue of tradition, it would have to be recovered artificially. The Flemish painter Jan Gossart received permission, probably in 1526, to make tracings of the crowning enthroned figures of John the Baptist, Christ, and Mary of van Eyck's great altarpiece in Ghent, normally off limits to copyists, according to the sources. His faithful painted copy of these century-old figures was most likely commissioned by Margaret of Austria, Governor of the Habsburg Netherlands and a significant patron of the arts, powerful enough to countermand the prohibition on copies.

The place where ancient works of art were displayed side by side with modern works in both the "ancient" and "modern" styles was the collector's cabinet. These were private versions of a princely collection such as that of Margaret of Austria. Here a history of the arts was physically recreated. Scholars and princes collected antiquities and rarities: coins, gems, cameos, vases, statuettes, objects in bronze and gold, slabs of stone with inscriptions, but also illuminated manuscripts, tapestries, liturgical implements, painted or mosaic icons, reliquaries, not to mention prints, drawings, and paintings. Panel paintings, plaster casts, drawings accumulated naturally in artists' studios, as well as antiquities: according to Vasari, Lorenzo Ghiberti had collected marbles and bronzes. Increasingly in the sixteenth century the non-artist collector was gathering paintings not only to adorn the walls of his dwelling but also to satisfy a special taste for allegorical painting, for Flemish painting, for landscapes, or for round panels depicting the Madonna and Child.

Early sixteenth-century descriptions of art were often prompted by prestigious collections. The court historian Jean Lemaire composed a laudatory poem, the *Couronne margaritique* (1510, published 1549), dedicated to his patron, Margaret of Austria. Lemaire mentions the major Netherlandish painters as well as several lesser or unknown names, and two Italians, Donatello and the medalist Cristoforo de Geremia.

The notes of a Venetian patrician, Marcantonio Michiel, give us the best insight into the conversations that took place in early sixteenth-century collectors' studies. These notes were not published in their author's own time, and in fact until the twentieth century his name was forgotten. Michiel is interested in attribution and provenance: "The Miracle of St. Anthony with the Child and the Glass, a terracotta, is the model for the work that Master Zuan Maria made for the Santo [in

Padua]." "The painted heads on the ornamental ceiling [in the house of Alvise Cornaro in Padua] and the paintings on the bedstead are copied from Raphael's cartoons, by the hand of the Venetian Domenico, a pupil of Giulio Campagnola." Some pictures may be copies, and it all needs to be sorted out: "The portrait of Sannazaro is by the hand of Sebastiano Veneziano [del Piombo] and was copied from another portrait of Sannazaro." "The bronze figurine with the kneeling girl holding a basket on her head is a modern work"; the "standing nude bronze figurine, one foot tall," in Pietro Bembo's collection, "is an antique work." Michiel visits private collections in Venice, Milan, Bergamo. In a church in Cremona, he notes a "terracotta Pietà, similar to the one in S. Antonio in Venice, by the hand of Paganino or Turriano." Knowledge about art has extended beyond the artist's workshop and into lay circles. Michiel does not himself know how to paint, and yet he imposes on the paintings he sees no knowledge gathered from anywhere beyond the sphere of art, from literature or philosophy, for example, and for that reason his dry, laconic judgments are valuable, in fact are still prized by many moderns suspicious of academic art-historical scholarship.

On the question of the relativity of artistic style, Giorgio Vasari set the tone. At the beginning of his life of Fra Angelico (1550), Vasari contrasts the pious Dominican friar to painters of little faith and little reverence for religion, whose beautiful forms "call to mind indecent appetites and lascivious desires," such that the work is praised for skill but censured for immorality. But Vasari quickly adds that he does not mean to suggest that only homely paintings are holy:

> I would not wish to mislead anyone into thinking that devout painting must be clumsy or inept, as do those who when they see paintings with figures of women or youths more than ordinarily charming or beautiful or adorned, immediately judge them lascivious, not realizing how they condemn the good judgment of the painter who considers the saints celestial, and therefore that much more beautiful than mortal nature as heaven itself exceeds the earthly beauty of our works.

Vasari's argument is that piety alone cannot make a painting a good work of art, and that a sensual painting may well be pious. He anticipates and contests the puritanical preference for the works of the medieval Christian artists. This question did not yet seem closed to Vasari even when he rewrote the book eighteen years later. He added then the disclaimer that he did not, after all, approve of nearly nude figures in churches, conceding that the appetite for beauty must be subordinated to the principle of decorum, or adaptation to place and circumstances. In this way he justified his own evenhanded historiographical treatment of artistic depictions of pagan and Christian subjects, which meet on his pages with little discussion of religion; the passage on Fra Angelico is an exception. Vasari lifts art out of worldly history; art now has its own history, the history of its self-realization. Art flows from artist to artist, a constant metamorphosis.

The first edition of Vasari's book, 1300 pages in two quarto volumes, was published in Florence in 1550 by Lorenzo Torrentino and dedicated to the Duke of Florence Cosimo de' Medici. Vasari structured his material as a series of lives punctuated by three general essays on the history and the principles of art. Of course, Vasari wrote in Italian, not Latin. The book narrated the lives of some 140 painters, sculptors, and architects. In the indexes about 300 more artists are mentioned. A further twenty-nine-page index lists 2100 works of art, by city and repository. Where Michiel was spare, Vasari is prolix. His text ran to 290,000 words, the length of James Joyce's *Ulysses*. The book is a readable mix of fact, anecdote, description of paintings, and value judgments that plunges the reader into the company of the makers, the purchasers, and the judges of art.

Vasari was born in 1511 in Arezzo, where the fame of the Etruscan pots such as those admired by Restoro d'Arezzo persisted. The chronicler Giovanni Villani—uncle of Filippo who had memorialized the Florentine painters—had written at the start of the fourteenth century about the Aretine pottery "made in ancient times by the most subtle masters," red vases "with various subtly incised decorations in all forms, and when you see them it seems impossible that they could be the work of men, and you can still find them." Vasari himself, whose name means "potter," mentions the Etruscan pots found in his native Arezzo in the "Preface to the Lives": "you can easily see that art had not just gotten started in those times, on the contrary, for from the perfection of those works it would seem to be closer to the zenith than to the beginning. As one likewise sees every day from the many pieces of those red and black Aretine vases, made, if one can judge from the style, around the same time."

Vasari's greatest achievement is the establishment of a program for empirical scholarship. The weight of fact testifies to a will to probity and objectivity. He gathers information from all over Italy, interviewing artists and patrons. He tries to distinguish reliable from unreliable sources. Vasari began early on compiling notes; already in 1536 Pietro Aretino refers to him as the *historico*, "historian." He studied the manuscripts of Ghiberti; as an eighteen-year-old he had lodged with Ghiberti's great-grandson in Florence. He drew on all the prior compilers: Antonio Billi, mentioned earlier, and the notes on Florentine art assembled, probably in the 1540s, by the author known as Anonimo Magliabechiano, as well as the description of the treasures of Florence, the *Memoriale di molte statue et picture* (1510) by Francesco Albertini, an antiquarian and cleric (the same who commented on the monolithic columns moved by Nicholas V to St. Peter's). (In his guidebook Albertini had named over two hundred works by artists as old as Cimabue and Giotto; even Masolino and Masaccio were for Albertini already *antiqui maestri*; he also gave locations of works and mentioned patrons and costs.) Vasari was given access to manuscript notes on fifteenth-century painters by Domenico Ghirlandaio, the teacher of Michelangelo. He says that he does not judge a painting unless he has seen it with his own eyes, and he tells readers exactly where the paintings could be found. He attributes old paintings on the basis of documents and heraldics but above all on the basis of style, for as he tells his readers "long practice teaches attentive painters to recognize, as you know, the various manners of other artists just as a learned and experienced secretary (*cancelliere*) recognizes the diverse and various handwritings of his colleagues." He makes every effort to follow an artist's evolution year by year.

Vasari frames his *Lives* with an overall "Preface to the Work," where he discusses the origins of art and ancient art, as well as an overall "Preface to the Lives" and prefaces to the second and third parts in which he expounds his theory of art and art history. The three parts correspond to three phases in the life-cycle of modern Italian art: rebirth with Giotto and his heirs; maturation beginning with Masaccio; and the ascent to perfection beginning with Leonardo and culminating in Michelangelo. This scheme still structures many textbooks and university courses on Renaissance art. Vasari admired the same artists who are admired today. There have been no drastic corrections to his judgments, except that some northern Italian artists like Cosimo Tura, whom he considered eccentric, are now cherished, not to mention the Venetian painters—Giovanni Bellini, Giorgione, Titian—whose genius Vasari misunderstood.

The modern art historian Lionello Venturi criticized Vasari for giving us "too many origins": diligence, study, imitation, knowledge of science. The one origin point missing, according to Venturi, is the only one that counts: imagination. Vasari tells us too much about patrons and commissions, tells too many anecdotes about the artists' families and training and eccentric habits. But with his anecdotes Vasari was only trying to express his conviction that art emerges out of life. His character sketches reveal more about art than his descriptions of paintings, which are spare. Among the caprices of the "dreamy" (*fantastico*) and "solitary" Jacopo Pontormo, for example, was that the room in which he slept and sometimes worked was accessible only by a ladder that he would pull up behind him with a pulley so that no one could climb up and disturb him. Francesco Salviati, meanwhile, a melancholic, first welcomed his friends into the Audience Chamber of the Palazzo Vecchio, which he was decorating for Cosimo de' Medici, and then before long began overpraising his own work and censuring the work of others, so angering his friends.

Vasari's *Lives*, more than any other European text up to this point, established a feedback loop between writing and art-making. Artists, once they had read Vasari, had difficulty imagining themselves participating in any other history than his. The book made artists aware of the directionality of their art, where it stood on a curve. The book offered the history of art as a legitimating context for art, to compete with the honor of the Church or the glory of a dynastic house.

Humanistic and philological scholarship, with its encouragement of hermeneutical reading, introduced scholars into a transgenerational conversation, rhetorical, relative, attentive to local norms, preparing readers to respond to the questions raised in the sixteenth century by the schism in the Church and the political turmoil. Vasari was seemingly untouched by this project, taking no interest in the functions of art, even though those functions were being redefined year to year, across Europe, in his time. In the "Preface to the Lives" he says that the first arts to fall into decay in the centuries after Constantine were painting and sculpture, "arts that served more for pleasure than for use." Because he is interested mainly in the pleasure that art gives, and not its uses, his conception of art is nonrhetorical, that is, noncontextual. Since the eminence of great art is self-evident, in Vasari's view, art requires no interpretation. The conversation among artists that Vasari initiates is transhistorical, but it is carried out on only one channel. And that is why he introduces a confusing distinction between *ancient* and *old*: "the 'ancient' (*antico*) are those works made, before Constantine, in Corinth, Athens, Rome and other famous cities, up until the times of Nero, the Flavians, Trajan, Hadrian, and Antoninus, whereas what are called 'old' (*vecchie*) are those works made after the time of St. Sylvester [pope from 313–335] by some left-over Greeks who knew how to dye rather than to paint." This merely "old" and unregulated style was followed by the "modern" style, that is, we recall, the good but incompletely regulated manner introduced by Cimabue and Giotto, local and customary in Tuscany; and finally by the style called *antico*, a successful emulation of the ancient models. Vasari may multiply the discriminations, but in the end he is just an annalist.

Vasari's enterprise may be compared to the annalistic prefatory texts to the albums of calligraphy and painting compiled at the Safavid courts of sixteenth-century Persia. These prefaces list the names and comment upon the works of distinguished calligraphers and miniature painters. The most important is the preface by the painter Dust Muhammad to the Bahram Mirza album (1544–1545). Dust Muhammad names and praises many calligraphers of the fourteenth and fifteenth centuries, providing information about who studied with whom and, like Vasari, employing repeatable topoi of praise: "the tongue of the pen falls short of doing justice" to such and such a master; other masters were "jealous" of his skill. Some remarks give us an insight into Dust Muhammad's understanding of art. He valued beauty and charm, of course, but also originality: he reports that "with the pen of his fingertips, on the tablet of vision," the earlier sixteenth-century master Nizamuddin Sultan-Muhammad "has drawn a different version at each and every instant."

The text expresses its author's annalistic desire to be written into art history. But like the early Chinese scribes, Dust Muhammad also writes his own art back into a creation myth:

> The coalesced forms and dispersed shapes of the archetypes were hidden in the recesses of the unseen in accordance with the dictum, "I was a hidden treasure." Then, in accordance with the words, "I wanted to be known, so I created creation in order to be known," he

snatched with the fingers of destiny the veil of non-existence from the countenance of being, and with the hand of mercy and the pen, which was "the first thing God created," he painted [them] masterfully on the canvas of being.

This is more poetic than anything offered by Vasari or any other European writer on art. Dust Muhammad tells several more stories about the origins of the art of painting. He speaks of the Byzantine emperor "Hercule" who showed some Muslim visitors an authentic portrait of Adam. He goes on to report that God gave Adam a chest containing several thousand pieces of silk, each bearing a portrait of a prophet. Alexander the Great seized this chest and gave it to the prophet Daniel, who copied the portraits, including that of Muhammad, the most beautiful of all, so initiating the art of painting. The Persian writer offers a reverse perspective on European art that is not matched by Vasari, who seems unaware, for example, that Italian architects in his lifetime were studying the mosques built by the Ottoman sultans. Portraiture, according to Dust Muhammad, flourished in the lands of Cathay and the Franks (i.e., China and Europe) "until sharp-penned Mercury scrivened the rescript of rule in the name of Sultan Abusa'id Khudaybanda" (i.e., the fourteenth century). Dust Muhammad offers the history of art as a succession of painting traditions distinguished by their mastery of representational technology, in other words, realism. It is a continuous history, like the Chinese histories of art, but distributed across competing and succeeding nations.

Portraiture, or realism, is presented as the painter's basic aim, even if Dust Muhammad's poetic way of writing would suggest that he well understood that there is more to art than the transcription of the appearances of things. He describes few works and generally seems less interested in content than in painterly skill. But he values form even less than content, or so he says: the recent painter Mawlam Muhammad known as Qadimi, "who knows that content is more important than form, has painted and spoken things as they ought to be." In other words, he recognizes some concept of rightness that is more than formal; perhaps it is ethical or metaphysical. This opens up the possibility of replacing a convergent, technique-based quest for the real with a history of art as an open-ended quest for truth. Either way, there is no trace in Dust Muhammad of a puritanical preference for a pristine, unschooled painting manner.

1550–1600

Vasari's *Lives of the Artists* is so important to the modern discipline of art history that we will pursue it into its second edition, published in 1568 with Giunti, now expanded into three volumes, with woodcut portraits preceding every biography and indexes that include topics, themes, and names of patrons as well as artists, places, and works.

Vasari's attitude to art is aristocratic: he is interested only in the best art. He has no more sympathy for the bad art of the past than he has for the bad art of the present. Vasari stoops to praise the Last Judgment carved on the pulpit in Pisa by Nicola Pisano (c. 1260), today hailed as a masterpiece: "He made many figures, if not perfect in design (*disegno*), at least with infinite patience and diligence." Co-opted into the *campanilismo* of the Florentines, who cherished Giotto as a naïve founder, the Aretine Vasari makes a half-hearted effort to indulge the Trecento painters. His admiration is less sincere than Ghiberti's, for by now the old masters have receded further in time. In the life of the painter Gaddo Gaddi, Vasari says he will not go on discussing his works, for the styles of those fourteenth-century masters "cannot be of much use to today's artists." Still, Vasari had something Ghiberti lacked, namely the example of his idol Michelangelo, who he knew admired Giotto. Thus, as we saw, Vasari condescends to judge the fourteenth-century artists not by the best standards, which would doom them, but by the standards of their own time. Vasari extended his contextualizing generosity to the skilled painters of the next century, the "second period." Vasari's descriptions of pictorial expressions of lived experience in fifteenth-century paintings are among his most animated passages, revealing a hidden enthusiasm. In the "Preface to Part Two" he mentions as a rare example of a surviving and admirable work by a master of the second period the depiction by Masaccio in the Brancacci Chapel of "a naked man shivering with cold." In his account of Piero della Francesca's *Legend of the True Cross*, a mural in his home town of Arezzo, Vasari says nothing about the painter's mathematics-based mastery of linear perspective but instead admires "the garments of the women of the Queen of Sheba, carried out in a sweet and novel manner" and "a peasant who, leaning on the spade in his hands, stands all attentive as he listens to St. Helen speaking."

In these passages the mediation of art melts away. Vasari's ekphrases are not so different from the descriptions of imaginary paintings by the third-century Sophist Philostratus, literary exercises that give you the scene itself, not the scene as painted. Philostratus was much read in the Renaissance, in the original Greek—first in manuscript and later in Aldus Manutius's edition of 1503—as well as in Latin and Italian translation. Here Vasari, like Pliny, who dealt out many anecdotes about the power of painterly illusion, is endorsing the preferences of the layman. Such descriptions are uncoupled from the craftsman's ideals of the well-made artifact. Vasari understands craftsmanship as the prerequisite of an expressive realism. A history of realism will tend to converge and in the long run conflict with the nonconvergent and annalistic "aristocratic" model that Vasari otherwise offers.

Vasari's treatment of the architecture of the past was more subtle. He has no praise at all for buildings built by architects whose names he does not know. The only architect in his book older than Brunelleschi is the thirteenth-century Tuscan Arnolfo di Cambio, better known as a sculptor. The Basilica of St. Francis at Assisi does not rate inclusion in Vasari's annals except as a place where one might see paintings by Giotto. (Vasari does report, however, that Pietro Cavallini stopped at Assisi "to see those buildings and those notable works made there by his master and by some of his fellow disciples." Vasari mistakenly believed Cavallini to be a pupil of Giotto). But Vasari himself was active as a renewer of medieval churches in Florence. At S. Maria Novella and S. Croce he removed the rood-screens, the structures that divided nave from choir. One may interpret his interventions not as arrogant corrections but as attempts to recover the historical buildings, fulfilling the original intentions of the builders—even if they go unnamed in his history—

by clearing out sightlines so that the interior structure could be seen. At S. Maria Novella, Vasari built an altar in front of Masaccio's fresco of the *Trinity* (1426–1428), which he had praised in his *Lives,* concealing but preserving the venerable masterpiece. But generally care was taken to preserve old works and cite old forms. The new façade of Santi Giovanni and Reparata in Lucca (1587) incorporated the old portal with its sculptures, signed by the master Villano in 1187. The architects of the Counter-Reformation designed new structures that cited medieval forms. The *confessio,* a reliquary chamber and space for prayer below the main altar but visible from above, an innovation of the Cappella Sistina at S. Maria Maggiore (1585), S. Susanna (1590), and other Roman churches, recollected the reliquary crypts of Romanesque churches. The twin bell towers at S. Anna dei Palafrenieri (from 1565), S. Trinità dei Monti (from 1567), and other new churches echoed the façades of Romanesque churches in northern Italy.

Like many painters, Vasari collected drawings. He mounted them on album pages with drawn frames and labels, gathering old and new on the same plane. Although his *Libro de' disegni* has long since been dispersed, many of the drawings are still attached to the original album pages. It is estimated that the work comprised 600 sheets with drawings attached to both sides. Among the earliest artists represented in the collection were Cimabue (or so Vasari thought—the drawing reproduced here is now attributed to the much later artist Spinello Aretino), Giotto, Gaddo Gaddi, Oderisi da Gubbio, Pietro and Ambrogio Lorenzetti, and Andrea Pisano. There were drawings by many fifteenth-century masters as well as engravings by Martin Schongauer and Albrecht Dürer—about 250 artists in all, possibly including Jörg Breu. The drawing attributed to Cimabue is a sheet of fine pen studies of scenes of martrydom, perhaps of a certain St. Potitus, copies made probably around 1400 after an older fresco cycle. On the verso there are similar scenes and Vasari's inscription of Cimabue's name, just visible in reverse at the bottom of the recto. Around the drawing Vasari drew a frame comprising a pointed arch and tympanum, two pinnacles, and somewhat classical pilasters and architrave. Above he pasted a copy of the woodcut portrait of Cimabue that appeared in the 1568 edition of his *Lives.*

For all his sympathy and curiosity, Vasari says at the end of the first edition that the purpose of making new art is to make the old art appear less beautiful and less illustrious. He is interested in the present state of

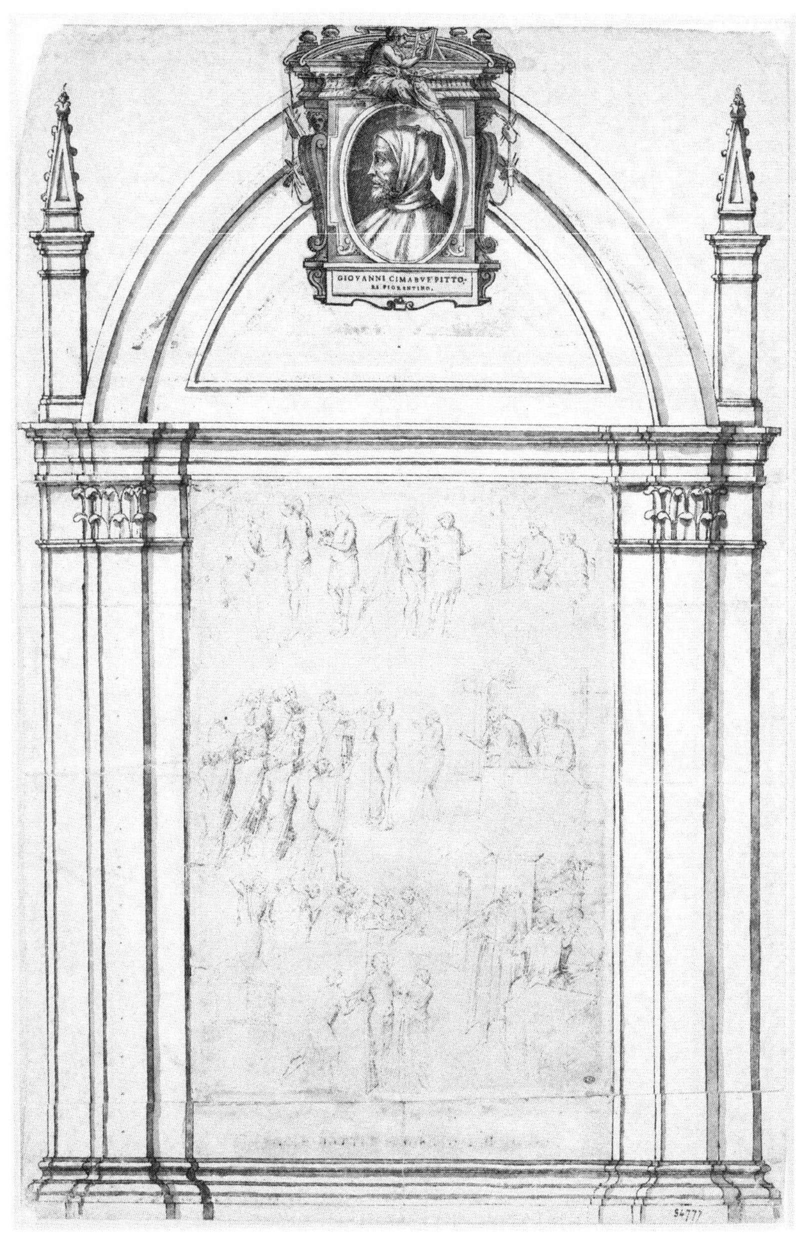

Spinello Aretino (?), *Scenes of the Martyrdom of St. Potitus* (?) (c. 1400). Pen drawing, 27.2 × 19.2 cm. Paris, École des Beaux-Arts. The drawing was mounted by Giorgio Vasari in the album he called his *Libro de' disegni*. The woodcut portrait pasted above the drawing is inscribed with the name of the artist Vasari believed had made the drawing: "Giovanni Cimabue, Florentine painter."

art, and at most the immediate preconditions for the present that had been established by Leonardo, Raphael, and Michelangelo between about 1490 and 1520. In short, his demonstrations of hospitality to the art of the past do not challenge the ideal of the best art.

The theorists of ideal or metaphysical art shared Vasari's scorn for medieval painting. Giovanni Battista Armenini (*De veri precetti della pittura*, 1587) derided the "strange paintings on the walls of many old churches and…those badly made puppets outlined on fields of gold which are seen scattered on many panels throughout Italy." Armenini thought Vasari's chronicles of the painters between Cimabue and Pietro Perugino (Raphael's teacher) served no purpose, for there was nothing to learn from those artists. Polidoro da Caravaggio, for instance, learned all he needed to know from studying the masters working side by side with Raphael on the loggie at the Vatican. Armenini considered Giotto overrated, mentioning Perugino as an artist "not inferior" to him. Gian Paolo Lomazzo, the painter and theorist, wrote in his treatise *Idea del tempio della pittura* (1590) that "painting languished and died, and remained buried from the time of Emperor Constantine until that of Emperors Maximilian and Charles V."

Vasari is suspended between several concepts of art. He is not interested in the liturgical functions of the religious painting or its contributions to theology. He is not interested in typological links to prestigious content or ur-forms. He does not treat public works differently from private ones. All contents for him are equally entangled in the riddles of form. He cannot explain art's relation to truth, or to the rest of life, nor does he speak any language that would permit him to describe art as fiction.

For all the idealist underpinnings, Vasari's descriptive vocabulary remains limited, and in the end his ekphrases begin to sound alike. If you do not already know the work he is writing about, it is difficult to visualize it. Although the technologies of woodcut and engraving were well established, no works are illustrated in Vasari's book. In fact, no published histories of art before the eighteenth century were illustrated. One is tempted to account for the coherence of premodern art theory with the bon mot of the twentieth-century art historian Erwin Panofsky: if you want to prove a point, don't illustrate it. Works by the early masters, who we are told in the prefaces were still very far from perfection, are described by Vasari as "beautiful" and "perfect." And so are the perfect works of Raphael and Michelangelo. When words fail him, Vasari resorts to the phrase *non so che*, meaning *je ne sais quoi*, a formulation of Saint Augustine (*nescio quid*) which had become shorthand for an ineffable quality. Vasari seems to understand that a depiction insofar as it is art-like is noncommunicative. Interestingly he uses the phrase *non so che* to describe a *religious* quality, an index perhaps of his confidence that the project of sacred painting is by no means inimical to artistic expression, that on the contrary Christian art had always been a generous host of creativity. In general one may have to read between the lines in order to detect Vasari's deeper insights. Julius von Schlosser read Vasari's bold interpretation of the twisted figures of the early fifteenth-century painter Parri Spinelli—the son of Spinello Aretino, and like Vasari a native of Arezzo—as a coded response to a traumatic experience of assault. Vasari described a painted Annunciation in a chapel at the Old Cathedral outside of Arezzo, where the Virgin Mary, "terrified by the angel, is all twisted, as if she were fleeing." He went on to report that the painter Spinelli

> was assaulted one day, while he was working on this painting, by some enemies and relatives, with a grievance about some money matter, with weapons to frighten him. He was immediately rescued, however, by some people who happened along. But surely the fear he experienced in this assault was the reason that he always painted his figures twisted toward one side.

Vasari raises the possibility that the real experience of this "solitary and melancholic" artist reaches into his work.

How poor Vasari's literary soil is, how uninspiring and unpoetic his comments on art. When he is faced with enigmatic modern pictures, he stalls. He reports with irritation that no one in Venice could help him decipher the frescoes by Giorgione on the walls of the Fondaco dei Tedeschi. Venetian pictures of this period, it is true, often seem to lack subject matter. Depictions of people lost in daydreams, thematizing the elusiveness of meaning, did not trouble the patrician fact-gatherer Marcantonio Michiel, who never puzzled long over subject matter. Instead of turning to theory, Vasari might have done well to say nothing at all, like Michiel.

Vasari's theoretical justification for the superiority of modern art established the hierarchy between the applied or decorative arts and the fine arts, which is the basis for the modern system of art and prevails to this day. Vasari deigned to write briefly about the arts he considered minor (engraving, manuscript illumination, intarsia, glass painting, embroidery) as well as about non-Italian art. Many of these arts were expensive and prestigious, above all tapestry, which he concisely praises as "the most beautiful invention…, offering comfort and grandeur, capable of transporting painting to any place wild or tamed." But the theory of *disegno* brings painting, sculpture, and architecture under a common denominator that excludes the minor arts—in fact, makes them minor. *Disegno* denotes the ability to extract from the natural data an improved scheme, an ideal form latent in the given. *Disegno*, which might be described as the correct ratio between the real and the true, enforces an invidious and in many quarters still active distinction between Italian art (guided, like the best ancient art, by the ideal) and non-Italian art (guided by the mere appearance of things or by caprice).

Disegno earns for art an edifying, reflective, and constructive function, justifying not only its status alongside poetry but also its prestige within society. The theory of art expounded in the *Lives of the Artists* was institutionalized by the Florentine academy, the *Accademia e Compagnia delle Arti del Disegno*, founded by Duke Cosimo de' Medici in 1563. The basis of training in this very first art academy, and for a long time in all subsequent such academies, will be drawn from those antique models understood to embody *disegno*. As for drawing directly from the live nude model, there is little evidence for it in the sixteenth century, though by the seventeenth century the practice was established. The rest of the curriculum was instruction in mathematics, especially Euclid; public lectures; and drapery studies.

Although nearly all the works in his topographical index of works are in churches, Vasari has little to say about the functions of sacred paintings. He admires modern churches and their architects; he notes the confraternities and other lay patrons of works in churches; he mentions sacred images associated with miracles. But when he discusses a chapel he says more about the artists who adorned it than the patrons who paid for it, the clerics who manage the liturgy, or the pilgrims who worship there. Vasari's ekphrases bring icons, altarpieces, decorated organ shutters, and worldly pictures displayed in banquet halls and bedrooms to a common plane. He would seem to have adopted a secular understanding of art, that is, a capacity to assign value to paintings independent of their referential claims (to a god or holy person) or their contribution to ritualized communications with divinity. If the sacred involves a stabilization of the valuation process, then the profane invites a ceaseless displacement of values. The comparative assignation of value to art, the preference for one work over another, represents an attempt to stabilize values but without any illusions that this will have any real impact, as a stabilization of values in the sacred sphere must. The secularization of art in the sixteenth century, a shift in mentality initially driven by the migration of a pragmatic artisan's attitude to art from the workshop into polite spheres, set in motion an endless proliferation of private evaluations and a shift of control of this process over to the non-artist.

Europeans routinely condemned as superstitions the artifacts and practices they encountered abroad: effigies, relics, miracle-working images. In fact such things were ubiquitous in Europe, and cult practices at the margins of the liturgy thrived right through Vasari's century and onward. Vasari mentioned ex votos, but indirectly, in the context of a discussion of the technical contributions to the art of sculpture by Andrea del Verrocchio:

> From this men came to make more perfect images, not only in Florence, but in all the places in which there is devoutness, and to which people flock to offer votive images, or, as they are called, "miracles," in return for some favour received. For whereas they were previously made small and of silver, or only in the form of little panels, or rather of wax, and very clumsy, in the time of Andrea they began to be made in a much better manner.

With Verrocchio's counsel the craftsman Orsino was able to construct life-size wax figures "portrayed from life, and painted in oils with all the ornaments of hair and everything else that was necessary, so lifelike and so well wrought that they seemed no mere images of wax, but actual living men."

Like a Protestant reformer, Vasari disdained illusionism in the service of superstition. Protestant zealots in many towns in northern Europe had destroyed quantities of medieval paintings and sculptures or banished them to the private sphere. This made effective political theater. Many citizens were unhappy with the overturning of the old ways and lamented the loss of what the works symbolized, and some few, presumably, lamented the loss of the works themselves. With time, a more circumspect attitude to old artifacts took shape. The painter and art historian Karel van Mander reported in 1604 that the painting of the Crucifixion in Bruges by the fifteenth-century master Hugo van der Goes was preserved, "even during the mindless fanaticism of the iconoclasm," "for the sake of art." But not for long: it was soon overpainted with black and the Ten Commandments in gold letters on a black background. A disgrace, in van Mander's view; luckily they were able to remove the overpainting later.

Around 1572 the Swiss artist Tobias Stimmer published a pair of chiaroscuro woodcuts representing the carved figures of Ecclesia and Synagoga on the portal of the south transept of Strasbourg cathedral (c. 1230). Stimmer does not reproduce the drapery or bodies faithfully but instead inflates his models into ample modern proportions. He lets them step forward out of their niches. Although they appear to be representations of real women, not sculptures, the verse below Ecclesia, probably composed by Johann Fischart, says, "These two beautiful old images / are found in Strasbourg / On the cathedral on the rear door / across from the Bishop's Palace / There you see the old art / And what they believed." The iconography of Ecclesia and Synagoga was rare after 1300. The verses under Synagoga offer two different reasons for preserving the old works. First, a theological reassurance: these images are after all consistent with Protestantism. But the verse goes on to offer a second justification: "For that reason and for their artistry (*Künstligkeyt*) we preserve such images today." Stimmer and Fischart, artists, introduce a concept that overrides doctrinal discontinuity.

Typology or continuity was the main concern of Counter-Reformation historians of the Church. The study of the catacombs of Rome, subterranean burial chambers decorated with simple wall paintings and inscriptions, set in motion the study of early Christian imagery and symbolism. There was plenty of awareness of the catacombs throughout the sixteenth century but little commentary on their contents. St. Filippo Neri used to bring his disciples. A breakthrough came in 1578, when the paintings in the catacomb of Priscilla on the via Salaria were discovered. These were incunabula of Christian iconography, austere, inexpressive, self-sufficient. The images were inexpertly drawn but authentic by virtue of their great antiquity. Torch-lit explorations of the Roman catacombs were undertaken, revealing the diagram-like paintings, gnomic Christian symbols, and unfamiliar portrayals of Christ and the early saints. The discoveries called into question the typological rights of succession of modern Christian art. One might guess that sixteenth-century Roman

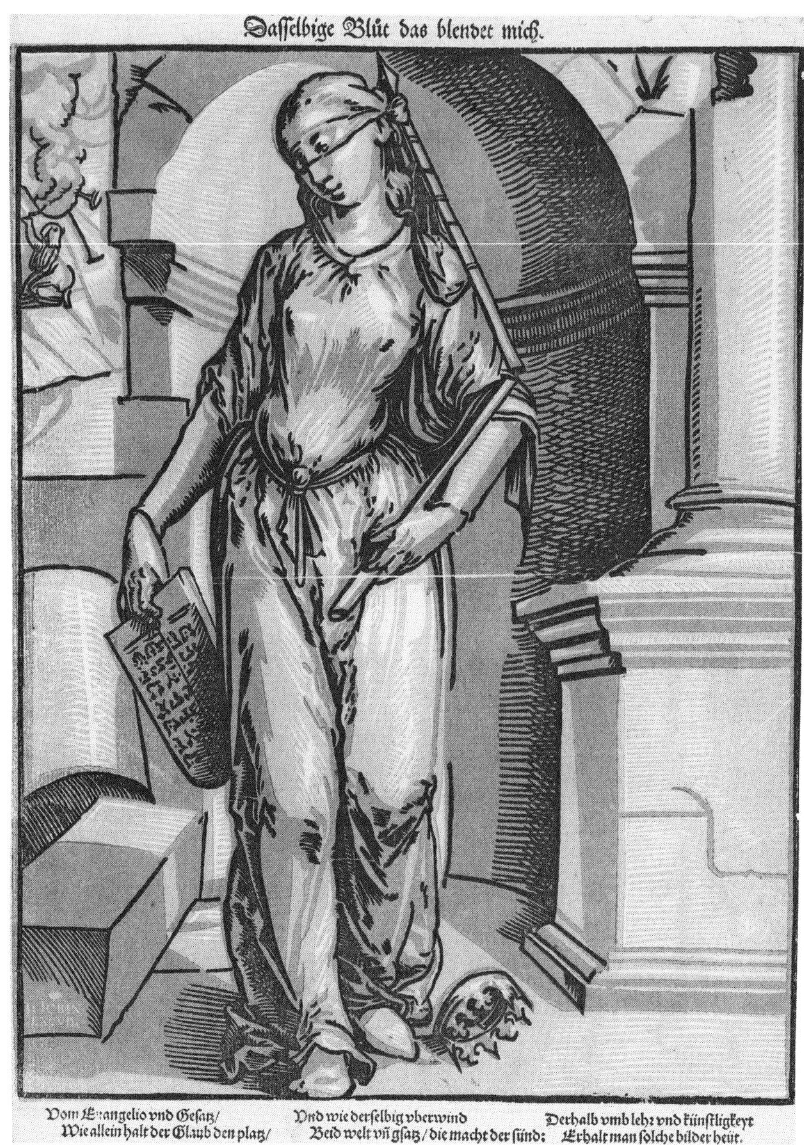

Tobias Stimmer, *Synagoga* (c. 1572). Chiaroscuro woodcut, 37.8 × 27 cm. Basel, Kunstmuseum. The inscription above, responding to Ecclesia's threat "With the blood of Christ I overcome you," reads: "The very blood that blinds me." The verses below explain that the pairing of Synagoga and Ecclesia illustrates the triumph of Christian faith over the Mosaic Law, Sin, and ultimately the World, and for that reason—as well as the artfulness of the works— we preserve them.

painters would be shaken by these uncouth witnesses, realizing how far the modern formulations of the sacred subjects had strayed from the venerable paths. Apparently they were not. The artistic shortcomings of the ancient Christian paintings were too blatant.

A modern painter was more likely to be drawn to another subterranean trove, the clandestine antitheses of the catacomb paintings, the *grotteschi*, ornamental flourishes on the ceiling vaults of the Roman palaces, long buried, and rediscovered in the late fifteenth century. Throughout the sixteenth century these images of hybrid animality flickered on the margins of the modern ideal style. The Dutch painter Karel van Mander, according to an ill-informed biographer, "was the first in Rome to rediscover the grottoes." "He made many copies from them underground, and of other objects, chiefly the antiquities; in short everything conceivable that was strange (*vreemt*)." These forms, rare survivals in the medium of painting from the ancient world, as if overcoming oblivion with wit and vitality, encouraged painters to animate and bend their figures, submitting them to invisible drives. *Grotteschi* teemed on the ceiling vaults of the galleries of the Uffizi, the palace designed by Vasari and today housing the very sequence of paintings that illustrates his history.

The *grotteschi* thematized monstrosity in an elegant, witty tone. Rough medieval figurations of the monstrous, however, in architectural sculpture or in the margins of illuminated manuscripts, which aimed not to stylize but to contain demonic and incomprehensible energies, were unassimilable to modern art.

Above ground, scholar-clerics cast a new eye on the medieval art of Rome, the mosaics and wall paintings of the fourth century or ninth century, stark, urgent forms that had not held the attention of Vasari for more than an instant. The art of early medieval Rome cut a poor figure next to the surviving pagan statuary and its expanding repertoire of shapely modern imitations. The antiquarian scholars who parsed the old paintings were interested in content, not form. The cardinal and historian Cesare Baronio in his *Annales Ecclesiastici* (12 vols., 1588–1607) noted that the Pseudo-Synode of 692 in Constantinople had prohibited the representation of Christ as a lamb. And yet in the New Testament Christ had been compared to a lamb, and thus had the paintings in the catacombs and later in the mosaics depicted him, in defiance of the Eastern Church's edict. Impressive evidence, to be sure.

The Church historians were disturbed, however, by the discrepancies between ancient Christian and modern Christian painting. The evidence of the catacombs seemed to confirm the contention of Protestant reformers that the Roman church had erred and to refute the Catholic controversialists who had insisted that the rituals and the images of the saints preserved by the Roman Church were rooted in primitive Christianity. Following the lead of scholars who collected and described the material remains of pagan antiquity, supplementing the evidence of the surviving ancient texts, the ecclesiastical historians took up the study of images, symbols, liturgical instruments, and the churches themselves. The Veronese cleric and historian monk Onofrio Panvinio published a description of the Roman basilicas (1570). His interest was mainly in patronage and inscriptions, his comments on the style of the buildings and images detractive—or at most grudging, making allowances for the time. The Dominican historian Alfonso Chacón, in pursuit of the true appearances of the popes and apostles, made drawings of the images in the catacombs as well as early mosaics. In his *Historia delle stationi di Roma* (1586) the antiquarian Pompeo Ugonio did offer some basic stylistic comparisons. But on the whole these scholars attended to iconography, in the original sense: whether this or that image delivered the true appearance of St. Peter and so forth. They did not assign value to the creativity of early or later medieval artists. None of them was able to envision a new, primitivist Christian art, as Martin Luther and Lucas Cranach in their way had.

Only the cleric Giovanni Andrea Gilio, sharply critical of the modern manner of painting represented by Michelangelo and Vasari, praised the pious style of the early Christian painters. Gilio urged a return to simplicity:

> The painting of decent and devout sacred images, with the traits they were given by the ancients, by the privilege of sanctity, has seemed to vile moderns something crude, plebeian, old-fashioned, lowly, without genius or art. And so these moderns, putting art before honesty, abandoning the custom of clothing the figures, instead made them nude; abandoning the custom of making them devout, they instead made them look forced, for to them it seemed a great thing to twist the heads, the arms, the legs such that they appear to be representing people dancing the moresca and other performances rather than people in a state of contemplation.

Gilio was pleading for more content and less form: a chastisement of art.

> And they have so debased the sacred customs with their new invention that one could hardly imagine paintings in brothels and taverns more indecent than these.

But Gilio had little influence on modern painting. It is possible, however, that some of the tranquility, gravity, and poise of early Christian art filtered into later sixteenth-century painting, for example in the works of Girolamo Muziano or Scipio Pulzone.

Although the scourge Gilio was insensitive to art, he was at least pointing to the possibility of a history of art not merely technical (i.e., convergent on high craft achievement) and not merely typological (i.e., dedicated to continuity of content at all costs). Unfamiliar content, the internal alterity of earlier phases of Christianity, could catalyze new thinking about the coordination of artistic form and content. The confrontation with external alterity—religious imagery beyond Christianity—had the same potential. Luxury goods imported from beyond Europe did not provoke such reflections. Non-European artifacts, purchases, plunder, gifts, dearly priced products of nature and artifice, were valued for workmanship and beauty. Lacking religious content, such objects generated no historical consciousness. With well-made objects, age as such was simply not an issue. The value of these objects was precisely their capacity to retain value beyond the original scenes of their fabrication and application.

Awareness of the contexts and histories of non-European forms opened only with travel and contact. Luxury goods arrived in Europe from the East, usually overland through a long series of relays. Few Europeans ever tracked the route back to the sources. Europeans knew Chinese luxury products but nothing about China. Nor did the Chinese know much about Europe. In the fifteenth and sixteenth centuries shipbuilding and navigation opened up new channels of awareness. The expansion of geographical reach brought more and more Europeans to remote shores. Some merchants and priests were curious enough to describe local customs, including architecture, cult images, and religious rituals; others made drawings. Travelers seek terms of comparison. European accounts of celebrants, dancers, costumes, carriages, and images in India, as well as temples, were carried by European terms such as shrine, altar, priest. Travelers and explorers often conceived the alterity of the peoples of the Americas and South Asia in historical terms, mapping unfamiliarity onto time. In his memoir of the conquest of Mexico (1568), the Spanish soldier Bernal Díaz del Castillo wondered whether the Americans had received their idols from the pagans or the Jews. The European came to understand the non-European as the prisoner of a nondynamic history; closer to the origin, but stalled.

When Europeans visited temples they saw a tradition- and ritual-bound art without history. Those with access to Chinese or Mughal courts soon learned, if they did not know already, that there were fine-art traditions other than the European. But they were unable to discriminate within those traditions.

A good witness is Antonio Monserrate (1536–1600), a Portuguese Jesuit who tried to convert the Mughal emperor Akbar to Christianity. His account of his travels in India between 1579 and 1582 includes many comments on artifacts and practices. In the city of Mandu in Madhya Pradesh, for example, Monserrate describes a half-finished royal tomb, "worth seeing for its architecture and huge size," and other buildings of "similar magnificence and costliness." He identifies a local style of architecture in Ujjain that "possesses a distinctive character of its own, and is not unpleasing to the eye, though it is infinitely inferior to the glories of the Roman workmanship." The European is more generous when he perceives a familiar pattern of the loss and recovery of historical material. In Mathura, in Uttar Pradesh, one of the cities associated with the origins of Hinduism, Monserrate sees ruins that "plainly indicate how imposing its buildings were. For out of these forgotten ruins are dug up columns and ancient statues, of skillful and cunning workmanship." Through excavation the Hindus write their own histories of sacred architecture.

When it came to the sacred image, possible target of worship, the European attitude was circumspect. The learned were aware that India was considered by some the seat of a pristine religion that predated the Egyptian and Greek religions. Gian Paolo Lomazzo described Michelangelo as a "gymnosophist," or an Indian "naked philosopher," a species known from the writings of Plutarch and Alberti. (Lomazzo also called Albrecht Dürer the "grand Druid," implying that the German artist had channelled native pre-Roman, precivilized pagan energies.) Yet the Hindu images had to be condemned as idols representing false gods. No European writing on South Asia fails to say this. The Jesuit Antonio Rubino in his treatise of 1608 on Vijayanagara (a city that included the modern site Hampi) combines detailed descriptions of idols and cult practices with contempt for the worshippers' belief that Peremal (Vishnu), who may appear as an elephant, a pig, or a bird, is a god. Rubino says that the Hindu images are so indecent that they cannot possibly represent gods. Christians believed that their own Church had vanquished both an older monotheistic (and iconophobic) religion and a plurality of interrelated pagan (but mostly iconophilic) cults. The Christian image-cult was a complex triage by which Christians tried to maintain the Judaic mistrust of image worship even while protecting a role for images in ritual. Christians recognized their own cult images as works of art—that is to say, beautiful as well as true—because they believed that their own god or holy personages had to be beautiful. They could postpone thinking about Hindu images as art, first, because the depicted gods were false (that is, either nonexistent or real but demonic and untrustworthy, claiming too many powers) and second, because those pretenders were anyway ugly (they had too many body parts, they were naked, their hindquarters were visible).

Europeans described the cult practices of the Hindus as immemorial customs, without history. Here a European could see a typological model of artifact production in its pure form. If you asked them who was the builder of a temple, Monserrate says, "the reply is sure to be 'Birbitcremas.' This is superstition." Birbitcremas, or Vikramaditya, was a legendary royal founder, possibly identical to the fourth- and fifth-century king Chandragupta II. It is as if a traveler to Rome were to ask who built the Church of the Gesù, and was told "Emperor Constantine." But why not? Constantine did after all introduce the type of the basilica. He may be a more significant origin point than the building's architects, Giacomo Barozzi da Vignola and Giacomo della Porta. The legendary origin is just another way of representing the history of architecture, not less true than Vasari's authorial version.

The theological riddles interfered with European perception of non-European art. It is instructive to compare the treatment of formal alterity in poetry, where there was no reference to the real and no entanglement in a cult. George Puttenham in his *Arte of English Poesie* (1589) said that travelers to remote lands report that archaic poetry is rhymed, thus providing a basis for his own cautious defense of rhyme. The context for this was the call by some humanist scholars for an English equivalent to the unrhymed quantitative meters of antique poetry. This was a version of the Ciceronian debate. Roger Ascham (1570), for example, had condemned "our rude beggerly ryming, brought first into Italie by *Gothes* and *Hunnes*, whan all good verses and good learning to[o] were destroyd by them, and after caryed into France and Germanie, and at last receyued into England by men of excellent wit in deede, but of small learning and lesse iudgement in that behalfe." Ascham's depreciation of the medieval manner is similar to that of Vasari or Baronio. Philip Sidney, however, in his *Defense of Poetry* (c. 1579), found the old poetry moving. He praised the "Ballad of Chevy Chase": "Certainly, I must confess my own barbarousness, I never heard the old song of Percy and Douglas that I found not my heart moved more than with a trumpet; and yet it is sung but by some blind crowder [fiddler], with no rougher voice than rude style; which, being so evil apparelled in the dust and cobwebs of that uncivil age, what would it work trimmed in the gorgeous eloquence of Pindar?" Even Sidney says that the ballad tells an affecting story but would be still more affecting if told by a modern Pindar.

The very discourse of idolatry, which sees the other not simply as a rival but as a mistaken rival, raises the possibility of conversion. We see this in Monserrate's comments on Hindu-Muslim relations. Although Monserrate reviled the Hindu cults, he distanced himself from what he saw as the excessive and hypocritical iconophobia of the local Muslims, who deprecated the Hindus as idol-worshippers and destroyed their temples. Monserrate pointed out that the Muslims had erected in the place of the temples "countless tombs and little shrines of wicked and worthless Musalmans," in which "these men are worshipped with vain superstition, as though they were saints." Such distinctions had been cultivated for decades in schism-riven Europe. A new Christian anthropology broached the possibility of "looking through" mere customs to an essential humanity. The reflexive arrogance of the Europeans was troubled by inner voices expressing relativist doubts (Las Casas, Montaigne). Protestant disrespect for the Church of Rome opened ironic perspectives on all institutions and finally on civilization itself.

These are more promising positions than Vasari's intra-European xenophobia. Vasari blamed the *tedeschi*, the Germans, for the graceless art of the Middle Ages, here echoing Filarete, who in his treatise on architecture (before 1465) had blamed the *barbari* for discouraging the art of building in Italy, such that customs and traditions from beyond the Alps were imported not by real architects but by "goldsmiths, painters, and stonemasons." Vasari may not have known who the *tedeschi* were, nor did he really know who the Greeks or the Romans were, or for that matter the Italians. But he is halfway to an ethnicist nationalism because he knows who are *not* Italians. Somehow, at some point in the late Middle Ages—it is unexplained in his account—this internal alien was overcome. Vasari's account of the Tuscans shucking off the bad influence of the Germans as well as the errors of the postclassical Greeks (who after the studies of the German historian Hieronymus Wolf in the mid-sixteenth century would come to be called "Byzantines") is the mirror image of the double fall of Rome to the so-called barbarians, first in the fourth century BC and then again in the fifth century AD. Vasari's noble approach, which does not trouble itself with alterity, cannot lead to relativism.

Vasari took little interest in the non-Italian art of his own time except as a source of technical innovation. By now there was much movement by artists across Europe, plenty of Netherlanders and French in Rome and Florence, and Italians in Prague and Brussels, plenty of informants. Vasari sought facts about the introduction of oil as a medium for colors, an innovation attributed by legend to Jan van Eyck and which even Vasari had to concede had transformed the art of painting. The Italians, who had used to paint with tempera, learned in the mid- and later fifteenth century to paint with oils. The older writers all credited the Netherlanders with this innovation (even if Bartolomeus Facius says van Eyck learned it from the ancients). Vasari seems to have asked the opinion of the Flemish painter Lambert Lombard, who had been in Rome from 1537. In a letter of 1565, Lombard provides Vasari with just the answer he desires. Lombard is critical of Italian art between Giotto and Donatello, saying that the things he saw in Italy dating from the period around 1400 were not pleasing. In the Netherlands, meanwhile, Jan van Eyck and Rogier van der Weyden had opened the eyes of painters to color. But color alone was not enough. The local imitators of Jan and Rogier, Lombard assured Vasari, filled our churches with gaudy panels *vestite de belli colori* but not resembling the good or the natural. Lambert Lombard was one of the many Flemish converts to the Italian manner of painting. The scholar, poet, and painter Domenicus Lampsonius also contributed information to Vasari's second edition.

Because of their reverse perspective, northern European readers of Vasari acquired a complex grasp of art history. Because historiography in the north was little developed, the past was theirs for the shaping. The northern painters also wanted a "descent," an annalistic record they could append themselves to. Although the primacy of van Eyck and van der Weyden was uncontested, it was unclear whether their achievement was artistic or technical. Philip Galle and Jan van der Straet in their *Nova Reperta* (1590), an illustrated account of modern inventions, published an engraving of van Eyck working in his studio. In 1563 the merchant and painter Cornelis van Dalem mounted sandstone portrait busts of van Eyck and Dürer, carved probably by Willem van den Broeck, on either side of the doors of his home in Antwerp, inscribed *Belgarum Splendor* and *Germanorum Decus*. But what could a modern painter like Lambert Lombard learn from van Eyck? In the 1550s the king of Spain, Philip II, commissioned from Michael Coxcie an exact copy of the more than one-century-old masterpiece by van Eyck, the *Adoration of the Lamb*, the altarpiece at Ghent, the first copy since Jan Gossart's of 1526. The azurite pigment for Mary's robe was borrowed from the workshop of Titian. Coxcie also made two copies of Rogier van der Weyden's *Descent from the Cross*, a fifteenth-century painting purchased by Mary of Hungary, Philip's aunt, in the 1540s. The practice parallels the copies of antique statuary made in this period. Coxcie's copies are exact, but they differ in kind from the copies of a generation earlier, such as Gossart's copies of van Eyck's Ghent altarpiece or *Virgin in the Church*. Whereas Gossart in 1526 was still contending with van Eyck, by 1550 a gap had opened up between the style of the patriarchs and the modern style. Michael Coxcie's own paintings were not in the style of van Eyck. A similar case in Italy was the copy, in actual size but on copper, commissioned around 1570 by Pius V from his court painter Bartolomeus Spranger of Fra Angelico's *Last Judgment* triptych (1425–1430), to be mounted above the pope's tomb. To reproduce the sweet restraint of the pious Angelico, Spranger suppressed as best he could his own sensual torque, his natural style.

Unparalleled in Italy were the Netherlandish prints reproducing the venerable masterpieces of the local painting tradition. In 1565 Cornelis Cort made an engraving of Rogier van der Weyden's *Descent from the Cross*, adding a landscape background. Hieronymus Cock published a large engraving, attributed to Cort, of a Last Judgment triptych by

Hieronymus Bosch, reproducing not the composition but the painting itself, a central panel and two wings, complete with frames. The painting is signed "HIERONYMUS BOS INVENTOR." No such painting by Bosch is known, however. Cock and Cort created a pastiche of Boschian motifs and forms. The engraving is not a substitute for an absent original but rather a completion, a rounding out, of the history of art. Print detaches information from presence and so creates in the beholder a sensation of intellectual choice.

As time passed, more painters slipped into the past and became canonical. Bosch's singularity was protected by adaptations and quasi-copies by Pieter Bruegel. The masters of the early sixteenth century, Gossart, Quentin Massys, and Lucas van Leyden, were rediscovered. In 1589 Marten de Vos tried to prevent the export of an altar by Massys. In the same year Crispijn de Passe made an etching reproducing the *Virgin and Child*, the Vienna painting or one of its copies, by Gossart. Around 1615 Simon Frisius made an etching depicting the *Mass of St. Gregory* in an old-fashioned manner, inscribed with Gossart's name. No such painting by Gossart is known.

Meanwhile the doctrine of *disegno* created an Italian "inner north." Vasari's peninsular artist-readers, gripped by his judgments on art, crammed the book's margins with comments. Some Paduan artists who marked up a copy of Vasari expressed resentment of his dismissive treatment of northern Italian painters. One artist says he undertook a trip to Ferrara just to see an altarpiece by Francesco Francia, praised by Vasari, and found it a "shoddy piece of work" compared to the paintings of the "modern" Lombards. Federico Zuccaro, El Greco, and the Carracci were avid readers of Vasari. This is the circuit between art-making and the annals of art that produced modern art itself.

1600-1650

It was inevitable that a northern European artist would imitate Vasari. But it took half a century. Karel van Mander (1548–1606) was born in Flanders to a noble family and migrated to the northern Netherlands during the Spanish war. Between 1573 and 1577 he travelled in Italy, where he learned firsthand what Italians thought about northern European painters who, provincial or stubborn, failed to adapt their locally acquired styles to the canons of beauty established in Florence and Rome. The historian Lodovico Guicciardini, in his *Description of the Low Countries* (1567), had praised the Antwerp painter Frans Floris but only because he had brought back from Italy—after a visit in the 1540s—"the correct way of rendering muscles and foreshortenings naturally and marvelously." No one described northern art in positive terms. Mostly, northern art figured as something like the "idea of the great alternative to the proper" that Henry James's Maisie slowly came to know (chap. 6).

Back in Haarlem, van Mander fell in with the painter Cornelis Cornelisz., the painter and printmaker Hendrick Goltzius, and the poet and scholar Dirck Coornhert. They styled their gatherings an "academy," one of the many informal artists' collectives to model themselves on the Florentine academy. Like Vasari, van Mander was a good but not a great painter. He was not erudite but acquired enough learning to write a comprehensive handbook on art, addressed, like Vasari's book, to other artists and to well-informed laymen.

Van Mander's *Schilder-Boeck*, the "book of painters," was published in Haarlem in 1604. It comprises six texts: a didactic poem in ottava rima, expounding the theory of painting; the "Lives of the Ancient Painters and Sculptors" (like Ghiberti's, cribbed from Pliny), the "Lives of the Italian Artists" (cribbed from Vasari), the "Lives of the Northern Painters" (the part that interests modern scholars; already the 1764 edition of van Mander is reduced to this section alone); a commentary on Ovid; and a lexicon of emblems.

Here emerges for the first time a coherent national or regional art history that is not Italian. The northern difference is incompletely theorized by van Mander, however, and his account is often bent by the magnetic pull of the classical style.

Van Mander's history of northern art begins with a drama that even Vasari could not match: Jan van Eyck appears on the scene, and without predecessors: for "it is to be assumed that there were few painters or good examples of painting known in those early days in that uncultured, isolated backwater." "Nowhere in High or Low Germany do I find earlier painters known or named." Because he knows no names, van Mander omits the entire history of art in northern Europe before van Eyck: no illuminated manuscripts, no painted or carved altarpieces, no sculpture at all, no Gothic churches. Suddenly there is the Ghent altarpiece, "excellent and admirable, considering its time." For van Mander, the "modern times" in painting began in the thirteenth century, with Cimabue; the fifteenth century is still the "old time" of the modern era. He ranks van Eyck's invention of oil painting alongside two other modern achievements of the northern Europeans that would have astonished the ancients: the invention of gunpowder by the Danish monk Berthold Schwartz and the invention of the printing press by Laurens Coster, in van Mander's own Haarlem. Local patriotism was one of the motors of van Mander's project. His history runs through some dozens of artists, culminating in his friend Hendrick Goltzius, who figures as an ambiguous counterpart to Michelangelo, and finally in his own autobiography.

Unlike Vasari, van Mander could draw on no local tradition of historiography. To assemble his biographies he relied in part on the information about northern artists that Vasari himself had already collected, for example from Guicciardini. He used manuscript notes made by the historian Marcus van Vaernewyck. Few other northerners had made any effort to collect material. Van Mander's own teacher, Lucas de Heere, had commenced a history of art in rhymed verse, but by van Mander's time it had already been lost. Van Mander adopted some of Vasari's methods. He interviewed, for example, the Haarlem painter Albert Simonsz. who had been a pupil of Jan Mostaert sixty years earlier, in the 1540s. Albert reported that Mostaert was around seventy years old at that time, that is, born in the 1470s, and had never met either Geertgen tot Sint Jans or Albert Ouwater. Van Mander reasoned that Ouwater must have been dead by the late fifteenth century and was more likely a contemporary of Jan van Eyck, indeed could be considered the northern Netherlandish or Dutch counterpart to the great Fleming. Elsewhere he complained that the artists he interrogated were not especially cooperative. Van Mander learned little about fifteenth-century art, and he made plenty of mistakes. Repeating Vasari's confusion, he splits one of the major Flemish painters into two people, Rogier of Bruges (presumably Hans Memling) and Rogier van der Weyden, who died however in 1529 (some sixty-five years after the real Rogier). He described Albrecht Dürer's *Four Witches*, in fact Dürer's first dated engraving, as a copy after Israhel van Meckenem.

Lacking sources on German artists, van Mander drew inferences from engravings. He says that we may guess on the basis of their prints what the paintings of Martin Schongauer, Israhel van Meckenem, Lucas Cranach, and Sebald Beham were like. Van Mander, like other northern commentators on art, was more aware than Italians were of the crucial role played by engravings in the creation of modern art. Prints were a network, a library, a laboratory. Van Mander put forth the engraver Goltzius not only as a peer of Michelangelo but also as a successor to Michelangelo's near-contemporary Dürer.

The German geographer Matthias Quad von Kinckelbach in his treatise *Teutscher Nation Herligkeit* (The Glory of the German Nation) (1609) composed an initial, concise history of printmaking. Quad also names the famous German and Netherlandish painters, describes several works, and recounts some anecdotes, including one about Dürer recorded nowhere else. He introduces an interesting opposition between artists oriented directly to life (the painters of Dürer's generation) and artists who work with their minds (Dürer's followers). Quad counts Virgil Solis as an artist of *Geist* or mind, and Jost Amman as an artist who recovers the immediacy to life. With Tobias Stimmer, whose reflections on the cathedral at Strasbourg we encountered, it is yet more *Geist*.

Van Mander tries to see the old painters as denizens of their own times, singling out in their antiquated art what is worthy of praise or even emulation. He says that Dirk Bouts lived "a good many years before the birth of Albrecht Dürer and [his works] are nonetheless very different from the hard or angular modern manner which looks so unattractive (*de harde oft cantighe onwelstandighe moderne maniere*)." The capacity to break down a style and abstract from it what is valuable will be the key to the ironic art history of the future. In his didactic poem van Mander says, "We see how our forebears, when they wanted to paint a devout history, placed the main figures clearly in the foreground, so that beholders can easily figure out the story; this is useful and we should imitate it." This is not a relativizing apology for the deficiencies of the old painters but an ironic overturning of the modern norm: van Mander is saying that the old compositions *really were* better, simpler, more effective. Vasari never said anything like this, though Michelangelo might well have, if we can trust the opinions relayed by the Portuguese artist Francisco de Holanda in his treatise *Da pintura antigua* (1548).

By giving Netherlandish painters a past, van Mander gave them a choice, and so shaped the history of art-making itself. His history allowed Netherlandish painters to decide whether to perpetuate the local tradition, as did Pieter Bruegel, the great Flemish painter who had died in 1569 when van Mander was twenty-one years old and whose legacy, in the custody of his sons and grandsons, cast a long shadow; or abandon it and join the Italian flow, as did most of Bruegel's contemporaries. Some later Dutch artists, like Rembrandt, engaged with Italian art while maintaining a native center of gravity. The artist who most subtly folded awareness of the history of painting into the basically realist modern Dutch mode was Jan Vermeer, whose attentive depictions of women and men in bourgeois interiors were guided by careful study of van Eyck and of the sixteenth-century Netherlandish painter known as the Master of the Female Half-Lengths.

Van Mander, who drew up the first chronological list of Dürer's paintings, contributed to the intensification of interest in this first German artist of European reputation. A topos of the sixteenth-century art-historical literature was to wonder how great an artist Dürer would have become if he had been exposed to Italian art and antiquities. Lambert Lombard posed the question in a letter to Vasari in 1565; the apology is repeated by Francisco de Holanda and Nicholas Hilliard. We can speak of a Dürer "Renaissance" only when we encounter Dürer without apologies: when Quad von Kinckelbach, for example, writes that "Dürer's manuscripts and paintings, his smallest pieces of paper are worshipped like relics nowadays; they are held up like jewels, yea, you have to pay just to look at them." Elector Maximilian I bought paintings. Thomas Howard, Earl of Arundel, brought Dürer's 1498 self-portrait and his portrait of his father to Charles I, gifts from the city of Nuremberg. Arundel himself bought paintings and had them engraved by Wenzel Hollar. Hollar also published two etchings after drawings he believed to be by Martin Schongauer, both dated 1646 and inscribed "Martin Schön inv.": a woman with wreath of oak leaves, a subject known only through copies after Schongauer in Munich and Karlsruhe; and a woman with turban, probably unrelated to Schongauer. Dürer was mentioned by Francis Bacon, John Donne, John Dee, Richard Haydocke, and Henry Peacham, as well as Nicholas Hilliard. "Dürer revived" was the subtitle of the *Book of Drawing, Limning, Washing and Colouring* published anonymously in London in 1660. Meanwhile, ten editions of Dürer's writings were published in Germany between 1592 and 1622.

Lucas Cranach, or his son, was once commissioned to copy an altarpiece by Hieronymus Bosch. Now Cranach, too, was copied, or closely imitated: a *Venus and Cupid* on a black ground in Munich, long attributed to the artist's son, was recently redescribed as a pastiche by the early seventeenth-century Bayreuth court painter Heinrich Bollandt.

Karel van Mander was contributing to a wider European correction of Vasari's Tuscan bias. Among Vasari's imitators and critics across the peninsula, one must mention the Sienese physician and amateur of art Giulio Mancini; the Roman painter Giovanni Baglione, who in his *Lives of Painters, Sculptors, Architects and Engravers, active from 1572–1642* (1642) picked up where Vasari had left off; and the Venetian painter Carlo Ridolfi, author of *Le maraviglie dell'arte, ovvero, Le vite degli illustri pittori veneti and dello stato* (1648). None of them, however, challenged either Vasari's basic premise that art rose to its highest level in the first decades of the sixteenth century or his confidence that once reoriented by academic study, art would maintain and even, paradoxically, improve upon its new perfection.

The best collection of paintings in Europe was assembled by Charles I of England, who as a young man had seen the collections of Charles V and Philip II in Spain. He made purchases, he received gifts, and the posthumous inventory of 1651 listed 1,570 pictures. The highest valued was the *Holy Family* by Raphael, known as "La Perla," at £2000, or more than 5 percent of the total value of the collection; a painting now usually attributed to his pupil Giulio Romano (this work, it seems, was mentioned by Antonio Maria Mazzoleni in his letter to the councilors of Salò, with its original cost, 1200 *scudi*, as a benchmark against which to measure the appropriate price of his own work). Charles I owned many modern works, for example Caravaggio's *Death of the Virgin*, now in the Louvre, and many early Netherlandish paintings, among them Jan van Eyck's triptych dated 1437, now in Dresden, and the panels by Geertgen tot Sint Jans now in Vienna. He had pictures by Dürer, as we know, Hans Holbein the Younger, Jan Gossart, Lucas Cranach, and Pieter Bruegel. He owned the Wilton Diptych, a French or English masterpiece of around 1400. The northern paintings were exempted, as it were, from the requirements of admission to the academic canon. And yet there was still no theoretical justification of northern art: taste runs out ahead of language. Charles owned nothing by any Italian artist older than Andrea Mantegna, whose series of *Triumphs of Caesar* on canvas were the second most highly valued work in the collection, at £1000.

Again, concern with content raises the question of the past. The iconographers, testing the typologies that had long governed the adornment of the churches, looked through historical variation of form. For this class of writers, artistic beauty did not so much matter. The English antiquarian and *curiosus* Thomas Browne in his *Pseudodoxia epidemica* (meaning vulgar errors) (1646) corrected conventional iconographies. After establishing on the basis of scripture that Christ was recumbent at the Last Supper, for example, Browne says of Mary Magdalene:

> That she stood at Christs feet behinde him weeping, and began to wash his feet with teares, and did wipe them with the haires of her head; which actions, if our Saviour sate, she could not performe standing, and had rather stood behinde his back, then at his feet; and therefore it is not allowable, what is observable in many pieces, and even of Raphaell Urbin, wherein Mary Magdalen is pictured before our Saviour, washing his feet on her knees, which will not consist with the strict description and letter of the Text.

Unlike Thomas Browne, Cardinal Federico Borromeo (1564–1631), archbishop of Milan and prolific defender of orthodoxy, knew fine art. He collected paintings, and he sponsored the restoration of Leonardo da Vinci's mural painting of the Last Supper in S. Maria delle Grazie.

Borromeo was interested in older Christian art but mainly for doctrinal reasons. He monitored the continuity of Christian art. He also corrected profane tendencies in modern art: in his treatise *De pictura sacra* (1624) he dispraised "images of sphinxes, a crowd of satyrs, men shaped like trees, and other vanities of the pagans" in churches. He was impatient of iconographical errors, not granting Michelangelo license, for example, to include Charon's boat in the *Last Judgment*. Borromeo hesitates to subscribe to the legends of wondrous portraits of Christ made "not by human hands" but by divine agency. He notes as iconographic touchstones, however, a marble sarcophagus excavated in the Vatican depicting Christ as a shepherd "holding a staff with one hand and stroking a lamb with the other" and a painting in the catacombs of St. Zephyrinus (now St. Domitilla) in which "the Savior is shown as Orpheus and can be seen standing among beasts." He reviews an array of early Christian images in order to determine whether Christ was crucified with three or four nails. He included in his treatise an engraving of the mosaic portraits of St. Peter, Pope Leo III, and Charlemagne, based on a drawing by Alfonso Chacón, from the wall of the Triclinium of Leo III, the apse of the eighth-century banquet hall in the old Lateran, or papal, Palace.

Borromeo judged the older Christian paintings deficient in style. In his own museum, the Ambrosiana, which he described in his treatise *Museum* (1625), Borromeo housed no works by any artist prior to Titian and the Milanese Bernardino Luini. He did make appreciative comments about the curious art of his friend Jan Bruegel the Elder. Borromeo's concerns often exceeded what orthodoxy demanded. He felt that even the pagan artists could not be forgiven their errors: Hercules must not be depicted killing the lion by ripping its muzzle open but rather, for example, as history attests, by inserting his hands into the jaws.

The pedantic eye of the antiquarian, when trained on the oldest Italian churches, was able to draw distinctions that were invisible to the ideologists of academic art. A biography of Cardinal Stefaneschi (1642), by the physician Sebastiano Vannini, disputed Vasari's attribution of the mosaics at S. Maria in Trastevere to Pietro Cavallini, pointing out that some sections were clearly newer and attributing them (wrongly) to Simone Martini. Giulio Mancini in his *Considerazioni sulla pittura* (1617–1621) apologized for the "imperfection" of the paintings in the catacombs "because their aim was not adornment but devotion and piety." Although Mancini's manuscript remained unpublished until the twentieth century, other scholars knew it well. Again and again he warns against judging painting without considering the period. The miniatures and the script of the Vatican Virgil (c. 400) "correspond to their time." The Roman mosaics of the eighth century are good because they resemble contemporary mosaics in Greece, where the art had been perfected. To see the Byzantine works as the realization of a medium is halfway to seeing them as simply good. Miraculous images, the icons "made without hands," "have no time." The thirteenth-century murals at Santi Quattro Coronati, however, are rather good "for those unhappy times." Mancini locates the *primo rinascimento*, or the "childhood of painting," in that thirteenth century, the time of Guido da Siena, an artist unmentioned by Vasari. The researches of Antonio Bosio on the catacombs, meanwhile, including their wall paintings, were published posthumously as *Roma sotterranea* (1632). But there was little interest on the part of the Christian antiquarians in the evolution of style.

The aristocratic collector and antiquarian Cassiano dal Pozzo (1588–1657), secretary to Cardinal Francesco Barberini, commissioned drawings after antiquities as well as geological, botanical, and zoological specimens. His 200 folio volumes containing c. 4200 antiquarian or architectural drawings, known as the "paper museum," were later purchased by King George III and are now at the Royal Library at Windsor. This scholarship is both ahistorical, in the sense that it does not pretend to trace the shape of history, and non-normative. Antiquarian history, deferring assessment, is simply inclusive. The deficiency of antiquarian history is also its merit: a lack of concept.

The medium of painting marked constant approaches and retreats from good form. There was more inertia in architecture, fewer challenges to good form. The normativity of Greek and Roman architecture was encoded in modern building practice by the architects and theorists Sebastiano Serlio and Andrea Palladio. Heterodox approval of the non-classical mode was occasionally voiced in the national contexts. The architect Philibert de l'Orme opined in his *Premier tome de l'Architecture* (1567) that "French" or pointed Gothic vaults were not all that bad. But the illustrated treatises of the sixteenth and seventeenth centuries provided a limited alphabet of acceptable forms. The history of architecture was always present before the eyes because the progression from simple, powerful beginnings to florid maturity was inscribed in the system of the orders. The Doric order was the symbol of primordial, unadorned authority. The system of the orders raises the possibility of its own permanence. Already the letter of Raphael of c. 1519 on the Arch of Constantine had distinguished between the architecture and the sculpture of the late empire. The fourth-century arch itself was still correct, still complying with the best formulas, but the sculpture on its faces had descended into rough ineptitude.

Typology, with its power to repeal the laws of form, was still in force in architecture and in proximity to the Church. Compliance with the type ferries content forward through a variety of forms. The typological content of a building is a link to an origin secured by ground plan and other structural elements. The typological content of an icon is the person portrayed, a reference sustained by a presumed system of reliable copying, more or less mechanical. This limits formal variation registering the personal contribution of the artist, *pace* Filarete's observation that personal style is legible even in portraits. Typology is profiled against personal style. The capacity of art to reflect on its own origins and conditions becomes a content of modern art. Art is now broadcasting on several channels at once.

It is sometimes said that all art was once contemporary. That is not true: typological or substitutional art was never contemporary.

The Bolognese painter Domenico Zampieri, known as Domenichino (1581–1641), who emulated Raphael in his pursuit of a timeless style, is a good example of a painter who worked both with and against typology. The best style, Raphael's style, was not a transparent window onto content. Raphael's style holds up the gaze with its beauty. Can such a style fulfill the project of a typology? No: exactly this beautiful form had to be dropped because it interfered with primordial Christian content. Because Domenichino was unwilling to do that, he instead corrected for style on the level of depicted style, the style of buildings depicted in his paintings. In his frescoes at the Abbey of Santa Maria at Grottaferrata, in the Alban Hills southeast of Rome, Domenichino narrated the early, legendary history of the monastery. The Greek monk St. Nilus had founded the abbey in 1004. The fresco depicts Nilus's successor, St. Bartholomew, supervising the construction of the monastery at some point before 1024, when the abbey was dedicated.

The grand marble structures depicted in the background (the abbey, presumably) and on the right (the church?), with their fluted column

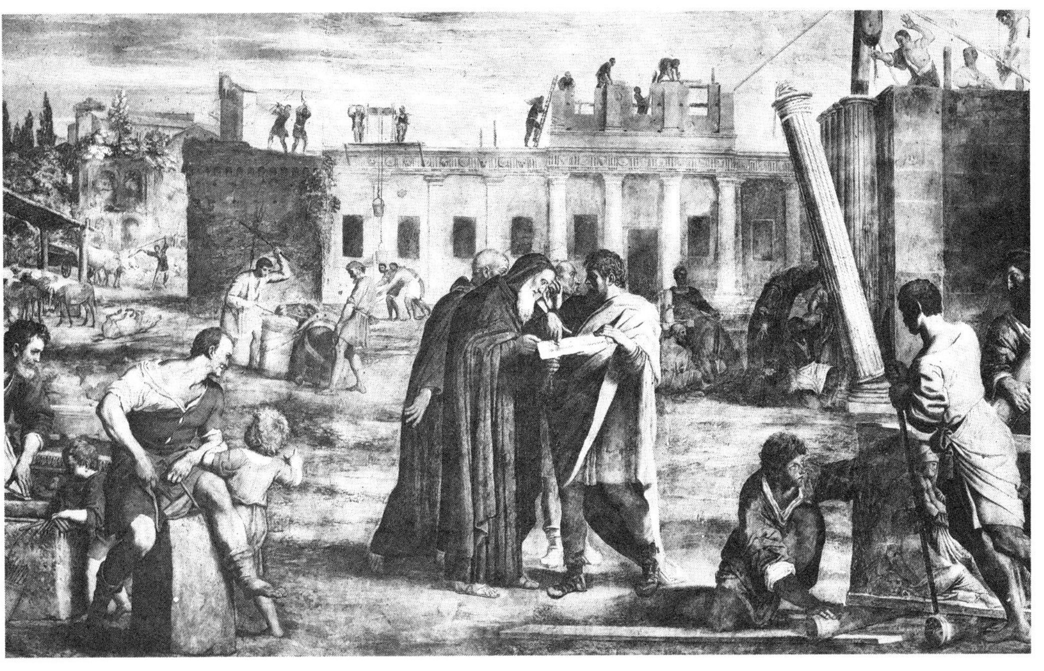

Domenichino (Domenico Zampieri), *Building of the Abbey at Grottaferrata* (1610). Fresco in the Abbey of Santa Maria, Grottaferrata. A scene of the eleventh century, imagined. At the center the architect or master builder shows the plans of the abbey to the monk Bartholomew. According to the legend the abbey incorporated eight marble columns from the villa of Cicero, presumably the brick structure under demolition in the background.

shafts and flat capitals, elements of the Doric order, do not much resemble eleventh-century buildings. Domenichino's abbey church recalls instead a pagan temple. He renders the eleventh-century building in classical form because the Doric order installs the archaic automatically. An eighteenth-century source relays a legend according to which St. Bartholomew rescued eight marble columns from the supposed villa of Cicero on the site (this must be the old brick structure that workmen in the left background of the fresco are tearing down). Those columns were in fact incorporated into Bartholomew's church, although they are no longer visible today. Domenichino's rendering of the abbey as a classical building asserted that the founders of Grottaferrata were still in contact with the ancient world and its ideals of beauty even if the church they managed to build was not very beautiful, apart from the salvaged columns. Domenichino asserted his freedom to tell the story in the most impressive way, unbound by pedantic cleaving to historical fact. He was aware that the history of art used to be typological. Even today, Domenichino is saying, typological substitution is a possible way of thinking about the history of art. He believed the history of art had started over again, recovered its footing on the path to perfection, with the painter and architect Raphael. Domenichino's aim now is not continuity with the whole past but a certain circling around ideal form.

The basic trend in Europe from now on is away from typology. The desire for artistic freedom outweighs the desire to profit from typology's antilinear but continuity-creating chronology. The desire for freedom coincided with the disengagement of art from politics. Architecture was slower than painting to extricate itself from typological systems because the meaning of architectural form was less specific and therefore did not interfere so readily with new functions and belief systems. This is exactly what Domenichino was proposing: a survival or "standing over" of the Doric order into the Christian era was less troublesome than the superstitious loyalty of the Swedes to their idols. (In fact, there is one, but only one, church in Rome that used Doric columns from a pagan temple, the fifth-century basilica San Pietro in Vincoli.) Architectural form was carried over the pagan-Christian threshold. Architecture is where the typological mode persists in modernity.

Even the strict classicist Domenichino knew that painting profited from the participation of ideal form in the non-ideal, so entering into an untimely time that evaded history but fell short of eternity. Christian iconography offered many occasions for the modern painter, inside the frame of his own painting, to multiply time frames. The co-presence within a single painting of saints who lived in different time periods was an obvious example of such routine anachronism. The author of a pamphlet on Giovanni Lanfranco's densely populated painted cupola in Sant' Andrea della Valle in Rome (1628), Ferrante Carli, had defended the work's "anachronism": for painting "fabricates images" and shares in the "fantasmatic power" (*virtù fantastica*). Painting enjoys the "privilege," exceeding the power of nature, of "adding" the past to the present. Anachronism, according to Carli, is a "license to take advantage, without blame, of the diversity of times in a single moment." Anachronism is the symbol of art's fictional nature. Yet this licence was not a new invention but one of the legacies of medieval and early Renaissance painting that the art of the rivals Lanfranco and Domenichino drew on, so obvious to any Christian—there were plenty of old paintings in the churches—that it went unacknowledged in writing.

The contest between typology and authorial performance is now the dramatic content of art. Contradictions become the matrix of artistic achievement. Artistic beauty engulfs the beauty of bodies.

Typology is of no use to the connoisseur, for whom the difference between original and copy is everything. Giulio Mancini in the *Considerazioni* tells us to look for the "boldness" (*franchezza*) of the master's touch, especially in passages where the artist is more likely to invent than to copy from other paintings, such as hair or eyes. The connoisseur values traces of the artist's fantasy and decisiveness more highly than the production of verisimilitude. The Dutch philologist Franciscus Junius (1591–1677) wrote a treatise on ancient painting, *De pictura veterum* (1637; his own English translation appeared in 1638 as *The Painting of the Ancients*), in which he asserts that those who study art, "discerning a perfect and natural force of grace in the originalls," "doe most readily discerne originall pictures from the other that are copied," suggesting the gratuitousness—with respect to typology—of authorial difference.

The reciprocal, self-perpetuating relationship between the production and the commentary of art is the legacy of this period. This was the system that the Chinese had developed and that Europeans were just now beginning to rival in complexity. It is still the system that prevails today in the West and increasingly worldwide. Closed off, art cultivates its untimely quality, and this explains the paradox that Italy in the seventeenth century is one of the strongest periods of painting and one of the weakest periods of art-historical writing. The historiography of art in the seventeenth century was still basically annalistic, and ideality had replaced workmanship as the criterion of inclusion. The only art history that can flourish within such a system is the fable about form.

The circling around the ideal is sustained by formal citations. Alternative art histories disturb this dream from the outside, threatening the citational closure. Everyone closes ranks around the idea of decorous art, as if in conspiracy against indecorous pasts. One might well wonder whether the memory of profane and non-eternal art disturbed the dreams of eternity. Did those dreams not leave negative impressions? Can one learn to read seventeenth-century art this way? The agreement to equate artistic achievement with technical accomplishment (by now a mere condition or necessary foundation) and approximation to the ideal (which by now overlaps with aristocratic codes sustained by the idea of decorum) casts to the margins all other modes of art. Materialist, non-evaluative antiquarian scholarship flourishes, but few paths lead from antiquarianism to the painting workshops of the day, apart from the odd citation of a weapon or costume. Northern art and Italian art are locked into a binary opposition that suits both parties; both the northern realistic and the Italian idealizing modes are valued. Northern art acquiesces in its second-class status. When a northern artist writes at all in this period, he inevitably succumbs to the authority of the Italian mode, deferentially writing himself out.

The most brilliant figure of the artistic culture of the Ming period was Dong Qichang (1555–1636), an official, scholar, calligrapher, painter, collector, and art historian. Dong Qichang shaped all subsequent histories of Chinese art by inventing a pair of opposed schools of painting, the Northern and Southern schools, embodying two approaches to the art. These terms are not geographic but conceptual; they are transferred from Zen Buddhism where there is a similar dichotomy of schools of thought. The Northern school comprises the professional painters who favor a rule-guided approach to representation. The Southern school comprises the so-called literati painters, often retired officials, who occupy their leisure with poetry, calligraphy, and a freer, more imaginative style of painting. Quoting the supposed founder of the Southern school, Wang Wei (eighth century, the same painter praised by Zhang Yanyuan), Dong Qichang says "the clouds, peaks, and cliffs should be formed as by the power of Heaven, then, if the brush-work is free and bold, the picture will be penetrated by the creative power of Nature."

For Dong Qichang, the true artist is not the professional painter, who must earn his bread with his brush, but the gentleman-scholar, often a retired bureaucrat who now views society from a disinterested, ironic, or spiritual distance. The gentleman's paintings will never appear rule-bound or labored. There is no equivalent to this in Europe. Leonardo da Vinci and Vasari would have liked to elevate painting to the prestige of poetry, but they did not quite succeed. Gentlemen in Europe at this point do not draw or paint, an old prejudice found in Pliny and not challenged until the late eighteenth and nineteenth centuries, when amateur drawing flourished.

Dong Qichang himself, the modern champion of the Southern school, made many copies of old paintings as well as original compositions, mainly landscapes. He imitated the masters of the Song period (tenth to twelfth centuries) as well as even more prestigious models from the Yuan dynasty (thirteenth and fourteenth centuries), who had themselves been imitating still more ancient painters. *Shaded Dwellings Among Streams and Mountains* is a hanging scroll, a landscape in ink on paper, imitating a composition by the tenth-century Southern-school master Dong Yuan, himself an imitator of Wang Wei. The humped hillocks at the base, modeled with so-called hemp-fiber strokes, support ramifying trees. The rocks and the trees climb to the sky, engulfing the houses. Dong Qichang's style in this late phase of his career has been described as abstract, additive, and allusive. The inscription in six columns, in his own hand, reports that the artist saw the painting by Dong Yuan "at the eunuch Zhu's palace in the Imperial Academy. I made a sketch copy and kept it in my satchel, and have just now completed [the painting]. It shows quite some resemblance." Shall we call it a copy, a pastiche, an homage? This is the rough equivalent of Domenichino imitating Raphael, who was studying Roman statuary, itself based on Greek models: a cascade of imitable classicisms.

Dong Qichang's landscapes are unintelligible outside their web of citations and borrowings. "Someone has said that each one must form his own school, but that is not right. Thus for example, the willow trees should be made after Chao-Po-chü, the pine-trees after Ma-Ho-chih and the old trees after Li-Ch'eng." His own paintings describe mountains

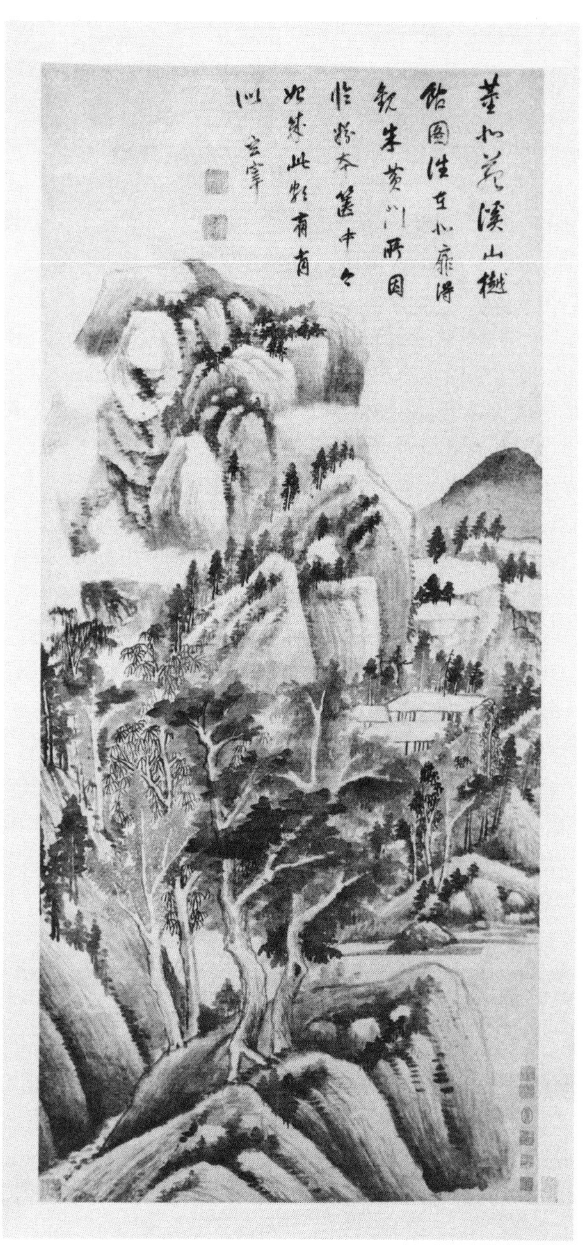

Dong Qichang, based on Dong Yuan, *Shaded Dwellings Among Streams and Mountains* (c. 1622–25). Ink on paper, 158.4 × 72.1 cm. New York, Metropolitan Museum of Art. The inscription in the artist's hand explains how the work came about: he made a quick copy of a painting by the tenth-century master Dong Yuan which he saw in someone's collection, and later made this more finished imitation, or homage.

with flat, ribbon-like bands, self-evidently conventional. They are only meaningful if you realize that they are pictures of a style, pastiches. They are markers of stylishness as such. The ability to imitate styles is the most refined personal style. Everything is in the difference: "Those who study the old masters and do not introduce some changes are as if closed in by a fence. If one imitates the models too closely one is often still further removed from them." The comparison with the Mannerism of sixteenth-century Europe, keyed to Raphael and Michelangelo and yet valuing idiosyncrasy, is obvious.

Dong Qichang the theorist is as original, and at the same time as dependent on his predecessors, as Dong Qichang the painter. Throughout the overlapping corpus of Chinese art history and art theory, the exhortation to imitate the old masters is accompanied by a discourse of immediacy: good painting, fresh and spontaneous, grasps the "spirit of things." The painter who seeks to put "life-breath and movement" in his works must wait for inspiration.

Quoting the sixteenth-century painter Mo Shih-lung, Dong Qichang says, "Painters of the past usually took the old masters as their models, but it is preferable to take Heaven and Earth as teachers. One should observe every morning the changing effects of the clouds, break off the practising after painted mountains and go out for a stroll among real mountains." But in the end Dong Qichang trusts the old pictures. "If one discusses painting with a view to its faculty to render distance, one must admit that it does not equal real landscape, but if one considers the wonders of brushwork, it becomes evident that real landscapes do not equal paintings."

Good copying, paradoxically, channels spirit. Dong Qichang, again quoting Mo Shih-lung, writes about the rebirth of the style of the ancient calligrapher Wang Xizhi in the Tang period. The more modern painters altered his manner, and yet the old and the new styles are alike. "These works may be difficult to understand, because close copying is quite easy but to transmit the spirit and meaning is difficult."

Just as in Europe in this period, the retrospective gaze is not necessarily primitivist. It is true that some Song and Ming artists cultivated rustic or grotesque styles they found among the archaic painters. But others saw in antiquity simplicity, spontaneity, and a generative power unknown to moderns. "Who can abandon the old forms and create new ones quite independently?" It is as if all painters were still alive, an apprentice-master system spread out over centuries. Only an artist can speak this way.

Such cryptic comments must be read in the context of the canonical Six Principles of painting, formulated in the late fifth century by Xie He, which call for fidelity to nature; spirit and vitality; and the copying of models.

Dong Qichang also wrote art history, assessing priority in the development of techniques. "The painting of cloudy mountains," he asserts, "did not begin with Mi Fei: such things were done already in the T'ang period by Wang Hsia who used the *p'o mo* manner."

Not every critic of the day was in tune with this. Hsie Chao-chih, scholar and official, not a painter but a generalist, in his *Five Jars of Potpourri* (c. 1607) disparaged modern painters who "amuse themselves with brush and ink" but would do well to study the old masters (though not the Six Principles, none of which "touches upon the secret of painting" and are only good for painting portraits, flowers, and birds). Hsie Chao-chih says, "We often laugh when eunuchs and women ask on seeing a picture, 'What story is it about?'" But they are right to ask, for the old paintings all told stories, whereas "modern painters concentrate on mood and flavour." "As for pictures of the gods and spirits, Buddhas and hell, hardly one percent of the pictures deal with them."

These would seem elite concerns, but in China there is also an opening to a wider public. Painting manuals since the Yuan period already included woodcut images. A publication of 1603, *Master Gu's Pictorial Album*, reproduced 106 woodcuts of works attributed to notable artists beginning with Gu Kaizhi (fourth century) and stretching to the present, including Dong Qichang. This was the first collection of independent printed reproductions of old art works. The compiler of the album is a certain Gu Bing, otherwise little known. He includes copies of the traditional lives of the painters, still basically encomia. It is not clear that all the reproduced paintings actually existed. Very little pre-Song painting had survived to the Ming period, as Dong Qichang himself conceded. Gu Bing may have invented the pictures, lending them what he saw as appropriate styles.

There is a tension in every advanced painting tradition between the ineffable qualities that cannot be learned (the reproduction of life, the grasp of the spirit of things) and the economical principle of imitation of the best masters, who in principle had already worked out how best to do this. The question is: does imitation of nature by way of someone else's rendering of it inevitably fall into falsehood? The same question imposes itself in Europe. Such impasses are not resolved, or even thought of as impasses, until a technological breakthrough reorganizes the canon or encourages a bypassing of the old masters altogether: modeling, light, perspective, photography, film. These technologies give art history a convergent shape. Until then, it is back and forth between nature and tradition.

Dong Qichang's works were soon copied and forged. It has been estimated that only 10 percent of works attributed to him are really his. But in China, where the frontiers between copy, imitation, and forgery were constantly shifting, such ambiguities were not new. Through these replicas Dong Qichang exerted a great influence. Four of six volumes of a calligraphic album published in 1747, *San xi tang fa tie*, will be devoted to works by the Ming master.

Parallels may be drawn between the scholarly and critical culture around Dong Qichang and conversations and writings in Italy, especially in Rome and in the circle of the Carracci in Bologna. The content of the art of the Carracci is art. How does Europe achieve this, given that many paintings are still destined for altarpieces and so contribute to active liturgical rituals? and that art in Europe—no longer in China at this point, except as a topos in the writings—is still understood by some as a form of knowledge? For form to become content, iconography needs to be neutralized. As in China, landscape is best for this, a field for the imagination created by the evacuation of subject matter. But the landscape tradition starts slowly and late in Europe.

Franciscus Junius's treatise on ancient painting was not really a history of art, for so little ancient painting had survived, but rather a history of ancient ideas about art, based on texts. As in the Chinese tradition, it is easier to defend archaic simplicity when the old paintings do not actually exist. Franciscus Junius provided much information on ancient image-cults. Junius, a philologist, nevertheless had a clear sense of what art was. He suggests that the most sophisticated art is the art that feigns simplicity, paraphrasing a passage in the preface to Edmund Spenser's *Shephearde's Calendar* (1579) by "E. K." (who is possibly Spenser himself): "The most curious spectators find themselves singularly delighted with such a disorderly order of a counterfeited rudeness." This is a pastoral fable of art. "Picture therefore must follow a bold and carelesse way of art, or it must at least make a show of carelesnesse in many things. Philostratus propoundeth unto us a lively example of this same secure and unlaboured Facilitie." Franciscus Junius trusts the "free spirit of the Artificer" before he trusts the "rules of Art."

Franciscus Junius associates artificial simplicity with the earlier periods of ancient art, before vice had set in:

> These Arts being anciently perfited [perfected] by the study and care of many and most consummable artificers, came so low about the times of *August*, that they were ready to give their last gasp: for in that very time, the vices prevailing, the Art perished; and when the Artificers, leaving the simplicity of the ancients, begane to spend themselves in garnishing of their works, the art grew stil worse and worse, til it was at last overthrowne by a childishly frivolous affectation of gaynesse.

This is a completely new history of art: decadence sets in already in early imperial times. By an internal logic—not by intervention of barbarians and not by decline in workmanship—art declines into immorality.

The doctrine of an artificial simplicity breaks with the idea that art is a kind of knowledge. The only valuable knowledge is the knowledge required to paint well (perspective, iconography); the rest is an unlearnable flair.

At the very moment when painting in Rome, Bologna, and Venice has found its niche in modern life; when the French were also planning an academy; and when painters are granted knighthoods (Rubens and van Dyck), a blow is struck against the legitimacy of the arts. Empirical science breaks with ancient science and so alters the very understanding of what knowledge is. A new idea of knowledge emerges that will alienate art from knowledge once and for all. Even antiquarianism will no longer count as knowledge, for it is too much driven by random curiosity, an undisciplined quality much valued by Franciscus Junius.

The spokesman for empiricism is Francis Bacon (1561–1626), the statesman and philosopher who urged the readers of his *Novum Organon*, published in Latin in 1620, to turn away from history, which is variable, and instead focus on nature. This was the second part of Bacon's unfinished *Instauratio Magna* (Great Restoration), a sketch of a more thorough "renaissance" or rejuvenation of civilization that is not so tied to the past. "The wisdom of the Greeks," in Bacon's view, "was rhetorical and prone to disputation; a genus inimical to the search for truth." "Anyone who has turned his attention from workshops to libraries and conceived an admiration for the immense variety of books we see around us will surely conceive a stupendous change of mind once he has given the matter and content of the books themselves a careful examination and inspection." For it is all repetition, thin and impoverished. Bacon's aim "is to open up a completely different way to the intellect, unknown and untried by the ancients." Opinions, words, theories, and abstractions are nothing but illusions, idols. We need to start the work of the mind all over again—and this time entrust it to a machine: in other words, to experiment, to a disembodied protocol of observation and recording, for the human sensorium cannot be trusted, nor is imagination the friend of objectivity. For Bacon, observation and experiment were the only ways to elicit knowledge from nature. He called this way the "interpretation of nature." The opposite approach, a "risky and hasty business," the forms of reasoning in current use, he derided as "anticipations of nature."

Theodor W. Adorno and Max Horkheimer began their treatise *Dialectic of Enlightenment* (1947) with a long quotation from Bacon. For them, he represented the overconfidence of the Enlightenment project, and the way of error, away from philosophy. But that was exactly Bacon's point: he believed that philosophy, beginning with the philosophy of the Greeks, had yielded nothing of value. "All the philosophies that men have learned or devised are, in our opinion, so many plays produced and performed which have created false and fictitious worlds"; they are the Idols of the Theater. The mechanical arts, by contrast, founded in nature and experience, "constantly quicken and grow as if filled with spirit…always progressing." These are the arts Bacon trusts, the ones that solve practical problems.

Do the mechanical arts have a history? In his "Outline of a natural and experimental history," an essay published in the same volume with the *New Organon,* Bacon says that "the most useful of the parts of history…is the history of the arts; it shows things in motion, and leads more directly to practice." He goes on to list 128 possible Histories including "Painting, Sculpture, and the Plastic Arts etc." "The manipulations of art…reveal the ultimate strivings and struggles of matter…. Therefore we must put aside our arrogance and scorn, and give our full attention to this history, despite the fact that it is a mechanics' art…illiberal and mean." The sole purpose of such a history, however, is to reveal more about nature itself, which is eternal and has no history ("truth is not to be sought from the felicity of a particular time," as he says elsewhere).

For Bacon, such mechanical histories are convergent: at some point people learn how to solve the problems, and then they move onto new problems. The history of art we have been considering up to now, by contrast, is not convergent but emergent. Although Vasari and others wrote as if painting were a technology for capturing nature, the art of painting was in fact continually exceeding nature, generating new and unheard-of forms. Now suddenly there is the possibility that art is not knowledge at all. John Dewey would say it again three centuries later, but the principle is already in Bacon. "A man cannot tell," he wrote, "whether Apelles or Albert Durer were the more trifler: whereof the one would make a personage by geometrical proportions; the other, by taking the best parts out of divers faces, to make one excellent.... The painter must do it by a kind of felicity...and not by rule." Moreover there is a danger that "outstanding and admirable works of art,...which seem like the peaks and high points of human endeavour, may stun the intellect, bind it, and cast their own peculiar spell on it so that it becomes incapable of further knowledge."

Bacon's lack of respect for the fine arts, for the lessons of the academies, for the passions of the collectors, and for the lucubrations of the theoreticians resonates to this day. The technological mentality cannot grasp what art has to offer other than solace and distraction. Modern art in the West, or art under the conditions of technological modernity in general, accepts Bacon's partition, agreeing that art opens a view not onto what *is*, but only at best onto what is *not*; not yet, perhaps not ever. Modern art history, meanwhile, Baconian at its core, is obliged to carry on delivering knowledge, knowledge about a kind of non-knowledge.

1650–1700

A century after Vasari's first edition: the moment for a new draft of the history of art. The modern exponents of the perfect manner, the masters of the early sixteenth century, remained fixed, like the constellations in the sky: Leonardo da Vinci, Michelangelo, and Raphael, but also Andrea del Sarto, Correggio, Pontormo, Bronzino, Parmigianino, and Titian. No academicians had any interest in displacing these paragons. But how did all the artists since measure up? What is the shape of a normative history?

A new entity challenged the Italian monopoly on judgment: the French Academy, an art school established by the crown in 1648. A group of artists led by Charles Le Brun approached the king and asked for protection from the restrictions of the guilds. The crown obliged, several years of rivalry with the guilds ensued, and by 1656 the Royal Academy was installed in rooms at the Louvre. Basic training, the mastery of tools, materials, and techniques, still took place in workshops, by the inveterate system of apprenticeship. At the Academy the pupil learned geometry, perspective, and anatomy; heard public discourses analyzing single exemplary paintings; and competed for prizes. To unify taste, the Academy exposed its pupils to only three sample sets of beautiful form: nude male bodies, posed; ancient statuary, mostly mediated by plaster casts, engravings, and drawings; and masterpieces of modern painting and sculpture, many known only through engravings, and no more than a century and a half old. The Academy discouraged idiomatic expression and recognized no national or local art histories, instead framing art as a universal project.

A century and a half after its establishment, because of its association with the aspirations of the monarchy, the French Academy became the symbolic target of all modern artists' rebellion against authority. Without the French Academy, there would have been no anti-academic momentum and a less disruptive, more piecemeal launch of modernism in art.

The Italian authorities by no means ceded their prerogatives. The most influential shaper of modern discriminations was the Roman academician Gian Pietro Bellori (1613–1696), a sometime painter, secretary of the Accademia di San Luca, antiquarian, and biographer of the recent artists. In Bellori's picture of modern art history, painting declined after Michelangelo and had to be revived in the seventeenth century. His *Lives of the Modern Painters, Sculptors, and Architects* (1672), protective of the legacy of antiquity and Raphael, instead of adding to the mountain of data, reduced the canon of modern artists to twelve: Annibale and Agostino Carracci, Domenico Fontana, Federico Barocci, Caravaggio, Pieter Paul Rubens, Antony van Dyck, François Duquesnoy, Domenichino, Giovanni Lanfranco, Alessandro Algardi, and Nicolas Poussin, all dead by that time.

Bellori's idealism is simplistic: he says that nature as we find it is imperfect and must be emended by the upward-oriented mind of the artist. The artist should be guided by the best models of antiquity, though not too closely. Bellori's doctrine of nature purified by mind is formulated against two negative examples developed throughout the sixteenth century: the mode of formal dissonance that we now call Mannerism and the realism associated with northern European and some northern Italian painting. Bellori counsels against both errors. His normative, nonevolutionary model of art is imposed upon a real history. Bellori counsels a forgetting: he is anti-art historical. Bellori does not perceive the rhythm of history that Wölfflin would two centuries later, the movement of the classic to the Baroque, from harmony to dissonance. He sees instead a recovery of harmony.

Academic norms shaped the so-called secondhand art market, the buying and selling of artworks beyond their initial commission. The basic reflex had always been to buy the latest thing. Interest in older painters was still new and not widespread. In the sixteenth century only in Florence with its intense focus on local history was there any market at all for dead painters. The market for works by all but a few fifteenth-century artists was soft. The value of a painting by Botticelli was about 10 percent of the value of a Raphael; Perugino, however, fetched 30 percent of the price of his famous pupil (Rubens owned a painting by Perugino). As time went on the supply of pictures by approved modern painters increased, whereas the tally of approved dead painters, although also increasing, was increasing more slowly. By the late seventeenth century, however, the highest prices for dead painters were higher than the highest prices for living painters, at least in Italy. In France and the Netherlands, where taste was less sophisticated, the highest prices were still fetched by works bought directly from the artist.

Art-historical knowledge was transferred from expert to amateur then as it is now, by tours and guidebooks. The wealthy came to Italy to learn and to buy. The concierge of the Palazzo Barberini, weary of repeating his explanation of the iconography of the ceiling frescoes by Pietro da Cortona, published a pamphlet in 1640. One Pietro Rossini set up shop in Rome as a professional cicerone or tour guide for noblemen, especially Germans and Austrians. In 1693 he published his descriptions of the collections and interior decoration of the great palaces. There was much debate about how much value to place on fine copies of celebrated paintings. There were plenty of forgeries on the market, and well-intentioned copies that became forgeries when dealers offered them as originals. Many travelers hesitated to plunge into this overheated market, preferring instead to buy landscapes or scenes of everyday life by living, nonfamous painters. The painters of such paintings had little chance of being written into the annals of art history, or so it seemed then. If more European gentlemen had been themselves painters, as was the case in China, they would not have been so diffident.

Reality was not disparaged by antiquarianism, or the study of the material remains of antiquity. Antiquarianism, unlike painting, was often pursued by gentlemen or clerics. Local antiquarians made neat and careful drawings after reliquaries or chalices found in church treasuries. The antiquarians were also prone to error, however, for the mosaic of knowledge was still too incomplete and access to books, or already-acquired knowledge, still too inconsistent. The notes of the architect Inigo Jones, for example, were edited and published posthumously as *The Most Notable Antiquity of Great Britain, vulgarly called Stone-Heng on Salisbury Plain* (1655). Here Jones made the mistake of trying to fit the monument into a philologically based history of art, the version of ancient art extracted from texts, the very one that Vasari and everyone else was so dependent on and that was only now slowly being adjusted on the basis of archeological findings. Jones construed Stonehenge as a kind of British Doric, an archaic building mode installed by the Romans, so misdating the monument by three thousand years. The research method of John Aubrey was unsystematic in the extreme, dependent on hearsay and the judgment of others. In his manuscript *Remaines of Gentilisme and Judaisme* (c. 1688–1691), for example, in the section on stained-glass windows, Aubrey writes: "Sir William Dugdale told me, he finds that the art of painting in Glasse, came first into England in King John's time." The Swedish antiquarian Olof Rudbeck, meanwhile, entered into the question of the antiquity of Gamla Uppsala, the site of the cult practices described by Adam von Bremen in the eleventh century. A German scholar had recently contested the traditional identification of Gamla Uppsala with Adam's pagan temple. Rudbeck made his contributions to that debate but then launched his own campaign to prove, in his four-volume treatise *Atlantica sive Manheim* (1679–1702), that Uppsala was the legendary city of Atlantis mentioned by Plato.

Lacking any method, the antiquarians' approach was opposed to both the idealists and to the empiricists. Guided by curiosity and passion, the antiquarians compiled, labeled, described, compared. For Bacon, the scholar's sensibility could only interfere with the accumulation of knowledge: "Our method of discovery in the sciences is designed not to leave much to the sharpness and strength of the individual talent; it more or less equalizes talents and intellects." For their blunders, however, the antiquarian scholars should not be dismissed but cherished. The lesson of antiquarianism is, contra Bacon, that imaginative musing and brooding were not incompatible with scholarship. The practice of scholarship—the gathering and sifting of data or facts, the submission of the material to the structures of language, the craft of publication—is private, introverted, pleasurable. The antiquarians often seem to lack a sense for beauty, and yet in their obsessiveness and fantastical imagination they duplicate aspects of the artist's creativity. Thus was the incompleteness of the academic understanding of art made good in the private sphere.

The *curiosi* of the mid- and later seventeenth century were eccentric also in the geographical sense, setting their sights on the remotest targets. The collection of Egyptian artifacts, scientific instruments, and ethnographic material of Athanasius Kircher (1602–1680), polymathic compiler and exegete, filled a 300-foot-long hall in the Collegio Romano. Among the thirty-five volumes of Kircher's writings, it was the studies of the ancient Egyptian language and religion that had the most lasting value. But Kircher himself took no interest in art. The antiquarian Filippo Buonarroti, however, the great-grandnephew of Michelangelo, in his publication *Osservazioni istoriche sopra alcuni medagli antichi* (1698), devised an ingenious apology for the supposedly coarse sculptures of the Egyptians: he says they must have been imitating, out of piety, the even greater coarseness of their revered predecessors.

A theater of antiquarian knowledge was the *Kunstkammer*, or art-cabinet, the antiquarian's storage and display device, a spatial assemblage of the products of nature and art. Kaleidoscopes of familiar and unfamiliar forms, the *Kunstkammer* or *Wunderkammer* (cabinet or chamber of marvels) were counteracademies, where the gentleman-scholar reasserted himself against the professional artists and judges. The *Kunst- und Wunderkammer* contained gems, coins, clocks, astronomical instruments, bronze statuettes, bits of coral or amber, animal specimens, dried flora, fossils, skeletons, paintings of freaks; scientific instruments, mechanical devices, automata; objets d'art, works of artifice: goldsmith's art, clocks; works of glass, miniature carvings; paintings, prints, drawings; furniture; relics and prodigies; mummified crocodiles and stuffed birds, dried scorpions and fish; turtle shells; fossils; arrowheads; dried ears of maize, coconuts, and jewelry from the New World. Some collections filled only a shelf or two, others filled rooms. The largest became famous through published inventories and engraved illustrations: the collections of the Danish physician Ole Wurm, for example, or the Milanese Manfredo Settala. None of these collections has survived intact, although the collection of Emperor Rudolf II now at Schloss Ambras near Innsbruck comes close.

Both the Academy and its opposite, the antiquarian *Kunst- und Wunderkammer*, supported an idea of art located outside of history. The criteria of selection of the *Wunderkammer* were rarity, unfamiliarity, divergence from pattern and from local custom; fine workmanship; brilliant color. The *Kunst- und Wunderkammer* staged the uncheckable flow of imagination, nature's and mankind's. Works of art and marvels of nature, old objects and recent, were housed under the same ceiling. All objects in the collection possessed qualities of ingenuity, beauty, or mystery. No one was collecting old farm tools, no one salvaged old religious paintings just because they were old. Some collectors had a physicalist bias, others were drawn to magic, that is, the possibility of connecting to the invisible forces behind experienced reality through the manipulation of objects and formulas or divination of forms. But most *Kunstkammer* were guided by no concept at all. The *Kunstkammer* is in the present tense. In these rooms one could not perceive the arc of history, as one did in the mythic accounts of Vasari and Bellori.

A neutral machine, unprejudiced and lacking a theory of itself, the *Kunstkammer* was a portal for the extra-European, one of the few in this period of European self-absorption. The academic art system was obviously not receptive to unfamiliar forms. Information and artifacts were arriving every month from distant coasts, but few beyond Athanasius Kircher knew how to read them. The *Kunstkammer* ingested these objects greedily.

In the 1640s the Dutch ousted the Portuguese from the west coast of Africa and set up a trade. The Dutch merchants were often frustrated by the local people's unwillingness to do business, even to agree on what was valuable. The people seemed to have little regard for gold, the Dutch complained, but were instead attached to worthless trinkets, which they wore about their bodies. Many travelers' accounts reported that Africans touched and spoke to such objects. Europeans could or would not understand these practices. Some spoke of the African objects as "toys" and as "idols." But neither term fit. Unlike an idol, the African objects did not represent anything. The concept of the idol, derived from Biblical and Greek religious discourses, involved a spectatorial distance that was adaptable to modern concepts of art. Here there was no such distance. Out of the interaction between Europeans and Africans, a completely new term emerged, the "fetish," a word derived from a Portuguese word, *feticao* or *feitiço*, itself derived from the Latin *factitius*, meaning "manufactured." With this word the Europeans tried to capture the somatic, familiar relation between person and artifact that they found in Africa. Whether the concept of the fetish as it emerges in these writings described real practices of the people living on that coast cannot be known. The term was prompted by an interaction between peoples and has no significance outside the discourses that managed that interaction. The term can be directed back upon the ones who introduced it and so may also help us interpret the relationship of the European collectors to their objects. The travelers were trying to describe something that seemed alien but was in fact near. European travelers were able to write of the votive uses of objects in Africa because they knew the collections of votive objects at European shrines. Pilgrims to tomb shrines, grateful for or hopeful of cures and rescues, brought offerings, small objects of value, statuettes, small paintings on panel (the Mexican ex votos interpreted by Anita Brenner in the twentieth century are the descendants of such objects). The offerings accumulated, producing crowded displays attesting to the power of the saint and prompting further gifts. The European votive shrines were vernacular and democratic versions of the *Wunderkammer*, with the difference that the meaning of the displayed objects was personal, in fact biographical. Like the African artifacts described as fetishes, the Christian votive offerings were linked to specific incidents, perhaps an illness, an accident, or predicament. Both kinds of object were expected to operate practically within local, personalized contexts. There will never be a history of votive objects or a history of fetishes, for too little data survives to permit generalization about their forms and meanings across such spans of time and space. And yet because it originates in experience, each fetish and each ex voto is more securely anchored in historical time than any work of art. The artwork is distinguished from other artifacts by the multiplicity of its origin points both within and beyond historical time.

The fetishistic approach to display was not unknown in the sphere of the fine arts. The new genre of the gallery picture presented the private collection of painted masterpieces as if it were a *Wunderkammer*, all crammed together and creating an effect of abundance and variety. David Teniers II (1610–1690) was court painter to Archduke Leopold Wilhelm, Habsburg governor of the south Netherlands. The painting shows Leopold Wilhelm among his paintings in Brussels. The archduke is in the center, wearing the hat. He also owned ethnographic artifacts and natural specimens, but they are excluded from the painting. This collection is the basis for the Italian holdings of the Kunsthistorisches Museum in Vienna. For his paintings Leopold Wilhelm built a pavilion—described by Teniers as a *pinakothek*, from the Greek word for picture gallery—in the garden of his palace. He showed the paintings to guests; they looked at drawings, engravings, and books, as do the figures in this painting; he allowed painters to work there; and he gave the gallery pictures by Teniers (fourteen survive, each different) to friends. In 1660 Teniers published the core of his patron's collection, an album illustrated with engravings after 243 paintings, all Italian, entitled the *Theatrum Pictorum* (there was also a Dutch version and many further editions). In all the archduke owned 517 Italian and 880 northern pictures.

The organization of the pictures according to size and not date or subject matter symbolizes the collector's control over the material. The historical range of the paintings depicted here is little over a century, with nothing older than the Giorgione. It is the equivalent of a collector or scholar today who is intensely engaged with modern art but uninterested in any art prior to Cubism—a perfectly common attitude, by the way. Leopold Wilhelm understood that too much history is suffocating. The problem of evolution that had preoccupied Vasari is disguised here: the gallery picture does not reproduce the history of art, though a well-informed person would be able to read it off from the picture. Art, now that it had arrived, was not going anywhere; it was instead only turning endlessly on itself, commenting on itself, just as this painting depicts a painting that depicts a sculpture, Titian's portrait of Jacopo Strada (1567/68), the architect, numismatist, and collector, the painting in the top row in Teniers's work, second from the left. A gallery picture can represent this infinite regress better than a written narrative can.

The picture gallery, governed by conventional academic taste, was not an open system like the *Kunstkammer*. The whole was *not* greater than the sum of the parts: most paintings depicted by Teniers were worth more than Teniers's painting itself. Still, the diminishment, the reframing, and the enforced painting-to-painting sociability suggest a certain ironization of academic idealism. Teniers offers no hypothesis of why paintings in this collection were so valuable, or what idea of art might embrace his own art and that of Titian.

For new accounts of the historical life of form, we will have to read the successors to Vasari, the historians who extended his account, dedicated to academic norms, to be sure, but often resentful of Vasari's biases. Carlo Cesare Malvasia, an aristocratic scholar and amateur painter and poet, published in 1678 the *Felsina pittrice, vite de' pittori bolognesi,* a passionately partisan history of the Bolognese school of painting, which had produced the Carracci, Guido Reni, Domenichino, Guercino, and Francesco Albani. (*Felsina* was the Etruscan name for Bologna.)

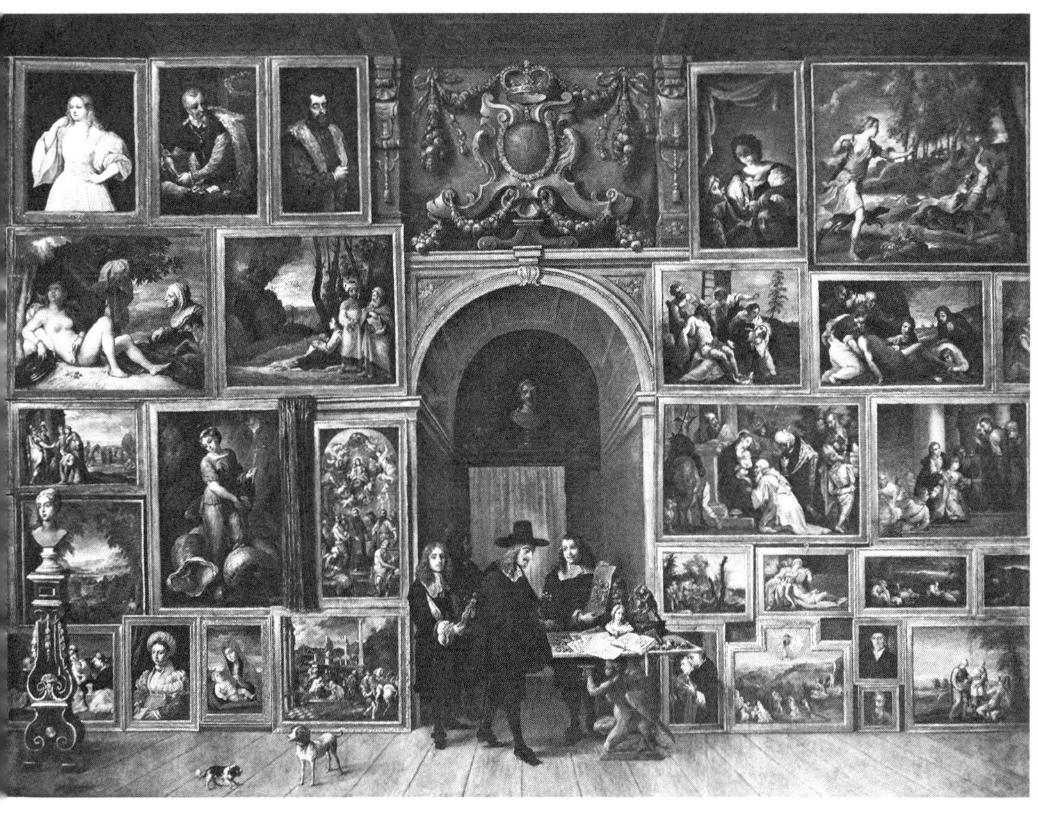

David Teniers II, *Picture Gallery of Archduke Leopold Wilhelm* (1651). Oil on canvas, 96 × 129 cm. Brussels, Musées royaux de Belgique. The curtain on the left side is meant to cover the especially precious *St. Margaret and the Dragon* by Raphael, now in the Kunsthistorisches Museum in Vienna.

Malvasia, mentioning several fine Bolognese frescoes of the twelfth and thirteenth centuries by way of refuting Vasari's claims of Tuscan preeminence, quotes him word for word: "You see how these works expose the lies of the author who writes that back then, 'on account of the infinite flood of evils that had undermined and submerged poor Italy, the art of painting, which was not merely lost but had disappeared altogether, was reborn first in Florence rather than elsewhere.'" Malvasia's resentment of Vasari's chauvinism, he himself notes, was shared by the Sienese Mancini, the Venetian Ridolfi, and the French historian André Félibien. He commends Félibien for writing about a twelfth-century French manuscript with fine drawings. According to Malvasia, Vasari had no excuse, for "Bologna is neither beyond the Alps nor placed in the Indies, and thus he could easily have observed such ancient paintings here, reported on the artists who signed them, and added the date placed beneath, and in conclusion, with due integrity and sincerity, published all this in his history of painting." This is the origin of critical historiography: the exposure of the biases and omissions of the predecessors; the imputation of unreliability; the mistrust of the authority of the printed page; in short, the origin of the present book.

Malvasia's sympathy for the early painters, however, Bolognese or not, was limited. "To tell the truth, the figures of these four artists [of the fourteenth century: an artist known by the initials p.f., Guido da Bologna, Ventura da Bologna, and Orso] have always seemed to me so feeble and dull, not to say stupid and flawed, that I can only wonder that our [Bernardino] Baldi [a local historian] exalts them as much as Vasari celebrates his first compatriots." Malvasia is insisting not on the absolute merit of the early Bolognese but only on parity with the Florentines. None of them measures up to the noble modern standards:

> I will always say that what was first heard coming from the hammers and resounding from the anvils of Tubalcaine was still just a noise, not a concert and harmony. Even the peasant (*il villano*) argues, and you hear him making inductions and enthymemes with the other dolts on the threshing floor. Does this naturalness, however, seem to you worthy of the name of a consistent logic? Come on! Until the arts show some small degree of excellence, one does not consider their beginning, one pays no regard.

We are not yet ready for a *villainous* concept of art.

For the painters of the fifteenth century, Lippo di Dalmasio, Marco Zoppo, and others, Malvasia mounts an apology on the grounds of their earnestness and piety. He praises the "most diligent" miniatures of the female religious the Blessed Caterina de' Vigri, whose depiction of Christ still has the power to heal the sick. But the artists of the fifteenth century were not yet free: "They painted more from necessity than from ambition, for the sake of truth, not for adulation, in the sincere taste of that pure and blessed century, and with the ingeniousness and sometimes excessive affectation of ours." "One should forgive them for their prudent choice and holy purpose, which today are mistaken for dryness and hardness." It is precisely bad art that requires historicization; the good art of our own time needs none, it is absolutely and not just relatively good. And yet not quite—for Malvasia's remark about modern "affectation" will one day become the basis of an apologetic contextualization and historicization of the art of his own time, the late seventeenth century, a period of art little esteemed in our own time.

The most significant extension of Vasari's *Lives* was undertaken by Filippo Baldinucci (1625–1697), a Florentine businessman, bookkeeper, and secretary, in his *Notizie de' professori del disegno da Cimabue in qua* (three volumes—1681, 1686, 1688—and two posthumous volumes). Baldinucci also found time to publish several pamphlets on art theory. He collected drawings and even drew a little himself. Incensed by Malvasia's critique of Vasari's patriotism, Baldinucci defended the styles of the early Florentines, Cimabue and Giotto, so emending Vasari's insufficiently admiring account. He included more non-Italian artists than any Italian predecessor had. Baldinucci organized his lives by decade, the decade in which the artist first flourished, Italian and northern artists alike—much like the present book. So, for example, Ghiberti and van Eyck both appear in 1400–1410, and Hans Memling and Andrea del Verrocchio in 1450–1460. The decade of 1550–1560 is populated almost exclusively by Netherlandish artists.

Among many other works on a range of topics, the court historian André Félibien (1619–1695) published *De l'origine de la peinture* (1660) and the *Entretiens sur les vies et les ouvrages des plus excellents peintres anciens et modernes* (1666–1688), in which he defended the French role in the rebirth of the arts, just as Malvasia had noted. Although on the whole conventional in his tastes, Félibien did draw some fine distinctions among the Italian primitives, remarking about the carved wooden crucifix in San Paolo fuori le mura in Rome, attributed by Vasari to Pietro Cavallini: "The drawing in this work is not very exquisite. There is something rather bold in the disposition of the body: I recall that the head of Christ is turned in a certain proud manner, and the attitude of the whole figure is extraordinary." This is the crucifix alleged to have spoken to St. Bridget in 1370. Whereas Vasari had made no stylistic comments on the work at all, Félibien discerned in Cimabue, the Florentine predecessor of Giotto, "a perfection somewhat greater than that of those old gothic painters who are noteworthy only by virtue of their antiquity."

A more likely place than Bologna, Florence, or Paris to find sympathetic attentiveness to the non-ideal was Nuremberg, Albrecht Dürer's town and the locus of the first German art academy, founded in 1674 or 1675 by Joachim von Sandrart (1606–1688), a German painter who had worked for many years in Italy and the Netherlands. Sandrart absorbed the entire historiographical tradition, from Vasari through van Mander and the later Italians. His monumental publication (in two parts, 1675 and 1679; translated into Latin in 1680–1684) was entitled *Teutsche Academie der edlen Bau-, Bild- und Mahlerey-Künste*, a printed supplement to or surrogate for an academic course. Between the covers of this book one met with descriptions of famous collections and museums; a treatise on art; a translation of Ovid's *Metamorphoses*, following van Mander; and a history of European art, to that point the most comprehensive. Like Baldinucci, he included a history of printmaking. More exceptionally, he added a brief chapter on Chinese art (Sandrart knew Athanasius Kircher). He says that among the barbarians of Asia, the Chinese are the most notable as artists and hold painting in high esteem. But they paint without rules and know nothing of shading, modeling, or perspective and so are at the mercy of their own deceptive eyes. Sandrart reports that he himself owns many samples of Chinese painting and compares them interestingly to the "primitive and inept figures that one finds in the first printed books of two hundred years ago, or in the old tapestries."

The only part of Sandrart's opus still read is the lives of the northern artists. Notable is the sheer quantity of painters he discusses, including minor Netherlandish and German artists of the later sixteenth and early seventeenth centuries. Although he is supposedly an exponent of the ideal style, Sandrart in fact had no prejudice against painters of landscapes or everyday life. He held his exact contemporary Rembrandt in high regard. He is indispensable for his researches into the early German painters, whose memory, apart from Dürer, and despite Sandrart's best efforts, was about to be extinguished, for a century or more. But for Sandrart's report, the mysterious figure of Matthias Grünewald may never have reemerged in the late nineteenth and early twentieth centuries. Sandrart reports that Grünewald was still remembered and praised but that there were few documents. He had been shown marvelous chalk drawings by the painter Philipp Uffenbach of Frankfurt, who had received them from his teacher Hans Grimmer, who had studied with Grünewald. Sandrart was overwhelmed by Grünewald's art but had no language for what he saw.

Sandrart reasoned like an art historian. Intent on establishing the priority of the Germans in printmaking, he adduced the oeuvre of Israhel van Meckenem. Sandrart conceded that none of Israhel's 136 copper engravings is dated, but he believed that Dürer had copied one, and he noted that two drawings in the early seventeenth-century collection of Johann Aegidius Ayrer in Nuremberg, attributable to Israhel, were dated 1490 and 1498.

The demand for drawings had augmented since Dürer's time. Sandrart admits that he once offered to pay 200 guilders for a single drawing by Hans Holbein the Younger. He himself sold a Dürer drawing to a Dutch collector for 300 guilders, or about a year's wages of an unskilled worker. Sandrart purchased the grave monument of Dürer, a metal tablet with an inscription by the artist's great friend Willibald Pirckheimer, and bequeathed it to the Academy of Nuremberg, adding an inscription.

By now the historians of art anticipate readers who wish to consult compilations and lists, to guide their travels or their collecting or their own researches. Karel van Mander had already undertaken to list all the paintings he knew by Dürer, in chronological order (though he only knew a few dates). Decades later, more systematic, Carlo Cesare Malvasia published a list of the engravings, more than 900, by the artists of the Bolognese school from Marcantonio Raimondi to the Carracci. Because it provided dimensions this may be considered the first catalogue raisonné of a corpus of prints.

By the start of the Qing dynasty in 1644, there was a massive accumulated palimpsest of the written record of Chinese painting, layer upon layer of lists and comments. Even specialists find it challenging, today, among the many compilations of source material and painting manuals—above all the *Mustard-Seed Garden Manual of Painting*, printed in color in 1679, made famous by many later reprints—to sort out historiographical tradition from innovation. Overburdened by patrimony, some painters developed spontaneous, wilder styles. The painter who also expounded in writing the new subjectivity was Shitao Daoji (1642–1707). Shitao studied the older masters, including Dong Qichang. He wrote an abstruse treatise on art, *The Sayings of the Monk of the Bitter Cucumber* (or *Friar Bitter Melon*), published in 1728. This a speculative and cosmic theory of art suffused with Taoist teachings and the I Ching. For our purposes it is remarkable for its extreme confidence in the authority of the individual artist. Shitao recommends abandoning the old masters—and all method. Paintings must instead express the essence of life and the artist's creative spirit. The painter must be immersed in art and detached from worldly cares. In this way he escapes the refined but suffocating historicism of Dong Qichang. Shitao made many cryptic pronouncements: "The most ancient had no method; their state of natural simplicity had not been shattered." Their method was the "all-inclusive creative painting," a mode of art that "lies open to the gods but is hidden to men." The ideas of the painter who grasps this non-methodical method "will be clear and his brush will be bold, whereas poor pictures reveal a lack of spiritual force in the wrist. The movements of the wrist must be freely revolving, they must transmit the richness of the ink and dominate the open spaces." The value of study of the past is limited: "When the superior man borrows from the old masters, he does it in order to open a new road." He who imitates does not know himself. "I am always myself and must naturally be present (in my work)." "When one has mastered the union of brush and ink, one can…open up chaos, transmit everything old and new and form a school of one's own." No such unequivocal assertion of artistic independence can be found in a European writer, not this early. The vehemence of Shitao's expressions is the measure of the psychic obstacles he faced, the ennui of historical consciousness. Shitao, already a modernist, gives a premonition of the countervailing forces that a modern art history will have to contend with. The historiography of art in modernity bends into the tenacious headwinds of modern art itself.

1700–1750

Until 1729 no one had ever mentioned in print a pictorial representation of the conquest of England by William of Normandy in 1066, the 231-foot-long embroidery known today as the Bayeux Tapestry. The Benedictine historian Bernard de Montfaucon (1655–1741) learned of a painted copy of this singular artifact among the papers of a government official, one Foucart. Aware that Foucart had worked in Normandy, Montfaucon made inquiries among his clerical colleagues in Caen and Bayeux and learned that the original of the painted copy was an embroidery preserved at the cathedral of Bayeux and exposed every year in the month of July, at the Feast of Relics. He published engravings based on the copy in the first volume of his *Monumens de la monarchie françoise* [sic], *qui comprennent l'histoire de France, avec les figures de chaque regne que l'injure des tems a epargnées,* a history of medieval France told through images.

Montfaucon, a pioneer of archeology and paleography, had published between 1719 and 1724 a fifteen-volume survey of everyday life in antiquity based on artifacts: weapons, costumes, vessels, and so forth, under the title *L'Antiquité expliquée et representée en figures.* This was succeeded by the five volumes of the *Monumens de la monarchie françoise* (1729–1733), gathering the evidence of cathedral sculpture, tombs, mural painting, stained glass, and miniatures, or manuscript illuminations, as well as brooches, buckles, and inscriptions. He published many illustrations, based on drawings made by an earlier antiquarian, Roger de Gagnières.

Montfaucon saw these artifacts not as artworks but as traces of life itself and so discounted the dependency of form on prior form, or the ambitions of an artifact to veil its usefulness with beauty. Montfaucon was looking for evidence, and he considered artifacts more trustworthy than texts. The study of material things liberated historiography from hearsay and rhetoric, the accumulated tangle of words. Montfaucon does think typologically about medieval portraits, however. Like the Church historians of the preceding century, he is confident that sacred portraits copy older portraits and so can be relied on to deliver ancient likenesses. He believes mistakenly that the figures on the façades of Notre-Dame and Chartres are portraits of the Merovingian kings, Sigebert, Chilperic, Fredegund, Dagobert. But this is only the shell of the typological approach, for by the 1720s it hardly matters what the Merovingians looked like; they no longer bear down on the present. This is typological thinking taken offline, converted into an instrument of art-historical research.

Montfaucon laments that the earliest testimonials or "monuments" of French history, from the Merovingian and Carolingian periods, have mostly perished, for our ancestors did not realize that "as crude as they are, they instruct us on many things that we cannot find elsewhere." Later monuments, from the fourteenth and fifteenth centuries, the reigns of Charles V or Louis XI, do often survive but are less valuable because they were designed to be monuments, or sources for historiography. They are propaganda, in other words, and leave little room for interpretation. Montfaucon's commentaries here are uninspired.

When he approaches a miniature or book illumination, or a stained-glass window, Montfaucon is aware of stylistic layering. In the section on the monuments of Charlemagne, he reproduces a circular glass painting, a supplicant figure, and part of a jewelled sword. The painting, now lost, belonged to a cycle of paintings in the apse of St. Denis, commissioned by Abbot Suger. It depicts a legendary meeting between Charlemagne and the Byzantine Emperor Constantine V at the gates of Constantinople. "The clothes and the crowns of the two emperors are pure caprice," Montfaucon remarks. He decided to reproduce the image anyway, he tells us, because it shows us how the people of the twelfth century imagined Charlemagne and Constantine. The praying cleric below is a portrait of Suger himself. On the right is the so-called sword of Charlemagne, then at St. Denis and now in the Louvre.

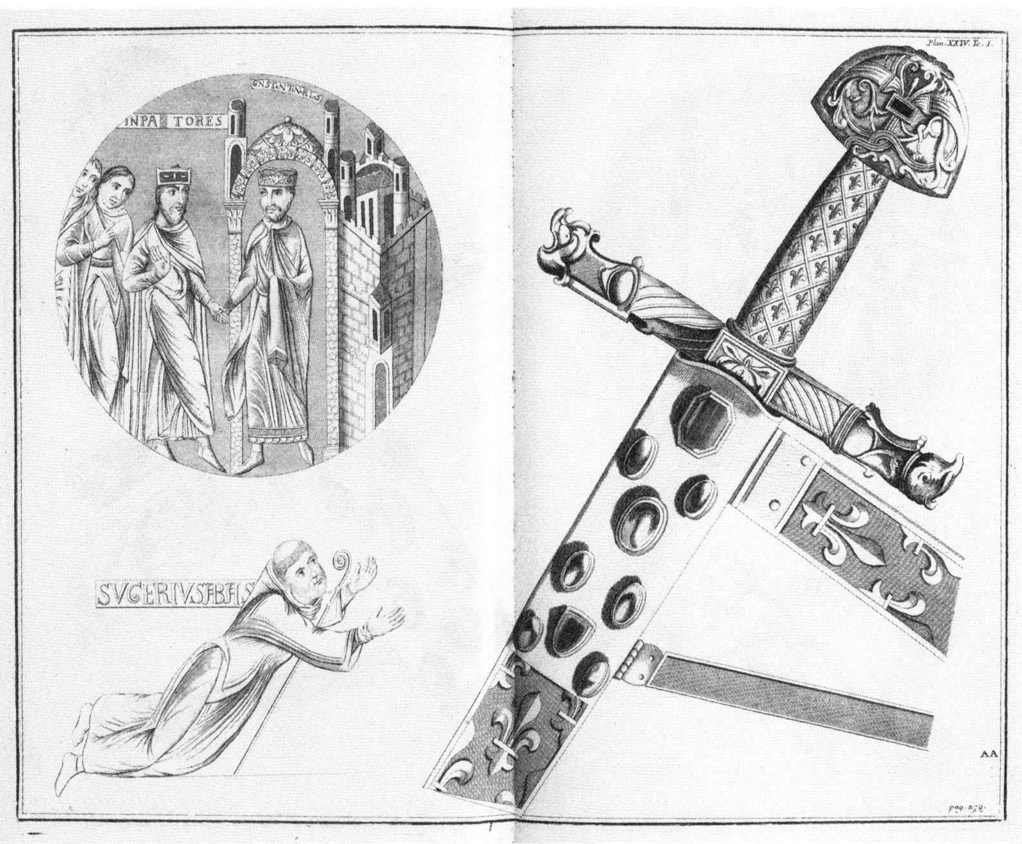

Glass painting once at St. Denis depicting a meeting of Charlemagne and emperor Constantine V; a portrait of Abbot Suger; and the sword of Charlemagne. Reproduced as engravings in Bernard de Montfaucon, *Monumens de la monarchie françoise*, vol. 1 (1729), plate 24. Paris, Bibliothèque nationale de France. Montfaucon observes that only the pommel and the guard on the sword of Charlemagne are old while the grip and all the rest are more recent. In fact, the pommel is tenth century, the guard is twelfth century, and the grip is thirteenth or fourteenth century.

Montfaucon reads the historical events off the Bayeux Tapestry without comment on style. As a philologist he knows that any element of a text might bear meaning. The old painted copy of the Tapestry that Montfaucon published had added shading to the embroidered figures, giving them shape in space. By the time the second volume of his history appeared, in which he continued his commentary on the Tapestry, Montfaucon had commissioned a new copy made directly from the work, and without shading.

Montfaucon's reproductions generally are attentive to medium, distinguishing relief from round sculpture, for example. He does not omit framing elements, such as the decorated margins of manuscript pages, even when they do not contribute to the subject. But he has no love for these forms. His eye is cold. Montfaucon could not grasp the representational mode of embroidery, which gives the figures only in outline. He guessed wrongly that the work had been left unfinished. He says that the taste of the time of the Bayeux Tapestry was barbaric but that he instructed his copyist to preserve the style because the decline and rise of the arts is an aspect of history. His idealism is implicit. Montfaucon would probably say that the history paintings, often battle scenes, of Charles Le Brun were the Bayeux Tapestries of our time: monuments supplemented by artistic value.

The riddle of modern sensibility is that modern viewers are more likely to take pleasure in contemplating the Bayeux Tapestry than a battle scene by Le Brun. They are similar in function; they each offer a strong interpretation, neither is true to life; and yet Le Brun seems entangled in stylistic ambitions, and he does not escape his own time. The Bayeux tapestry, though for a long time unrecognized, does.

Montfaucon is a dead end, leading to an impoverished art history that reads artworks only as traces of past customs and mentalities. For sympathy for the coarse forms of the Middle Ages, we have to look elsewhere. Filippo Buonarroti, as noted, was one of the first to articulate a proclivity for the simple, rough, and archaic. His apologies for early Christian art easily rolled over into admiration. In his *Osservazioni sopra alcuni frammenti di vasi antichi di vetro ornati* (1716), he wrote of the simple forms of the earliest Christian painters, "unskilled craftsmen … with no experience of good design." Yet "the very crudity (*rozzezza*) of the artists did much to achieve the true purpose of sacred images — that is, to give fruitful instruction to the faithful." The "natural simplicity" of these works, "unmixed with anything extraneous, inspired in those who beheld them stronger sentiments of devotion." Scipione Maffei (1675–1755), also an Etruscologist, was a patriotic defender of the Veronese antiquities. In his writings on the Mausoleum of Theoderic at Ravenna and on Verona he expressed appreciation for the archaic and the bizarre. He tried to understand the painting of Lorenzo Veneziano in terms of his era, the fourteenth century. This is the apology or the excuse as a basis for art history.

Ironic and contrarian thinking emerged out of scholarly rivalries. In 1749 Antonio Francesco Gori (1691–1757), Maffei's adversary, published *Storia antiquaria etrusca*. Here he quoted at length the description of the Etruscan vases by the thirteenth-century cosmographer Restoro d'Arezzo. Gori's treatise is a history of Etruscan culture framed as a history of Etruscology. Already people were writing histories of scholarship, scholarship at one degree removed.

Sometimes provincial or local scholarship is the best. Johann Friedrich Christ (1701–1756), a professor in Leipzig and pioneer of classical archeology in Germany, published a short life of Lucas Cranach in 1726. Christ developed a vivid and precise descriptive language. His *Anzeige und Auslegung der Monogrammatum* was the first independent dictionary of monogrammists, or artists known only by their initials (1747, already translated into French by 1750). The pioneer in this field was the cleric and amateur Michel de Marolles, who in the second edition of the catalogue of his collection (1672) had listed and reproduced 163 monograms.

What was the impact of the shifting historical perspectives on the production of new art? It was unthinkable in the early eighteenth century to paint a new painting in the Gothic style. Yet Gothic buildings were built well into the eighteenth century: rarely in Italy, where the system of the orders banished the Gothic or "German" manner in architecture that Vasari had deplored, but frequently in England, France, and Germany. Before the eighteenth century no German writer directly disavowed medieval architecture. In northern Europe the array of classical orders was nested within a larger binary system, Gothic versus classical, introducing a choice that was also a choice about how or whether to orient the present to the past; a choice that figures the classical as an historical possibility rather than, as in Italy, a nonhistorical ideal. Some architects accomplished in the classical mode also worked in the Gothic manner alongside their main practice, when they were involved in restorations, for example. There are many modes of Gothic survival and partial revival in the seventeenth and eighteenth century. Only the most parochial builder was unaware by 1650 of the challenge of neoclassicism, the system established by Serlio and Palladio. Gothic from that point on takes on diacritical meaning, as *not neoclassical*, and therefore suited to regionalist aims, ecclesiastical purposes, other reasons for continuity.

The scholar and architect Christopher Wren (1632–1723) worked easily with the Gothic language. Wren had no interest in recovering an authentic Gothic but simply in carrying an established language forward. He considered Gothic a misnomer, preferring to derive the style from the Arabs, who did not have access to the vast quarries from which the Romans had drawn their heavy stones and who anyway preferred smaller, lighter stones that could be carried on the backs of camels. The so-called Saracen manner was imported into France, according to Wren, because it suited northern European climates and geology. Alongside his original neoclassical churches Wren was occupied with many preservation and restoration projects in London, Oxford, Windsor, and elsewhere. He was often willing to suspend his own classical aspirations in order not to interfere with existing construction. So, for example, at Westminster Abbey he was prepared to "agree with the original scheme of the old Architect … to deviate from the old Form, would be to run into a disagreeable Mixture, which no person of good Taste could relish." In his report on Old St. Paul's, however, he expresses no admiration for the oldest or Romanesque parts, any more than Montfaucon had admired the style of the Bayeux Tapestry: the first builders were negligent because "they valu'd not Exactness.… Nor were they true in their Levels." They used spoils, which interrupted stylistic themes, and "they made Pillars without any graceful Manner; and thick walls without Judgment." But he gives them credit for staying true to the ancient ways of building, for "they had not as yet fallen into the *Gothick* pointed-arch … but kept to the circular Arch; so much they retained of the *Roman* Manner, but nothing else."

French, German, and English architects realized they had formal languages at their disposal beyond the classical orders. Perhaps they found Doric not sufficiently primitive, Corinthian not sufficiently extravagant. The survival of Romanesque and Gothic forms shades over into revival. A remarkable case is the Moravian architect Johann Santini Aichel, who built Gothic churches of astonishing originality in the 1710s and early

1720s. Although raised on medieval foundations, these are not restorations but new constructions in a fantastical Gothic manner and yet not unrelated to his churches in more conventional Baroque style. In his address of 1741, *Mémoire sur l'architecture gothique*, Jacques-Germain Soufflot, the architect of the Panthéon, compares the principles of Gothic construction to "our" or post-Renaissance churches, and finds nothing to reproach in the older buildings. He is ravished by the "spectacle" of the luminous upper reaches of the cathedral of Notre-Dame, a kind of "second church" mounted on the arcades of the nave. In a church such as the Deutschordenskirche (Church of the Teutonic Order) in Vienna, meanwhile, it is impossible to draw the line between Gothic survival and Gothic revival. Additions to the fourteenth-century church were made in the 1720s *auff die Alt gottische Form,*" but with subtle differences. The church is an essay in Gothic, drawing on the long intimacy between the local and international modes in the southern German and Austrian region. The Gothic qualities of Baroque had permitted Sandrart to esteem Grünewald's paintings.

The Austrian architect Johann Fischer von Erlach published in 1721 the eccentric *Entwurff einer historischen Architectur* (Sketch of a Historical Architecture), a pictorial menu of the styles of world architecture: Jewish, Babylonian, Egyptian, Persian, Ottoman, Chinese. Gothic architecture, too familiar, is omitted but participates in the leading idea of the anthology, expressed in the preface:

> In building one must reckon with ruleless custom, as for example in Gothic the little carvings and the pointed arches and the towers, etc., or in the Indian dragon motifs and crooked roofs; whereby one can no more dispute a people's freedom of choice than their taste.

His own architecture, taking up hints dropped by Francesco Borromini, was combinatorial, citational. Fischer was interested only in styles generated by the great civilizations. In his view, these were all classical orders. He looks through local content to the shared principles of good building—symmetry, statics—that unite the best of all times and all places. "Some things please in any circumstances."

A parody holds a style at arm's length, makes it opaque. Parody makes you aware of the mechanisms hidden within a style by reproducing them. Literary parody flourished in this period. This is Alexander Pope's youthful parody of Geoffrey Chaucer:

Women ben full of Ragerie,
Yet swinken nat sans secresie.
Thilke moral shall ye understond,
From Schole-boy's Tale of fayre *Irelond*:
Which to the Fennes hath him betake,
To filch the gray Ducke fro the Lake.
Right then, there passen by the Way
His Aunt, and eke her Daughters tway.
Ducke in his Trowses hath he hent,
Not to be spied of Ladies gent.

This is an amusing but also subtle reading of the venerable antiquated model, a comic mask placed before a deep-structural engagement with Middle English poetry. Parody is by no means an unmixed expression of disdain; it is often the inverted indicator of envy. There is nothing comparable in European art. It is hard to plant, in a painting, the markers that signal ironic intention or tone. For a true equivalent to Pope's exercise in the visual arts, one must look to China, to Dong Qichang; unless we recognize miniature sculpture in porcelain—and more generally the so-called chinoiserie of the eighteenth century—as a mode of historicizing wit. The technology of hard-paste porcelain, permitting fine detail and long known to the Chinese, was finally mastered in Europe in the early eighteenth century, at the royal court in Saxony. The pastoral subjects in Meissen porcelain, impious, suave, could be understood as a parody of the antique ideal embodied by classical sculpture. Chinoiserie, meanwhile, European imitations of motifs and forms found in Chinese art, could be understood as a defensive, parodic reaction to the threatening authority and sophistication of the Chinese tradition. The thematics of leisure and everyday life, sensuality and appetite, in both pastoral and Chinese subjects, ironized the rhetoric of virtue and public service and the epic pretensions of academic art. Susan Sontag, seeking the origins of the camp sensibility, wrote that

> the dividing line seems to fall in the eighteenth century; there the origins of Camp taste are to be found (Gothic novels, Chinoiserie, caricature, artificial ruins, and so forth). But the relation to nature was quite different then. In the eighteenth century, people of taste either patronized nature (Strawberry Hill) or attempted to remake it into some-

thing artificial (Versailles). They also indefatigably patronized the
past. Today's Camp taste effaces nature, or else contradicts it outright.
And the relation of Camp taste to the past is extremely sentimental.

Chinoiserie was possible only because it was unthinkable in Europe to
paint or build straightforwardly in the Chinese manner. The history of
Asian art could only be looked at askew, as a species of caprice. Stylistic
difference within the main European tradition of painting was too laden
with meaning for such performances. The lack of a culture of parody is a
sign that people took such differences too seriously.

In art theory and connoisseurship in these decades, the groundwork
was laid for a revolution in art theory that would eventually support a
relativization of historical form. The subjective basis of the assessment
of art was now for the first time articulated. Since Plato, the artwork
had been judged on the basis of the adequacy of its rendering of reality
(earthly or heavenly). Now reality recedes and the artwork is instead
judged by its impact on the beholder. The writer and painter Roger de
Piles had published influential treatises, the *Dialogue sur le coloris* (1673)
and *Conversations sur la connoissance de la peinture et sur le jugement
qu'on doit faire des tableaux* (1677), including a biography of Rubens,
in which he defended the sensuous painterly manner of the Venetian
painters and of Rubens against the academic orthodoxy favoring line or
disegno as the theoretical basis of the art. In the *Conversations* de Piles
lays the groundwork for a reception-oriented theory of art. He says
that the best works have been left incomplete to give the beholder the
pleasure of imagining what the artist intended. "It is not necessary that
everything appears in the painting, but that everything is there without being there." In his last work, the *Cours de peinture par principes*
(1708, translated as *Principles of Painting* in 1743), where he reaffirmed
that the aim of art is "to seduce our eyes," de Piles invited every beholder
to participate in the shaping of the canon, reducing judgment to a kind
of parlor game. He published in tabular form a set of numerical rank-
ings of the great artists, assigning fifty-seven modern painters, among
them the old Germans Dürer and Holbein, scores from zero to twenty
in the categories of composition, design or drawing, color, and expression, or "la pensée du coeur humain." Raphael and Rubens end up with
the highest overall tallies. This is a trivialization of the public culture of
judgment established by the lists of leading painters perused by Antonio

Maria Mazzoleni in the 1550s. Domenichino is awarded 17, second only to Raphael, for expression. Giovanni Bellini gets zero in this category, and Guercino only 4. Even Titian gets only 6 for expression, well behind Rembrandt, who is however awarded only 6 for drawing. And so on.

On the unreliability of subjective judgment, Bacon had invoked Heraclitus: "Men seek knowledge in lesser, private worlds, not in the great or common world." Sentiment as the basis for evaluation democratizes but also, paradoxically, stabilizes taste. This was the insight of Jean-Baptiste Dubos, the Abbé Dubos, whose *Réflexions critiques sur la poésie et la peinture* (1719) contributed to the long-running Querelle des anciens et des modernes, the debate about whether modern poets and thinkers should defer to ancient models. Dubos was on the side of the ancients, but his views are in fact closer to those of de Piles. People are less likely to be duped in poetry than in philosophy, he argues. They disagree in matters of reason but agree in matters of sentiment. No one doubts that Raphael's *Transfiguration* is a marvelous painting, he points out, and that Corneille's *Polyeucte* is an excellent tragedy. But philosophers are contantly disagreeing. From a relativist's point of view, the *Querelle des anciens et des modernes* was a false quarrel because both sides agreed that some artworks or ideas are objectively superior to others. Dubos introduces a new criterion that cuts across the ancient-modern divide, namely that the subjective response has its own objectivity. People are never closer to one another than in their emotional or precognitive responses. It is reason that divides. Here the modern estrangement of the arts and the sciences is already in effect.

The judgments invited by de Piles and Dubos are disengaged from the content and function of artworks. The Academy had preserved those links, underwriting an idea of the social and political utility of art, not to mention the ritual function of religious paintings. Raphael himself, who died in 1520, lived in a world in which an altarpiece was still essentially a supplement to a ritual sacrifice. For that matter, such altarpieces could be found even in the churches of de Piles's Paris. The Counter-Reformation scholars like Borromeo had been trying to pull art-making back toward this central ring of meaning. From their perspective, the subjectivization of evaluation was reducing the engagement with art to a private luxury, participating in nothing but itself. The annalistic and typological approaches to the past had public functions. The proper context for the cultivation of private or idiomatic judgments, however, was the private

sphere. This completes the process of privatization and deprofessional-
ization that began two centuries earlier with the conversations in Venice
and Padua that we overheard in Marcantonio Michiel's notebooks.

Connoisseurship threatened the academic system. The connoisseur
aimed to know the mind, the sensibility, of the artist, graphed most sen-
sitively by the pen or chalk drawing. The axiom of the irreducibility of
the individual was implicit in the biographical approach to the history
of art, in Europe or anywhere. The connoisseurs may have packaged
their intuitions in precise and referential statements. But the attribution
of works on the basis of style is an imperfect science that also serves as
an arbitrary field in which to exercise taste. The Abbé Dubos himself
had described connoisseurship as *le plus fautif de tous les arts après la
médicine*. The nonscientific character of connoisseurship, involving elements of trust and performance, earned it an insecure reputation. Connoisseurship nevertheless challenged the academic system because it
was practiced outside the circle of teachers and pupils, by well-informed
laymen. Connoisseurship of drawings opened a window onto the fabrication process, for drawings were stages in the flow of creativity. The
penchant for the medium of drawing suggested an interest in pure art,
untainted by considerations of content or function. The high value put
on individual sensation implied a withdrawal from public life. This
is private valuation, not celebratory. Connoisseurship was a protest
against the instrumentalization of art for the state. The cultivation of
judgment through attribution was in accord with de Piles's principles:
art was a matter of individual judgments, somatic, inalienable, evading
custom. Connoisseurship brings out the antisocial character of art, its
escape from rhetorical and political projects.

Traditionally, drawings were handed down from artist to artist. This
was still the basis for Joachim von Sandrart's access to drawings. But
already Marcantonio Michiel had attested to lay collecting of drawings.
Many Dürer drawings were inherited by the Imhoff family of Nuremberg, one of whom had married the daughter of Willibald Pirckheimer.
There is evidence that drawings were framed under glass as early as the
1580s. As the mass of paper accumulated, the task of sorting it mounted.
In 1732 the first auction catalogue with descriptions of individual drawings was published. In 1741 the collection of the financier Pierre Crozat
was put on sale, an unimaginable 19,000 drawings. Pierre-Jean Mariette
was commissioned to prepare the catalogue, and with this labor he made

his mark. Mariette spent the rest of his life making notes toward an encyclopedic dictionary of artists, the legendary *Abecedario*, corrections of prior scholarship accompanied by spare comments on style; a work published only in the mid-nineteenth century. Mariette's *Abecedario* is the ne plus ultra of the connoisseurial ineffable. Mariette does little more than gesture to the artists he likes, inviting his readers, who can imagine they are in a closed cabinet with him, bent over a box of drawings, at one of the weekly meetings with Crozat and Marolles, either to accept his judgment or demur. His notes are muted echoes of person-to-person communication, the horizons of two subjects blending into one another over a drawing. Mariette's comments are elliptical, general, only helpful if you already know the artist. For example, he says of Antoine Watteau: "His color is pure and true, his figures have all the delicacy and all the precision one could desire." Out of context such an analysis is useless for it could be applied to many artists. But such observations, each modifying the other, add up. Mariette's critical achievement was enormous, and he was much esteemed in the nineteenth century and in some circles to this day, because like Marcantonio Michiel and Carl Friedrich von Rumohr (whom we will meet later) he exerts an elegant counterpull on academic scholarship.

Mariette himself had no fondness for the primitives. The major stage for connoisseurship in the early twentieth century, however, will be the study of the primitives, the Italians of the fourteenth and fifteenth centuries and the Netherlanders of the fifteenth century; the lifework of Bernard Berenson, Max J. Friedländer, Richard Offner; one would not wish to omit John Beazley, who sorted out the Greek vase paintings. These scholars' affinity for the prevenient and the anonymous is a clue, for it reveals that connoisseurship is finally the construction of excuses. If it were merely a rhetoric of admiration it would be too easy to dismiss. Because it personalizes, tries to understand, connoisseurship tends toward sympathy, catching the artists when exposed, not fully dressed. Thus connoisseurship contributes to the emergence of relativism.

1750–1770

Four major figures of the third quarter of the eighteenth century, each representing a different approach to the coordination of present and past: Johann Joachim Winckelmann, Denis Diderot, Horace Walpole, and Giovanni Battista Piranesi.

Winckelmann (1717–1768), the son of a provincial Prussian cobbler, excelled at his studies. His break came at the age of thirty: an appointment as court librarian to a Saxon nobleman. In 1755, before he ever set foot in Italy, and lacking any deep knowledge of modern art, he published the *Reflections on the Imitation of the Greeks*, an impassioned and soon widely discussed pamphlet calling for a reform of art on the basis of the ideal forms of ancient art. At the core is a reading of the Laocoön group, the iconic sculpture excavated in Rome in 1506, as an account of the Trojan priest's heroic, stoical suffering, his calm fatalism.

Winckelmann saw that modern artists were entangled Laocoön-like in a double past: they were expected to imitate both the masterpieces of Greek and Roman sculpture and the superlative artists of the early sixteenth century. Although some modern critics were steadily adding names to the roster of greats, others believed that Raphael and Michelangelo could never be equalled and that modern art was doomed to a perpetuity of repetition and pastiche. Winckelmann suspected that modern art had no content other than itself. By losing touch with meaning, painting had become merely decorative: "Paintings on ceilings and above doors are mostly only there to occupy the space and to cover those bare spots that couldn't be filled with some kind of gilding." Winckelmann insinuates that patrons want stable value and that is to be found in gold. It fell to the historian to explain once again why the ancient statues were in fact more valuable than gold. Winckelmann's answer is that behind the agitation of the Laocoön group is a clear apprehension of the ideal. This is the "noble simplicity and quiet greatness" (*edle Einfalt und stille Grösse*) that Winckelmann perceived in the figure of Laocoön in the serpent's grip. Modern art, or what we now call Baroque art, looked to Winckelmann like mere restless energy and limitless abundance, lacking gravity and soul. Later he described the overstimulated art of modern times as an "epidemic."

The art of Raphael and Michelangelo was grounded in antiquity, yet at the same time they were "originals," for their works are not predicted by their predecessors' works. How could a modern artist, without abandoning the surety that antiquity was the high point, again be original? Winckelmann's riddling answer was: "The only way for us to become great, maybe even inimitable, is through the imitation of the ancients."

The *Reflections* made Winckelmann's name and won him a stipend from the elector of Saxony, allowing him to go to Rome. He found employment with several patrons, including a papal official whom he had met at the library in Saxony, and finally as secretary to the antiquarian and collector Cardinal Alessandro Albani. He was close to the painter and theorist Anton Raphael Mengs. We call Mengs and Winckelmann "neoclassical." What does that mean, given that the classical models had been continuously present for two or three hundred years? "Neoclassical" conveys the sense of a correction of an errancy, perhaps a decadence, perhaps the vanity of de Piles's sensualist subjectivism.

Cardinal Albani purchased the albums of Cassiano dal Pozzo in 1714. Winckelmann knew them well but did not succumb to the charm of the early medieval forms. Winckelmann shared the taste of the architect James Adam, who in 1762 wrote to his brother Robert (a friend and admirer of Winckelmann) about Cassiano's "Paper Museum": "In such a vast collection much rubbish must be expected. The mosaics, paintings, and bas-reliefs of the primitive church or the first stages of Christianity will entertain you little."

In 1764 Winckelmann published his magnum opus, the *History of the Art of Antiquity*. The book was instantly hailed and soon translated into French. Winckelmann broke with all previous histories of art on his very first page: "The principal object is the essence of art, on which the

154

history of the individual artists has little bearing." The field of ancient art permitted Winckelmann to write what had never before been written—a history of art that is not a history of artists. Virtually all the facts about the ancient artists were already available in Pliny, and there was little hope of adding to them. Instead, Winckelmann could analyze individual works and so bring out the "cause of their beauty." The description of form contributed to the characterizations of the successive styles of ancient art. Although the *History of the Art of Antiquity* is a survey of ancient Mediterranean art, beginning with the Egyptians, the core is the story of Greek art. Winckelmann describes four styles: archaic, grand, beautiful, and decadent. Winckelmann's narrative of ancient art is not much use any more to scholars of ancient art because his idea of Greek art—his ideal—was excessively shaped by the image of Greek art that Roman copies had bequeathed. He was in no position to sort out this confusion, never having visited Greece, not to mention the Near East. The first illustrated description of the Greek monuments, James Stuart and Nicholas Revett's *Antiquities of Athens*, was only published in 1762. Nevertheless Winckelmann's book has reverberated, especially in Germany, down to the present day.

Winckelmann advanced something like a nonphilosophical hyperidealism, a direct aesthetics of the body. In his *Erläuterung der Gedanken von der Nachahmung der griechischen Werke* (1756, as an appendix to the second edition of the *Reflections*), a "clarification" or response to his critics, Winckelmann makes direct comments on the body types in Raphael's compositions: the Venus in the *Banquet of the Gods* in the Villa Farnesina is too heavy, the women in the *Massacre of the Innocents* are too full in the breasts and the men too scrawny. His later scholarship, more subtle, opens a door onto a substratum of desires and drives hinted at but ultimately masked by the more polite early eighteenth-century discourse of taste and sentiment. Winckelmann, a nonbeliever, despite an opportunistic conversion to Catholicism, is often described as a pagan, a coded reference to his conviction that erotic desire cannot be subtracted from art through an overly strict distinction between artistic beauty and natural beauty. Thus his fixation on sculpture, which delivers the beautiful body, even as his own culture is devoted to painting. Art theory since the nineteenth century, as we will see, pries artistic beauty apart from natural beauty. To the enigma of aesthetics, Winckelmann contributes some answers; for historiography he creates only problems.

And yet Winckelmann's book is often described as the first modern history of art. Modern in Winckelmann, in the sense of pointing forward to nineteenth-century art-historical writing, are at least the contextual explanations he provides for style, rudimentary as they are. He coordinated the styles with political events, with the entire Greek way of life, with real Greek bodies. There is no mention of smallpox in the Greek texts, he points out; that is why the skin of the sculpted beauties is so clear. He coordinates style with political liberty: "As the mind of a man accustomed to reflection is usually more elevated in the broad fields, on the public highway, and on the summit of an edifice, than in an ordinary chamber, or in a confined space, so, also, the manner of thinking among the free Greeks must have been very different from that of nations living under more arbitrary forms of government." The beauty of the gods as they appear in Greek sculpture is captured by Winckelmann with the strange word *Unbezeichnung*, his coinage: "lacking character," a pure flavorless quality, no longer historical, no longer symptomatic of anything. Art approaches this ideal; reality drags it back. Ideally, there would be no history of art, just great art. A *history* of art will always end up having to face up to failure or incompleteness. Unlike us, the Greeks were "conscious of their own grandeur up to the fall of art" and so remained true to the principles of the great masters. The Greeks ignored the history of lesser art.

The key to Winckelmann's achievement was the intensity of his personal engagement, pulsing on every page; his inhabitation of antiquity. There is no note of irony and no hospitality to the other. He is too conscious of himself as an other, an other to the ideal, as a savage northerner. He records with chagrin the surely hyperbolic story that the paintings by Correggio seized as war booty by Gustav Adolphus were used to cover windows in the royal stables at Stockholm. The last page of the *History* strikes a note of hysteria:

> I have in this history of art already gone beyond its set bounds [i.e., he has ventured into the very late imperial period], and although contemplating the collapse of art has driven me nearly to despair, still, like someone who, in writing the history of his native land, must touch upon the destruction that he himself has witnessed, I could not keep myself from gazing after the fate of works of art as far as my eye could see. Just as a beloved stands on the seashore and follows with

tearful eyes her departing sweetheart, with no hope of seeing him again, and believes she can glimpse even in the distant sail the image of her lover—so we, like the lover, have as it were only the shadowy outline of the subject of our desires remaining.

He decides to remain behind in the land he wishes were his native land, antiquity. Modernity lies under a cloud of failure.

Happier in his own epoch was Denis Diderot (1713–1784), the essayist, novelist, and editor (together with Jean Le Rond d'Alembert) of the massive *Encyclopédie*, a compendium of modern practical and secular knowledge. Diderot was the liveliest mind of his day. In his *Salons*, which admittedly were distributed through Baron Grimm's *Correspondance* only to a super-select readership of twelve European monarchs and not published until 1798, he invented modern art criticism. The *Salons* were witty, opiniated accounts of the Royal Academy's biannual exhibition of new painting. In his *Salon* of 1765, Diderot mocked the obsession with ancient Greek art that led Winckelmann to project onto the Belvedere Torso, Don Quixote–like, whatever fancies he pleased. Diderot compares the "charming enthusiast" Winckelmann to Jean-Jacques Rousseau, who in similarly fanatic fashion pretended to disdain the study of letters and philosophy that he had cultivated his entire life as well as the corrupt society whose approbation he craved. Diderot points out that Winckelmann attributed the superiority of ancient art to the superior morals and acquaintance with nature of the Greeks. Since we moderns lack those advantages, Diderot wonders, will our faithful imitations of the Greeks not be cold and lifeless, ignorant as we are of the concealed truths of nature?

Diderot is so modern that he can dismiss Rousseau and Winckelmann, who reject the present in favor of an overrated past, as mere fabulists. How do they differ, Diderot is asking, from the partisans of the quaint styles and customs of the Dark Ages?

For Diderot approves of modern painting. He promotes the still lifes of Jean-Baptiste-Siméon Chardin and the genre scenes of Jean-Baptiste Greuze, praising their simplicity, straightforwardness, and edifying character. He is pleased to see in Greuze and Chardin the deflation of the overblown courtly style. Diderot shared Winckelmann's contempt for Baroque art and his preference for the severe and simple. Diderot wonders why modern painters are unable to make portraits or busts, the proper origins of art. "They should be honored by a republican people accustomed to having citizens' attention focused on the defenders of their laws and their liberty. In a monarchical state things are different. There's only God and King." Writing in the *Salon* of 1761 about François Boucher, exponent of "such agreeable vice," Diderot could only wonder how one may resist "the bulges, the roundnesses, the nudities, the libertinage, the epigrammatic in Boucher (*au saillant, aux pompons, aux nudités, au libertinage, à l'épigramme de Boucher*)." The key is that Diderot looked to overcome the agreeable vice by promoting a new art rather than a return to an old art. Diderot mocked the obsession with ancient statuary in an ironic passage on nudity. Diderot asks why modern sculpture is so much more prepared than painting to expose the body. The answer, perhaps, is that its morals, more savage and more innocent, are superior to the morals of painting. Sculpture "thinks less of the present moment than of the time to come. Men have not always been clothed; who knows if they always will be?"

Diderot was not out of tune with his time. The relativization of antiquity was already underway. The pupils at the French Academy in this period, alongside their exercises in drawing from plaster casts of antique statuary, were also conducted on sketching tours in the country involving old buildings and picturesque scenery. This is what Winckelmann had to contend with.

Because the *Encyclopédie* was basically a dictionary "of sciences, arts, and crafts," that is, of technics, it is not surprising that the entry on modern painting reproduces the received opinion that painting remained in a primitive state until the arrival of Raphael in Rome in 1508. That entry was written not by Diderot but by Louis de Jaucourt, an unoriginal compiler. The reborn art of modernity is excellent, however, not because it recovers ideal form—an Encyclopedist would recognize no metaphysics of form—but because it is technically proficient. The article concedes that several painters of the fourteenth and fifteenth centuries achieved a certain mastery, but it does not name them, for in fact "none of them proves himself to be excellent. The works of these painters so praised in their own time have suffered the fate of the poetry of Ronsard—no one any more seeks them out." Late medieval painters were incapable, for example, of representing strong emotions: "Before Raphael and his contemporaries, the martyrdom of a saint did not affect any of its beholders. The witnesses to this tragic action introduced by the painter were only there to fill the empty space on the canvas [sic] beyond the saint and the executioners."

So what was Diderot's criterion of artistic value, if it was not the ideal style perfected by the ancients and recovered by Raphael? In art he admired immediacy, feeling, sincerity, truth; direct action, not posturing. In the *Salons*, he responds directly to the subject matter, recording his own seemingly unreflected responses. This is "uninformed" criticism because unencumbered by awareness of the history of form. Diderot never notes a pictorial citation, an echo of Raphael or Michelangelo, of Annibale Carracci or Guido Reni, by a modern painter. He is no longer participating in the game of allusion and recognition. In fact, Diderot is not so far from Winckelmann, who for all his erudition was dreaming of an art of immediacy, an art without iconography. Greuze's *Accordée du Village* represents an aged father handing over a dowry to his daughter's bridegroom. The youth harkens attentively to the old man's emotion-laden words of wisdom; the family gathers round in pious ceremony. Diderot had praised the picture in his *Salon* of 1761. The painting was purchased by the Marquis de Marigny and on Marigny's death by the king. A source of 1769 reports that "before the year was out, players of the Italian Comedy had represented it as a tableau vivant in *Les Noces d'Arlequin*": the direct imitation of the painting with the body.

Diderot does often know the artists personally, and his commentary drifts easily from the abstract to the anecdotal, a measure not of his lack of seriousness but of his intuition that we grasp the artists better when we glimpse them off guard, rather than in their works, where they have control. Diderot's criticism, which reproduces patterns developed by now over decades, in conversation among insiders, is closer to the spirit of the collection of letters by and about artists, *Raccolta di lettere sulla pittura scultura ed architettura*, published in 1754 by the Vatican librarian Giovanni Bottari. This is a somewhat random anthology of letters dating from the early sixteenth century to the 1660s, many by well-known artists, including Michelangelo, Annibale Carracci, Guercino, and Artemisia Gentileschi, many others merely mentioning artists. Few contain any significant content; many are involved with commissions. But Diderot liked anecdotes about his contemporaries, not about the old artists. Pleasure in art is pleasure in modern life.

Plato in the *Timaeus* (c. 360 BC) had told of an Egyptian priest who chided the Greeks for their lack of historical sense, their amnesia:

> O Solon, Solon, you Hellenes are never anything but children, and there is not an old man among you. Solon in return asked him what he meant. I mean to say, he replied, that in mind you are all young; there is no old opinion handed down among you by ancient tradition, nor any science which is hoary with age.

Instead of rushing into old age by acquiescing in traditional wisdom, the Greeks cultivated mathematics, physics, metaphysics, with the eagerness of youth. The studies of the Greeks are innocent, objective, sustained by the arts of writing and reckoning, and for that reason limited to the elite; knowledge is not carried by the community as a whole. If the advanced arts of learning are lost, then

> you have to begin all over again like children, and know nothing of what happened in ancient times, either among us or among yourselves. As for those genealogies of yours which you just now recounted to us, Solon, they are no better than the tales of children.

The Greeks were unburdened by history and that is what Winckelmann ultimately envied, though he could not say it. Bacon, however, who by the way figured prominently in the program of the *Encyclopédie*, had quoted just this passage from the *Timaeus* approvingly; and Nietzsche a century later would say the same thing about the Greeks. By this measure, the true Greek was not Winckelmann but Diderot.

Horace Walpole (1717–1797), Winckelmann's exact contemporary, was the son of Robert Walpole, the dominant political figure in England during the first half of the century. Horace was also active in politics, but art interested him more. He bought a villa at Twickenham, near Alexander Pope's, and had it thoroughly renovated in a medley of Gothic styles. Walpole stocked Strawberry Hill, as he called his house, with a miscellany of objets d'art, statuettes, miniature portraits, enamels, porcelain, medieval architectural fragments, and illuminated manuscripts. His architects, Richard Bentley and John Chute, copied the forms, but not the functions, of medieval monuments. The poet Thomas Gray was under the impression, for example, that the chimney in Strawberry Hill's so-called Holbein Chamber was a copy of the high altar in the cathedral of Rouen. Walpole himself, however, said that its forms were borrowed chiefly from the tomb of Archbishop Warham at Canterbury.

Walpole wrote directly on art: the biographies of the English artists (1758); *Some Anecdotes of Painting in England* (1762); a catalogue of engravers (1765). In 1774 he published a description of his villa and its contents. The house also served as the setting for Walpole's novel, *The Castle of Otranto* (1764), the very first so-called Gothic novel, an historical romance involving crypts, trysts, and ancient prophecies, presented as a translation of a text published in Naples in 1529. *The Castle of Otranto* gives us a clue: for Walpole, history provided atmosphere. His house is irregular and heterogeneous, imitating no real model but rather history itself, the piecemeal process of building, only loosely guided by rule or ideal. This is what appealed to Walpole: in medieval forms he sought freedom from idealism, which had become a convention. The architects William and John Halfpenny, in *Chinese and Gothick Architecture Properly Ornamented* (1752), had identified variety as a principle common to both the European medieval and the Asian building systems. This is more or less the position of Walpole, who in a letter once confessed himself just as happy with the "sharawaggi" or Chinese manner (*sharawadgi*, a term of uncertain origin introduced by Sir William Temple in the late seventeenth century, referred to planned irregularity in garden design). For all his devotion to the pointed arch, Walpole could also write, "When men enquire, 'Who invented Gothic buildings?' they might as well ask, 'Who invented bad Latin?'" He was not even so certain that he admired medieval painting. Walpole describes a fifteenth-century painting in the chapel at Strawberry Hill, apparently a wing of a triptych depicting the Nativity of Christ, but he knows so little about premodern Christian art that he cannot decide whether the person in the attitude of worship in the stable is St. Joseph or a donor. Even Walpole feels he must defend the style of the painting by asserting that it transcended its historical period and so could fairly be compared to modern painting, that is, painting since Raphael: two of the figures in this group of panels, including the possible St. Joseph, "are painted in a style very superior to that age, and the folds of their garments loose and large, not unworthy of the Bolognese school." (He is thinking of Annibale Carracci or Guido Reni.)

Walpole admitted visitors to Strawberry Hill and even set up a system whereby they could buy tickets in London before making the boat trip upriver to Twickenham. This was new: anyone (except children) was welcome; you did not require an invitation. The outing to Strawberry Hill is one of the original scenes of middle-class tourism, a modest, class-equalizing version of the visits to the Roman palaces by touring noblemen.

For Johann Fischer von Erlach, the panorama of historical buildings had been a testament to permanent ideals. The great buildings of China, Babylon, the Ottoman empire, and ancient Greece and Rome overwhelm anyone's mere preferences. With Walpole it is the opposite. Only his own fanciful imagination bestows unity on the "assemblage of curious trifles." The project is a monument to a subjectivity. It is true that when it came to old oil paintings, Walpole felt obliged to apologize for their deficiencies, a testimony to the special prestige of painting. Throughout the rest of the house, Walpole took refuge in the miniature, the decorative, anything but the forceful mimesis of the body. Likewise he was happy to immerse himself in the Middle Ages because he did not have to contend with the outsized personalities of artists. It is worth comparing him to Pierre-Jean Mariette, whom he met in Paris in 1765. They both made room for ordinary sensibility. Mariette did it by communicating with artists when they were in dishabille, as it were. By focusing on drawings he levelled the artists, brought them down from the ideal, and made it possible for a bourgeois and non-artist to approach them. Walpole's domestic approach was just to stay clear of the body and the artist altogether. Mariette appreciated his English friend and translated him, in fact reportedly learning English in order to translate Walpole.

Finally Giovanni Battista Piranesi (1720–1778), the printmaker and polemicist, an architect who was only ever entrusted with a single commission but who learned to channel his extravagant visions, and his passionately held ideas about the history of ancient architecture, into a two-dimensional medium, engraving, and into somewhat overheated writing. Piranesi was trained in Venice as an architect by his uncle Matteo Lucchesi. In Lucchesi's circle Piranesi was exposed to heterodox opinions on the priority of Etruscan architecture to Greek and on the unreliability of the first-century BC architect Vitruvius, who in his treatise *De architectura,* a text intensively studied in the Renaissance and beyond, had assigned only a minor part to what he called the Tuscan temple. In Rome Piranesi learned the crafts of engraving and etching, and in 1743 he published a set of views of Rome, the *Prima parte di architetture e prospettive,* the first in a series of publications combining textual and visual argument. His descriptions of Roman buildings veered ever farther from reality: "These speaking ruins," he explained, "have filled my spirit with images that accurate drawings, even such as those of the immortal [Andrea] Palladio, could never have succeeded in conveying." (The sixteenth-century architect Palladio was an eminent interpreter of Vitruvius.) Over time Piranesi's combinatory fantasies on themes furnished by the surviving fragments of ancient Roman architecture became ever more extravagant.

The Temple of Vespasian (first century, with later improvements) at the northwest end of the Roman Forum, its three surviving columns from the pronaos, with their entablature, is familiar to every tourist. In Piranesi's depiction of the Temple the columns are still embedded in earth, earth removed only in 1811 by the architect and restorer Giuseppe Valadier. Piranesi has greatly magnified the columns, for in reality they are only 1.57 meters in diameter. There are no checks on Piranesi's imagination. Unlike a real builder, he heeds neither function nor a patron's wishes; unlike a painter, he is never reined in by the proportions and scale of the body.

Piranesi's system may resemble a typology, an accumulation of citations from Roman architecture and design, but it lacks content. Piranesi's chimerical buildings are packed with symbols, but they deliver no message other than their own plentifulness. This is not so different from the visual survey of world architecture of Fischer von Erlach, who was also protective of the architect's license but who does not commit himself chauvinistically to one tradition as Piranesi does.

Like Walpole, Piranesi cultivated an aesthetic of *copia:* abundance and variety. He extends the Baroque style; indeed he is one of the few of his day—and here again he is in tune with Fischer von Erlach—who grasped the idiosyncratic architecture of Borromini. He was enraged by the calls for austerity from the anti-Baroque party, which included Mariette and Diderot as well as Winckelmann. Incensed by fashionable Hellenophilia favoring chaste Greek forms over the fertile native Italic heritage, Piranesi was one of the first to challenge the purism of the

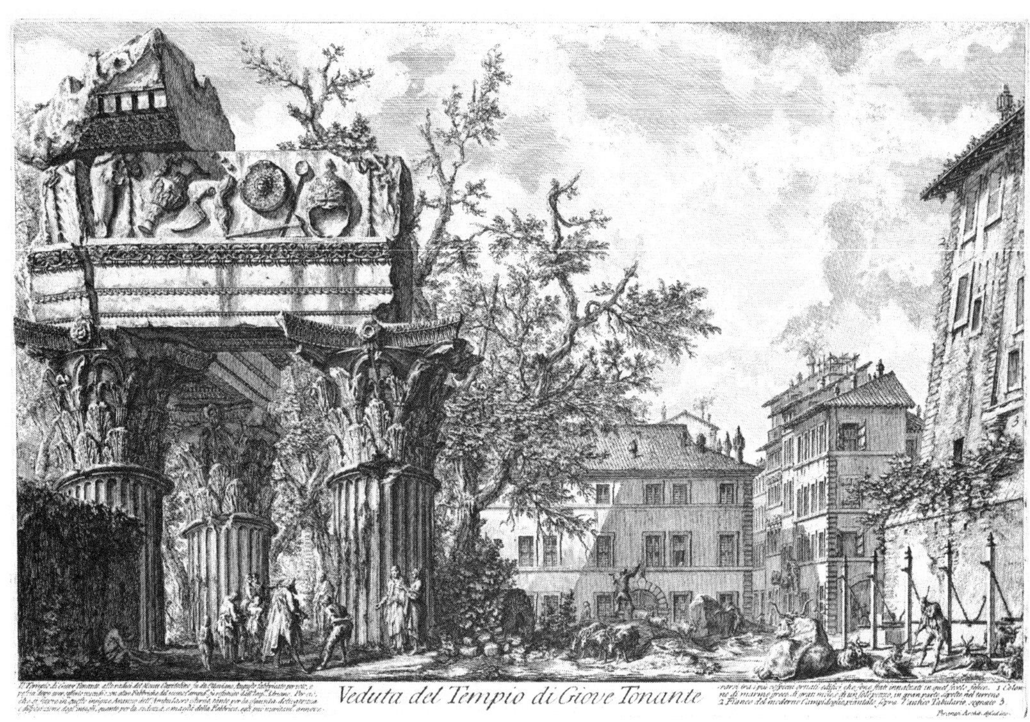

Giovanni Battista Piranesi, *View of the Temple of Jupiter Tonans* (c. 1756). Engraving and etching, 38 × 60 cm. New York, Metropolitan Museum of Art. Piranesi misidentified his subject: this is the Temple of Vespasian and Titus. The artist has also wildly exaggerated the dimensions of the temple: the depicted capitals are nearly twice the height of a person.

foreigner Winckelmann. Creativity and imagination, according to Piranesi, ought to be valued higher than compliance with abstract rules of proportion, rules that anyway cannot possibly have been derived from Greek buildings:

> Students have long since made their way in a steady stream to Greece, Asia Minor, Syria, and all those other lands where the Greeks sowed the seeds of their art; and every one of them has returned with the same things. All have brought back the same drawings of disfigured and deformed architecture and sculpture.

Piranesi also objected to the theses of the Jesuit and theorist Marc-Antoine Laugier, who in his *Essay on Architecture* (1753) had derived architecture from wooden huts (already mentioned by Vitruvius) that are later represented by the Greek Doric temple.

In his architectural etchings Piranesi makes no attempt to narrate a history of art. The structures he describes stand outside history. His views make the case that Roman building practice is an inexhaustible trove of forms. Piranesi redesigns the past in order to promote the manner of modern building he longs to realize. He shows us not what he sees but what he envisions. This is not a new way of depicting history, for painters of the fifteenth and sixteenth centuries had already inserted images of unbuilt and unlikely buildings in the backgrounds of their paintings. Piranesi's difference is his occupation of the genres and formats of modern archeological description. He is an artist wielding the tools of truth. Imposing on his contemporaries a counterhistory driven by obscure grievances, Piranesi adjusts reality to his vision. Many contemporaries were outraged, if not by Piranesi's designs then by his intemperate polemics. Luigi Vanvitelli said, "It is really amazing that the lunatic Piranesi dares to become an architect; I can only say that it is not an occupation for madmen."

Winckelmann gives us a picture of ancient art as an edifying paragon. The study of history is implicated in the cultivation of a public self. His narrative feeds into the production of new art, for example by his close friend Mengs. Winckelmann's project is founded on a base of knowledge established by the methods of the archeologist and the antiquarian. But then he more or less concedes that his narrative is shaped by a sensualism, a concession that an idealist critic true to Neoplatonic dogma, such as Bellori, would never have made. Winckelmann, his reputation as the founder of art history notwithstanding, does not really think historically. His hypotheses about the shaping role of climate or form of government on the styles of Greek art are so empty as to be worthless. Decoded, Winckelmann's art history amounts to: What a magnificent place ancient Greece was, I wish I had lived there. Greek culture was great *because* art was totally integrated into life. This is more or less what Hegel will say later. It is neither an idealist nor an historicist position, but it does give history a form.

Diderot meanwhile asks of art little more than present-tense pleasure and edification: "art" for him is "contemporary art," as it is for many today, even for critics and theorists of art whose job description is "art historian." For Diderot, art reflects us back to ourselves. Just as for Winckelmann, the role of the arts in public life is a fundamental concern, whereas Horace Walpole browses among subjective trifles, taking pleasure from the process of seeking, finding, installing artifacts in his dwelling. His aesthetic emanates from the body outward. An amateur, private, and disengaged from the production of new art, Walpole can mix styles as he pleases.

If Diderot and Piranesi are right and the Hellenophiles were after all ironic fabulists, choosing a limited, jejune manner over the natural and affecting style of the present, then there is no great distinction between the fond vagaries of the amateur medievalist, Walpole, and the yearnings of the professional neoclassicist Winckelmann.

1770–1790

Johann Wolfgang von Goethe (1749–1832) left his native Frankfurt at the age of twenty-one to study law in Strasbourg. Two years later, in 1772, he published a short essay on that city's Gothic cathedral, fashioned as a paean to the building's putative architect, Erwin von Steinbach. This essay was the first modern expression of wholehearted admiration for a medieval work. Such a building was the product of collective labor over many years, as Goethe well realized, evoking in his essay the "thousand willing hands" that "conjured up the steep heights." But to sustain his thesis—namely that the cathedral of Strasbourg is the paradigm of a work of art generally—Goethe needed an artist, the source of the idea that sets the many hands in motion. So Goethe begins by describing his search for the tomb monument of the stonemason Erwin von Steinbach, who seems to have directed the building campaign for several decades beginning in the 1270s. Goethe's model is the pious visit to the reliquary shrine of the saint. His pilgrimage is thwarted when he cannot locate the tomb. Already this is a sign that Goethe intends to disenchant the Christian building and then re-enchant it on his own terms.

How surprised he was, he reports, when his prejudice against the Gothic building manner was confronted with this great work:

A great and whole impression filled my soul, one that, because made up of a thousand harmonizing particulars, I could savor and enjoy, but by no means recognize or explain. They say it is that way with the joys of heaven, and how often I have returned to enjoy this heavenly-earthly pleasure, and to comprehend the gigantic spirit of our ancient brothers through their works.

In a subjective sensation of plenitude, he overcomes the objective discontinuity of the building, a conglomeration of forms that defeated the eye schooled in neoclassical principles. Experiencing and writing he recreates the architect's herculean gathering of perception and feeling into a whole.

With an impetuous gesture Goethe has swept away the entire literature of art: philosophical aesthetics, archeology, the connoisseurs, art history. He is impatient with experts and tastemakers, with those who measure, compare, wield stylistic labels. Although Goethe found the text of the inscription to Erwin von Steinbach in a guidebook published in 1744, he did not mention his source. He is dismissive of the vogue for antiquity, which he associates with the French and the Italians. Instead, he strips the confrontation with the building down to a communion of two great souls:

> Then in quiet intimations the genius of the great master builder revealed itself to me. "Why are you so surprised?" he whispered to me. "All these measurements were the necessary ones—don't you see them in all the other old churches of the city? I have only brought their arbitrary dimensions into the correct proportions. See how the broad circle of the window opens above the main portal…: what was otherwise just an aperture for daylight now responds to the nave of the church. See how the belfry high above calls for smaller windows. All that was necessary: and then I made it beautiful."

The origins are historical and local, but the destination is eternal:

> How the vast and grounded building rose lightly into the air; how everything was perforated and yet made for eternity.

Goethe's recommendation is: stop copying the templates of beauty fashioned elsewhere; return to the local truths of practice, circumstance, and necessity; and beauty will follow. Winckelmann, too, had felt oppressed by the compounded refinements of modern art. Winckelmann sought relief in his adopted homeland, classical antiquity, but what he found there was no more than what Raphael and Michelangelo had led him to find. Goethe seeks another homeland, and it is proximate. Strasbourg cathedral, the Gothic cathedral, was the pyramid in their midst that the

Germans could not see. Even for Johann Gottfried Herder (1744–1803), the eloquent philosopher of culture and partisan of vernacular poetry, "Gothic" remained a term of opprobrium. For "Gothic" still mainly signified a useless piling on of ornament at the expense of clear and simple meaning. Goethe's essay on Strasbourg was republished by Herder in 1773 in a pamphlet entitled *Von deutscher Art und Kunst* (On the German Manner and Art). In this very volume, in an essay on the recently published and widely admired verses attributed to the Celtic bard Ossian (in fact archaizing fabrications of the modern Scottish poet James Macpherson), Herder depreciated the "artificial, overburdened, Gothic manner of the recent so-called philosophical and Pindaric odes of the English," contrasting them with the plain sincerity and force of the Ossianic verse. It was difficult to get any perspective on Gothic cathedrals, even literally, for in Strasbourg and elsewhere they were hemmed in by lesser structures. Only in the first great age of art history—in the century following Goethe's text—would space be cleared so that everyone else could step back and at last behold the church.

Goethe was able to pierce the fog of prejudice because he had not yet been to Italy or France. Goethe's taste is "forged": it is all based on reading. He knows the *Essay on Architecture* (1753) by Marc-Antoine Laugier, for instance, mentioning Laugier's theory of the primordial hut and seconding his critique of a church in Paris that combined German vaults with a Greek temple colonnade. One passage in Laugier that Goethe overlooked, or repressed, was his praise for Strasbourg cathedral. On the whole, however, Laugier did indeed believe that Gothic or "modern" architecture had been the "delight" of Europe for too long and regretted that most of our great churches will bear its traces into the most far-flung posterity. Pace Strasbourg, Laugier musters only grudging praise for the cathedrals: "Although in their most magnificent productions there reigns a completely shocking heaviness of spirit and coarseness of sentiment, may one not admire the boldness of the forms, the delicacy of the chisel, the air of majesty and freedom noted in some passages which everywhere have something dreadful and inimitable about them." Fortunately in the Renaissance the architects abandoned "the ridiculous baubles of the gothic and the arabesque, substituting for them the masculine and elegant finery of the Doric, Ionic, and Corinthian orders."

Like Diderot, Goethe derided the soft hedonism of recent fashionable painting: "our painters of painted dolls" (*geschminkte Puppenmaler*). But as countermodels he offered not Greuze or Chardin but a native archaic figure, the "manly Albrecht Dürer, mocked by the neophytes: 'your most rough-hewn figure is to me more welcome.'" Goethe's patriotic aspersions on French and Italian art echo earlier poets like the much-admired Friedrich Gottlieb Klopstock, who had responded in 1760 to Winckelmann's *Reflections on the Imitation of the Greeks* by reasserting the primacy of Christianity and the fatherland: "Interesting as it may be, how does the history of the Greeks and Romans concern me?" Aware that the historical is conditioned and cannot be repeated, Klopstock also advised against copying: an imitation (*Nachahmung*), he said, is like the shadow of a tree, "which is always either too short or too long or misshapen."

Goethe is not averse to striking the Tacitean chord—ironic under the ancient Roman historian's hands, no longer so in Strasbourg in 1772— of approval of the rough manly virtue of plainness:

> Do not let the soft doctrine of modern beautification (*Schönheiteley*) spoil you, until roughness has no more meaning, until finally your sickly sensibility can tolerate only meaningless polish.

He associates ornament and refinement with femininity. But Goethe will not develop this polemic and will not retreat into xenophobia. The local and the familiar—the lifeworld—are the starting point, but art must transcend them, just as Erwin von Steinbach overcame the limits of the Christian Middle Ages:

> Here stands his work: approach, and acknowledge the deepest feeling for truth and beauty of proportion, emerging out of the strong, rough, German soul, on the constrained and gloomy and priestly stage of the *medii aevi*.

In fact, Goethe was no great admirer of the Middle Ages as such. He was interested in organic harmony, and it mattered little to him when and where you found it. He ignores the manifest content of Strasbourg cathedral, never mentioning its Christian functions, liturgical and pastoral, a remarkable aspect of the essay. The English architect John Carter offered the more conventional defense of the Gothic manner in 1774 when he said that Gothic was more affecting to the religious sensibility. Goethe's capacity to discount content in favor of form, a dimension of the work more immediately in contact with being or eternity, is the hallmark of a sophisticated culture of art, as we learned from Cicero's letters.

Goethe pushed the principle further. Now any two buildings can be compared, any church with any temple. Already Fischer von Erlach had proposed a similar leveling of the multiple alterities, although he omitted the Gothic, which in his time and place had not yet receded into alterity or invisibility. Goethe created a language to address alterity by melding several languages. He discusses the technical achievement of the cathedral, even if this aspect is not as decisive as it was for Christopher Wren. He speaks of proportion, invoking a classical or idealist criterion. He describes Erwin's creativity as a maieutics, a bringing forth of the latent content in the earlier buildings in Strasbourg, Romanesque or early Gothic—an art-historical judgment. Goethe echoes the Psalms but ends on a pagan note, comparing the youthful German artist of the future to Prometheus.

By 1772 Goethe had conceived his *Faust*, and Faust's unquenchable desire for experience and immediacy already burns in the Strasbourg essay. Like Don Juan, Faust was a myth devised in the sixteenth century but one that did not unfold for another two centuries. Goethe is restless and reactive. We recall that in 1786, only fourteen years later, arriving at Assisi, Goethe was ready to bypass St. Francis's hulking "Babylonian" basilica, a Gothic building, in favor of the classical Temple of Minerva in town.

Goethe does not believe that the dilemmas of the modern artist can be resolved by ransacking the past. He offers no image of the shape of art history that would militate in favor of one form over another. He is uninterested in the Gothic style as an element in a binary system, deriving its significance only from its oppositional position. He entertains no myth about the origins of art. In rejecting Laugier's attempt to recalibrate the history of architecture to its presumed origin in huts, he exposes such thinking as nothing more than an anthropologically expanded version of the typological thinking that had governed Christian church building. Goethe offers an alternative anthropology: the "savage" who fashions his own environment:

> Art is plastic, shaping, long before it is beautiful, and true and great art is often truer and greater than the mostly beautiful art. For it is in man's nature to shape things, and this nature is activated as soon as his existence is secure. As soon as he is free of worry and fear, the demigod, efficient in his ease, casts about for material into which he can

breathe his spirit. And so the savage models with fantastical strokes, hideous shapes, and gaudy colors his woven mat, his feathers, and his body. And even if this artistry involves the most arbitrary forms, they will nevertheless harmonize even without any mutual formal relation, for a single feeling made them into a characteristic whole.

This most important passage in the essay breaks with all previous European thinking about art. The references to the woven mat and the hideous forms, which echo the dismissive logbooks of the European travelers and colonists, obscure the radical content of the passage. For Goethe is the first writer to provide a basis for judgment that levels the arts across cultures:

> This characteristic art is the only true art. If it takes effect through inner, unified, distinctive, and independent feeling, unimpeded by, in fact unaware of, anything foreign to it, then it will be whole and living, regardless whether born out of a rough savagery or a cultivated sensibility.

He is saying that the basis of judgment cannot be the sensation of beauty, a deceptive guide because it is susceptible to local pressures. One society places the desirable nude body at the center of its art; another goes to great lengths to discourage eroticism in art. One society looks to art for accommodation and ease; another looks to art for inspiration and agitation. There is no form or style that leads more directly to artistic truth than any other. The key is the creative impulse that raises every artist in any time or place to the level of a demigod, an impulse that cannot be taught by rules and copying of models. Goethe shifts away from a decorative conception of art: art is not meant to beautify our environment, but to create an environment. Finally there is no rule, no standard measure, that can be held up to art. The creative impulse has to be felt by another creative subject. That is why it was so important for Goethe to identify the architect. Erwin von Steinbach is a fiction, but he clinches the point that the artist is the one who succeeds in synthesizing the parts into a harmonious whole. The building emerges organically from Erwin's sensibility like a tree out of the mind of God.

Goethe understands the bulk and complexity of the Gothic cathedral as the colossal projection of a personality, Erwin's, in all its heterogeneity. The juxtaposition of forms defies all conventions and yet is endowed with unity by the personality. There is no respect for codes, for every work reinvents the code anew. Erwin von Steinbach's pile stands behind the bildungsroman and the Romantic symphony.

Goethe used the image of the savage to overcome the maddening superiority of the aesthetes, whose exclusivity is sustained by the mystique of taste. Modern painters are the derivative imitators of already derivative models. The scholarly arbiters of artistic judgment are obsessed with lifeless rules and measurements. Goethe sees that Gothic and barbarian are mere slurs, ways of designating forms that don't fit. This is the resentment of the outsider, a somewhat feigned tone that rhymes with Rousseau's critique of civilization.

Goethe expresses contempt for the feeble aesthete of the collector's cabinet, bereft of any ambitions to create in his own right. This sterile creature is "dizzied" by the Colossus. Yet Goethe's aesthetic, in truth, is not so far from that of Pierre-Jean Mariette: the individual soul is the tuning fork; art brings about communication between two similarly tuned sensibilities. Goethe's break with Mariette is his demand for a new social frame. He is unwilling to adapt his project to the ethos and the economics of a noble class.

Among Goethe's contemporaries it is not hard to identify partisans of medieval form. The writer Wilhelm Heinse in his epistolary novel *Ardinghello* (1787) praised Gothic cathedrals over Greek temples. The Italian painter and scholar Ignazio Hugford produced a close copy of the thirteenth-century Madonna dell'Impruneta. The librarian Jean-Joseph Rive in his *Essai sur l'art de vérifier l'âge des miniatures* (1782) published twenty-six etchings reproducing miniatures from medieval French manuscripts in the collection of the duc de la Vallière. Each illustration was hand colored. The oldest miniature in the volume is a page from one of the greatest manuscripts of the early fifteenth century, the Rohan Hours. It depicts St. John the Evangelist bent over his own manuscript, the baldachin-like room in which he writes itself distorted as if pressed down by the rays of divine inspiration. On the right, God receives the elect. The transcription of pictorial form is exact.

In his text *Deutsche Geschichte*, published in 1773 in Herder's *Von deutscher Art und Kunst*, side by side with Goethe's Strasbourg essay, the jurist and historian Justus Möser (1720–1794) sketched a vision of a total cultural history whereby every aspect of life from law and institutions to poetry and art is shaped by the same hidden forces:

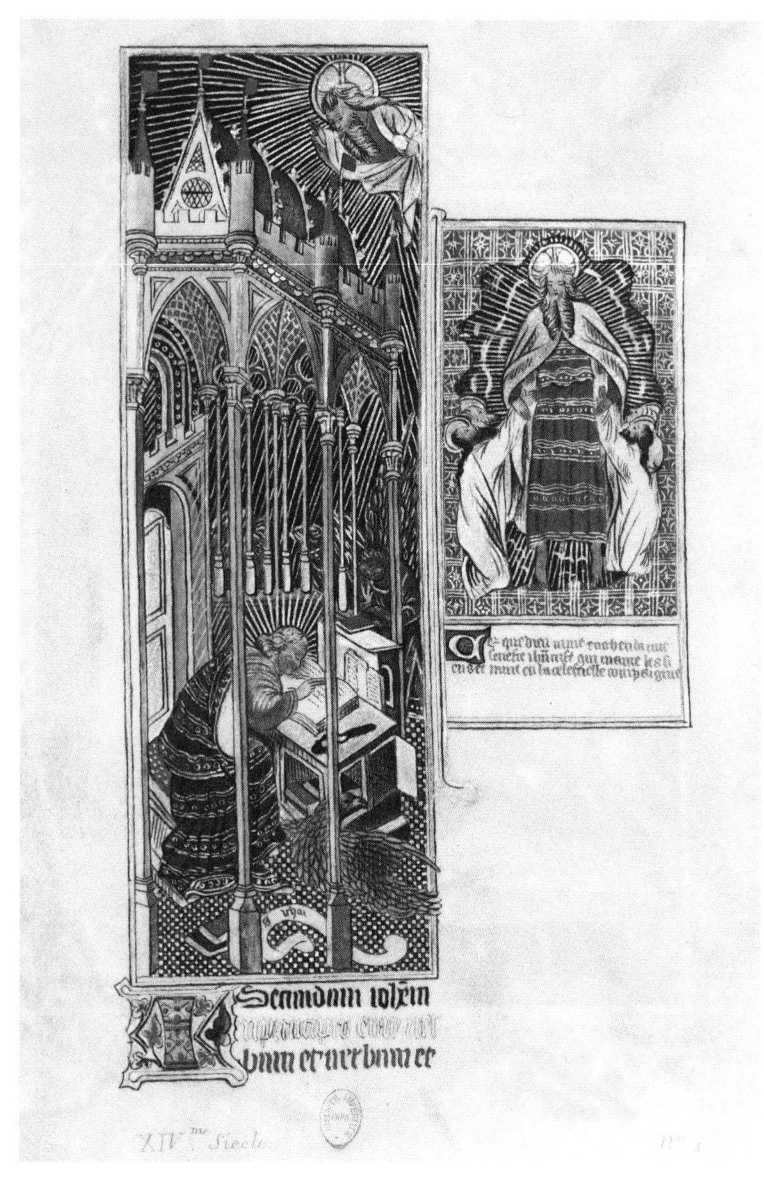

John the Evangelist at his desk, and God receiving the elect into Heaven, from Rohan Hours, lat. 9471 (1420s?), fol. 19r. Paris, Bibliothèque nationale de France. Hand-colored etching in Abbé Rive, *Prospectus d'un ouvrage: Essai sur l'art de vérifier l'âge des miniatures* (Paris, 1782), plate 1. Paris, Bibliothèque nationale de France. Rive, more interested in the painting than the book, included the six lines of text but not the foliate decoration that filled the rest of the page.

The custom of the times, the style of every constitution, every law, I would even say every ancient word, must please the amateur of art. The history of religion, of jurisprudence, of philosophy, of the arts and the fine sciences is certainly inseparable from the history of states.... One sees the hands of the master. The style of all the arts, even the memoranda and the love-letters of a Duc de Richelieu, stand to one another in a single relationship. Every war has its own tone and diplomatic negotiations have their own coloring, their custom, and their manner in relation with religion and the sciences.

Möser understands "style" as a formative dynamic pervading all creative production:

The historian will feel this, and each time take as much from the history of the arts and sciences as he needs, in order to account for transformations in the modes of states.

Many modern scholars would consider this a possible basis for the study of history *as* art history and a program for scholarship applicable to all cultures of all times. The historian of style is a connoisseur who perceives likenesses and patterns.

This is not quite what Goethe was proposing. Goethe also believed in the vital unity of a period, as did Winckelmann, but he imagined that its source was in the great soul of an individual artist and not evenly distributed across the collectivity. He also believed that he could distinguish art from other shaped things.

1790–1810

On August 10, 1792, several thousand volunteer militiamen and insurgents drawn mostly from the Jacobin political club of Paris, radical republicans frustrated by the failure of the Legislative Assembly to broker a royal abdication, attacked the Tuileries Palace. Louis XVI abandoned the palace of his own volition, walked straight through the crowd, and presented himself to the Assembly at the Salle du Manège, the royal equestrian academy commandeered by the legislature in 1789 and located only a few yards from the palace. The king was made a prisoner and the Revolution entered into its most radical and bloody phase.

On August 19, 1792, only nine days after the effective fall of the monarchy, and in the midst of political chaos, the Assembly recognized "the importance of bringing together at the museum"—a museum that did not yet exist—"the paintings and other works of art that are at present to be found dispersed in many locations." A commission of five artists and a mathematician was given the task of gathering paintings and preparing the Grande Galerie of the Palais du Louvre, the former royal residence, for their display. This was to be the museum of the French people. It is hard to believe that in these weeks and months of turmoil, when state and nation were being ripped apart and stitched together again at the cost of thousands of lives, an art museum could assume such significance. And yet on August 10, 1793, on the first anniversary of the assault on the Tuileries, on the occasion of the first of the great revolutionary festivals, the Muséum Français, also called the Muséum Central des Arts de la République, opened its doors to the people.

At that festival the people beheld the statue of an Egyptian goddess of nature whose breasts spouted the regenerative water that washed away the shameful history of aristocratic entitlement, arbitrary royal authority, and religious superstition. But were not the 537 paintings and 124 sculptures and other objects now on display in the Grande Galerie of the Louvre, drawn from the royal collection and confiscated from noble private collections, the most conspicuous souvenirs of privilege and luxury and the most eloquent testimonies to the vitality of religious faith? The roster included all the approved masters of the Italian and French schools, beginning with Perugino and Raphael and extending to Rubens and Rembrandt, and not excluding Pieter Bruegel the Elder. There were many French painters including Pierre Subleyras and Claude-Joseph Vernet. Both Boucher and Greuze were excluded, however. Three paintings by Hans Holbein the Younger made the selection as well as one by Dürer and two works attributed to the Limburg brothers, the Netherlandish minaturists who worked for the French crown in the early fifteenth century. These works, too, betokened the entitlements of the ancien régime. Why were they exempt from the Revolutionary cleansing of the Augean stables? Some commentators did worry that images of the frolics of the pagan gods or the spiritual intoxication of the saints would corrupt the public. The painter Jacques-Louis David, a Jacobin, questioned the value of paintings that "could only encourage bad taste and error." Casimir Varon, author of the 1794 report of the Conservatoire, as the arts commission was known, admitted the temptation to destroy the tokens of "superstition, flattery, and debauchery," products of "long centuries of slavery and shame." Medieval art, too, the product of the darkest superstition — and rightly absent from the Grande Galerie — was vulnerable to revolutionary resentment, as were the statues on church façades that Montfaucon had identified as portraits of French kings. Many were destroyed in 1792 and 1793.

The museum commission ignored these concerns and offered the works not as negative but as positive examples. The arts would edify the nation. The paintings of Raphael, Guido Reni, and even Holbein were unassailable, like household gods rescued from the catastrophe, carried over the threshold of the Revolution and into modernity.

The paradox is easy to explain: the five artists on the commission were academic painters. They believed that the arts flourished through continuity, skills and sensibility passed down from master to pupil. The works themselves, however, grounded in but improving upon nature through convergence on ideal beauty and expression of abstract ideas, overcame the local circumstances of their making. The lessons of the greatest works of art, according to academic theory, were eternally valid. It did not matter that the paintings had been paid for by pampered noblemen and clerics and had adorned salons and churches. As works of art they dominated the world around them, even after they had been translated from the spaces they were made for and into the public domain. And this remains the principal thesis sustaining the public art museum to this day.

The display of Holbein and the Limburg brothers in the Muséum Français suggests, however, that the content of the story told by the career of form, the mythos that painting itself wrote, was unclear.

Although the idea of the public museum was realized in the regicidal passions of 1792 and 1793, already between 1750 and 1779 royal paintings had been on display in two galleries of the Luxembourg Palace. There was no admission fee, though in practice visitors were well-informed insiders, not a general public. For decades there had been discussion of what form a permanent royal museum would take. Other European princely collections offered semipublic access, sometimes to buildings constructed as picture galleries, such as Frederick the Great's picture gallery at Potsdam (1755–1763). The more comprehensive Fridericianum in Kassel, meanwhile, housing the collections of the Landgrave Frederick II of Hesse-Kassel (1779), was the first building ever conceived as a public museum. The Muséum Français did not represent new thinking about art. What was new was unrestricted public access. The social range of the visitors to the Grande Galerie of the Louvre was immediately remarked upon. Middle-class families from the provinces came to Paris and admired the spaces and the canvases just as they do today. The key to the experience of the museum is freedom of movement. In a museum you are not a participant in a ritual and you are not a guest.

On the walls of the museum at the Louvre hung the products of a continuous modernity that had begun shortly before 1500 and extended in an unbroken chain of adaptations to the present day. The royal and noble collections were not mired in the past but had long since been admitting the most innovative art of the present: Greuze's *Accordée du Village*, praised by Diderot; David's *Oath of the Horatii*; the genre paintings of Chardin, all eventually absorbed into the national art museum.

Some artists and writers were dissatisfied with the image of continuity between past and present that the museum projected. The Revolution, after all, had proved that it was possible to "correct" history. The Jacobins had disrupted the orderly handing down of values that knit the generations together. The Revolution altered everyone's sense of their own place in time, and not least the poets and artists born around 1770, who experienced the Revolution in their youth. The Revolution had failed to disrupt the story of form, so encouraging art's recoil from politics.

In 1802 the critic and theorist Friedrich Schlegel (1772–1829) visited Paris, now accessible to foreigners after the fires of the first Napoleonic wars had cooled, though not the memories of the Revolution itself. He spent days in the galleries of the Louvre, renamed in November of that year the Musée Napoléon, and now stocked with the spoils of victory, paintings and statuary confiscated from the collections and churches of the Netherlands, Germany, and Italy by the armies of the Directory. Schlegel published his impressions in his quarterly, *Europa*. "I am sensible only to the old painting," he confessed; "only this I understand and grasp, and only about this can I speak." He refused to write about the French school or the more recent Italians. Even the Carracci, Guido Reni, and Domenichino left him unmoved. Who could linger over these cold, too-perfect works with the paintings of the early Italian and German schools hanging so close at hand? Schlegel describes what he is seeking:

> Not confused piles of people, but rather few and isolated figures, and accomplished with that assiduous study to which the feeling of the value and sanctity of that highest of all hieroglyphs, the human body, is natural.

He is speaking about bodies—soon exclusively about form:

> rigorous, even lean forms with sharp contours, which stand out decisively, no grimy chiaroscuro painting in darkness and shadow, but pure relations and masses of colors in clear harmonies.

Nearly everything painted in the previous two and a half centuries is dead to Schlegel. Only ten years after it had opened, the Louvre was already a morgue.

Some few foreign artists working in Italy in the 1790s, outside the academic system, for the first time began to make drawn copies of medieval works, and not for antiquarian purposes. William Young Ottley (1771–1836) came to Rome in 1791. Ottley purchased the *Mystic Nativity* by Botticelli and in 1798 sent it to London; it was the first painting by Botticelli to leave Italy. Ottley made drawings after still earlier works, such as the thirteenth-century sculpture of the Pisani or the fourteenth-century frescoes at Assisi and Pisa. Ottley was allied with David Pierre Humbert de Superville (1770–1849), a Dutch artist of Swiss origin who had arrived in Rome in 1789 and whose infatuation with the fourteenth-century painters earned him the sobriquet Giottino. Ottley and Superville made outline drawings in a spare, clean style meant to capture the simplicity and gravity of the forms. This flouted the drawing manner taught in the academies, which was designed to capture the volumes and masses of the nude human body, and especially the body in tension. The new linear drawing manner had nothing to do with life drawing. Ottley and Superville learned it from older artists in Rome such as the sculptors Antonio Canova, who also made drawings after fourteenth- and fifteenth-century works, and John Flaxman, who copied the frescoes at Orvieto and the Camposanto at Pisa. They had studied the publications of William Hamilton's collection of vases, and they knew the pottery of Josiah Wedgwood. The new reproductions of antiquity—not Winckelmann's three-dimensional, desire-generating antiquity but flat images—taught them to see medieval art. They knew the many antiquarian publications from Montfaucon on, including the facsimiles of manuscripts, that reproduced medieval art in linear engravings.

The young artists may have been reading the appendix to the Florentine edition of Leonardo da Vinci's notes on the art of painting, the so-called *Treatise on Painting* (1792): this was the *Dissertazione* of the Florentine antiquarian Giovanni Lami (1697–1770), a short essay defending the reputations of the Italian painters of the eleventh to the thirteenth centuries. This text had been written in 1757, ahead of its time. Here Lami ignored the technical deficiencies of medieval art in hopes of detecting some quality proof against invidious narratives of progress. In his *Dissertazione* Lami criticizes Cennino Cennini's statement that Giotto "translated painting from Greek into Latin." The rebirth of painting in Florence, Lami is convinced, was a myth invented by the early followers and admirers of Giotto. Lami himself finds that the painters before Giotto, the so-called Greeks, were "relatively praiseworthy from the point of view of *disegno* or the vivacity and nobility of the colors."

He mentions some eleventh-century miniatures in Florentine libraries that are possibly better than those by the two miniaturists praised by Dante in the *Divine Comedy*, Oderisi da Gubbio and Franco Bolognese. He invokes ivories, icons, the Crucifix from the church of San Miniato al Monte, the mosaics by Jacopo Torriti in the Lateran Basilica, and many other works and artists who rose above the rough, ungainly manners of the time. Admittedly he has little to say about these works except that Cimabue must have envied them. Lami has no language at his disposal to express his intuitions. He grasps that technical accomplishment is the collective achievement of a society and cannot be held against the individual artist, who floats on a rising or falling tide of technical capacity.

The prolific historian and collector of medieval paintings Alexis-François Artaud de Montor (1772–1849) published a catalogue in 1808 of his collection of 110 panels attributed to thirty-eight different artists, the *Considérations sur l'état de la peinture en Italie, dans les quatre siècles qui ont précédé celui de Raphael*. Remarkably, forty-five of the pictures were thought to predate 1300. In the accompanying essay he says, for example, about the thirteenth-century master Guido da Siena that "the attitudes of his heads, especially of his saints and bishops, are very noble." Artaud de Montor considered the two Guidos in his collection—as did some well-known Florentine experts—preferable or at least equal to the works of Cimabue, their style "as frank, as determined" as that of the latter's Madonna at S. Maria Novella (presumably he meant the Madonna Rucellai by Duccio).

Ottley and Superville aimed to escape the recent history of art as it had been packaged for them by the academies. One might point out that the academic program, through the practice of life drawing, did after all route art through observation of a real fact in the world, whereas the exponents of the new outline drawing manner were turning their eyes away from the world. Ironically it was they who began to produce the most purely art-historical art. Their line drawings sought to recover the unself-consciousness ascribed to early classical or medieval art. The thirteenth-century sculptures of the Pisani were, in truth, anything but naïve. They were the products of an intense synthesis of local traditions of stone carving with careful study of the Roman sarcophagi in Pisa. Giotto, too, achieved miraculous effects of simplicity and necessity but only by deflecting a native tradition of mural painting that reached back into Carolingian times, through study of ancient and modern sculpture. The line draughtsmen of the 1790s hoped to find their way somatically back to a state of oneness with the world, contriving their own naturalness. The poet, playwright, and philosopher Friedrich Schiller (1759–1805) expressed this paradox in his influential essay "On Naïve and Sentimental Poetry" (1795). Here Schiller described art as a contrivance that is put to shame by the necessity, autonomy, and nontemporality of nature. Schiller then claims that the ancient poets enjoyed such intimacy with nature that their works are for us moderns like nature itself. We can only envy the capacity of the ancients to extend nature:

> Poets have at all times…been the *keepers* (*Bewahrer*) of Nature. When they can no longer entirely be such and already experience in themselves the destructive influence of arbitrary and artificial forms…, then they become the *witnesses* and the *avengers* of Nature. They will either *be* Nature or they will *seek* the lost Nature.

Today, Schiller says, we can only behold nature as an object and as the exemplar of a moral idea. The relation to nature of the witnesses and the avengers is no longer naïve but sentimental.

Ready to dream his way back into the envied state of naïveté was the youthful author of a bouquet of essays and poems published anonymously in 1796 under the title *Herzensergiessungen eines kunstlieben-den Klosterbruders* (Outpourings of the Heart of an Art-Loving Friar). Wilhelm Heinrich Wackenroder (1773–1798) was a law student who had visited not Italy but Nuremberg, where he fell under the spell of the art of Albrecht Dürer. Wackenroder studied with the artist and art historian J. D. Fiorillo at the university of Göttingen and was exposed to the history of early German art written by Matthias Quad von Kinckelbach. In the preface of the *Outpourings*, Wackenroder, a Protestant from Berlin, assumes the voice of a (modern-day) cleric who once practiced art but now has retreated to a monastery. He professes tearful admiration for the great painters of the past, who are as saints to him. The next section, entitled "Raphael's Vision," is Wackenroder's attempt to invent a language adequate to his impressions of that painter's art, which he knew only from reproductive engravings. He had been disappointed by all previous writing on art, and with some justification. For as Wackenroder points out, "The so-called theorists and systematizers describe to us the inspiration of the artist from hearsay…. They speak about the artist's inspiration as if it were something right before their eyes; they explain it and tell us a great deal about it; and they should rightly blush to pronounce the holy word, for they do not know *what* they are expressing by it." Many writers before Wackenroder had recognized that artistic creation is a mystery. The confession of the inability to account for a judgment complements the connoisseur's mute gesture of discrimination or approval. Friedrich Schlegel noted as much, with shrewd ambivalence, in one of his *Critical Fragments* (1797): "If some mystical amateurs of art who take every critique to be a dismemberment, and every dismemberment to be a destruction of pleasure, were to think the problem through to its logical conclusion, then the best judgment of the most worthy work would have to be 'upon my soul!' (*Potztausend*). There are in fact critiques that say nothing more than this, but take longer to say it."

Wackenroder is not content with the laconic ejaculation—"wow," as we might say today—and turns to the language of revelation. He quotes the famous passage in the letter supposedly written by Raphael to Baldassare Castiglione where the painter explains that, because he cannot always find in nature the ideal models he needs, he relies instead on *una certa idea*, a kind of idea. Wackenroder then interprets this principle through a fictional text by the architect Donato Bramante which he, the art-loving friar, had found among the papers of his monastery. Here Bramante recounts that Raphael had told him in confidence that his image of the Madonna had appeared to him in a dream, sent by God and projected as if by a magic lantern onto the wall. Wackenroder deduces that art, which appears to come from nowhere, and whose provenance Raphael himself had declined to guess at, is sent to us by God.

In the next section Wackenroder writes of Italy as a new Holy Land, a pilgrimage destination. He relates the anecdote, found in Vasari, about the death of the Bolognese painter Francesco Francia, where the older artist dies of grief when he beholds the beauty of Raphael's *Ecstasy of Saint Cecilia*. Wackenroder then offers fictional exchanges of letters between Raphael and his (fictional) pupil Antonio, and between Antonio and his friend Jacopo in Rome. And so on, in a series of biographies of artists and brief essays on art.

In 1798 Wackenroder's friend Ludwig Tieck published *Franz Sternbalds Wanderungen* (Franz Sternbald's Travels), an historical novel and art-historical fantasy. Franz Sternbald is an imaginary pupil of Dürer who leaves Nuremberg and sets out first to the Netherlands and eventually to Italy in search of the new, sincere mode of painting. Dürer writes him a letter, urging him to spend time with peasants and children as an antidote to pedantry and manner. Though convinced that a new age of art is dawning, Franz nonetheless catches himself admiring the old paintings he finds in out-of-the-way chapels:

> Whether it is my inexperience or my predilection for the old times, I rarely see a really bad painting. Before I discover the faults, I see the merits…. I often feel a pious reverence for our honest ancestors, who now and again expressed really beautiful and elevated thoughts in such uncomplicated ways.

Wackenroder's and Tieck's fictional letters and romanticized biographies are more sincere and searching versions of the invented lives of artists published by the Orientalist and collector William Beckford in 1780, *Biographical Memoirs of Extraordinary Painters*. Beckford claimed that he produced these pseudoscholarly and somewhat hysterical sketches after having overheard the tales told by his own housekeeper to visitors to his own house. Beckford gives us the life of Aldrovandus Magnus, for example, born in Bruges in 1473, who painted the Apotheosis of the Princess of Bohemia, draped in a saffron stole. This master's pupils, Andrew Guelph and Og of Basan, held a public debate in Venice with the Viennese painters Sucrewasser and Soorcrout about the comparative merits of egg-based and oil-based paint. And so on.

In his "Description of Two Paintings," meanwhile, Wackenroder observes that the old chroniclers were perhaps wise not to try to describe paintings, instead simply characterizing them as "excellent" or "incomparable." He offers a pair of poems about paintings, like little plays. These poems, and the theory of divine inspiration that lies behind them, may or may not be a satisfying account of the mystery of creativity. This is how Wackenroder escapes the dogma of academic theory and instead rehearses finally a poetic mode of address comparable to what we have long since found in the Chinese and Safavid traditions.

Poetic here is to be understood as the opposite of prosaic. Friedrich Schlegel develops the same thought in his essay of 1803 on Italian paintings at the Louvre. "Poetry" is the criterion of great art, he writes, and the example of the older painters best reveals this to us. "Admittedly if we limit ourselves to poetry in the sense of words and poets, then only a few paintings of old times are 'poetic,' and these few are actually rather thoughtless and not the loftiest. Instead we mean the poetic view of things, and the old masters had this view, and had it closer to the source." After contemplating the early German panel paintings in Cologne, Schlegel wonders whether the present day is capable of producing another "true" painter. Probably not, he concludes, because "the deep and inward feeling" (*das innige and tiefe Gefühl*) is wanting.

The poetic theory of art—art as authentic expression—bears on the historicist project developed by Winckelmann, Goethe, and Herder. The latter had written in "Conclusions Drawn from the Comparison of the Poetry of Diverse Peoples of Ancient and Modern Times" (1796):

> In poetry's gallery of diverse ways of thinking, diverse aspirations, and diverse desires, we come to know periods and nations far more intimately than we can through the misleading and pathetic method of studying their political and military history. From this latter kind of history, we rarely learn more about a people than how it was ruled and how it was wiped out. From its poetry, we learn about its way of thinking, its desires and wants, the ways it rejoiced, and the ways it was guided either by its principles or its inclinations.

The Revolutionary Louvre, by this measure, was antihistoricist: the great art of the past was carried forward into modernity precisely because it did not merely express the desires and rejoicings of a corrupted aristocracy and clergy.

Wackenroder and Schlegel altered the shape of history by at once de-objectifying the past (again, Schlegel builds on Winckelmann) and defamiliarizing the present. The aim was to enter into a more confidential relation with the past. Schlegel warned: "One should never appeal to the spirit of antiquity as if to an authority. It's a peculiar thing with spirits: they don't let themselves be seized and shown to others. Spirits reveal themselves only to other spirits."

Wackenroder's intuition was that the subjectivized piety of the late Middle Ages provided a working model for a new approach to art. And yet he could find no words of praise for any artist older than Dürer and Raphael—the mirror image of Schlegel's unwillingness to praise artists younger than Dürer and Raphael. Despite all the accumulating scholarship on medieval art since the late sixteenth century, no one, it seems, apart from Félibien, as well as Mancini, Muratori, Lami, and a few others, each in a few phrases, had found a way to express admiration for medieval art. The most eloquent critical passages to this date are found in Schlegel's reports from Paris. We recall that Schlegel in 1802 had praised the "Egyptian sublimity and constraint," the "forbidding sobriety," of the altarpiece of the Adoration of the Lamb by Jan van Eyck. One may or may not agree with Schlegel that van Eyck's world was greater and stronger than the modern world. Still, it is the case that he was the first writer not only to assign van Eyck's work to the towering, indeed nonpareil, status it enjoys to the present day but also to try to explain why it deserves that status.

In a further essay on the art treasures of Paris, published in 1805, Schlegel describes works he saw in the Musée des Monuments français assembled by Alexandre Lenoir. Lenoir, erstwhile painter, had been put in charge by the National Assembly of the depot of medieval sculpture and other artifacts confiscated from churches and monasteries. The depot was located at the former convent of the Petits-Augustins, today the site of the École des Beaux-Arts on the Left Bank. By 1795 Lenoir had imaginatively transformed his depot into a museum of medieval French art and culture. Lenoir himself was interested in medieval artworks mainly as historical documents. Scholarship, however, even of a nationalist orientation, can serve as the matrix for poetry. Schlegel was impressed by Lenoir's specimens of thirteenth-century glass painting with their "burning" colors. "Just as grating dissonances in music are often momentously used by the greatest masters as the expression of the highest passion, almost approaching despair, so are the nearly screaming colors of glass painting ideally suited to impress the whole profundity of the highest passion and passion-stories with full force into the eyes and hearts of the beholders."

Herder had recommended the study of folk ballads. Here the English antiquarians had preceded him. Thomas Percy had published a collection of ballads as *Reliques of Ancient English Poetry* in 1765; Robert Burns published *Poems, Chiefly in the Scottish Dialect* in 1786; in 1798 appeared Coleridge and Wordsworth's collection of modern artificial folk poetry, the *Lyrical Ballads*. The Germans soon followed. Achim von Arnim and Clemens Brentano published a volume of discreetly improved folk poetry as *Des Knaben Wunderhorn* in 1805. Yet writers on art were unable to follow them. Even Schlegel seeks not simplicity but sublimity, awe, and powerful expression. He is listening not for the collective voice of the common people but for the distinctive tones of the strong author, even if he is able to praise the anonymous painter of the altarpiece of the cathedral of Cologne (the very altar Dürer had visited) because he was not driven by vanity but only by devotion or love (*Liebe zum Werk*). No one at the time had an eye for what later came to be called folk art. The churches were still full of simple paintings and wood carvings, but not a word is written about them.

The key to a total expansion of the horizons of criticism, to the very edges of space and time, is already at hand. It is the doctrine of the subjective response as the basis for judgment, already formulated by Roger de Piles. Wackenroder expressed this in his section entitled "A Few Words on Universality, Tolerance, and Human Love in Art." Here he adopts a celestial point of view. God hears the Babel of languages and sees the strife and misunderstanding, but

> He knows that each person speaks the language which He has created in him, that each expresses his inner feelings as he can and should;—if in their blindness they dispute with each other, then He knows and recognizes that each is, for himself, in the right.

Wackenroder has solved an historicist riddle by positing that the late Middle Ages, now accessible to the sympathetic historian, was itself the epoch par excellence of subjective feeling. As the not yet institutionalized art of subjectivity, late medieval art could be grasped both as timeless and historical at once. It is the same move that Winckelmann made, with the values switched. This does not quite match Herder's purer doctrine of relativism. Herder in his "Conclusions Drawn from the Comparison of the Poetry of Diverse Peoples of Ancient and Modern Times" wrote: "Poetry meant something very different to the Roman and the monk; to the Arab and the crusader; to the scholar who uncovers other ages and to the poet and the people in diverse periods of diverse nations.... This is why the quarrel about the *superiority of either ancient or modern literature* was meaningless." Herder is saying that poetry serves different purposes to different people and that there is no platform outside the human sphere, no perspective beyond perspective.

And yet a little later in the same text Herder takes up a botanical metaphor, envisioning the artwork as fragile, self-contained: the "natural" approach to poetry is "to leave each flower in its own context and from here to study it from its roots to its top just as it is, in reference to its own time and nature. The truly humble genius hates ranking and comparison. Genius prefers to be first in the village rather than the second in rank behind Caesar. Lichen, moss, fern—each plant flourishes in its own context in the divine order." In his "Yet Another Philosophy of History" (1774) Herder had already written: "Each nation has its *own center* of happiness within itself (*Mittelpunkt ihrer Glückseligkeit*), just as every sphere has its own center of gravity."

Wackenroder also thinks perspectively, imaging an angelic point of view from which judgment is unthinkable:

> Stupid people cannot grasp that on our globe there are antipodes and that they are themselves antipodes. They think of the place where they are standing as the center of gravity of the universe,—and their minds lack the wings to fly around the whole earth and take in with a *single* glance the integrated totality.

In approaching art emotionally, they fail to recognize their bias:

> They regard their *own* emotion as the center of everything beautiful in art and they pronounce the final verdict on everything as if from the judge's bench, without considering that no one has appointed them judges and that those who are condemned by them could just as well set themselves up as judges.

Wackenroder draws out the implications for art history:

> Why do you now condemn the American Indian, that he speaks his own Indian language and not our language?—
>
> And yet you want to condemn the middle ages for not building such temples as they did in Greece?—
>
> O, find a way through intuition into these foreign souls and note that you have received the gifts of the spirit from the *same hand* as your misunderstood brothers! Understand, too, that every being can only create things out of himself with the capacities which he has received from heaven and that each person's creative works are in proportion to his talents. And if you are not capable of *feeling* your way into all unfamiliar beings and *experiencing* their works in your soul; then try, at least, to arrive at this conviction indirectly, through the intellect's chains of reasoning.—

There was no more vivid way of expressing such paradoxes than by invoking the most remote art conceivable to a European:

> If your soul had arisen several hundred miles further to the East, on the soil of India, then you would feel the secret spirit which exists,

concealed from our senses, in the little, strangely shaped idols with many arms and, if you were to see the statue of the Venus of Medici, you would not know what you should think of it. And had it pleased that One, under whose power you stood and are standing, to cast you into the multitudes of southern island dwellers, then you would find in every wild drumbeat and in the crude, shrill shocks of the melody a deep significance, of which you now comprehend not a syllable.

Although Wackenroder arrives at the conviction of the relativity of customs and beliefs by reasoning, he implies that there is also an inner route to this insight: a sympathetic participation in the feelings of the unfamiliar ones. One ought to be able to enter into the mentality of the other and at that point the once-rebarbative idol or melody will be reborn into beauty. The capacity to feel overcomes all the possible uses of image, effigy, and melody and overcomes class, for he is describing a new nobility of soul. The image of the god had once been the focus of a collective ritual. The votive image had been a token in an exchange. The temple had framed a real or symbolic sacrifice. The music had generated a second state of collective emotion, inviting the revisitation of the ancestors. The European artist of 1800, the receptive soul, has no desire to participate in any of these rituals. He is drawn to the prelapsarian sincerity of the late fifteenth-century painters, and he is mesmerized by the image of the many-armed Hindu god. In his fascination he retains his sovereignty.

Wackenroder's fantasies of sympathy remind us that European knowledge of South Asian art and religion was accumulating at a rapid rate. Notable publications were Pierre Sonnerat, *Voyage aux Indes Orientales et à la Chine* (Paris, 1782), with engraved renderings of the Hindu deities, and William Hodges, *Select Views in India* (London, 1786), an album of aquatints after Hodges's own drawings of Indian monuments. The Society of Antiquaries of London, an entity dedicated since its establishment in 1707 to the antiquities of Britain, turned its attention to the monuments of South Asia. Joshua Reynolds and John Flaxman took an interest in Indian art. The retired military officer Edward Moor published a handbook to the deities of South Asia, *The Hindu Pantheon* (London, 1810), supplemented by 105 engravings based on lucid line drawings by an academic artist, one Haughton, after pictures, sculpted reliefs, and bronze figurines. Moor had no Sanskrit but he gathered intelligence from many sources, structuring his account of Hindu myth and symbolism around an iconography, the images of the gods. His image of the goddess Devi, an avatar of Parvati, is typical.

The engraving is based on a marble sculpture. Moor tells us how deeply cut the relief is and how worn the ornament is; he says the work is painted and gilt; he compares the illustration to the original. Although he is somewhat baffled by the image, he provides clues to its meaning by comparing its elements to other works.

The "Orient"—a cluster of half-understood but passionately clutched forms and ideas—had come to stand for a state of poetic suspension, a state of creative readiness. Schlegel addressed these words to the poet Friedrich von Hardenberg, known as Novalis, in 1800:

> *To Novalis*: You don't hover on the margins, but rather in your spirit poetry and philosophy inwardly pervade one another. In these images of the uncomprehended truth your mind stood closest to me. What you have thought, I think; what I have thought, you will think, or have already thought. There are misunderstandings that only confirm the highest agreement. Every doctrine of the eternal Orient belongs to all artists. I name you instead of all the others.

The phrase "images of the uncomprehended truth" could also describe the harvest of the new outward-directed scholarship. Angelic relativism does not always sponsor historicist piety for the humble native flower. Not every scholar and artist was committed to protecting the local, irreducible characters of Hindu art or medieval Christian art. Some translated images of those art worlds into their own sphere. History writing fashions a reality, remote in time or space, as a world, and then inserts that world into another world, my world. The scholarly study of medieval art extracted a reality from oblivion and gave it a shape, propelling medieval art into a second life, now embedded within the modern world. The antiquarian scholars of the eighteenth century who collected and published material, like Montfaucon, entertained no particularly vivid fantasies of fusion with the past. The mind of the scholar may well be prosaic. But the products of prosaic scholarship, even archeological data, can be fed into a picturesque dream machine. The lush views of Indian monuments, color aquatints, published by Thomas and William Daniell as *Oriental Scenery* (in six parts, from 1795–1808), which for many Britons fixed the image of the Hindu monuments, may be compared in

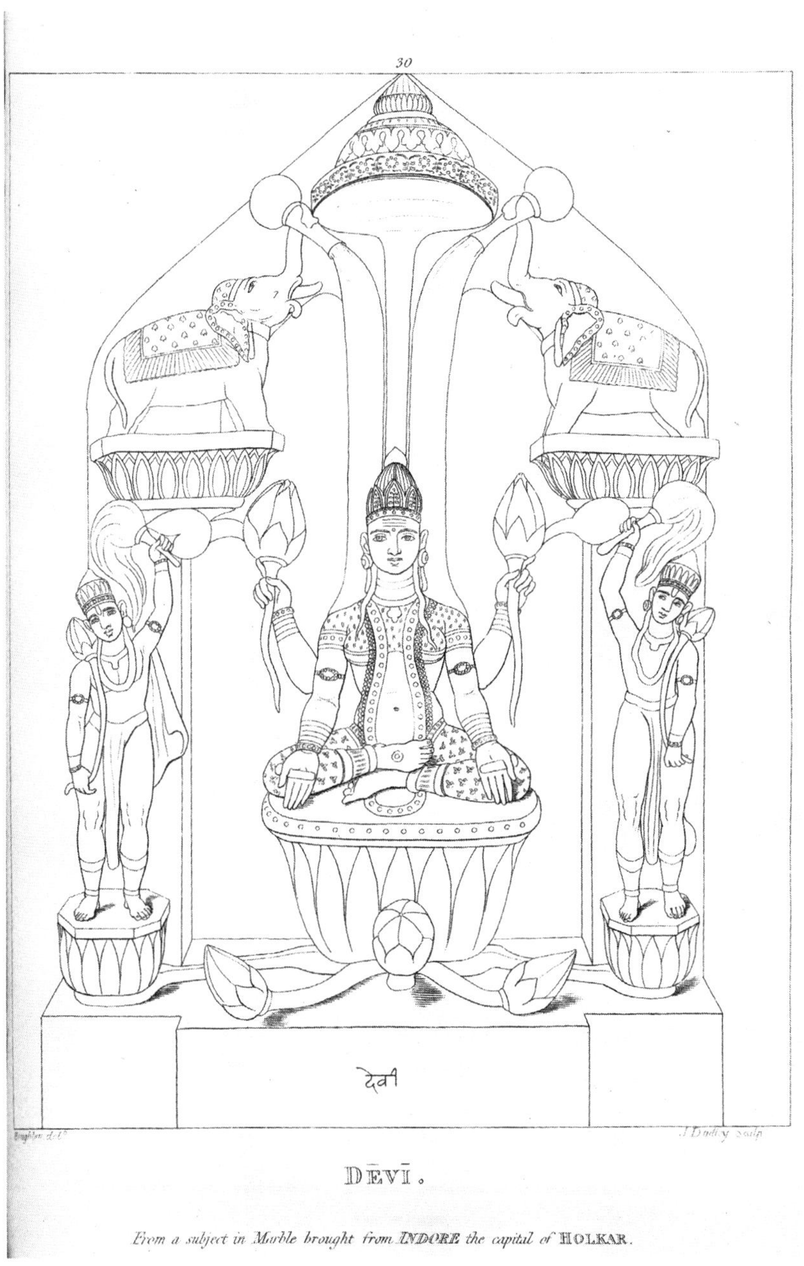

The Goddess Devi. Engraving in Edward Moor, *The Hindu Pantheon* (London, 1810), plate 30. Moor archives the iconography of the Hindu gods; the medium of engraving suits his purpose. Yet in his text he describes aspects of the marble sculpture not captured by this image.

their holistic and atmospheric approach with the color engravings of the rooms of Alexandre Lenoir's museum. The European recovery of European medieval art was both a sympathetic rapprochement with a half-forgotten world and a misreading of that world. The abuse was as it were self-inflicted. The European misreadings of Indian art, Japanese art, African art, no matter how attentive and well-intentioned the scholarship, were another matter.

In 1805 Goethe together with the painter Johann Heinrich Meyer and the philologist Friedrich August Wolf published a volume entitled *Winkelmann* [sic] *und sein Jahrhundert*, comprising a selection of Winckelmann's letters, biographical notes by Goethe, an essay on the art of the eighteenth century by Meyer, and an essay on Winckelmann as philologist by Wolf. Meyer's views on the revival of the arts around 1500 were anti-academic. He considers the high point of art the religious art of the years around 1500; after that, art declines into the secular. "To the Catholic religious zeal of the thirteenth, fourteenth, and fifteenth centuries we owe the foundation and the growth of the visual arts. "Obscure monkish ideas seem to have little hindered the artist, for he adapts, brightens, and beautifies them." Once arrived at the beautiful level of the late fifteenth and early sixteenth century, the arts could have continued progressing indefinitely, were it not for the intervention of the great worldly patrons, who desired but did not urgently need the arts. Instead of the "stillness and freedom" of altarpieces, Raphael found himself painting halls and rooms, Michelangelo the sculptor squandered his genius on tombs.

Goethe, independent-minded, his youthful enthusiasms cooled, is by now already a step or two beyond the progressive view. Now he is orienting everyone once again to the classical. Goethe, impressed by the undivided quality of Winckelmann's antiquity, says that modern man heads off in reflection toward infinity, whereas the ancients remained within the actual. Goethe says contemplation of the extrahuman world brings the "division of our powers and capacities, a fragmentation of the previous unity." Winckelmann had avoided all this, remaining centered and earthbound: "An antique nature of this kind…appeared once more in Winckelmann…. From the very moment when he won the freedom he required, he appeared whole and complete, entirely in the spirit of antiquity." Goethe envied Winckelmann his capacity to escape his time and Christianity and to *become pagan*: a delayed fulfillment of the Renaissance project.

Schlegel in the *Athenaeum Fragments* (1798) had already credited Winckelmann with the recognition of the integrity of antiquity: "The systematic Winckelmann, who read all the ancients as if they were a single author, who saw everything as a whole and concentrated all his powers on the Greeks, laid the foundations, through his perception of the absolute difference between the ancients and the moderns, of a material doctrine of antiquity." But this was only a foundation. Scholarship requires a fusion of horizons: "Only when we discover the attitude and the conditions of an absolute identity of ancient and modern, as it was, is, and will be, will one be able to say that at least the contours of such a course of study have been sketched and one can now contemplate carrying it out in a methodical way."

Goethe's reflections laid the groundwork for the cult of Winckelmann in the nineteenth century. Since Winckelmann was neither a philologist nor a university professor, it is unclear why he was celebrated in the nineteenth century as the patron saint of *Altertumswissenschaft*, or the scholarly study of antiquity. The custom of marking Winckelmann's birthday, December 9, with festivities and speeches began in the 1820s and is recorded over the course of the century at the universities of Kiel, Bonn, Berlin, Greifswald, Göttingen (and even today in Salzburg and Graz). Yet already Friedrich August Wolf—notwithstanding his own involvement in the volume—wondered why Goethe and his Weimar circle were so taken by Winckelmann, given that he made few significant contributions to philology. But the Weimar classicists, despite Wolf's involvement, were not so impressed by philology. They were also antiphilosophical, and here Winckelmann seemed an ally. Goethe and his colleagues were not convinced by Friedrich Wilhelm Joseph Schelling, who had proposed in the *System of Transcendental Idealism* (1800) that it is the artist who makes us aware of the Absolute. What is the Absolute? The Absolute is the universe as whole; it is one substance; it is dynamic and developing; it is rational and teleological, that is, it is governed by an archetype or primal idea. Schelling was not satisfied with Immanuel Kant's critical philosophy, which arrived at a compromise between the challenge of the world to resist our efforts to know it and the power of the mind to construct reality. Schelling's speculation was that the mind, or the I, was finally one with the world, or nature, and that our destiny was to intuit that oneness, so dissolving the subject into its object. He was led to this by his insistence on the freedom of the subject, which he saw as the key to politics and art. If the subject will be free, then it must either deny the reality of the external world, or become or fuse with that world. Only artistic genius can bring us there. The product of genius flows both from conscious activity and from something beyond consciousness, something unknown:

> This unknown, however, whereby the objective and the conscious activities are here brought into unexpected harmony, is none other than that absolute which contains the common ground of the pre-established harmony between the conscious and the unconscious.

Art is where freedom and necessity (i.e., the Absolute) are resolved:

> That incomprehensible agency which supplies objectivity to the conscious, without the cooperation of freedom, and to some extent in opposition to freedom (wherein is eternally dispersed what in this production is united), is denominated by means of the obscure concept of *genius*.
>
> The product we postulate is none other than the product of genius, or, since genius is possible only in the arts, the *product of art*.

Goethe said that the *Altertumsforscher*, the scholars of antiquity, were the only ones who ignored the Kantian revolution—which laid the groundwork for Schelling—and got away with it. He meant that Winckelmann's real contribution was not to have secured the metaphysical credentials of ideal form but rather to have anchored ideal form in ancient life. The presence of Winckelmann's person in his own writing, as well as his insistence that all involvement in art is framed by desire, is exactly what proposed him as a countermodel to the objective scholarship developed in the nineteenth century. The Winckelmannians could not quite say this, could not recognize the nature of their own fascination, could also not acknowledge that antiquity for its modern votaries is not an historical epoch but a form of life, thus both very near and very far. "Antiquity" is a project of self-cultivation and exceeds any role it may play within historiography.

In a brooding passage in his *Phenomenology of Spirit* (1807), the idealist philosopher G. W. F. Hegel, the colleague of Schelling, assigned to his own post-Winckelmannian contemporaries the subordinate task of tending to the works of historical art:

> The works of the Muse now lack the power of the Spirit, for the Spirit has gained its certainty of itself from the crushing of gods and men.

They have become what they are for us now—beautiful fruit already picked from the tree, which a friendly fate has offered us, as a girl might set the fruit before us. It cannot give us the actual life in which they existed, not the tree that bore them, not the earth and the elements which constituted their substance, not the climate which gave them their peculiar character, nor the cycle of the changing seasons that governed the process of their growth. So Fate does not restore their world to us along with the works of antique Art, it gives not the spring and the summer of the ethical life in which they blossomed and ripened, but only the veiled recollection of that actual world.

This confutes any confidence in the reinhabitation of ancient paganism. The sculptures in the museums are not delivering their "world." Historical scholarship, Hegel believed, cannot revivify but only at best provide pictures of lost worlds. We cannot "worship" those sculptures, he will say, implying that our modern cult of art has no proper object, no plenitude to meet its cravings:

> Our active enjoyment of them is therefore not an act of divine worship through which our consciousness might come to its perfect truth and fulfilment; it is an external activity—the wiping-off of some drops of rain or specks of dust from these fruits, so to speak—one which erects an intricate scaffolding of the dead elements of their outward existence—the language, the historical circumstances, etc., in place of the inner elements of the ethical life which environed, created, and inspired them. And all this we do, not in order to enter into their very life but only to possess an idea of them in our imagination (*in sich vorzustellen*).

Hegel describes an historical scholarship whose purpose is deferred, and is perhaps still unknown to us; whose discoveries are not in themselves significant. A shadow of inadequacy falls on modern art history at the moment of its birth.

1810–1830

On the last page of his monumental survey of the medieval, Renaissance, and Baroque *Kunstliteratur* or "literature of art" (1924)—the corpus of treatises, handbooks, academic theory, and art histories—the Viennese art historian Julius von Schlosser called upon an unlikely figure to speak the envoi: the German artist Philipp Otto Runge (1777–1810). Runge produced few works and his career was brief, but his concept of art as a direct cognition of nature was much admired in the early twentieth century. Runge studied at the art academy in Copenhagen with neoclassical masters and met with little success. After periods in Dresden and Hamburg, he retreated to his family home in the far north, on the Baltic coast. Except for a treatise on color, which earned the admiration of Goethe, Runge formulated his ideas on art mostly in long letters to his brother, published in 1840.

For Schlosser, Runge was an authentic witness of the closing of a tradition of writing on art because, unlike some superficial enthusiasts of his generation—Wackenroder and Tieck, principally—and unlike the art theorists and the professors, Runge wrote from the "secure terrain of his *métier*." Runge believed that the crucible of art was not the study of Raphael and other paragons of the high style but rather the study of nature by means of introspection. The creative mind, for Runge, must shelter itself from history by participating in nature. This artist rejects tradition, looking beyond temporal "becoming and passing (*vergehen*)," even as he concedes that art is only a sample of the "eternally marvelous of all times" and perishes like a flower. Runge wrote that "the permanent rhythm within the temporal event is the alpha and the omega." To grasp this rhythm the artist must take a completely new approach to historical works of art. When such an artist, "with the deep sensibility animated, in a state of rapture, by the inner configuration of the spirit," stands before a work of art,

> the inner connection of the work with nature will dawn on him; he will as it were reproduce the work within himself, and all the splendor of the design will appear to him as a means for expressing himself more purely and comprehensively in that very connection which he inwardly and outwardly perceives.

Runge's words persuaded Schlosser that there is no vantage point on the history of art outside the creation of art. Only an artist who sees the most beautiful artworks of the past as "products of nature raised to a higher power" can grasp the meaning of art history. The rest of us are watching a puppet show.

Schlosser's history was infiltrated by his own increasing loss of confidence in the capacity of modern writers on art to say anything significant about art. Throughout his account he depreciated his own book's protagonists—Leon Battista Alberti, Giorgio Vasari, Gian Pietro Bellori—as text-bound, dogmatic pedants who had forgotten what it meant to make art, if they ever knew. They were good for nothing but writing books. Runge takes the stage at the close of Schlosser's pessimistic history, briefly, as if to bid adieu to the long tradition of academic art and at the same time to deliver an ironic greeting to the emergent discipline of scholarly art history, the succession of university instructors that a century later yielded Schlosser himself; a tribe who can only be more alienated from art, not less, than their ancien régime predecessors. In invoking Runge, Schlosser was indulging a kind of academic death wish.

Runge fled the academy in favor of the kitchen table, recovering a childlike state of receptivity. At home in Wolgast he cultivated together with his sisters the domestic art of cutting paper silhouettes. Although Runge's drawn lines, schooled in the manner of John Flaxman, remember forms handed down from classical art, the repetition is deceptive. In fact, Runge was trying to begin art history over again by identifying the essential lines of nature and by tracing new, unseen subjects. His drawings might be compared to the engravings accompanying Edward Moor's *Hindu Pantheon* (1810; see p. 191). Runge's "Morning," an emblematic composition, recalls Plutarch's description, in the *Oracles at Delphi*, of an Egyptian image of dawn: a baby perched on a lotus flower; as if to note that only the Egyptians, who felt the full burden of the past, had invented an adequate symbol for the forgetting of history.

In Paris voices had asked why the Academy should survive the Revolution. In Germany there were many local academies, none with the weight and power of the French Academy. Young painters began in the 1790s to rebel against their teachers. Some headed for Rome, the source, as if the problem were not Rome itself but the repetitions of Rome, the diaspora of good form. They wanted to see the works of Raphael as they really were, unfiltered by the layers of copies, reproductive engravings, and citations.

The artists of the day who most flamboyantly acted out the recovery of innocence, making a mark where Runge had not, were a band of six painters, led by Johann Friedrich Overbeck and Franz Pforr. They called themselves the Brothers of St. Luke (Luke was the patron saint of painting), quit the Academy in Vienna in 1810, and moved to Rome. They occupied some buildings at a secularized Franciscan monastery on the Pincian hill and adopted an archaizing, long-haired mode of dressing that earned them the sobriquet "Nazarenes," or men of Nazareth, a term referring to Christians generally already in Acts 24:5 and later, in the fourth century, the name of a Christian sect. They were the first band of artists to withdraw from an academy. But their radicalism was limited, for they only replaced one discipline with another, drawing not after ancient statuary but medieval mural and panel painting, up to and including Raphael. They were joined in 1812 by Peter Cornelius, in 1813 by Wilhelm Schadow, and later Philip Veit, Ferdinand Olivier, and Julius Schnorr von Carolsfeld.

The Nazarenes painted figural compositions with religious content, in legible and nubile outline and in soft, bright colors. In the sacred stories they discovered a bashful eroticism. Overbeck's *Finding of Moses* (1822–1824), a panel painting, is more subdued, less joyous and agitated, than its model, Raphael's fresco of the same subject in the Vatican Loggia. The painting knows too much. Every gesture is burdened with meaningfulness.

The Nazarenes received two substantial commissions in Rome: a series of murals illustrating the story of Joseph in the Casa Bartholdy, and murals illustrating scenes from Dante, Ariosto, and Tasso in the

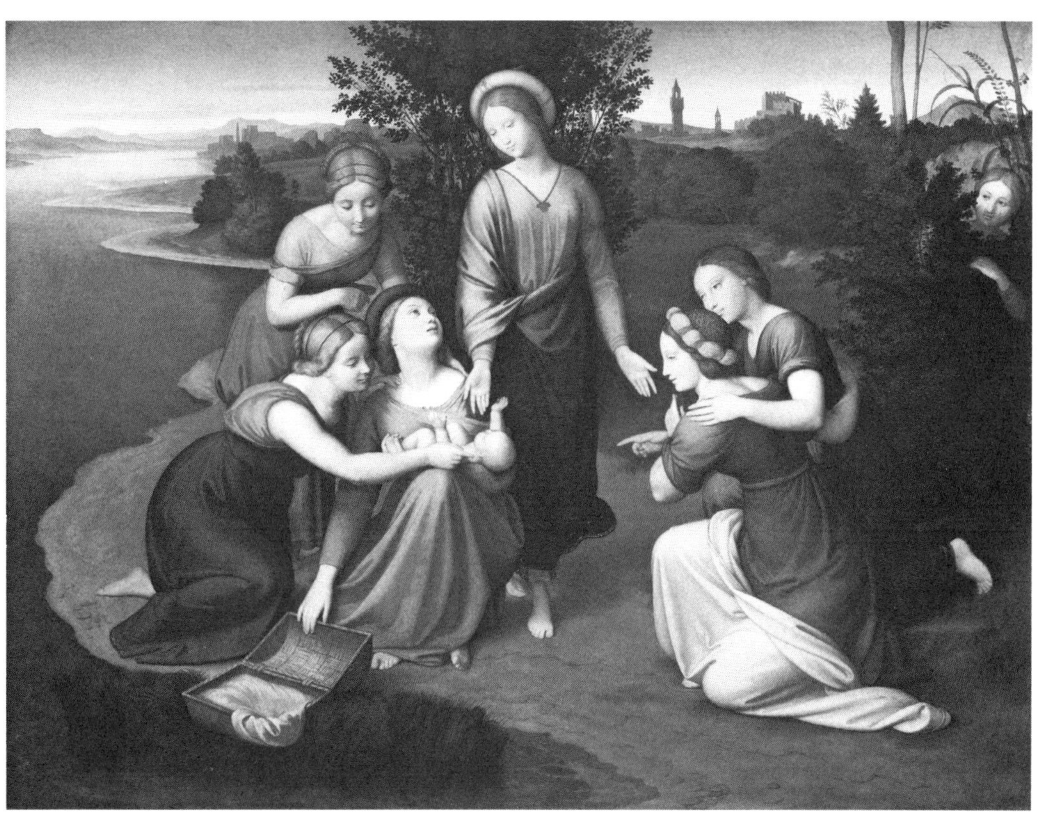

Johann Friedrich Overbeck, *The Finding of Moses* (1822–1824). Oil on panel, 44 × 59 cm. Bremen, Kunsthalle. The six women in their bafflement are barely distinguishable one from another. Which is Pharoah's daughter? Only the sister of Moses, hiding in the bushes, and the painter grasp what is happening.

Casa Massimo. They oriented their art to the suave, disingenuous style of the early Raphael as well as of his teacher Perugino. But they were also steeped, as was Raphael himself, in the style of Albrecht Dürer. From the torrent of Wackenroder's *Herzensergiessungen* they drew their sentimentality. The generation of Goethe had brooded over the dichotomy between Gothic and classical style. The Nazarenes tuned their work to the binarism of Raphael and Dürer—Italia and Germania, south and north—which was in fact no binarism at all. For Dürer and Raphael had in a similar fashion, and the Nazarenes were the first to see this, recalibrated the relation of painting to the body. The figures of Dürer and Raphael were rooted in attentiveness to simple attitudes and gestures, and this is why their art seemed to anti-academic artists not fully to belong to the historical succession of painting manners.

The engagement of the Nazarenes with historical art was ardent. In 1829 Johann Friedrich Overbeck painted a mural on the façade of the Porziuncola, the ancient, diminutive Franciscan chapel englobed since the sixteenth century by the basilica of Santa Maria degli Angeli, a couple of miles from the church of St. Francis at Assisi. This was the third church repaired by Francis. The mural, depicting the legendary granting of the Porziuncola Plenary Indulgence to Francis, echoes the styles of Giotto, Fra Angelico, and Raphael. Here Overbeck is the colleague of the architect and theorist Heinrich Hübsch, his near-contemporary, who would rebuild the west end of Speyer cathedral in the 1850s. Their approach extended the typological attitude to the past that had for so long dominated European art, whereby buildings and images were permitted to live in time, retaining their identity through sanctioned interventions, substitutions, and revisions. It was also continuous with the practice of conservation, now in the new century increasingly scientific. The conservators, who adapted to the practical sphere the neutral, value-free mentality of the bookish antiquarians, protected whatever was old, without strong prejudices for or against one style or another. Between 1818 and 1824 the architects Raffaelle Stern and Giuseppe Valadier restored the first-century Arch of Titus in Rome. To replace missing material they cut new blocks in the ancient Roman manner. Until then, buildings had been repaired along practical lines, or in a modern style, and no one worried about the formal integrity of the structure. The modern conservator who matched his additions to the existing fabric perpetrated a forgery supported by archeological knowledge. The writer

Stendhal, for one, registered a complaint, describing the Arch of Titus in 1828 as the "most elegant of the triumphal arches until the fatal epoch when it was redone by M. Valadier."

The landscape painter Caspar David Friedrich, who like Runge hailed from the far north and never visited Italy, recommended the study of nature over the emulation of other artists. The Nazarenes' path to the state of innocence, by contrast, led through the art-historical past. The art of the Nazarenes, paradoxically, proved completely compatible with the academic mentality. In the 1820s Peter Cornelius took over the directorship of the academy at Düsseldorf and later of the academy at Munich. The Nazarenes' reversion to the academy, their spurious radicality, might have made it clear that citational painting was a dangerous vortex. But not all contemporaries, including for example the exponents of the French *style troubadour* and many Victorian painters, steered clear.

Friedrich Schlegel remained unconvinced that one could simply escape history. In 1804 he suggests that a modern painter might indeed be capable of creating completely original works, "hieroglyphs" or divine symbols, out of his feeling for nature; but maybe not, maybe tradition is after all the best source. In 1823, preparing the edition of his collected works, Schlegel added a footnote on Philipp Otto Runge, whom he had met in Dresden in 1802. He adduces Runge's "allegorical" drawings as an example of how badly it can go when even a talented artist turns his back on tradition. Runge's art was to Schlegel a warning that a modern art unmoored would be as directionless as the new society projected by the French Revolution. The modern hieroglyphs of nature are in the end empty; symbols should be based on old symbols, "consecrated by tradition." For the artist, "tradition is the solid mother earth which he can never abandon without peril and without irreparable damage to himself."

Schlegel converted to Catholicism in 1808 and drifted towards conservatism. By 1812 he was certain that there was no new beginning for art. "The best theory of art is its *history*." he wrote. "In art, just as in other areas of human activity, a sudden tearing of the threads of tradition, the discarding of the rich capital of the work of past epochs, and the desire to create a new art as if out of nothing never go unpunished."

Julius von Schlosser made few comments, in print at least, on the art of his own day. Yet he must have recognized that Runge's desire to tune his art to the "permanent rhythm within the temporal event" prophesied the ideas of Wassily Kandinsky and Piet Mondrian, artists of Schlosser's generation.

The university professor of art history did not yet exist when Runge died in 1810. At that point scholarship was practiced by gentleman amateurs, librarians, conservators, and instructors in academies of art. Or artists: one of the few admirers of medieval art was the French painter Jacques-Nicolas Paillot de Montabert, who praised in his *Dissertation sur les peintures du moyen âge* (1812) the magnificent simplicity of the Italian paintings of the thirteenth, fourteenth and fifteenth centuries. The early Italians, he believed, invented oil painting—before van Eyck, of course—but immediately and wisely rejected it. After Raphael, according to Paillot, painting fell into arid academicism.

One of the favored modern formats was the monograph, or the account of the life and works of a single artist. Vasari's history had been a sequence of monographs, of varying length. To write a single such text was to extract the artist from a narrative of the progress of the arts and recreate him as a paragon of self-sufficiency. The favored subjects of the monographs of the early nineteenth century were the artists of the early Renaissance, the pioneers who broke with the Middle Ages but were not yet enlisted in an academic program. The polymath Carlo Amoretti published a monograph on Leonardo da Vinci in 1804. Luigi Pungileoni wrote the life of Correggio (1817–1821). Gustav Friedrich Waagen, later director of the Gemäldegalerie in Berlin, published a monograph on Hubert and Jan van Eyck in 1822. In the same year the writer Johanna Schopenhauer, acknowledging the influence of Goethe and his circle as well as of Schlegel and the brothers Sulpiz and Melchior Boisserée, collectors of fifteenth-century northern painting, and with an epigram from Wackenroder, published *Johann van Eyck und seine Nachfolger*, a history of northern art from the beginning through the end of the sixteenth century. More than one woman writer of distinction took up the form of the monograph. Maria (Dundas) Graham (Lady Callcott) published *Memoirs of the Life of Nicholas Poussin* in 1820, translated into French the following year. The Irish novelist Sydney Owenson (Lady Morgan) published the *Life and Times of Salvator Rosa* in 1824, more life and times than art despite the author's conviction that by the late seventeenth century the "long list of illustrious masters…was closed for ever, and terminated" in Salvator Rosa himself, "well worthy of the splendid but melancholy preeminence."

Joseph Heller's *Life and Work of Albrecht Dürer* (1827) was the first catalogue raisonné of his works. Johann David Passavant, a painter who had spent several years in Rome with the Nazarenes, now curator of the Städelsches Kunstinstitut in Frankfurt, published a monograph on Raphael (1839). Already in the first three decades of the century twenty books had been written on Raphael.

The monograph combined the work catalogue with the biography, diagramming a continuity between art and life. The life-and-work model solved the dilemma of historicism: the life provided a shelter for the art, as if the art—once bottled up inside the life—could finally be exempted from history. The artwork is shifted out of general history and into the special history of a life, so preserving its art quality.

Biographical or monographic art history often downplays the historical functions of art, the framing institutions, and the pressures of politics. The monograph was designed to bring out everything that managed to resist those constraints, that is, art as such. The monograph is best suited to painters and sculptors, where the concept of authorship is manifest. The authorship of prints, which often involve several individuals—designer, engraver, publisher—is more complicated. Prints can be treated like paintings if the designer is a strong artist, and especially if the designer also prepares the plate. Adam von Bartsch, the curator of the graphic collection of the Court Library in Vienna and advisor to Duke Albert von Sachsen-Teschen, invented the concept of the *peintre-graveur* or painter-engraver, a peremptory elevation of some but not all printmakers to the status of artists. His twenty-one-volume catalogue (1803–1821) created a lasting order within the vast corpus of European prints but also a lasting problem, a split within the inventory, since most printmakers were not like Rembrandt.

Few of the earliest monographists had any connection with a university. One who did was Johann Dominik Fiorillo (1748–1810), an Italian painter, born in Germany, who held a professorship in philosophy at Göttingen but also taught drawing and art history (he was the teacher of Wackenroder). Fiorillo's edition of the poem on painting by Salvator Rosa (1785) was prefaced by a life of the artist. He published a *Geschichte der zeichnenden Künste* in nine volumes (1798–1821), a history of European art from the Middle Ages to the eighteenth century. Fiorillo mostly compiled the findings of Italian scholars such as Leopoldo Cicognara. This was art history with a low intellectual profile, basically a collection of facts based on primary sources or communicated by earlier authorities such as Vasari, and observations on works laced with critical judgments. Fiorillo and most other art historians of the early nineteenth century have faded from view and, in truth, are not very interesting to read.

Carl Friedrich von Rumohr (1785–1843), however, a polymath much admired by his contemporaries, enjoys even today a secret cult. Rumohr's scope exceeded art history. He wrote a travel book on northern Italy with many notes on agriculture; he wrote a philosophical cookbook; he anthologized the Italian *novelle* of the late Middle Ages and himself wrote prose fiction; he was an accomplished draughtsman. His main contribution to art history was the three volumes of *Italienische Forschungen: Zur Theorie und Geschichte neuerer Kunstbestrebungen* (1827–1831), a history of Italian art from the early Middle Ages through the fifteenth century, crowned by a monograph of Raphael. Rumohr studied with Fiorillo at Göttingen and at the art academy in Munich. He was welcomed into the progressive circles of Ludwig Tieck and the brothers Riepenhausen, of Runge and Friedrich Perthes. In 1808 Rumohr travelled with Achim von Arnim and the Brentanos. He saw the Boisserée collection in Heidelberg and published his first study of medieval art in Schlegel's *Deutsches Museum*. In 1816 Rumohr settled in Italy, where he found companionship among the Nazarenes. In the 1820s he was involved in sorting out, with Waagen, the art collections of the Prussian state.

Rumohr's art-historical writing is characterized by a mistrust of the literary tradition, including Vasari. Instead he sought out documents. Rumohr's account of thirteenth- and fourteenth-century Tuscan art is built on documents about the guilds or artistic commissions found in the archives. He admired the Sienese master Duccio's "lovely expression of goodness and mildness." But generally Rumohr's remarks on style are spare. Breaking the religious mood conjured by the Nazarenes, he describes Giotto as a secularizer. Rumohr will not join the chorus of praise for Giotto, finding Friedrich Schlegel's admiration overblown. He himself considers Giotto merely a "lucid, judicious, hard-working master" (*der klare, besonnene, werktätige Meister*). Giotto may have "steered art toward the lively and the active," but he also "encouraged that…alienation from the ideas of Christian antiquity which marks and distinguishes the Florentine school all the way to Leonardo and Raphael…though one might except Fra Angelico and Masaccio."

The other cause of the decline was the excessive power of the guilds, who enforced a democratic "levelling of masters," "dangerous for the arts." Too many lesser artists were involved in decisions; aristocratic principles were suppressed in favor of the common good.

In 1844, a year after his death, an eighty-three-page biography of Rumohr was published by his acolyte Heinrich Wilhelm Schulz: a monograph not on an artist but on an art historian. Art history doubles back upon itself almost as soon as it begins. The peculiar self-regard of this discipline has its psychological origins in fear: fear that modern scholarship is alienated from art and fear that modern art is alienated from power. Schlosser will admire Rumohr, identifying him as the first interesting art historian who was not himself an artist, just as he identified himself as the last academic art historian who was still intimate with art. Carl Friedrich Rumohr is the library-bound art historian's own better image of himself, namely as a gentleman with a discerning eye and an empiricist with no tolerance for *Schwärmerei* or mystical nonsense, a man of the world, perhaps an amateur draughtsman, an ideal combination of empirical and critical sensibilities. He is the doppelgänger of the free artist depicted by the early nineteenth-century monographs. He figures even today in a patrician fantasy of the discipline.

Even more isolated than the Nazarenes in his own day, and much more admired than they are in ours, was William Blake (1757–1827). Blake was trained as an antiquarian engraver. As an apprentice he made drawings and prints after the tombs in Westminster Abbey. He brought the linear style of Flaxman to his tasks, but, like Piranesi, spurned all that was Greek. Like Runge, Blake was a reader of the Baroque mystic Jacob Böhme, whose cosmological diagrams purified his line and reintroduced him to symmetry. Blake allied himself with James Barry, John Hamilton Mortimer, and Henry Fuseli against Joshua Reynolds and the Royal Academy. He sought savage and rude but also lithe and fluid forms. Blake found in Edmund Burke's theory of the sublime as well as in older eccentric accounts of world architecture sustenance for his belief that everything of value had been invented by the ancient Jewish tribes. He believed that the Greeks had cribbed their architectural orders and their sculptural manner from the Temple of Solomon. His early engraving of *Joseph of Arimathea among the Rocks of Albion* (1773, reworked in the 1810s), based on a figure in Michelangelo's Pauline Chapel, known to Blake through a print, bears the inscription: "This is One of the Gothic Artists who Built the Cathedrals in what we call the Dark Ages." Blake saw and copied fifteenth-century paintings in English collections. In his late works he introduced Indian and Asian motifs, including the child perched on a lotus leaf.

Blake despised the Royal Academy and the margins of his copy of Reynolds's *Discourses*, which had brought the academic gospel to Great Britain, are crammed with expressions of acid outrage. Reacting to Reynolds's condescension to Dürer in *Discourse III* (1770), Blake scribbled: "What does this mean, 'would have been one of the first painters of his Age?' Albert Dürer *Is* not would have been. Besides, let them look at Gothic figures & Gothic Buildings & not talk of Dark Ages or of any Age. Ages are all equal. But Genius is Always Above the Age." We encountered already in the sixteenth century the thought experiment of imagining how wonderful an artist Dürer would have been had he received a proper artistic education. André Félibien extended the topos when he said that Dürer, "closed in his own knowledge and not seeing anything around himself which would give him more noble and elevated ideas, did not notice that in painting there is an infinite number of other faculties [beyond skillful imitation of nature] that he must know in order to achieve perfection." Roger de Piles said much the same thing; Winckelmann opined that Dürer and Holbein had talent and that if they had been exposed to the ancient works they might have surpassed the Italians. Blake was contesting the conventional wisdom of centuries.

Blake was a skilled, in fact radically inventive, engraver. The project of conservation, with its desire to publish findings—there was affinity with antiquarianism—was tied to reproductive technologies. For three centuries the task of the reproduction of Renaissance and Baroque paintings, with their infinite gradations of shade and color, had taxed the capacities of the print media: engraving and etching, later mezzotint and now aquatint, reproducing analogue tones. The preferred medium for the reproduction of pre-Renaissance paintings, however, was the simple line drawing, both to clarify the unfamiliar forms and to symbolize an innocent nondependence of their purity on the blandishments of color. Karl Joseph Ignaz Mosler had already made line drawings after paintings in the Boisserée collection before 1808, but they were never published. Fifteenth-century works, not to speak of older works, were rarely featured in the great anthologies of engravings after historical paintings published in these years. Jean-Baptiste Seroux d'Agincourt, whose attitude was antiquarian, reproduced medieval works in outline in his *Histoire de l'art par les monumens, depuis sa décadence au IVe siècle jusqu'à son renouvellement au XVIe* (1810–1823), the first illustrated history of art. The outline drawings reported on composition and iconography but not much more. Seroux d'Agincourt was obliged to illustrate the invention of oil painting with line drawings of a group of figures from van Eyck's Ghent altarpiece, a portrait of van Eyck, and the *Dead Christ* by Antonello da Messina. At this point lithography became available, a medium, like woodcut, well suited to line drawing. The lithograph sent the artists in search of suitable works to copy. From 1821 Johann Nepomuk Strixner made lithographs after works in the Boisserée collection and after Maximilian I's *Prayer Book*, the emperor's personal copy of a printed Book of Hours whose margins were hand-decorated with drawings by Dürer, Altdorfer, Baldung, Cranach, and Burgkmair.

Goethe, in an article of 1816, says that the readers should be given at least reproductions of outline drawings of the paintings discussed, "otherwise it is mere rhetoric and versifying (*Rederei und Verselei*), requiring neither nature nor an artistic object." This was not the norm, and in this respect the European tradition lagged well behind the Chinese and Japanese tradition, which for centuries had accompanied art-historical and critical texts with woodcut illustrations.

The painter William Young Ottley, as we noted, was in Italy in the 1790s making drawings after medieval paintings. In 1826 he published a volume of engraved plates after drawings by himself and by Humbert de Superville, dedicated to Flaxman and to the hope that viewers would share his admiration for the "beauties dispersed" among the works by the "Most Eminent Masters of the Early Florentine School." These specimens attest to the "intrinsic and peculiar excellence" of that school before the corruption of style that set in after Raphael. Something about the early masters, Ottley muses, made them "safe teachers," unlike Raphael and his generation, whose perfection only led to ruin. He praised the early painters and sculptors, including Cimabue, Giunta Pisano, and Nicola Pisano, but above all Giotto, whose "ingenious distribution of the figures" develops subjects "with a degree of perspicuity seldom equalled, and perhaps never surpassed, by painters of later times." These paintings are "almost ever exempt from affectation of manner."

For all the gloomy eloquence of Paillot de Montabert and the enthusiasms of Ottley, most observers at the start of the nineteenth century either deplored or patronized paintings more than three hundred years old. The portraits of the Virgin Mary, Christ, and the saints were considered documents of obscurantism. The efforts of the northern painters in the wake of van Eyck to describe the world as they saw it were reminders of the poverty of depiction unsustained by an ideal. There was as yet little taste for realism. In *The World as Will and Representation* (1818/1844), the philosopher Arthur Schopenhauer, son of the novelist and art historian Johanna Schopenhauer, dismissed the idea that the description of nature could ever generate beauty: "We see how far the old German [read: Netherlandish] painters arrived at beauty by imitating nature. Let us consider their naked figures. No knowledge of the beautiful is at all possible purely *a posteriori* and from mere experience." No one had any language yet to justify the ugly, the deformed.

Relativism, or the redescription of the universe as an infinity of local and incommensurable truths, already proposed as an intellectual ideal by Herder, proved difficult to realize. Art historians of the early nineteenth century took almost no interest in the functions of images, in rituals, in the performance of sacraments and vows, in the political agency of images, in the meaning of images to collectivities, and generally in the existential investments that once animated past or distant images. Art history bought its relativism at the price of a diminishment of the idea of art. Stylistic eclecticism betokens a loss of confidence in art, because it signals acceptance of a split between form and content. Relativism on the level of style is relatively easy; relativism on the level of custom, ritual, and belief is hard to achieve. Eclecticism exposes an incomplete relativism.

The desideratum of relativism, because so difficult to realize, paradoxically encouraged the extraction of works from their historical and local contexts. It was easier to admire the flowers of Indian art when those flowers were removed from their ritual beds and transposed to the printed page or, ultimately, to the museum. Wackenroder, we saw, embraced medieval and Indian art on the same page. Protestant eyes rested benignly on the very images, Popish or Hindu—once they were translated into black lines on paper—that had not so long before been abominated as props for superstitious cults.

The European desire to protect, in the name of Enlightenment, the freedom of aesthetic judgment from the pressures of custom, ritual, and politics, swaps one misreading for another: disapproval of the alien belief-system gives way to a universal aestheticism. The translation of the Indian artwork into an alien language of art revealed aspects about the work not seen before, but also aspects that were not really there. It is not clear which attitude to prefer: the generous but superficial curiosity manifested in Edward Moor's compendium of Hindu iconography, or G. W. F. Hegel's exclusion of Indian art from the narrative of the progress of spirit, on the basis of its lack of historical sense:

> The Indians have proved themselves incapable of an historical inter-pretation of persons and events, because an historical treatment requires sang-froid in taking up and understanding the past on its own account in its actual shape with its empirical links, grounds, aims, and causes.

Hegel is ready to concede that the European's perspectival view of history, which aims for objectivity, is cold-blooded. The European historian's "prosaic circumspection"

> is at variance with the Indian pressure to refer each and everything back to the sheerly Absolute and Divine, and to contemplate in the commonest and most sensuous things a fancifully created presence and actuality of the gods.

The Indians cannot keep poetry and prose, infinite and finite, apart, and so

> fall, despite all their exuberance and magnificent boldness of conception, into a monstrous extravagance of the fantastic which runs over from what is inmost and deepest into the most commonplace present in order to turn one extreme directly into the other and confuse them.

Hegel's tone is censorious, and his understanding of Indian art distorted by his historical philosophy of art, his own nonconfused partition of the finite and the infinite, which will be discussed in the next section.

In 1808 Schlegel recommended to Goethe Karl Mosler's drawings after the early Netherlandish and German panel paintings of the Boisserée collection. In his long essay of 1816 entitled *Kunst und Altertum am Rhein und Mayn*, Goethe discussed the Boisserée collection (in that same year, by the way, Sulpiz Boisserée discovered or rediscovered the tomb of Erwin von Steinbach that the youthful Goethe could not find). This text contains one of the earliest sketches of a true contextual history of art, an art history that suspends present-tense observances and instead tries to grasp unfamiliar forms on their own terms. We must not, Goethe warns, mistake early northern panel painters for rustic naifs and so exclude them from our study of art. Instead we must understand the world that produced them. He begins by outlining a complete history of Christian art in five pages. Goethe gives historical reasons for the emergence of the Rhineland as a cradle of art: the Roman garrisons and the arrival of the saints, which provides local myths. For a long time, though, painting is imprisoned in the stiff "Byzantine" style. Only in the fifteenth century does it break free, shrugging off conventions—symmetry, the gold ground—and instead learning simply to observe the world around it. The painters develop a free and natural style. This is a compact alternative to Vasari's narrative of the rise of the new art in Tuscany. Goethe says that it is otiose to attempt constantly to explain where the artistic way of seeing came from, for the original artist finds it all around him:

> The man who emerges from childhood and raises his eyes does not find nature, as it were, pure and naked around him, for the divine strength of his forebears has created a second world within the world. He is so enclosed within imposed acclimatizations, conventional usages, favourite customs, venerable traditions, treasured monuments, beneficial laws, and so many splendid products of art that he never learns to distinguish what is original (*ursprünglich*) and what is derived. He helps himself to the world and has a perfect right to do so.

Goethe is saying that fifteenth-century Netherlandish art is valuable not because it transforms the world, nor because it invents a new world, but because it successfully reproduces the craftsman's experience of a world that has already been shaped. The value of the painting is its continuity, guaranteed by the craftsman's integrity and freedom from the interference of aesthetic ideas, with a world shaped to human needs. The beauty of the painting is the beauty of a social world collectively constructed over time.

According to Goethe, even the artist's most original creations are fabricated out of preformed materials: "One may call that artist original (*original*) who treats the objects around him in an individual, national, and above all traditional way, and shapes them into a well-knit whole." The world is itself already such a well-knit or well-established whole. This is the basis for the idea of context. Goethe's conceit is that northern art is a felicitous parody of academicism. For he does not say—as Schopenhauer and many others would—that they simply copied what was before their eyes. Rather, he says they copied an already artificial world, a fabricated environment sedimented with life, experience, and craft. Art is best, Goethe knows, when it copies art. And yet this is very far from academicism. The academy by nature establishes criteria for education other than the naïve transmission of skills. Goethe trusts, or pretends to trust, in such transmission. It is a weak concept of art, for in Goethe's account the work of art only repackages the social world, which is not a "first world," a ground, but only a "second world." Art adds nothing to that world but a frame.

Goethe, ironist and illusionist, incompletely occupies his own words. His strategy here is in part to discredit the religious or neo-Christian or Romantic interpretation of these works, in particular the recent Schlegel. He stresses the secular dimension as the key to the works' liberation into the aesthetic sphere. He tacitly breaks with the theses of his own colleague J. H. Meyer expressed in the publication on Winckelmann of 1805. The angels in the painting of St. Veronica holding the sudarium attest to a local "feeling for nature" developed since the thirteenth century. The Medusa-like head of Christ on Veronica's veil is a universal, no longer Christian, symbol of the horror of death and the misery of the human condition.

Goethe's other witness is Jan van Eyck's *Adoration of the Magi* triptych from the church of St. Columba in Cologne, which the Boisserées had purchased in 1808 (the picture is now in the Alte Pinakothek in Munich, the attribution corrected to Rogier van der Weyden). The picture leads him to the thesis that every community has an essential character that is expressed in a great individual or artist. He wishes upon every province or city the patriotism it is entitled to. Relativism has often served as a cover for chauvinism, for it sanctions nonstandard perspectives. Goethe's counterchauvinism is a way of unmasking what he saw as the chauvinism of the influential art historian Cicognara, who had said in 1808 that Italians and Greeks have the *bello ideale*, whereas the foreign schools can only be rescued by the concept of a *bello relativo*. The opposite of aesthetic absolutism, in 1816, is localism. The rootedness of Netherlandish painting supplies Goethe with a general model of what art should be. The provinciality of Netherlandish art is a virtue because it allows for more authentic self-expression. This argument upends the values of civilization in the name of the essential project of modernity, namely, to assert the right of the living to express themselves without worrying about whether they measure up to the past. Modernity protects the freedom of the present to sink into temporal provinciality.

Goethe is not proposing that modern painters imitate early Netherlandish art. He is saying, first, that their art expresses its own lifeworld, and to bring this out is the task of an art history; and second, that expression of the familiar world is not such a bad recipe for art today. Artists would do well to take up their own experiences as subjects and not attempt to select their preferred forms and subjects from the past, as the neoclassicists and the Nazarenes had been doing. The aim of a modern art is to offer itself, as early Netherlandish painting had done, as the ready-made object of a contextual art history.

A paradox looms. Goethe assigns art history an infinity of tasks. It must show how all styles in all times have reflected their respective worlds. This is a supposedly nonevaluative task. It will soon emerge, however, that some styles reflect their worlds more effectively than others, and these styles are to be praised precisely for their humility, lack of aesthetic pretensions, and readiness to be drafted into a contextual history of art. This is the basis for the admiration for fifteenth-century Flemish and seventeenth-century Dutch art by modern beholders, pious, bourgeois, rational, and urban, who see in this art the prehistory of their own mentality. Herder had offered a glimpse of a deep relativism that would relativize art itself. This relativism yielded a concept of art as no more than an unusually eloquent form of expression. Goethe's exposition of Netherlandish art seems in tune with this teaching. But realism is also an artistic style, even if no one could quite see this before the middle decades of the nineteenth century. The art historian Lionello Venturi has gone so far as to propose that the historicist project itself—defined as the encompassing within historical study of "all phases of human activities from heroic deeds to the minutiae of everyday life"—actually created pictorial realism. The emerging openness to the ordinary registers a deep political shift that can be summarized as skepticism about authority. It permits Protestants like Goethe to greet pre-Reformation cult images with the same patronizing generosity that they display toward African or Indian works. The original ritual functions are forgotten and the depictions can be met on another plane. Iconoclasm, the original Protestant riposte to icons, will eventually be condemned, even by Protestants, as meaningless vandalism.

In a traditional society images are expected to deliver real pictures of the cosmos or of history. Styles might change from one decade to another, but content remains stable, for reality itself is stable. In a traditional society, art is much more than style. Vasari and the academicism that came in his wake reversed this formula. For Vasari, the content of art was its style. But that is not because style was now disengaged from reality. For Vasari, an accomplished and beautiful style reproduced ideal and eternal forms. He took for granted the ideality of the content of both Christian and mythological art and had in fact invested in style only because he was confident of the ideality of the contents chosen by his preferred painters. Manifestation of the ideal style was the project of civilization and the proper occupation of the ruler and the ruling class. Vasari combines the craftsman's annalistic conception of success with the courtier's flattery of power, offering little sense of what the content of art should be. Sacred and profane subjects, if treated with a beautiful style, are equally praiseworthy. The so-called Mannerist styles were unacceptable because their dissonant forms seeped into the level of content.

The *sermo humilis* of the Romantic medievalists, their cultivation of a pious homeliness, can be understood as a rejection of both aristocratic consonance (the classic style) and aristocratic dissonance (Mannerism). One response to this challenge, the challenge of the Nazarenes but also that of the many unrealized counteracademic impulses, was the futuristic cosmic spiritualism of Philipp Otto Runge. But no one would heed his call until the early twentieth century. Another response was the aesthetics of the ugly and the everyday, and Goethe does provide some preliminary language for this. But Goethe is complex: he has high regard for the early Netherlanders for non-pious reasons, and yet he is still drawn to the grand. He delivers Strasbourg cathedral but later switches his allegiances to the classical and the balanced.

Less ambivalent, no less untimely, are the poet Heinrich Heine's critical remarks on the Nazarenes. In his *Reise von München nach Genua* (1828) Heine unfavorably compares the ex-rebel and now academician Peter Cornelius to the seventeenth-century Flemish master Peter Paul

Rubens. To the affectation of the Nazarenes, Heine prefers a "Hellenist" sensualism and a Saint-Simonian materialism. Perhaps Heine, if not Karl Marx, would also have appreciated the project of the utopian socialist Charles Fourier, had it been realized. In the section "Orgie de Musée, ou l'omnigamie mixte en ordre composé et harmonique" in his unpublished tract *Le nouveau monde amoureux* (1816), Fourier proposed a completely new kind of museum. Instead of painted and sculpted simulacra of admirable human forms, the stock-in-trade of the Louvre, he suggested staging exhibitions of live people exposing their best and most beautiful body parts—"simple nature" instead of art. This was the museum of the society already envisioned by Diderot, who wondered whether modern man would go on wearing clothes. This would have been a museum liberated once and for all from history, a museum that removes objects from time, as a collection should, rather than inducting them into the constructed time of art history.

1830–1850

The theses of the philosopher G. W. F. Hegel (1770–1831) on the meaning of art in world history have exerted a magnetic pull on the project of art history for nearly two centuries. Hegel offered lecture courses on aesthetics at the University of Berlin four times over the course of the 1820s. The art historian H. G. Hotho synthesized Hegel's lecture notes as well as notes taken by students, including Hotho's own notes. He published the text in 1835 as part of the posthumous edition of Hegel's works; an improved version appeared in 1842. Although there has been much dispute about Hotho's fidelity to Hegel's original words, his version of the lectures has furnished an unavoidable framework for all subsequent art-historical scholarship. They were translated into French beginning in 1840 and into English beginning in 1879. By the late nineteenth century Hegel's narration of art's registrations of the emergence of spirit (*Geist*) or ideality into history was familiar to all German-speaking art historians, even if only in broad outline. In the twentieth and present centuries Hegel's thesis that "art in its highest vocation has become a thing of the past" and can only be contemplated indirectly, through historical scholarship, has vexed art historians because it gives them a project and at the same time licenses them to disparage the art of their own time.

Hegel's knowledge of the history of art was uneven but far from superficial. He was close to the Boisserée brothers and visited their collection in Heidelberg at least twice. He imparts insights of astonishing penetration into styles and works. Hegel's innovation is to have expounded his philosophy of art in the form of an historical fable. The first part, some three hundred pages, is a systematic investigation into artistic or ideal beauty as opposed to natural beauty. For earlier idealists up to and including Immanuel Kant, natural beauty was the place where one was mostly likely to glimpse the ideal. The second part narrates the history of western or Mediterranean art from the Egyptian kingdoms to the present, with asides on Indian and Chinese art, as the "development of the ideal into the particular forms of art." The third part reframes the argument through analyses of the individual art forms, namely, architecture, sculpture, painting, music, and poetry.

Hegel's basic thesis in the *Lectures on Aesthetics* is that art began by failing to recognize the ideal and ended by recognizing that it was unable to make the ideal manifest. The ideal or spirit for Hegel is similar to the Absolute of Friedrich Schelling, or the irreducible and unconditional essence of reality. Hegel, Schelling, and the poet Friedrich Hölderlin had been roommates at the Protestant seminary at Tübingen in the late 1780s and early 1790s. They held that the material world as we know it through our senses is finite and alienated from spirit. In its early phases, when it was still tied to myth and authority, art made no effort to reconcile matter with spirit. The Egyptian pyramids are Hegel's example. This mode of art Hegel calls symbolic because it is the result of religion forcing animals and other natural objects to symbolize the gods, an approach that fails because the gods end up looking grotesque. In art's "classic" phase, exemplified by Greek sculpture of the fourth century, the gods are symbolized by beautiful human bodies, so placing matter and spirit in equilibrium. This is Hegel's explanation for why the art of this period is felt to represent the high point of world art. Christianity, however, upset the balance by excessively valuing spirit. In the Christian era, art is stripped of the role it played in pagan culture, because the "content of romantic [i.e., Christian] art is already present explicitly to mind and feeling outside the sphere of art," that is, in religion. Painting, a material medium, is eventually felt under Christianity (read: Protestantism) to be incapable of providing full access to spirit. From that point on painting is asked only to represent spirit negatively, as it were, by representing withdrawal from the external world. The external or contingent world "is regarded as an indifferent element in which spirit has no final trust or persistence." Therefore,

> the mode of actual configuration in romantic art, in respect of
> external appearance, does not essentially get beyond ordinary real-

ity proper, and it is by no means averse from harbouring this real existence in its finite deficiency and determinacy.

Because romantic art has such a low opinion of art, it does not mind hosting reality, so losing its privileged relation to the ideal:

> This means the disappearance of that ideal beauty which lifts the contemplation of the external away above time and the traces of evanescence in order to give to existence the bloom of beauty instead of its otherwise stunted appearance.

The romantic art of the Christian era, in Hegel's view, reached to his own day. The lofty style initiated by Raphael, for Hegel, was not an approach to the absolute but rather an extension of the mixed, contaminated, but poetic painting of the late Middle Ages. This is an innovative argument. It reproduces the position of the Nazarenes but with the values reversed. In short, Hegel was not persuaded by the claims of the academic idealist theorists of the sixteenth to eighteenth centuries, for they had misrecognized the limits of painting in the modern world. In Hegel's schema the Middle Ages had never ended. The romantic art of this long Middle Ages would in the end be constrained by its own principles to abandon the visual arts in favor first of music and then of poetry. In the end, poetry too would give way to spirit's unobstructed reflection on itself in the form of philosophy. Art's role in history is diminishing.

How did the visual arts, which trade in illusion, *ever* contribute to the unveiling of spirit? Hegel defends art by saying that it gives us at least a glimpse of the truth, a glimpse that neither reality itself nor what he calls historiography, or direct writing about reality, offers:

> If the mode in which artistic forms appear is called a deception in comparison with philosophical thinking and with religious and moral principles, of course the form of appearance acquired by a topic in the sphere of *thinking* is the truest reality; but in comparison with the appearance of immediate existence and of historiography, the pure appearance of art has the advantage that it points through and beyond itself, and itself hints at something spiritual of which it is to give us an idea.

And yet it is the limits of art that will dominate his account:

> It is on the other hand just as necessary to remember that neither in

content nor in form is art the highest and absolute mode of bringing to our minds the true interests of the spirit.

The pagan statuary of the fifth and fourth centuries BC is supreme because the gods of the Greeks were at home in the realm of the senses. The Greek gods, in effect, walked straight into art:

> In order to be a genuine content for art, such truth must in virtue of its own specific character be able to go forth into [the sphere of] sense and remain adequate to itself there. This is the case, for example, with the gods of Greece.

But that was not enough for Christians, whose incarnated god was never really at home among humankind. And for Hegel, to be Christian is to be modern:

> There is a deeper comprehension of truth which is no longer so akin and friendly to sense as to be capable of appropriate adoption and expression in this medium. The Christian view of truth is of this kind, and, above all, the spirit of our world today, or, more particularly, of our religion and the development of our reason, appears as beyond the stage at which art is the supreme mode of our knowledge of the Absolute. The peculiar nature of artistic production and of works of art no longer fills our highest need. We have got beyond venerating works of art as divine and worshipping them. The impression they make is of a more reflective kind, and what they arouse in us needs a higher touchstone and a different test. Thought and reflection have spread their wings above fine art.

But Hegel is mistaken, misled by his Protestant instincts. The older religions did not worship images, they worshipped gods. If anything, it is the moderns, since Vasari, who worship pictures. Hegel's narrative resembles the history of art proposed by the Reformers of the sixteenth century. John Calvin as well as some radical followers of Martin Luther had argued that sculpted and painted representations of the human figure distracted worshippers from Christian teachings, if not from God himself. Reformed congregations removed the offending depictions from their places of worship. The Reformers did not insist on the destruction of every last painting. Even Calvin conceded that art in the private sphere brought pleasure. The Reformers assigned art a supple-

mentary, optional role in modern life. This rhymes with Hegel's dicta on
the end of art:

> Art no longer affords that satisfaction of spiritual needs which ear-
> lier ages and nations sought in it, and found in it alone…. The beau-
> tiful days of Greek art, like the golden age of the later Middle Ages,
> are gone.

Of course, the Protestant Reformers did not condescend to pagan art by
admiring its cult images as art.

The inexorable destiny of art, according to Hegel, is dematerialization. One may respond to this thesis, as did many Christian artists in
the European communities that ignored the Protestant Reformation,
by piling on sensuality in the confidence that beauty and the stimula-
tion of affective identifications would only enhance the worshipper's
apprehension of the mysteries, which Hegel conceded was art's special
faculty. Or one may acquiesce in Hegel's program, as did many artists
of the twentieth century, by denying art its rhetoric of delectation and
instead summoning a concept to shine through a reduced material scaf-
folding. Today art is often understood not as a special category of object
fashioned by a special class of people (artists) but rather as a system of
initiatives and actions, orchestrated by artists, in which non-art objects
and non-artist people take part. The end of art is often envisioned by
avant-garde artists not as a disaster but as an ecstatic fusion of art and life
in which the meaning and promise of life is finally revealed through art;
an "apocalypse," literally.

It is not clear what Hegel meant by "art" because although architecture, sculpture, and painting provided the basic scheme of his narrative, he also assigned key roles for music and poetry. Yet historians of
music or poetry have been much less enthralled by Hegel's account of
the history of the arts than have art historians. Composers, musicians,
poets, and novelists, as well as historians of music and literature, are less
likely in modernity to allow their work to be shaped by an intuition of an
imminent musical or literary apocalypse.

Many modern readers have dismissed the idealism of Hegel and
Schelling as a regression to the metaphysical dogma of the ancien
régime, the very target of Kant's critical philosophy. At the same time,
there is an important difference between Schelling and Hegel. Hegel
had been persuaded by Friedrich Schiller and Friedrich Schlegel to think

historically about art. He breaks with idealist aesthetics and in fact with all prior theories of art, from Plato and Aristotle to Diderot, Kant, and Schelling, in that he vindicates his theory of art by a history of art. In this respect Hegel's approach is complementary to Vasari's. If Hegel was a theorist who supported his theory with history, Vasari was an historian who supported his narrative of the rebirth of the arts in Tuscany with a theory of art, namely as *disegno*, or a ratio between reality and artistic form. Both Vasari and Hegel wrote biographies of their ideal modes of art.

The obsolescence of all prior theories of art, according to Hegel, opened up a space in modern life for the historiography of art:

> Art, considered in its highest vocation, is and remains for us a thing of the past. Thereby it has lost for us genuine truth and life, and has rather been transferred into our *ideas* instead of maintaining its earlier necessity in reality and occupying its higher place.

Art is kept alive as a project in modernity through its absorption into the more meaningful project of thought. Art is now understood as a ratio not of reality to form but of content to form, in other words, as a local and relative quantity:

> What is now aroused in us by works of art is not just immediate enjoyment but our judgement also, since we subject to our intellectual consideration (i) the content of art, and (ii) the work of art's means of presentation, and the appropriateness or inappropriateness of both to one another.

There are two ways to go about this "consideration," he argues: on the one hand, the assemblage of individual works of art into groups and patterns on the basis of historical scholarship, so framing an inquiry into the nature of art; and on the other, an abstract philosophy of the beautiful, detached from actual works of art. These are the inductive and deductive methods, basically. The purpose of the first method, art history, is to grasp what art is, and that method requires

> a precise acquaintance with the immeasurable realm of individual works of art, ancient and modern, some of which (α) have already perished in reality, or (β) belong to distant lands or continents and which the unkindness of fate has withdrawn from our own inspection.

This is where scholarship is called for:

> Every work of art belongs to its own time, its own people, its own environment, and depends on particular historical and other ideas and purposes; consequently, scholarship in the field of art demands a vast wealth of historical, and indeed very detailed, facts, since the individual nature of the work of art is related to something individual and necessarily requires detailed knowledge for its understanding and explanation.

Hegel sees that art once served different purposes, and our knowledge of those purposes must bear on any assessments of a work. He opens a new topic for art history: the study of the historical functions of art within public and private life, what one might call the anthropology of art. Theorists of art, neglectful of the history of art, all go astray. Hegel had no kind words for any premodern philosophers of art, neither Aristotle, nor Horace, nor Longinus, nor any of the post-Renaissance idealist theorists:

> The prescriptions which these art-doctors wrote to cure art were even less reliable than those of ordinary doctors for restoring human health.

Possibly Hegel, a reverent reader of Goethe, recalled the passage in the novel *Wilhelm Meisters Lehrjahre* (1795), where the protagonist, a stand-in for the youthful author, casts a skeptical eye on the shelves of his own library, well supplied with books on art, poetry, and criticism. Wilhelm remarks drily that the pages of the "theoretical" books remain "mostly still uncut."

Hegel is a messianic thinker, his vision of world history teleological, that is, governed by a conviction that historical events point to their own destiny. Teleology is the study of final causes, or the goals toward which not only human beings but, according to Aristotle, nature itself strives. Modern scientific thought since Bacon does not recognize final causes in nature. Hegel's philosophy of history from the point of view of Bacon or any empiricist is simply a rationalized form of mythic thinking.

Yet Hegel himself grasps the threat to abstract theorizing posed by empirical scholarship. His error is to have considered his own philosophy to be a philosophy not like any other and therefore exempt from empiricism's corrective. A true relativism is incompatible with such progressive fables as Hegel's. As a result his *Lectures on Aesthetics* supports two different kinds of historicism, and both have thrived in modernity. On the one hand, historicism is defined as the faith that one day history will all add up and make sense. On the other hand, historicism is defined as the will to understand every society, every event, every work of art on its own terms, without prejudice; what Erich Auerbach called the "largeness of our [modern, historicist] aesthetic horizon." From the point of view of an historicism of the second sort, the first sort leads to the fabrication of a *necessary* past, a betrayal of the dead. From the point of view of an historicism of the first sort, the second sort neglects the demands of the present and the promise of the future, and so betrays the unborn.

The crack in Hegel's golden bowl is impossible to ignore. The same faultline, between emancipatory aspirations and empiricist compunctions, runs right through the discipline of art history today.

In his willingness to look steadily at "tangible examples," Hegel musters sympathy for the humble art forms of the centuries after the collapse of Rome, and even partial sympathy for Indian and Chinese art. He goes well beyond the demands of evenhandedness, for he does not merely accept but also tries to explain the ugliness of medieval Christian art. Romantic—i.e., medieval—art "intertwines its inner being with the contingency of the external world and gives unfettered play to the bold lines of the ugly."

In moving beyond a neutral or antiquarian open-mindedness about unfamiliar forms and remote forms of life, and instead seeking to enter them imaginatively, Hegel is not so far from the Nazarenes. The Nazarenes were drawn to the art of the late Middle Ages because they sensed that the idealist theorists of art since the sixteenth century had misidentified the location of spirit in art.

In the decades following Hegel's death, art history was installed in the German universities. The first person to receive a PhD in art history was Franz Kugler, in Berlin in 1831, with a dissertation on the illuminations of an eleventh-century manuscript. He was criticized by his examiners, who were of course not professional art historians, for giving too much description and not displaying enough knowledge beyond his topic. Kugler, needing to satisfy his fact-minded colleagues, was an empiricist and anti-Hegelian. His *Handbuch der Kunstgeschichte* (1842), translated early into English, was a panorama of world art history. Kugler drew on the pioneering *Essay on the Architecture of the Hindus* by the Indian civil servant Rám Ráz, published posthumously in 1834. Rám Ráz's treatise revealed to readers of English the principles, based on sacred texts, of Indian architecture. The global perspective was popular in the nineteenth century, dovetailing with research in etymology, philology, comparative religion, ethnology, so-called *Völkerpsychologie* or psychology of peoples, and the study of ornament. There is some similarity to the present moment, though in that comparative-minded century there was more tolerance for broadly limned patterns and less disapproval of national, ethnic, and racial bias.

On the whole the first academic art historians were happy with the framework Hegel had offered. Hegel had cleared out conceptual space for a new discipline, encouraging art historians, who would have to fight for their ground over the next several generations alongside the long-established professoriates in history and philology, not to mention archeology, the most immediate threat because so unimpeachably empirical.

H. G. Hotho, Hegel's editor and now professor in Berlin, published in 1842–1843 a *History of German and Flemish Art*. This was no rudimentary sketch but a dense narrative that already closely resembled the stabilized accounts of northern art produced in the twentieth century, raising the specter of a scholarship of diminishing returns. Hotho had sufficient perspective, for example, to discuss the decline of the reputation of Jan van Eyck in the sixteenth, seventeenth, and eighteenth centuries, and its resurrection in the early nineteenth, as a historical phenomenon. Karl Schnaase, not a professor but a jurist, was the most thoughtfully Hegelian of the early art historians, with a poetical-spiritual sensibility and a reach to the Orient. He published his impressions of northern painting in the *Niederländische Briefe* (1834) and, in eight volumes, the *Geschichte der bildenden Künste* (1843–1864), a survey of world art.

The philosophical riposte to Hegel's historical approach to art was delivered by his antagonist and one-time colleague Arthur Schopenhauer. In his magnum opus, *The World as Will and Representation* (1818, revised 1844), Schopenhauer described a clash between historical scholarship founded on scientific or empirical principles and the idea of the work of art as an exception to those principles. His articulation of the event-like character of art countered the systematic study of art as recently established in the universities, with its allegiance to historical thinking and its bias toward the material artifact. Science, Schopenhauer wrote, proceeds "according to the principle of sufficient reason in its different forms, and its theme remains the phenomenon, its laws, connections, and the resulting relations." His metaphor for history is a constant flow of causes and effects. He then recognized an alternative mode of apprehending reality:

> What kind of knowledge is it that considers what continues to exist outside and independently of all relations, but which alone is really essential to the world, the true content of its phenomena, that which is subject to no change, and is therefore known with equal truth for all time, in a word, the *Ideas* that are the immediate and adequate objectivity of the thing-in-itself, the will? It is *art*, the work of genius. It repeats the eternal Ideas apprehended through pure contemplation, the essential and abiding in all the phenomena of the world.

The historical, or scientific, method is incomplete. At the very least it must acknowledge its other:

> The method of consideration that follows the principle of sufficient reason is the rational method, and it alone is valid and useful in practical life and in science. The method of consideration that looks away from the content of this principle is the method of genius, which is valid and useful in art alone.... The first is like the mighty storm, rushing along without beginning or aim, bending, agitating, and carrying away everything with it; the second is like the silent sunbeam, cutting through the path of the storm, and quite unmoved by it.

The tumultous rush of a tempest is Schopenhauer's metaphor for the chain of causes and effects. The historian, in his view, describes the storm well. But historical method, which is a practical way of thinking, reads everything as a trace or an effect and so cannot grasp the sunbeam, a pure event, an exception to the total environment created by the storm, and an anti-monument. The sunbeam for Schopenhauer was a metaphor for a glimpse of the ideal. This metaphor is hard to sustain. But his model, in which the storm is unable to deflect the sunbeam, has the merit of suggesting the limits of historical reason and the superiority of the mind to reality. Schopenhauer reminds the art historian not to let art history devolve into a history of things. His metaphorical combination invites the conclusion that art is the event that proposes a reorientation, and the response to that proposal, and the response to the response, and so on. Art is an ongoing cascade of events whose disciplining by writing is always incomplete.

By 1830 Europe was already prepared, like a specimen, for art-historical scholarship: an archive of works was on display in galleries and museums and churches, as well as the works of architecture under the open sky. Art history contributed to the social mnemonics of projects like Heinrich Hübsch's rebuilding of Speyer cathedral or the completion of the cathedral of Cologne. Begun in 1248, Cologne was destined to be one of the loftiest Gothic cathedrals. Construction stalled in 1473, leaving a westwork and an apse but nothing in between. Not until 1846 was the project revived, guided by the original design; the last stone was laid in 1880. Restorations in this period were aggressive, as we saw with Valadier at Rome. Vincenzo Camuccini invented the entire center of the Bacchic mosaic at the round church of Santa Costanza in Rome (1834–1840). By now there is a feedback effect whereby art history helps conservators craft the material for future art histories.

Art-historical knowledge reverberated in social life. In 1840 the people of both Munich and Nuremberg mounted festivals on "Old German" themes, collective costumed celebrations of the vitality of urban life, self-government, and the self-assertion of the trades and crafts, the emergence out of the feudal night, all revolving around the folk hero Albrecht Dürer.

At this point no one was speaking of Dürer's moment as a Renaissance. That word and concept was introduced in the 1830s by French writers who had experienced the Revolution and its repercussions. The Romantic generation saw the age of Louis XIV and Classicism as a long episode of repression and so identified the sixteenth century, the moment of Pierre Ronsard and François Rabelais, as a moment of élan, free expression, the flouting of rules, a polymorphic liberation of the drives, abundance and fertility, love and war, an interlude between scholasticism and absolutism. This was the Renaissance admired by the writers Charles-Augustin Sainte-Beuve (*Tableau historique et critique de la poésie française et du théâtre français au XVIe siècle*, 1828) and Théophile Gautier (*Les grotesques*, 1844). The pen of Gérard de Nerval, in his masterpiece *Sylvie* (1854), detached the word from its historical referent and limned the 1830s in France as a period "of activity, of hesitation and laziness, of brilliant utopias, of philosophical or religious aspirations, of vague enthusiasms, mixed with certain renaissance instincts." The

Renaissance invented by the French writers contested the picture painted by the German Romantics, who also thought of the period around 1500 in terms of rebirth, but stressed the innocence and vulnerability of the infant; weakness read as spirituality; the antithesis of Rabelais's Gargantua. From the Nazarene point of view, the secularized sixteenth century was a decline into vulgar health.

By now the principles of classical archeology, a discipline launched in the sixteenth century—one could even say in the fifteenth century with the measurements of the ruins of Rome by Donatello, Brunelleschi, and Alberti—were well established. The keys were good record-keeping of excavations and conscientious publication of findings. Excavations and publications imposed a linear sense of time on monuments that had been constructed under different principles. Archeology was also a discipline prone to sensationalism, then as now, and nineteenth-century archeological expeditions were too often little more than quasi-criminal treasure hunts. East Asia was off limits to European diggers, but not the Near East or Central Asia. A well-crafted published account of an expedition, supplemented by good illustrations, could catalyze an entire field of study. Such was the case with John Lloyd Stephens and Frederick Catherwood's *Incidents of Travel in Central America, Chiapas and Yucatán* (London, 1841), a description of Maya sites and monuments.

The limits on archeology were not only imposed by political reality but also self-imposed, by the framing questions. Archeologists were mostly looking for temples and palaces, the art of royal and priestly power. It is as if the archeologists were venturing beyond Europe not to understand something alien, but rather to find imaginary surrogates for the European paragons of civilization, whose symbolic resources seemed exhausted. From Tangiers the painter Eugène Delacroix wrote, in a letter of June 4, 1832, "The Romans and the Greeks are there at my door.… If the painting school persists in setting the fledglings to paint the Muses or the family of Priam or Atreus, I am convinced they would be infinitely better off sent as ship's boys on the first boat to the Barbary Coast than to spend any more time working the classic lands of Rome. Rome is no longer Rome." In the event, Delacroix never went to Rome.

In antiquity the emperors had shipped statuary and splendid columns from Greece and Egypt to Rome. In the nineteenth century the form that spoliation took was the citation of architectural styles. Cities became heterogenous outdoor museums of world architecture. Assyrian, Egyptian,

"Moorish," and above all Byzantine forms proliferated on churches and all manner of public and private buildings. Anachronic architecture had always existed, but now the cross-referencing is stalked by doubt. Not until recently have we been able to see eclecticism not only as a waking nightmare of a pile-up of history but also as a modern style with its own content, namely, the shape of form in time.

The Gothic style more than held its own. The Old Palace of Westminster in London burned down in 1834. The competition to build a new quarters for Parliament was won by Charles Barry, proposing a synthesis of Perpendicular and Tudor Gothic. Barry enlisted the architect Augustus Welby Pugin, who already had credentials in this field. The construction stretched from 1835 to 1868 and involved not only the fabulous exteriors but elaborate polychrome interiors. The development of the Gothic Revival style was so advanced in England that Pugin could include as one of the engraved plates in his polemical tract of 1836, *Contrasts, or, A parallel between the noble edifices of the fourteenth and fifteenth centuries and similar buildings of the present day*, a mock advertisement for industrially made Gothic architecture.

The new parti-color cityscape was reproduced inside the museums. Crown Prince Ludwig of Bavaria, who on visiting Rome in 1821 engaged Carl Friedrich von Rumohr as his cicerone, had for decades been planning a museum for ancient sculpture in Munich; that opened finally in 1830 as the Glyptothek. Ludwig bought the works himself and was involved in every aspect of planning and construction. His architect Leo von Klenze designed a square structure with the façade of a temple. Two rooms were decorated with frescoes of scenes from mythology by Peter Cornelius, whom Ludwig had met in Rome in 1818. In 1826 Ludwig had begun construction of the Alte Pinakothek or "Old Picture Gallery"; it was completed in 1836. The oldest work it housed was a painting by Giotto purchased by Ludwig in Rome in 1805.

Ludwig's projects were sustained by patriotic sentiment and piety for the past. The Austrian historian Joseph von Hormayr, who advised Ludwig, articulated in 1830 the double goal of the Bavarian museums: first, art translates the knowledge of the past into terms that everyone can grasp; second, art selects what is valuable from the past:

> Art—and only art—transplants history out of the memory and into
> the heart, out of the scholar's study and into the minds of women,

youth, and the people. Art winnows the old from the antiquated. It clarifies, refines, quickens.

Friedrich Wilhelm III of Prussia also opened a museum in 1830, the Kunstmuseum, now the Altes Museum, in the Hofgarten in Berlin. The architect was Karl Friedrich Schinkel; Peter Cornelius also painted frescoes for this museum. The first floor housed 451 sculptures, the second floor nearly 2000 paintings, mostly of the Italian schools. There was a debate between those who wanted the displays to depict art history as a continuous span, even if the gaps had to be filled by mere reproductions or plaster casts (the archeologist Alois Hirt), and those who saw artistic excellence alone as the criterion of selection (Schinkel, Waagen, and Rumohr).

There was one important sense in which art-historical scholarship was out of rhythm with the museums. The museums and galleries were well stocked with late Renaissance and Baroque paintings, the products of the age of academies. And yet the scholars of the early and mid-nineteenth century were not writing the art history of these eras. Rumohr, for instance, stopped with Raphael. There were few nineteenth-century monographs on any artist later than Raphael. It was as if the canon as established by the academies were history enough. More in tune perhaps with scholarship was the National Gallery in London, which had opened in 1824. A Committee on Arts and the Connection with Manufacture reported in 1836 that pictures acquired for the national collections should date from the period before Raphael, "such works being of a purer and more elevated style than the eminent works of the Caracci [sic]."

One did write on celebrated recent artists, however, especially those identified as neoclassicists. Leopoldo Cicognara wrote a monograph on his friend Antonio Canova (1823); Karl Ludwig Fernow wrote on the painter Asmus Jacob Carstens (1806). Just Mathias Thiele launched a multi-volume biography and catalogue of Bertel Thorvaldsen in 1831. In 1838 Thorvaldsen returned from Rome to Copenhagen; the city created a museum whose exterior walls depict the return of the sculptor with his works as an epic event. The neoclassical artists were already classic in their lifetimes. In 1848 modern German artists demanded a museum for modern art. In Munich the Neue Pinakothek, dedicated to the recent schools of southern Germany and the first public museum of modern art, opened in 1853.

Few critics, however, and even fewer academic art historians, held the Nazarenes in high regard. This despite the vogue for anachronism. Schnaase remarked of Schnorr's Barbarossa-Saal in the Residence at Munich that the costumes were all wrong (1840). Kugler dismissed the Nazarenes as aristocrats alienated from life (1843). The art historian Anton Springer said that the Nazarenes, obsessed as they were with tedious synods and coronations, had botched the medieval content (1845). The art historian Anna Jameson in her *Visits and Sketches at Home and Abroad* (1834) expressed admiration for the early German painters — she saw the Boisserée pictures at Schleissheim — but wondered whether it was wise for modern painters to imitate them: the results are a "hardness of manner" and a "tendency to violent colour and high glazy finish, which interfere too often with the beauty, feeling, and effect of their compositions." "'You English have no school of art,' was often said to me; I could have replied — if it had not been a solecism in grammar — 'You Germans have *too much* school.'"

Hegel had already inveighed against anachronism:

> The modern artist, it is true, may associate himself with the classical age and with still more ancient times; to be a follower of Homer, even if the last one, is fine, and productions reflecting the medieval veering to romantic art will have their merits, too; but the universal validity, depth, and special idiom of some material is one thing, its mode of treatment another. No Homer, Sophocles, etc., no Dante, Ariosto, or Shakespeare can appear in our day.

Content can persist, but an artificially adjusted style is an error. This is more or less what Philip Sidney had said about the "Ballad of Chevy Chase." But even content was not infinitely translatable. What was expressed has been expressed. "Only the present is fresh, the rest is paler and paler." For Hegel, "all materials, whatever they be and from whatever period and nation they come, acquire their artistic truth only when imbued with living and contemporary interest." "Artistic truth" must "provide [man] his own mirror-image." In calling for a synchronization of form and content Hegel is only asking European modernity to match what he sees as the internal consistency of the great civilizations of the past.

Hegel was unable to draw the obvious conclusion from this, namely, that modern art should represent modern life directly. He admired seventeenth-century Dutch art for its realism, but he believed his own age had fallen into the merely prosaic. Hegel saw the modern subject striving for freedom but mired in the "prose of the world": finitude and mutability, entanglement in the relative, the pressure of necessity. This subject lacks opportunity for ideality and independence. The modern prosaic mentality is wrapped up in the parsing of means and ends, instrumentality and function. Here Hegel proves himself the child of Winckelmann, who would have agreed that an unmediated image of a prosaic world could serve as the basis only of a prosaic art.

The Nazarenes, in the mocking account of the writer Friedrich Theodor Vischer, did deliver that contemporary fallen reality, but inadvertently and so ridiculously. Of the Madonnas of the Nazarenes, Vischer said: "One sees in them a time in which there are scrapbooks, mirrors, fashion magazines, and frontispiece engravings of paperback books…. They have read in the 'Hours of Devotion,' they grew up in a pension, in a boarding school."

Heinrich Heine wrote of the end of what he called the *Kunstperiode*, the "period of art"; or the age of the "art idea" (*Kunstidee*), in short, the age of Goethe. Art and literature used to give us the "beautiful objective world." This trust in art seemed to Heine an irretrievable artifact of the ancien régime. Now art is under pressure from modernization and politics and at the same time cultivates inwardness. Art will have to invent a new set of symbols to match a new world. Yet neither Heine nor anyone else in 1832 could quite envision a modern art of the real. The unhesitating embrace of imperfect reality was not yet an option for European artists, and no theorist was calling for it, unless we include a fictional art critic, the eponymous protagonist of the fragmentary story by Georg Büchner, *Lenz* (1836), a character based on the unstable and unrealized eighteenth-century writer J. M. R. Lenz. In discussion with another character, Kaufmann, the fictional Lenz expounds his anti-idealist aesthetics. By "idealism" he means Schiller. The artist, for Lenz, is nothing more than an historian recording reality, undistorted, not improving on or transfiguring it:

Let us for once try and sink ourselves into the life of the most humble people and then reproduce it…. They are the most prosaic people under the sun; and yet the pulse of feeling is in almost everyone the same, only the shell that it has to pass through differs in thickness. You only need eyes and ears.

What does Büchner mean? He is saying that humanity conceals itself beneath defensive layers of ineloquence. Civilization produces ready-made subjects for great art. But the uncivilized are human, too, just as medieval art is art:

> Yesterday as I walked up the valley I saw two girls sitting on a stone: one was tying up her hair, the other was helping her; and her golden hair hanging down, and a pale serious face, and yet so young, and her black dress, and the other one so attentively occupied. Even the most beautiful and fervent paintings of the old German school give hardly any sense of all this.

The Flemish painters of the fifteenth century, van Eyck and van der Weyden and their followers—that is what Lenz meant by the "old German school"—humble and truthful as they are, come close to grasping this. The homely and the unprepossessing are the proper objects of the not-yet-realized art of a common humanity:

> You have to love mankind in order to arrive at the particular being of every person; no one is too lowly, no one too ugly, only then can you understand them; the most insignificant face makes a deeper impression than the mere sensation of beauty.

The artistic supplement to reality needs to be reduced to the minimum:

> I prefer those writers and artists who give me nature as it really is, so that their creations make me feel something; everything else upsets me. I prefer the Dutch painters to the Italians, they are also the only ones who make sense to me.

Büchner writes just prior to the invention of the representational technology that would overturn the entire edifice of European art theory, removing the burden of the accumulated tradition of painting and so changing the meaning of art-historical knowledge; namely, photography.

1850–1870

The historian Leopold von Ranke, following Giambattista Vico and Johann Gottfried Herder, and rejecting Hegel, formulated the ne plus ultra of relativism in 1854, clarifying the ethical stakes of historical study. Ranke conceded that progress was not evenly distributed across all epochs. "Art," for example, "flourished most in the fifteenth century and in the first half of the sixteenth century; in contrast, it declined most at the end of the seventeenth century and in the first three quarters of the eighteenth century." But it is unjust, Ranke asserted, to assess each generation only in relation to the preceding or succeeding generation. Nor should earlier generations be valued only for their success in anticipating the most recent. Instead,

> each epoch is immediate to God, and its value is not at all based on what emanates from it. On the contrary, its value emanates from its own existence and its own identity … necessitating the consideration of each epoch as something valid in itself and extremely worthy of scrutiny.

To express his disapproval of historiography, Ranke introduces the metaphor of a divine point of view:

> I conceive the deity in such a manner that, since no time lies ahead of it, it surveys the entire history of mankind in its totality and finds equal value everywhere. The idea of the education of the human race admittedly has something true in itself; but the generations of mankind appear before God with equal rights, which is also how the historian must regard the matter.

This passage resonates with Herder's image of the plant flourishing in its own context in the divine order, as well as with Ralph Waldo Emerson's essay "History" (1841), so important for Nietzsche. Ranke, however, more sober-minded than they, associates the divine point of view with the impersonal perspective of the empiricist. To neutralize the biases of the historian, scholarship externalizes knowledge. The researcher extracts facts from archives or objects and translates them into more accessible formats, gathering knowledge into such compendia as encyclopedias, dictionaries, manuals, and guidebooks, hedges against the wasteful repetition of scholarly labor. An early landmark was the *Manual of Iconography* (1855) by Anton Springer, the first art historian to be appointed ordinarius or full professor of art history (at the University of Bonn in 1860). In 1858 G.K. Nagler published the first of five volumes of a dictionary of artists known only by symbols, initials, or abbreviations, *The Monogrammists*, eventually running to 15,000 monograms by 12,000 artists.

Empiricism is a collective project, drawing on the experience of others. Samuel Johnson defined empiricism as "dependence on experience without knowledge or art; quackery." In the eighteenth century the word "empiric" referred to the medical charlatan who relied on his own observations and practice treating patients rather than on theory, that is, the treatises of Galen and Vesalius. Today, it is fair to say, a physician is more likely to trust experience than theory, but—and this is all the difference—not exclusively her own experience but the accumulated experiences of many other physicians, recorded, compiled, and published. As Leon Battista Alberti, precociously skeptical of theory, said in his treatise *The Art of Building* (c. 1450), "Medicine, they say, was developed by a million people over a thousand years; sailing, too, as almost every other art, advanced by minute steps." Historical scholarship is equally dependent on diachronically shared knowledge.

The pragmatic approach is also the modern approach to architecture. Because buildings are functional, the form of their cladding can be chosen from a catalogue or from the exhibits at an exhibition, such as the Great Exhibition of 1851 at the Crystal Palace in London. The treatise of Owen Jones, *Grammar of Ornament* (1856), an album or sample book, displaces easel painting from its cosmic, orienting role in society. The Enlightened discrediting of mindless adherence to tradition, and the Romantic repudiation of normative authority, had invited, perhaps even obliged, nineteenth-century architects to choose from a worldwide menu of forms. For a building had to be built in some style. This was not quite true of painters, for a painter can always retreat from style altogether by turning back to nature.

In 1852 the Germanisches Nationalmuseum was established in Nuremberg, a new kind of museum that pries medieval paintings away from the category of art and reclassifies them, together with furniture, costumes, weapons, and vessels as the objects of new fields of study: ethnography, folk art, domestic arts. The South Kensington Museum, later the Victoria and Albert Museum, dedicated to the mechanical and applied arts, opened in 1858.

Knowledge about art was once handed down from artist to artist, shared perhaps with privileged patrons who eavesdropped by collecting drawings or reading anecdotes or letters. Now anyone could buy a pocket-sized descriptive guide to central Italy or Belgium and Holland published by John Murray or Karl Baedeker. Baedeker's 1832 guide to a Rhine journey launched the concept. Murray soon followed, introducing the term "handbook" and distinctive red covers. Baedeker also adopted the red binding in 1854; his guidebooks were translated into English beginning in 1861. Murray later became the Blue Guides. The guidebooks described public monuments, churches, and picture galleries, secularizing the manuals that had steered the medieval pilgrims. They reinforced the clichés of cultural geography and the fading memories of European history learned at school. They channelled the esoteric knowledge collected by scholars back into the exoteric sphere, in effect restoring knowledge about art to oral circulation patterns, linking the generations by the old mechanisms of showing and telling: for there was always one in the group who best recalled what she had read in the guidebook on the train and so was able to recite and point in the presence of the altarpiece. The guidebooks in this period reached many more people than did the university lecturers.

In modernity the venerable city is the surface of an art history, the image of a process. The construction of the façade of the Duomo of Florence had stalled in the late Middle Ages, half-finished. In 1587 Grand Duke Ferdinand I had it removed in preparation for a new façade in an up-to-date neoclassical style. Five architects submitted proposals, all of them involving classical orders, pediments, niches, and windows. Nothing happened. Another competition was held in the seventeenth century, and again the menu was classical, although one of the entries, responding to concerns that the façade would clash with the building's Gothic body, introduced slender octagonal side towers, an understated allusion to Giotto's Campanile. Again nothing was built. Finally in the 1860s they tried again; ninety-two projects were submitted. The successful entry, constructed between 1875 and 1887, was in the neo-Gothic style, blending with the existing fabric. The process is disguised. The guidebooks reveal this secret, but it is not clear how many visitors to Florence even care, typologists that they are.

The conservation of artworks in the mid-nineteenth century went far beyond the discreet wiping off of specks of dust imagined by Hegel in his prose poem about the loss of historical art. In 1852 or shortly thereafter the painter Gaetano Bianchi invented the figure of Saint Louis more or less out of whole cloth for the Bardi Chapel in S. Croce in Florence. In the 1860s Giuseppe Molteni gave a portrait by Lorenzo Lotto in the National Gallery in London an entirely new face, more in line with the style of the sixteenth century.

Baedeker's guidebooks reached almost as many people as did the writings of the polymath and barely secular preacher, John Ruskin (1819–1900), an unavoidable figure, a Christian moralist whose medium was art history and art criticism. Ruskin was a champion of the Pre-Raphaelite Brotherhood, the English successors to the Nazarenes. In his *Modern Painters* (1843–1860) he promoted modern art generally but especially the landscapes and seascapes of J. M. W. Turner. Ruskin depreciated the Old Masters, especially the "false" landscapists of the seventeenth century, Claude Lorrain and Gaspard Dughet, who must not be confused with the earlier "historical" painters Leonardo and Michelangelo. *Stones of Venice* (1852) is not a history but a moralized analysis of Italian Gothic architecture: the materials, the parts, the building types. Ruskin hoped that modern architecture would recover the grace of the non-instrumental relation to nature that urbanized modern society had lost. Beyond its practical functions medieval architecture was also called upon to speak, to record, to narrate, and all with graceful and pleasing expression, or "loveliness." Walls and arches and roofs are like living organisms, means responding to ends. But the decorative is not to be disparaged: "All noble ornamentation is the expression of man's delight in God's work." Northern buildings are grotesque, Italian buildings charming.

Later, Ruskin notes that his own comment on noble ornamentation implies that there is an ignoble ornamentation, the expression of man's delight in his *own* work. "There is such a school, chiefly degraded classic and Renaissance, in which the ornament is composed of imitations of things made by man." The function of modern architecture is to repair our broken ties with nature, "to possess us with memories of her qualities; to be solemn and full of tenderness, like her, and rich in portraiture of her." He prizes a lovable "mystery and unity" in the convolutions of Byzantine style, and the "strange disquietude" of the Gothic spirit.

Ruskin finds in Gothic exactly what man is supposedly always seeking in the world around him, a balance between love of "facts" as perceived by the eye and mind and love of "design," or the power to arrange lines and colors nobly. He recommends obedience and reverence, rejoicing in sacrifice. He praises "healthy, proper, and ennobling" labor in contrast to manufacturing. Ruskin is an attentive student of historical form, but his approach is not historicist. "Gothic" for Ruskin is a universal quality that was most perfectly realized in the thirteenth century.

Ruskin invents a completely new fable of form, an inversion of the academic canon. Bad form is now good form. Ruskin uses the language of nobility, but the coordination of this concept with social class has now changed. With William Morris, the poet, designer, and socialist ideologue, he shared the idea that the life of the people, the collectivity, is the matrix of art. For Morris, too, the years 1160 to 1300 were the high point.

The best nineteenth-century scholarship on historical art, with few exceptions, was non-academic or even leisured scholarship. Landmarks in the study of historical sources were the translation of Cennino Cennini's *Treatise on Painting* (1844) and the edition and translation of *Original Treatises on the Arts of Painting* (1849) by the polymath Mary P. Merrifield. This latter collection, nearly 900 pages long, made available the texts of Latin, Italian, and French painters' handbooks or recipes over several medieval centuries. Merrifield found the manuscripts mainly in northern Italian libraries. She supplemented her editions with accounts of her conversations in Verona and Venice with Signori A, B, C, D, and E, elderly painters and restorers whose memories of the old painting techniques, passed down by word of mouth, seemed to reach back to the Renaissance itself. Merrifield was told, for example, "that Titian began by painting in the flesh in chiaroscuro with a mixed tint, formed of biadetto [azurite], biacca [white lead], and a very little terra rossa [red ochre]. He then painted the lights with flesh color, and laid by the picture to dry. After five or six months he glazed the flesh with terra rossa and let it dry." Charles C. Perkins (1823–1886), meanwhile, a wealthy Bostonian who had studied painting in Paris and art history in Leipzig, published *Tuscan Sculpture* (1864). Perkins edited for publication writings by the English painter Sir Charles Lock Eastlake (1793–1865), president of the Royal Academy, first director of the National Gallery, and champion of the Italian and northern primitives. Eastlake had translated Goethe's *Treatise on Color* and written *Materials for a History of Oil Painting* (1847). Elizabeth (Rigby), Lady Eastlake, translated Passavant, Waagen, and Kugler. Her own anti-Ruskinian essays on Italian Renaissance artists were collected and published in 1883.

Ruskin himself was not an architect. Two major theorists who were, Gottfried Semper and Eugène Viollet-le-Duc, looked to historical knowledge to point the way out of the modern predicament of freedom of stylistic choice.

The German architect Semper (1803–1879), in exile after the revolutions of 1848, was looking for work. He designed several national pavilions at the Great Exhibition at the Crystal Palace. In London Semper came face to face with the full chaos of eclectic historicism. He found a politicized scene; an engagement with the questions posed by technology and industry; the dubious enterprise of colonization. In this period he wrote a short treatise proposing solutions to the conundrum of historicism, *Science, Industry, and Art: Proposals for the Development of a National Taste in Art at the Closing of the London Industrial Exhibition* (1852). Semper saw the "Babylonian confusion" of styles on display at the "world market" as an opportunity to radically rethink building. The exhibition inspired him to propose a new way of ordering the arts, with architecture as the base. All the arts, he argues, derive from "the elements of the domestic settlement: *hearth, wall, terrace, and roof.*" Embracing these elements is a fifth, "high art." All objects and forms descend from these "primordial motives (*Urmotiven*)." But today, he says, these simple principles are obscured by the mechanical inventions that have alienated us from necessity and from the properties of materials. Our own modern handmade Gothic now suddenly appears eccentric, affected, devoid of meaning or idea: "Have not the new Houses of

Parliament in London been made unbearable by the machine?" "The recognized triumphs at the Exhibition [of 1851] of the half-barbaric nations, especially the Indians with their magnificent industries of art…show us that we with our science have until now accomplished very little."

A new doctrine of style will call upon on art history to show us how the primordial motives govern the later development of forms. The divisioning and ornamentation of walls, for example, the coloring, all the arts in contact with the walls, all follow from the original spatial dividers, the mat and its successors, the woven or embroidered carpet.

Semper's thought is complex, twisting. He notes that an unintended consequence of the proliferation of citational ornament on modern buildings is a disintegration of the traditional building types. This, he says, is our opportunity.

In 1853 Semper was given a major commission in Zurich, the Polytechnikum, today's Eidgenössische Technische Hochschule. He thrived from this point on, building the Opera in Dresden and the Kunsthistorisches Museum and the Burgtheater in Vienna. These mighty buildings occupy space, dominate, swell, assert themselves, symbolize the gravity and permanence of institutions and communities. They do not seem revolutionary; in fact they are historicist, riveted together out of modules of classical form. Their style is best described as neo-Renaissance or neo-Baroque. Yet Semper's writings reveal a mind uncowed by the authority of tradition, a mind moving at liberty between cosmic and practical thought. In 1860–1863 he published the two volumes of *Style*, his magnum opus, an amplification of the ideas in the 1852 essay. Again Semper refuses to choose between the anthropological and the symbolic interpretations of the primordial motives, or between historicist freedom of choice and technological reason. The elements of building precede social organization and so exist outside of history. "Style theory is not art history." Semper reveals genetic, not real, sequences. The hearth calls upon the basic technical arts to protect the flame, symbol of society: textiles (cladding), ceramics (enclosing), tectonics or carpentry (or covering), and stereotomy or masonry (protecting). The development of form is driven by the pursuit of eurythmy, or pleasure in nature. After hundreds of pages of analysis of the survival and recombinations of the basic forms established in prehistory by the textile arts, the Greek monuments so admired by Semper's readers can only appear belated, composite, secondary. It is true that the Greeks were able to apprehend the forms as symbols of form, lending them a higher sense. Yet Semper is ready to consign the fine arts to a protected zone of irrelevancy. In *Science, Art, and Industry* he said that the fine arts have no role in the modern marketplace because they must be autonomous. The plastic arts were once rooted in public functions but are no longer. In his sketch of world art history in *Style*, he assigns painting a minor role. The significance of Semper's account is that he ignores the high points and thresholds that had once seemed significant: Greek art, Gothic art, Renaissance art. He discusses the tectonic arts of Polynesia, China, and India. But in the end we are made to feel that the real story is the advent of machine technology in the nineteenth century, completely altering our perspective on the past. Technology, which cannot be ignored, allows us the opportunity to halt the decline into dislocation and stultification that all prior art histories had narrated.

A less ambiguous thinker than Semper, and equally fundamental, was the French architect, historian, and theorist Eugène Viollet-le-Duc (1814–1879). He was the nephew of Étienne-Jean Delécluze, the painter and biographer of Jacques-Louis David. Viollet-le-Duc's many restorations at the invitation of Prosper Mérimée were and remain controversial, for they involved creative additions; they are not reconstructions but fantasies on the theme of Notre-Dame, the Sainte-Chapelle, Saint-Denis, and most notoriously the walled city of Carcassonne. But Viollet-le-Duc was no vandal. On the basis of his notes and drawings, he published a ten-volume *Dictionnaire raisonné de l'architecture française du XIe au XVIe siècle* (1854–1868), not a history but an encyclopedia of medieval architecture. Viollet-le-Duc was appointed professor of art history at the École des Beaux-Arts in 1863. Among his many publications the most significant was the *Entretiens sur l'architecture* (two vols., 1863–1872), a total theory of architecture, already translated into English by 1875.

Despite his immersion in medieval and neo-medieval building practices, and unlike Ruskin, Viollet-le-Duc is free of any nostalgia for bygone ways of life. He considers the medieval worldviews no longer real or living. With his admiration for the rational, lay spirit of the cathedral builders, he would seem to have little patience for liturgy and theology, though he would not have dared to say it.

Viollet-le-Duc deplores "the current anarchy in the matter of art" and wonders whether the nineteenth century is condemned to end without ever possessing an architecture of its own. Our education is nothing but an "undigested jumble of old traditions that no one believes in any more";

we must stop living as if Charles Le Brun were still *surintendant des Beaux-arts*. This is hardly preferable to the submission to tradition, enforced by theocracy, characteristic of ancient Egypt and the Near East, involving the typological imitation of inveterate building materials. Europe is supposed to have given up typology when the Greeks introduced the critical spirit.

Like Semper, Viollet-le-Duc had a strong sense of a break with the preindustrial world. This allowed him to reject the three centuries preceding his own. From his point of view, the eclectic nineteenth century, "abounding in reminiscences," had already begun by 1500. And yet Viollet-le-Duc was unwilling to jettison the past. "If it is difficult for man to learn, it is even more difficult for him to forget." In fact, he said, it is impossible to invent a new architecture; one can only analyze, recombine, appropriate.

Viollet-le-Duc sees medieval architecture as "progress" over the ancients because it put the "idea" above doctrine and tradition and, against the egoism of antiquity, resituated man in nature. Viollet-le-Duc admires the rational Gothic cathedrals. At the same time he is a relativist: "It is the *nature* and not the *degree* of civilization which produces the epochs of art." As a disciple of Mérimée, he is able to cast a sympathetic eye even on the ungainly buildings of the late antique or early Christian period and develops a new apology. The passive imagination of the primitive peoples is imperfect. They saw antiquity as in a dream, exaggerated and distorted. The poetic active imagination of civilized man "seizes" the passive imagination of the primitive, and the crude forms lose their savage traits. Civilization needs the barbaric; it provides contrasts, dissimilitudes, moral fermentation, the cross-fertilization of ideas, movement, struggle, obstacles.

Compare Ruskin on "The Nature of Gothic," in *Stones of Venice* (1852):

Go forth to gaze upon the old cathedral front, where you have smiled so often at the fantastic ignorance of the old sculptors: examine once more those ugly goblins, and formless monsters, and stern statues, anatomiless and rigid; but do not mock at them, for they are signs of the life and liberty of every workman who struck the stone; a freedom of thought, and rank in scale of being, such as no laws, no characters, no charities can secure; but which it must be the first aim of all Europe at this day to regain for her children.

Ugliness is redeemed by freedom. Gothic form emerges directly out of the lifeworld of the craftsman, his direct and intuitive experience of life.

Unexpectedly, Viollet-le-Duc sees in Greek and Roman society a harmony among the *génie du peuple*, the *moeurs*, and the institutions (even if for Greeks everything is subordinated to a rational form, and for Romans everything is subordinated to a public reason). Whereas, in the Christian Middle Ages there was contradiction between the genius of the people and the institutions—and for this reason, he says, the Middle Ages are worth studying! Presumably because his own century shared this problem.

Viollet-le-Duc recommends not the revival of past forms but knowledge of the principles of past architecture. Architecture would finally be scientific. In architecture "we are only now at the point where the West in science was at the time of Galileo." The superiority of the lay or critical spirit to tradition is what the cathedral builders of thirteenth-century France had established. Gothic architecture, the "triumph of intelligence," defies tradition. Gothic form corresponds to structure—a necessity, just as in an animal or vegetal organism.

Ruskin's sanctimonious Christian aesthetic—at once invigorative and neurasthenic—is insufferable, but at least he is seeking a language to account for the appeal to the senses of Gothic architecture, or any architecture. Semper and Viollet-le-Duc give up on this—their approach is unpoetic. Their functionalism opens the modern fracture between art history and architectural history.

In practice, Viollet-le-Duc's rationalism, translated from the thirteenth to the nineteenth century, meant iron vaulting. Semper and Viollet-le-Duc are partially betrayed by the buildings they built, or by the buildings inspired by their teachings, for the symbolic associations of neo-Baroque and neo-Gothic forms will press through. Like Semper, Viollet-le-Duc was unable to envision the future architecture that would be founded on his principles.

The sophisticated tourist carried, if not Ruskin's *Stones of Venice* or *Mornings in Florence*, then the companionable handbook to Italian painting by the Swiss scholar Jacob Burckhardt (1818–1897), *Der Cicerone: eine Anleitung zum Genuss der Kunstwerke Italiens* (1855), already translated into English as *The Cicerone: A Guide to the Enjoyment of the Artworks of Italy* by 1873. Here Burckhardt retailed his observations on

241

schools and artists from antiquity to the seventeenth century, culminating in two French painters, Nicolas Poussin and Claude Lorrain. Precise but judgmental, rarely enthusiastic, he discusses attributions, subjects, styles, compositions, coloring. He offers miniature essays on Giotto's narrative style, for example, or Raphael's *School of Athens*. Burckhardt developed the first post-idealist and affirmative account of what came to be called—because of Burckhardt—Renaissance art. His Renaissance is not the academic treasure house of authorized form, nor is it the cradle of an innocent sentiment that could relaunch modern art, nor is it the merely imitative and incomplete classicism derided by Winckelmann.

The youthful Burckhardt, under the spell of the historians Ranke and Johann Gustav Droysen, still believed in the providential shape of history. But already by 1842 he speaks in a letter of the breach between his own era and the ancien régime, striking a pessimistic note that would only deepen with age. In the early 1840s Burckhardt also studied art history, with Kugler in Berlin. He came to insist on seeing things for himself; he mistrusted concepts. Burckhardt believed that philosophy subordinates, while history coordinates. Burckhardt was nothing if not an anti-Hegelian, which is why he is idolized by so many historians to this very day. The seven-volume biography by Werner Kaegi, published between 1947 and 1982, is by a considerable margin the longest biography ever dedicated to a scholar whose life beyond the study, the library, and the lecture hall was no more eventful than yours or mine, dear reader. Burckhardt's later books and lectures paint a flat, dry picture of history; in his letters he expresses a bitter fatalism.

Burckhardt's *Die Cultur der Renaissance in Italien* (1860), a title mistranslated by S. G. C. Middlemore in 1878 as *The Civilization of the Renaissance in Italy*, is a reanimation of primary textual sources, organized thematically. There is no historical arc: *The Culture of the Renaissance in Italy* is a portrait of an epoch, Italy between the mid-fourteenth and the early sixteenth centuries.

The first writer to describe the regeneration of painting, sculpture, and architecture in Italy as a rebirth (*rinascita*) after centuries of neglect had been none other than Vasari (although the architect Filarete had said that he himself felt "reborn" when he saw the new Florentine structures built in the ancient manner [*mi pare rinascere a vedere questi cosi degni edifici*]). But Burckhardt in his book did not explain the vitality of fifteenth-century Florence as a reactivation of ancient energies. He was uninterested in reconstructing the genealogy of modern scholarship and so downplayed the philological and archeological achievement of the Renaissance. Burckhardt took his cue from Jules Michelet's *Histoire de France*, whose seventh volume was entitled *Renaissance* (1855) and covered the period from the Italian War of 1494 through the reign of François I. Michelet began by noting that the word "Renaissance" means something concrete for aesthetes, scholars, and jurists. The "revolution" of the sixteenth century was profounder even than this, for like no era before it the Renaissance discovered the world and discovered man. Michelet meant exploration and astronomy; and he meant the penetration into the "moral mystery" of man in Protestant theology, in jurisprudence, and in literature. For Michelet, as for Burckhardt, the Renaissance appears to emerge out of nothing, willing itself into existence. And just as for Michelet, the "spirit of renewal" for Burckhardt permeates all aspects of life. The signatures of Burckhardt's Italian Renaissance are spectacle, power, possession, conquest, and personality. Christianity plays a minor part. Burckhardt's protagonists are pragmatic, lucid, ruthless, and yet virtuous businessmen, statesmen, warriors, though also scholars. Burckhardt celebrates the creative energy, the flow of life, that united potentate, merchant, and poet. The modernity of the era is its dynamic responsiveness to evolving economic and social conditions and its commitment to civic virtue and political action. Burckhardt's Florentines were driven by curiosity, a will to heroism, and a bold and skeptical spirit.

Michelet's earlier book, *Le Peuple* (1846), an impassioned, sentimental, anti-authoritarian, and anticlerical tract, had closed with a denunciation of the Romantic cult of the Middle Ages, that Middle Ages "where I have spent my life, whose affecting, futile aspiration I have reproduced in my histories, I have had to say to it: '*Stand back!*' now that impure hands rip it from its tomb and place this stone before us trying to make us stumble on the path to the future." Burckhardt would surely have concurred. Is it then fair to say that with Burckhardt finally the Middle Ages is murdered, for the second time; that Burckhardt completes the project of the Enlightenment? Yes and no, for Burckhardt also creates modern medieval studies—negatively. The first principle of medieval studies, a principle that no historian or art historian of the European Middle Ages contests, is that Burckhardt was wrong.

As noted, the concept of a festive, affirmative Renaissance had been established in France in the 1830s. The term referred almost exclusively to the French sixteenth century and to a modern style of furniture that imitated Renaissance forms. Burckhardt was the first to transfer the word from France to Italy. He enshrined the word, untranslated, in his title. His use of the French word established "Renaissance" as the unquestioned period label both in German and in English. Italian art historians, overtaken by Burckhardt, had to activate an old word, *rinascimento*—*rinascita* and *rinascenza* seemed too limited—to translate his title (that translation appeared in 1876) and his concept. *Rinascimento*, echoing *Risorgimento*, immediately became the Italian term for the Renaissance.

The advent of the Renaissance as the overall designation of an historical period, and more importantly as a concept, marks the end of Europe's reconciliation with its own Middle Ages, the reconciliation dramatized by Goethe. For the positive valuation of the Middle Ages of course persists in the twentieth century and beyond, sometimes as a cover for varieties of anti-modernism.

The materialist, even Epicurean or Lucretian, tradition of thought that Burckhardt identified with and the libertinism of the free-thinking and sensualist princes are allied with realism and the defiance of conventions, academic and other. Burckhardt is a bridge between Goethe (see the essay on Florentine history that he appended to his translation of the *Autobiography of Benvenuto Cellini*, 1803) and Nietzsche.

A close reader of Burckhardt was the French historian Hippolyte Taine, whose *Lectures on Art* (1867) proposed an invigorated contextualism, a calibration of art to the realities of *race, milieu, moment*. Taine's writings were immediately translated into English. In *La Philosophie de l'art en Italie* (1867), Taine recreated the milieu of mysticism of the fourteenth and fifteenth centuries, and then the milieu of paganism of c. 1500. He laid out the "intellectual conditions" or "conditions of existence" of Italian painting, aiming at "a complete explanation of the Fine Arts, and of art in general." Our philosophy of the fine arts or aesthetic system, Taine asserts, "is modern, and differs from the ancients, inasmuch as it is historic, and not dogmatic; this is to say, it imposes no precepts, but ascertains and verifies laws." "My sole duty is to offer you facts, and show you how these facts are produced." Science "neither pardons nor proscribes; it verifies and explains. It does not say to you despise Dutch art because it is vulgar, and prize only Italian art; nor does it say to you despise Gothic art because it is morbid, and prize only

Greek art. It leaves everyone free to follow their own predilections, to prefer that which is germane only to one's own temperament." "Science has sympathies for all the forms of art, and for all schools." Like Herder, he turns to a vegetal metaphor: "It is analogous to botany, which studies the orange, the laurel, the pine, and the birch, with equal interest." Even Henri Focillon, who deplored Taine's unpoetic spirit, would praise his evenhanded generosity of spirit: Taine no longer uses time as a scythe to destroy, he pointed out, but instead offers a plenitude of culture, almost mythological.

One of the features of Burckhardt's Renaissance was the easy interaction between elites and common people. Taine, too, had spoken of the animated beauty of sixteenth-century sculpture not as a mere ornament but as a force emerging from a layer of appetite below the surface of social life. Burckhardt puts great store in the festivals, religious and profane. He must have read the novel by his countryman Gottfried Keller, *Der Grüne Heinrich* (1855), which describes the hero's experience of the festivities and procession staged by the artists' association in Munich in 1840 (here translated to Nuremberg):

> The best opportunity to cheer oneself through the conjured-up splendor of earlier German magnificence was the coming together of the whole richly styled band of artists to depict the lost imperial grandeur; and it was a real production, not with canvas, brush, stone, and hammer, but rather with their own persons used as raw material; and, joining forces in a hundred ways, each was a vital part of the whole, and the life of the whole pulsed in each, beamed from eye to eye, and a short night dreamed itself into reality.
>
> Old Nuremberg was to be resuscitated, at least insofar as it could represent itself in moving human figures; and how it was in those times when the "Last Knight," Emperor Maximilian I, celebrated feast-days there and decked with honors and coats-of-arms the city's greatest son, Albrecht Dürer.

(In fact, Keller himself arrived in Munich in spring 1840, two months too late to have witnessed either the carnival festival on an "Old German" theme in Munich, or the Dürer festival in Nuremberg of that year.) Historical art is an occasion for national or ethnic pride. Remnants of popular festival culture merge with modern art-historical knowledge. In the next decades other artists completed Keller's transfer of the "renaissance" concept to Germany. The last act of Richard Wagner's *Meistersinger von Nürnberg* (1868) recreated a competition at the *Johannisfest*. The "German Renaissance" was libidinal, Falstaffian, and profane, a post-1848 picture of harmony among the social classes, a celebration of crafts and trades.

But the festivals are repetitions of repetitions, soon empty of content. Keller himself is perplexed:

> Strange times, when people who wish to joyously rise up must don the garment of the past simply to appear respectable! And certainly it is a thrilling sensation to know that posterity will adopt our contemporary dress only when they wish to go about in a mocking manner, the way we do now with the garb of that eighteenth century which felt so good about itself.… When will a time come again when we will turn on our own axis and be satisfied with our own present tense?

There is a second unfamiliar word in Burckhardt's title: *Cultur* (or *Kultur*). Early in the century the word had often meant "heritage," the patriotic or even tribal patrimony, the traditional ways. The Schlesische Gesellschaft für vaterländische Cultur was founded in 1809; the Verein für Cultur und Wissenschaft der Juden in 1819. *Kultur* had been associated by Herder with the people, and by mid-century the word had come to denote the object of a kind of history-writing dedicated to society as a whole, high and low, and to the life of the people, as opposed to great men and notable events. Immediately preceding Burckhardt were the books by Wilhelm Wachsmuth, *Allgemeine Kulturgeschichte* (1850–1852) and Gustav Klemm, *Allgemeine Culturwissenschaft* (1854–1855). Burckhardt, retaining Herder's holism, used the word to mean a way of life, mentality, the sum of the ways that a community represented reality to itself.

For Burckhardt *Cultur* meant the exact opposite of tradition. Culture was the zone of spontaneity. In his university lectures on the theory of history, published posthumously as *Weltgeschichtliche Betrachtungen* (1905), Burckhardt described the "constants" of history as three *Potenzen* or powers: state, religion, culture. Culture comprises social exchanges, technologies, arts, literature. Culture is a natural state, emergent and creative, which state and religion try to suppress:

> Culture may be defined as the sum total of those mental developments which take place spontaneously and lay no claim to universal

or compulsive authority. Its action on the two constants [i.e., State and Religion] is one of perpetual modification and disintegration.

Burckhardt believed that modernity lacked culture:

> The man of culture who earns his living would gladly pick up as much learning and pleasure as he can, but must regretfully leave the best for others: others must be cultivated for him, just as others prayed and sang for the great lords of the middle ages.

The accelerated pace of modern life and the competition for goods was accompanied by an increased desire for knowledge and taste, for culture:

> Admittedly a good number of these are the American men of culture, who for the most part have renounced history, that is, spiritual continuity, and wish only to go on sharing in the enjoyment of art and poetry as forms of luxury.

Burckhardt was not a nationalist but a European chauvinist. Both Henry Adams and Henry James internalized the refined European's contempt for America. Adams (1838–1918) embarked for Europe after his studies at Harvard. He soon realized that he could not match his experiences on the Continent to any respectable behavioral model. The proliferation of guidebooks and the swelling tide of middle-class travelers, especially to Italy, were already a target of mockery. Adams saw himself neither as a dandyish *flâneur* in search of sensation nor as an earnest Goethean in search of *Bildung*. The episode is recounted in his autobiography, written in the third person, *The Education of Henry Adams* (1907):

> Henry Adams…chose the path most admired by the best judges, and followed it till he found it led nowhere. Nothing had been further from his mind when he started in November, 1858, than to become a tourist, but a mere tourist, and nothing else, he had become in April, 1860, when he joined his sister in Florence. His father had been in the right. The young man felt a little sore about it. Supposing his father asked him, on his return, what equivalent he had brought back for the time and money put into his experiment! The only possible answer would be: "Sir, I am a tourist!"

The word "tourist" was introduced into the language in the late eighteenth century and had from the start a pejorative connotation. The tourist profanated not sacred precincts but the shrines of art. Ambivalence about tourism persists to this day. Tourism has become a major element of many people's aspirations, emblematic of an expansion of internal horizons.

In the late 1850s the James family sojourned in Europe, principally Paris. Later Henry wrote of his adolescent encounter with the pictures of the Louvre: "The beginning in short was with Géricault and David, but it went on and on and slowly spread…as so many explorations of the house of life, so many circlings and hoverings round the image of the world." The boy looked at pictures and pictures, at Veronese, Murillo, Leonardo's "unholy dame with the folded hands," looked

> at France and looked at Europe, looked even at America as Europe itself might be conceived so to look, looked at history as a still-felt past and a complacently personal future, at society, manners, types, characters, possibilities and prodigies and mysteries of fifty sorts.

This was Henry's version of the Dürer Festival in Nuremberg: "The house of life and the palace of art became mixed and interchangeable."

Burckhardt assigns an ambiguous role to historical consciousness. He says that historical memory staves off the self-indulgent fancy that culture can simply be acquired and consumed (the American version of culture, according to Burckhardt). And yet the society that really is a culture, like the Italian Renaissance, was vital because it freed itself from history.

The open secret of Burckhardt's book is that it does not deal with the visual arts. In the first part Burckhardt describes the State as a "Work of Art." He often quotes and discusses poetry and drama. But he seldom mentions the fine arts, painting and sculpture. In fact, he frequently says that art tends to lag behind poetry and other cultivated practices (*Bildung*). In this way Burckhardt protects art, shields it from the cultural historian's expectation that the arts naturally "picture" history. It is as if he were taking his cue from Charles Baudelaire, who wrote in *L'art philosophique* (published in 1868 but already conceived in 1855):

> What is pure art according to the modern concept? It is the creation of a suggestive magic containing at once the object and the subject, the world external to the artist and the artist himself.
>
> What is philosophical art according to the concept of Chenevard

and the German school? It is a form of visual art which purports to replace the book, that is, to compete with the printing press in the teaching of history, morals, and philosophy.

"Philosophical art," which Baudelaire associates with the French painter Paul Chenavard and with the "German school"—Hegelians, basically—is art "destined to paint the historical archives of a people and its religions and beliefs." Such was the art of the past. But modern art is not easily coordinated with anything else—that is its nature:

> For several centuries now in the history of art there has been an ever more marked separation of powers: there are subjects that belong to painting, others to music, and still others to literature.

Baudelaire is saying more or less what Burckhardt had said: that art in the Renaissance—and since the Renaissance—is out of sync with the rest of culture.

The artwork once served as a monument. A society displays its own heroic history in images; these are intentional monuments, like the Egyptian pyramids. Later, a society becomes interested in monuments created by *other* societies: Herodotus writes about the pyramids. Eventually someone realizes that even non-monuments, exactly because they are not intentional and therefore more reliable, can serve as witnesses to the past, as "the abstract and brief chronicles of the time." Archeologists and antiquarians gather and collate such non-monuments. The credo of the modern historian is that any relic can be read as a trace of a past reality.

Pictures, however, like poems or folk tales, are already stylized and so camouflage their own potential usefulness as traces, or evidence. To read them as evidence is to read them against themselves. An artwork is simply an image that acquiesces in the dreamwork carried out by any image. The artwork does not just deliver but generates meaning. The implication, spelled out by Baudelaire, is that the modern artist, who has no will to counteract the intrinsic fictionality of the image, will fail to archive his own present, even if he wishes to. The modern artist mistrusts the image as evidence because the image arrests, suspends, mortifies; it condenses and reduces; it is unstable in time. The image is always already an artwork: opaque, enigmatic, self-contradictory, allegorical, anarchic even when it appears most composed. Qua art, the image reveals truths unknown even to the one who made the image. The image "knows better"; what kind of evidence is this? The recognition of the image leads to the recognition that premodern art was also art.

Art history in England, France, and Italy was less academic than in the German-speaking societies. Access to libraries was not yet the decisive factor it would later become. The gentleman or lady scholar with leisure and taste made real contributions. Art criticism flourished in mid-century France. Théophile Thoré-Bürger (1807–1869) wrote several books on Dutch painting and is especially remembered for having rediscovered Jan Vermeer, a painter held dear today but completely forgotten in the eighteenth and early nineteenth centuries. The pedagogue and scholar Charles Blanc was the first editor of the *Gazette des Beaux-Arts*, a magazine pragmatic, materialist, and elitist, oriented to collectors, amateurs, and artists. Its run extended from 1859 to 2002. Théophile Gautier, Baudelaire, Champfleury; the reviews of the annual salons—the future president of the Republic Adolphe Thiers wrote about the Salon of 1822: this was the matrix of artistic modernism. An impatience with the past and with memory, a low tolerance for Romantic historicism, a nonphilosophical, anecdotal, subjective, sensation-oriented spirit of contradiction, an ease with the events of the day, all of this descended from Diderot.

The brothers Edmond and Jules Goncourt, novelists, wrote a series of monographs on eighteenth-century painters that appeared in periodicals between 1856 and 1875 and were collected later as *Art du XVIII siècle*. Their tone is conversational, a salon tone, easy on erudition, espousing a contextualism that does not go far beyond the idea of the painters "expressing, personifying, embodying" "an airy moment of history." The history of art plays no greater role than it played for the artists themselves. One of Watteau's figures is described as "posed as if by a penstroke of Parmigianino." The Goncourts are doing more or less what the historians are doing, except with more grace. They do not go very deeply into form, but not because they do not see form. There is still no special language to describe pictorial form, so they draw on literary language, a parallel language. They believe in the person behind the artwork: the artist is the reality, the plenitude. This is the conviction behind the flourishing of the genre of the artist's monograph in the nineteenth century.

The Goncourts took an interest in Rococo in order to ignore realist tendencies in contemporary art. Anti-moderns (and anti-Semites), they reassert the element of fantasy, planting seeds that will grow later in the century, in the Symbolist milieu. Subject matter is irrelevant for them. Christianity in the Renaissance had already accepted a leveling with paganism, a leveling of the subjects of art on the basis of the idea of fiction. Romantic medievalism had countered this, reasserting the primacy of subject matter. The Goncourts represent not so much a decadent royalist fantasy as a non-pious response to Romantic and ironic historicism. This is related to the enthusiasm for the forms of world art: one can like it all, because it is all just so many myths.

The canon of European art was virtually closed by this point, out of inertia. There were no Goncourts writing about sixteenth- or seventeenth-century art. With few exceptions, the artists most admired by Vasari are still the ones most admired even today. The assessments of post-Vasarian painters have been more labile, mutable: the reputation of Guido Reni has declined since the nineteenth century, while that of Orazio Gentileschi has increased. The nineteenth century learned how to look at the Dutch painters. It is striking how few tasks the nineteenth century left us. Already in his "Notes on Leonardo da Vinci" (1869), the English essayist Walter Pater said that we know all there is to know about the artist: "Antiquarianism has no more to do." Erich Auerbach in his late book *Literary Language and Its Public* (1958) discussed the attempt by the historian Konrad Burdach, around 1900, to identify a humanistic proto-Renaissance at the court of Emperor Charles IV in Prague in the fourteenth century, an episode, in Burdach's view, that would stand as a counterpart and rival to Burckhardt's Florentine Renaissance. But such an attempt was doomed, Auerbach wrote, because "great intellectual centers and literary works capable of molding a national language cannot very well be so thoroughly forgotten that they have to be rediscovered by so late a scholar; their full significance would have been recognized at the very latest by nineteenth-century historicism."

1870–1890

In his essay on the hazards of historical consciousness, "On the Use and Abuse of History," one of the four "untimely meditations" he published in 1874, Friedrich Nietzsche asserted that Europe was "suffering from a debilitating historical fever." Things would get worse before they got better. The machinery of academic scholarship was only beginning to bulk up in the 1870s. In the preceding decades the number of full professors (Ordinarien) in all disciplines, in all German universities, had risen only about 10 percent between 1796 and 1864, from 650 to 725. Then between 1864 and 1890 the sum increases by 50 percent; and then again by 50 percent between 1890 and 1920. The student population, meanwhile, reached 12,000 in 1835 and stayed at this level until the late 1860s. From this point on the number of students rose precipitously. By 1902 there were 35,500 students; by the start of World War One 61,000. (Today the number of students enrolled in German universities is about two million; the population of Germany is only double what it was in the 1870s.)

In these decades the academic discipline of art history took on its modern contours. By 1875, the year of Charles Eliot Norton's appointment as professor at Harvard, there were twenty-one Ordinarien in art history at the twenty-nine universities in Germany, Austria, and Switzerland. Most of these taught classical archeology, however; only four taught the history of "modern" or post-medieval art, and only one taught medieval art, at the University of Vienna. In these years Vienna played the leading role. In 1871 the Viennese scholar Rudolf Eitelberger launched a series of compilations and editions of art-historical source material, the *Quellenschriften für Kunstgeschichte und Kunsttechnik des Mittelalters und der Renaissance*. The series included editions of the Carolingian sources on art, edited by Schlosser, as well as theoretical texts by Cennino Cennini, Leon Battista Alberti, Filarete, Albrecht Dürer, Lodovico Dolce, and others. The first art-historical congress, or professional meeting, was staged in Vienna in 1873. Three years later the first scholarly journal of art history, the *Repertorium für Kunstwissenschaft*, was established in Vienna. The article addressed to specialists is now the basic unit of scholarship.

In the winter semester of 1888, August Schmarsow took a leave from his teaching position at the University of Breslau and set up shop in Florence. Among the students who followed him to Florence, and attended his lectures, seminars, and excursions, were Aby Warburg and Max J. Friedländer. This extramural academy, dedicated to the study of works in situ and to archival research, was the embryo of the Kunsthistorisches Institut in Florence, founded in 1897.

The protocols of publication and professional self-monitoring meant that scholarship was now less likely to be practiced by gentleman amateurs and more likely to be a collective enterprise, and a career. The fact-gathering and fact-sorting, the drive to relativize, the induction of the laws of history, the triage of norm and anomaly, and the pedagogic imperative all tended to generate coherent pictures of past societies, pictures that became mirrors for present societies. Art history as cultural history—and Burckhardt played a role here—seemed suited to the lecture hall just as connoisseurship was suited to the salon (and now the print cabinet in the museum). Friedländer, the eminent connoisseur and director of both the print cabinet and the painting gallery in Berlin, reportedly boasted that he never once in his life gave a public lecture.

The Kunsthistorisches Museum in Vienna, designed by Gottfried Semper and opened in 1891, was the first museum to offer itself explicitly as a walk-in textbook of art history, like a supplement to the lecture courses offered at the Institute of Art History in Heinrich von Ferstel's university building, built in 1884, a little further along the Ringstrasse. The painters Hans Makart, Gustav Klimt, Franz Matsch, and Mihály Munkácsy adorned the stairwell of the museum. In the lunettes Makart portrayed the masters of the sixteenth and seventeenth centuries with their female models, in imitation of their own styles: Raphael, Titian, Dürer, and so forth. Art-historical knowledge was now so widely shared among the public that the styles alone of these pastiches could function as portraits of the historical artists. Exceptions were made for Rembrandt and Velázquez, whose portraits appeared in cartouches, that is, not represented through scenes rendered in their styles but directly as portraits. It was as if their realistic styles—styles imitated by painters of the third quarter of the nineteenth century—would not be recognized as their own.

On April 27, 1879, a festive parade of costumed citizens representing the traditional professions and trades—goldsmiths, clockmakers, bankers—that sustained the bourgeois society established in the German-speaking lands in the sixteenth century rotated slowly along the Ringstrasse, the perimeter of the old city of Vienna. The "Historical Procession" was mounted by the city in honor of the twenty-fifth wedding anniversary of the Habsburg emperor and empress Franz Josef and Elisabeth. Some paraders rode on floats resembling the chariots in the printed *Triumph of Emperor Maximilian* (1515–1518) by Dürer. The procession was designed by the painter Makart. The costumes, in sixteenth-century styles, are recorded in posed photographs. In 1855 Gottfried Keller had described the 1840 Dürer festival in Munich as if it were the last manifestation of a culture of festivals that stretched back to the fantastical princely and royal entries of the late Middle Ages. But the taste for costumed public festivals was to linger for a few more decades. Nietzsche asked in 1882: "What is the point of all the art of our works of art if we lose that higher art, the art of festivals?" The brief moment of intoxication lures us off the *via dolorosa*. Such spectacles also asserted the underlying continuity of European society since the Renaissance, despite steam engine, train, and telegraph. Such was the confidence in the homology between the present day and a supposedly integrated and self-assured sixteenth century that people were still willing, in donning costumes, to turn themselves into living works of art. (This was the bourgeois response to the fantasy of the socialist Fourier, who thought people could become living artworks if they disrobed.) The contrast between the costumes and the black-and-white everyday garb of 1879, a way of dressing as if designed to be photographed, was sharp. Fourteen thousand citizens took part in Makart's extravaganza, 300,000 more looked on.

The enthusiasms that fueled Makart's festival had been stoked by the nine volumes (1871–1888) compiled by the Graz architect August Ortwein, the *Deutsche Renaissance: eine Sammlung von Gegenständen der Architektur, Decoration und Kunstgewerbe in Original-Aufnahmen*

(German Renaissance: A Collection of Architectural, Decorative, and Craft Objects Based on Original Photography). "German Renaissance" became a fashionable style, worthy rival to the French Renaissance, not to mention the Italian, a style of costume and interior decoration. Art in bourgeois life tends to the middle space between the body and the walls of the dwelling: the range of somatic sensory experience. Art readjusts the body to the environment. "Renaissance" is comfort.

The reoccupation of a supposedly national style was a riposte to the "world's fair" approach to styles, the total availability of all forms that our "historical artists prepare for us," in Nietzsche's derisive words. Now the European Renaissance is celebrated as an ideal interwovenness of art and life, standing for a transcending of ideological or confessional difference, an end to superstition. The term "Renaissance" names precisely the end of anxiety about the "standing over" of obsolete beliefs. In 1879 the nostalgia for the sixteenth century was also standing in for regret for the lost enthusiasms of the peaceful second quarter of the century, before the crises of 1848; as if Makart's festival were remembering 1828 as much as 1528.

In his text "On the Use and Abuse of History," Nietzsche described three kinds of modern history-writing. The first he called "monumental history," or the hope that instances of past greatness will elevate the present. Makart's mobile spectacle was an example of this. The monumental historian, according to Nietzsche, believes "that the greatness that once existed was at least possible at one time, and that it will probably be possible once again." Through "the occupation with the classical and rare accomplishments (*mit dem Classischen und Seltenen*) of earlier times" he becomes a "connoisseur of greatness" (*Kenner des Grossen*). Monumental history, however, will tend to "diminish the differences between motives and causes in order to present, to the detriment of the *causae*, the *effectus* as monumental—that is, as exemplary and worthy of emulation." In other words, the historian neglects his duty to explain how things came about. We may describe monumental history as "a collection of 'effects in themselves,' of events that will have an effect on every age. What is celebrated at popular festivals and at religious or military commemorations is really just an 'effect in itself.'"

Nietzsche believed that the study of history encourages an individual, a people, or a culture "to develop its own singular character out of itself, to shape and assimilate what is past and alien, to heal wounds, to replace what has been lost, to recreate broken forms out of itself alone." Monumental history is one of the ways that historical study may serve the present, as it should, in the view of Nietzsche, who in the early 1870s, as a young professor of classical philology at Basel, was attending the lectures of his older colleague Burckhardt. Nietzsche suspects, however, that the monumental historians have little admiration for the present. This applies especially to the historians of art: "Thus they are connoisseurs of art because they want to do away with art altogether; thus they masquerade as physicians, while in fact they intend to administer a poison." "For they don't want great art to come into being; their strategy is to say: 'Look, great art already exists!'" Their admiration for the past barely conceals their contempt for the present: "They act as though their motto was, 'Let the dead bury the living.'" In the end, this is morbid history. Nietzsche makes it clear that Hans Makart and his temporary actors neither admire the art of their own time, nor see any need to evolve.

The second variety of history described by Nietzsche, the antiquarian, is characterized by an unselective reverence for bygone customs and obsolete forms of life. The antiquarian withdraws from "the fresh life of the present": "The scholarly habit…revolves with self-satisfied egotism around its own axis. Then we view the repugnant spectacle of a blind mania to collect, of a restless gathering together of everything that once existed. The human being envelops himself in the smell of mustiness."

The third and most dynamic approach to the past, according to Nietzsche, is critical history. "Only those who are oppressed by the affliction of the present and who wish to throw off this burden at all costs sense the need for critical history—that is, for history that judges and condemns." Nietzsche favors getting on with life and not bothering excessively with the past. Yet he concedes that "at times this very life that requires forgetfulness demands the temporary suspension of this forgetfulness; for when it is supposed to become absolutely clear precisely how unjust the existence of certain things—for example, a privilege, a caste, or a dynasty really is, and how much these things deserve to be destroyed, this is when its past is viewed critically, when we take a knife to its roots, when we cruelly trample on all forms of piety."

History, ironizing the present through a restructuring of memory, should be either critical or monumental. Nietzsche prefers the critical mode, but even this can go awry. "Human beings or ages that serve life by passing judgment on and destroying a past are always dangerous and endangered human beings and ages. For since we are, after all, the products of earlier generations, we are also the products of their aberrations, passions, and errors—indeed, of their crimes." The critical historian, in other words, tries to disengage himself from a chain of influences and dependencies. Critical history is the futile "attempt to give ourselves *a posteriori*, as it were, a new past from which we would prefer to be descended, as opposed to the past from which we actually descend." Critical history becomes the dishonest fabrication of the desired history.

One of the modes of critical history that we are familiar with by now is the discrediting of accomplished styles, the accumulated results of civilization, in favor of half-forgotten earlier stages, unfulfilled, rude, but direct and expressive. Nietzsche lists this fallacy among the risks of antiquarian devotion to the past, but the import of his observation exceeds his treatment of that mode. Nietzsche considers the re-creation of the archaic style a mark of decadence, for that style corresponds only to archaic forms of life: "In the plastic and graphic arts even the Greeks tolerated the hieratic style alongside the free and great style; indeed, later they not only tolerated pointed noses and frosty smiles, but even turned them into a sign of refined taste."

"The surfeit of history (*die Übersättigung einer Zeit in Historie*)" encourages "the belief that one is a late-comer and epigone" and "throws an age into the dangerous attitude of self-irony." Here Nietzsche echoes Michelet's warning in the closing pages of *Le Peuple* about the cult of the Middle Ages. Costume dramas and historical novels, neo-Gothic architecture, but also scholars projected an illusory picture of an organic, pious, or stably hierarchical European medieval culture, *or* Renaissance culture—but anyway pre-industrial and predemocratic.

The best artists—not the superficial pseudo-Impressionist Makart, but the free thinkers, the originals—did not participate in such self-serving fantasies. Unwilling to decorate the social environment, unwilling to archive their own times in the manner of Baudelaire's "philosophical art," unwilling in short to become the easily legible source material for future art histories, they understood the museum as a refuge. The painter Anselm Feuerbach admitted that "sometimes my life is like a dream in which, one hundred years from now, I wander through the galleries and see my own works hanging in quiet gravity on their walls." The museum, Feuerbach recognized, protected a premodern, annalistic approach to art history. The painter gains entry into the museum not by meeting society's expectations but by dismissing them, or creating new expectations. Historicist scholarship, meanwhile, aims to ease artworks back into their settings, ignoring the works' own drive to escape those settings. Feuerbach imagines exactly that escape.

Historicism provoked a counterpull back toward a nonhistorical concept of art. The resistance to historicist dogma came from beyond the university. The painter Eugène Fromentin (1820–1876), in *Les maîtres d'autrefois* (The Masters of Past Time) (1876), tried to restore the original scene of talk. In his preface, as if responding directly to Hippolyte Taine, he wrote: "I warn you that there will be no method of any kind, no course pursued in these studies." They are not really studies but just "notes," and so "more specialized than previous studies," just notes "where philosophy, aesthetics, terminology, and anecdotes will play a lesser role and questions of technique—shop-talk—a greater role. It will be a sort of conversation about painting, where the painters may recognize their habits, and where practical men may get to know painters and painting a little better." He is positioning himself in both camps at once. "For now, my method will be to forget everything which has been said on this topic," code for: don't pay any attention to the scholars. Fromentin goes on to offer observations on Dutch paintings in the museums at Brussels, Antwerp, and the Hague as well as the Louvre; musings, ruminations, judgments. He dwelled on the absence of subject in Dutch painting. The Dutch artists seem untroubled by the times, by history. "What reason has a Dutch painter to make a picture? None whatsoever; and notice that no one ever asked him to give such a reason." Fromentin identified a content that was a non-content, and so outside politics.

Another quotable voice who reasserted civilized talk as the scene of art-historical good sense was Giovanni Morelli (1816–1891), an Italian physician and parliamentarian, a liberal patriot who contributed to the founding of the Italian nation-state and ascended to a seat in the Senate in 1873. Like so many other seekers in this period, he was oriented toward Germany, where he had studied and travelled as a young man; and he was well versed in the scriptures of Romanticism. In late middle age Morelli devoted himself to writing on Renaissance painting, at first hiding behind a pseudonym, in fact behind a double mask. In the mid-1870s a series of articles on the paintings in the galleries of Munich, Dresden, and Rome appeared in a German review under the name Ivan Lermolieff.

The series, later published as books, begins with a dialogue between the narrator, a naïve Russian visitor to Florence, and a Florentine gentleman who undertakes to develop his taste in art. In the dialogue Morelli lends his own opinions not to the young Russian, his anagrammatic doppelgänger, but to the unnamed Italian cicerone. The older scholarship on art, the Italian gentleman concedes, was weak, practiced mostly by "aesthetic literati or pedantic archeologists." Today there are professors of art history in Germany who year by year train able new scholars to follow in their steps. But the new experts, warns the Florentine, are often no better than the old. They pore over written documents, they propound abstract theories, and they even trust their intuition, but in fact they are unable to look directly at a work of art:

> The man whose enthusiasm for art has been stimulated in the lecture hall—how does he behave in a picture gallery! Very much like a rustic in a menagerie; or, if he be one of the learned and cultivated, he approaches the pictures in a kind of aesthetic abstraction, not knowing exactly what to make of them. The lecturer's elaborate definition of the "beautiful" debars our scholar from seeing any beauty in the painting before him, whether by Titian or Correggio.

If the experts were to look closely at the characteristic forms of the human figures painted by the great masters, however, observing with the attentiveness of a scientist, they would "discern in the features, in the form and movement of the hand, in the pose of the figure—in short, in the whole outward frame—the deeper qualities of the mind." Morelli is extending the basic concept of the artistic monograph. The aim of the study of art, he believes, is to gain access to the mind and being of the superior artist. There is no concern with history at all, only with the overcoming of history.

The next day the pair meet at the Uffizi. The connoisseur, Morelli's spokesman, imparts a lesson in close looking to his Russian acolyte. He moves through the galleries, from painting to painting, contesting and adjusting the attributions of the works on the basis of anatomical observations. A depiction of *St. Augustine in His Study* attributed by the catalogue to Filippo Lippi is revealed to be a masterpiece by Botticelli: "Among Sandro Botticelli's characteristic forms I will mention the hand, with bony figures—not beautiful, but always full of life; the nails, which as you perceive in the thumb here, are square with black outlines, and the short nose with dilated nostrils, which you see exemplified in Botticelli's celebrated and undisputed work hanging close by—'The Calumny of Apelles.'" That is the end of the analysis. Morelli gives us no real reason to admire the painting. He then demotes a female portrait attributed to Raphael. The painting is "unfortunately so much repainted that we can only form an opinion of it from the scale of colour in the dress, and from the drawing of the face, and more especially of the hand, with the first finger extended." "Does [that finger] bear any resemblance to the hand of the 'Fornarina,' or to that of the 'Madonna del Cardellino'?" Like a philologist, Morelli "chastises" the pictorial text, mentally, to arrive at a fair copy that can be assessed and appreciated. And yet this appreciation is postponed. In this case, Morelli refrains from guessing at the work's true author. He practices attribution but only in order to identify the works really painted by the greatest masters. He leaves it to you to derive profit from the works.

This is Nietzsche's monumental history, brought to bear against not only the present—Morelli seems to have little admired the art of his own day—but all art of the preceding three centuries. Morelli's taste in art was conventional, Vasarian. Students "should be taught to feel at home among the dry, archaic, *quattro-centisti* painters, and to hold intelligent converse with them. By this means their enjoyment would be heightened when they came to see the glorious works of Raphael, Titian, Giorgione, or Correggio." His scientific method of attributing paintings is not scientific at all but corrupted by judgments about the inner qualities of the persons depicted in the paintings. Morelli's fictional connoisseur refutes a "professor of painting at the Academy," a fellow visitor to the galleries of the Pitti, who believes that the Donna Velata, a female portrait (c. 1516), is not a work by Raphael but a copy:

> Just look at the painting with your own eyes, my dear sir, and never mind what the critics in Berlin or Paris see fit to tell us about it. A copyist, indeed! to have painted those eyes, with their wonderful expression, that proud mouth, that noble brow—never!

Form has content, it would seem. That content flows forth from people—the sitter, the painter. The painting is edifying because the Donna Velata herself had a proud and noble spirit and because Raphael himself possessed sufficient nobility of spirit to reproduce this character. Such a judgment is the desired result of the study of art. Logically, however, admiration for Raphael really should not be both the basis of the attribution and the outcome of the attribution.

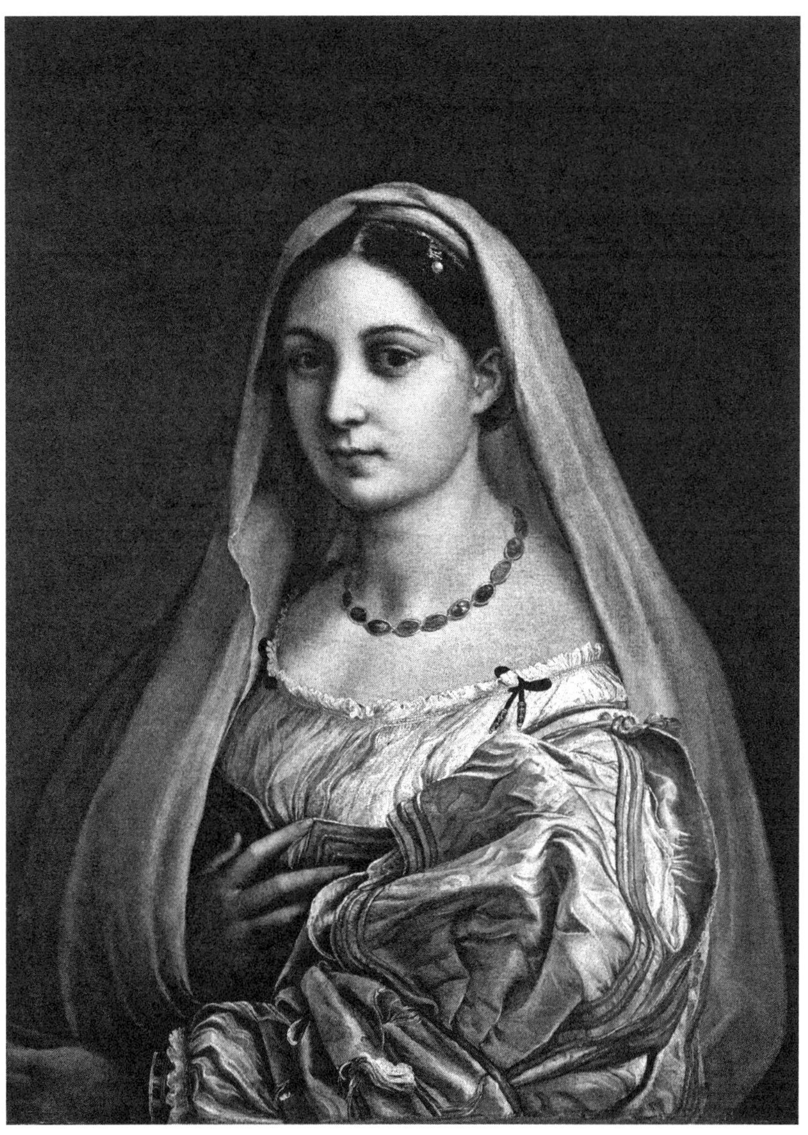

Raphael, *Donna Velata* (c. 1516). Oil on canvas, 82 × 60.5 cm. Florence, Palazzo Pitti. Although the painting had entered the Palazzo Pitti by 1622, its attribution to Raphael was doubted for at least the next two centuries.

So Morelli is a circular thinker. On one page he says that the "art-historian will gradually disappear (no great loss either, you will admit), and in due course of time, as the larva develops into the butterfly, the connoisseur will emerge from his chrysalis state." On the next page he says that "it is absolutely necessary for a man to be a connoisseur before he can become an art-historian." His conception of "knowledge" of art—for that is what the connoisseur, the *Kenner*, possesses—is holistic, existential. He derides the flocks of tourists, "armed with red and brown guide-books," who are unable to achieve a moment of contemplative repose. Books are useful for the study of the art of remote cultures, Egyptian, Hindu, Assyrian, and so forth. But the authority of these and all other books is sustained by a superstitious reverence for the printed word: "The public, who have the greatest respect for everything in print, have no discrimination—resembling the peasant, who, when a parrot called out to him 'Good morning,' from a window, took off his hat to it." The conversation in the gallery, without the safety net of portable books, restores the original scene of the discourse of art. "Discourse," late Latin *discursus*, literally meant conversation. Talk is plastic, interactive, the medium of a free convergence of subjects unsustained by external authorities. Ideally talk about art happens on site—or in more recent modernity in the one-way formats of the lecture hall, guided tours, or television.

The young man returns to Russia, or to be precise Kazan, in Tatarstan. When he revisits Florence some time later the old man is no longer in view, having retired in his misanthropy to the country. Armed with the precepts of his guru, Ivan Lermolieff undertakes to visit and describe the picture collections of Rome.

Morelli's strangest comment is his recommendation to begin with the study of the fifteenth-century Florentine painters, for in their works "the bones and muscles are less hidden by the flesh, and the distinctive and characteristic forms of each master are therefore more apparent, than is the case with the painters of the *cinquecento*." As if to perceive the bone structure in the depicted figures were to perceive the essential nature of the painter! Morelli does not see the entire painting, the composition. He grasps the painting as a place to encounter other people: the artist, but also the people depicted in the painting. In the end the engagement with art becomes an engagement with portraits, just as inquiry into historical art becomes a matter not of inscription of fact but of interlocution in real time.

Morelli boasts at one point that the Goncourts have adopted his method. It is true that his method of attribution, involving the comparison of overlooked details, is effective even if you do not share his prejudices. Freud will invoke him in his essay "The Moses of Michelangelo" (1914). Morelli cleared out a space that many people wished to occupy. He believed that the connoisseur who learns to look at nature and the world with a "trained and cultivated eye" becomes himself a kind of artist. And so he reconstituted, and remystified, that priesthood of art that the lecture halls and the libraries had been trying to discredit. This metamorphosis is recapitulated today, except that the curator, not the connoisseur, is the artist-like butterfly who emerges from the art-historical cocoon.

Another anti- or even post-historiographic writer was the English essayist Walter Pater (1839–1894). Suspected of irreligion and homosexuality, and not without reason, Pater nevertheless secured a post as a nonclerical fellow at Oxford. Pater published his essays on poetry and painting in 1873 as *Studies in the History of the Renaissance*. The term "Renaissance" for Pater, as for Burckhardt, designates not a period but a unique flowering of culture in Italy, "that solemn fifteenth century" esteemed for its "positive" results, its "concrete works of art, its special and prominent personalities." His object is not an abstract concept of beauty, but the impression made by beauty on the temperament of the critic. In his rejection of Ruskinian moralism and in his bodily paganism, Pater is in tune with Nietzsche, his junior by five years. "Renaissance" is Pater's code word for intense feeling, for the critic's identification with genius, for the rejection of the crassness of the present. Relativism is drab.

Confident that this "outbreak of the human spirit may be traced into the middle ages," Pater begins with an essay on "Aucassin et Nicolette," a French prose fable of the thirteenth century. Already here the "care for physical beauty, the worship of the body," challenge the "limits which the religious system of the middle age imposed on the heart and the imagination." In this simple tale he finds an "assertion of liberty," "a strange rival religion" of love, a hidden paganism, a rebellious and noble antinomianism. In his essay on the humanist scholar Pico della Mirandola, Pater speaks of the "natural charm of pagan story" reasserting itself against barbarism. He invokes the Romantic poet Heinrich Heine, who as we saw was a partisan of sensuality and who in his essay "The Gods in Exile" had described with humorous literalism the retreat of the pagan deities, during the Christian centuries, into hiding and ignominious disguise. The *Birth of Venus* by Sandro Botticelli, according to Pater a "quaint design," gives us "a more direct inlet into the Greek temper than the works of the Greeks themselves even of the finest period."

The Renaissance meant a return to antiquity, but it also meant "realism, its appeal to experience," its curiosity, which was often but not always in conflict with the desire for beauty. Thus Leonardo da Vinci, the experimenter, also learned in the studio of his teacher Andrea del Verrocchio "the love of beautiful toys, such as the vessel of water for a mirror, and lovely needlework about the implicated hands," and of reliefs, and cameos, and "bright variegated stones," and "a hieratic preciseness and grace, as of a sanctuary swept and garnished."

It is customary to say that Pater is one of the greatest prose stylists of our language, but his deep purple is shot through with golden threads of insight. He is a student of history; he is writing what he thinks should be written when the fact-gathering and sorting is done. After history, we recover the poetry. The advantage enjoyed by the folk of the fifteenth century was their lack of "the very rudiments of the historic sense, which by an imaginative act throws itself back into a world unlike one's own, and judges each intellectual product in connection with the age which produced it." Pater signals a new layer of modern nostalgia: envy of the prehistoriographic age, when there was theory of art but not yet history of art. Like Johann Joachim Winckelmann, whom he considers the last writer of the Renaissance, and with whom he identifies, Pater would seem to be one who is wise only too late, *ophimatheis*. He seems to know too much ever to experience anything immediately. But this is not the case, for the study of history prepares experience and multiplies worlds.

Jacob Burckhardt knew that a roll call of great artists was not an art history, any more than was a history of art's meanings and functions. In a letter written from Rome in 1875, late in his career, he lamented: "As far as the scholarly outcome of the trip is concerned, I am rather distressed, for there was by no means enough time to accomplish what I had foolishly hoped for: I wanted to get away from the old nonsense of a history of *artists* and instead undertake the studies which would have put me in a position to transform the teaching of art history into a pure history of styles and forms (*zu einer reinen Geschichte der Style und der Formen*)."

Laying his own grievance at the door of academic art history, and as if answering Burckhardt's regrets, the aesthetician Konrad Fiedler (1841–1895) worried that scholarship was "explaining everything about a work of art except what makes it a work of art." In his essay "Observations on the Nature and History of Architecture" (1878), Fiedler sketched a new evaluative history of architecture based on the fantastical premise that the function of buildings was to express ideas through their form. Here Fiedler goes beyond Gottfried Semper and Viollet-le-Duc, who were interested in the rational principles of good building, not in architecture's participation in a history of artistic form. He does invoke Semper, who had spoken of the inherent "striving" in architecture as an expression of mind's domination of matter. Fiedler looks for the signs of creative aspiration rather than mere pleasure in the "massive, ornate, fantastic, eccentric" (this is Asiatic and Egyptian). A Greek building "presents nothing to our view except its form." The Romans ruined this by recombining forms without any inner necessity, and the Renaissance resumed the pointless project. Gothic was only an aberrant byway that exploited the technical capacities of the pointed arch but neglected its artistic qualities. And so, inexorably and with breathtaking irrealism, Fiedler arrives at the same conclusion that Heinrich Hübsch had offered exactly half a century earlier, albeit for a different reason: Romanesque or round-arched architecture was the most artistic because the promotion of the vault from a substructure into the main formal content of architecture displayed the origins of ideated form in the material unformed: "only when there is awareness of a given, unformed material that is given form can we speak of artistic activity."

Fiedler believes that in writing about a twelfth-century church as if it were a work of art he is performing the most difficult trick, namely the forgetting of the work's original function. But it was not such a hard trick because that church's function by 1878 was moribund, half-forgotten. It would be much harder to rewrite the history of *painting* as a meditation on form, at least until someone invented abstract painting, because it is harder to forget the content of painting. When looking at a painting of a garden by Claude Monet, it is impossible not to think about how pleasant it is to sit in a garden in the summertime. When looking at a medieval church, it is quite possible to forget about eschatology, or the nave as a metaphor for the Christian community. The school for abstraction, and for the art history of form, was architecture.

Fiedler, who was close to artists, prepares modernism, when artists will take control again of art history. The best art history for the next generation will place form in the foreground. The precondition for this was a postponement of the question of the historical origins of art. Semper had written about the origins of art in the primordial dwellings, a speculative prehistory. Vitruvius, Laugier: the first dwelling is a topos of architectural theory. The protoformalists were content to locate the origin in the human mind. Fiedler maintained that "all reality is nothing other than the result of a sensuous and mental process (*eines sinnlich-geistigen Vorgangs*) whose origins recede into the dark zone of sensory perception (*dunklen Gebiet der sinnlichen Empfindung*) and which out of these beginnings, withdrawn from the light of consciousness, develops and expands into manifold and shifting determination and the plenitude of phenomena." Franz Kugler had already tried to deal with the prehistory of art, hinting at the psychological riddle of creativity. The philosopher Robert Vischer spoke of the "unconscious" in his writings on empathy, invoking the book by Karl Albert Scherner on dreams. Nonplussed by the enigma of origins, the art histories of the nineteenth century did not stretch back beyond ancient Egypt.

In 1879 a Spanish gentleman, Don Marcelino Sanz de Sautuola, together with his daughter, cast the light of a lantern on the walls of a cave on his property at Altamira, near Santander, and made a discovery that ought to have represented a *catastrophe* in the historiography of art, in the original sense of the word: an overturning of discourse. Don Marcelino saw teeming herds of buffalo painted on the walls of the cave in vivid colors. These paintings were unconnected in style to anything ever seen. They were a thousand miles and ten thousand years removed from the oldest known paintings. They were assimilable to no art-historical narrative. They seemed to emerge out of nothing, connect to nothing. They matched no principle of morphology, no conventions of representation.

The shock was so great that many archeologists and art historians judged the paintings at Altamira a hoax. Don Marcelino recognized similarities with the prehistoric bone carvings of Aquitaine that he had seen reproduced in the book by Édouard Lartet and Henri Christy, *Reliquiae Aquitanicae* (1865–1875). But these splendid paintings did not match the spare image of the beginnings of art represented by those humble carvings. The paintings, many experts believed, must have been painted by a modern painter. The discovery of Don Marcelino was dismissed. Only decades later was the significance of Altamira grasped. In the twentieth century the painted caves would replace the early Middle Ages as the primal scene of art history. Modernism and formalism alike would be shadowed by Altamira, an excess of content.

1890–1900

No art historian other than Vasari has written texts with a longer life-span than Alois Riegl (1858–1905). Riegl's first post was at the Österreichisches Museum für Kunst und Industrie in Vienna, founded in 1863 on the model of the South Kensington (later Victoria and Albert) Museum in London. Here he was responsible for oriental textiles. The carpets became Riegl's textbook of form. His *Stilfragen: Grundlegungen zu einer Geschichte der Ornamentik* (Questions of Style: Foundations of a History of Ornament) (1893), narrates the development of ornament, based entirely on the acanthus leaf, from ancient Egypt to the arts of Islam, as a continuous unfolding of form independent of function, materials, symbolism, or representational content. By focusing on patterns woven in textiles or painted on vases, void of subject matter, Riegl opened a direct vista onto form. Riegl saw that the representational art that had dominated European art for centuries had the power to govern its own interpretation—too much power. In the premodern "applied" arts, paradoxically, he found the absolute abstraction that had not quite yet been invented, in 1893, on the stretched canvas.

Riegl was a careful observer, trained in the Morellian method, but he left questions of authenticity or dating in the background. Riegl's vases and carpets were authorless, so there was no interference from imputations of psychological states. His own prose is dry and factual.

Riegl explained the evolution of form neither as approach to or retreat from nature, nor as a symbolic response to the physical conditions of dwelling, as Gottfried Semper had done, but rather as an internal development, work to work, as the form-making mind altered the already-shaped forms it encountered in prior art, leaving reality long behind. The impulse to create forms is most directly registered in the free play of vegetal ornament.

Riegl's assertion of the autarky of form opened a path back to a certain classicism, classicism understood as the state of not having to choose. The classicism of pure form was guided by nature, not external nature but form itself as a second nature. Riegl contrasted the organic development of the tendril in ancient art to the deliberate selections, "unimaginative transcriptions of nature," of the modern Arts and Crafts movement. Scholarly attempts to explain "new" ornamental motifs in ancient art by identifying actual plants as their sources are the "pure product of the most modern artistic sensibility, even in part the modern perplexity about art." The classicism of form had the potential to awaken the late nineteenth century from the double nightmare of an excess of choice (in architecture and design) and not enough choice (in painting, now more and more acquiescent in the meaningless task of verisimilitude, oppressed by all the reality waiting to be pictured).

Riegl's book signals the arrival of art history's culminating moment, the years when the project of art history most perfectly realized its possibilities. Riegl's art history was impersonal and erudite, as scholarship must be, and yet was responding to pressures from outside scholarship, in particular the development of a quasi-philosophical discourse of form. Riegl develops the art history that responds to Konrad Fiedler, whose text of 1878 on architecture we encountered in the last section. In his essay "Moderner Naturalismus und künstlerische Wahrheit" (Modern Naturalism and Artistic Truth) (1881), Fiedler had contested the assumption of painting's naturalist destiny. It was the doomed competition with photography that had led painting to lose its way in the mindless transcription of reality. Admittedly the scorn for realism had been a traditional theme of premodern art theory, often mapped onto a geographic distinction. The direct imitation of reality was the northern European weakness, a limitation to be countered by an idealism cultivated in the Mediterranean realm. But Fiedler was not just reproducing that debate, as if to complain that the northern mode had prevailed. Fiedler's main aims, like Riegl's, were to safeguard autonomy, to justify the fictive quality of art's propositions, and to protect art from functionalist thinking.

Fiedler argued that the role of art in modernity was to restage the mental and physiological processes that construct reality: "The truly artistically gifted nature…brings forth in itself so to speak that process, now arrived at a new freedom, in which reality is generated for man." Fiedler was recovering the epistemology of Kant, who latterly had been overshadowed by Hegel and Hegel's antagonists, Schopenhauer and Nietzsche. Kant's critical philosophy licensed Fiedler to credit the true artist or poet not with reproducing the world but with creating a world. The sufficient content of modern paintings is therefore vision itself. Fiedler represents a transitional phase between the intuitions of artistic autonomy of the mid-nineteenth century (Baudelaire) and the philosophies of autonomy of the twentieth century, those of Benedetto Croce, Suzanne Langer, Gaston Bachelard, and Theodor W. Adorno.

The short treatise on relief sculpture by the artist and theorist Adolf von Hildebrand, entitled *Das Problem der Form in der bildenden Kunst* (The Problem of Form in the Visual Arts) (1893), had immediate influence. Like his friend Fiedler, Hildebrand could not see where realism or naturalism was heading. Hildebrand did not accept the idea of representation as the mechanical reproduction of the results of perception, a fallacy only encouraged by the realist tendencies of modern painting. Hildebrand defined artistic vision instead as the apprehension of an idea of form (*Formvorstellung*) abstracted from the shifting phenomena perceived by the eyes. The work of art, he argued, offers the "form of existence" (*Daseinsform*) as a pure visual effect.

Hildebrand asserted that we apprehend objects in the world either by moving around them and assessing their plastic form, or by gazing straight at them from a fixed distance. Artists work with these two approaches: the painter delivers a flat view of the world that nevertheless tries to reproduce plastic form and even movement, while the sculptor delivers a plastic form that nevertheless resolves into satisfying picture-like views. The artist clarifies nature by comparing it to imaginary pictures and sculptures. The resulting artwork is an independent entity that stands beside nature, liberated from mutability and accident. The ideal was the relief sculpture of ancient Greece, which alone "places us as observers in a secure relationship with nature." Therefore relief is "a way of viewing things that in all times has been the mark of artistic sensibility and the expression of its unchanging laws."

Hildebrand challenges his own theory by asking: If the artwork is a pure product of the artist's mind, how can we explain the illusionistic power of paintings? The answer is that each of us, not only the artist, assesses nature by comparing imaginary moving and stable views, or pictures. Perception is always already artistic. It is no surprise then that the painted landscape resembles the landscapes we see outdoors. Real existence reemerges inside the artwork as pure effect. The mind of the ordinary viewer dominates nature, but the artist dominates that viewer. Hildebrand tells the artist: your destiny is in your hands, you are free, art is a present-tense problem involving your own mind and body. The critic, meanwhile, is one who oversees perception and its reenactments, and who corrects the history of art.

Because he perpetuates the cult of ancient Greece, and because he offers the Greek relief as a recipe for the ailments of modern art, Hildebrand is today less serviceable than Fiedler. Still, the aim of his text was the same, as was its grounding in Kantian critical philosophy. Fiedler and Hildebrand created a new language for analyzing form, so revealing the impoverishment of nineteenth-century historical scholarship. Without this language, art history remains stretched between the ingratiating narratives of the historians (Taine) and the pathos of the critical word-poets (Pater). Taine has little to say about artworks that is not plainly visible to any sentient person. Pater has plenty to say, but his graceful sentences, relaying reverberations of the soul of the artist, sometimes obstruct the view onto form.

Fiedler and Hildebrand, paradoxically, recovered form in order to give the art of their time a renewed sense of its own meaning in history. The very idea that art might evolve seemed threatened by realism, a style unlike all other styles because it cedes authority to the motif in reality. Fiedler and Hildebrand's redefinition of vision as the content of art guarantees that the content of art is always *other art*, because art and only art delivers a picture of vision that can serve as a starting point for new art.

Fiedler and Hildebrand's focus on form entailed no relativism; they were in effect trying to maintain Gian Pietro Bellori's high standards. Fiedler wrote about medieval architecture, but by 1878 that was hardly controversial. They were not much interested in anything but masterpieces. The recentering of art history on form does not invite an egalitarian approach to cultural artifacts. And yet the principle of autonomy allows for a canon of art more open or more closed as the historian sees fit, for it allows the historian to extract applied art from its original functions and settings and to treat it *as art*. This is exactly what Riegl did in his books on carpets and the acanthus ornament. Formalism prepares a recognition of a larger population of artifacts as art: the third-century brooch or the ancient Chinese bronze vessel alongside the oil paintings lauded by Bellori. This is the principle of the modern encyclopedic art museum.

The theory of pure visibility, however, also protects a not fully acknowledged normativity. In the *Problem of Form*, Hildebrand speaks of the unchanging laws of art. As a modern, Hildebrand invokes no metaphysical authority. Yet his idea of form is not neutral, but ennobling. The contingent forms of nature, according to Hildebrand, must become *form*, that is, complete form. In the way of seeing expressed in relief

> the visual sense, stimulated in a thousand ways, finds its center of gravity, its stable relations, and its clarity. The method is essential for all artistic forms, whether a landscape or a portrait; everywhere it orders perception, combines it, and stabilizes it.

It is fair to ask whether artistic freedom secretly oriented to even a post-metaphysical idealism is freedom at all. A closer reading of Fiedler reveals a similar hidden idealism. In his essay on architecture of 1878, Fiedler had written, "Creation of form must be imagined as a thought process in which the architectural forms themselves are the content." Form is already the content of the artist's form-producing (*gestaltende*) thought. The artist thinks about form while he is transforming bad or contingent form into good or artistically lasting form. The given forms—the forms of existing buildings—are unsatisfying because they are trapped in their materiality: Greek architecture was the effort "to free form from its earlier dependence on the requirements of construction and material, so that 'when we look upon the work of art, the means and the materials are forgotten and it is satisfying in itself as form.'" Fiedler is actually quoting Semper, exposed here as an idealist. Fiedler's recruitment of Semper is an indication of how difficult it was for nineteenth-century thinkers to escape teleological thinking. The form of the building, "which is a thing of the mind, develops an increasingly autonomous existence (*selbständigeren Dasein*)."

At some point the process ends: "Only when the building has become a pure expression of form is the intellectual work of the creation of form complete."

The late nineteenth-century and early twentieth-century adherents of form as beautiful order assigned form two prestigious positions within narratives of artistic creation. "Forms," in this view, are packages of sensible reality that perception, drawn to beauty, picks out of the totality of what there is to be perceived. The artist then assembles the forms into a new package, creating beauty at a higher level of organization. Form, therefore, is both the starting point and the endpoint of the artwork.

A residual idealism reaches into the thought of Fiedler and Hildebrand. And yet it proved possible to look through this idealism: Riegl's studies, which we will pursue into the next section, took up this challenge.

The power of the mind over reality was expressed in a different way by Oscar Wilde, who called Pater's *Studies in the Renaissance* his "golden book" and yet did not himself write poetic art criticism. Wilde is deceptive: his gifts for paradox and aphorism and the absence of philosophical reference points mask the radicality of his thought. Wilde identified the destination of Fiedler's and Hildebrand's doctrines, for once art is no longer evaluated by comparison to nature, there are no limits to the critic's power to shape the evolution of art. In Wilde's dialogue of 1890, "The True Function and Value of Criticism," the straight man Ernest contends that "the Greeks had no art-critics": "By the Ilyssus, my dear Gilbert, there were no silly art congresses, bringing provincialism to the provinces and teaching the mediocrity how to mouth. By the Ilyssus there were no tedious magazines about art, in which the industrious prattle of what they do not understand." The ironist Gilbert, who speaks for Wilde, contradicts him:

> I assure you, my dear Ernest, that the Greeks chattered about painters quite as much as people do now-adays, and had their private views, and shilling exhibitions, and Arts and Crafts guilds, and Pre-Raphaelite movements, and movements towards realism, and lectured about art, and wrote essays on art, and produced their art-historians, and their archæologists, and all the rest of it.

According to Gilbert, the Greeks were in fact "a nation of art-critics." The critic is the one who filters art and literature through a sensibility and a prose style. The critic, for Gilbert and Wilde (and Pater), is anything but a parasite on art. The critic only completes the work of repetition and combination begun by the artist: "I would call criticism a creation within a creation. For just as the great artists, from Homer and Æschylus, down to Shakespeare and Keats, did not go directly to life for their subject-matter, but sought for it in myth, and legend, and ancient tale, so the critic deals with materials that others have, as it were, purified for him, and to which imaginative form and colour have been already added." Art is secondary from the start. The artist is a critic, for does he not also dominate nature with his subjectivity, which has itself already been shaped by art? "The very landscape that Corot looked at was, as he said himself, but a mood of his own mind."

This was Wilde's way of closing the gap between art and life. In Europe art had been stripped of its central role in religious ritual and public life. Most nineteenth-century churches were outfitted with nineteenth-century paintings. But the best nineteenth-century painters had no interest in painting for churches. The modern painter was on his own. The illusions of art were exposed to the pitiless reasonings of commerce and engineering. The artist, dependent on the historians and critics, the authors of immortality, could only hope that his works would find refuge, one day, in the museum. Wilde understands that it is the writers who patrol the frontier between art and life. He strikes back against modern naturalism or realism by arguing that reality itself is generated by a combinatory artistic creativity. Art colonizes life. If life itself is already a work of art, then the artist will never find himself on the outside of life.

Fiedler posited a radical incompatibility of art and life. Life was like art only in the sense that perception was already creative; through this channel alone did life reach into art. The English writers Ruskin, Pater, and Wilde saw life itself as a work of art in a more complete sense, as a project, collective or individual, potentially free, self-realizing, and imagining. Art, in their view, only needed to catch up with life.

In mocking the modern business of art, including historical scholarship, Wilde was striking back, as Nietzsche had done almost thirty years earlier, against the great accumulated pile of writing that loaded the burden of the past on the back of the present. The weight of learning in 1890 seems light when one struggles today, deep in the stacks of an art-history library housing half a million volumes, to part the mobile shelves creaking on their runners. Wilde's solution was economical. Both the judgment of value in the present and the shaping of a narrative of the past would be entrusted to the critic. Historiography is reborn inside the critic's project, and so redeemed:

> To realise the nineteenth century, one must realise every century that has preceded it and that has contributed to its making. To know anything about oneself, one must know all about others. There must be no mood with which one cannot sympathise, no dead mode of life that one cannot make alive.

Can the academic discipline of art history be measured against Wilde's criterion of sympathy? The most innovative art-historical books published in Germany and Austria in the 1890s pushed relativism into new territory. In his *Anfänge des monumentalischen Stils im Mittelalter* (1894), Wilhelm Vöge, professor at Freiburg, defends the French cathedral sculpture of the twelfth century. It is hard to imagine today that the sculptures of the portals of Chartres ever wanted defending. But with their taut robes and vacant expressions they had played only a marginal role in the imagination of the nineteenth century. Vöge quotes the approving comments of Prosper Mérimée in 1836 on the portal of the cathedral of Angers. Vöge addresses directly the supposed problem of the sculptures' ugliness, their "peculiar, eccentric, or degenerated" style.

Vöge was an opiniated but scrupulous scholar, attentive to detail both in the archival record and to the stones. He addressed the Christian subject matter of the works, the worldviews of the patrons, materials and technique, the evolution of styles, and modern restorations. Vöge did not believe that iconography, or the recovery of the lost code that permits us to read medieval art like a book, could help the scholar grasp medieval art as art. The study of medieval Christian iconography had been inaugurated by the French historian Alphonse Didron in his *Iconographie chrétienne: Histoire de Dieu* (1843–1844) and would culminate in the treatise *L'art religieux du XIIIe siècle en France* (1898) by Émile Mâle, which in effect reproduces the theological manual guiding the construction of the cathedrals, a manual that did not in fact exist. Vöge's inspiration was instead Mérimée's accomplice Viollet-le-Duc, whose "incomparable contribution" it was to have "translated archeology into aesthetics," so rediscovering "artistic instincts and ideas." "What would history be, if we were unable to greet the living spirit among the remains of past centuries!" Most remarkable is Vöge's readiness, and by extension the readiness of empiricist art-historical scholarship, to peer into what he called "the hidden process of style-formation." He wants to track art back to its source in the artist. At this deepest and most hidden level, any form can be compared to any other form. From the crypt, he says, all cathedrals look alike. In these shadowy places one has a chance of understanding the "singular beauty" of the early Gothic sculptures.

Vöge's attempts to identify creative individual masters embarrass later art history, perhaps because they prevent medieval art from fitting snugly back into its niche in medieval life, the very niche in life that modernist art renounced. One might describe the contract struck between the nineteenth-century historian and the nineteenth-century art historian as follows: the historian constructs a picture of twelfth-century life with an art-sized gap in it. The art historian is invited to fill that gap. Vöge accepts but emends the contract because he is no longer sure that art will fit tightly into that gap. He detects some quality of art—a quality shared by the severe schematic sculpture of the twelfth century and, say, the sleek wraith-like figures of Puvis de Chavannes—that escapes its historical moment.

The flexibility of this new contract between historical scholarship and aesthetic evaluation recommended it for export. The United States, whose patrician elite were all too aware of their youthful nation's lack of a worthy artistic past, had kept open channels to German, French, and English learning and criticism. American colleges and universities had been offering instruction in the theory and history of art for decades. The New York Free Academy, later City College, held lectures on aesthetics and art history from 1856. The first advanced degree in art history awarded in the United States was given to Elizabeth R. P. Coffin of Vassar College in 1876, for her master's thesis on ancient art. Specialization came quickly: by 1903 the University of Chicago offered a graduate seminar on Botticelli. Multilingualism, or at least reading knowledge of German, was expected of students. The curriculum at the School of Fine Arts at Yale University for 1894–1895 included texts by Hegel, Schnaase, and Kugler as well as Winckelmann, Lessing, Lanzi, Ruskin, Charles Blanc, and John Addington Symonds.

Charles Eliot Norton (1827–1908), a Bostonian who had lived in Europe and cultivated friendly relations with Ruskin and other luminaries, and a translator of Dante, was appointed professor of art history at Harvard in 1875, the first professorship of art history outside a German-speaking country. Norton published *Historical Studies of Church-Building in the Middle Ages* in 1880. His Ruskinian teachings made an impact on the student Bernard Berenson (1865–1959). With his aptitude and taste Berenson won the patronage of the collector Isabella Stewart Gardner, and he set off for Italy with the aim of writing a monograph on the sixteenth-century Venetian painter Lorenzo Lotto, today admired but in the late 1880s not very much. The book was published in 1895.

Berenson evokes in his preface the word "connoisseurship," the eighteenth-century term for lay expertise on art, the knowledge of one who neither makes art nor theorizes about it. With its quaint, partially French spelling the word preserved a link to the ancien régime, to the world of Pierre-Jean Mariette. In 1895 the word "connoisseurship" cast a spell of amnesia, a forgetting of the learned nineteenth century with its seminars, journals, and congresses.

The connoisseur, Berenson says, "pounces upon" the trivial recurring details in a painting—ears, hands, ringlets of hair, bits of landscape, awkwardnesses of attitude—because here the painter relies on learned habit. The details will reveal the master's training, his antecedents, the riddle of his novitiate—for we cannot trust the written sources on matters like this, they are worth little more than gossip. Even Vasari, who knew Lotto's works and a few stories about his life, is untrustworthy. The ostensible aim of Berenson's book is to disprove, on the basis of observation alone, Vasari's statement that Lotto was the pupil of Giovanni Bellini. This he does by deriving Lotto's treatment of ears, hands, and hair from Alvise Vivarini.

Then the real project of the book begins. Berenson's aim is not to trace artistic genealogies but to sympathize with the artist, to know his mind. One begins by bracketing out not only those acquired habits of execution, precisely mindless, but also habits of attention, habits of "visualization," habits of thought, in fact all habits—anything that Lotto acquired not only from his teacher but from his contemporaries, from society, from books. "All of them the spectator must be able to deduct before he is approximately sure of having before him an idea of the master." Art is the direct confrontation between an irreducible individual soul, unreachable by society, and the facts of nature and human nature. The critic, not the connoisseur, reconstructs this confrontation.

Berenson is uninterested in the original functions of Lotto's paintings—the role of altarpieces in ritual, for example, or the role of portraits in family politics. He is uninterested in the worldviews of Lotto's patrons. He in uninterested in materials and techniques. He is interested only in psychology. He revels in the revelations of a lucid portrait of a young married couple. He finds in a family portrait a "trace of the 'bitterness of things,'" comparing it to Tolstoy's novel *Katia, or Family Happiness* (1859).

Berenson savors the neurotic gestures of the characters in the Recanati *Annunciation*: the angel "filled with the awe of his own message," the leaping cat, and flustered Mary, hand raised, wheeling as if to appeal to the viewer. "As execution, this is one of Lotto's best works [as usual Berenson does not tell us why], and as interpretation—well, nowhere else has a

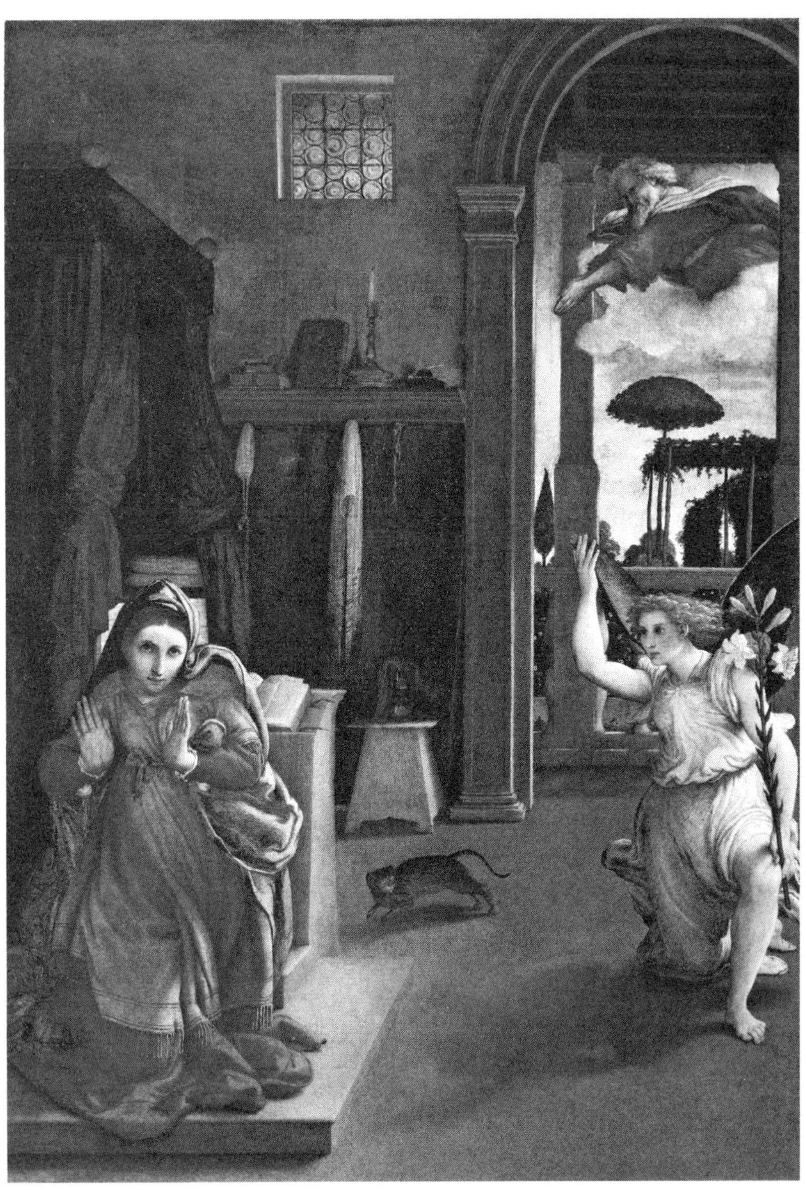

Lorenzo Lotto, *Annunciation* (c. 1534). Oil on canvas, 166 × 114 cm. Recanati, Pinacoteca Civica. The cat is either a symbol of evil, driven from the scene by the holy visitor, or merely a cat.

painter of this subject ventured to portray the woman in the Virgin." It is a chain of high-strung temperaments communicating one with another: Lotto the psychologist finds what he is seeking in the inner life of his contemporaries, of his models; Berenson clambers among the chapels and sacristies of the Marches in search of the then-obscure artist Lotto; Berenson makes his appreciation, which can only be a sincere "confession," in his book. There is a woman at the beginning of the chain, and no doubt at the end as well, as reader. Women played a greater role in Berenson's world than in academia, where gender was a formidable, in fact in the 1890s still an impenetrable, barrier. Among the aesthetes and connoisseurs, by contrast, class was a greater obstacle than gender.

Lotto, once free of his teacher's influence—just as Berenson was free of the university—proved an improviser, an eccentric, an individualist. He was "endowed with an exquisite sense for decoration, not of the architectonic, monumental sort, but…of the more personal, Gothic, or Japanese kind." "Gothic" or "Japanese" in the 1890s are code words for indifference to classical proportions and to the mainstream tradition of academic form rooted in the idealized nude body. "Decoration" is a code word for the taste for fragments of form and color detached from illustration or content. Berenson associates Lotto with the anti-academic painters Edgar Degas and Édouard Manet. In his attentiveness to deviation from the norm, Berenson resembles a medical pathologist, a forensic scientist, or a detective. But his aims are the reverse. Since art is not life—at least not until we are all living in a world designed by Oscar Wilde—non-observance of the norm can be treasured rather than corrected.

"The perfect masterpiece…must give us the attitude of a typical human being toward the universe. The perfect criticism should give us the measure of the acceptability at a given time of the work of art in question." By "a given time" Berenson means the critic's own time. For Berenson, as for Wilde, art inhabits two time frames only: eternity, or the present. What lies between—the historical lives of the artwork, the work in its original settings and in its multiple receptions across time—they leave to the academic scholar.

Beyond the Lotto monograph Berenson was basically an attributionist. His main project and source of income was identifying the authors of early Italian paintings and drawings. In 1890 he met Giovanni Morelli, who gave him letters of introduction that gave him access to the more remote Lotto paintings. He began work on his magnum opus, the

Drawings of the Florentine Painters (1903), a three-volume catalogue consisting entirely of descriptions, attributions, and concise but evocative phrases. It is highly opinionated, a mesh of deep familiarity. Berenson's connoisseurship is unmediated and practical, a kind of craftsman's knowledge raised to the second degree. The knowledge of the connoisseur was not so much parasitical on the painter's knowledge as a successor to it, for connoisseurship emerges just as in painting the process of de-skilling sets in. Connoisseurship is fetishistic, private, inalienable, and evasive of custom. Berenson was learned, but his approach to pictures was "pre-alphabetical," a kind of somatic thinking. He intuits, he thinks by seeing. He sees family resemblances, for he is a familiar of the artist. He mistrusts ideas, systems, narratives, and rules. Connoisseurial writing tends in two directions: either toward mutism or toward poeticizing singularity. Berenson points and gestures, just as Mariette had; as if he were simply indicating to the collector which work to bid on. It is a binary gesture of approval or disapproval; criticism (*krinein* = to separate) in its purest form. But Berenson, a disciple of Walter Pater—"the greatest writer," he says in his Lotto book—is a prose poet. He marks his own prose as neurotic, singular; Lotto-like, with weird quasi-neologisms like "embogged" or "pronest." He is anyway never professorial.

The idea that knowledge about art is a personal, bodily knowledge would seem to align with a humble conception of craft. In fact, connoisseurship reassociates art-historical scholarship with social privilege. The museums offered art to the people. The publications of the academic scholars with their increasingly effective illustrations were just that, a "making public." Connoisseurship stresses the limits of teachability. Ability to judge is intuitive and not easily acquired. Even given aptitude, one requires access. An American at that point could not become a connoisseur of European art without spending long years in Europe in constant contact with works. "Vicarious" experience, as Berenson says, will not suffice.

Collectors, eager to connect through works of art to other distinctive individuals, to artists, to a natural aristocracy, were happy to hear this. Collectors also know that works of art are good investments, attractive furnishings, status symbols. Art historians, too, know that works of art function this way but prefer to think of this as something that happened mostly in the past. This is the subject matter of the study of artistic patronage. Historians of premodern artistic patronage like to think of anti-academic modern artists as liberated from patronage. But this was only a half-truth, as Berenson knew. Degas and Manet were nearly as dependent on their patrons as Lotto had been. Still, the modern Maecenas is on the defensive and craves a redemptive account of what art was and is. Berenson could be found at the heart of this paradox, as both the generator of the redemptive story and as the beneficiary of the free market of art, through commissions on sales where he had provided counsel. Berenson was much admired by many academic art historians, Heinrich Wölfflin for example, for his good judgment. But the prospect of a commission (as much as 25 percent with the dealer Joseph Duveen, who sold pictures to Isabella Stewart Gardner!) could not but exert a magnetic pull on an attribution.

A great reader of both Pater and Berenson, and a rival as stylist and as poetic historian of art, was Violet Paget (1856–1935), who published among many other books and essays *Renaissance Fancies and Studies* (1895), a sequel to her collection of essays entitled *Euphorion: Being Studies of the Antique and the Mediaeval in the Renaissance* (1884). Like Giovanni Morelli, she wrote behind an authorial mask, a pseudonym that hid her gender: Vernon Lee. In "The Imaginative Art of the Renaissance," one of the essays in *Renaissance Fancies and Studies*, Lee divides art into two broad categories. There is the art "which, beyond or independent of the charm of visible beauty, possesses a charm that acts directly upon the imagination" through the impressions and thoughts it summons. It is created by an "imagination which delights the mind by holding before it some charming or uncommon object, and conjuring up therewith a whole train of feeling and fancy; the school, we might call it, of intellectual decoration, of arabesques formed not of lines and colours, but of associations and suggestions." Lee was also a theorist of art who introduced to English readers the teachings of Robert Vischer and other German psychologists and aestheticians on empathy, or sense-based identification, as the source of pleasure in art.

But there is also a narrative art that imagines "how an event would have looked; the power of understanding and showing how an action would have taken place, and how that action would have affected the bystanders; a sort of second-sight, occasionally rising to the point of revealing, not merely the material aspect of things and people, but the emotional value of the event in the eyes of the painter." Lee's aim is to turn conventional taste inside out by developing a new basis for the appreciation of the frescoes of Giotto and of his fourteenth-century followers, neglected by Burckhardt and Pater.

To the first category of imaginative art, she assigns Fra Angelico, Benozzo Gozzoli, Botticelli, and the Venetians. Her emphasis on the associative qualities of the depicted objects, rather than on the style, allows her to connect these artists, with some condescension, to a wider world of art:

> This is one of the peculiarities of rudimentary art—of the art of the early Renaissance as well as of that of Persia and India, of Constantinople, of every peasant potter all through the world: that, not knowing very well its own aims, it fills its imperfect work with suggestion of all manner of things which it loves, and tries to gain in general pleasurableness what it loses in actual achievement; and lays hold of us, like fragments of verse, by suggestiveness, quite as much as by pictorial realisation.

Such judgments, however, cannot be disentangled from Lee's freethinking dismissals of the beloved treasures of the Florentine Quattrocento, for example the many anodyne Annunciations, a "crowd of unimpressive, nay brainless, representations of one of the grandest and sweetest of all stories":

> It never seems to have occurred to any one that the Virgin and the Archangel might be displayed otherwise than each in one corner of the picture. Such a composition as that of Rossetti's Ancilla Domini, where the Virgin cowers on her bed as the angel floats in with flames round his feet; such a suggestion as that of the unfinished lily on the embroidery frame, was reserved for our sceptical and irreverent, but imaginative times.

The Quattrocento painters are impoverished as narrators, in comparison to the Pre-Raphaelites like Dante Gabriel Rossetti, because the monumental paintings of Giotto and his followers left them nothing to do. The Giottesques narrate so well that "to describe the picture, it almost suffices to narrate the story, no arrangements of different planes and of light and shade, no peculiarities of form, foreshortening, colour, or texture requiring to be seen in order to be fully understood."

This narrative gift is also the art sought after by the crowd: "the recognised commodity: artistic imagination, as bought and sold in the market, whether of good quality or bad." The Quattrocento painters will instead develop the other, lesser gift. Vernon Lee writes a refined art criticism that is also a sketch of a never-written history of Renaissance art.

1900–1910

In the second chapter of E.M. Forster's novel *A Room with a View* (1908), the upper-middle-class heroine Lucy Honeychurch wanders into a famous church in Florence without her guidebook:

> How could she find her way about in Santa Croce? Her first morning was ruined, and she might never be in Florence again. A few minutes ago she had been all high spirits, talking as a woman of culture, and half persuading herself that she was full of originality. Now she entered the church depressed and humiliated, not even able to remember whether it was built by the Franciscans or the Dominicans. Of course, it must be a wonderful building. But how like a barn! And how very cold! Of course, it contained frescoes by Giotto, in the presence of whose tactile values she was capable of feeling what was proper. But who was to tell her which they were? She walked about disdainfully, unwilling to be enthusiastic over monuments of uncertain authorship or date. There was no one even to tell her which, of all the sepulchral slabs that paved the nave and transepts, was the one that was really beautiful, the one that had been most praised by Mr. Ruskin.

Lucy Honeychurch, if we are to trust the modern novelist's free indirect discourse, which opens a window directly onto her thoughts, is a well-read tourist, for the phrase "tactile values" had only been introduced to writing on early Italian art by Bernard Berenson in 1896. It is less surprising that she frets about John Ruskin, whose *Mornings in Florence* (1875–1877) had supplemented many a Baedeker and Murray. In that book, in his description of the Bardi Chapel in S. Croce, Ruskin had taken the figure of St. Louis, brazenly invented by the restorer Gaetano Bianchi in 1852, to be a masterpiece by Giotto. In Forster's novel Lucy visits the Peruzzi Chapel right next door. Ruskin goes on and on for pages about the St. Louis, the subject Giotto was most likely to take up with the maximum of "care and delight." He concedes that "your Murray's guide" tells you the figure may have been restored, but he is undaunted: this is "Giotto in his consummate strength, and nothing lost, in form, of the complete design." Raimond van Marle as late as 1924 attributed the St. Louis to Giotto: "His round face is not very beautiful but full of individuality." The extent of Bianchi's interventions was not revealed until 1937.

Historical scholarship sets traps for itself. To avoid the traps is not necessarily to arrive at art. Scholarship filtered into the guidebooks and guided the tourist's encounters with the paintings.

Henry Adams, the reluctant tourist of 1860, pondering the forty-foot dynamos in the Great Exposition of 1900 in Paris, sensed with alarm their "moral force, much as the early Christians felt the Cross." He saw "only an absolute *fiat* in electricity as in faith." Physics was occupied with a "supersensual world" of "chance collisions"—physics was "stark mad in metaphysics." The pragmatic and human-scaled thinking that had sustained the fond narratives of nineteenth-century historians seemed feckless, disoriented.

In 1904 the philosopher Henri Bergson wrote a memoir of his teacher Félix Ravaisson (1813–1900). Ravaisson had written a thesis on Aristotle's *Metaphysics*; in Germany he sought out Schelling. Later he developed a new pedagogy of drawing. He studied archeology and ancient Greek sculpture. Inspired by Leonardo da Vinci's writings, Ravaisson believed that art gave access to a real realm of permanent forms hidden behind visible reality. Through Ravaisson, Bergson glimpses a counterfactual world, another modernity in which art history plays a different role, a picture of a different configuration of art, research, and thought. There is limited compatibility between Ravaisson's and Bergson's metaphysics and professionalized, matter-of-fact scholarship. Art for the metaphysician either belongs to the deceptive screen, and so can be set aside; or is the portal to the unseen. Only one who already has an idea of what lies behind can even recognize the portal.

The convulsive reaction to the earthbound quality of nineteenth-century thought took many forms. Aby Warburg (1866–1929), whom we glimpsed in Florence among August Schmarsow's pupils, was the eldest son of a Hamburg banking family. He defied his parents by pursuing art-historical studies, enrolling at the universities of Bonn, Munich, and Strasbourg, where he wrote a dissertation on Sandro Botticelli's *Primavera* and *Birth of Venus*. In 1895 Warburg undertook a journey to the American Southwest in search of the secrets of ritual and gesture. He saw this as time travel, historical distance mapped onto space. The origins of art in traumatic experience became Warburg's great topic. Later he would write of "the experience of religious ritual as the primal mint for the expressive systems of tragic passions." In 1898 Warburg settled in Florence, where he pursued his studies of fifteenth-century Florentine art. Here he saw Adolf von Hildebrand, but also Bernard Berenson, whom he did not like. To Berenson he preferred Herbert Horne, an English scholar, like himself walking a non-academic path, who was preparing a magisterial monograph on Botticelli. Horne's study, published in 1908, is built on archival documents, reproduced in the book as an appendix. He provides much political, social, and literary context and only very few but precise comments on the pictures, evocative assessments of quality and originality. Warburg, too, immersed himself in archives and books, but his relation to art, unlike Horne's, was not sensuous. Warburg did not collect art and took little interest in the art of his own time. Schmarsow's thinking on art as an encounter between bodies in space may have convinced him that the nineteenth century had overrated the visual character of art.

Herbert Horne was one of the real-life people after whom Marcel Proust drew his character Charles Swann, a Parisian gentleman who filled his leisure hours writing a monograph on the seventeenth-century Dutch painter Vermeer. Others who inhabit the character of Swann are the *mondain* Charles Haas, *habitué* of the studio of Edgar Degas; Théophile Thoré-Bürger; and Charles Ephrussi, a banker, editor of the *Gazette des Beaux-Arts* and author of a major study of Albrecht Dürer's drawings. In the first volume of his *In Search of Lost Time*, which he began to compose in 1909, Proust compares Charles Swann's obsessive attempts to reconstruct the mysterious social life of his lover Odette to the passion of the aesthete ransacking the Florentine archives in hopes of penetrating the soul of the Primavera, the central allegorical figure of Botticelli's painting. With Aby Warburg it was just the opposite. He was not interested either in the soul of the Primavera or in the soul of the artist who imagined her.

Instead he was interested in the patrons and scholars who conceived and paid for the picture. He was struck by the power of the figures in the *Primavera* with their swirling draperies and tangled tresses—Venus, Spring, Flora, the Graces—to emerge from the past and seize the present. Artist, patron, and modern beholder alike, in Warburg's account, are at best only coping with the living force of such images.

In 1902 Warburg moved back to Hamburg. He published an essay, entitled "The Art of Portraiture and the Florentine Bourgeoisie," about the frescoes in the Sassetti Chapel in Santa Trinita in Florence, painted in the early 1480s by Domenico Ghirlandaio, the teacher of Michelangelo. Warburg focused on a represention of a historical event, the Confirmation of the Franciscan Order by Pope Honorius III in 1223. Ghirlandaio introduced into the scene lifelike portraits of the patron Francesco Sassetti, a banker, together with his family and his own patron, Lorenzo de' Medici, the Magnificent, as well as Lorenzo's sons together with their tutor, the poet and scholar Angelo Poliziano, whose works were the basis for the *Primavera*. These latter personages, vivid and alert, climb a flight of stairs and emerge upon the ceremony that took place a quarter of a millenium earlier. Through archival study Warburg identified and so revived these people.

Warburg saw that the Italian painters' new ability to render exact likenesses in oil paint, which they had learned from Netherlandish painters, had changed the rules of the game of fifteenth-century art, just as photography had changed the rules of the game of nineteenth-century art. The portraits of the Sassetti and the Medici are direct, unmediated links to the lived experience of fifteenth-century Florentines. By insisting upon the portraits' domination of the work of art containing them, Warburg dismissed the idea that the calling of art was to improve upon reality. The raw portrait did not want redeeming by the surrounding subject matter, which for Warburg was empty, because already historical in Sassetti's time. From Warburg's point of view, Fiedler and Hildebrand, for all their updated terminology, had only been extending the theoretical project of the Renaissance itself, namely idealism, which had supported the invidious comparisons between Italian and Netherlandish art. Warburg does not recognize a distinction between matter and spirit. In general he was uninterested in philosophy, and at university he studied psychology and medicine. For this reason, perhaps, he was not captivated by the tension between freedom and rule; and in the rivalries between the real and the fictive, or the body and the mind, he tended to side with the former terms.

Warburg shared with Jacob Burckhardt and Hippolyte Taine, and by now many others—Robert Browning, George Eliot, John Addington Symonds—a predilection for the Quattrocento. The obsession of the bourgeois northern European with Florence was easily satirized, as for example by Thomas Mann in his short story "Gladius Dei" (1902). Undeterred, Warburg described the poetry and painting of the Quattrocento as an "art of life" (*Lebenskunst*), an "occasional art" with "the power to draw nourishment from its roots, which rest in the soil of everyday life." Like Burckhardt, Warburg was partial to the mentalities of the merchant and the potentate, but he was also interested in the emergence of the laboring classes into representability in French tapestries and in popular printed broadsheets, coarse woodcuts that until now had played no role in histories of art. These were the very years when the Milanese scholar Achille Bertarelli began to assemble his vast collection of popular prints, now in the Castello Sforzesco in Milan.

Warburg was impressed by the fervid embrace of religious superstition and astrological determinism not only by the people but also by the elite. Warburg interprets the painted portraits in the Sassetti Chapel as transpositions into two dimensions of an archaic devotional practice, a survival of ancient pagan customs: the placing of wax effigies in sacred spaces to guarantee the connection between the votary in this world and the other world. A wax effigy of Lorenzo de' Medici, for example, outfitted with real clothes and hair, was mounted in the nearby church of Santissima Annunziata only a few years before Ghirlandaio undertook his painting:

> Only a comparison with this ceremonial, legitimate, and long-enduring barbaric custom of displaying the wax figure in the church itself, in fancy dress, defiant and mouldering, allows the portrait-like quality of the historical figures in the fresco in the church to appear in a truer and more favorable light: in comparison to the fetishistic magic of the wax images this attempt to approach the divinity through merely painted images was relatively discreet.

The art of portraiture is sustained not only by sublunary pragmatism and the desire to memorialize but also by a dread of the unknown and a desire to tame hidden forces.

For Warburg, mastery of nature, in life or in paint, was only ever a fantasy. The true source of creativity is the loss of self, in fear and ecstasy. Warburg was prompted by the evolutionary theorist Tito Vignoli, who argued that primitive man reacted to a dimly comprehended environment with the "phobic reflex of cause projection," a defensive warding off of malevolent forces. Warburg believed that the traumatic experiences of archaic man were imprinted in pictorial symbols, concretizations of "emotionally heightened gestures" (*pathetisch gesteigerte Mimik*) provoked by loss of composure in self-defense, confusion, ecstasy, inspiration, or anger. The gestures are transferred to the agitation of limbs, drapery, tangled tresses of hair, even foliage, as the projection of emotional states. He called these gestures and displays *Pathosformel*, or "pathos-formulas." The most striking examples are the nymphs of the agitated gait and fluttering drapery that reappear in the paintings of Ghirlandaio and Botticelli. These hieroglyphs of strong emotions are passed down from picture to picture through history. The pictures within which the hieroglyphs appeared were only accidental way stations, stopping places. As direct registrations of the past, they dominate any context they appear in. Gestures are not culturally coded, or only minimally so, and beholders do not need keys to read them. Warburg was a close reader of Charles Darwin's *Expression of the Emotions in Man and Animals* (1872), which weighed the innate and learned components of facial expressions and gestures. The pathos-formulas are dense focal points of nonconventional, nonarbitrary signification, like the realistic portraits embedded in the historical frescoes. The pathos-formula has the power to persist through all the corruptions of contingent history, including the history of art. The pathos-formula arrives from antiquity, but not the antiquity that so preoccupied Warburg's century.

The notion that we are governed by images from a primordial past is a cheerless one, not so far removed from the mentality of the Ferrarese prince who had planetary gods painted on the walls of the ceremonial hall of his palace, including avatars of Indian demons, the subject of Warburg's article "Italian Art and International Astrology in the Palazzo Schifanoia, Ferrara" (1912). Warburg's sympathy for the superstitious could not be more remote from the liberal rationalism of Fiedler, Hildebrand, and Riegl.

Warburg, like Fiedler or Wilde, was not satisfied to let art stand alongside life either as an ornament or as a reflecting mirror, the subordinate functions to which modern life had seemed to relegate art. Each of these thinkers instead wanted to let art and life flow into one another. But Warburg's model is the reverse of Fiedler's and Wilde's. They see life as already shaped by the mind. Warburg, by contrast, sees the work of art as already paralyzed by the force of real life, which arrives unbidden in the form of the agitated gesture. The work of art is saturated by life before the mind can even begin to contemplate it. The pathos-formulas were potent long before they ever appeared in paintings. Warburg believes that the mimic gestures or fluttering drapery represented in the paintings would have the same effect on beholders if they were perceived in real life.

Since he was not interested in a stable encounter between beholder and artwork, Warburg did not accord the art of painting any privilege. He had no concept of the work of art as a synoptic unit. He took no interest in describing the relationships between figure and ground or framing devices that might structure painted forms as a composition. For Warburg, the human figure and its immediate accessories—drapery, hair—are the alpha and the omega of the artwork. In his dissertation on Botticelli, Warburg traced the drapery effects in theatrical pageants and in poetry, as much as in the paintings. He adopted the point of view of anthropology, at that time a new discipline or not yet a discipline: namely, that art is continuous with other forms of symbolic behavior.

Warburg downplayed the input of the painter: "If one assumes that the dramas of the time placed those figures physically before the eyes of the artist, as elements of a truly animated life, then the process of artistic shaping seems obvious." Warburg was uninterested in master-pupil genealogies and in attributions. His art history speaks neither to the academic artist, nor to the anti-academic artist, nor to the aesthete who hopes to commune with the artist. But this does not mean he discounted the past—quite the opposite, for images travelled through artists. Collective memory for Warburg was not a hermeneutic process of choosing to remember only what "interests" or engages us, a process invoked by the nineteenth-century historians Johann Gustav Droysen and Wilhelm Dilthey. History is not a conversation with the past. Instead, in Warburg, memory is carried forward to us, objectively, by the sequence of pathos-formulas. We do not choose our past, it chooses us.

This was not an entirely direful story. The pathos-formulas register danger but they also ward it off, apotropaically. Art creates the psychic distance that gives mankind a chance in its struggles with hostile nature or with the gods.

288

The historical relativist is the one who adopts an eagle's-eye view on the past, lofty enough not to need to prefer one epoch to another. Warburg was no such relativist. For him the European Renaissance, Burckhardt's Renaissance, the fifteenth century, held the keys to the present. He was fully absorbed by the epic of Europe. The "Orient" figured for Warburg only as a mystifying threat to Mediterranean reason, a passive source of fascination, coded as female. The non-Western here is the image of a hidden weakness within the West. America, meanwhile, sheltered the remnants of the archaic societies it destroyed and at the same time promised a telecommunicational future of "instantaneous electric connection" where "mythical and symbolic thinking," which once formed "spiritual bonds between humanity and the surrounding world, shaping distance into the space required for devotion and reflection," would no longer be needed.

Warburg refused an academic appointment and instead built his library, installing it in a townhouse in Hamburg and later transforming it into a research center.

Less unnerved by the past's hold on the present, it would seem, was Warburg's older contemporary Alois Riegl, who in 1901 published *Die spätrömische Kunst-Industrie, nach den Funden in Österreich-Ungarn* (The Late Roman Art Industry Based on the Finds in Austria-Hungary). This was the first installment of a research report commissioned by the Austrian state responding to recent archeological discoveries in the eastern parts of the Austro-Hungarian empire, the lands corresponding to the ancient Roman provinces of Pannonia, Dacia, and Illyria. Riegl was supposed to report on excavated metalwork and jewelry. The first 250 pages of the book, before he arrives at the jewelry, are dedicated to the architecture, sculpture, wall paintings, and mosaics of the Roman empire. All of the book's twenty-three full-page plates are dedicated to material from the last chapter: buckles, clasps, pendants, and brooches dating from the third to the sixth centuries. The chapter classes the objects not chronologically but by formal modes: perforated or open-work, chip-carving, garnet-settings, enamel, and so forth.

Ornamental and applied arts had been much in view since the mid-nineteenth century. The "art industry" (*Kunstindustrie*) of the title was not a coinage of Riegl's but a term generally in use. Gottfried Semper in his treatise *Style* had used it to refer to jewelry, weapons, weaving, pottery, and household utensils, whether handmade or industrially produced. Riegl's aim in planting the term in his title was to disorient: there was no surer way to demystify the prestigious art of antiquity than to label it the product of industry.

No one had written an art history that so tightly braided all the arts together into a single narrative. Riegl refused to depreciate the graceless forms of the late imperial and Byzantine period. His account of the mosaics of Ravenna was a final overcoming of Vasari (even if Vasari had praised the worksmanship of the mosaics in his introduction). Riegl's Viennese contemporary, the painter Gustav Klimt, went to see them in 1903. The late imperial buildings are not treated as a decline from the still-Greek earlier imperial structures. But most significant was his account of the reliefs on the Arch of Constantine in Rome (AD 315). These were the very works that the painter Raphael had chosen, in the letter of c. 1519 attributed to him and (usually) Baldassare Castiglione, and addressed to Pope Leo X, to make a point about the decline of ancient style. Raphael differentiated, on the basis of style, between two sets of reliefs on the arch, one group dating from the Trajanic period (spoils, in effect) and the other from Constantine's time. Raphael was introducing difference into the image of ancient art, asserting that one period was capable of great art while another no longer is. Riegl notes the same difference, but then points out that each period had its own aims. To judge the Constantinian reliefs on the arch for their non-ideal bodies is to impose criteria from another time and place and to misunderstand the aims of that period. Here Riegl was following his colleague Franz Wickhoff, who in 1895 had published a monograph on the the fourth-century miniatures in the Austrian National Library known as the Vienna Genesis. Wickhoff detected in the manuscript's loose, disintegrating treatment of form the origins of modern coloristic, impressionistic painting, from Diego Velázquez to the Impressionists themselves.

Wickhoff and Riegl's redemption of the early Christian works overturned the standard narrative of European culture set in place by Petrarch, in which the arts declined together with the empire into ruin and confusion. Even in the flush of Romantic enthusiasm for Gothic architecture, and later for Gothic sculptural form, no one had eyes for the art of the earliest Middle Ages or of late antiquity. Jacob Burckhardt, who in his account of the Italian Renaissance downplayed the classical revival, maintained conventional disparaging views about late antique art in his book *The Age of Constantine the Great* (1853).

Riegl deduced from morphology, or the itineraries of form, an impulse or drive to satisfying form, which he called the *Kunstwollen* or "art-will." It suits him not to locate that drive too literally in the psyche of an artist or craftsman. Nor does he anthropomorphize artifacts by endowing them with will. Instead, *Kunstwollen* is a property of forms that permits the historian to attribute meaning to relations among forms.

Riegl's basic axiom is that each epoch, each society, each artist seeks satisfaction in form:

> All human will is directed toward a satisfactory shaping of man's relationship to the world, in the most comprehensive sense of this word, within and beyond the individual. The plastic will-to-form (*Kunstwollen*) regulates man's relationship to the sensorily perceptible appearance of things. Art expresses the way man wants to see things shaped or colored, just as the poetic *Kunstwollen* expresses the way man wants to imagine them. Man is not only a passive, sensorily recipient being, but also a desiring, active being who wishes to interpret the world in such a way (varying from one people, region, or epoch to another) that it most clearly and obligingly meets his desires.

In proposing that the mind shapes reality in its own image, Riegl echoes Fiedler. But Riegl's historical "man" is more acquisitive and self-serving than Fiedler's aesthete. The *Kunstwollen* recreates the world as the world it wants.

Riegl's analytical tools respect no distinction between a brooch and a painting. Each work is a closed system operating with limited variables. Manipulations of the variables generate an infinite range of responses in beholders. From the traces left by the *Kunstwollen* in form the historian reads worldviews and sensibilities.

For Riegl it was the late Roman metalwork and jewelry that made the crucial break with the ancient Mediterranean conception of art that had persisted in stimulating the "tactile" imagination, both in its imperious and auratic figurative art and in its ornamental art, tied through figuration and symbolism to the natural world. The early medieval artifacts abolished any clear distinction between figure and ground through light and dark contrasts shimmering in a shallow plane. This happened especially in the jewelry of the fourth, fifth, and sixth centuries.

The new opticality implied a new and modern format: the framed tableau. For Riegl, the tableau is received by the beholder as a layer of light and color hovering perpendicularly in the middle distance. This layer, a dematerialized apparition, proposes a virtual reality and invites the beholder to participate in that reality intellectually. In the "colorism" of these artifacts—their fusing of pattern and ground into a single integrated apparition—he sees the template for the purely optical constitution of the modern work of art. This is the template of the modern Western artwork, the one that Warburg rejected: the framed and stable field, cut off from the world, where figure and ground can forever switch places, ground becoming figure, figure becoming ground; a conceptual space where forms and colors enact a miniature drama for the attentive gaze of the individual beholder. The breakdown of the distinction between figure and ground allows the artifact as a whole to cohere and detach itself from the rest of the world, as if the work itself were now a figure set off against the ground of life. The optical objectivism of the metalwork was the key step in the historical establishment of the autonomy of the artwork.

Riegl smooths out the tangles of Roman history. But Riegl's relativism is limited. He is always on the side of history's winners—that is, with the barbarians, against Rome. As is so often the case, shapings of history designed to bring out lost sources of vitality call upon fictions of ethnicity or race as their medium. Riegl also believes that each epoch and each artist is contributing to a vaster story that they themselves are unaware of. Riegl's formal analyses feed into a narrative of Mediterranean and northern European art history stretching from prehistory to the Baroque, with implications for the art of his own time. The shape of this story is more or less Hegelian, though without the prospect of a metaphysical apotheosis. This is a narrative of the increasing authority of cognition, for the mind profits from the dematerialization, which seems to license a disengagement of art from practical functions. It is also teleological, as Riegl says in *Late Roman Art Industry*: cultures and peoples that are unable to participate in this history are shunted aside:

> Byzantine art, which continued to adhere to the ancient notion of the closed individual isolated form as the goal of all plastic arts, thereby excluded itself from that future and so from the second half of the middle ages lost all significance within the progress of the European art development.

No one is free; we are not even free to react to the environment. Only the art historian can see the overall pattern, from his vantage point at the end of history, that is, after the proliferation of historical citations in the nineteenth century had dismembered the history of art.

The art academies had offered a story of art as the conquest, loss, and finally reconquest of nature through the mastery of illusionistic technology, improved by a grasp of ideal beauty. Romanticism replaced this with the story of art as an acquisition and then loss of wisdom, warning us not to mistake naturalism or technical skill for such wisdom. Historicism proposed that each period expresses its view of the world through its own forms; no art form can be preferred for they are all true registrations of the evolving mind. Materialism, finally, a version of historicism, told the story of art as a series of local responses to conditions, materials, tools, and functions. The immediate purpose of Riegl's teleology was to counter the crass reductionism of the materialist version. He did this by insinuating that there was something animating the history of form, a ghost in the machine, a will to form that overrode pragmatic needs. There is a tension in Riegl's art history between the anthropomorphic concept of *Kunstwollen*, which locates the motor of history in the individual, and the teleological shape of history, the inexorable dematerialization and intellectualization of art, a schema inherited from Hegel and never justified philosophically by Riegl.

For Riegl, all art is naturalistic; it is simply that each epoch sees nature differently. *What* they see is the true object of art. This transforms art history into a history of seeing, and therefore of thinking. Riegl corrects Hildebrand by identifying—implicitly—impressionistic painting, not relief sculpture, as the task of the present. Dispelling any lingering nostalgia associated with the Romantic embrace of medieval art, Riegl reinstated the progressivism of the ancien régime. Riegl also solved a paradox of academic doctrine, wedded to the ideal: its tendency to summon its own subversion by reality, or by lowly life. Now that the story line is the movement from touch-based art to vision-based art, the future is open-ended, for art can always be further intellectualized without worrying about a surfeit of sublimity or transcendence, just as low subject matter does not threaten to drag art back into the weeds of practical life. Riegl's dematerialization "saves the appearances": what appeared to some as technical decline in the Middle Ages, and to others as authenticity, was in fact underground work on the overall project. What appeared to be the pomp and decadence of the Baroque was actually the pursuit of formal disintegration. Instead of a conquest of nature tempered by idealism, which periodically fails and has to be restarted—or the opposite, an apprehension of spirit periodically pulled back to earth by mere creaturely life—we are presented with a steady, unidirectional process without real regression, pauses, or catastrophes.

Riegl was a rationalist, and yet his overall narrative is a fantasy. It was just the combination of the fantastical and the objective in Riegl that appealed to twentieth-century readers. Some of his modern commenders, like Georg Lukács and Walter Benjamin, shared his confidence in the meaningfulness of historical evolution. Others, like Henri Maldiney or Gilles Deleuze and Félix Guattari, have not shared that belief in evolution but have been able nonetheless to extract from the dematerialization narrative the principle of art's underivability from non-artistic material. It is as if the dematerialization narrative—haptic to optic, body to mind—were only one possible picture of art's historical life and could be replaced by any number of others, or even no picture at all, as long as the basic principle of art's autonomy was safe.

Riegl redeems the museum and at the same time puts it in its place. The academic discipline of art history sets itself up as a superior discourse that justifies, through historicization, the ideal attentiveness that the museum solicits. Academic art historians since Riegl are apt to consider the museum an atavistic institution attached to a primitive conception of art as possession. As if the museum that hoards ancient gold and garnets were no more than a treasury until the art historian succeeds in explaining why jewelry and oil painting belong under the same roof. The art historian crafts a new, conceptual roof and so crowns the museum.

Riegl's *Dutch Group Portrait* appeared in 1902 as a long article in a scholarly journal and was reprinted as a book in 1931. Although focused on one of art history's fortunate epochs, Holland of the seventeenth century, the book dealt neither with the Biblical narratives of Rembrandt van Rijn nor with Jan Vermeer's domestic meditations but with a kind of applied art: the group portraits that documented bourgeois society. The paintings were unpromising because they seemed to offer nothing beyond simulacra of men seated at tables in dark rooms, involved in no meaningful action. There seems to be no content beyond the objective transcriptions of physiognomies. Riegl's series of patient analyses of paintings starts in the fifteenth century and culminates in the great works of Frans Hals and Rembrandt. His terms of analysis are subordination—the imposition of an ordering principle from outside upon the gathered company—and coordination—the composition's internal self-governing through depiction of the sitters' awareness of the other sitter's presences, through body language and glances. The historical life of the men, their social existence, is unmentioned in Riegl's analyses, because it is all already there in the paintings.

These were militia companies, civic brotherhoods of citizens who gathered to eat and drink and celebrate the national liberty that their forefathers had won in the revolt against the Spanish crown. The portraits were hung in the clubhouses of the companies. The visitor to the quarters of the Companies of St. George or St. Adrian in Haarlem in 1627 saw hovering before him a virtual feast, in life-size. The militia companies were now idle, merely festive institutions. The militiamen reveled in the prosperity of their young nation, commerce-oriented, proto-democratic, and Protestant. They cultivated the arts of peace, poetry, and painting. The portrayed individuals, senses heightened, are relaxed but alert to one another, watching, questioning, enjoying one another. Aesthetic experience itself is figured in the pictures, in the many miniature dramas of mutual attentiveness. The realism endows the portrayed individuals with fictional interiority so that they are able to engage in fictional psychic interactions with each other and with the beholder.

Riegl adds a dimension to the doctrine of pure visibility. He acknowledges a content of art superior to all other contents, more meaningful even than perception, to wit, the possibility of communication with the minds of others. When painting can represent attentiveness and sympathy, then the circuit between beholder and painting is closed. The beholder takes over art history. Art history as a discipline now has a social task: to form these beholders—and not only by exposure to paintings but also by historical study.

The militia company interior space was distinguished from the rest of society as an ideal theater of sympathetic and coordinated intersubjectivity. It became one of the indispensable cells of this balanced and harmonious polity. Seventeenth-century Dutch society for Riegl is corporatist, communitarian, and antihierarchical, an ideal liberal society. The corporatist society sampled in the Dutch group portrait is an unfolding of late medieval northern European urban culture, the cradle in some nineteenth-century political mythologies of modern civic liberty and individualism. The fragile canvases and softly molded oil paints that Riegl describes with such deliberation figure a stable, appealing model for European society, which in Riegl's time was coasting on a long run of peacetime not unlike the Dutch of Hals's time.

Liberal, bourgeois society had developed an art of sensations, Impressionism, that folded easily into the realist program and yet with every iteration—so aware was it of its own recent history—resembled more an art of sensations of sensations, ever further removed from a natural, external fact. Impressionism was undercoded, a mode of painting that only gently guided perception—perception of what? of anything: city life, vegetation, the body. Thinking with the Impressionists, Riegl was unafraid of realism or naturalism. Like Warburg, Riegl recognized that the development of realistic portraiture in the second quarter of the fifteenth century had irreversibly altered the history of painting, initiated its long slide or progress toward uselessness. The black-and-white reproductions in Riegl's text, which only augmented an effect of achromatism that the Dutch portraitists themselves strove for—not to mention the drapers and tailors who clothed the Dutch burghers—made the comparison between the historical group portraits and modern photographic portraiture obvious.

In Riegl's lifetime European painting was ascending to its high point, an accumulation of adjustments and refinements—the last stretch, in the last quarter of the nineteenth century, provoked by photography. Painting was the pursuit of a balance between the claims of the world, processed by perception, and the claims of all the previous paintings to have found that balance. Art history was designed for painting; its self-adjustments were always coupled with the development of new languages to describe painterly form, from Vasari on.

Riegl's writing raises the question of whether art history as a project can survive the end of painting—or the beginning of painting. The parietal images at the cave of La Mouthe near Les Eyzies, in the Dordogne, were discovered in 1895, beneath layers of paleolithic material that decisively proved the site's antiquity. Font-de-Gaume and Les Combarelles were discovered in 1901. In 1902 the great antiquity of Altamira itself, which had been discovered in 1879 but doubted, was finally accepted.

But paleolithic painting in the end proved unassimilable to art history. The twenty-three years that it took to establish the authenticity and date of the paintings at Altamira only gave the discipline of art history a kind of reprieve.

Riegl had discussed the origins of art in the opening pages of his book of 1893, *Stilfragen*, ignoring Altamira. Riegl might well have introduced the paleolithic paintings without upsetting his hypotheses. For the bone carvings and the paintings alike only reinforce his theory that art begins in naturalistic representation of animals, in an apparent attempt to seize directly the principle of life itself, and only later tends toward the representation of plants, toward the establishment of a picture plane, toward ornamentation, toward stylization. Riegl never abandoned this principle: the glint of the brooch, the gleam of the eye of the Dutch burgher. He simply relocates life from animal to artifact to people. Riegl saw that in their vitality the prehistoric images did not support a story of art that begins with technology, function, and ornamentation and only arrives at figuration and imagination much later. For Riegl, the prehistoric images disclosed the "primacy of creative thought." Altamira and the Aquitaine make it seem as if the subsequent history of art were not so much a learning of plenitude and vitality as an unlearning.

All this was very far from the questions prompted by paintings in Florentine chapels. It is as if art history had undertaken to narrate a history of mural painting stretched too thin.

Wilhelm Worringer (1881–1965) wrote the most successful of all art-historical dissertations, *Abstraction and Empathy: A Contribution to the Psychology of Style* (1906, published 1908 and still in print today, though translated into English only in 1953). Lacking footnotes, *Abstraction and Empathy* did not resemble academic scholarship. But it also lacked illustrations. The book was read by scholars and thinkers, including artists, well beyond the field of art history.

The concept of empathy enjoyed great currency in the last decades of the nineteenth century. Empathy was the tendency of the embodied mind to tune itself to the shapes and rhythms of the environment. In the context of aesthetics, empathy was the susceptibility of emotions to the cues of form. Theorists of empathy accepted the Kantian doctrine that the mind makes sense of reality by imposing its own categories on it, but only in part, because empathy theory allowed the body to play a greater role. Use of the word signalled a desire to move away from philosophy and toward psychology, perhaps even to submit aesthetic responses to controlled experimentation. Theories of empathy recovered and updated the aesthetic theory of the eighteenth century with its stress on the senses. Like eighteenth-century aesthetics, empathy theory was non-normative, for each individual will have her or his own empathic relationship to things. The theory of empathy exceeds aesthetics, however, because the mind and body adapt not just to artworks but also to the shapes of things in the world and because a psychology based on empathy need not generate a prescription for art-making. Worringer himself cleaved close to the question of art. He did not trust empathy as a basis for an aesthetics because the history of art, he believed, taught that empathy tended to seek out only satisfying experiences. Empathy, as it was cultivated by art and protected by art-historical scholarship, amounted to a merely comfortable cooperation with the physical world. Worringer, quoting Theodor Lipps, described empathy as "objectified self-delight," corresponding to naturalism in art. Worringer invoked Riegl constantly and adopted his coinage *Kunstwollen*. But he tests the implications of Riegl's premises that the *Kunstwollen* always seeks satisfaction and that man is pursuing analogies of his own body.

Worringer, like Burckhardt and Warburg, believed that the nineteenth-century bourgeoisie had inherited the participatory relationship to nature achieved by Europeans in the Renaissance. The Renaissance and what Worringer calls its "parallel phenomenon," antiquity, struck the keynotes for the entire standard narrative of Western art. "Both periods represent the efflorescence of naturalism. But what then is naturalism?" Here Worringer changes the terms of the debate. To define naturalism he will focus not on the product (as did classical art theory) nor on the response (as did the aesthetics of sensibility introduced in the eighteenth century) but rather on the process of creation. This is aesthetics for artists:

> The answer is: the approach to the organic and the true to life, but not
> because the artist wished to represent an object in nature, faithfully
> and in its corporeality, not because he wished to create the illusion
> of life itself, but rather because the feeling for the beauty of organic
> and true-to-life form had been awakened and because the artist

wanted to satisfy this feeling, which dominated the absolute artistic volition (*Kunstwollen*).

Worringer adds that these theses "naturally take no account of content, which is secondary in every artistic representation." Worringer detects in Renaissance art and all its variants an evasion of the truth in favor of simple satisfaction. Only this ingratiating art, whose culmination is the Naturalism of the nineteenth century, deserves the name "art" and yields to the analyses of aesthetics (Fiedler and Hildebrand would have objected to this argument!): "naturalism alone belongs to the domain of pure art and is therefore accessible to aesthetic evaluation":

> Its psychic precondition…is the process of empathy, whose object nearest to hand is always the familiar and organic; that is, formal processes play out within the artwork which correspond to the natural organic tendencies in human beings and permit him, in his aesthetic perception, to flow without restriction with his inner vital feeling, with his inner need for activity, into the felicitous current of this formal happening.

This art encourages a quasi-pantheistic investment of trust in nature, a pleasure in organic lifelike form, and a confidence in the immanence of meaning in things. Technology is just the extension of empathy. Empathy was Worringer's code word for the materialism and consumerism of nineteenth-century life.

The paradox is that Worringer sees aesthetics as perfectly matched to Naturalism, and yet he will reject Naturalism. Instead he clears a path to a post-aesthetic art. For the new century Worringer foresaw—but wisely did not attempt to describe—an art of truth. He had pointed out that the theory of empathy cannot explain why some people are drawn to inorganic beauty. He offered an aesthetics founded on a different principle, abstraction. By abstraction Worringer did not mean nonfigurative painting—that had not quite been invented yet—but rather a tendency to flee the terrifying chaos of the natural world and seek refuge in the discipline of style. The art of abstraction is for Worringer a more honest project than Renaissance or naturalist art because it fabricates a stylized alternative to nature instead of vainly attempting to appease nature by mimicking it.

When Worringer states that abstraction is born of a troubled relation to nature, including the fear of space, he is not so far from Warburg. The pathos-formulas are also abstractions, evasions. For Worringer, however, abstraction means not the body in extremis but a turning away from the body entirely. Worringer gives some examples, but the real heart of the book is the chapter on northern European animal ornament. The rhythmic, intertwined bands and lines of early medieval Scandinavian and insular art had been the subject of intense art-historical interest over the previous decade. Riegl had published on the topic. The authors of these forms were Europe's semi-mythical internal savages, the peoples living in disharmony with nature, clasping to paganism deep into modern times, restlessly seeking an outlet into the absolute. The abstract form, whether crystalline or curved, was detached from accident, temporality, and unclarity. This tendency culminated finally in Gothic. The architecture of the cathedrals, which was liberated from all natural models—it no longer drew its proportions from the human body—was a pure mechanism, like a marionette. Gothic was uncanny. The same struggle to escape expressed itself in the sculptural drapery of the Gothic period. But in the end sculpture turned back to the natural model and so began the episode of falsehood that we call Renaissance.

Modern man, according to Worringer, finds himself again alienated from nature, not by his incapacity but by an excess of capacity, namely by technology. He finds himself in the situation of the primitive. Rationalism has failed; now we again want a stable relationship to things. Abstraction was both the primordial attitude toward nature and the advanced approach that under the conditions of modernity was once again appropriate. Abstraction is both a starting point and a final psychic contrivance.

What kind of art history is this? Worringer handles the past roughly, does not let the past assert itself. This is history written from the point of view of the present.

In Riegl's model, ancient Mediterranean art sought to isolate objects, to remove them from space. Since the early Middle Ages, European art reinserts those objects into a virtual space, a space shared by (depicted) objects and (depicted) beings. Worringer reverts to the ancient project, isolating objects to bring out their implacable objecthood, reintroducing them to the haptic plane. Worringer will isolate objects from one another to give them their necessity and eternity. Here he speaks the same language that the painter Wassily Kandinsky will. Worringer breaks with Hildebrand and Riegl and their logic of dematerialization, which favors concept over sensation. But if his efforts to escape it are more strenuous, Worringer is still basically defined by the naturalism/idealism binary that had structured all thinking about art in the late nineteenth century.

The avant-gardes of the first two decades of the new century were also shaped by nineteenth-century assumptions, exactly to the degree of vehemence with which they sought to overturn them. This, too, is a "standing over," a superstition. Art history, the knowledge, the writing, the museums, is inscribed in the avant-garde mentality.

Worringer rewrites but does not overturn the dominant art-historical fable of modernity, the truth of medieval art. In some ways nothing has changed since 1800: the art praised by Vasari and Bellori is still being challenged, as are Winckelmann's statues. The difference is that the antidote to the false promise of worldly satisfaction is not the sweet sincerity of Dürer's Madonnas but malign twisting serpents. Worringer rejects pleasure as the basis for the experience of art and instead identifies a higher kind of pleasure, art-pleasure, that involves recognition of pain and loss. This concept was latent in Warburg's art history, too, and remained latent. Worringer's teaching casts a shadow over all subsequent art. From this point on affirmation is suspect. The moral of the new fable is no longer the superiority of the rude to the civilized but of the hideous to the beautiful.

Worringer in his sympathy for the barbarians was taking up a theme of Riegl's. For Riegl, however, barbarianism was ultimately sublimated in liberal democratic society. Out of the chaos of the Middle Ages came new political structures. People organized themselves beyond the reach of central authority, learning the arts of negotiation and democracy. To relativize civilization itself, as Worringer did, was a dangerous game to play.

1910-1920

In only a single field of our civilization has the omnipotence of thoughts been retained, and that is in the field of art. Only in art does it still happen that a man who is consumed by desires performs something resembling the accomplishment of those desires and that what he does in play produces emotional effects—thanks to artistic illusion—just as though it were something real.

This is Sigmund Freud in *Totem and Taboo* (1913), a collection of four essays drawing comparisons between the spiritual life or mentality of "wild" peoples and modern neurotics. Characteristic of wild or prescientific societies, according to Freud, is the confidence that magical procedures carried out properly will relay mental states outward to reality. Modern, civilized peoples have lost confidence in such techniques. Magical thinking survives only in art. Already around 1800 the Romantic poets had asserted their dominion over reality. A century later artists, poets, and composers reasserted that ambition, describing themselves as an "advance scouting party," an avant-garde, that would show the way forward. In 1910 magical world-shapers faced even longer odds than in 1800, for the illusions generated by art—which are by no means limited to the simulations of appearances created by the painter's skill, as Freud implied—could hardly compete with the industrial and military technologies beleaguering the minds and bodies of laborers and consumers as well as the wild people visited by Aby Warburg, the undertechnologized on the Indian reservations of the American Southwest.

Not to mention the ingratiating entertainments devised for the uncultivated and unsophisticated, the popular forms of art mostly, though not always, disdained by the avant-garde artists.

Some artists in France and Germany called themselves "savages": the Fauves and "die Wilden." But the vanguard was also labeled, at least in Germany, in the field of literature, a New or Neo-Romanticism (Neu-Romantik). In the manifesto he published together with Franz Marc in 1912, the *Blue Rider Almanac*, the painter Wassily Kandinsky asserted: "At a certain point the necessities are ripe. That is, the creative *spirit* (which one could characterize as the abstract spirit) gains access to the soul, later the many souls, and brings about a longing, an inner impulse." This impulse has "the power to create in the human spirit a new value." The new value is then given material form. "This is the positive, the creative. This is the good. *The white, fertilizing ray.* This ray leads to evolution, to elevation." So art will transform the world through form.

Franz Marc associated the artist with the misunderstood witches and seers of Europe's past. As an example of a modern unheeded prophet he named, however, not an artist but an art historian: Julius Meier-Graefe, an influential German champion of the French Impressionists, who had tried to introduce "a completely unknown great master" to his contemporaries, the Greek painter of the late sixteenth and early seventeenth century, El Greco. According to Marc, Meier-Graefe's rediscovery of El Greco, a painter admired in his own day but ignored in the nineteenth century, was greeted either by indifference or by enraged indignation. Also in this sense artists of the early twentieth century saw themselves repeating the project of the Romantics, who had rediscovered the painters of the late Middle Ages and early Renaissance so disesteemed by the ancien régime academies.

The attitude of the avant-gardes to art historians was ambivalent. They relied on scholarship to deliver the overlooked examples from the past, not only El Greco but also the primitive woodcuts of late medieval Germany, as well as the treasures of the wide world. Marc, in a review of an exhibition of the Neue Künstlervereinigung (1910), mentions another recent exhibition in Munich, "Meisterwerke muhammedanischer Kunst," a huge collation of over 3600 objects, influential on the modern historiography of so-called Islamic art. Marc ventures a comparison that no historicist would make: "It is a pity that one can't hang Kandinsky's great Composition [*Composition II*, 1910, now in the Solomon R. Guggenheim Museum, New York] and other works next to the Islamic carpets in the exhibition." Marc believes that no European decorative work can hold its own next to the carpets, yet he is prepared to make the thought experiment of juxtaposing the carpets to a painting by Kandinsky—and not to test the carpets but to test Kandinsky, who did in fact visit the exhibition. The result: "What artistic insight this rare painter contains! The great consistency of his colors is balanced by the freedom of his drawing." Marc's imaginary comparison is historically careless, but that was exactly the point. Marc did not fear the reproach of the scholar who would point out that the carpets had symbolic functions in the societies that produced them and that their patterns were not freely chosen like Kandinsky's forms but handed down by tradition and governed by rules of combination. The Blue Rider artists admired so-called folk art, for example the Bavarian reverse paintings on glass, as samples of a past embedded in the present. Kandinsky and Marc reproduced on the first page of the *Almanac* a woodcut from the *Ritter vom Turn*, a profane text published in Basel in 1495, which they had seen reproduced in Wilhelm Worringer's book on early German book illustration (1912). In the *Almanac* everything was gathered on the same level, as if pinned to a bulletin board. Page layout was a new museology, new again, new as the early printed books, like the *Ritter vom Turn*, combining type and image. Marc in an essay of 1912 named Worringer's *Abstraction and Empathy* one of the two books, alongside Kandinsky's *On the Spiritual in Art*, laying the groundwork for a "new dogmatics of the 'republic of the soul.'"

Marc saw the previous century as purely negative. It produced no style of its own. Scholarship had undermined the collective beliefs that sustained powerful styles: "Scholarship works negatively, *au détriment de la religion*.... Artistic style…, the inalienable possession of the old times, collapsed catastrophically in the mid-nineteenth century." Bereft of their myths, the creators of the nineteenth century could only rummage through history, trying on styles as if they were costumes. No avant-garde artist wished to produce stylized rebuses of prior art. Futurists, Cubists, and Constructivists were even more thorough than Kandinsky and Marc in their repudiation of the past. The least pious were the protagonists of the various Dada moments. Marcel Janco said that Tristan Tzara was accustomed to begin his morning prayers with the words "I don't even want to know whether there has been anyone before me." "We aimed," Janco wrote, "to make a fresh start, beginning with the babble of infants, and to constitute a new plastic language." Hugo Ball imagined language starting over again: he said in the *Dada Manifesto* (1916): "I don't want words that other people have invented." In comparison, the destruction of the forms developed by centuries of painting was child's play. Dada could be interpreted as the effort of art to spring the grip of art-historical thinking, once and for all. Dada exceeds the capacities of the discipline.

The Blaue Reiter artists were still participating in the life of historical form, as were Picasso and Matisse. A Dada artist, by contrast, would have asked what distinguished Kandinsky and Marc's predilections for the primitive, the vernacular, and the exotic from nineteenth-century eclecticism. The difference was that the historicists of the previous century were interested in alternative systems of art. Gothic architecture had a system; Japanese woodcuts had a system. But Marc and Kandinsky were drawn not to systems but to anarchic representation—the early woodcuts, the folk art—where nothing interfered, supposedly, with the expression of the artist's intuition of spirit. Kandinsky objected to all rules and blamed art history for sustaining them: "All those rules that were discovered already in the earliest art as well as the rules discovered later, and to which the art historians assign such exaggerated value, are not general rules: they do not lead to art." Kandinsky is saying, in effect, that modern art-historical scholarship amounted to nothing more than a perpetuation of premodern academicism. The way to escape the rules was to abandon representation. Magic required form. Traditional magic—the Persian carpets, for example—looked to rules to generate the correct forms. The new magic—Kandinsky's—recreated the form anew each time.

Kandinsky, like the Impressionists before him, and like the avant-gardists in France or Russia, was not intimidated by the loss of an unquestioned collective style. He believed that the nineteenth century lacked a style of its own because it lacked a content of its own. Now there was a content: newness itself, the promise of the new century. That content dictated the style. Kandinsky did not hesitate to designate his own style as the "necessary" style of his time. Each epoch, he conceded, even his own, has at its disposal a limited repertoire of forms. But he was prepared to convert the relativity of style into an opportunity: "Form is always temporal, that is, relative, because it is never more than the medium currently necessary through which today's revelation makes itself known, sounds forth." This style did not emerge out of the collectivity, it was his very own style, and yet it was as authentic as the Gothic.

The art of the Blaue Reiter was accessible to many art historians, as was Cubism to the extent that it derived from Cézanne, and as was Picasso's engagement with African tribal masks. Wilhelm Worringer was well aware of the Blaue Reiter artists' interest in his writings. In 1911 a group of German artists published a protest against recent critical tendencies, including favoritism of French art and primitivism. Worringer was asked by the Blaue Reiter artists to contribute a text to their formal response, a pamphlet entitled *Im Kampf um die Kunst* (In the Struggle for Art). In Worringer's, Riegl's, and Franz Marc's schemas, primitives and Orientals play similar roles. Worringer's repudiation of European naturalism basically repeats Schopenhauer's invocation of the Vedic and Buddhist concept of the "Veil of Maya" or illusion. The West turns to the East in order to expose Western blindness. The arts of the early Middle Ages or of Asia reveal that the sensible world is a deception. This is a twist on Kantian constructionism. If the world is only our own mind projected outward, then that world is to be rejected—not because it is alien to us, as it was for primitives, but because it is too familiar. Abstraction is an attempt to replace the naïve or Kantian magical thinking of the modern Europeans, who do not even know they are thinking magically, with a sophisticated artistic thinking that is prepared to venture into self-alienation.

The response of Hans Tietze, the Viennese historian of Renaissance art, to the Blaue Reiter is instructive. In a text published in 1912, Tietze gave the Blaue Reiter his blessing but also hoisted a warning flag about the artists' unscholarly wanderings in the past, which he interprets, wrongly, as their attempt to reassure us that their campaign is not so innovative after all, that they "weave threads that lead back into the darkest depths of mankind." In their attempt to construct an ancestry, they do not seem to realize that the "overrunning (*Überwuchern*) of form by expression" in folk art is a result of incompetence. Primitive and Gothic art are connected in myriad ties to spiritual worlds completely alien to modernity. Thus are marked the limits of the historian's sympathy for avant-gardist sovereignty over the entirety of experience. Freud, too, was wary of regression. In 1917 he said that trench warfare was only possible because the primitive in man had not yet been subdued. But even

Freud and Tietze would have agreed with Worringer that the wild seeing graphed by the rebel artists was not the sign of technical deficiency but of a reoriented artistic will.

Hans Tietze and his wife Erica Tietze-Conrat were the most likely of scholars to embrace the new tendencies in art. They were close to the major Viennese modernists including Oskar Kokoschka, from whom they commissioned in 1909 a double self-portrait. Exiled, the Tietzes sold the picture to the Museum of Modern Art upon arriving in New York in 1939. A pupil of Riegl and Wickhoff, like her husband, Erica Tietze-Conrat was the first woman to receive a doctorate in art history from the University of Vienna, in 1905. Of course, no teaching position was open to her. (Not until 1971 was a woman, Renate Wagner-Rieger, appointed professor of art history in Vienna.) In 1911 Tietze-Conrat published an essay on an exhibition of women artists at the Wiener Secession, mostly painters of the sixteenth to nineteenth centuries. Here she reflected on why women had been so long excluded from the history of art, and on why that need not be the case in the future.

The art historians most likely to learn from the new art were those who saw form as the key to art history's self-differentiation from general history. Form, they believed, is what art history knows. The inquiry into form postpones a decoding of the artwork that would reveal content as merely local. The Swiss art historian Heinrich Wölfflin (1864–1945) put it this way: art history typically understands art as expression. The artist, the society, the epoch express themselves in paintings and buildings and furniture and fashion. Every individual, every nation, every period has its own style. But an art history that understands art as expression or communication will end up depreciating form as mere rhetoric, the clothing of content. The description of historical styles, paradoxically, is biased toward content. To correct this bias, heeding the reproaches of the artists, Wölfflin wrote the *Grundbegriffe der Kunstgeschichte* (Basic Concepts of Art History; usually translated as Principles of Art History) (1915). Here he concedes that the art historian will be unable to assess artistic quality, which is never a variable of an extra-artistic term. For this reason "it is not easy to interest artists in historical questions about style." The artistic problem, from their point of view, is always the same. The artists scorn the art historians who compare finished products but do not enter imaginatively into the crisis of the artistic problem and so "cling to the non-artistic side of human nature." His *Principles of Art*

History is the most influential book by the most influential art historian of the twentieth century.

Wölfflin was converted to art history by the lectures of Jacob Burckhardt at Basel. His dissertation of 1886, *Prolegomena to a Psychology of Architecture,* was a brief, urgent meditation on the psychosomatic processing of form, in tune with the empathy theorists of the day. Here Wölfflin cultivated a youthful, "pathetic" mode of writing matched to a disquiet he detected in bodies and forms. Wölfflin's first full-scale book, *Renaissance and Baroque* (1888), introduced the theme that structured all his writings, the riddle of the two "high points" on the curve of European art, the early sixteenth century and the mid-seventeenth century, the one disrupting the equilibrium achieved by the other and yet both equally eminent. Wölfflin taught at Munich, Basel, Berlin, Munich again, and finally Zurich, reaching thousands of listeners, including many susceptible students—among them Worringer—as well as a general public. His books reproduced the relaxed, conversational tone of the lectures as well as the strictly formal and comparative approach to the works. These were practical exercises in seeing, expecting of the audience—like Impressionist and Post-Impressionist painting—no learning or preparation. Wölfflin's pages were uncluttered by erudition or exchanges with other scholars. The fantastical, anthropomorphizing descriptions and the notes of anxiety struck in the dissertation are banished. Now the tone is as sovereign and balanced as the very paintings and buildings discussed in *Classic Art: An Introduction to the Italian Renaissance* (1899). The originality of Wölfflin's readings of form is masked by the rhetoric of authorial mastery.

The book of 1915, the *Principles,* calls out five aspects of form, each structured by a pair of opposed terms that chart an irreversible development from relative harmony to relative dissonance, from the tactile to the visual, from rule to freedom. The sets of terms are: linear and painterly, plane and recession, closed and open form, multiplicity and unity, absolute and relative clarity. The book expounds each set of paired terms, one by one, through descriptive comparisons of paintings, drawings, prints, sculptures, and buildings. The terms are presented as the "most general forms of representation" or beholding, as if they would serve for any possible art-historical task. The examples, though, are all drawn from the stock of European masterworks, Italian, German, Flemish, Dutch, and French, of the sixteenth and seventeenth centuries. The first term in each pair corresponds to the art of the High Renaissance and the second to the art of the Baroque. Wölfflin expresses few preferences; every work he adduces is a work of high quality.

The *Principles of Art History* was published in wartime, and in the teeth of an artistic revolution stalled by that war. One might well interpret the two-note melody of Renaissance and Baroque, Wölfflin's constant narrative theme, as a model of the entire history of post-medieval European art, from the Renaissance to the early twentieth century: once there was harmony, now there is dissonance. The new art of modernity, since Impressionism, would be cast as another unsettled "Baroque" that follows the lengthy career of composed or good form, from 1500 to 1800. The avant-gardes repudiated all closed or balanced systems. The "bad" form they developed was the grimace of a new artwork open to a new society, to new viewers, to new realities. Such a reading would seem to expose Wölfflin as an anti-avant-gardist, for his narrative corrals the avant-gardes within a preestablished narrative schema, so questioning their claims to absolute singularity. But the same reading also supports the avant-garde project, for it reveals apparent bad form to be a modality of good form.

The span of Wölfflin's own career, beginning in the late 1880s and extending into the new century, embraced the third high point on the curve of art history, even if Wölfflin himself never put it that way. The art of painting in Europe attained its zenith with Manet, Degas, Cézanne, Monet, and Renoir (all born between 1832 and 1841), with van Gogh (born 1853), with Wölfflin's contemporaries Matisse, Munch, Kandinsky, and Mondrian (born between 1863 and 1872), with Picasso, Klee, and Beckmann (born in the 1880s). Wölfflin did not recognize photography as a catastrophe for painting, and understandably so, for the great painters of this epoch, his own, met the threat either by intensifying their own scrutiny of given form, leaving the lens far behind, or by delivering the results of new, nonobjective ways of seeing. Nor was Wölfflin troubled by painterly naturalism, for he saw that success in rendering the look of things was only a surface phenomenon and was more often than not only a reform of content, with no bearing on the underlying modes of representation. Wölfflin arrives finally at a formula recapitulating the premodern academic principle of *imitatio*, this time not as prescription but as description: "The effect of picture on picture is a much more important factor of style than what comes directly from the observation of nature." His point is that even a modern artist, no longer academic, no longer respectful of pre-established styles, "finds certain 'optical' possibilities before him, to which he is bound. Not everything is possible at all times."

Wölfflin's fourth pair, multiplicity and unity, can exemplify the book. In primitive or pre-Renaissance art, he says, the parts do not yet function as free members of an organism. This only happens when the single detail—a feature in a face, a figure in a composition—comes to seem necessary to the whole. Renaissance art gathers the parts into a whole but represents the articulation and separateness of the parts. In Baroque art, by contrast, the individual component "loses its privileges." If the classic work subordinates the parts, the Baroque work pulls them into an "endless flow." Wölfflin's use of these terms acknowledges his debt to Riegl. "All our previous categories have prepared this unity. The painterly is the deliverance of the forms from their isolation; the principle of depth is no other than the replacement of the sequence of separate layers by a uniform movement into depth, and the taste for the atectonic dissolves the rigid structure of geometric relations."

In Albrecht Dürer's woodcut of the *Death of the Virgin* (1510), Wölfflin observes, "the parts form a system in which each in its place appears conditioned by the whole and yet comes across as completely independent." This "relationship of (relative) co-ordination of independent values" he calls the principle of multiple unity. A Baroque artist "would have avoided or made inconspicuous the meeting of pure horizontals and verticals." "The component parts, whether the bed canopy or one of the apostles, would have been melted into an overall movement governing the whole picture." Wölfflin's contrasting example is Rembrandt's etching of the same subject (1639):

> The play of contrasts does not cease, but it hides itself away. The patently juxtaposed and clearly opposed are replaced by a single interwovenness. Pure oppositions are broken. The finite and the isolable disappear. From form to form, paths and bridges open over which the movement hastens forward uninterrupted.

The local perceptions yield general insights. "Classic art does not know the concept of the momentary, the pointed emphasis, or of intensification generally: it has a leisurely, broad quality. And though it proceeds from the whole, it does not reckon with first impressions." You can excise the classic figure from its context and it does not collapse, whereas "the very existence of the baroque figure is thoroughly bound up with the other motives in the picture." Such observations could easily be folded into a history of the functions and meanings of art. The indifference of the classic mode to the momentary and the subjective, for example, could be connected to the persisting alliance of early sixteenth-century painting with painting's immemorial sacred functions, with chapels, altars, and liturgies. Wölfflin knew that, and as the adviser of dozens of dissertations of every methodological stripe knew that not all histories of art could or should be pure histories of form. Wölfflin was a great reader of art-historical scholarship: he wrote more than 150 book reviews. (Aby Warburg, book-oriented, wrote none.) Wölfflin's observations also contribute to iconographical analysis. There are many remarks on content embedded in the *Principles*. Wölfflin points out for example that Renaissance depictions of the story of Susanna show the prurient Elders watching or approaching. Only in the Baroque is the emphasis shifted to the drama of their arrival and address. It was the same with Samson and Delilah: first the hero sleeps in the lap of the temptress, later the attack itself is shown. But Wölfflin understood that the power and reach of his concept of form depended on its indifference to local content. He also knew that a contextual history of art that is blind to form is, finally, of little worth.

Two paradoxes maintain the tension in Wölfflin's system. Without that tension his book would not have earned the recognition it did beyond art history, among historians of literature and music, for instance, throughout the middle decades of the century. *Principles of Art History* was translated into Spanish (1924), Russian (1930), English (1932), Japanese (1936), French (1953), Italian (1953), and seventeen other languages. There have been twenty German-language editions. Wölfflin's unbalanced pairs mark out a theory of art. Yet he himself denied that his book was about art. This is the first paradox. He aimed to resolve the antitheses of expression versus quality, or imitation versus decoration, by taking as his topic not art but modes of representation. His books may resemble histories of art but in fact amount to a history of seeing: "It was not the art of the sixteenth and seventeenth century which was to be analyzed—that is something richer and more alive—only the schema and the visual and formal possibilities within which art had to remain." This latter sentence is a masterstroke. Wölfflin pretends to hold no

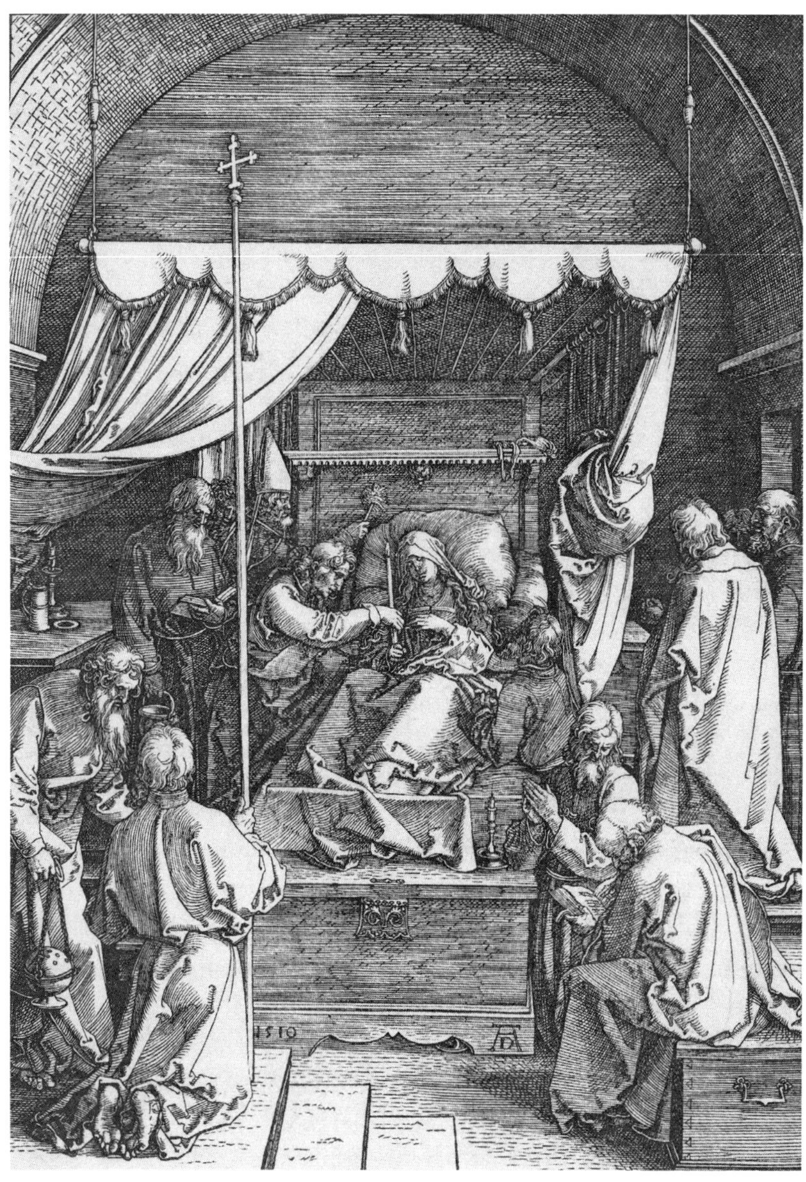

Albrecht Dürer, *Death of the Virgin* (1510). Woodcut, 29.3 × 20.8 cm. Washington, National Gallery of Art. Dürer depicts the twelve apostles who, according to tradition, witnessed the death of the Virgin.

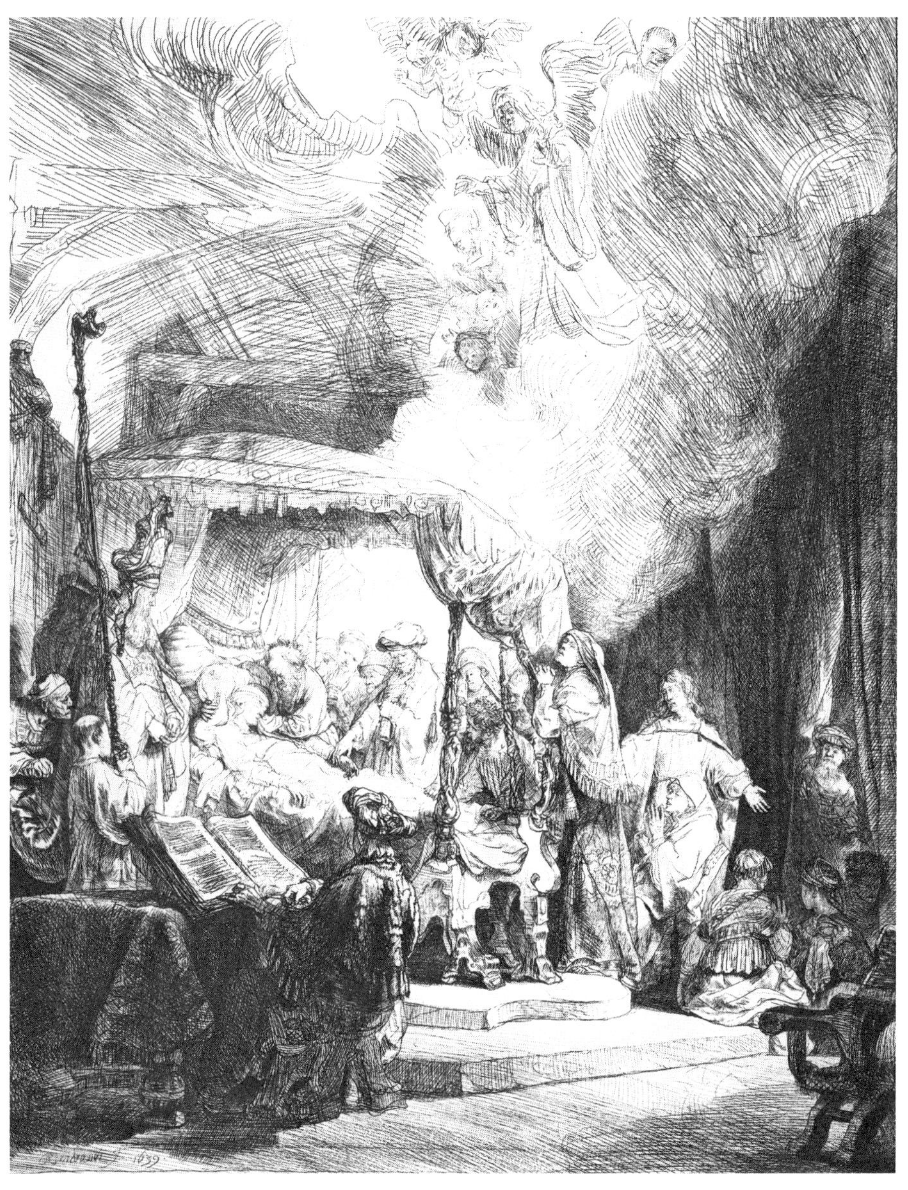

Rembrandt van Rijn, *Death of the Virgin* (1639). Etching, 41 × 31.4 cm. New York, Metropolitan Museum of Art. Rembrandt adds to the household.

special stake in art, as if he had just happened to choose famous artworks to illustrate his history of seeing but could have chosen any depictions. In this way he deflects the objection that he is only offering lessons in art appreciation. To those who do not wish art history to be anything less than art appreciation, meanwhile, he sends a secret signal. The phrase "something richer and more alive" indicates that he is well apprised of art's rarity, well aware that art is more than the mere reflection of the mental and perceptual habits that his book has been chasing. He defers the real project of art history. For now he is content to assert that "vision itself has its history and the uncovering of these 'optical layers' must be considered the most elementary task of art history." This sentence, too, is a masterstroke, connecting Wölfflin to Riegl and opening a clear path to an historicist scholarship aiming to coordinate ways of seeing with the deep structure of collective life, or what could be called mentality. Wölfflin, classicist and elitist, formulates the basic axiom of a future visual culture studies. He manages to keep faith with the relativism of the nineteenth century even as he recenters art history on beautiful form.

Wölfflin in the *Principles* was not saying that form is timeless, but neither was he saying that form is bound to the rest of life. He was saying that form is all the content you need; and this is why his art history is the classic art history.

The second paradox structuring Wölfflin's thought is built on the first. "People at all times see what they wish to see." In other words, vision is not innocent, like the poor camera lens, but interested, selective, empathic. And yet "that does not exclude the possibility that through all the changes a law remains operative." In each pair of "modes of representation," the second mode follows logically from the first. This is exactly what Theodor W. Adorno said in the passage from his *Aesthetic Theory* quoted at the beginning of the present book. Harmony devolves into dissonance, and never the reverse. This law of the declension of form provides the internal resistance to an expressionist or cultural historical approach to art. It makes no difference whether forms are delivering ideas or stories, picturing lived life, or registering mentality, as a "history of seeing" would have it. Form in each case will march to its own drummer.

In the conclusion to the *Principles*, Wölfflin notes that the art of the years around 1800 seems to defy the law. He is speaking of the medieval revival as much as of Neoclassicism. Here order—the linear styles of Flaxman, Canova, the Nazarenes—appears to emerge out of disorder. Wölfflin's answer to this puzzle is that the career of form was interrupted by an unnatural emphasis on content. The art of 1800 was the result of a "revaluation of being, in every domain." Ethical and political preferences were allowed to shape the assessment of form. "Diderot contests in Boucher not only the artist but also the man. Pure human sentiment seeks the simple." Wölfflin quotes Friedrich Schlegel, who also favored the "good-natured simplicity…which I am inclined to regard as the original character of mankind: that is the style of the old painting, the only style that pleases me." Content, or a real principle fetched from a place outside of art, is set up as a rival to the form-creating imagination.

Wölfflin considers historicism, or imaginative sympathy with obsolete forms and the forms of life they register, a distraction from the project of art. The year 1800 was marked by an excess of ambition. The artist-magician believed that he could intervene in reality. Wölfflin's stance on the art of his own moment is now clearer. One can read his words on the art of 1800 as a warning. The nineteenth century had acquiesced in the claims of extra-artistic content; the twentieth century risked an unconditional surrender. The modern conviction that artistic form could shape reality had just been described by Freud as a neurotic superstition about the magical potency of form. Freud was well aware that the artist, the "man," as Wölfflin puts it, could persist into the artwork. Leonardo da Vinci's childhood traumas left traces in his paintings (Freud's "A Childhood Memory," 1910). Michelangelo's biography penetrates upward into his style, giving psychoanalysis a chance to identify the enduring or mythic meaning of his art (Freud's "The Moses of Michelangelo," 1914). But Freud was also wary of art's tendency to confuse reality and unreality. If Leonardo was a neurotic, then he needed to be cured. Freud, like his near-contemporary Wölfflin, was biased toward order and composition: composition of the artwork, composition of the personality. This bias supported a sequestering and marginalization of avant-garde art, whose basic principle was mistrust of composition. But then Freud was not an avant-garde thinker. Like Aby Warburg, he saw the potential for disorder in the human personality but sought to contain that potential.

Heinrich Wölfflin, like Alois Riegl, believed that art realizes its possibilities when ethical and political exigencies are kept at bay. For much of history, reality was encroaching, taking up too much room. Power was assigning imagination its tasks. Liberal modernity cleared out a free zone for the imagination, promising an end to the conflict between content and form. In modernity, the threat of hostile belief systems had been neutralized; superstitions had been scattered; secularization had quenched the last religious wars. Alterity was easily absorbed into the modern European philosophies. To make his point about order and disorder, Wölfflin did not need to summon Romanesque art or Hindu art. One might guess on the evidence of his writings that Wölfflin was ignorant of art before Dürer, or beyond western Europe. His books draw on the contents of the great princely collections of the seventeenth and eighteenth century. But of course Wölfflin was well aware of what he excluded. Historical awareness is written into the aesthetic of dissonance, for only by passing through clarity does one come to value unclarity.

Wölfflin contrasts rule and misrule. But the second term in each of his pairs is only an image of misrule. This is clear with architecture, which must be tectonic if it is to stand up. Atectonic architecture is a fiction. So is atectonic painting. "The tectonic style is the style of constrained order and clear adherence to rule: the atectonic, by contrast, is the style of more or less concealed adherence to rule and of unrestrained order." Atectonic art "plays with the semblance of lawlessness. It plays, for in the aesthetic sense, of course, all artistic form is necessary form." The analysis of form takes art offline. The first avant-gardes made the mistake of taking aesthetic play too literally.

This is the moment when art history and art begin to diverge. Art historians will not be able to keep pace with art; artists will drift out of the range of premodern art. The modern artists who forget the history of art are the successors to Diderot and the Encyclopedia. They accept the modern world as they find it and react directly to it. Freud urges the individual to correct her own history; the avant-garde artist wants to correct our collective history.

Wölfflin did not invest in painterly abstraction, but those who did, all around him, believed that abstraction released form into a free flow, from picture to picture, as Wölfflin had written. The painter and writer Roger Fry said as much in his influential essays of the 1910s; so did Clive Bell in his book *Art* (1914). The literary theorist Roman Jakobson in an essay of 1919, "Futurism," mocked a critic who misunderstood abstract painting. That critic did not grasp that there is nothing to grasp but perception itself. "For him, perception that is valuable in and of itself does not exist. He prefers paper currency to gold: currency, with its conventionally assigned value seems to him more 'literary.'" Representation is deception, according to Jakobson, while abstraction recuperates real value and restores art to an honest relation to reality. Avant-garde art defictionalizes.

A third and unexpected paradox presents itself. Wölfflin's formulas would seem to prepare an indictment of modernism—all the art produced since 1915, basically—as a giving way of form in the face of the suddenly more urgent claims of reality. Form defers to content. Art answers non-artistic reality; artistic reality is diminished. But the same formulas also vindicate modernism by supporting the axiom of the irreversibility of the avant-garde rupture. For Wölfflin's principle of principles is that once there is disorder, order can never be restored. The reverse entropy of 1800 was unartistic. So too would be a twentieth-century return to wholeness and clarity. This paradox is resolved once one recognizes that the declension from discipline to indiscipline has been fatal for the art of painting, but not for art.

1920–1930

The students of the 1920s were the first to profit from the documentation projects launched in the late nineteenth century: biographies, bibliographies, corpuses of paintings, museum catalogues, topographical handbooks, yearbooks with reports on archival discoveries. Now every major library stocked transcriptions of unedited primary sources and good editions of the old printed texts. Universities and research institutes built huge collections of photographic reproductions. The authoritative *Allgemeines Lexikon der bildenden Künstler*, a biographical dictionary of artists edited by Ulrich Thieme and Felix Becker (thirty-seven volumes, 1907–1950), was well underway. Georg Dehio's *Handbuch der deutschen Kunstdenkmäler*, a series initiated in 1900, was a travel guidebook for professionals. The editing and compiling encouraged two tendencies: the adoption of a hierarchical conception of scholarship, whereby interpretation builds upon facts; and a precocious turn to historiography, or the reflection on the genesis and development of the discipline itself.

In 1921 and 1924 Wilhelm Waetzoldt (1880–1945), professor at Halle, author of a treatise on the art of portraiture, published a two-volume history of art-historical writing in Germany entitled *Deutsche Kunsthistoriker*. This was the first major study of the history of the discipline. Waetzoldt told his story as a series of lives. The first volume began with the spare comments on art by sixteenth-century German writers and reached to Rumohr; the second volume extended the sequence of the lives of the German art historians to Carl Justi, professor at Bonn in the

Gründerzeit, with a sentimental cast of mind, who had himself stuck to biography as the basic principle of art history and who had died in 1912, the very year in which Waetzoldt launched his historiographical project. Justi's first book had been a three-volume life-and-times study of Winckelmann.

It is often said that art history is more absorbed with its own origin and history than any other academic discipline. This is hard to measure; there were other disciplinary histories in this period, including the *History of Classical Scholarship* from antiquity to the nineteenth century by the Cambridge classicist John Sandys (three volumes, 1903–1908) and *Geschichte der neueren Historiographie*, a history of the writing of history since the Renaissance, by the Swiss historian Eduard Fueter (1911).

Art historiography, or the history of the history of art, seemed to symbolize the autarky of a discipline no longer auxiliary to art instruction. Yet beyond Germany there were still plenty of major universities without a professorial chair or a degree program in art history. The occupant of the first chair of art history at Oxford was Edgar Wind, appointed in 1955; Cambridge has offered degrees in art history only since 1970. At Yale University art history was taught in the art school until the 1940s when several students of Henri Focillon, who for some years had been engaged as a visiting professor, established an advanced-degree program.

Historiography also marked a self-distancing of the discipline from the image of the belletristic art historian: from the lethargic pursuits, as it were, of Charles Swann. By writing a genealogy of the German historiography of art that stretched back to the sixteenth century, Waetzoldt was distinguishing his discipline from the newcomers sociology, anthropology, and psychology. He was also constructing a German tradition to rival the Italian. Still, Vasari is present in the book's principle of organization: neither Sandys nor Fueter thought to organize his history as a series of Lives. The format of the scholar's biography invited identification and hero worship, an overrating of individual innovation and underrating of the collective nature of scholarship. The vita reminded the reader that scholarship was rooted in existence, subject to social and other real conditions, and that the history of a discipline was not an abstract succession of ideas. Waetzoldt writes the annals of art historiography.

Waetzoldt sketched a tripartite history. He characterized the first period, running from Winckelmann to Rumohr, as Hellenophile and aestheticizing and the second, running from Passavant to Justi, as historicist and scholarly. Waetzoldt cut short his account just before art history became interesting. But he grasped well that the third period of art history, coextensive with his own lifetime, taking for granted and therefore emancipated from the mass of fact, had introduced the free analysis of form. The history of art, according to Waetzoldt, will become a mere auxiliary discipline not to training in painting but to the higher interpretation of art. It is thus ironic that Carl Justi should have been the figure to crown this phase, given the embarrassing exposure, in 1905, of a fabricated document in his Velázquez monograph, which had appeared in 1888. Justi had introduced into his narrative the text of a letter supposedly written by Velázquez about his experiences in Rome. He did not indicate that he had invented the letter, nor did he pretend that he had found it in an archive. One could charitably see this episode as an imaginative but misfired attempt to transcend mere historicist probity and venture instead that higher criticism.

Waetzoldt's note of condescension toward the historical scholarship of the nineteenth century, and the desire to rid himself of the prejudices of his father's generation, resonates with Bloomsbury; as if *Deutsche Kunsthistoriker* were a milder, more prosaic *Eminent Victorians*, the ironic unmasking of Victorian pretentions published in 1918 by Waetzoldt's exact contemporary Lytton Strachey.

Waetzoldt, like other art historians of his day, was reminded constantly by artists that artworks exceeded the factual worlds they emerged from. The moment had come to stand back and assess, to convert data into meaning. Many German and Austrian art historians in the early 1920s believed in the special intellectual promise of the discipline.

The term *Kunstwissenschaft*, meaning "systematic study of art," or better yet "artology," had already been used in the early nineteenth century. The frequency of use of the term increased sharply in the 1880s. By the 1920s it signified recognition of the limits of a strictly historical approach to art. The use of the term would decline after the Second World War, rise again in the 1970s, and then fall again.

Historiography also signalled a turn away from collecting, custodianship, museums, and generally art history's sensuous involvement with art. The authors of art histories from this point on are less likely themselves to be collectors or painters. Still, *Kunstwissenschaft* was prepared to account for the aesthetic, to factor it in, anticipating the objections from beyond the university. No one wanted to make the blunder of mis-recognizing the artwork. The academic discipline, invested in empiricism, compensated by introducing the aesthetic at another level of analysis: engagement with art was sublimated as engagement with form.

A discipline enters into a state of self-consciousness, writes its own history and theorizes its practices, when something is unresolved. A prehistory of good empirical practices would be of limited interest, a chronicle of false starts, of trial and error. The practicing physician has no need to know the history of medicine. That history is valuable only when profiled against an alternative history: Asian medicine, for example. The art historians proceed by importing attitudes alien to them, provincializing their own scholarship as a hedge against the possibility of their own fatal detachment from possession and beauty.

The doyen of the Viennese school of art history, Julius von Schlosser (1866–1938), a student of Wickhoff, and a more original scholar than Waetzoldt, published in 1924 his magnum opus, *Die Kunstliteratur: ein Handbuch zur Quellenkunde der neueren Kunstgeschichte* (The Literature of Art: A Handbook for the Study of the Sources of Modern Art History). This was a history, with commentary, of writing on and about art from the Middle Ages to the dawn of the modern age. Across more than 600 judgmental and most readable pages Schlosser described texts by several hundred authors in a range of genres: medieval treatises on painting, treatises on perspective and proportion, treatises on architecture, and the early histories of art, principally Lorenzo Ghiberti.

A disciple and friend of the philosopher Benedetto Croce, Schlosser was dissatisfied with art history and felt that academic scholarship was alienated from its true object, namely creativity or intuition. Schlosser's guide to the sources undermined its own subject matter. Schlosser dismissed many of the most notable as excessively "literary," a strange reproach given that the title of the book is *Kunstliteratur*. The only witnesses to the genesis of the artwork whom Schlosser trusted were the artists themselves—some artists. We have already noted his admiration for Philipp Otto Runge. He did not trust Leon Battista Alberti or Giorgio Vasari. Schlosser sometimes treats Alberti as if he were a mere rhetorician. Vasari, although a painter, had according to Schlosser an impoverished artistic imagination and could only think in terms of influences, dependencies, and technical progress. Schlosser dismissed Gian Paolo Lomazzo as a "pedant."

Schlosser brings his history to a close around 1800, leaving the impression that he saw no meaningful task left for the modern historian of art other than a pointless sifting through the written testimonies and a circling round the taciturn artworks. For Schlosser, nineteenth-century academic art history subjected a living tradition of writing about art to the conventions of the university. Nineteenth-century art history was not the beginning so much as the beginning of the end.

The one fixed point that anchored all of Schlosser's work, and the only text he truly trusted, was Ghiberti's *Commentaries*. For Schlosser, only Ghiberti was sufficiently *sachlich*, or "to the point." Only Ghiberti gave access to the artist, the true source of art. Schlosser would have admired the writings, had he known them, of Dong Qichang and Shitao.

Schlosser's recursive handbook presents the writing of art history as the possibility of a belated contribution to an already alienated tradition of writing. Why was he so pessimistic? Riegl, whom he revered, was dead, but Schlosser's own students Otto Pächt and Hans Sedlmayr were tending to Riegl's legacy. In 1923 Riegl's lecture notes on Baroque art, first published in 1908 as *Die Entstehung der Barockkunst in Rom*, were reprinted. *Late Roman Art Industry* and *The Dutch Group Portrait*, as noted, were re-edited. In 1929 Sedlmayr prefaced a collection of shorter writings with an essay entitled "The Quintessence of Riegl's Teachings." Heinrich Wölfflin was also very much still present; Schlosser expressed great admiration for his 1905 monograph on Albrecht Dürer. Schlosser made out the true physiognomy of the discipline between the wars: the academicization of the classic mode of art history. The readership from now on will mostly be other professors of art history. The same thing happened to sociology and anthropology, disciplines whose classic moments (Durkheim, Weber, Boas, Malinowski) were similarly brief.

Erwin Panofsky (1892–1968) published several early essays assessing the theoretical achievements of Riegl and Wölfflin. His *Habilitation* or second thesis (1920; the only typescript was lost in the war and rediscovered by accident in 2012), entitled *Die Gestaltungsprinzipien Michelangelos*, was an exercise in formal analysis in the mode of Wölfflin, philosophically fortified. (The term *Gestaltungsprinzipien*, or "formal principles," had been introduced to art history by August Schmarsow in his *Grundbegriffe der Kunstwissenschaft* [Basic Principles of the Study of Art] [1905], a book that extended the project of formal analysis to architecture, in particular to the problem of space, more thoroughly than anyone had before.) Panofsky argued that Michelangelo's art cannot be assimilated to the sequence of styles Quattrocento—High Renaissance—Baroque. That first style Panofsky characterized as an unfree lawlessness, the second as a freely chosen lawfulness, and the third as the equally free negation of the law. Michelangelo's style, by contrast, expressed an inner struggle between freedom and law. In crafting a fable about form, Panofsky hoped to correct his own bias toward humanism, or edifying content. Panofsky's conscientious form-biographies, however, did not derive from mistrust of the referential claims of the pictorial signifier, such as to support an aestheticism, but rather from the plausible conviction that content has a better chance to survive the vicissitudes of history when it is carried by beautiful form.

In 1920 Panofsky took a chair at the university of Hamburg and soon fell under the spell of Aby Warburg, his library, and the community of scholars and thinkers drawn to the library. Panofsky's essay "Perspective as 'Symbolic Form,'" delivered as a lecture at the Warburg Library in 1925 and published three years later in the library's publication series, shared with Schlosser's book its recursivity. This tour de force of art-historical writing, an ambiguous text that still generates debate, redescribes in seventy-two pages (more than half given over to footnotes) the entire sweep of European art history from Greco-Roman antiquity to the seventeenth century. Panofsky's thesis is that painters' perspective, or the projection of three-dimensional reality onto a plane surface, is never true to reality. Every perspectival method distorts reality in one way or another. The question facing the historian, then, is not whether a given artist or artistic culture can paint in perspective, but which sort of perspective they use.

This is a relativist history of perspective. Still, one system of perspective emerges as special, namely, the *perspectiva artificialis* or *costruzione legittima* invented by the Florentines Brunelleschi and Alberti in the fifteenth century and systematized by artists and mathematicians over the next two centuries. Alberti's linear, central, or one-point perspective measures the diminishment in apparent size of objects as their distance from a stationary beholder increases. Panofsky believed that curvilinear perspective, of the sort used by some ancient Roman painters, produced a more accurate representation of optical impressions. He reasoned that the success of the less accurate method, Alberti's linear perspective, must reflect the peculiar demands of Renaissance and post-Renaissance

European culture. Panofsky saw each perspectival system as an expression or "symbolic form" (a concept borrowed from the philosopher Ernst Cassirer) of a mentality, of an approach to reality. According to Panofsky, the linear perspective invented in fifteenth-century Florence, and perfected over the next two centuries, negotiated between the objecthood of the viewed scene and the subjecthood of the beholder. The model for this epistemological reconciliation was what Kant would not until the eighteenth century describe as the "category," the cognitive framework that makes possible the mind's apprehension of the world.

In later writings Panofsky built upon this thesis to argue that Renaissance painting provided the metaphor of the very "intellectual distance between the present and the past" that "enables the scholar to build up comprehensive and consistent concepts of bygone periods." The perspectival metaphor implies charity toward both the claims of the researcher and the claims of the past, a past that included Renaissance painting. In this way Panofsky turns the history of art back on itself. He offers an image of equilibrium between scholar and artwork. The modern person, according to Panofsky, thinks perspectivally. Events in the foreground appear too large, events in the background too small. The writing of history acknowledges the distortion but does not necessarily correct for it.

The German academic model of relativist art-historical scholarship guided by critical philosophy, and tracked by a disciplinary self-consciousness, is powerful. To find countermodels to *Kunstwissenschaft* one must venture to the margins of academia.

As a student in Berlin, Carl Einstein (1885–1940) heard the lectures of Heinrich Wölfflin and like many others first absorbed and then rejected his teachings. The main lesson stuck, however, namely, that artistic form alone—not the depicted subject, not the function of the work, not the historical circumstances—has a chance of opening onto something real. An account of the subject matter of an artwork, Einstein wrote in his book *Negerplastik* (Negro Sculpture) (1915), "moves beyond the given object, by treating it not as a formal construct but appropriating it as guide to some practice outside of its proper domain. Formal analysis, on the other hand, remains within the domain of the immediate.... [F]orms serve the analysis better than individual things because they also contain information about ways of seeing and laws of vision, and so precisely compel us to practice a kind of knowledge that remains within the sphere of the given."

In Paris in 1912, Einstein discovered Cubism as well as a political calling. Later he would participate in the revolutionary fighting in Berlin in 1919 and in the Spanish Civil War. In Cubism he witnessed what he interpreted as an irreversible break with conventional seeing, with the orientation of the European subject to reality, that he believed prefigured an overall rupture in history.

Einstein did not follow an academic career but wrote independently. In 1928 he left Germany for Paris where he developed close ties to the Surrealists; he was involved as well with the Russian avant-garde and with the Bauhaus.

Einstein wrote on Picasso and Braque in 1912 and 1913 and then found his voice as a visionary ideologist of a new art with *Negerplastik*, a short tract on African sculpture. The African artifacts were cult objects, Einstein asserted, which did not signify or represent the gods so much as make them real. The sculptures "will never mingle in the process of human life." They achieved this "unentangled" and "unconditional" status by excluding human subjects, sculptor and beholder alike. The African work "absorbs time by integrating into its form what we experience as movement." It renders three-dimensionality not by way of the representation of objects, as European art does, but directly with form. European sculpture was ruined when it submitted itself to mere "pictorial surrogates" for form—planar and perspectival arrangements of form. Cubism opens a path out of this overly psychological, experiential concept of artistic form.

In 1926 Einstein published the volume *Art of the Twentieth Century* in the *Propyläen Kunstgeschichte*, a handbook for a general readership. In 1929 he cofounded the periodical *Documents* with Georges Bataille. In the first issue Einstein published an essay entitled "Methodological Aphorisms," clarifying his project. European art imposes a stable world picture and offers artworks only as epistemological objects ensuring the stability of subject. This is exactly what Panofsky was saying in his perspective essay, where the presence of time in the perspectival model is unaddressed but is implicit: the picture will change the moment the subject moves. The intertwining of form with experience and psychology acknowledges that time is the medium of existence and so creates the possibility of a biography of form as empathetic, existential, and linear; form coordinated with other aspects of life, namely, form as style. African sculpture revealed that the true medium of art is space, because only here can it establish its own time beyond mere psychology, which is the time of metamorphosis or "revolt." The first step is the rejection of historical art: the African works encourage "skepticism [which] brings the dissociation of vision from the visual heritage." Einstein had already predicted in *Negerplastik* that the modern artist would have difficulty extricating himself: "The artist of today is not entirely a partisan of pure form. He still senses its opposition to his own prehistory."

Einstein believed that the art of his own time had transformed human nature and expanded human powers. "During the past twenty years," he wrote in 1929, "the grip of mechanized reality has diminished, and hallucinatory and mythological invention has increased." The new art, he wrote in his *Art of the Twentieth Century*, is rebelling against reason:

> We constantly experience elementary and unverifiable processes such as the dream and the miracle, where the psyche apparently acts oblivious to the correctness of physics or to a superficially formal correctness. Reason imposes on man an idiotic monotony of existence and of the gestalts, of which he will at best produce variations or rearrangements; this is a fatal limitation.

But the old tactics no longer suffice: "In earlier times, myths had served as a means of defense against such gestalt monotony; gestalt formation was not a matter of aesthetics but of religion." Today art takes up that challenge:

> This same impulse is at work today in the experiments with new gestalt structures; the fundamental drama of metamorphosis, of gestalt transformation, is being played out anew. That's easily possible in a painting, for any one form can signify a great number of things.

Profiting from the intrinsic ambiguity of the depicted object, the painter creates an interplay between the painting as object and the objects it depicts, attempting to configure space directly. They are "free, autistic figurations." A conventional history of art, which must discover or create temporal order, can only account for those artworks that fix reality. The works that instead strive to capture the invisible flux will escape historiography. Reality is a "pluralistic complex":

> Beyond a reality that has been fixated there exists a sphere of permanent creation and metamorphosis, that is, of the continuous revolt against the imposed world picture.

Art delivers the real by recreating that "continuous revolt." Art is an event in the sense that it signals a break in what is self-evident. That event inhabits multiple present tenses because it is capable of reproducing that break over and over again. Such events elude storytelling, or the construction of cause-and-effect chains. Form is closed but not autonomous, for it joins art to other metamorphoses, other revolts.

Like Anita Brenner, Einstein compared artworks to miracles. In a letter of 1923 to Daniel-Henry Kahnweiler, he defined the miracle as "two moments in time that our contemporary sensation is unable to align into congruence. Which simply means that one had the courage to come up with experiences that transgress the psychological method that's habitual nowadays. Nobody will deny that these people actually did experience miracles. But that means that these forces must have been displaced somewhere." They have been displaced, according to Einstein, into art. Art is the place where the points in time that reason holds apart are reunited.

This is the moment of the fission of art-historical thinking, the moment of the ascendancy of the formal method together with its countermodel. Einstein exposed the inadequacies of Wölfflin's concept of form, and by extension Riegl's and Hildebrand's, not to mention the concept of form of such historians as Panofsky who could educe their synthetic, consolatory lessons from history only by remaining on the surface of the artworks. Einstein's approach to art history is not historical at all. Instead he brings to bear on the art of his own day an art that supposedly lies outside of time: African art (just as the *Documents* authors will look to paleolithic painting). The only alternative to Einstein is a retrenchment in historicist scholarship, even for African art, an approach that has thrived in the academy but may well appear, from the outside, to represent a retreat into a state of non-knowing about art, inexcusable after Modernism. This is the divide in the discipline that prevails even today.

Both Anita Brenner and Carl Einstein were saying that the Enlightenment's teaching is an incomplete teaching. History does not converge on understanding as a life might. Art discredits the Enlightenment's discrediting of the miracle. Even some academic art historians shared these doubts. Wilhelm Pinder in an article of 1926 on the problem of art historical generations wrote of the temporal clusterings of form as unintelligible, as nature's "casts of the dice." Erwin Panofsky in 1927 wondered whether it still made sense, given the stylistic disparities among contemporaneous works, to reflect on art-historical events as if they were temporal occurrences: it is possible, he continued, that "the very idea of a historical and temporal relation [among artworks] is practically unrealizable and even a logical contradiction."

The theologian Karl Barth in an essay of 1920, "Biblical Questions, Insights, and Vistas," wrote of the modern sense of standing "outside," expressed in "our naturalism, our soulless historism, our estheticism." The "history of religion," he remarks disparagingly, had already gotten underway with Aaron. "At the moment when religion becomes conscious of religion," as a "psychologically and historically conceivable magnitude in the world," it falls into idolatry. Barth is saying that there is no external vantage point on the soul, for you are it. That is what Brenner was saying about the ex voto. The painted miracle cannot participate in histories of art because it is too close to disorderly experience. It emerges out of a non-time where no one has control. The ex voto involves you in the miracle and offers you no vantage point outside a history of life, suffering, and death.

If you are speaking from a position *within* art, within the circle of creation, you do not see the reality outside, or do not recognize it as reality. If you are speaking from *outside* the circle of art, as art historians do, you cannot grasp the anarchic, miraculous quality of art. Brenner and Einstein were standing right on the border between inside and outside. They were not artists, but they were not art historians either. For Einstein, the history of art converged on the definitive discrediting of self-evidence—with decisive political stakes, he believed—carried out by early twentieth-century European art. For Brenner, the history of art was a nonhistory because for her art was always already modern, more true to reality as people experience it than the ideologies, cults, and sciences devised by civilization.

1930–1940

Already in 1931 Paul and Felix Warburg, who had been living in New York for decades, were seeking a new home for the private library and research center established in Hamburg by their brother Aby, who had died in 1929. They foresaw, under a National Socialist regime, repression and eventually closure. That would be exactly the fate of the Bauhaus, the art school founded by Walter Gropius in Weimar in 1919. Erwin Panofsky, who was teaching as a visiting professor at New York University in the fall and winter of 1931–1932, was involved in the conversation and in the efforts to bring the Hamburg institution to the attention of possible American sponsors. In a letter to Panofsky of January 5, 1932, Fritz Saxl speaks of moving the Warburg library to Rome, possibly to the American Academy; or to an American university such as Johns Hopkins, Harvard, or Princeton. In April 1933, again teaching in New York, Panofsky received a telegram informing him that he had been stripped of his professorship in Hamburg. At that moment he was, along with Adolph Goldschmidt and Paul Frankl, one of three Jewish *Ordinarien* or full professors of art history in the German-speaking nations.

In Germany and Austria in 1933, about one thousand individuals held professorships or lectureships in art history or curatorial positions in museums. A quarter of them were Jews, or were identified as such by the Nazis. They lost their positions and over the course of the 1930s left their countries, ending up in the United States, Great Britain, and elsewhere. Those who went to France were forced to move on. Among the exiled art historians there were fourteen non-Jews, some of whom were married to Jewish women. Non-Jewish academics deemed unsuitable for political reasons were also dismissed. By 1939, 45 percent of all university posts in Germany had been reassigned.

It is perhaps an accident or a paradox, or perhaps neither, that several of the most original art-historical thinkers of this period were sympathetic to the National Socialists. They took advantage of the illiberal climate to amplify the chauvinistic, racist, or primitivist aspects of their projects, often winning large readerships. The most widely read art historian in Germany in these years, and unfortunately also one of the most incisive and original, was the vitriolic reactionary Wilhelm Pinder. Remembering, or more likely forgetting, the last page of Schlosser's *Kunstliteratur*, Pinder closed his own *Deutsche Kunst der Dürerzeit* with a hymn to the pure landscapes of Albrecht Altdorfer, "one of the few who survived [the end of the *Dürerzeit*] unscathed. While the others cooled off, he remained warm. He did so, because he was a *devoted* man. Three hundred years later Philipp Otto Runge saw in landscape the last possibility of the European. Altdorfer was the first to conquer it."

In 1931 all Italian university professors were obliged to take an oath of fealty to Benito Mussolini's Fascist regime. Among some 1200 professors only twelve refused and were forced to resign, among them the art historian Lionello Venturi. Venturi, who was not Jewish, moved to Paris where in 1936 he published the first catalogue raisonné of Cézanne's work. He moved on to New York where he published *History of Art Criticism*, in effect a history of art history, in 1936. Venturi's book *Il Gusto dei primitivi* (The Taste for the Primitives, 1926), was the first study of the eighteenth-century rediscovery of Italian medieval painting.

After his dismissal Panofsky returned to Germany; returned to New York the following winter; returned once more to Germany; and in the summer of 1934 emigrated, via England, to the United States, first taking a position that had been created for him at New York University and a year later moving to the Institute for Advanced Study in Princeton. Not all of the exiled art historians found permanent posts abroad, and many of those who did found themselves teaching in outposts where art history had never been recognized as a subject of study, at state universities or liberal-arts colleges far from major research libraries and art museums. With his curiosity and his shrewd eye Panofsky, whose correspondence has been published in five volumes, is an informative guide to these dismal times.

The German and Austrian emigrés had an immediate impact on the American and British scenes. American art history in 1933 was provincial and anti-intellectual; in England knowledge about art was bound up with class and collecting and had little foothold in the universities. The emigrés built the libraries, trained the students, gave lectures. Americans were quick learners. The winter public lecture program at the Philadelphia (then Pennsylvania) Museum of Art in 1935 offered a lineup of seven speakers: Dewitt Parker, John Dewey, Alfred North Whitehead, Erwin Panofsky, Meyer Schapiro, Ananda Coomaraswamy, and Gustav Pauli. Pauli, a pupil of Jacob Burckhardt and a friend of Aby Warburg; a contributor alongside Kandinsky, Marc, and Worringer to the pamphlet *Im Kampf um die Kunst* (1911); and the longtime director of the Kunsthalle in Hamburg, dismissed in 1933 for his sponsorship of modern art, must have been surprised to find himself, in an American lecture series, one of the *least* distinguished speakers. Parker, an aesthetician, is admittedly now forgotten. Whitehead, the British logician and metaphysician whose wide-ranging thought reverberates again today, was enjoying a brilliant second career since his appointment at Harvard in 1924 at the age of sixty-three. Dewey, the most eminent American philosopher, had published in 1934 his *Art and Experience*, which presents art as an edifying form of social conversation. Dewey was a mentor to the chemist Albert C. Barnes, whose collection of French modernist painting, located in the suburbs of Philadelphia and opened to the public as a study center in 1922, promoted the Deweyan idea of art. Coomaraswamy, the key mediator of Indian art and its philosophy in the West, had arrived in the United States in 1917 to take up the post of curator of Indian art at the Boston Museum of Fine Arts. Schapiro, finally, only thirty-one years old, had already made a mark with his bold dissertation on Romanesque sculpture and his engagement with Marxist and Freudian thought.

Such ambitious public lecture programs, ministering to Dewey and Barnes's vision of art integrated into society, did not acknowledge a tension between study of the art of the past and criticism of the art of modernity. Modern art, which Dewey understood as converging on reality, the way things really are, as well as a therapy, was the framework. Dewey saw the study of historical art as at most an auxiliary to the aims of pedagogy and art appreciation. Coomaraswamy espoused the "perennial philosophy" of the sages. Whitehead was not interested in history at all. Pauli was a champion of modernist painting. Schapiro, whose studies of medieval art ran in parallel with his critical writings on modern painting, had updated the study of Romanesque sculpture by proposing his own present-day concerns—profane, popular, psychological—as the framework of interpretation. Schapiro's writing on Romanesque art arrived at one of the vanishing points of relativism: the unlovely forms now finally recognized as prophecies of modernist truth.

In such company a historicist scholar such as Panofsky might well have been inclined to underrate the irreversibility of the avant-garde mutiny. In the 1933 article "Classical Mythology in Medieval Art," Panofsky and his colleague and friend from Hamburg, Fritz Saxl, at that point attempting to reestablish the Warburg Library and research institute in London, wrote that "we can understand why…down to the crisis of our own days, which, among other phenomena, has given rise to the classicism of Picasso, almost every artistic and cultural crisis has been overcome by that recourse to antiquity which we know as classicism." This seems very far from Warburg, not to mention Schapiro. In a long footnote to his essay on perspective of 1927, Panofsky had corrected the supposed error of El Lissitzky, the Russian suprematist and constructivist artist, who in an essay of 1925 had asserted that his artworks involving mechanically rotating bodies introduced art to a non-Euclidean, "imaginary" geometry. Panofsky, by pointing out that even modernist art was still rational, and so not necessarily in conflict with perspective, was trying to stitch art history back together again before it was too late.

Historicism was the mid-century creed. Erich Auerbach, in his classic *Mimesis: The Representation of Reality in Western Literature* (1946), paraphrased Friedrich Meinecke's recent study of the eighteenth-century origins of historicist thought, *Die Entstehung des Historismus* (1936): to think historically is "to realize that epochs and societies are not to be judged in terms of a pattern concept of what is desirable absolutely speaking, but rather in every case in terms of their own premises"; "to reckon among such premises not only natural factors like climate and soil but also the intellectual and historical factors"; "to develop a sense of…the incomparability of historical phenomena and of their constant inner mobility"; "to accept…that the meaning of events cannot be grasped in abstract and general forms of cognition and that the material needed to understand [the epoch] must not be sought exclusively in the upper strata of society and in major political events but in the depths of the workaday world and its men and women, because it is only there that one can grasp what is unique, what is animated by inner forces, and what is universally valid." For historicists, the precepts of Meinecke and Auerbach *are* the perennial philosophy, incontrovertible. From this point of view, the momentum of reality is too powerful and avant-gardism can never be more than a symbolic gesture of protest.

Warburg's own writings registered modernity at best indirectly, and yet Carl Einstein and Walter Benjamin both responded to the innovative dynamic of the projects generated by his research center. Einstein wrote to Fritz Saxl in 1929 in hopes of entering into an alliance with the scholars around Warburg. He was rebuffed. Panofsky's response, which does not survive, to Benjamin's *Habilitation* on German Baroque drama (submitted in 1925, published 1928), which dealt in part with a topic close to Panofsky, melancholy, was described by Benjamin as "cool and resentment-laden." Einstein wrote to Panofsky in January 1933, apparently in response to a letter from Panofsky that has not survived, expressing his sympathy for his project, which he understood as an antidote to what he called the "Wölfflin-hype" (*wölfflinrummel*):

Form as the beyond, and with its own "proper motion," gratis, the bleak remains of the dead metaphysics, always disgusted me. We always found the broad-brimmed aesthetes, who blather about triangles and quadrangles and so on and who are still trapped in the dualisms of form and content, rather repugnant. It is not so simple, you can't obtain the autonomy of the artwork just by a thorough chemical cleansing.

Panofsky's response was somewhat formal and noncommittal.

Benjamin had attended, and later professed not to have been impressed by, Wölfflin's university lectures in Berlin. In 1933 he wrote a largely favorable review of the first volume of Otto Pächt and Hans Sedlmayr's journal *Kunstwissenschaftliche Forschungen*. Here Pächt had repudiated writing that sought to render the aesthetic qualities of works of art in prose, while Sedlmayr had distinguished between a first, empirical art history that need not recognize the artifact as an aesthetic construct, attending instead to attribution, dating, iconography, patronage, function, and the social context. The second, interpretative art history adopted the attitude or point of view (*Einstellung*) toward the work of art that would reveal its aesthetic nature, what he called not *Kunstwollen*, as

Riegl had, but *Struktur*. Sedlmayr, whose political views were conservative if not reactionary, in a letter of January 12, 1933, to Meyer Schapiro listed Benjamin as someone he hoped to recruit to write for the journal *Kritische Berichte*. Sedlmayr tried in these years to cultivate a relation with Schapiro, who reviewed the second volume of *Kunstwissenschaftliche Forschungen* perceptively but critically; the correspondence later broke off in acrimonious misunderstanding.

Not until the 1970s would Walter Benjamin and Martin Heidegger figure among the tutelary deities of art history, that is, the small group of modern philosophers and theorists to whom historical scholars turn for orientation. Yet in their writings of the 1930s, both Benjamin and Heidegger articulated, more incisively than any art historian of the time, the problem of the historical treatment of art. Both turned to the metaphor of the origin, *Ursprung* in German, meaning literally "primal leap." To speak of an artwork as an *Ursprung* is to assert its autopoetic character, that is, its quality of having self-started, set itself into being. The primal leap is unconditional; it is not produced by a chain of events or any past at all but instead commences something. The title of Heidegger's text on this topic, delivered as a lecture in the mid-1930s though not published until 1950, embraces the two meanings, the wrong and the right: *Der Ursprung des Kunstwerkes* (The Origin of the Work of Art). At first it sounds as if he will speak about where the artwork comes from. By the end we learn that the sense of the title is that the artwork is itself an origin. He calls this "founding" quality of art "historical": "Art is historical, and as historical it is the creative preserving of truth in the work. Art happens as poetry. Poetry is founding in the triple sense of bestowing, grounding, and beginning. Art, as founding, is essentially historical." By this he means that the place where art sets truth into being is ordinary human existence in bounded, historical time. Here art makes truth available to us. He is not saying that an artwork has a life of its own or that it is subject to the ravages of time, for that is true about any artifact or fabricated thing: "This means not only that art has a history in the external sense that in the course of time it, too, appears along with many other things, and in the process changes and passes away and offers changing aspects for historiology [*Historie*, his disparaging term for what commonplace or positivist historians write]. Art is history in the essential sense that it grounds history." This ability to "ground history" does distinguish artworks from tools and other useful artifacts:

Art lets truth originate (*entspringen*). Art, founding preserving, is the spring that leaps to the truth of what is, in the work. To originate something by a leap, to bring something into being from out of the source of its nature in a founding leap—this is what the word origin means.

The origin of the work of art—that is, the origin of both the creators and the preservers, which is to say of a people's historical existence, is art. This is because art is by nature an origin: a distinctive way in which truth comes into being, that is, becomes historical.

Here Heidegger strikes a dissonant note that reveals his political investments beyond the task of the definition of art: he speaks of those who make the artwork and those who receive it as "the people," *das Volk*. This was gratuitous: the origin-quality of art could well have been established without further specification of its social "address." But it is more than a slip. Heidegger explains:

Whenever art happens—that is, whenever there is a beginning—a thrust enters history, history either begins or starts over again. History means here not a sequence in time of events of whatever sort, however important. History is the transporting of a people into its appointed task as entrance into that people's endowment.

In a later, wartime text, much less well known, Heidegger makes explicit his doubts that conventional scholarship can place art properly in history. Like Nietzsche, he thought little of the cult of monuments, dead witnesses to a dead past, sustained by the historical sciences. He was interested instead in a past that was still active and that might well include a "remembered" artwork. He invoked this artwork near the beginning of his long manuscript *Besinnung* (Mindfulness), written in 1938–1939 but not published until 1997. Here Heidegger extends the basic argument of *Being and Time* of 1927, namely that the task of philosophy is at once to reveal the finitude and historical boundedness of human existence and to guide human beings toward some acquaintance with Being itself, a given that precedes and exceeds mankind. In *Mindfulness*, he says: "Insofar as in this art, too, being of beings takes shape, one can initially interpret what being-historically sways in art from out of the historical remembrance, whereby this interpretation already no longer thinks metaphysically, but being-historically." Heidegger's writings from the war years verge on unintelligibility. He seems to be saying that historical art—the art of the Renaissance and the succeeding centuries—was still metaphysical, that is, still organized as an encounter between a subject and an object and mistakenly trusting in representation to mediate between the two (this is exactly what Panofsky's perspective essay maintains). And yet even this incomplete historical art, according to Heidegger, points toward its modern and future vocation, its real identity, as a site of revelation of Being. In this way the art of the past, produced by people facing quite different challenges than our own, can yield truth.

Heidegger doubts the academic discipline of art history will guide us to the encounter with past art because art historians are not really interested in art, but only in embellishing man's image of himself and securing his autonomy and comfort in an increasingly technological, pragmatic world. Here he harmonizes with the note that Worringer had already struck in 1908. "The explicit regard for art," Heidegger wrote, "and the preoccupation with art (all the way to the industry called art-history) are animated by entirely different 'categories' of thinking, namely those that are required by the pre-eminence of man as subject.... 'Art' counts as an 'expression' of 'life' and is valued to the extent that it succeeds in being such an expression." With these contemptuous phrases Heidegger is saying that the whole enterprise of art history, which he derides as a mindless "industry," depends on an artificial distinction between the forms generated by the creative imagination and the bed of experience or life out of which they supposedly emerge. It is convenient for art history to keep those separate, so that it can celebrate art as a sublimation of mere life—as what Panofsky's mentor Ernst Cassirer would call "culture."

Heidegger—and Sedlmayr would have concurred—dismissed the relativistic approach to art as a missed appointment with art and a reduction of art to the status of mere expression of something else more fundamental. He describes a discipline that cultivates a principled relativism and yet inconsistently allows that relativism to stand alongside and not interfere with a covert aestheticism. This is what he means when he asserts that

> there is a "historical" continuation of the "art-industry" of the nineteenth century which is now assessed in terms of cultural politics, but remains unreal and only indicates the historicism that shimmers in all its possible colors. Besides, parallel or lingering next to this

historicism there is a cultivation and an enjoyment of the "historical" traditions of Occidental art that are aesthetically sure of their taste and mostly supported and guided by the educationally motivated dissemination of historical research into art.

Heidegger's *Kunst-Industrie* stretches a malign bridge between Semper and Riegl's term and Max Horkheimer and Theodor W. Adorno's "culture industry," a coinage of their book *Dialectic of Enlightenment* (1944). It would be hard to formulate a more devastating judgment than Heidegger's on the modern project of art history.

As noted, Heidegger lists art history among the practices that prop up a metaphysical conception of art, that is, an idea of art as a processing of objects by subjects that permits the subject finally to surpass a merely straightforward engagement with things, with life. This supposed movement from matter to spirit is achieved by a series of substitutions that go by the name of "representation" or "symbolization," involving the exchange of lower for higher, concrete for abstract. These operations and the transcendence they bring about permit, finally, a set of value judgments that sit alongside, even if they logically clash with, the foundational relativism of the discipline. He is basically describing Cassirer and Panofsky's project. In pointing to the cohabitation of relativist and transcendentalist tendencies within modern scholarship, Heidegger seeks to force us to recognize that historicism hesitates before the problem of origins, the double enigma of the artwork's source in the collectivity and in individual creativity.

Remember that Auerbach, following Meinecke, said that to understand an epoch we must descend to the level of ordinary experience. "The depths of the workaday world and its men and women" is where the new and the unique is forged; from here the authentic products of imagination and artifice emerge to form eventually a society. Only on this level will we discover what about the period is "universally valid." Hidden in the relativist research program is a universalist aspiration.

Many societies have not looked downward to common bodily experience as the starting point, but upward or outward to some better reality beyond human life: the gods, or the ideal, or nature. Traditionally art has been understood as an overcoming of the everyday. The distance between ordinary experience and art has seemed to count most. It is in fact difficult to track a path backward from a work of art, or a poem, into experience. An artwork wanders away from its site of origin, from the matrix of circumstance and intention that brought it forth.

Heidegger is saying that the modern study of art proceeds as if it already knew in advance what art was and what it was good for. He suggests that modern elites value art, long after it has lost its complicity with state, church, and other mythically sustained potencies, because it gives us a sample of an involvement with reality that is not merely pragmatic and material; an involvement all the more precious in technical modernity.

Walter Benjamin's approach was to locate the origin within the artwork itself. This places him not so far from Freud and Warburg. Benjamin said that in the historical study of art, the origin of an artform, its *Ursprung*—the very primal leap that Heidegger invoked when describing the artwork—must be conceived not as a new beginning but as a kind of midstream event like a whirlpool that devours and so eliminates the traces of its own preconditions. In his *Origin of German Tragic Drama* (1928), Benjamin writes:

> Origin (*Ursprung*), although an entirely historical category, has nevertheless nothing to do with genesis (*Entstehung*). Origin means not the becoming of what has sprung up, but rather the becoming and the vanishing of what is springing up. Origin stands in the flow of becoming as in a whirlpool, pulling into its rhythm the materials of its genesis.

Benjamin made this claim just after having argued that Benedetto Croce's definition of art as intuition prevented Croce from discerning the compatibility of an idealist account of the modes of art (*Ideenlehre von den Kunstarten*) with reflection on history. The key to a properly historical treatment of art, according to Benjamin, is the concept of *Ursprung*, a concept that contains both the aspect of innovation and the aspect of incompleteness:

> The original is never revealed in the naked and manifest existence of the factual; its rhythm is apparent only to a dual insight. On the one hand it will be recognized as a restoration, as re-production, and on the other hand, precisely because of this, as incomplete, unfinished.

Benjamin is saying that history is not exterior to art. The artwork alone is capable of revealing its own historicity. This spells the end of the container-contained model of the relation between history and art. Art can no longer be coordinated with a fixed time scheme. Benjamin's theory of the origin also foretells the breaking of the pact between art history and liberal politics, which depends on objective and linear time. From this point on, the only politics that art can connect to is a fabulous, unrealistic politics.

Benjamin and Heidegger's mystified theories of the historicity of art are responses to art's gradual estrangement from power since the Renaissance. This special European anxiety helps explain the limitations of European art history's capacity to articulate the art-quality of art beyond Europe, where the relations of art to real power have been differently calibrated. The obstacles to a universal art history were masked by the relativist historian's complacent relish in the exotic, which Heidegger rightly mocked. Only a nonrelativist like Carl Einstein had a chance with African art.

Relativism, the enlightened fairness, the reluctance to favor one perspective over another, had been sustained but also suspended by the inquiry into form. The concept of art as a hypothesis about vision forestalled a final relativization of values. No one really wanted absolute relativity, not Heidegger, not Benjamin.

Only in art history is the relativity of values—where it appears in diminished form as a relativity of taste—pursued. The last great apostle of pure visibility, and the last most eloquent defender of the stark, simple art of the eleventh and twelfth centuries, was the French scholar Henri Focillon (1881–1943), whose aphorisms on the incommensurability of art with the rest of life were quoted in the opening pages of the present book. Focillon wrote on a wide range of topics, including Buddhist art, Japanese art, and the engravings of Piranesi. He came late to medieval art and architecture, succeeding the iconographer Émile Mâle at the Sorbonne in 1924. In his short treatise on art, *Vie des formes* (1934), he stressed the independence of art from social time: "We have no right to confuse the state of the life of forms with the state of social life." "The artist inhabits a country in time that is by no means necessarily the history of his own time." Focillon is always crafting poetic definitions of art and at the same time clearing away fallacious theories and misguided art histories. He dismisses Hippolyte Taine, the nineteenth-century contextualizer of Renaissance art, because he considered art "a masterpiece of *external* convergence." "Taine's merit lies in having been, as it were, a kind of interior decorator of time: that is, he disregarded it as a force in and of itself, even though time, like space, is nothing unless it has been really lived." Focillon was a reader of the philosopher Henri Bergson.

Art history as it was organized in the previous century could not grasp that nothing external to art explains art. Even architecture, which seems so tightly bound to environment and history, is free: "The architect engenders new conditions for historical, social and moral life. No one can predict what environments architecture will create. It satisfies old needs and begets new ones. It invents a world all its own." Focillon rejects any interpretation—typological, iconographic, or Warburgian—that revisits an originary scene: "Sometimes form…will not only survive long after the death of its content, but will even and unexpectedly richly renew itself." He rejects all realisms: a form can "create a picture of the world that has nothing in common with the world." Focillon's concept of art as event is compatible with Heidegger and Benjamin's theories of art as origin as well as with Einstein and Brenner's concepts of art as miracle (Focillon: If an artwork is put to practical use its ancient "privilege of working miracles is revoked").

Focillon is apt to stretch a point: "Nothing could have determined the astonishing height of the naves of those cathedrals save the activity of the life of forms: the insistent theorem of an articulated structure, the need to create new space." Neither Riegl nor Wölfflin resorted to such exaggeration, nor did they attempt to define art, even negatively. By 1934 the biography of form had become an improbable project. Even the art of the day no longer seemed to be adding to the story of form.

Architecture told a different story. The most original art-historical thesis of the decade was the short tract *Von Ledoux bis Le Corbusier* (From Ledoux to Le Corbusier) (1933) by Emil Kaufmann (1891–1953), a Viennese-Jewish student of Dvořák, Schlosser, Tietze, and Strzygowski who later emigrated to the United States and enjoyed little more than a *succès d'estime* on either continent. In his book Kaufmann set off the architecture of Claude-Nicolas Ledoux against the foil of a "heteronomous" Baroque architecture whose only content was the maintenance of the social hierarchy. Even before the French Revolution Ledoux conceived of a riposte to this established architecture enthralled by tradition and by rules, which according to Kaufmann are always foreign to the nature of building. Ledoux's autonomous architecture, true to elementary geometry and at the same time true to materials, predicted the projects of the twentieth-century form-givers. Even more insightful is Kaufmann's apology for the eclectic "art historical" architecture of the nineteenth century: the buildings of the Ringstrasse in Vienna, supposedly representational and so heteronomous, stand in fact in "absolute isolation" from one another, indifferent to the overall effect, engrossed in their respective pasts, and as such already rehearsing an aestheticist autonomy.

The faith in pictorial form retreated to unlikely garrisons: the great corpuses of premodern prints and paintings, for example, pictures described, attributed, and dated, the archives of the accumulated achievements of connoisseurship. Many such corpuses were completed or initiated in the 1930s. Encrypted within these most positivistic projects was a conviction, as robust as Focillon's, of the independence of form. In the accompanying essay to his catalogue raisonné of Cézanne's paintings (1936), Lionello Venturi asserts his artist's absolute freedom, from both tradition and nature: "No one was more aware than he that art and nature must travel in parallel tracks." Cézanne created a second nature, purified of "all elements foreign to art." He was a pure painter, comparable to Giotto, Titian, and Rembrandt, even if today the "harmony" of his art is misunderstood or misused.

Less obvious is the claim for the art status of the early northern European engravings implicit in Max Lehrs's *Geschichte und kritischer Katalog des deutschen, niederländischen und französischen Kupferstiches des 15. Jhs.* (History and Critical Catalogue of the German, Netherlandish, and French Engravings of the Fifteenth Century) (10 vols., 1908–1934), the basis of all modern scholarship on these not always winsome objects. Lehrs's descriptions are spare, as are Max J. Friedländer's attribution notes in his *Altniederländische Malerei* (Early Netherlandish Painting) (14 vols., 1924–1937), the corpus of fifteenth-century Dutch and Flemish panel paintings. But Friedländer accompanied his lists with poetic but precise essays on his artists, many of them anonymous. In 1930 Richard Offner, born in Vienna but raised in New York, with a doctoral degree from Vienna under Max Dvořák, and later professor at New York University, launched his *Critical and Historical Corpus of Florentine Painting*.

A new genre of the 1930s, perhaps influenced by Friedländer's prose and certainly by that of Berenson, whose *Drawings of the Florentine Painters* and lists of the Florentine, Venetian, central Italian, and north Italian paintings had set the mark, was the minimalist monograph, cautious and at the same time eloquent, striving to translate perceptions into language. A good example is the monograph on the fifteenth-century Sienese painter Giovanni di Paolo by the youthful John Pope-Hennessy (1937). Like his model Herbert Horne, Pope-Hennessy assembled an oeuvre and a chronology on the basis of documented facts and observation of the works, adding a layer of vivid, judgmental commentary. He achieves an opiniated intimacy with art and artist that recalls the felicitous years in Florence at the end of the previous century. The monograph is by definition structured by an artist's life. It is easy to forget that the real protagonist of Pope-Hennessy's study is form itself: "In a vain search for forcible expression the later Sienese Trecento, while it adhered to primitive mediums and iconography, had abandoned the primitive ideal of contour which was expressive because it was unbroken. Simone in his last Passion scenes had prepared the way for this renunciation. The decision—it was general, voluntary and unconscious—was disastrous." Horne would never have struck this epic tone. Horne had not yet read Wölfflin, presumably. In Pope-Hennessy's narration of the struggle between the artist's will and the logics of form, there is little room for the subject matters or the functions of Giovanni di Paolo's sacred painting. Unshakeable is the conviction of the unity of life and work. The author chose his subject, surely, as Berenson chose Lorenzo Lotto, for his nervous susceptibility: "Giovanni di Paolo's visual pecularities seem to have been directly dependent on and indeed to have acted in the ratio of the emotional impact on his mind of the episode he portrayed." He was an expressionist *avant la lettre*. But "emotional stress was not uncommon at the time." Religious mysticism drove the painter beyond "aesthetic dictates" (read: the Academy, which of course did not exist in Giovanni di Paolo's time) toward a purely personal art, a "style heated to receive the impress of a vital and candescent personality."

Non- or even antiphilosophical, the connoisseurs believed in artistic intention. Focillon did not. His skepticism of all reductive explanations led him to reject even the authority of the author: "A work of art is not the outline or the graph of art as an activity; it is art itself.... Art is made up, not of the artists' intentions, but of works of art."

The most insightful of the Italian historians was Roberto Longhi (1890–1970), a critic and academic, author of monographs on Piero della Francesca and Caravaggio as well as several unorthodox works such as a book-length commentary on an exhibition of Ferrarese painting of the

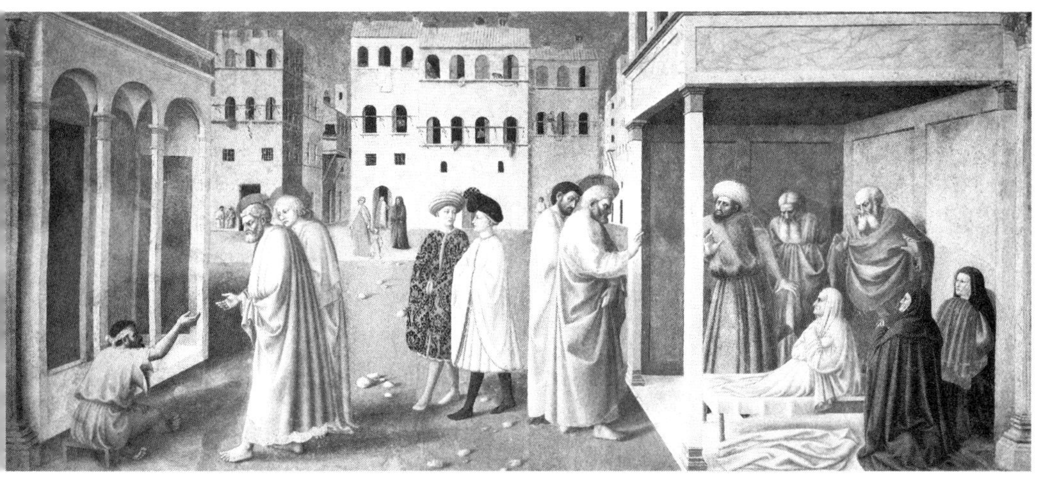

Masolino, *St. Peter Healing a Cripple and Raising Tabitha* (1427). Fresco in the Brancacci Chapel, Santa Maria del Carmine, Florence, 247 × 588 cm. The miracle on the left occurred in Jerusalem, the one on the right in Jaffa.

Renaissance, the *Officina ferrarese* (1934). The atmosphere of intimacy—in a "workshop" now, not a salon—is all the more intense because in the borderlands and early stages of Renaissance art real data is scarce. Psychobiography takes on a speculative quality, an irrealism that reads as an acknowledgment of the antinomian nature of art itself, or as a secret sign to the reader, a guarantee, like the stranger passages in Wölfflin. Longhi, like many other connoisseurs, clothed his genial perceptions in idiosyncratic prose. In a long essay of 1940 on the relation between the early fifteenth-century Florentine painters Masolino and Masaccio, Longhi actually invents comic dialogue to illustrate his theory of the genesis of the fresco of St. Peter healing the cripple and raising Tabitha in the Brancacci Chapel, a "truth which has, in fact, been arrived at by measuring everything to the millimeter."

Behind the material evidence of the more gifted younger painter's interventions and corrections, Longhi hears an improbable psychodrama:

> Think first of Masolino's untrammeled happiness in the 1423 *Madonna*, and again of how that bliss returns in the frescoes of 1435 in the Baptistery at Castiglione. One is immediately prompted to say that the period of Masaccesque terror had ended for him.... During the time he was painting the two deeds of Saint Peter, however, that terror was at its height.

This is because Masolino had decided to depict two separate events in a single urban space unified by linear perspective. On the left, St. Peter, accompanied by St. John, heals a lame man seated before the Temple in Jerusalem (Acts 3:1–8). On the right, the same St. Peter, rotated 180 degrees, raises the good woman Tabitha from the dead (Acts 9:36–42); this actually happened in Jaffa. Masolino is still thinking like a medieval painter, and according to Longhi he must have dreaded Masaccio's censure:

> Masaccio, like Christ, was waiting for him at the shore, and was not about to grant him a moment's peace: "Don't you think that if you made the space more definite, you'd be able to join the two episodes, but keep them distinct at the same time? Or would you really rather 'tell' all your stories in a single breath, like Hail Marys on a rosary, and have Peter following Peter?"

And so forth. Perhaps Longhi had read Paul Valéry, who in his essay *Degas Danse Dessin* (1936) called for a more biographical art history. Valéry chided modern historians for their lack of curiosity about the relations between the young and the old: "admiration, envy, incomprehension, encounters; precepts and procedures handed on, disdained; reciprocal judgments; negations that respond to one another, contempt, returns"; the transmission of secrets; all the aspects of what Valéry calls "the *Comedy of the Intellect*" that must not be passed over in silence.

The French root of "connoisseurship," *connaître*, holds the sense of personal knowledge as opposed to the impersonal knowledge of *savoir*, cognate with *science*. *Connaître, kennen, gnosis* are ripostes to science and *Wissenschaft*. The connoisseur knows art that, if it knows anything, knows no more than what a person knows. The aim of Lionello Venturi's catalogue raisonné had been simply to show how "Cézanne's way of feeling is realized in painting."

The connoisseurs, inhabitants of an endless nineteenth century, were still drawn to the "primitives," the shade-like masters of the early Renaissance. This was still the pastoral fable. Focillon, like Schapiro, went all the way back to the Romanesque, absorbing the shock of its rough forms in the soft bed of his aphoristic prose. Riegl had embraced the late Roman and barbarian styles and the ungracious pragmatic style of the Dutch group portraitists. Wölfflin, for his part, abandoned the pastoral fable. He saw that once there was consensus that art could be found in any time or place, once Vasari's annalistic and noble theory of art was overcome, then one is liberated again to focus on the art of the Renaissance and Baroque.

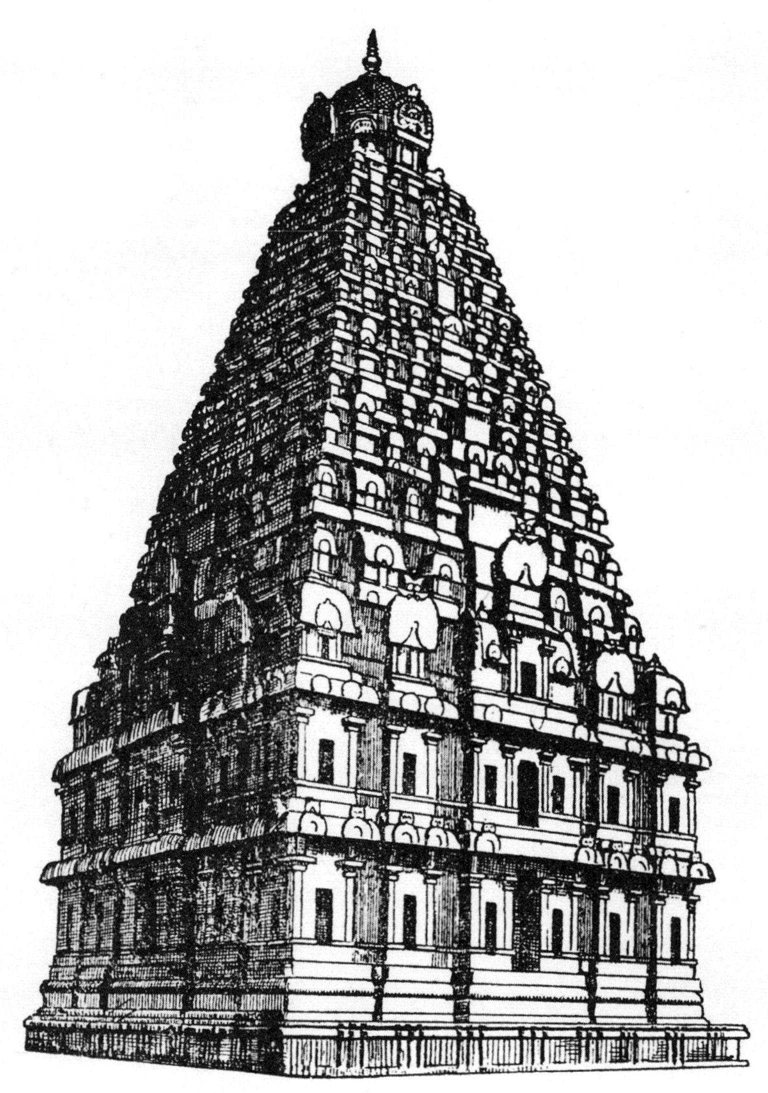

Śikhara of the Brihadisvara or Great Temple at Thanjavur. In Stella Kramrisch, *The Hindu Temple* (Calcutta, 1946), vol. 1, p. 187, fig. h. The pyramid is 66 meters high; the temple-like structure on top is a single granite block more than seven meters square.

1940–1950

The career of Stella Kramrisch (1898–1993) spanned three continents. She wrote a dissertation in Vienna in 1919, under Alois Riegl's archrival Josef Strzygowski, on early Buddhist imagery in India. Only four years later she was appointed professor at the University of Calcutta, at the age of twenty-five, the only woman and the only European on the faculty. In the late 1930s she taught half-time at the Courtauld Institute, founded in 1932, the first institution in the United Kingdom to award doctorates in the history of art. She worked with Fritz Saxl in 1940 on an exhibition of photographs at the Warburg Institute. In 1950 Kramrisch moved one last time, from India to the United States, where over three decades she held positions at the University of Pennsylvania, the Philadelphia Museum of Art, and New York University. Her magisterial two-volume study *The Hindu Temple* (1946), written in Calcutta on the basis of profound knowledge of ancient religious texts, builds upon the approach introduced into English by Rám Ráz's *Essay on the Architecture of the Hindus* (1834) more than a century earlier.

The Hindu Temple covers a vast range of buildings, stretched across centuries and the entire subcontinent. But the book tells no story. Instead, it interprets the temple as the symbolic form of reintegration with the cosmos. Kramrisch shows that a sacred diagram, the Vastupurusamandala, provides the essential plan of the temple. Because the construction of any temple is always a reconstruction, and so every Hindu temple is the same, it makes no sense to write a history of temple-building. Each temple writes its own history, for its origins are inscribed in its form. Forms and designs encode myths, just as do rituals. "The Hindu temple," wrote Kramrisch, "is the sum total of architectural rites performed on the basis of its myth. The myth covers the ground and is the place on which the structure is raised." The structure translates into relative permanence the rites and their rhythmic formulas (*mantra*).

For Kramrisch, the Hindu tradition draws no real distinction between art and ritual, any more than it distinguishes between art and dance. The same essence is expressed in different media, at different paces. Her book opens up a vista onto an infinity of alternative art histories—and not only of Indian art—that will embrace rituals and dance and not merely still, silent things.

The origin of the temple is sacrifice. In "the pedestal, Adhisthana, the socle, and the Vedika is embodied the memory of the sacred ground (*vedi*) with its piled altar (*citi*) whence the sacrificial offerings were carried up by the flaming fire. The place of the flame is now taken by the structure on its socle; it arises with perpendicular walls and pointed superstructure." The origins of the temple in ritual and sacrifice—the only history that counts—is concretized in the building itself.

"Period and place," she concedes, influence the temple while it is being built, "leave their mark on its style." But such contingencies are not her subject matter. The symbol of the exemption of the temple from history is the fire-altar, whose "shape is independent of time and place, independent even of extensiveness. One of the types of the Vedic Altar is prescribed to be made of rhythms only (*chandasciti*) and not of bricks which are their representatives." The symbol of "concentration on the divinity and the elation that accompanies it," meanwhile, and "the zenithal pole of realization where this world ends and that world begins," is the pyramidal superstructure, the Śikhara. Kramrisch reproduces a drawing of the great tower of the Brihadisvara Temple at Thanjavur in Tamil Nadu (eleventh century).

The curvilinear pyramid, sixteen stories high and crowned by a miniature temple, is mounted on the walls of the symbolically determinant earthbound enclosure and so is the "inevitable form" of the superstructure. The superstructure serves no sacred function but only shows the purpose of the temple. Its form "cannot be mistaken for, or derived from a palace or any dwelling of man."

Each building material carries its own meanings. When a material is not available or must be replaced, another material can stand in. Brick, with its ties to Vedic rites, altars, and metaphysical knowledge, is best, but stone can stand in for it. Wood, too, is symbolic, and form can be made to retain a memory of the wood, for example in the bent form of an arch, even when it is replaced by more durable materials. Because the substituted materials put up resistance, it falls to the craftsman, guided by tradition and piety, to handle these resistances, to counteract them with sensibility and so preserve the qualities of the original materials, "severed as they are from their natural life and habitation, in a more permanent body which has but one destination." In this way "the memory of the building stones of the temple is retentive."

The building exceeds the will and imagination of any patron or architect. One inscription records the exclamation of the builder upon completion of the project: "Oh, how was it that I built it?" A history of building based on a succession of architects would be meaningless, for "the science of architecture having its origin in Brahma and being transmitted by an unbroken series of sages preserves its integrity in the planning and building of every temple. Thus it is said that 'Brahma himself is the Sthapati [master architect].'"

The realities of the availability of materials, the relative skill of craftsmen, local stylistic variations, the will and wherewithal of local patrons, the actual day-to-day use of the temple: all this is legible in the bodies of the temples. But Kramrisch, breaking with the archeological mentality, chooses to ignore the evidence. The form of the temple "settles" history.

That form may be read, or it may be experienced, but it cannot really be seen. Abandoning the pictorialism of the European art historian, who studies pictures of buildings and not buildings, Kramrisch points out that "a monument stands in space, it does not face it. The Hindu temple, too, has strictly speaking, no façade; the four orients and the intermediate directions of space step forth in buttresses and images form the body of the temple in a continuous integrity of the mass." She acknowledges that pilgrims will visit the temple, as if remembering the human insufficiency that makes the temple necessary in the first place. But that pilgrim sees the building with "the sight of knowledge (*darsana*)."

The Hindu Temple is like no other book of the century. It is as if Kramrisch had to escape to the other side of the globe to break with the mental habits of European art history. For Kramrisch, there can be no profane history of sacred architecture. Nor does she acknowledge any tragic advent, within the Hindu tradition, of an historical self-consciousness that would threaten to break time in two, or give it any shape at all. No modernity impinges on her book, except insofar as the book itself is a negative inscription of a European's response to the Indian Independence Movement and Partition. Kramrisch's husband, a Hungarian economist employed in Pakistan, was murdered in 1950, prompting her emigration to the United States.

The closest equivalent in the European tradition to Kramrisch's book was not perhaps Émile Mâle's *Art religieux du XIIIe siècle en France* (1898) but rather the nearly contemporary study by another Austrian, Hans Sedlmayr: *Die Entstehung der Kathedrale* (1950), a radical and controversial experiment in art-historical scholarship, still untranslated into any language. In this book Sedlmayr interpreted the Gothic cathedral, on the basis of a somewhat forced Augustinian reading of the liturgy, as a literal copy of the celestial Jerusalem mentioned in the Apocalypse. The book is a collage of quotations; like Kramrisch's treatise, it tells no story. Sedlmayr was interested in identifying a mode of representation stronger than mere symbolism and depicting not a mere worldview, that is, one perspective among many, but a true picture of the cosmos, in order to remind his readers that modernity can no longer consult a cosmology that includes us. The cathedral itself mocked historicism, for the cathedral "cannot be repeated, cannot be re-collected [*wieder-geholt*, a hyphenization that breaks the word, in English just as in German, into two meanings, remembering and recovering]." The author took the incommensurability of the cathedral, resisting typologies and explanations alike, as a license to select the data that matched his thesis.

Kramrisch's teacher Strzygowski had been less interested in what was happening in heaven than in the horizontal exchanges among peoples. Strzygowski's map of world art was shaped by the racist myth of the destiny of the Aryans. For all that, Kramrisch remained true to Strzygowski, translating his essays rather late, in 1933. In her scholarship Kramrisch masked the European sources of her thought. In conversation later in life she acknowledged her debt to the intellectual-historical speculations of Max Dvořák. She was less impressed by Riegl, whose art history affirmed the ascendancy of the secular. Kramrisch belonged to a tradition of European predilection for Hinduism that extended from Schopenhauer to Rudolf Steiner and Wassily Kandinsky. The basis is a nondistancing respect for cosmologies that locate the real beyond human sensory experience. Art is in contact with this realm, Kramrisch believed; and in turn she believed that the Hindus believed that this is art's only meaningful function. Her tendencies and her scholarship found sympathetic Indian readers, above all her patrons Rabindranath Tagore and Ananda Coomaraswamy. One might wonder whether Tagore and Coomaraswamy in their roles as transcultural emissaries were not sometimes meeting the West halfway, thus predetermining Kramrisch's assimilation to Hindu thought. And yet there is her book, a unique monument of modern scholarship. *The Hindu Temple* may not show us the alternative to European art, since no European book could ever do this, but it may show us an alternative to European art history.

Stella Kramrisch spoke late in life of childhood memories of angels carved in a vault on her family estate in Moravia, "superhuman figures," in her eyes, "appearing from an invisible realm that was made real by art." One is reminded of the later reminiscence of Ernst H. Gombrich, who like Kramrisch was Jewish and raised in a secular home, on the allegorical paintings of the Baroque era, the ceilings of Austrian churches and palaces that he knew from childhood, personifications of Platonic ideas that to his eyes appeared "anything but bloodless." These images, Gombrich reported, did not merely point to an ideal reality but became it. In the midst of secular modernity the angels and the allegories nevertheless "spoke through" all the obstacles, as if art could not help but deliver, if not another reality, at least the hypothesis of another reality. The distinction between reality and the hypothesis of a reality may mean little to children, which is why they are the subjects of these anecdotes told by adults to adults.

In Europe, academic scholarship was paralyzed by the war. Some mavericks outside the university plunged into the arcane or the mystical, detecting unfamiliar rhythms of thought without traveling, like Kramrisch, to another continent. Wilhelm Fraenger, for example, forced out of his position as a library director by the Nazis, published in 1947 an eccentric interpretation of Hieronymus Bosch's painting *The Garden of Earthly Delights* as the image of the utopian society envisioned by a millenarian cult; a Thousand-Year Realm perhaps parodying the delusions of the Third Reich. Emigré scholars were less likely to avert their gaze from actuality. In 1938 Sigfried Giedion (1888–1968), the Swiss architectural theorist and historian, exponent of the International Style, gave lectures at Harvard that became his classic *Space, Time, and Architecture* (1941), a masterful survey of the origins and emergence of the modern movement. This was the opposite of Kramrisch and Sedlmayr: Giedion downplays the symbolic content of architecture in favor of the "organic" quality of buildings, the relation of their elements to one another, and free extension in space.

At the end of the war, the discipline enters into a convalescence. Art history as such is fatigued, no longer confident in what had always been its principal object, the object that gave it meaning: painting. Architectural history has its moment. The emigré scholar Rudolf Wittkower presented in his *Architectural Principles in the Age of Humanism* (1949) a defense of neoclassicism. He writes against interpretations of Renaissance architecture as expressions of profane impulses and against formalist analysis. The result of formalist reasoning, he says, is that forms become available for any purpose and we will no longer be able to distinguish between Renaissance and nineteenth-century eclecticisms, for after all both episodes were derivative, not original as Gothic had been. Wittkower's question opens onto an abyss: if he is right, he has found the key to the redemption of the historicist architecture of the nineteenth century. The key is there for the taking, but no one yet has dared to seize it—and least of all Wittkower himself. Instead of equating the nineteenth century and the Renaissance, he restores the old imbalance. The nineteenth century was unsure of its content; the Renaissance by contrast had stable content that according to Wittkower we risk forgetting: like all great architecture it was "based on a hierarchy of values culminating in the absolute values of sacred architecture." All Renaissance forms had symbolic value. Wittkower's response—which resonated for decades—to the manifest lack of robustness of modern civilization was to reassert the absolute difference between the past and the present: premodern societies were oriented, and they knew hierarchy. Wittkower argued, on the basis of the texts by Alberti and Palladio, that the architecture of the Italian Renaissance materialized a mathematical program: a system of ratios that pictured the invisible structure of the cosmos. Architecture placed the human body within this system. It is hard to see the difference between this and Sedlmayr's views except that the one believes that man's image was best framed by forms based on the divinely measured proportions of the human body, and the other believes that man's image was best framed by an image of divinity itself. Wittkower recovers a religious conception of architecture but detached from Christianity: the Renaissance church as a Hindu temple, as it were.

Giedion's *Mechanization Takes Command: A Contribution to Anonymous History* (1948) is another matter entirely, a pessimistic book that seems to have been written under the shock of technologized war, viewed from the far side of the Atlantic, but also in full realization of the meaning of the assembly line. Handicraft, fondly nurtured by intellectuals in the nineteenth century, was now dead. *Mechanization Takes Command* is a history of the accommodations between the body and machines. Giedion's focus on the body in work and leisure is a sketch of an alternative art history. His freedom from conventional theories of art and from conventional narratives of art history, for example, allows him to present the early eighteenth century as the turning point toward modernity, and on a completely new basis: the comfort of the Rococo chair.

Giedion's history of furniture brings out the tension between the perfect configuration of space and the accommodation to the body. Europe and later America abandon pattern in favor of the satisfaction of the desires. This is the anthropomorphism of European art first detected, perhaps, by Roger de Piles, theoretical prophet of the Rococo. Both Riegl and Wölfflin had identified satisfaction or pleasure as the basis of art's place in life. Giedion's account of the chair literalizes this dictum. Giedion was in no mood, it would seem, to indulge Worringer's aesthetic of pain, now an obscene luxury after two wars. Giedion sets aside the question of whether the collaboration between machine and man excludes the soul, or whether the prosthetic functions of the machine liberate the soul. The book steps back from every possible abstraction. Giedion's thought moves once again in the opposite direction to Kramrisch and Sedlmayr, not toward but away from constancy, stasis, and integration. He sees no equilibrium in the Gothic cathedral, only a "stream of movement." Movement was already represented graphically in the fourteenth century, leading to the dissection of labor into its component principles, the basis for mechanization. Giedion's history offers a role for America, where in the nineteenth century the mechanization of the complex crafts—milling, harvesting, locks—was developed.

Fiske Kimball was the founder of the Institute of Fine Arts at New York University and later the director of the Philadelphia Museum of Art who had invited Panofsky and the other luminaries to speak in 1935. His history of Rococo ornament, *The Creation of the Rococo* (1943), is revealing. This is an empirical account, based on archival research, of the emergence of the Rococo style in Paris in the 1720s. Kimball mistrusts any theory of art and rebuked even Semper and Giedion. He says he will beat back the German theorists with facts. Kimball's topic is also the interior, the salon. He is interested in how it was furnished but not in what it was like to inhabit it.

Temple, cathedral, and salon represent three places of refuge, three solutions to disorder and entropy, whose extreme form is war. In France, a diverse group of thinkers took the first steps into a new mythic space, a primal scene of creativity and belief: the decorated cave of the paleolithic era. The subterranean chambers at Lascaux in the Dordogne, with their parietal depictions of beasts, were discovered in 1940. The revelation of this mysterious temple after 25,000 years captured the imagination the way the discovery of Altamira in 1879 had not. Suddenly there was no difficulty seeing paleolithic painting—not enough difficulty, in fact. It was precisely the resemblance of the murals at Altamira to the great tradition of European painting that had led the specialists initially to reject them as modern hoaxes: their apparent frieze-like quality, their dramatic energy and heroic narrative pull, their expressiveness; an illusion of familiarity. Now the paintings won a privileged position at the very beginning of all art histories. Altamira and Lascaux are not really beginnings of anything. They come at the end of a tradition of at least 300,000 years of mark-making and image-making. Nevertheless the cave paintings appear in art histories in isolation, as symbols of a permanently unknowable bursting forth of creativity in the attempt to control natural forces through images.

In his essay "Primitive Art," published in 1930 in *Documents*—the periodical he founded with Carl Einstein—Georges Bataille had asserted that art began with the destructive alteration of surface. Only later does imagination substitute a new object that is assimilated to the original; art moves toward resemblance. Resemblance and naturalism are today the great obstacles that art must overcome. Bataille picks up again the avant-gardist themes of Worringer. Art today, he says, has returned to decomposition. Bataille was wary of what he called Vitruvian or mimetic architecture, which naturalized power. This is why it suited him to seek the origin of art in painting rather than architecture.

The German art historian Max Raphael (1889–1952) fled to Paris, where he published *Proudhon Marx Picasso* (1933); and then New York, where he published *Prehistoric Cave Paintings* (1945). Raphael had studied art history in Paris and Munich, where he also encountered the Blaue Reiter group. His thesis on modern painting was not accepted by his teacher Wölfflin. For an evolutionary, indeed Marxist, thinker like Raphael the topic of the cave paintings was ideal because it cannot be solved by historical scholarship. The paleolithic painting is cut off from later history. There is evolution only within what he called "realistic monumentalism." Raphael, like the other Surrealist-oriented intellectuals lured into the caves, took seriously the magic, totemism, and shamanism that seemed the likeliest contexts. Raphael stressed the ethnographic use value of the paintings rather than the exchange value of aesthetics and formalism.

History-writing is the modern mode of expression because modernity has given up hope of ever knowing, through myth and prophecy, the beginnings and the endings. For those supermoderns already fatigued with history, the paleolithic paintings re-opened the question of origins. The caves were a space for philosophical, mythic, and psychoanalytic truth. Thus art is mobilized against art history.

One might describe this as a primitivism stretched to its maximum extent. But as Max Raphael points out there is nothing primitive about paleolithic art, for it perfectly expressed its world. Carl Einstein, too, was no primitivist: the art he champions creates a new reality.

Most mid-century Marxist theorists of culture were, like Bataille, scornful of both realist and idealist aesthetics, each in their own way based on exchange value. They did not count on realism, a style forever locked in its own present, to restore the lost collectivity. The Soviet Russian writer Maxim Gorky, writing in 1934, made it clear: art will have to create its own future. It will need to *add to* realism. "If to the idea extracted from the given reality," Gorky proposed, "we add…the desired, the possible, and thus supplement the image, we obtain that romanticism which is highly beneficial in that it tends to provoke a revolutionary attitude to reality." This is naïve but at least a plausible theory of art.

Gorky's words were quoted by Francis Klingender, a German art historian of British parentage, living in England from the 1920s, in his book *Marxism and Modern Art* (1943). Later in the decade he published *Art and the Industrial Revolution* (1947). From a Marxist point of view, all negativity, perhaps especially Worringer's, was bourgeois. Life must be affirmed. Klingender chastised Roger Fry's non-negative but formalist art history for seeking the roots of the sense of form in the mind or the body rather than in the plain daylight of everyday life and ordinary awareness. The "sub-conscious" and the "pre-social," according to Klingender, were irrelevant to a progressive aesthetics. Klingender dismissed "sterile" avant-garde art in favor of vital "war painting": the painting of 1914–1918, or the Blitz paintings of 1940–1941, art that was unafraid to confront death, its other. The social art historian who intends to stand by the new artwork that leaves the past behind, a different avant-garde, has no interest in holding conversations with the dead and risking a plunge into the vertigo of memory. The twentieth-century Marxists did not peer very deeply into the past; Max Raphael's caves, again, existed outside of time. For Karl Marx, in the *German Ideology*, the "poetry" of all previous political revolutions was suspect because it came from the past. The political revolutions referred to one another and so repeated one another. The poetry of the *social* revolution, according to Marx, will instead come from the future.

Klingender's book, striking notes both desperate and defiant, is not typical of the long British tradition of Marxist and Marxist-inspired histories of art that would extend into the 1980s. The so-called social history of art interpreted art as the expression of the interests of communities or classes. In the past, art was paid for and shaped by the elite and the powerful. In the future, art would express the vision and will of democratic collectivities. The reality that art delivered was the reality of economic relations. There is no need to look for any other origin.

A social history of art was a desideratum before it was a practice. Nikolaus Pevsner (1902–1983), who had emigrated to England from Germany in 1933, averred in the preface to his book *Academies of Art, Past and Present* (1940) that the parlous times called for a turn away from style history and toward the "changing relations between the artist and the world surrounding him." "Only a social history of art can help." He then apologized for the limited aims of his own book. Arnold Hauser (1892–1978) arrived in England from Hungary in 1938. He was asked in 1940 by the sociologist Karl Mannheim, who had been teaching at the London School of Economics since 1933, to write the foreword to an anthology of texts on the sociology of art. The result, published in 1951, was the four-volume *Social History of Art*. Frederick Antal (1887–1954) emigrated to the UK in 1933, like Mannheim and Hauser from Budapest, and in 1948 published *Florentine Painting and Its Social Background*.

The concept of a social history of art appealed to scholars who had lost all patience, under conditions of war and forced emigration, for the study of the formal relations among works. The study of art history as a study of culture, or *Kulturwissenschaft*, as conceived by Warburg, was too subject-centered and lacked political urgency. Such an art history considers lived life itself as something like a representation, a performance, or a text. In this way *Kulturwissenschaft* reconnects art in a sensible way to life—text to text, like with like. The artistic performance is shown to be continuous with the social performance: this was Warburg's Botticelli. An art history that levels the artistic products of all times and cultures by conceiving them all as representations permits them to be compared. This is already the art history that Goethe had sketched out in his essay "Heidelberg" of 1816. But from a Marxist standpoint such an art history is not *social* but merely *sociable*.

The real enemy, what the social art historians wrote against, was hidden from view, or nearly so. Hans Sedlmayr's book *Verlust der Mitte: die bildende Kunst des 19. und 20. Jahrhunderts als Symptom und Symbol der Zeit* (1948) was a screed against modern art and culture based on wartime lectures and journalism. Sedlmayr laments the lost integral image of man of the twelfth century, man in the image of God, sustained into modern times despite the profanizations of the Renaissance but since the French Revolution irreversibly discredited. Emil Kaufmann, the champion of the autonomous revolutionary architecture of Ledoux, is the anti-Sedlmayr: his vision of history is identical but with all the values reversed. Likewise *Verlust der Mitte* is a mirror image of the avant-garde myth. Revolution and reaction agree on the meaning but not the worth of modern art. Sedlmayr, who was stripped of his chair in Vienna in 1945, is reminding his readers between the lines that some had put hope in Nazism as the last chance to restore this image. No one missed this; the covers of the British and American translations (1957) were red and black. Sedlmayr was also saying that conventional art history, with its empiricist probity and fictions of cause and effect, was incapable even of picturing the lost center. His own radical response, as we have seen, was the book on the Gothic cathedral.

The social history of art generally worked with a model of the artwork that was cut off from its possible origins in the person or in experience. Wary of the integrated image of man that they saw in both Sedlmayr and Burckhardt, the social historians postponed the question of the transmutation of reality, within the body and the mind, into plastic constructs. The social history of art worked with too simple a model of creativity. The mentality of Marxist history of art was often literal-minded and scientistic, unequipped to solve the enigmas of art or religion.

Marxist theories of culture flourished in the United States in the 1930s and 1940s. The narrator of Edmund Wilson's novella, "The Princess with the Golden Hair," published in 1946 in the volume *Memoirs of Hecate County*, is an ex-academic with Marxist leanings trying to write a book about style and economics: "I had, also, with no talent of my own, a very great enthusiasm for art; and what I really wanted most to work on and what the categories of college had no place for was an historical study of painting in relation to its social-economic roots." Wilson's character had been a devotee of the formalist critic Clive Bell's doctrine of "significant form," but "saw now how impossible it was for me to accept his Platonic idealism which made art represent a reality independent of the vicissitudes of life":

> For Clive Bell, the school of painting that began with Cézanne was the herald of a great rebirth; to me, it seemed already to reflect the human decadence and the mechanical tyranny of a dying social system.

In 1946 the most influential art critic of the day was no longer Clive Bell but Clement Greenberg (1909–1994). Greenberg won his reputation with two articles published in the *Partisan Review* in 1939 and 1940, "Avant-Garde and Kitsch" and "Towards a Newer Laocoon." Greenberg was not an historian of art, but his avant-gardism carried with it a theory of history. European bourgeois society in the middle of the nineteenth century, Greenberg argued in "Avant-Garde and Kitsch," produced for the first time an avant-garde art whose aim was to break out of the "motionless" academicism toward which all "formal cultures" had always tended. "A superior consciousness of history—more precisely, the appearance of a new kind of criticism of society, an historical criticism—made this possible." But art itself was not suited—is by its nature not suited—to carry out this historical criticism. Instead, "retiring from public life altogether, the avant-garde poet or artist sought to maintain the high level of his art by both narrowing and raising it to the expression of an absolute in which all relativities and contradictions would be either resolved or beside the point." The avant-garde artist rejects realism, symbolism, allegory, and finally content itself. The advanced artist, seeking a "constraint" that he can obey in pursuit of the absolute, takes as his subject matter "the medium of his own craft," "the very processes or disciplines" of art. He imitates imitation itself.

Greenberg was disappointed by what the nineteenth century became. Avant-gardism drifted too quickly into an ingratiating realism. He wanted to start the project all over again; to pick up where Konrad Fiedler left off, as it were. Greenberg's equation of kitsch with academicism, which ignores the possibility that there might be a legitimate art of "the many," beyond "formal culture," allows him to replay the painters' break with the Academy, in his view incomplete. Once that break is made, art can disengage from social and political reality entirely and pursue its own internal, self-relational history.

In his purist conception of the art of painting and his distaste for realism, Greenberg adhered to the doctrines of the early twentieth-century British formalists Fry and Bell. Greenberg's insistence on medium-specificity, meanwhile, recovered the eighteenth-century critique of the doctrine of *ut pictura poesis*, or poetry as a model for painting. His essay "Towards a Newer Laocoon," which basically asserts that art is not communication, descends from the Beaux-Arts system. This anachronistic teaching provided a way for American artists to seize for themselves a role in art history, by picking up the abstractionist thread, dropped in Europe in the time of calamities.

A significant figure in the intellectual life of mid-century New York was the medievalist Meyer Schapiro (1904–1996), whose early writings on Romanesque sculpture, as we have seen, dared to trace outlines of class conflict in those uncouth forms. In his article of 1947, "On the Aesthetic Attitude in Romanesque Art," he identified passages of freedom and conflict, hinting at a latent secular spirit, in the religious art of eleventh- and twelfth-century France. In the monstrous carvings denounced as profane by the Cistercian abbot Bernard of Clairvaux, Schapiro saw "a world of projected emotions, psychologically significant images of force, play, aggressiveness, anxiety, self-torment and fear, embodied in the powerful forms of instinct-driven creatures, twisted, struggling, entangled, confronted, and superposed." This willingness to peer into the psyche is just what was missing from British Marxist art history, more skeptical of psychoanalysis. Schapiro defended the thesis that the freedom of art, legible in the formal dissonances of Romanesque art, was later suppressed by Gothic art, underwritten by the Scholastic theologians, the successors to Bernard of Clairvaux, and—counterintuitively—by Renaissance art, the style that sought the ideal, the integral, and the universal. The emigré art historian Rudolf Berliner, in his essay "The Freedom of Medieval Art" (1945), said much the same thing.

Schapiro found in the past an image of the present. The twelfth-century texts on art reveal a world that knows "rapture, discrimination, collection; the adoration of the masterpiece and recognition of the great artist personality; the habitual judgment of works without reference to meanings or to use; the acceptance of the beautiful as a field with special laws, values, and even morality." Schapiro is not ironically elevating the humble, for he does not see Romanesque art as humble. The historicizing and relativizing medievalists of the nineteenth century had done their job too well. Schapiro now feels licensed to abandon historicism and to practice instead an archeology of the present.

In seeking a model for an art that emerged directly from the life of the people, bypassing institutions and the elite as well as theories of art, Burckhardtian and Marxist historians alike looked to profane iconography and to the circulatory vitality of the public square. This was art, it seemed, that was securely embedded in life. Such an art was contrasted both to the official religious art of the Middle Ages, harnessed to doctrine and liturgy, and to the supposedly superficial role of art in modern life. If premodern art expressed mostly the ideology of the powerful and the wellborn, then modern art, free to explore the vagaries of subjecthood or simply to be beautiful, expressed the ideology of a powerless elite. Premodern art can *only* be dealt with by a social history of art (Hauser might say), whereas modern art can *never* be grasped by a social history of art (Greenberg might say). Schapiro avoided both traps with his presentism, arguing, first, that modern art is in fact "bound up with modern experiences and ideals," and so is the potential object of a social history of art; and second, that medieval art was in many of its modes *also* free, like modern art. What profane or profane-leaning medieval art and all modern art both express is the agony and the ecstasy of subjecthood once it comes out from under the shelter of dogma and convention. As for the rest, the obsolete ideologies affirmed by the Gothic cathedral—or for that matter, Schapiro would have been forced to say, the Hindu temple—there was no need to hear, once again, all about them. The social history of art only has one message to deliver, and it is affirmative. The message does not respect the difference between historical cultures.

360

1950–1960

Art history made a new pact with modernity in the 1950s, a pax aesthetica. Form was asked to reconcile modern art and the modern forms of life.

In 1955 Arnold Bode, an artist and curator, staged an ambitious exhibition of modernist and contemporary art, called the Documenta, in his hometown of Kassel, a city in the middle of Germany that had been one of the headquarters of the Nazi army and severely bombed in 1945. Among the few barely intact historic buildings was the Fridericianum of 1779, which we recall was the first building in Europe designed to be a public museum. Documenta was a relaunch of modernism, a rebuke and *damnatio memoriae* of the National Socialists' popular traveling exhibition of 1937, *Degenerate Art*, an obscene denunciation of Cubism, Expressionism, Abstraction, and Dada. In that first Documenta—the exhibition is staged roughly every five years in Kassel, most recently in 2017—there was mostly painting, with little sculpture, the latter medium suspect because favored by the Nazis. The exhibition was curated by Bode, Will Grohmann, Werner Haftmann, and Werner Schmalenbach and included 570 works by 148 artists. There were 130,000 visitors. Some exhibits attempted to identify an enduring image of human nature that could serve as the basis for repair. Others reverted to abstraction. By the 1950s critics across a wide ideological spectrum saw abstract painting as the covenant of a new spiritualism, austere or romantic, in the face of the brutal literalisms and delusionary mythologies that had together wrecked the century. The bourgeois amateur of art could congratulate herself for apprehending a modern art that, according to André Malraux, writing in 1949, "has liberated painting which is now triumphantly a law unto itself." The neo-Thomist theologian Étienne Gilson, who delivered the A.W. Mellon Lectures in the Fine Arts in Washington in 1955, asserted that painters could never again indulge in "the easy pleasures of imitational or representational art." Since Cézanne, Gilson affirmed, painting had been forced to submit to a "cure of abstractionism." Not everyone liked this complacent tone: the American art historian Leo Steinberg reminded readers in 1953 that the ambitions of the major modern artists, including Manet, van Gogh, Cézanne, and Matisse, had been "adequately summarized in [John] Constable's dictum which defines the goal of painting as 'the pure apprehension of natural fact.'" There was an elitist dimension to postwar abstraction, especially in Europe.

Avant-garde and conservative art histories of this period are symmetrical: both stress the cosmic or order-endowing functions of art. That point of view encouraged scholarly study of the art beyond Europe and did not discourage a therapeutic medievalism. The catalogue of the large 1950 exhibition of early medieval art in Munich under the rubric *Ars Sacra* invited comparison and contrast with "spiritual tendencies of our own day." The exhibition revealed the "cultural unity of Europe in the early middle ages." So did the popular series of magazines and books dedicted to Romanesque architecture and sculpture, *Zodiaque*, published by the Benedictine priest Angelico Surchamp at his abbey in Burgundy. The *Zodiaque* publications, especially the series of topographic handbooks inaugurated in 1953 under the rubric *La Nuit des temps*, gave pride of place to the monuments of Burgundy, Poitou, and Anjou, but *Zodiaque* was not nationalist in spirit so much as Christian-international. Surchamp had studied with the Cubist painter Albert Gleizes, a disciple of the neo-Thomist philosopher and aesthetician Jacques Maritain. The photographs printed in lush, grainy heliogravure extracted the bare shaped stones from their liturgical and historical contexts. Christian art supported the hope that art in general could shepherd sensibilities to a higher altitude. The pain of the war is internalized, and the Romantic taste for dissonance democratized. Hypertrophied disciplines of formal organization, whether those of Renaissance and Baroque art or those of the late nineteenth century, are now seen as screens blocking our access to the universal wisdom.

Disappointment in the unfulfilled promises of the avant-gardes led to a divergence between histories of architecture and histories of art.

Building is always cosmic, if cosmic is understood as a placing of man in nature, including the second natures he builds, above all, society. Whereas art, made by individuals, is noncombinatory, noncumulative, nondialectical, and not anchored to anything real. Mistrustful of art because it deals in illusion, many art historians looked to architecture as a reliable vehicle for content, any content, signalling a willingness to trust again in ancestors. After Sedlmayr's book on the Gothic cathedral, there was Günter Bandmann (*Mittelalterliche Architektur als Bedeutungsträger*, 1951), Otto von Simson (*The Gothic Cathedral*, 1956), and Hans Jantzen (*Kunst der Gotik*, 1957). Architectural history is always orienting itself to the production of new buildings. Rudolf Wittkower's ideas about proportion fed straight into practice; architects figured out quickly how to translate past to present.

In his posthumously published book *Gothic vs. Classic: Architectural Projects in Seventeenth-Century Italy* (1974), Wittkower devoted several pages to the sixteenth- and seventeenth-century debates about how to complete the façade of the cathedral of Florence, left unfinished, mostly bare, an episode we discussed earlier in the context of nineteenth-century restorations. He reviews a series of never-realized proposals, from 1589 to 1636, by the major architects of the day, all of them classical in style, with pilasters, windows, and niches designed by the book, the orthodox system of the orders—that is, completely indifferent to the Gothic style of the rest of the building. Wittkower marvels that the Florentines did not respect the "principle of conformity," as had those postmedieval builders in Bologna and Milan who "had far outpaced Florence in progressing toward a positive historicizing attitude in relation to the Gothic style." By the third quarter of the nineteenth century, Wittkower says, the Florentines finally came to their senses and built a pastiche of a Gothic façade, the one we have today and which is taken by many visitors to be Gothic. Wittkower's idealism needs nineteenth-century historicism as a foil. And indeed in architecture idealism could thrive alongside the understanding of architecture as living in time. Art and architecture are not symmetrical. Wittkower's approbation of the nineteenth-century façade of the Duomo, a forgery, is patronizing. Surely he would not condone Gaetano Bianchi's 1852 pastiche of a Trecento painting of St. Louis in S. Croce to supplement Giotto's figures. Why? Because painting has been expected since 1800 to march in step with its own time, but architecture only since 1920? Wittkower asks sincerity of the nineteenth-century painter; of the architect he asks only competence.

Wittkower consigned the nineteenth century to limbo and cast his lot with his own century. He must have envisioned some rebirth of civilization, perhaps not as the Futurists had planned it, but a renewal anyway. Born with the century, he still believed in it.

Wittkower did not agree with his contemporary Hans-Georg Gadamer that art was lost to us moderns. From the vantage point of the philosopher's cathedra, it was impossible, apparently, to articulate what had happened to art except in negative terms. The philosopher is not easily persuaded that our wounds could be healed by an abstract painting. In 1960 Gadamer asserted placidly that

> no one can doubt that the great ages in the history of art were those in which people without any aesthetic consciousness and without our concept of "art" surrounded themselves with forms whose functions in religious or secular life were understood by everyone and gave no one exclusively aesthetic pleasure.

In other words, artistic beauty is wanton unless it is steered by an extra-artistic purpose. A cult of art is not the answer. Gadamer was an anti-modernist in the sense that he believed that the idea of art was a decoy, even an idol, that distracts us from the work that works of art properly do. Gadamer believed in antiquity and the Middle Ages but not in the Renaissance and its degraded aftermath. Yet his doctrine is compatible with the avant-garde ambition of escaping the aesthetic sphere and recovering a political rhythm.

Gadamer also believes—and here he is in tune with the artists—that historical scholarship misrecognizes art. Like his teacher Heidegger, Gadamer considers historical scholarship an aspect of modernity's plight, not its salvation. Gadamer detected dimensions of art that will always escape capture by scholarship:

> The scholarly investigation conducted by so-called *Kunstwissenschaft* is aware from the start that it can neither stand in for nor exceed the experience of art. That an artwork offers an experience of truth attainable in no other way constitutes the philosophical significance of art, asserting itself against all reasoning. Thus the experience of art, alongside the experience of philosophy, is the most forcible admonition to the scholarly consciousness to acknowledge its own limits.

He is saying that the humanities should not bother competing with the natural sciences. Art eludes objective analysis because it is never fully historical. Even the art of the past is always pointing forward, opening up unseen paths leading to unanticipated places.

Melancholy is palpable in Theodor W. Adorno's brief essay of 1952–1954, "Valéry Proust Museum." Back in Germany at this point, and evidently as depressed as he had been while living in Pacific Palisades during the war, Adorno used the contrasting attitudes of Paul Valéry and Marcel Proust (who were both born in 1871 and so represented for Adorno the generation of the father—his own father had been born in 1870) toward the imprisonment of the masterpieces of painting in the museums of Paris. Valéry saw painting and sculpture as the forlorn children of architecture. His reaction to the chaos and superficiality of the museum was simply to stay home. Proust, according to Adorno, solved the dilemma by introducing the works into his own consciousness, so avoiding "idolatry" and offering his own literary art as the ideal modern gallery of historical art. Adorno sees some cause for hope in Proust's quietist withdrawal from the world, his resigned devotion to a promise, his willingness to postpone. Valéry by contrast

> is a bit too ingenuous in his suspicion that museums alone are responsible for what is done to paintings. Even if they hung in their old places in the castles of the aristocrats…they would be museum pieces without museums. What eats away at the life of the art work is also its own life.

Relieved to be back in Europe, Adorno resigns himself to the art museum. "Works of art can fully embody the *promesse du bonheur* only when they have been uprooted from their native soil and set out along the path to their own destruction." Anything important is going to have to happen in consciousness, the real laboratory of form. This is the opposite of the point of view of the architectural historian who wishes to see the life of forms staged in public.

It is easy to imagine what Gadamer and Adorno thought of the European cities now partitioning themselves into an *Altstadt* or *centro storico*—a nucleus of authentic medieval structures, heavily restored—surrounded by an inauthentic nineteenth-century fabric, at best invisible, at worst hideous. This is art history written in stone, a triage of good (reflective) and bad (functional) modernities. The philosophers would have disapproved for the wrong reason: that the *Altstadt* only makes the bad modernity more conspicuous. Most everyone agreed that historicist buildings quoting past styles were now unacceptable; they belonged to the world that had begotten the two wars. The protagonist of Heinrich Böll's novel of 1959, *Billard um halb zehn* (Billiards at Half-Past Nine) is a German architect whose father, also an architect, had built a much-admired neo-Romanesque monastery in the 1920s. Near the end of the Second World War, the British army decided to destroy the monastery for strategic reasons. The British compelled the son, whose knowledge of statics, or the science of making things stand up, was easily reversible, to dynamite his father's building: "Demolition is only the reverse of statics. So to speak its reciprocal."

After the war the son is unable to build anything at all; his architectural practice now consists of nothing but verifying other people's measurements. Architecture in Böll's 1950s is reduced to engineering, adjustment, precision, adaptation to circumstance; a damaged and self-protective approach to creativity. The father, meanwhile, absorbs the blow of the destruction of his masterpiece with phlegmatic, ecological wisdom: "I could never take buildings seriously; dust, baked and concentrated dust, transformed into structure; an optical illusion, fata morgana, meant to become rubble." The father arrives at a final anthropomorphization of architecture as something made by people for people and that must share in human fortunes. He no longer takes any interest in the thesis that a monument might concretize the values of a civilization. The civilizations that call on art and architecture to endorse their hierarchies of value will end up destroying what they create. Civilization winds down by creating anti-monuments: "Dynamite, a few formulas, that was his opportunity to erect monuments." The monument, in principle its own historian, instead persists only on the page: finally a task for the historian.

The British officer apologizes to the son for destroying the twelfth-century Crucifixion group that his father's monastery had housed but not for destroying the modern neo-medieval structure—and most certainly not for the death of the son's wife in an air raid. The Nazis set in motion a destructive cycle that in the end drew in their adversaries. The British officer has surrendered to an impious logic of war that is able to displace the reckoning of loss from the plane of life itself onto the plane of civilization, a psychological economy. The officer's conception of civilization involves a distinction in value—between the authentic twelfth-century

Crucifixion and its ersatz neo-Romanesque container—that in the fires of war has come to seem meaningless. The officer probably believes that maintaining that distinction is the way to prevent the next war. He knows the difference between original and substitute because his Baedeker or even Dehio handbook has pointed it out. But by what criterion is the twelfth-century artifact more precious? Because it is irreplaceable, more difficult to reproduce technically, than a building? Yes, to some extent. Because it is more beautiful? But the twelfth-century church is not necessarily more beautiful than its twentieth-century simulacrum. Because it is older and rarer? This is not a reliable criterion: there is plenty of old junk not worth keeping. Because it is a relic of a superior civilization—the civilization that begat the Crusades? Because it reminds moderns that art once had a lofty purpose? Yes, this certainly.

The officer's dubious distinction reveals what could not be seen before the war: that the neo-medieval churches of the nineteenth and twentieth centuries entered into a flow of building that had always, from the beginning, involved repetition and citation, compliance with types, and a concept of the true origins of a building that exceeded the bare, punctual date of its construction. From that point of view, the Romanesque monastery of the 1920s was still a medieval building. Although not a relic of the twelfth century like the Crucifix it housed, it was nonetheless connected to the past by a chain of structures conforming to a flexible but symbolically dense program. At the same time the monastery of the 1920s, which no doubt took advantage of reinforced concrete, was a modern building. Many of the forward-pointing buildings of the nineteenth century also emerged out of historical matrices: Karl Friedrich Schinkel's plans for a department store, for example, a Renaissance palazzo in steel and glass, or Henri Labrouste and Viollet-le-Duc's iron-framed architecture.

Symbol-laden and technologically-driven histories of building were historically interwoven and conceptually compatible. National Socialism adopted just this convergence of the symbolic and the technological as a program, and this made it impossible ever after to pursue such a program.

Rudolf Wittkower's Renaissance had appeared to obliterate not only the nineteenth century but also the Middle Ages, completing what he believed to be Alberti's own project. Wittkower condescended to both the Middle Ages and the nineteenth century—they were perfect for each other. Panofsky, by contrast, plunged back into the Middle Ages in his short treatise *Gothic Architecture and Scholasticism* (1951). He took advantage of the historical distance that, in his own account, was the principal intellectual achievement of the period that succeeded the Middle Ages, the European Renaissance. The Renaissance pictured the world in perspective, while we moderns picture the past in perspective. The Renaissance bequeathed to us the conceptual tools to excavate the very historical period that the Renaissance itself had buried. Panofsky argues that the principles of construction of the great French cathedrals between 1130 and 1270 followed from "mental habits" established by the teaching of the Scholastic philosophers. The narrative content of a sculptural program on a portal, for example, is clarified by framing devices and compartmentalization. The building itself is limitlessly "fractionized" into parts. Panofsky points out that these are the very principles of argumentation and presentation of Scholastic doctrine. The cathedral, he shows, reconciles in its plan and its structure seemingly irreconcilable architectural principles. Such syntheses were also characteristic of a school of philosophy bent on preserving the authority of the supreme authorities—Aristotle, the Church Fathers—at all cost. Like Wittkower, Panofsky succeeds by excluding. For he focuses not on the content of the Scholastics' thought but the form. He is describing the house of God, but an empty house. He performs a double abstraction—on the buildings and on the texts—and arrives at the essential structure underlying them. This was also Riegl's method.

In his afterword to the French translation of Panofsky's *Gothic Architecture* (1967), the sociologist Pierre Bourdieu argued that Panofsky's vision of a "structural affinity" between different aspects of the historical totality was more intuitive than positivist, and therefore laudable. Panofsky, according to Bourdieu, discerned the schemata (habitus, customs, rules) that serve as the matrix for all typical thoughts and perceptions. To discern the deep grammar of the Gothic worldview, Panofsky had to mask out the history of building, the typological aims, the symbolic programs coordinated with liturgy, the availability of techniques and materials, and the movement of artisans. Panofsky ventured to the frontiers of empiricism in order to produce a partisan interpretation of a world. He anticipated methodological objections by claiming that he was correlating a building style with a mentality that, if not shared by everyone in the society, was prevalent among Parisian professors. Scholasticism enjoyed in this period a monopoly on education. Everyone in the urban professional milieu of the cathedral's designers and builders was exposed to the thinking of the Scholastics. Panofsky contextualizes the buildings not by constructing laborious causal chains but by pointing out that everyone in 1951 speaks of "vitamin deficiencies" or "inferiority complexes" without knowing much about biology or psychology. This is a rather breathtaking argument, for it implies that the cathedrals themselves, noble piles, were grounded in garbled lay misconstruals of the Scholastic teachings. A cultural conservative like Panofsky suspected that the glories of modern culture were built on half-understandings. Perhaps Panofsky was slyly dismissing the cathedrals. After all, his book may be read as a preemptive strike against the thinly disguised eulogies for medieval civilization by the even more conservative von Simson and Jantzen, or as a direct response to Sedlmayr's *Entstehung der Kathedrale* (1950), discussed in the previous section and later noted by Bourdieu as Panofsky's foil. Unlike Sedlmayr, who did not condescend to the Middle Ages, Panofsky depicted a thirteenth century bereft of an all-knowing father.

The discipline settled on a basic consensus around form. Every painting, figurative or abstract, is read as if it were abstract, though not always as inventively as Lionello Venturi, whose deft narration of *The Bridge at Narni* (1826) by Camille Corot slips from motif to form and back again:

> The river Nera is turbid and sandy until, through the shadow of the bridge in the middle distance, appears the clear blue of the water flanked by the gray-greens of the hills and the blues and shadows, until in the far distance appear the blue mountains veiled in mist under the pale blue of a sky broken by white clouds. With a few intense blacks the painter plunged right into the battle of light and shade over the broken ground and the ruined bridge, a battle which finally spends itself in the distant azure of the sky. From the neighboring tumult of life, to the distant, yearned for peace, this is the theme of the picture.

Meyer Schapiro, meanwhile, reverts to pure form. In his magisterial essay "Style" (1953), explaining art history to non-art historians, Schapiro says that all art can be reduced to a simple algorithm modeled on the framed painted tableau:

> Basic for contemporary practice and for knowledge of past art is the theoretical view that what counts in all art are the elementary

aesthetic components, the qualities and relationships of the fabricated lines, spots, colors, and surfaces. These have two characteristics: they are intrinsically expressive, and they tend to constitute a coherent whole. The same tendencies to coherent and expressive structure are found in the arts of all cultures.

This is not so different from what Alois Riegl had said in *Late Roman Art Industry*, which although not yet translated into English enjoyed a secret esteem in the United States: classical archeologists, Riegl had insisted, must learn "to see the ancient artwork first of all, and with their own eyes, with regard to its material apparition as outline and color in space and plane." The art historian Robert Goldwater reviews Riegl's ideas and influence in his book *Primitivism in Modern Art* (1938). Schapiro discusses him directly in the essay "Style."

Where in Schapiro's framed aesthetic system does the real leave its trace? He has described nothing but the interrelation of signs. Riegl's relativizing formalism, even before it was formulated, had been refuted by photography. Riegl met this challenge with his study of the proto-photographic group portraits of seventeenth-century Holland. Art in a cosmic or hierarchical society—and Sedlmayr is saying nothing else than this—is a real act in the world. In the seventeenth century it is realistic painting that makes this gesture; in modernity it is the photograph. But the avant-garde artwork, photographic or not, is also a real gesture. Schapiro does not seem to grasp this. Form-based paintings in the twentieth century can mimic such gestures, but they are no longer cosmic.

Schapiro says in 1953: "Art is now one of the strongest evidences of the basic unity of mankind." All right, but to maintain this claim Schapiro has to make the following assertion about art: "There is no privileged content or mode of representation." But we know that for Schapiro there are privileged contents. Riegl had not been a relativist of values any more than Schapiro was. Riegl was looking for the sympathetic mutual attentiveness that was the basis of liberal democracy just as Schapiro was looking to Romanesque sculpture for early signs of the profane fertility of the collective life. Schapiro wants to have his cake and eat it, too. All art can be judged by a common set of criteria, he says, but some art is more important than other art. "This approach is a relativism that does not exclude absolute judgments of value; it makes those judgments possible within every framework by abandoning a fixed norm of style." So it is not quite the end of the pastoral fable, the primitivism, the wielding of the past as a lever against the present.

Panofsky in his 1927 essay on perspective had been equally ambivalent. Every era has its own way of seeing, he said, and none of them is more faithful to reality. And yet, the European linear perspective is different because it anticipates Kant, whose account of the mind is not relative but simply true, in all times and places.

For Wittkower and Panofsky, war brought the pastoral fable to an end. Now the present needs lessons from the past. That is the basic split after the war, even today: who is confident any longer that modernity can manage its own affairs? Wittkower looked to architecture, seeking to historicize the impression of permanent validity conveyed by some fifteenth- and sixteenth-century European buildings. In painting, that stability was provided by the frame. Thus Schapiro's reassertion of painting as the paradigm of art at the very moment when painting was losing its unquestioned primacy. Schapiro writes as if the framelessness of much avant-garde art (readymades, the various Dada and Surrealist found and other objects—little of that at the first Documenta!) were responsible for all the troubles. The picture counteracted such disorientations. The stable frame contained all forces: gestural painting, Art brut, Art informel, outsider art, neo-Dada combines. No amount of formlessness could destabilize the framed picture. Painting can even afford to discard its frame. The frameless canvases of Abstract Expressionism are only a tribute to the power of the frame.

Where Schapiro as a modernist and as an American was not yet ready to give up on the twentieth century, Panofsky had no high opinion of his own era. Panofsky looked not to architecture for ballast but to the improving content of premodern philosophy and literature. Iconography originally meant the sequence of portraits that writes the life of a great man. Iconography in the context of art-historical scholarship was the study of the coding of theology in medieval Christian art. Aby Warburg, de-Christianizing, coined the word "iconology" to designate a general scholarly study of images in history and in society. Panofsky created a postwar research program by narrowing the concept of iconology to the study of allegorical and other images informed by theology, philosophy, or literature. The books that established iconology as a scholarly program in the United States were Panofsky's *Studies in Iconology: Humanistic Themes in the Art of the Renaissance* (1939) and *Meaning in the Visual Arts* (1955), both collections of closely focused studies of Renaissance art. Here he argued that the aim of art historical interpretation in general was the apprehension of "those underlying principles which reveal the basic attitude of a nation, a period, a class, a religious or philosophical persuasion—unconsciously qualified by one personality and condensed into one work." The art historian could improve on the mere stylistic and thematic analysis of the work by applying what Panofsky called "synthetic intuition," or "familiarity with the *essential tendencies of the human mind*," and then by tempering this intuition with "insight into the manner in which, under varying historical conditions, *essential tendencies of the human mind* were expressed by specific *themes* and *concepts*." Iconology sounds neutral but it was not. It began as an alternative to the social history of art but ended as a reverse primitivism, that is, the recognition that *we* have become the primitives and yet have nothing to teach the civilized past. The pretense to iconology's value-neutrality was thin or nonexistent. Iconology was designed as a hermeneutic of paintings produced in Italy in the fifteenth, sixteenth, and seventeenth centuries, when paintings could be expected to encipher edifying content prepared by the study of ancient Greek and Roman texts as well as by modern poets and thinkers.

Panofsky's faith in historical scholarship was completely opposed to Gadamer's fatalism. But then his attitude to the century was completely different. Gadamer was born in 1900, Wittkower in 1901, Adorno in 1903, and Schapiro in 1904 (and Arnold Bode in 1900). This was the first generation born into the teeth of the avant-gardes, who never knew a world without Cubism. Panofsky shared neither Gadamer and Adorno's pessimism (they saw no way backward and no way forward) nor Schapiro and Wittkower's confidence in the new century. Panofsky, born in 1892, just wanted to go backward.

Humanism was not a loss of confidence either in art or in art's capacity to exceed historical scholarship. For Panofsky humanism meant dedication to a balanced ideal of human nature. As such, it was a formal concept. Humanism sees asymmetries and imbalances in human nature as deformations. Humanism is the form classicism takes after the discrediting of the Idea.

Panofsky's picture-readings were inspired not by the old outward-pointing idealism of Platonic pedigree, whose intellectual fortunes in the art theory of the ancien régime he had traced in his book *Idea: A Concept in Art Theory* (1924), but a new "inner" idealism, customized to the imperfect postwar pax, venturing again the thesis of the perfectibility of human nature. In his essay "Art History as a Humanistic Discipline," written in 1940, as Europe plummeted into war and the year he obtained American citizenship, Panofsky had conceded the ahistoricity of humanism: as if the moment had arrived to draw the limits of the once totalizing—as recently as Meinecke's treatise of 1936—historicist project. The stakes were suddenly too high: historicism seemed like a peacetime luxury, the slowly brewed product of a century of European prosperity and conquest interrupted at home only by distracting clashes among the social classes. There was no leisure now for the fables that had ironized civilization.

Iconology responded to the public expectation that the art historian decode historical artworks that had receded into illegibility. Modern art, meanwhile, was swinging between undercoding (Impressionism, naturalism, or the more recent objects that seemed to rebuff interpretation altogether, the readymade or the monochrome painting) and overcoding (abstruse Symbolist allegories or their Surrealist parodies).

If iconology offered allegories of reconciliation of art and culture, then it was the so-called social history of art that might have been expected to produce allegories of division and disappointment. The social history of art as conceived in the years before and during the war, however, was losing momentum.

Ernst Fischer, an Austrian Communist intellectual and politician, active in exile in Moscow in the war years, wrote *Von der Notwendigkeit der Kunst* (On the Necessity of Art) (1959). For Fischer, the task of the art of the present and the future is to re-create the lost collectivity that was once the ground of art. This was a left-wing version of the postwar restorative impulse. How does an artwork, a fabrication, mediate a collectivity? According to Fischer, through a "possessed" individual who paradoxically exists at the margins of collective life and shared experience. In early societies the sorcerer was the "representative" or "servant" of the collective. When the sorcerer entered into a state of demoniacal possession, he "forcibly re-created the collective, world unity." "The content of demoniacal possession," Fischer argued, "was the collective reproduced in a violent manner within the individual, a sort of mass essence." This is indeed a theory of art, as Heidegger had been asking for, and not a theory of representation: the collective reproduced in a violent manner within the individual.

Pierre Francastel, in *Peinture et société: naissance et destruction d'un espace plastique de la Renaissance au cubisme* (1950), offered the artwork as a means of communication. Interpreting perspective as a system of signs, he rewires art history as a species of cultural anthropology. In *Art et technique aux XIXe et XXe siècles* (1956), Francastel presents art and technology as equivalents, differing only in their ends: they both transform nature. Technology, however, does not establish values. Although born in 1900, Francastel still believes that the avant-garde is modern, that is, in tune with modern life.

Even Arnold Hauser appears in his 1958 *Philosophy of Art History* to repudiate his own *Social History of Art,* published only seven years earlier. "We are living now in the day of the sociological interpretation of cultural achievements. That day will not last forever." "A work of art is a challenge; we do not explain it, we adjust ourselves to it." Here he sounds more like Croce or Warburg. Social art history always seems to be putting water in its wine. Hauser is conceding that the work comes at us from history, that we are dominated by it; he casts historical explanation as a kind of defensive manoeuvre. "In interpreting it, we draw upon our own aims and endeavours, inform it with a meaning that has its origins in our own way of life and thought. In a word, any art that really affects us becomes to that extent modern art." The converse is: any art of the past that *doesn't* affect us is just bric-à-brac. He also redeems Panofsky and Wittkower, revealing them to be presentists who mask the creative violence they do to the past behind scholarly protocols.

Art history did not respond to the proliferation of new forms of art—how could it? it was all happening too quickly. The past was receding at a swifter pace. And yet a moving lens still sees in perspective. José Ortega y Gasset began his essay "On Point of View in the Arts" (1949) with the assertion that "when history is as it should be, it is an elaboration of cinema." History gives "the image of a movement." "'Vistas' which had been discontinuous appear to emerge one from another, each prolonging the other without interruption." But a shifting point of view also generates new overlappings and blockages, new perspectival distortions to be overcome.

This is the moment of art history's consolidation within the framework of mass education. Art history finds its berth within the American university. Alfred Neumeyer, a German-Jewish emigré and professor of art history at Mills College in Oakland, California, published in 1956

374

a short report on art-historical study in the United States. Neumeyer paints a nondepressive picture of American scholarship that reveals much about the German art-historical establishment that he left behind in 1935. Neumeyer listed the innovative interdisciplinary approaches that had transformed art history: psychoanalysis, anthropology, economic analysis, as well as the opening onto art beyond Europe, including the colonial New World, and finally folk art. Neumeyer downplayed the contribution of his fellow emigrés, crediting them with introducing the iconological method (Panofsky) and the topic of the migration of symbols (Wittkower). He feared that the iconologists were apt to neglect style, form, and creativity. Neumeyer's survey is surprising because it was the perception of the closure of art history in the 1950s to anything beyond its traditional frontiers that would later drive the self-reform of the discipline in the 1970s. Of 430 articles published in the *Art Bulletin* between 1923 and 1948, Neumeyer had to concede, only thirty-two covered art since 1800, and only twenty-two the arts of Asia. Still, in Europe an article on Asian art would have been found only in a specialized journal, not in the general periodicals of the discipline. That is still largely true today. These articles bear witness to an increasing submission of the study of world art to the common principles and procedures of empirical scholarship. Sometimes this dovetailed with indigenous traditions of connoisseurship and historiography, principally with Chinese or Japanese art, sometimes not.

The survey course, or series of lectures introducing students to world or Western art, had been around a long time. Charles Eliot Norton's course at Harvard was the model. Survey courses build art history's financial base and they still initiate thousands. The aims and style of such courses have been much altered, but many still rely on the textbook published in 1962 by the emigré scholar H. W. Janson, *History of Art*. Janson distilled the century's art-historical knowledge. His treatment was evenhanded across time and place yet keyed to the concept of the timeless and placeless masterpiece, a concept that met students' expectation that the purpose of a liberal-arts education was improvement through exposure to the best. The survey course protected the idea of art as rarefied and esoteric, salvaging remnants of aristocratic ideas of decorum and grace by translating them into the idiom of modern sociology. The premise of the survey course was that form was the medium of achievement and expression. The biography of form preserved the continuity of the present with the by now multiple ancien régimes, reconnecting with those distant societies that preceded computers, decolonization, two World Wars, photography, the French Revolution, and even the steam engine. This was the continuity that had been explicitly asserted by Burckhardt and Riegl, but really by all art historians of the nineteenth and twentieth centuries. In its proudest, least ineffectual versions, the life of form overcomes barriers of language and mistrust, the most bitter memories of injury and betrayal, overcomes also the Renaissance, finding common cause with the illiberal and misguided societies of the Middle Ages. This is Janson on the twelfth-century portal sculpture at Moissac: "Human and animal forms are treated with the same incredible flexibility, so that the spidery Prophet on the side of the *trumeau* seems perfectly adapted to his precarious perch…. He even remains free to cross his legs in a dancelike movement." The praise is unstinting; the emphasis is not on limits but on freedom, freedom even from tradition: "intense expression, unbridled fantasy, and a nervous agility of form that owes more to manuscript illumination and metalwork than to the sculptural tradition of antiquity." In Janson's textbook there are no breaks and no sense that art in the modern world has either lost its way or come into its own.

Contrast this with Ernst H. Gombrich's *Story of Art* (1950), which had told the story of art as representation, a story neither homogeneous nor uninterrupted. Art beyond representation escapes Gombrich. He narrates medieval art but his heart is not in it. For Gombrich medieval art is applied art. This is Gombrich on the late twelfth-century church of St.-Trophime in Arles. In the tympanum above the door, the sculptor has carved an implacable enthroned Christ, as if sitting in judgment, flanked by four creatures, as described in the book of Ezekiel and later interpreted as symbols of the four Evangelists. Gombrich apologizes for the style: "We must not expect such sculptures to look as natural, graceful and light as classical works. They are all the more impressive because of their massive solemnity. It becomes much easier to see at a glance what is represented, and they fit in much better with the grandeur of the whole building." Is that all he can think of to say? He musters about as much enthusiasm for this masterpiece of Romanesque art as could be expected from an open-minded antiquarian of the early nineteenth century.

Gombrich (1909–2001) wrote a dissertation under the supervision of Julius von Schlosser. In 1936 he was called to London by Fritz Saxl to put Aby Warburg's papers in order. This project, interrupted by the war, generated an intellectual biography of Warburg (1970) that, though often criticized by defenders of Warburg's legacy, comes closer to grasping the essence of Warburg's thought than many other studies. Gombrich stayed on at the Warburg Library, by now a degree-granting branch of the University of London, and from 1959 to 1972 served as director. Gombrich published important studies on iconographic topics in Renaissance art and mostly ignored his British art-historical colleagues (Anthony Blunt, Kenneth Clark) or quarreled with other emigrés, notably Otto Pächt. Gombrich eventually aimed his writings beyond the discipline or even over the heads of the professoriate, at an educated lay public. All his books had their origins in public lecture series except one, the most widely read of all, *The Story of Art*. In that book, still in print and widely read, Gombrich addressed everybody. He is the most widely read of all art historians, even more than Burckhardt, and possibly the most widely read scholar of the twentieth century in any field.

Gombrich cannot take modern art seriously, whereas Janson did. Modern art was too concept-driven for him. Gombrich, in a later book, would disparage even Renaissance art of the Neoplatonic sort for its submission to the concept. He deflated the enterprise of the early modern art academies by suggesting that Neoplatonism, which "held sway...for at least three hundred years, from 1550 to 1850" and which ascribed to the painter the gift of perceiving "eternal patterns," hardly represented a break with the Middle Ages at all. For Neoplatonic aesthetics was basically "a continuation of Villard's [Villard de Honnecourt, a thirteenth-century artist] conceptual art, with a slightly specious philosophical halo." Now, in modernity, art seems to regress to medieval conceptualism. Conceptual art, modern or medieval, seemed to Gombrich a useless luxury, for it is so much easier to make than nonconceptual art.

If Gombrich points to an obscure future where art may be unrecognizable, and where the entire modern project of art history breaks down, Janson tells a story that need not ever end. Janson's narrative of a continuity of purpose carried by form is still the invisible framework for most art historical research.

CONCLUSIONS: *NOVISSIMA*

Today more and more students of art history, at every level, beginning and advanced, focus on modern and contemporary art, the art of our own moment and its immediate antecedents. Students are often unwilling to peer back in time any farther than 1960 or 1970 or 2000. The study of premodern art appeals to ever fewer. The academic discipline has only partly adapted to this rearrangement of passions. The gamut of expertise of the faculty of a typical art history department does not align with the demand of the students. The absorption in the fortunes and prospects of present-day art could possibly be explained sociologically: a new category of student has emerged who may well be susceptible to the lures of wealth and glamour but is no longer in a competition for social status in which admiration of premodern art—the canvases of the great Dutch painters, the cathedrals of the Île-de-France—is a marker. The obsession with the contemporary may also be explained as an aspect of an overall cultural amnesia. History is, after all, always adding to itself, and if there is too much to learn, one can simply abbreviate history. The *New York Times* reported on June 22, 2018, that the College Board, the entity that administers placement exams for admission to universities and colleges, would henceforth hold students taking the Advanced Placement World History exam responsible only for history since AD 1450. After a modest outcry the College Board compromised with a starting point of AD 1200.

The real reason that students and increasingly teachers of art history are ready to jettison the past, however, is that the refusal of the authority of the past is the very program of modern art. To invest in modern art existentially is to agree to carry out that program. The investment in modern art entails contempt for the past. The inverse is true as well, although some would deny it. I would maintain that it is only possible to say something insightful about contemporary art from a standpoint well inside the magic circle. The rest of us on the outside, who do not live but only look at contemporary art, always misrecognize it.

With the perspective of a century, it appears that early twentieth-century modernism's break with the past was irreversible, just as advertised, but was realized only belatedly. The breach announced in 1910 took half a century to open up inside art, and another half century for anyone other than artists to comprehend. This created an irreparable split within the discipline, for everyone other than the partisans of the modernist project still believes that the present is involved with the past. The discipline also splits on the question of evaluation—evaluation of artworks as art. Whereas the study of contemporary and modern art is mainly evaluative, the study of non-modernist art has become mainly nonevaluative. The archive of premodern art history has opened to non-art, such that many art historians no longer consider art their principal object of study, just as many literary scholars no longer brood about "literariness." There is plenty of precedent for this in the nearby fields, old fields, of antiquarianism and archeology, as well as the study of material culture, which has deep roots in the nineteenth century. The studies by Julius von Schlosser on wax portraits and the *Wunderkammer* and Aby Warburg on the German woodcuts that in the period of the Reformation published news of alarming portents and astrological lore, were already building on decades of holistic, inclusive, and relativist cultural history. *Only* scholars in the premodern and non-modernist fields, however, frame their work as the study of images, objects, and practices (rather than art). Historians, theorists, and critics of contemporary art do not directly study the proliferation of non-art images and things in contemporary society, nor do they examine from a sociological or anthropological point of view the interactions of modern people with art. They do not need to because advertising, fashion, celebrities, television, tattoos, toys, comics, pornography, politics, iPhones, and stuff in general, as well as all the many modes of beholding and possessing are already the content of so much elite contemporary art. The images, things, and practices have already been filtered and framed by art, absorbed into artworks whose autonomy—unlike the autonomy of the premodern works—remains unchallenged. The main task of the art historian of the modern and contemporary is to justify the value of those works. The paradoxical result is that the art history of the present has nothing to say about mass culture that art itself doesn't already tell us. So-called mass or popular culture ought to be art history's topic, but it proves too difficult to grasp. The image-surfaces enfolding us will not take on density; they melt or disintegrate too quickly, such that art is everywhere but nowhere. How should art history, with its specialized conceptual toolbox, solve the puzzle of entertainment, when society itself has two or more minds about everything, admiring, for example, Hollywood movies that break box-office records on their first weekend and at the same time revering Vincent van Gogh because he was unappreciated in his own time—and yet not knowing exactly what, if anything, differentiates a painting by van Gogh from a well-crafted movie.

Classic art history and its belated avatars are poorly equipped to deal with most of this, gravitating as they do toward dense and stylized artifacts, marked off from the rest of reality and from other classes of things that they resemble, such as messages or machines or entertainment, by a certain disability, an excess or deficit of form that interferes with communication or efficiency.

The main shift, and it has been obvious for decades, is that art history can no longer occupy itself in an innocent fashion with the biography of form because art itself is no longer preoccupied with form. The generation of classic art history, from the 1890s to the 1920s, was by no means out of tune with an artistic modernism that, for all its rhetoric of rupture, still reckoned in ratios of good form to bad form, form to nonform, form to content. That early twentieth-century paradigm has long since broken down as art redistributes itself in events, vectors, emotions, ideas, clusters or swarms of artifice. Art today is less about form than about the conditions of possibility of effective speech and action, the tension between enunciation and performance, the virtues of images. Today creativity itself is differently distributed in society: in the mass media and social networks, in amateur or outsider art, in fashion elite and democratic, in the proliferation of recognized but little-esteemed aesthetic categories—"the zany, the cute, and the interesting," for example. Even the sophisticated discourses of modernism that have dominated art-history departments over the last three decades—the "classic art history" of our time—are not keeping pace. They are still organized by master-disciple chains reaching back into the 1960s, chains of psychic involvement that bind generations, despite everything, to the old discourses of form.

Those chains will slip, finally, and the history of art as the history of the tension between good form and bad form will be replaced by the history of art as the history of the tension between truth-telling in the guise of fiction, and mere fiction.

Already Ernst Gombrich and George Kubler, in the early 1960s, sketched art histories of the future, histories barely recognizable in their own time as art histories. They disbelieved the parables that sustained the histories of form, and they switched out the avant-garde concept of reality and replaced it with another that was not so much constructed by illusions as following upon disillusionment.

For much of the twentieth century, modernism still saw itself as the latest phase in a ongoing series of contestations of harmony by dissonance, a logic that led nowhere. Heinrich Wölfflin recognized this when he conceded that his cycles of open and closed, tectonic and atectonic, came to a halt in 1800; as did the literary historian and theorist Renato Poggioli to whom in 1962 the project of the avant-garde already seemed historical. Avant-gardism in art and literature only made sense, Poggioli argued in his book *Theory of the Avant-Garde*, when profiled against the recalcitrance of classicism. Poggioli was not wrong when he stated that an avant-garde defining itself through form devolves into an endless cascade of negativities. The real content of the secessions, and the pastoral fables, was deformation, and there is no way to go on deforming deformation. The tension builds, is soon unbearable. It would have been possible to follow the path forward, toward reality, as charted by Carl Einstein only if artists were still making art like African sculptures or Cubist paintings, that is, with an extremely high degree of attention to infinitesimal inflections of visible form, and with great discipline. But that is not how it turned out. The Cubist paintings analyzed by Einstein, flickering between representation and abstraction, were still governed by the paradigm established in the Renaissance and characterized by Niklas Luhmann as "double-framing": oil paint and perspective, like the proscenium stage, trading in illusions that are always unmasking themselves as illusions as soon as they are created, so introducing doubt about the coordination of truth and beauty. This double game was sustainable only by the incompleteness of the pretechnological representational devices, paint and theater.

Wölfflin and Poggioli and many others wondered: whither art, once it is no longer preoccupied with form? They might have heeded Einstein or Wassily Kandinsky, who hinted that the proper destiny of good form was not to generate more good form but to disclose reality. Kandinsky wrote in the *Blue Rider Almanac* of 1912 that "*in principle there is no question of form*." "It makes no difference," he said, "whether the artist uses a real or an abstract form. Inwardly, both forms are equal. The choice must be left to the artist, for he knows best by which means he can most clearly materialize the content of his art." For Kandinsky, form may become a medium for art, but art does not need any particular form. That was true when Kandinsky said it, if hard to perceive at the time; since Poggioli wrote in 1962 it is patently true. Form in art has given way to "possibly form," so ending the sequence of clashes between harmony and dissonance. And now the image, too, is mistrusted as a basis for art, the image with its bias toward integration, or completeness at every level. So one may read an enigmatic passage by Robert Klein, the Romanian-French historian of Renaissance art, in his "Notes on the End of the Image" (1962), suggesting that the stable work as the criterion of art is now being replaced by a vector of will or a fabricating mechanism that precedes it. At every stage in art's history up until now, Klein argues, artworks were compared to something beyond themselves that was more stable, more continuous: academic idealism, but even the modernist modes of Impressionism, Symbolism, Expressionism: "There, too, something that was not of the work surfaced within it. Admittedly, that something presented itself as a lived instant, an immediate encounter, a revelation, an act; but, independently of the represented, we recognized the experience as something already beyond all art—a memory, an archetype, a key on our keyboard which only waited that hand." The artwork continually absorbed that alien element—the real real thing—and managed, at least until now, to maintain its own art-like quality, that for Klein seems to involve an immanent "division," against the "monistic demand" from beyond art.

Art's relation to form, to the image, to the monistic fantasy that provoked its defense of its own dividedness is today, as Klein predicted, intermittent and embarrassed. There are modes of art now that resemble activism or protest, pure and simple; modes of art characterized by a refusal to structure themselves around subject-object relations. The visual itself, the image, is questioned as the normative framework of art. Art is often not a product, not a precious trace, not a singularity, but rather a dynamic, multipolar interaction that creates temporary publics who are public to one another. Art does not have to add anything to the world, for technology and entrepreneurship already do that. Art is an irreality opened up inside the world. Art is the refusal of complicity in any form of domination. You are not trapped by the collectivity, but you are not entirely free either, for freedom, even the anarchic mode of the artwork, is suspected to be a mode of evasion of responsibility. Art is a quasi-event: it is not there all the time (like a book), but it is also not there only at an assigned time (like a theatrical play). This has become a comparative advantage for art over the other arts, which have more trouble intervening in reality. Much art today is coordinated with long-term eschatological or emancipatory projects, with projects as such. Art aims at such positive goals as synchrony, participation, inclusion, and sympathy, concepts hard to reconcile with the once-prized, exclusive qualities of art.

Art in the past always seemed to be transforming content into form. When form becomes content, however, then you only have forms transforming themselves: metamorphosis, namely, a subordination of content to form. Art today, which values content highly and which cultivates skill and hones form only when it pleases, tries to put the brakes on that process and postpone the descent into mere formalism. In this way the avant-garde momentum has been sustained. Art today is as modern as it ever was.

Avant-garde art of the first third of the twentieth century projected ideas outward, onto form. The moment of that first avant-garde was the moment of form. The adjustments, the recombinations, the microvibrations; the exteriority or spacing of art in form, the self-distancing from reality, were the keys to the avant-garde's self-rule but also to its political availability. The avant-gardes of the early twentieth century, as well as its antic or negational doppelgängers, were left wing, right wing, or neither. Externalization in form hedged against all instrumentalizations. Today, form-based noncommittal versions of the avant-garde are held in some suspicion.

The final theorizations of the formal approach to art were formulated in the 1970s. According to Umberto Eco (*A Theory of Semiotics*, 1976), art or the aesthetic text asserts its difference from ordinary communications by introducing constant deviations from conventional coding, such that every work of art can seem to confront us with a private code. Eco argued that deviation on one level of the work compelled rereading on every other level:

> Insofar as the aesthetic text has a self-focusing quality, so that its
> structural arrangement becomes one of the contents that it con-
> veys…the way in which the rules are rearranged on one level will
> represent the way in which they are rearranged on another.

The permanent self-recoding and deliberate ambiguity that distinguishes
art, and drives it inexorably forward into novelty, entangles form and
content:

> The ambiguous arrangement on one level that provokes a reassess-
> ment on another: in /a rose is a rose is a rose/ the puzzling redun-
> dancy of the lexical level stands for a semantic complication on the
> definitional one.

The emphasis is no longer on *what* form, but on the ratio between
form and content—and the gap between today's ratio and yesterday's
ratio. Art is innovation, and its history cannot be written except from
a distance sufficiently great to perceive form and form-ratio. One might
answer that art today is still an incessant violation of codes. But how are
those violations legible if no one code ever settles into common use, that
is, starts to behave like a language or another convention-based system
for getting things done; like a style, in other words? There can be no
artistic innovation unless someone else is not innovating.

Siegfried Kracauer in his book *History: Last Things Before the Last*,
published in 1969, three years after his death, made one last effort to justify form-history. Kracauer saw a threat not from the artists' diminishing
patience for form but from the simplistic linear model of time endorsed
by technology. He notes that J. G. Herder had proposed that every kind of
phenomenon had its own time, uncoordinated with all the other times.
Art, in that case, cannot be clocked because it is itself a clock. From the
form-ratios you used to be able to deduce the shape of history. The modern envisions time, Kracauer said, as an "immanent continuous process,"
a "homogeneous medium indiscriminately comprising all events imaginable." Kracauer wonders whether art might not instead "invalidate our
confidence in the continuity of the historical process":

> It is noteworthy that [today] it is precisely anthropologists and art
> historians—not any historians or philosophers of history—who are
> aware of the problematic character of chronological time.

He recalls that Henri Focillon had identified an "inherent logic of the unfolding of art forms" and shown that "simultaneous art events often belong to different 'ages.'" Art has its own time table. "Focillon also has the concept of the emergent 'event' which determines its environment rather than being produced by it." The art historian disbelieves "in the magic spell of simultaneity, the effectiveness of an alleged Zeitgeist." Focillon in the 1960s was no more, but his American student George Kubler, according to Kracauer, extends his thinking. The Mayanist Kubler reorganizes artworks into sequences representing successive solutions to formal problems. "The date of a specific art object is less important for its interpretation than its…position within the sequence." Each sequence has its own "time schedule." "Its time has a peculiar shape."

Kracauer hoped that general history would learn from the special history of art to grasp the "relationships and meanings" of events, outside of chronology. But his envisioned undermining of rationalist time through form-histories would never come about, because by 1969 the history of form had been discredited, in retrospect irreversibly so. To a realist, the anachronic biography of form can be no more than a reverie. Fredric Jameson, the contemporary and complement of Umberto Eco, in a passage in his book *Marxism and Form* (1971) reproving art history, contends that the strengths and weaknesses of any "theory of history" are clearest when it "deliberately limits itself to a single cultural sphere or level of the superstructure." (It is as if he were responding directly to Kracauer. This was also exactly the argument of Friedrich Engels—recall Benjamin's essay "Eduard Fuchs, Collector and Historian," on the limits and possibilities of histories of the arts, discussed in the opening pages of the present book.) Heinrich Wölfflin's art history does just this, Jameson says, an art history "which has long seemed to offer a paradigm for other cultural cross sections such as the history of literary form." "Media, theories of perspective, the relationship between line and color, iconography: such topics mark out a kind of lost innocence of purely formal content for which the literary critic, faced with the more ambiguous phenomena of linguistic significance and of forms in time, yearns in vain." Jameson exposes what he sees as art history's foundational delusion that art succeeds in processing meanings (stories, subject-object relations, desire) such that they are entirely woven into the formal fabric of the image. The work neutralizes meaning by converting it into visible form, so making it available for comparison with other forms, and for the writing of histories of form. Literary studies can only envy this luxury of evasion, because whereas the image is always a refuge, language is always routing you back through reality. Perhaps that is where art, and in pursuit art history, finds itself today: refusing, like Jameson, the alibi of fictionality.

Jameson speaks of "a kind of ultimate vanity of art history which oppresses us whenever we feel too strongly that it is the art historian himself who wields a free shaping power over his historical data—raw materials which, elements of the superstructure with no inner resistance or reality of their own, are at one with his own substance." When form no longer has an "inner resistance or reality" of its own, then we are left with mere formalism. That is the key; and it is not easy to go on believing, as did Umberto Eco and Claude Lévi-Strauss and other structuralists, in the "inner resistance" of form and so in the approach to art-making, to writing, to the analysis of works or texts that accepts a reversal of the flow: instead of form following content, content follows form.

Ernst Gombrich saw the dead end of formalism. He began as a relativist, but ended as a realist (as did Panofsky, we recall, within the seventy-two-page span of his essay on perspective). Gombrich instead targeted what he saw as formalism's hidden normativity. In his essay "Norm and Form" (1963) Gombrich attacked Wölfflin's crypto-idealism. By inserting the classical style into a series of contrasted pairs—linear and painterly, plane and recession, multiplicity and unity, etc.—Wölfflin appeared to be relativizing the classical. Gombrich objected that Wölfflin's pairs were not true binarisms but only points on a scale, like hot and cold. What does painterly, *malerisch*, really mean? Gombrich answers: "We can safely translate it as a term of exclusion and call it 'less linear.' Less than what? Less than Wölfflin's hidden norm, the classical." Gombrich was refusing to see form as relational; relationality was Wölfflin's disguise. Instead Gombrich takes good form literally and so politicizes it.

Gombrich confronts formalism with a postwar realism amounting to the conviction that reality will crush all hopes. That is far removed from the avant-garde realism that discerned in artistic form a more real reality.

Novissima is an ambiguous Latin word, summoned by the title of Kracauer's book. In Catholic theology, *novissima* translates the Greek *eschaton*, or end times, the "last things." The term implies that the sequence of events, the content of history, has been a meaningless show and once time comes to an end there will be an unconcealing or *apocalypse* of what really is, beyond time. The last things, the topics of eschatology, are death, judgment, heaven, and hell. But the Latin word suggests that the end is also the very newest, the very youngest, such that nothing newer or younger can be conceived. In art today, and in its accompanying discourses including art history, there is no sense at all of an impending endgame. On the contrary, everything is opening up, expanding. Perspectives multiply; outsides become insides; art eschews all norms.

The *novissima*, the newest, the last—how do you know where you are in the sequence, until the sequence has come to an end? The unintelligibility of the trajectory for those who are on it rattles the still widespread confidence that things are, should, must get better. I used to teach in a so-called "great books" program that introduced freshmen, over the course of two semesters, to classics of Western literature from Homer to the twentieth century. One year, as the end of the syllabus approached, a student expressed relief when we finally arrived at T. S. Eliot's poem *The Waste Land* (1922). Finally an author, she said, who "got it right" about human nature, about life. I was surprised and discouraged. Did the student, an excellent student, really believe that Dante, Cervantes, Shakespeare, Goethe, and Tolstoy had been wrong about life?

There are two ways to interpret the student's comment. Either she was tired of making allowances for historical authors, tired of reading them in perspective, and was glad finally to read a poem of her own time (a poem nearly a hundred years old!), a poem she could read straightforwardly without having to correct for its otherness. She might well have conceded that her own convictions about reality and human nature were historically conditioned and that the reason she found it so easy to recognize herself in Eliot is because she had been raised in a world shaped by many of the same forces that had shaped Eliot's world: rationalization, secularization, urbanization, the acceleration of communication and transportation technologies, the mass media, depth psychology, and so forth. If so, then she was expressing her limited willingness to make the effort to shift her point of view and see things from an unfamiliar angle, to relativize her own modern assumptions.

That is vexing enough. But there is another way to interpret the student's comment. She was willing, under pressure from her teacher, to adopt a historian's perspective in order to profit from the premodern writers as literary artists. Successful as the old poets may have been as artists, however, she did in the end believe that they were mistaken about life, really mistaken, and not just by our modern lights. And why shouldn't she believe this? A modernist is convinced not only that modern art is the most adequate response to modern conditions but also that modernity itself offers the best possible solutions, so far, to the enigmas of human nature and human possibility, even if societies and polities do not always avail themselves of those solutions. The project of modern life, modern life conceived as a project, believes in its own correct orientation. Sigmund Freud proposed not just a new account of human personality but what he was sure was the true account. Even Theodor W. Adorno, who repudiated the Enlightenment as a betrayal of philosophy, nevertheless believed that modern art was moving in the right direction. The "emancipation" from the classical ideal in the twentieth century, for example, is an aspect for Adorno of the "unfolding of the truth-content of art."

Modern art has until now believed categorically in its own superiority to earlier art, and perhaps it still does. The new forms inducted into the world in the early twentieth century grasp reality better than premodern art had, supposedly, and not just social reality but the nature of the self, the properties of things, the ways of power.

The unapologetic preference for the now, and the voluntary embrace of the role of chroniclers and publicists of successful living artists, is a regression to the mode of the annalist, as we encountered it in Giorgio Vasari. Like today's publicist-historians, Vasari reconstructed workshop genealogies of the art of the generation before his own birth and at the time of his own childhood (the late fifteenth and early sixteenth century), but had little patience for the art of the time of his more distant ancestors (the Middle Ages). The neo-annalistic approach that characterizes much art history today means an end to the reversals of historical perspective, to the pastoral or ironic switching of the signs, the parodies—at least on a grand scale, for on a local, compressed scale there is plenty of historical consciousness. Art today is so self-referential and citational that unless you are keeping up month by month you will not be able to assess it. Within the telescoped recent history, and the democratization of cultural research, there is if anything a heightened historical consciousness. Refined abilities to date melodies, dance steps, cuts of clothes, shapes of furniture, styles of humor, and so on and so forth, to the decade, to the half-decade, are widely shared across society. The capacities to detect parodies, pastiches, citations, allusions, archaisms, and stylistic innovations rival those of the cognoscenti of painting in Italy or China in 1600. Without the long vista across time, however, neither the amateur nor very many of the professional art historians possesses any longer a "philosophy of history," a picture of the overall shape of history such as was developed by the Jewish and Christian Bible, for example, and later in the German philosophical tradition.

In breaking with history, art has broken with all primitivisms. Art may still seek plenitude and participation, therapies and ceremonies, a repeal of the dissociation of sensibility, but not routed through the past. Today the challenge to an obtuse and callous classicism is no longer mapped onto a rejection of tradition, nor does it ironically re-embrace traditions previously rejected. Now classicism, or intellectual vassalage, is internal to the present. The ancien régime targeted by modernism is no longer found in the past but rather embedded within our own society: mass culture, entertainment, the superstitions and stupidities, the half-hearted democracy, the disguised cruelty of the modern economy. It is just as in the era of religious conflict: content provides the resistance. Art is a struggle against false content.

This struggle gives history its shape. Since the content of contemporary art is often topical, basically current events, there is a constant obligation to keep up the pace. This is consistent with the overall project of Enlightenment, whose successor is modernism. Within the project of emancipation, there is finally no tolerance for relativism. The Enlightenment was antirelativist; we saw that with Diderot, who did not allow historical perspective to deflect his present-tense opinions. Historicist relativism was allied instead with the neo-Christian reaction to Enlightenment. The Enlightenment critiques itself, of course, pointing out that the Enlightenment of the *philosophes*, or last year's enlightenment, was not enlightened enough. Ongoing self-castigation is the very shape of the Enlightenment project. However, anyone today who dares to revive the Romantic critique of the Enlightenment, namely, to take up again the illiberal call for remystification and recovery of trust in myth or ritual—anyone who dares to exit the Enlightenment—is vilified.

In his book *Von Ledoux bis Le Corbusier* (1933) Emil Kaufmann contended, in an aside, that the relativist generosity of the nineteenth century that "recognized the right to existence of every style," that at first purged old buildings and paintings of their anachronistic encrustations and later simply preserved them as they were—all this was simply the extension of the principle of aesthetic autonomy to the works of the past. We may infer from Kaufmann's observation that when the dogma of aesthetic autonomy collapses, relativism, too, will be questioned. The relativist is profane because he can live with a plurality of values.

The ambiguity of the *novissima* remains. The artist points the way forward. Or does the artist trail history behind him? Nietzsche expressed this doubt with his paradoxical assertion that artists, like preachers, orators, and writers, are "late-born": thoughtless heirs who squander the communicative gifts that society with its accumulated practical wisdom has bequeathed them. "All of them people who always come at the end of a long chain." This reverses the logic of the avant-garde: according to Nietzsche art is a harvest, late but rich, telling us more about its past than about its present. This untimely quality of art is incompatible with a convergent modernism. Note that according to the philosopher the artists are heirs to form, not to content. This is the bequest they have squandered: the ability to express things. They have so much to say; there is always more present and future; but they don't know how to say it.

The confidence in a permanent amelioration that petrifies the past, a conviction that may have been learned from the technological sphere, recasts the historian either as a pessimist about the plasticity of human nature—a classic conservative, one might say—or as a relativist who hesitates to favor one perspective over any other and so never develops any convictions at all. Modernism calls a halt to the proliferation of values and perspectives that the relativist fosters and instead stabilizes value. This is a resacralization of ethics, if the sacred in general designates a stabilization of the valuation process while the profane designates a nightmare of ever-shifting values.

A paradox impends. Modernism is also commonly understood as secularization, or the loosening of ties and traditions in favor of the multiplication of individual points of view and a breakdown of the collective basis for value-assignment, value in life, value in art. Under the pressure of artistic innovation, anomie and pluralism mount. Good form, or the stabilization of value—the sacred—can only reassert itself pathetically against bad form. In modernity, art becomes an emblem of the subjectivization of value. The entropic dynamic is built into art. Secularization is a limitless ecology of new perspectives and shifting values, and in art, an infinite expansion of the repertoire of form.

But if the renunciation of form is the emblem of art's secularization, then the stabilization of content, in the spirit of a convergent progressivism, seems to represent a countermovement, a resacralization. This paradox is not easy to resolve.

Artistic form, traditionally, was the key to artistic longevity: contents fade but form survives. But then relativism held that forms can only artificially survive—none has any intrinsic staying power. This is in tension with the modernist idea of progress, or convergence. Convergence is the opposite of proliferation. Is there also an infinity of legitimate contents? Are all contents—values—equally valid? What happens if you push the logic of relativity of values to its limits?

Nietzsche already travelled far down the path of relativism, and the result was troubling, to say the least. The infinite perspectivalism and ceaseless revaluation of values that he himself had called for he found finally intolerable. Nietzsche drew a line: an elite, finally, the Übermensch, would decide things. He was unwilling to defer permanently the possibility of value-assignment. This deferral would result in the community of value-assigners constantly expanding such that the very possibility of finding common basis for valuation vanishes. Nietzsche proposed to arrest that chaotic process by cordoning off a new elect who would establish new values, leaving the mass or herd to their heterogeneity or individualism (mutual respect, negotiation, democracy, free market). Nietzsche attacks traditional valuations but does not finally doubt the possibility of valuation and is ready to limit the sphere of valuation in order to defend that possibility.

So what do we have now in art? Something similar: an imperative to think perspectivally about form, yes, but a willingness to think perspectivally about values that *goes only so far*. Art banks on content, so confident is it that it has arrived at the content of contents. Value must stabilize around the true value, call it justice or human rights, else we are lost. These values are nonrelativizable. Modernism is thus committed to a retreat from the profane and a quest for a protected place inside life where values may be stabilized, as if to demonstrate the possibility of a oneness, as promise or as memory.

In the twenty-first century only an artwork can picture an end to relativism, a standing face to face in the full presence of the other who is no longer an object, such that there is no difference and instead simple recognition. It does this better than theology, rationalist ethics, or politics. Only an artwork can be entrusted to chaperone us into the circle of justice, for only art is nonmetaphysical—it is not guaranteed by anything beyond our ken—and yet still normative.

Much art is a mode of political expression, taking the shape of indignant protest or exposure of hidden iniquities. Much art today—not all—is characterized by pessimism and dread. The postwar mentality has given way to a prewar mentality. Artist and critic embrace the ancient value of *parrhesia*, the duty to speak the truth, openly, and in one's own name. *Parrhesia*, an ancient Greek term explicated by Michel Foucault in his late writings, opposes itself to rhetoric, or speech that values form over content.

Inquiry into modern art is now inextricable from modernism's own confidence in its own content. There is no way out of this loop. This is why the study of modern art is still awaiting its heresiarch.

Modernism conceived as emancipation is convergent. Our model for the convergent process, which generates a sense of an ending, is problemsolving: social problems, technical problems, also artificial problems like chess. This is a species of realism, and one way of thinking about art as realist is to treat depiction as a technology of representation.

Art history since 1800 has been hostile to descriptions of its project as realist in this sense. That is the true intent of the academic doctrine of relativism: to stave off a technical-realist account of art history. The autonomous history of form served that same purpose. Untimeliness as an ideology signalled that art is not a technology. Art history protects art as one of the few places in modern life where disparate ways of thinking about time are protected: eternity, flow, reversals, and switchbacks. All around art is linear time, directed and convergent, the time of mere experience that governs modernist progressivism. This is realist time—time as just what it seems to be. Classic art history with its discontinuous, anachronic story lines was in this respect antirealist: Riegl, Wölfflin. Form-based art history guarantees itself a permanent project.

Art history today is different. The contemporary art paradigm *is* convergent, because it is problem-solving, with the problem being lack of freedom. If freedom were achieved, there would be no need for art or art history.

The art historian who broke with the antirealism of established art history was Gombrich. His break with his Viennese teachers, if not clean, was thoroughgoing, such that he can almost be said to be not an art historian any more. Of course, Gombrich did not believe that the problem that art was meant to solve was society's ills. His disillusionment in the face of liberal society's abject collapse in the 1930s made him a realist in that other sense, the skepticism about progress. His response was to retell the entire story of art as a convergence on representational realism, a reduction that allowed him to postpone any articulation of what else art might be, an articulation that inevitably exposes itself to further disillusionment.

Gombrich commenced his project with the eleven-page essay of 1951, "Meditations on a Hobby Horse." The basic idea of this pithy text is that art begins with the creation of a workable substitute for the horse, in a child's playroom as much as in ritual. The impression of lifelikeness is generated not strictly by resemblance but by efficacy within a "context of action," a ritual or a game. The resemblance of the hobby horse to a real horse is an afterthought, an excess. In this essay Gombrich shows that representational realism is spurious. Real realism was the hobby horse. The hobby horse is just what modernist art was trying to achieve: special access, by nonfictional means, to something more real than what we merely perceive with our everyday eyes; the realism that we modern Europeans have lost. So far Gombrich is consistent with Kandinsky or Picasso.

Gombrich's lectures given as the 1956 A.W. Mellon Lectures in the Fine Arts at the National Gallery of Art and published in 1960 as *Art and Illusion: A Study in the Psychology of Pictorial Representation*, were a kind of sequel to the "Meditations on a Hobby Horse." Here as always Gombrich's radicalism is disguised by his accessible, non-mandarin writing style. Unconvinced by Kandinsky and Picasso, finally, he reorients the history of Western art to an epic history of representational technology that overrides the weak histories of form devised in the nineteenth century in order to justify art's continued existence. Here Gombrich introduced his formula "making precedes matching." "Meditations on a Hobby Horse" had stressed the first part of the formula, the capacity of the imagination to select or fashion objects that stand in for other things in ritual and play. *Art and Illusion* develops the theory of "matching," the process of comparison of the hobby horses to real horses. "Making and matching" transforms "art as reality"—the axiom of avant-garde, anti-fictional art—into "art as (mere) realism." The humble hobby horse will eventually be replaced by a photograph of a horse. The reduction of art to a representational technology is exactly what artistic modernism had been designed to overcome.

In *Art and Illusion* Gombrich showed how artists make pictures by manipulating ready-made representational devices, inherited schemata that designate reality by force of convention. At some point an artist compares a pictorial schema to the evidence of the eyes and on that basis presumes to correct it. The new schema enters the stock of available shortcuts until some later artist holds it up to the world and ventures a further adjustment. Beholders, in turn, make their own sense of pictures by collating what they see on the canvas with what they know about the world and with what they remember of other pictures. Perception, in Gombrich's account, is learned, bodily, interactive, and cumulative. Gombrich says that the artist is not free but faces a limited array of choices. He says that cultures determine what is possible. It would seem that art historians already knew all this. Wölfflin in the *Principles of Art History* had already recast art history as a history of seeing. Making and matching may recapitulate the old academic opposition between *imitatio* (fidelity to the received models) and realism (slavish copying of the natural data). Gombrich's mechanism of making and matching would seem to allow for an endless relativism, and this is how he was read by such radical relativists as the philosopher Nelson Goodman. Resemblance to reality, Gombrich says, is an effect generated by the interplay between the expected and the unexpected. Pictures are "relational models" of reality. But neither the academic theorists nor Wölfflin nor Goodman could imagine how their stories would wind up, whereas stories about technology do end. The match of form to reality is a soluble problem. There is no endless oscillation between real and ideal. A problem-solving process is a kind of externalized reason. Technology does not depend on human virtue, only competence. Gombrich is speaking here not exactly of progress, but rather of an emergent process that seems, from the inside, to have a structure even if it is not clear where it is headed. It is like learning: not mastery of a skill, like riding a bicycle, but learning as the development of deep familiarity with a subject. Learning is a convergent process that nevertheless has no endpoint. We may feel that we are learning more and more and yet, paradoxically, not have any idea what it might be like to have nothing more to learn. European art has at times appeared to be a convergent process, and yet no one ever has imagined that art would one day achieve its ends and cease to change. Unless that end was utopia, or a life in which nothing needed to be disguised. Since Gombrich held out little hope of such a destiny, doubting that modernity had many prospects to improve upon the past, he offered instead his ironic parody of an emancipatory art history.

His story, paradoxically, clears out room for the very no-longer-modernist art that he himself lived long enough to despise. So long as artistic realism is cultivated within the sphere of form, it will involve illusion, and here there can be no competing with photography, film, and virtual reality. The only way to salvage the project of realism and yet avoid a convergent, creativity-discouraging illusionism of the sort described by Gombrich is to withdraw art from the project of form. And that is just what has happened.

It was observed earlier that Gombrich's critique of Wölfflin was political. But Gombrich's realism, like all technological realisms, is apolitical: it just shows things as they are, letting the chips fall where they may. There is a symmetry with formalism, which is also apolitical, but for a different reason. Formalism is apolitical because form disengages from reality and veers into tropology, disfiguration, or rhetoric, courting error and counting on misrecognition, such that art would never be expected to decide about content. So Gombrich politicized formalism and depoliticized modernism.

The ongoing self-writing history of art can never again be a history of form and cannot be appended to the histories of premodern form. The pax aesthetica of the postwar moment is finally rescinded. Form-histories are mythic. The lives of forms circled around something imponderable, undiscoverable. But it is no longer possible to write such lives.

Siegfried Kracauer was right that Henri Focillon, with his ideas about the untimeliness of art, poses a challenge to conventional historiography, that is, his history of form is of limited value to historians but for that reason reveals something about art. He was wrong about George Kubler, Focillon's pupil. Kubler was not the answer, for unlike Focillon (and like Gombrich) he was fallen, a realist. Kubler believed that the time of making, the fabrication of objects, was immanent to making. But he did not know how to distinguish artworks from other made objects.

Kubler (1912–1996) studied under Focillon at Yale University and in 1948 translated his teacher's *Vie des formes* (1934) into English. Kubler became an authority on the ancient and modern arts of Central and South America. In the field of Maya art, he was a pioneer, one of the first to address this material from an art-historical point of view. The study of Maya art in the mid-twentieth century, in some ways even today, was still in an archeological phase, literally unearthing its palaces and temples—at the stage of the study of ancient Greek and Roman art in the sixteenth century. Kubler also wrote a standard account of the colonial art and architecture of Spain and Portugal.

The study of Maya art was much preoccupied with archeological sorting and sequencing and with chronology. This gave Kubler the core idea of his own short tract, *The Shape of Time: Remarks on the History of Things* (1962), the most original and enduring art-historical text of its decade, in any language. Here Kubler argued that the history of art would look entirely different if we conceived it not as a relay of expressive utterances by gifted artists (that was Focillon), but rather as inclusive populations of things, mere artifacts as well as works of art, replicas and originals alike. He prefers "history of things" to the "bristling ugliness of the phrase 'material culture.'" These populations will be "portraits" of collective identity. If that is all he were saying the book would not have endured. It would just be historicist art history without the trouble that art brings. For the whole challenge of art history is that artworks are every time original and so are only imperfect portraits of collective identity. Kubler realized this and made place in his system for the artwork. He placed it at the head of sequences of replicas and called it a "prime object." His paradigm was the corpus of Maya pots. The invention is succeeded by a "mass" of reproductions, reductions, transfers, and derivations.

Kubler is completely in the mainstream of European art history since Romanticism in that he neutralizes alterity by inviting it inside. He performs a kind of "inverted colonial action"—this is his own phrase for the twentieth-century historicisms that reanimate obsolete forms. His examples included Frank Lloyd Wright renewing Maya "form-classes" of the fifteenth century (corbel-vaulted compositions) and Henry Moore's citations of Toltec-Maya recumbent figures. Kubler compares this to the Renaissance, when "the unfinished work of Greco-Roman antiquity took possession of the entire collective mind of Europe," so reversing the usual flow by which the present continually engulfs the past. In the Renaissance—and now again in the twentieth century—it is the past that commands us by a "mortmain action" to round out the contours of its unrealized possibilities. A dead, negative cosmos works on the living. This is not the fluid time of Bergson, but a spatialization of time. "The replication that fills history…prolongs the stability of many past moments." Kubler's replicas mortify, the dynamic life of the artwork in its reception is sacrificed.

Kubler is writing about sequences that failed to produce art. The "masterpiece" appeared at the beginning of the sequence (it is the opposite of Nietzsche's late-born). Kubler had no sense that the masterpiece itself is produced by accumulation, layering, and citation. He had forgotten what his teacher Focillon would have said, namely, that art is produced by a sequence's self-awareness, and not only that but it is the artwork at the end of the sequence that produces the sequence.

To offset the historians' excessive emphasis on *meaning*, Kubler urged a reacknowledgment of *being*; in place of assigned meaning (which he called the "adherent signal"), he favored the "self-signal" or the "mute existential declaration of things." At times Kubler seems to lean into the threat of meaninglessness, to acquiesce in it. The "mosaic of pieces in different developmental stages," he says, does not permit us to assign an overall character to an historical period. The "cultural bundles" that make up a period "are juxtaposed largely by chance."

Elsewhere he allows that we do need meaning after all: "Existence without meaning seems terrible in the same degree as meaning without existence seems trivial." Yet recent art (Abstract Expressionism), he says, stresses self-signals alone while recent art history (humanistic iconology à la Panofsky) stresses adherent signals alone.

Although Kubler's paradigm was Abstract Expressionism, his theses resonate more with minimalism, which was on the horizon. The minimalist attitudes, which were shared in part by pop art, included ironic transpositions of center and margin; the mistrust of conventionally coded sign systems; the disabling of the matter-spirit dichotomy through the introduction of a third term, a quantity neither matter nor spirit, namely, information; and the acceptance of iteration as the basic condition for difference and meaning.

Kubler's austere but poetic text was read by artists. Lawrence Alloway, Robert Smithson, Al Held, Ad Reinhardt, Michael Heizer, Donald

Judd, and Robert Morris, among others, expressed interest in Kubler. The artists may have underread him as a neo-formalist providing an antidote to Abstract Expressionism and kitsch existentialism.

John Baldessari's *Painting for Kubler* (1966–1968), depicts a sequence of statements about art in block capitals on a neutral ground, composites and paraphrases drawn from *The Shape of Time*. The painting responds to Kubler's argument that works derive meaning from their position within a sequence. Baldessari knows that Kubler is right, and not only about clay pots but also about authored paintings. His *Painting for Kubler*, a droll protest, points out that Kubler's story is not the whole story.

Kubler's *The Shape of Time* echoed in format, tone, and metaphoric language the tract of his teacher. The book ends up saying the opposite of Focillon. Whereas Focillon was a liberal humanist who trusted in artworks as portals to a universal shared human experience, Kubler stressed the ways that sequences of artifacts function as a kind of exoskeleton, an outsourcing of memory and experience that promises no way back. He is gloomy about the possibility of grasping the moment of actuality, "which slips too fast by the slow, coarse net of our senses."

This is very close to Gombrich's making and matching, except that since Kubler will not deal with representation, there is no matching—it is all making. His replica chains were formalist morphologies like those of Riegl or Focillon, pushed to an extreme, except that there will be no sublimation of the thing as artwork. The key to Kubler is his lack of reverence for art.

Kubler seems to open up onto mass culture but doesn't. Mass culture is not just subartistic or understylized art, that is, poor replicas of the prime object. It is no different with Gombrich. After the war Gombrich had envisioned an "ambitious work of which actually *Art and Illusion* and *The Sense of Order* [his book of 1979 on ornament, in effect an extended reading of Riegl's *Questions of Style*] are only fragments: a general book on images and the different functions of images. It was to include illustration, symbolism, emblems and decoration." He even submitted to a publisher "a long project…which I called *The Realm and Range of the Image*." *Art and Illusion* itself, with its reproductions and analyses of posters, advertisements, popular prints, optical illusions, and scientific illustrations, prophesied the fields of study that would later be called *Bildwissenschaft* in Germany, and "visual culture studies"

PAINTING FOR KUBLER

THIS PAINTING OWES ITS EXISTENCE TO PRIOR PAINTINGS. BY LIKING THIS SOLUTION, YOU SHOULD NOT BE BLOCKED IN YOUR CONTINUED ACCEPTANCE OF PRIOR INVENTIONS. TO ATTAIN THIS POSITION, IDEAS OF FORMER PAINTING HAD TO BE RETHOUGHT IN ORDER TO TRANSCEND FORMER WORK. TO LIKE THIS PAINTING, YOU WILL HAVE TO UNDERSTAND PRIOR WORK. ULTIMATELY THIS WORK WILL AMALGAMATE WITH THE EXISTING BODY OF KNOWLEDGE.

John Baldessari, *Painting for Kubler* (1966–1968). Acrylic on canvas, 173 × 144 cm. Private collection. None of these sentences is a direct quote from *The Shape of Time.*

in Britain and America. The student of visual culture believes that the study of images has been impeded by outmoded tastes for the fine arts, aesthetic experiences, and the recondite art of interpretation.

Kubler and Gombrich's versions of visual culture studies were apolitical—and for that reason open-ended—but incompatible with a convergent art history structured by the coordination of art with justice and ethics.

The "fallen," like Gombrich and Kubler, are realists about art. The fallen are those who have decided that they were not interested in art in the first place; that their real object of study is image, object, thing, matter, power, flow. Fallen art history accepts that the base, material world is all there is, which does not rule out entertaining the fancy that base material things are alive, or "want" something. Art, meanwhile, for the fallen, is made by humans for humans, it is edifying and pleasurable, but no more. The fallen are convinced that art alone is not enough, for it lacks any real connection to knowledge or power. Art history was always insecure about its relation to power. Art historians are no longer writing private art criticism for Catherine the Great of Russia, the duke and duchess of Saxe-Gotha, the royal house of Sweden, August III of Poland, and the princess of Nassau-Saarbruch, as Diderot was. Instead, to the extent they are not writing for each other, they cast flowers to the college-educated museumgoers, hoping a few will be gathered and pressed in books. Art history seems to them susceptible to the charge that art, and by extension the artwork, the discourse of art, and the discipline of art history, lacks something. What does art lack? Art lacks a strong tie to reality. Art is cut off from reality because it is merely fictional. The discipline's object of study, art, is a manufactured irreality. The fallen propose new objects of study that substitute for something that art is seen to lack.

Up until now, to be really radical as an art historian you had to not believe completely in art, you had to mistrust it, like Warburg, Gombrich, and Kubler. Today that unbelief is commonplace, especially among nonmodernists, and so no longer radical.

In the 1960s and 1970s, realist models of art history discovered broad audiences. John Berger, the British critic, was perhaps even more widely read than Gombrich. Berger's *Ways of Seeing*, the BBC television series and the subsequent reader-friendly book (1972), innovative in layout and exoteric in outlook, demystified the center of the art historical canon, the easel paintings of the sixteenth through nineteenth centuries. Gombrich had deflated the Old Masters by folding the story of oil painting into the story of technologies designed to reproduce perceptions. Gombrich's book had provided no reasons for the continued admiration of these works except as episodes in a process that eventually produced photography and film. Berger would have criticized Gombrich for naturalizing and depoliticizing representation. In other ways his project extended Gombrich's. He exposed the revered masterpieces by Titian, Bronzino, and Holbein hanging in the National Gallery in London as the mendacious toys of the "ruling classes," as the purveyors of images of sexually submissive women, and as cynical justifications for gross luxury and acquisitiveness. Modern society idolizes these paintings, according to Berger, because reproductions in coffee-table books and magazines and the illustrated lectures of art historians propagate the illusion that art "justified most other forms of authority, that art makes inequality seem noble and hierarchies seem thrilling." "The art of the past is being mystified because a privileged minority is striving to invent a history which can retrospectively justify the role of the ruling classes."

Berger exposes what had been thought natural—the relation between property and art—as a pernicious conspiracy. The last moribund form of the visual art of post-Renaissance Europe is finally "publicity," or advertising.

If the proximity of art history to the art market and to luxury and fashion is a curse, Berger casts a powerful countercurse. The hammer strokes of Berger's indignant polemic ring even today and, to a considerable extent, ring true. He maps no path forward for the student of premodern art: the paintings in the museums, once they are exposed as insidious baubles masking society's real visage, are no longer of any use except as shameful documents of European history. Berger is saying more or less what the Marxist art historians Arnold Hauser and Frederick Antal had said in the 1940s. This time the point came across. In 1972 everyone seemed to be learning to read all over again.

With Gombrich and Berger art history fulfilled its communicational promise, its natural interdisciplinarity and reach. Their demystifications of elite art met head-on the popularity of that very art, the art housed in museums and admired without bound by tourists and exhibition-goers. And yet the museum thrives, as if the cult of art and its debunking were natural complements.

Academic art history since the 1970s that adopts Berger's icono-clastic stance tends not to imitate his blunt language, however. Schol-arship—and here art history is not alone among the humanistic disciplines—has turned away from plain speaking and straightforward argumentation, turned away from the very concepts of the "plain" and the "straightforward." Art history is protected by household gods bor-rowed from other clans, the concept-makers, the "irrealist" thinkers forced to bend language because the language they inherit does not match the way things really are. The irrealists or, as they are called, "theorists" propose renamings and unnamings in order to interfere with assumptions about how the mind works, how language works, what reading or looking is, how one knows anything, how symbols work, what value to assign to experience, how power disguises itself, whether the body is destiny, whether nature is real or invented, how the exis-tence of objects differs from the existence of living things, how society functions at all. Some of these are traditional philosophical questions, but theory mistrusts philosophy, especially the academic discipline of philosophy, which too often aims at little more than a monitoring of the relation between concepts and language, a necessary activity but so lacking in love and wisdom that it hardly deserves the monopoly it claims over the word "philosophy."

"Theory" is a space within society where texts, images, performances, and other artifacts are cut open and exposed to the "world"—existence, ethics, politics—without relying on commonsense assumptions about how texts or images connect to the world. Theory's instrument is a not always lucid mode of writing that divides readers abruptly into the initi-ate and the uninitiated. The "parabolic" thinkers think "alongside," they speak in figures. In turning toward irrealist thought, art history dealt away any chance of winning back the giant readerships of Gombrich or Berger, not to mention the audiences of the museum exhibitions or the television programs about art. The hybridization of art history since the 1970s with the varieties of nonhistorical and often non-art-oriented thought has come at the cost of esotericism. Scholars may give the read-ing public what they need, but they forget to explain to the public why they need it.

The limitation and the hazard of irrealist, nonphilosophical thought is that it expresses itself in modules of language that when first formulated were innovative but when copied and reused are no longer. They are like images of innovative thought. The language quickly mortifies and needs always to be refreshed. Only an initiate can keep pace with the constant readjustments, cross-wirings, cross-references. This is a major weakness, but it is structural and cannot be remedied. The poor relations between irrealist thought and the extra-academic public cannot be repaired. Theory is not a menu of methods, or paths. There really is only one *method*, and it is empiricism. All the rest is existential. Theory is existential in the sense that it is a mode of living, tentative and situational.

If Gombrich, Kubler, and Berger were fallen, then we are by contrast gnostics, the ones who know that there is something to know, but cannot name it, or can express it only in negative terms. The gnostics know that the material world is a fallen world made by an ignorant demon whose gaze is bent earthward. Form-histories were metafictions that sustained the fiction of gnosticism.

Gnosticism is also the mode of the parabolic thinkers, the chimerical, nonconformist, demiurgic, marvelous, speculative, libertine theorists, often para-academic or exiled to the margins of academia. The emergence of new constellations of thinkers, like stars coming out at night, is one of the main features of the postwar period. The chimerical or antiphilosophical thinkers are mostly self-authorizing; they have no clear expertise, they do not appeal to the real world. Irrealist thought detects and works with (not against) misrecognition, transfiguration, dream, indirection. Speculative and nonconformist, as skeptical of the natural or experimental sciences as they are of philosophy, the theorists also know that art does not know anything either. In short, one cannot say that "theory" says in a baroque fashion what John Berger already said plainly. Theory leaves Berger far behind. Not until the moment of theory did the West develop a language adequate to art's combinatory, topological, dream-like nature. Parabolic discourse comes close to naming or rhyming with art. Parabolic thinkers are talking about art even when they are not.

Irrealism also entails skepticism about the possibility of writing a realist history of art. That skepticism is even more justified now that art is understood as something like a moral force, something like love or belief, and not as a set of things in the world. Art history that really keeps pace, and faith, with art cannot be a history any more.

From the point of view of the modernist, the historian can at best find the real, but not the true. A modernist reads the past, if at all, through the lenses provided *by* modernism: through Freud, for example, or Benjamin. The past lives in the idea-spheres built by those thinkers. For a modernist, there is no point to studying the history of premodern European art other than as a record of false beliefs. Unless exposed, the false beliefs will persist as superstitions. The modernist premise is that modernist thought is irreversible: the genie is out of the bottle; it is absurd to try to imagine the innovators away, painters and writers alike, and to carry on without their guidance.

Presentism, or the imposition of a pattern found in actuality onto the past, used to be the (art) historian's cardinal sin: now it is an unnameable norm. We have been "lured so far away from our ancestors that we believe they were like us." From the empiricist's point of view, presentism is a violation of hierarchy: the algorithm of forensic investigation is not supposed to be contaminated by biases filtering in from the command level. History, admittedly, is not laboratory science. Even the best art history is a little presentist. Art historians wrote vital histories of old and remote art only when they posed questions whose answers would matter to their own present. The new presentism is more explicit and has its lineage: Diderot; Nietzschean "critical" history—judgmental, moralizing, self-serving; American Pragmatist philosophy from Emerson to Dewey, which courted an insouciance toward the past, preaching a post-European freedom from the obligations of history; and Benjaminian "imagistic" history. Carl Einstein wrote that "what is effective in history is always a consequence of the immediate present." The last most powerful assessment of the presentist possibility was Michel Foucault's essay "Nietzsche Genealogy History" (1971), which concluded by summarizing the three modes of history described by Nietzsche: monumental, antiquarian, and critical. Foucault sees the three modes reappearing in his own time but in reversed, parodic form. The parodic, impious attitude was already partly present in Nietzsche's account, such that Foucault hardly needs to do more than restate the aims of the first two modes to remind us of their absurdity. Foucault's first mode, the parody of Nietzsche's "monumental" history, is "directed against reality, and opposes the theme of history as reminiscence or recognition." The second, which he calls the "dissociative," is the parody of Nietzsche's antiquarian approach. The dissociative mode is "directed against identity, and opposes history given as continuity or representative of a tradition." The third mode is the parody of Nietzsche's critical history—and the most delicate case because Nietzsche had come close to endorsing the critical, ironic, or presentist mode, the mode of history dedicated to truth and justice, as the only acceptable one. Who could reject "its just treatment of the past, its decisive cutting of the roots, its rejection of traditional attitudes of reverence, its liberation of man by presenting him with other origins than those in which he prefers to see himself"? But to be consistent Foucault has to complete his parodic sequence. The third mode he calls "sacrificial" because it sacrifices the very subject of knowledge. This mode is "directed against truth, and opposes history as knowledge." But critical history, Foucault insists, is sublimated and redeemed in its own parody. He calls on the authority of Nietzsche's own later writings to argue that history-writing, if it is ever to escape the cycle of injustice, must undercut even its own authority: "It is no longer a question of judging the past in the name of a truth that only we can possess in the present, but of risking the destruction of the subject who seeks knowledge in the endless deployment of the will to knowledge." Foucault cancels ordinary presentism by pulling it into an infinite regress of self-criticism.

Presentism has power when you have a choice, when it is voluntary, as it was for Nietzsche and Foucault in their tragic critical modes, and not merely a consequence of temporal provincialism.

The self-styled "new art history" of the late 1970s and 1980s aimed to bring the politics of historical art production into plain daylight. Art historians, adept solvers of pictorial ciphers, discriminated between the art that screened and the art that exposed asymmetries of power. The new art history followed John Berger, and not Ernst Gombrich or George Kubler, and so in no way challenged the traditional philosophy of history, which assigned to technologized modernity the task of realizing the redemptive ambitions of the Enlightenment. The "new art history" was an Anglo-American coinage, but the German-speaking countries ran on a parallel track. "Form" as an object of analysis was replaced by "representation," a concept that shifts the stress from the results to the process of art-making. Representation is the rearrangement and reassignation of elements of reality. Representation is not peculiar to art. To describe art-making as representation is to prepare the retreat of art history back into the fold of a general science of symbol- and meaning-making. Representation is not a simple operation, however, and is not so easily reverse-engineered. A picture or a configuration involves not only encoding but also doubling, substitution, and mimicry. Something is made present in a representation—what? The image possesses an ineluctable, self-sufficient quality that words do not. Many art historians who resented the ideological imperatives of the new art history and who had no interest in undermining the concept of art preferred instead to plunge into the labyrinth of representation, well realizing that they would never find their way out. Many influential art-historical studies of the 1970s or 1980s now look like late forms of the paradigm of art history established between 1895 and 1925, and not the early stages of anything. Michael Baxandall (1933–2008), the social historian of art, author of studies of Italian and German Renaissance art in their civic contexts, confided later in life that his aim really had been to "do Roger Fry over again but after nature." Baxandall insisted on eating and having his cake, and so should we all.

And yet—the newness of the new art history has by no means faded. The sense of unlimited intellectual possibility, the liberation—still far from complete—of art-historical research from the directives of class-based and propertied authority, the defiance of the anti-intellectualism that blanketed art-historical study in the first two or even three decades after the Second World War—all this is as real and as stirring as it ever was. Modern art, in the same way, will always be modern. Art history as a discipline became truly modern only in the 1970s. The critical program, the casting of searchlights, persists as the overall program of scholarship in the humanities.

Discouraging is the waning today of curiosity about the past, accompanied by a decline in language learning. This has happened, perhaps, because some historians and critics came to conclude that art in the past was mostly apologizing for repressive authority. Since we are all amply aware of this fact, it made sense to some simply to abandon the past and instead attend to the more urgent task of the triage of good and bad art in the most recent decades. Even more urgent, by that logic, is the maieutic project, the hatching of the just society of the future out of the critical art of the present.

The great merit of the commitment to critical contemporary art is that it reinforces confidence in art generally. That confidence is no longer shared by the rest of the discipline, the ones who work on everything other than "contemporary art." No longer transfixed by the Medusa effect of form, anxiously aware that European art-historical scholarship, no matter what its object, is always guided by European concepts of art, the historian of what was once called art enrolls in research programs that know little of art: environmental studies, urbanism, material culture studies, neurobiology, the histories of science and technology, the histories of conquest and commerce. (Not true about all disciplines: psychoanalysts, literary theorists, anthropologists, and historians of religion are very often in tune with art.) Why should an art historian answer questions posed by other disciplines? How will such an art history profile itself against those disciplines? What is the expertise of this art historian? Expertise is the minimum that society expects from the scholar.

Some persist in their pursuit of old or distant art because the art of our own moment and recent past seems too familiar, even self-evident. All the strangeness has been contrived by the artist, who is our contemporary and so never really foreign to us. Whereas the art of the past—just recall the stories told by Pausanias, at the beginning of this book, about the ancient image-cults—is automatically mysterious and needy of interpretation. The historians of the contemporary are devoted to art but are too confident that they know where to find it. They believe they are looking straight at art. But art wears many masks: beauty, piety, knowledge, justice. None of these masks is art itself, which is unavailable to reason and not fully involved with history, an unknown external to man even if produced by man. "The reason the artist puts on a different face, a role, is because Art has no face. And truly, every actor in his role does not sense the face but the sensation of the presented face," wrote Kazimir Malevich in 1927. "Suprematism is the end and the beginning, when the sensations are made bare, when art becomes itself, without a face." We are still waiting for that end that is a beginning, but never mind: the case was well-stated.

The new historian of old art, panicked by the cascade of masks, procrastinates, postpones the meeting with art. Perhaps the art historian hesitates in the spirit of Jacob Burckhardt, whose tendency to evade, demur, pull up short before art we noted in our discussion of his *Culture of the Renaissance in Italy*. Let us hope that is the case! In the phrase of his insightful younger colleague at Basel, who in a letter was telling a friend about a lecture he had just heard, Burckhardt tended "not so much toward distortions (*Verfälschungen*) but rather, it would seem, a withholding (*Verschweigungen*) of the truth." More likely, Burckhardt was circling around something he could not clearly see. Few others in the audience, surely—so the immodest colleague imagined—followed "the deep ways of his thought with its strange breaks and turns whenever it approaches something troubling (*das Bedenkliche*)." Burckhardt's writing kept pace with the hesitations and feints of art, not vainly striking out at, but protecting, like a moving shield, the sensed quarry: protecting the troubling unknown from a premature translation into a narrower existence.

In this list of references, I cite the sources of my quotes so that readers can seek out the passages in their original contexts. In some cases, when the page layout and typography are still of great interest, I have given page references to original publications, for example, *The Blue Rider Almanac* of 1912. Most significant texts, however, are found in modern critical editions, and there is no reason to cite the original versions: Gian Paolo Lomazzo's *Idea del tempio della pittura*, for example, or Hegel's *Lectures on Aesthetics*. I have in many cases listed significant translations into English, but for the sake of economy not into any other languages. If no translation is cited, then I have done the translation myself. When I do cite an English translation, I indicate whether I have quoted from it or have done the translating myself.

I do not give in the list of references a full citation for every book mentioned in the text. In the main text I give title and date of the first edition of every publication I mention. But if I don't quote directly from that book, then there will be no additional citation here at the end of the book. Readers should be able to track down editions of the mentioned books pretty easily. The Internet has changed the nature of research in this field. Many premodern books can be read online or even downloaded free of charge, either reproduced as page images or as searchable text files. Some important resources are the Internet Archive (archive.org), Hathitrust Digital Library, Gallica at the Bibliothèque nationale de France, and the digital platforms of the Bayerische Staatsbibliothek and the Universitätsbibliothek at Heidelberg. See also the specialized websites devoted to the primary sources of art history, *Fontes: Quellen und Dokumente zur Kunst 1350–1750* (https://www .arthistoricum.net/publizieren/fontes/) and *Fondazione Memofonte* (https://www.memofonte.it). The *Journal of Art Historiography*, an online periodical, publishes many primary sources in translation as well as scholarship on this material. See also the bibliography of the Historiography of European Art compiled by Thomas Da Costa Kaufmann in Oxford Bibliographies Online (DOI: 10.1093/obo/9780199920105-0001).

The quantity of writing on the principles and the multiple histories of the discipline has augmented massively since the early 1980s. It is truly a garden of forking paths, too vast to survey. The scholarly literature on the history of art history is underrepresented in these endnotes. I have tried to acknowledge at least my most direct dependencies on the interpretations and insights of my colleagues. When I was led to a little-known quote by another scholar, I have acknowledged this.

I wish to list some books of the last several decades which have been especially important for me: Heinrich Dilly, *Kunstgeschichte als Institution: Studien zur Geschichte einer Disziplin* (Frankfurt: Suhrkamp, 1979), Michael Podro, *The Critical Historians of Art* (New Haven: Yale University Press, 1982), Hans Belting, *Das Ende der Kunstgeschichte?* (Munich: Deutscher Kunstverlag, 1983), Michael Baxandall, *Patterns of Intention: On the Historical Explanation of Pictures* (New Haven: Yale University Press, 1985), Hubert Damisch, *L'origine de la perspective* (Paris: Flammarion, 1987), Georges Didi-Huberman, *Devant l'image: question posée aux fins d'une histoire de l'art* (Paris: Éditions de Minuit, 1990), Margaret Olin, *Forms of Representation in Alois Riegl's Theory of Art* (University Park: Pennsylvania State University Press, 1992), Francis Haskell, *History and Its Images* (New Haven: Yale University Press, 1993), Whitney Davis, *Replications: Archaeology, Art History, Psychoanalysis* (University Park: Pennsylvania State University Press, 1996), Henri Zerner, *Écrire l'histoire de l'art: Figures d'une discipline* (Paris: Gallimard, 1997), Philippe-Alain Michaud, *Aby Warburg et l'image en mouvement* (Paris: Macula, 1998), Georges Didi-Huberman, *L'image survivante: Histoire de l'art et temps des fantômes selon Aby Warburg* (Paris: Éditions de Minuit, 2002), Frederic J. Schwartz, *Blind Spots: Critical Theory and the History of Art in Twentieth-Century Germany* (New Haven: Yale University Press, 2005), Éric Michaud, *Histoire de l'art: une discipline à ses frontières* (Paris: Hazan, 2005), Gabriele Guercio, *Art as*

Existence: The Artist's Monograph and Its Project (Cambridge, MA: MIT Press, 2006), Margaret Iversen and Stephen Melville, *Writing Art History: Disciplinary Departures* (Chicago: University of Chicago Press, 2010), Whitney Davis, *A General Theory of Visual Culture* (Princeton: Princeton University Press, 2011), Alexander Nagel, *Medieval Modern: Art out of Time* (London: Thames & Hudson, 2012), Spyros Papapetros, *On the Animation of the Inorganic: Art, Architecture, and the Extension of Life* (Chicago: University of Chicago Press, 2012), Molly Nesbit, *The Pragmatism in the History of Art* (Pittsburgh, PA, and New York: Periscope, 2013), Peter N. Miller, *History and Its Objects: Antiquarianism and Material Culture since 1500* (Ithaca, NY: Cornell University Press, 2017). I would also mention the essays on historiography by Colin Eisler, Kurt Forster, Carlo Ginzburg, Werner Hofmann, Wolfgang Kemp, Alina Payne, Ulrich Pfisterer, Willibald Sauerländer, and David Summers.

Despite the growth of the historiographical field and the myriad studies of individual art historians (Riegl, Warburg, etc.), there are to my knowledge only a few synthetic or narrative treatments: Julius von Schlosser, *Die Kunstliteratur: ein Handbuch zur Quellenkunde der neueren Kunstgeschichte* (1924) (discussed in this book, section 1920–1930); Lionello Venturi, *History of Art Criticism* (1936); Udo Kultermann, *Geschichte der Kunstgeschichte: Der Weg einer Wissenschaft* (1966); Germain Bazin, *Histoire de l'histoire de l'art de Vasari à nos jours* (1986), and Hubert Locher, *Kunstgeschichte als historische Theorie der Kunst 1750–1950* (2001).

INTRODUCTION

1 On the Doberan altar: Ernst Badstübner, "Typologische Bildkunst im Münster zu Doberan," in Dirk Schumann, ed., *Sachkultur und religiöse Praxis* (Berlin: Lukas, 2007), 151–76, and the articles by Badstübner and Jens Rüffer in *Die Ausstattung des Doberaner Münsters*, Gerhard Weilandt and Kaja von Cossart, eds. (Petersberg: Michael Imhof, 2018).

4 Ernst Robert Curtius, *Europäische Literatur und lateinisches Mittelalter* (Bern: Francke, 1948), 22; *European Literature and the Latin Middle Ages* (Princeton, NJ: Princeton University Press, 1953), 14–15. According to Curtius it is only *Kunstwissenschaft* that achieves this "essence-intuition" (*Wesensschau*) into art; the mere "historical study of art" is blind.

5 Henri Focillon, *Vie des formes* (Paris: PUF, 1934), 1 (my translation); but see *The Life of Forms in Art*, Charles B. Hogan and George Kubler, transl. (1942) (New York: Zone Books, 1989), 31.

5 Stendhal, *De l'amour* (1822), vol. 1, chap. 17, n. 1. Note that according to Stendhal beauty is *only* the promise of happiness, and whereas beauty may well be absolute, happiness, he says, is historically relative. On this phrase, and the difference between the aesthetics of Kant and Stendhal, see Friedrich Nietzsche, *The Genealogy of Morals*, Third Essay, § 6.

6 On the eighteen art history professors in 1920: Christian von Ferber, *Die Entwicklung des Lehrkörpers der deutschen Universitäten und Hochschulen, 1864–1954* (Göttingen: Vanderhoeck & Ruprecht, 1956), 207–208.

6 Theodor W. Adorno, *Ästhetische Theorie* (Frankfurt: Suhrkamp, 1970), 168–69; *Aesthetic Theory*, Robert Hullot-Kentor, transl. (Minneapolis: University of Minnesota Press, 1997), 110. I have quoted this translation.

7 Mentions and discussions of Heinrich Wölfflin: José Ortega y Gasset, "The Dehumanization of Art" (1925), in *The Dehumanization of Art and Other Essays on Art, Culture, and Literature* (Princeton, NJ: Princeton University Press, 1968), n. at 45. Boris Eikhenbaum, "La théorie de la 'méthode formelle'" (1925), in Tsvetan Todorov, ed., *Théorie de la littérature: textes des formalistes russes* (Paris: Seuil, 2001),

32. Sergei Eisenstein, "Rodin and Rilke" (1945) as well as *Nonindifferent Nature* (texts written between 1937 and 1945) (Cambridge, UK: Cambridge University Press, 1987), 122, 340; see also M. B. Iampolski, *Memory of Tiresias: Intertextuality and Film* (Berkeley: University of California Press, 1998), 236 and 279n43, who states that Eisenstein's "search for abstraction" matches the thought of Riegl, Adolf von Hildebrand, and Wölfflin. Walter Benjamin, see below. Marshall McLuhan, *The Gutenberg Galaxy* (Toronto: University of Toronto Press, 1962), 41. Gilles Deleuze, *The Fold: Leibniz and the Baroque*, Tom Conley, transl. (Minneapolis: University of Minnesota Press, 1993), 28–29, and *Cinema*, vol. 1, *The Movement-Image*, Hugh Tomlinson and Barbara Habberjam, transl. (Minneapolis: University of Minnesota Press, 1986), 26 and n.25. Richard Wollheim, see below. Walther Rehm, *Heinrich Wölfflin als Literaturhistoriker* (Munich: Bayerische Akademie der Wissenschaften, 1960). René Wellek, "The Concept of Baroque" (1945) and "Concepts of Form and Structure in Twentieth-Century Criticism" (1958) in Wellek, *Concepts of Criticism*, 74–88, 63. Joseph Frank, "Formal Criticism and Abstract Art," *Hudson Review* 6 (1954): 481–86. Renato Poggioli, *The Theory of the Avant-Garde* (1962) (Cambridge, MA: Harvard University Press, 1968), 211, and Fredric Jameson, *Marxism and Form* (Princeton, NJ: Princeton University Press, 1971), 322.

7 Mentions and discussions of Riegl: see Christopher S. Wood, "Introduction," *The Vienna School Reader: Politics and Art Historical Method in the 1930s* (New York: Zone Books, 2000), 9–15; updated as "Formalismus und kein Ende: Die Einführung zu 'The Vienna School Reader' (2000) mit einem neuen Nachwort," in *Formbildung und Formbegriff: Das Formdenken der Moderne*, Markus Klammer, Malika Maskarinec, Rahel Villinger, and Ralph Ubl, eds. (Paderborn: Fink, 2019); and see also Eisenstein, *Nonindifferent Nature*, 367; and Balázs, "Problems of Style in Film" (1952), in Balázs, *Theory of the Film* (New York, 1972), 158.

8 Focillon on form intervening between man and nature: *Vie des formes*, 74; *Life of Forms*, 124.

8 Walter Benjamin on Wölfflin: "Eduard Fuchs, der Sammler und der Historiker" (1937), in Benjamin, *Gesammelte Schriften*, 7 vols. in 14

(Frankfurt: Suhrkamp, 1972–89), 2: 465–505, here 480–81; translated as "Eduard Fuchs, Collector and Historian" (1937), in Benjamin, *The Work of Art in the Age of Its Technical Reproducibility and Other Writings on Media* (Cambridge, MA: Harvard University Press, 2008), 119, 127, 149n34. The quote from Wölfflin is from *Die klassische Kunst* (Munich, 1899), 227.

9 Richard Wollheim on Riegl, Wölfflin, and Focillon: *Art and Its Objects* (New York: Harper & Row, 1968), 145.

11 Cicero on the relativity of style: *De oratore* 3. 7. 25–26; I have used the translation by H. Rackham, *De oratore*, Loeb Classical Library (Cambridge, MA: Harvard University Press, 1942), 3: 20–23.

11 The late medieval altarpieces came to the Landesmuseum when it opened in 1898; the Kunsthaus did not begin collecting the old paintings until the 1920s. See *Kunsthaus Zürich: Gesamtkatalog der Gemälde und Skulptur* (Ostfildern: Hatje Kantz, 2007), 10.

12 Zhang Yanyuan: see Susan Bush and Hsio-yen Shih, eds., *Early Chinese Texts on Painting* (Cambridge, MA: Harvard University Press, 1985), 66.

12 Zhao Mengfu: see Lin Yutang, ed., *The Chinese Theory of Art* (New York: Putnam, 1967), 109.

13 On the *Prayer of Enos and Vocation of Noah* at Saint-Savin: Mérimée, *Notice sur les peintures de l'église de Saint-Savin* (Paris, 1845), Plate 10, p. 106.

13 Mérimée on the superiority of the painter of Saint-Savin to Jan van Eyck: Mérimée, *Notice sur les peintures de l'église de Saint-Savin*, 53; reprinted as "L'église de Saint-Savin et ses peintures murales" in Mérimée, *Études sur les arts au moyen âge* (Paris, 1875), 165, and in Mérimée, *Études sur les arts du moyen âge* (Paris: Flammarion, 1967), 111–12.

15 Cicero on statues of the gods in his home: *Ad familiares*, VII, 23; I have used the translation by D. R. Shackleton Bailey, *Letters to Friends*, Loeb Classical Library (Cambridge, MA: Harvard University Press, 2001), Letter 209, 2: 266–67.

16 Northrop Frye, *The Secular Scripture: A Study of the Structure of Romance* (Cambridge, MA: Harvard University Press, 1976), 35–36.

17 Focillon, *Vie des formes*, 83, 2, 8, 100; *The Life of Forms in Art*, 137, 33, 42, 156.

18 The ex voto of Manuela Ybarra: *Agents of Faith: Votive Objects in Time and Place*, Ittai Weinryb, ed. (New York: Bard Graduate Center, 2018), 262, fig. 11.6, cat. no. 46.

18 Anita Brenner, *Idols Behind Altars* (New York: Harcourt, Brace, 1929), 167–68, 13.

22–23 Herodotus, *The Histories*, Robin Waterfield, transl. (Oxford: Oxford University Press, 1998), 2.124–31, pp. 145–47.

23 For the documents on the dispute between Mazzoleni and the town council of Salò, see *Romanino: un pittore in rivolta nel Rinascimento italiano*, exhibition catalogue, Trento, Castello di Buonconsiglio (Milan: Silvana, 2006), 424–25. The incident is discussed by Alessandro Nova, *Girolamo Romanino* (Torino: Umberto Allemandi, 1994), 33–34.

24 Giorgio Vasari, *Le vite de' più eccellenti pittori, scultori ed architettori*, Gaetano Milanesi, ed., 9 vols. (Florence: Sansoni, 1878–1885) (cited henceforth as "Milanesi"); *Le vite de' più eccellenti pittori, scultori e architettori*, Rosanna Bettarini and Paola Barocchi, eds., 6 vols. (Florence: Sansoni, 1966–1987) (cited henceforth as "Bettarini-Barocchi"). Searchable texts of both editions of Vasari are readily available online. See the Fondazione Memofonte, https:// www.memofonte.it/ricerche/giorgio-vasari/. On the English translations and partial translations of Vasari, see Patricia Lee Rubin, *Giorgio Vasari: Art and History* (New Haven, CT: Yale University Press, 1995), 415–16.

24 Vasari on Romanino, in the life of Vittorio Carpaccio (1550 ed.): Milanesi 3: 653; Bettarini-Barocchi 3, 1: 626; and in the life of Benedetto Garofalo and Girolamo da Carpi (1568 ed.), Milanesi 6: 504, Bettarini-Barocchi 5: 429.

25 Possible traces of Mazzoleni's paintings in Salò: Monica Ibsen, *Il Duomo di Salò* (Gussago: Vannini, 1999), 98.

25 Petrarch on the fame of artists: *Remedies for Fortune Fair and Foul*, transl. Conrad H. Rawski, 5 vols. (Bloomington, IN, 1991), bk. I, dialogue 41, vol. 1, p. 131.

26 Vasari on the dependency of fame on writing: Preface to the *Lives*, Milanesi 1: 222, Bettarini-Barocchi 2: 13.

27 Franz Boas, *Primitive Art* (Cambridge, MA: Harvard University Press, 1927), 156.

28 Barbara Isenberg, *Conversations with Frank Gehry* (New York: Knopf, 2009), 59.

29 Gaston Bachelard, *La poétique de l'espace* (Paris: PUF, 1958), 1; my translation, but see *The Poetics of Space*, Maria Jolas, transl. (New York: Orion, 1964), 1.

30 Eva Hesse, interview with Cindy Nemser, originally published in *Artforum*, May 1970, the month Hesse died; reprinted in *Eva Hesse*, Mignon Nixon, ed. (Cambridge, MA: MIT Press, 2002), 22, 10, 18.

31 Michel de Certeau, *The Writing of History* (1975), Tom Conley, transl. (New York: Columbia University Press, 1988), 2–4. Certeau borrowed a couple of phrases from the anthropologist Louis Dumont.

32–34 Pausanias, *Description of Greece*, Book VIII, xlii, 1–13, W. H. S. Jones, transl. (Loeb Classical Library) (Cambridge, MA: Harvard University Press, 1935), 4:109–17.

36 Claude Lévi-Strauss on "diachronic flavor": *The Savage Mind* (1962) (Chicago: University of Chicago Press, 1966), 241–42: the relic and the original document in an archive places a society "in contact with pure historicity." But our past "would not disappear if we lost our archives: it would be deprived of what one is inclined to call its diachronic flavor. It would still exist as a past but preserved in nothing but contemporary or recent books, institutions, or even a situation. So it would be exhibited in synchrony."

37 On Heinrich Hübsch at Speyer, see Arthur Valdenaire, *Heinrich Hübsch: eine Studie zur Baukunst der Romantik* (Karlsruhe: Braun, 1926), 50–54.

37 Heinrich Hübsch, "In What Style Should We Build?" (1828), in Wolfgang Herrmann, ed. and transl., *In What Style Should We Build? The German Debate on Architectural Style* (Santa Monica, CA: Getty Center, 1992), 63–101; quoted phrases on p. 99.

39 Herodotus on Philitis the shepherd: *Histories*, 2: 128, p. 146.

40 Zhang Yanyuan on the school of Ku K'ai-chih and Lu T'an-wei: Bush and Hsio-yen Shih, *Early Chinese Texts*, 52; on the painters of antiquity, 54; on Wang Wei, 68.

41 Vasari on Giotto in relation to his time, and his apology for the early Italian painters: Preface to Part Two, Milanesi 2: 102–3, Bettarini-Barocchi 3: 12–14.

42 On the *sermo humilis*, see Erich Auerbach, *Literary Language and Its Public* (1958) (Princeton, NJ: Princeton University Press, 1965), 25–66.

42 Erasmus on the Silenus statues: *Silenus Alcibiades* (III, iii, 1), in *Collected Works of Erasmus*, vol. 34, *Adages II vv 1 to III iii 100*, R. A. B. Mynors, ed. and transl. (Toronto: University of Toronto Press, 1992), 262–82. Margaret Mann Phillips, *The "Adages" of Erasmus: A Study with Translations* (Cambridge, UK: Cambridge University Press, 1964), 269–96 (the 1515 edition).

43 Friedrich Schlegel on the Ghent Altarpiece: "Nachricht von den Gemälden in Paris" (1802, publ. 1803), in *Ansichten und Ideen von der christlichen Kunst*, Hans Eichner, ed., *Kritische Friedrich-Schlegel-Ausgabe* (Paderborn: Schöningh, 1959), 4: 43–44.

43 Ralph Waldo Emerson, "History," in *Essays and Lectures* (New York: Library of America, 1983), 240–42.

44 Cornel West, *The American Evasion of Philosophy: A Genealogy of Pragmatism* (Madison: University of Wisconsin Press, 1989), 70.

44 John Dewey, *Art as Experience* (1934) (New York: Putnam, 1980), 142–43.

45 Art history in the German university: Ferber, *Die Entwicklung des Lehrkörpers der deutschen Universitäten und Hochschulen, 1864–1954*, 84.

45 On the interaction between Western and Asian models of art history: a concise account of the long trajectory of Chinese art history is Cao Yiqiang, "World Art History and the Historiography of Chinese Art," in Kitty Zijlmans and Wilfried van Damme, eds., *World Art Studies: Exploring Concepts and Approaches* (Amsterdam: Valiz, 2008), 119–33. For clues to the relations of the modern Japanese tradition both to China and to the West, see Yukio Lippit, *Painting of the Realm: The Kano House of Painters in Seventeenth-Century Japan* (Seattle: University of Washington Press, 2012), 217–29.

800–1400

47 On the pagan temple at Uppsala: Adam von Bremen, *Hamburgische Kirchengeschichte*, Bernhard Schmeidler, ed. (Hannover: Hahn, 1917), book IV, chap. xxv–xxvi, 257–59. *History of the Archbishops of Hamburg-Bremen*, transl. Francis J. Tschan (New York: Columbia University Press, 1959), 207.

49 St. Francis at San Damiano: Bonaventura, "Major Life," in Marion A. Habig, ed., *St. Francis of Assisi, Writings and Early Biographies* (Chicago: Franciscan Herald, 1983), 640.

52 On the Muslims and pagans in the Chanson de Roland and Mandeville: Michael Camille, *The Gothic Idol* (Cambridge, UK: Cambridge University Press, 1989), 146, 156.

52 On Giotto's depiction of the Temple of Minerva, see Francesco Benelli, *The Architecture in Giotto's Painting* (New York: Cambridge University Press, 2012), 40–50.

52–53 Goethe in Assisi: J. W. von Goethe, *Italienische Reise, Sämtliche Werke* (Munich: Hanser, 1985–1998), 15: 133–37. *Italian Journey*, Robert R. Heitner, transl. (New York: Suhrkamp, 1989), 96–98.

53 The handbook Goethe consulted was Johann Jakob Volkmann, *Historisch-kritische Nachrichten von Italien* (Leipzig, 1778), 3: 431–32.

53 Andrea Palladio in his *Quattro libri dell'architettura* (1570) described and reproduced with three engravings the temple in Assisi ("Scisi"). See Palladio, *Four Books of Architecture* (London, 1738) (available as a Dover reprint), Book IV, chap. xxvi, and for the elevation, plate 76.

53 The Etruscan vases excavated near Arezzo: Restoro d'Arezzo, *La composizione del mondo*, Alberto Morino, ed. (Parma: Fondazione Pietro Bembo, 1997), II.8.4 bis, 311–15.

54 Zhang Yanyuan on the origins of painting: *Early Chinese Texts on Painting*, Susan Bush and Hsio-yen Shih, eds. (Cambridge, MA: Harvard University Press, 1985), 49–50.

54 The Ming handbook was published and translated by Percival David, *Chinese Connoisseurship: The Ko Ku Yao Lun, the Essential Criteria of Antiquities* (London, Faber, 1971).

55 On medieval artists' signatures: Albert Dietl, *Die Sprache der Signatur: die mittelalterlichen Künstlerinschriften Italiens* (Berlin: Deutscher Kunstverlag, 2009), 4 vols.

55 On the signatures of the Maya scribes, see Michael D. Coe and Justin Kerr, *The Art of the Maya Scribe* (New York: Abrams, 1998), 89–90 and passim.

1400–1500

57 The icon Hans Tucher brought back to Nuremberg: *Constantine and Helena with the True Cross*, Nuremberg, Germanisches Nationalmuseum, inv. no. Gm 507. The work has never been properly published. For the documents, see http://objektkatalog.gnm.de/objekt/Gm507.

58 The fifteenth-century inscription on the twelfth-century ivory: *Descent from the Cross*, Dommuseum Hildesheim, *Medieval Treasures from Hildesheim*, exhibition catalogue (New York: Metropolitan Museum of Art, 2013), no. 15.

58 On the columns from the Baths of Agrippa moved to St. Peter's, see Carol M. Richardson, "Saint Peter's in the Fifteenth Century," in Rosamond McKitterick et al., eds., *Old Saint Peter's, Rome* (Cambridge, UK: Cambridge University Press, 2013), 331–33.

59 Cennino Cennini and Filippo Villani on Giotto and his pupils: Cennini, *Il Libro dell'arte o Trattato della pittura*, Fernando Tempesti, ed. (Milan: Longanesi, 1984), chaps. 1 and 67, pp. 30, 71; Villani, *De origine civitatis Florentiae* (1381–1382), in Julius von Schlosser, *Quellenbuch zur Kunstgeschichte des abendländischen Mittelalters* (Vienna, 1896), 370–71; see Erwin Panofsky, *Renaissance and Renascences in Western Art* (Stockholm: Almqvist & Wiksell, 1960), 14–15.

59 Leon Battista Alberti on modern Florentine artists: *On Painting*, John R. Spencer, ed. and transl. (New Haven, CT: Yale University Press, 1956), 39, or: *On Painting*, Rocco Sinisgalli, ed. and transl. (Cambridge, UK: Cambridge University Press, 2011), 18.

60 Alberti on the restoration of buildings: *On the Art of Building in Ten Books*, Book 10, § 1, Joseph Rykwert, transl., with Neil Leach and Robert Tavernor (Cambridge, MA: MIT, 1988), 321.

60 Pliny, *Natural History*, vol. 9, H. Rackham, transl. (Cambridge, MA: Harvard University Press, 1952); on the temples at Ardea: 35.vi.17.

61 On Pliny's sources, see the introduction by E.

Sellers to *The Elder Pliny's Chapters on the History of Art*, K. Jex-Blake, transl. (London, 1896), xiii–xciv.

61 Pliny on Iaia of Cyzicus: *Natural History*, 35.xl.147.

61 Giovanni Boccaccio on the painter Martia: *De mulieribus claris*, chap. 66.

61–62 Pliny on the sculptor Vulca: *Natural History*, 35.xlv.157; the list of firsts: 35.xxxiv–xxxvi; painting was once illustrious: 35.i.2; the victory of Pompey: 37.vi.12; on Apelles: 35.xxxvi.79; on Protogenes: 35.xxxvi.106; on the margin beyond realism: 35.xxxvi.96; on Aristides: 35.xxxvi.98.

63 Ghiberti on art ceasing and beginning again: *Lorenzo Ghiberti's Denkwürdigkeiten (I commentarii)*, Julius von Schlosser, ed., 2 vols. (Berlin: Bard, 1912), 1:34; Lorenzo Ghiberti, *I commentarii*, Lorenzo Bartoli, ed. (Florence: Giunti, 1998), 83.

63 Pliny on the rebirth of the arts: *Natural History*, 34.xix.52.

63 Petrarch on the dark ages: *Africa* IX, 453ff.

63 Boccaccio on Giotto: *Decamerone*, VI, 5.

63 Dante, *Purgatorio* 11: the translation is by Allen Mandelbaum.

64–65 Ghiberti on *provedimenti*: *I commentarii*, Schlosser, ed., 1: 37; Bartoli, ed., 85; on the goldsmith Gusmin: *I commentarii*, Schlosser, ed., 1: 43–44; Bartoli, ed., 90–91. On the mention of Gusmin by the Anonimo Magliabechiano, see Richard Krautheimer, "Ghiberti and Master Gusmin," *Art Bulletin* 29 (1947): 26.

66 Text and translation of the letter of Manuel Chrysoloras to John VIII Paleologue are in Michael Baxandall, *Giotto and the Orators: Humanist Observers of Painting in Italy and the Discovery of Pictorial Composition, 1350–1450* (Oxford, UK: Oxford University Press, 1971), 80–81, 148–49.

66 Leonardo on medieval painting: Jean Paul Richter, ed., *Literary Works of Leonardo da Vinci*, 2 vols. (Oxford, UK: Oxford University Press, 1939), 1: 331–32, no. 660 (= Codex Atlanticus, fol. 139r).

67 Giovanni Santi's rhymed chronicle: text and translation of the list of painters in Michael Baxandall, *Painting and Experience in Fifteenth-Century Italy* (Oxford, UK: Oxford University Press, 1972), 113–14. For the passage on perspective ("alta scienza acuta…invention del nostro secul nova"), see Lise Bek, "Giovanni Santi's 'Disputa de la pictura'—A Polemical Treatise," *Analecta romana danici instituti*

5 (1969): 75–102, with transcription of the verses in the rhymed chronicle on painting (vv. 73–142).

67–68 Quintilian, *Institutio oratoria* XII.10.3, *The Orator's Education, Books 11–12*, Donald A. Russell, transl., Loeb Classical Library (Cambridge, MA: Harvard University Press, 2001), 282–83. On Quintilian, see E. H. Gombrich, *The Preference for the Primitive: Episodes in the History of Western Taste and Art* (London: Phaidon, 2002), 30–32.

1500–1550

69 Martin Luther on the arts in modern times: Luther, sermon on the Gospel (Luke 21: 25–33) on the second Sunday of Advent, first published as *Ein christliche und vast wolgegrundete beweysung* (1522), in Luther, *Sämmtliche Werke*, 26 vols. (Frankfurt, 1862–1885), 10: 56.

70 Luther on Dürer and the simple style: Luther, *Werke, Tischreden* (Weimar: Böhlau, 1921), 6: 350, no. 7036, dating from around 1546.

70 On the altarpiece at S. Martino a Mensola, see Cathleen Hoeniger, *The Renovation of Paintings in Tuscany, 1250–1500* (Cambridge, UK: Cambridge University Press, 1995), 113–20.

70 On the Cimabue in Padua: *Der Anonimo Morelliano (Marcanton Michiel's* Notizia d'opere del disegno), Theodor Frimmel, ed. (Vienna, 1888), 20–21.

70 Vasari on the fresco by Giotto at St. Peter's: *Le vite de' più eccellenti pittori, scultori ed architettori*, Gaetano Milanesi, ed., 9 vols. (Florence: Sansoni, 1878–1885), 5: 625; *Le vite de' più eccellenti pittori, scultori ed architettori*, Rosanna Bettarini and Paola Barocchi, eds. 6 vols. (Florence: Sansoni, 1966–1987), 5: 152–53. The fragment was later discarded.

71 On Ludovico de Varthema, see Joan-Pau Rubiés, *Travel and Ethnology in the Renaissance: South India through European Eyes, 1250–1625* (Cambridge, UK: Cambridge University Press, 2000), 125–63, and 158 on Breu's woodcuts; and Stephanie Leitch, *Mapping Ethnography in Early Modern Germany: New Worlds in Print Culture* (New York: Palgrave Macmillan, 2010), 101–46.

73 Albrecht Dürer on the Mexican artifacts: Dürer, *Schriftlicher Nachlass*, Hans Rupprich, ed., 3 vols.

(Berlin: Deutscher Verein für Kunstwissenschaft, 1956–69), 1: 155. I have used the new translation by Jeffrey Ashcroft, *Albrecht Dürer: Documentary Biography*, 2 vols. (New Haven, CT: Yale University Press, 2017), 1: 560.

73–74 Bartolomé de las Casas on Mexican art: *Apologética historia de las Indias*; I have drawn the translated passage from *Las Casas, A Selection of His Writings*, George Sanderlin, ed. and transl. (New York: Knopf, 1971), 111–12; see also Alessandra Russo, *The Untranslatable Image: A Mestizo History of the Arts in New Spain, 1500–1600* (Austin: University of Texas Press, 2014), 85–87.

75 The letter by Petrarch on the exemplarity of the ancients: *Res Seniles* II, 3, quoted in Ulrich Pfisterer, ed., *Die Kunstliteratur der italienischen Renaissance: eine Geschichte in Quellen* (Stuttgart: Reclam, 2002), 242.

75–76 The exchange between Pico della Mirandola and Pietro Bembo (1512–13): *Ciceronian Controversies*, Joann Dellaneva, ed., Brian Duvick, transl. (I Tatti Renaissance Library) (Cambridge, MA: Harvard University Press, 2007), 32–33, 48–49, 96–99.

75 Filarete on portraiture: John R. Spencer, ed., *Treatise on Architecture* (New Haven, CT: Yale University Press, 1965), 12; *Trattato di architettura*, Anna Maria Finoli and Liliana Grassi, eds., 2 vols. (Milan: Il Polifilo, 1972), 1: 27f., quoted in Pfisterer, ed., *Die Kunstliteratur der italienischen Renaissance*, 244.

76 Carlo Lenzoni on Boccaccio and Giotto, quoted in Marco Ruffini, *Art without an Author: Vasari's Lives and Michelangelo's Death* (New York: Fordham University Press, 2011), 153–54.

77 Erasmus on the singularity of the New Testament: the epistolary preface to his edition of the New Testament. *Novum instrumentum omne* (Basel, 1516), 229, my translation. *The Correspondence of Erasmus: Letters 298–445 (1514–1516)*, R. A. B. Mynors and D. F. S. Thomson, transl. (Toronto: University of Toronto Press, 1976), no. 373, p. 204.

77 Sebastian Franck on progress: *Paradoxa*, Siegfried Wollgast, ed. (Berlin: Akademie, 1966), nos. 64, 65, 241, 63.

77–78 Michel de Montaigne, *The Essayes, or Morall, Politike, and Millitarie Discourses*, John Florio, transl. (London, 1603), chap. 30, "On Cannibals."

78 Jean-Jacques Rousseau, "Discours sur les arts et les sciences" (1750), Part Two, in *Oeuvres complètes* (Bibliothèque de la Pléiade) (Paris: Gallimard, 1964) 3: 22.

79 Dürer as art tourist: *Schriftlicher Nachlass*, Hans Rupprich, ed., 3 vols., 1: 155, 160, 168; *Albrecht Dürer: Documentary Biography*, 1: 560, 565, 577.

79 The Nuremberg drawing inscribed "very old": Berlin, Kupferstichkabinett, KdZ 2131. Elfried Bock, *Staatliche Museen zu Berlin: Die Zeichnungen alter Meister im Kupferstichkabinett: Die deutschen Meister* (Berlin: Bard, 1921), 89.

80 Jan Gossart's copy of van Eyck's Ghent altarpiece is in the Prado, Madrid; see *Man, Myth, and Sensual Pleasures: Jan Gossart's Renaissance*, exhibition catalogue, Metropolitan Museum of Art (New York: Yale University Press, 2010), no. 29.

80 Vasari on Ghiberti as collector: Milanesi 2: 245, Bettarini-Barocchi 3: 102.

80 Jean Lemaire, *La couronne margaritique* ([Lyon], 1549). The relevant stanzas are translated into German in Wolfgang von Löhneysen, *Die ältere niederländische Malerei: Künstler und Kritiker* (Eisenach: Röth, 1956), 80.

80–81 Marcantonio Michiel on the Miracle of St. Anthony: *Der Anonimo Morelliano (Marcanton Michiel's* Notizia d'opere del disegno), 30–31; on copies after Raphael's cartoons: 12–13; on the portrait of Sannazaro: 20–21; on bronzes: 24–25; on the Pietà in Cremona: 45.

81 Vasari on Fra Angelico and piety and beauty: Milanesi 2: 518, Bettarini-Barocchi 3: 273–74. On my citations from Vasari: the edition by Milanesi is basically the 1568 edition, as it had been handed down by previous editors, with some modifications based on discrepancies with the first edition. The edition by Bettarini and Barocchi gives both the 1550 and the 1568 texts, on the same page, one above the other.

82 Giovanni Villani on the Aretine vases: *Cronica di Giovanni Villani*, F. G. Dragomanni, ed. (Florence, 1844), 1: 72.

82 Vasari on the Etruscan pots: Milanesi 1: 220, Bettarini-Barocchi 2: 10.

83 Aretino names Vasari as "historico": in his introduction to the modern edition of the first version of the Lives, the "Torrentino," *Le vite de' più eccellenti architetti, pittori, e scultori italiani* (Torino: Einaudi, 1991), p. viii, n. 6, Giovanni Previtali mentions a letter but gives no reference.

83 On Vasari's sources, see Patricia Lee Rubin, *Giorgio Vasari: Art and History* (New Haven, CT: Yale University Press, 1995), chap. 4.

83 Francesco Albertini, *Memoriale de molte statue et picture sono nella inclypta cipta di Florentia* (Florence, 1510). *Memorial of Many Statues and Paintings in the Illustrious City of Florence*, Waldemar H. de Boer, ed. (Florence: Centro Di, 2010).

83 Vasari on judging works with his own eyes: Milanesi 6: 457–58, Bettarini-Barocchi 5: 409, and on recognizing styles like a secretary: Conclusion ("L'autore agli artefici del disegno"), Milanesi 7: 727, Bettarini-Barocchi 6: 411. These passages were cited by Alessandro Nova, "'Vasari' versus Vasari: La duplice attualità delle *Vite*," *Mitteilungen des Kunsthistorischen Institutes in Florenz* 55 (2013): 66, 68.

84 Lionello Venturi on Vasari's "too many origins": *History of Art Criticism* (New York: E. P. Dutton, 1936), 100; *Storia della critica d'arte* (1945) (Torino: Einaudi, 1964), 116.

84 Vasari on Pontormo and Salviati: Milanesi, 6: 279, Bettarini-Barocchi, 5:328; on Salviati: Milanesi, 7: 25, Bettarini-Barocchi, 5:522–23.

84 Vasari on "arts that served more for pleasure than for use": Milanesi 1: 228, Bettarini-Barocchi 2: 17.

85 Vasari on "ancient" versus "old" art: Milanesi 1: 242, Bettarini-Barocchi 2: 29.

85–86 Dost-Muhammad (Dust Muhammad), Preface to Bahram Mirza Album, in Wheeler M. Thackston, *Album Prefaces and Other Documents on the History of Calligraphers and Painters* (Leiden: Brill, 2001), 9, 16, 4, 11–12. On the Persian album prefaces, see David J. Roxburgh, *Prefacing the Image: The Writing of Art History in Sixteenth-Century Iran* (Leiden: Brill, 2001).

1550–1600

87 Vasari on the pulpit in the Baptistry at Pisa by Nicola Pisano: Milanesi 1: 304, Bettarini-Barocchi 2: 63.

87 Vasari on Gaddo Gaddi: Milanesi 1: 349, Bettarini-Barocchi 2: 84.

88 Vasari on the Brancacci Chapel: Milanesi 2: 105, Bettarini-Barocchi 3: 17; on Piero della Francesca: Milanesi 2: 496, Bettarini-Barocchi 3: 261–62.

88 Vasari on Assisi and Cavallini: Milanesi 1: 540, Bettarini-Barocchi 2: 187.

88 On Vasari as restorer of medieval churches, see Christian-Adolf Isermeyer, "Il Vasari e il restauro delle chiese medievali," in *Studi vasariani: Atti del Convegno internazionale per il IV centenario della prima edizione delle* Vite *del Vasari* (Florence: Sansoni, 1952), 229–36; and Marcia B. Hall, *Renovation and Counter-Reformation: Vasari and Duke Cosimo in Sta Maria Novella and Sta Croce, 1565–1577* (Oxford, UK: Oxford University Press, 1979).

89 On the medieval citations in Rome, see Claudia Conforti, "Roma: architettura e città" in Claudia Conforti and Richard J. Tuttle, eds., *Storia dell'architettura italiana: il secondo Cinquecento* (Milan: Electa, 2001), 44, 47.

89 On Vasari's "Cimabue," see Licia Ragghianti Collobi, *Il libro de' disegni del Vasari*, 2 vols. (Florence: Vallecchi, 1974), 1: 26, and Milanesi, 1: 258–59, Bettarini-Barocchi, 2: 44.

89 Vasari on making new art in order to make the old art seem less beautiful: Bettarini-Barocchi 6: 413.

91 Giovanni Battista Armenini on old painting: *On the True Precepts of the Art of Painting*, Edward J. Olszewski, ed. and transl. (New York: B. Franklin, 1977), 71, 299–300, 281.

91 Gian Paolo Lomazzo on medieval art: *Idea del tempio della pittura* (1590), chap. 9, Robert Klein, ed., 2 vols. (Florence: Istituto nazionale di studi sul Rinascimento, 1974), 1: 101–2; *Idea of the Temple of Painting*, Jean Julia Chai, transl. (University Park: Pennsylvania State University Press, 2013), 75.

91 On the early attempts to produce an illustrated Vasari, and the first illustrated histories of art, see Ingrid R. Vermeulen, *Picturing Art History: The Rise of the Illustrated History of Art in the Eighteenth Century* (Amsterdam: Amsterdam University Press, 2010).

92 Vasari on Parri Spinelli: Milanesi 2: 284, Bettarini-Barocchi 3: 120. Schlosser mentioned this passage, *La letteratura artistica*, 321, 327.

92 Vasari on the unintelligible frescoes by Giorgione: Milanesi 4: 96, Bettarini-Barocchi 4: 44.

93 Vasari on tapestry: Milanesi 1: 96, Bettarini-Barocchi 1: 16.

94 Vasari on wax ex votos: Milanesi 3: 373–74, Bettarini-Barocchi 3: 544.

94–95 Karel van Mander on the Crucifixion by Hugo van der Goes overpainted by Protestants: *Het leven der doorluchtighe Nederlandtsche, en Hooghduytsche schilders*, part three of *Het Schilder-Boeck* (Haarlem, 1604), 204r. The painting has not been identified.

95 Woodcuts of Ecclesia and Synagoga at Strasbourg: *Tobias Stimmer 1539–1584: Spätrenaissance am Oberrhein*, exhibition catalogue, Kunstmuseum Basel (Basel: Das Kunstmuseum, 1984), nos. 147–48. The woodcuts are discussed by Joseph Leo Koerner, *The Reformation of the Image* (London: Reaktion, 2004), 52–55.

97 Van Mander's visit to the "grottoes" is reported in an anonymous biography appended to the second edition (1618) of the *Schilder-Boeck*, reproduced in van Mander, *The Lives of the Illustrious Netherlandish and German Painters*, Hessel Miedema, ed., 6 vols. (Doornspijk: Davaco, 1994), vol. 2, fol. R3v–R4r.

97–98 On the church historians Baronio, Panvinio, Chacón, and Ugonio and their studies of older Christian art, see Giovanni Previtali, *La fortuna dei primitivi dal Vasari ai neoclassici* (Torino: Einaudi, 1964), chap. 7, "L'erudizione sacra"; Ingo Herklotz, "'Historia sacra' und mittelalterliche Kunst in der zweiten Hälfte des 16. Jahrhunderts in Rom," in *Baronio e l'arte: atti del convegno internazionale di studi, Sora* (Sora: Centro di studi sorani "Vincenzo Patriarca," 1985), 21–74; and Francis Haskell, *History and Its Images: Art and the Interpretation of the Past* (New Haven, CT: Yale University Press, 1993), 43, 101–11, 122–23.

98 Giovanni Andrea Gilio on the piety of older painting: "Degli errori de' pittori circa l'istorie," in Paola Barocchi, ed., *Trattati d'arte del Cinquecento*, 3 vols. (Bari: Laterza, 1960–1962), 2: 111.

100 Bernal Díaz on New World idols, quoted in Serge Gruzinski, *Images at War: Mexico from Columbus to Blade Runner (1492–2019)* (Durham, NC: Duke University Press, 2001), 23.

100 Antonio Monserrate on the tomb in Mandu, the temple in Ujjain, and the ruins in Mathura: *The Commentary of Father Monserrate, S.J., on His Journey to the Court of Akbar*, J.S. Hoyland, transl. (Oxford: Oxford University Press, 1922), 17, 19, 93.

100 Gian Paolo Lomazzo on the wisdom of Michelangelo and Dürer: Lomazzo, *Idea del tempio della pittura*, chap. 8, Klein, ed., 1: 97; *Idea of the Temple of Painting*, Chai, transl., 73.

100–101 Antonio Rubino on Hindu images and rituals: Joan-Pau Rubiés, "The Jesuit Discovery of Hinduism: Antonio Rubino's *Account of the History and Religion of Vijayanagara* (1608)," *Archiv für Religionsgeschichte* 3 (2001): 252. See also Rubiés, *Travel and Ethnology in the Renaissance*, 324–35.

101 Monserrate on "Birbitcremas": *Commentary of Father Monserrate*, Hoyland, ed., 19.

101 George Puttenham, *The Art of English Poesy*, Frank Whigham and Wayne A. Rebhorn, eds. (Ithaca, NY: Cornell University Press, 2007), 100.

102 Roger Ascham on rhyme: G. Gregory Smith, ed., *Elizabethan Critical Essays*, 2 vols. (Oxford, UK: Oxford University Press, 1904), 1: 29–30.

102 Philip Sidney on the Ballad of Chevy Chase: Sidney, *Miscellaneous Prose*, Katherine Duncan-Jones and Jan van Dorsten, eds. (Oxford, 1973), 97.

102 Monserrate on Muslim tomb-shrines: *Commentary*, Hoyland, ed., 27

102 Filarete on barbarians and architecture: *Traktat über die Baukunst*, W. von Oettingen, ed. (Vienna, 1890), 428; *Treatise on Architecture*, John R. Spencer, ed. (New Haven, CT: Yale University Press, 1965), 175–76.

103 On the contributions of Lambert Lombard and Domenicus Lampsonius to Vasari's second edition, see Schlosser, *La letteratura artistica*, 341–42.

104 The busts of van Eyck and Dürer on the house of Cornelis van Dalem: Antwerp, Museum Vleeshuis. See *Antwerp: Story of a Metropolis, 16th–17th Century*, exhibition catalogue, Antwerp, Hessenhuis (Ghent: Snoeck-Ducaju & Zoon, 1993), no. 16.

104 On Michael Coxcie, see Ruben Suykerbuyk, "Coxcie's Copies after Old Masters: An Addition and an Analysis," *Simiolus: Netherlands Quarterly for the History of Art* 37 (2013–14): 5–24.

104 The *Last Judgment* by Fra Angelico is in the Gemäldegalerie, Berlin; Spranger's copy is in Torino, Galleria Sabaudia. See the exhibition catalogue *Fra Angelico* (New York: Metropolitan Museum of Art, 2005), no. 32, pp. 165–71.

104–5 Cort's engraving of a Last Judgment triptych: Timothy A. Riggs, *Hieronymus Cock, Printmaker and Publisher* (New York: Garland, 1977), no. 17.

105 On the revival of the early sixteenth-century masters, see Larry Silver, "Marketing the Dutch Past: The Lucas van Leyden Revival around 1600," in Mia M. Mochizuki and Lisa Vergara, eds., *In His Milieu: Essays on Netherlandish Art in Memory of John Michael Montias* (Amsterdam: Amsterdam University Press, 2006), 411–22.

105 Marten de Vos's attempt to prevent the export of the altar by Massys: Ethan Matt Kavaler, *Pieter Bruegel: Parables of Order and Enterprise* (Cambridge, UK: Cambridge University Press, 1999), 50, citing J. Pauwels and P. Génard, *Verzameling von Oorkonden…Antwerp*, 1871–1872, 295–96, nos. 2149–52.

105 The etching by Simon Frisius after a supposed Gossart: *Man, Myth, and Sensual Pleasures: Jan Gossart's Renaissance*, exhibition catalogue, Metropolitan Museum of Art (New York, 2010), p. 426, fig. 324.

105 A list of the major marginalia and postils to Vasari's text is Schlosser, *La letteratura artistica*, 333–34. The Paduan artist's dismissal of Francia: Marco Ruffini, "Sixteenth-Century Paduan Annotations to the First Edition of Vasari's *Vite* (1550)," *Renaissance Quarterly* 62 (2009): 753.

1600–1650

106 Lodovico Guicciardini on Frans Floris: Wolfgang von Löhneysen, *Die ältere niederländische Malerei: Künstler und Kritiker* (Eisenach: Röth, 1956), 257.

106 Karel van Mander, *Het leven der Doorluchtighe Nederlandtsche, en Hooghduytsche Schilders*, part three of *Het Schilder-Boeck* (Haarlem, 1604). The edition by Hanns Floerke, *Das Leben der niederländischen und deutschen Maler*, 2 vols. (Munich: Müller, 1906), gives the original Dutch text and German translation. The edition by Hessel Miedema, *The Lives of the Illustrious Netherlandish and German Painters*, 6 vols. (Doornspijk: Davaco, 1994), gives a facsimile of the 1604 edition and English translation as well as extensive commentary. Here I quote from Miedema with the pagination of the 1604 edition.

107 Van Mander on the absence of any predecessors to van Eyck: *Lives*, Miedema, ed., 199r, 198v; on the Ghent altarpiece: 200v; on "modern" and "old" times in painting: see Miedema's commentary, *Lives*, 2: 186; on the invention of gunpowder by Schwartz: *Lives*, 200r.

107 On the history of art in verse by Lucas de Heere, see Schlosser, *La letteratura artistica*, 357.

108 Van Mander on Ouwater, *Lives*, Miedema, ed., 205v; on non-cooperative artists, 198v; on Rogier van der Weyden, 203r; on Dürer's *Four Witches*, 208r; his inferences about German printmakers, 204v.

108 On Matthias Quad von Kinckelbach, see Wilhelm Waetzoldt, *Deutsche Kunsthistoriker*, 2 vols. (Leipzig: Seemann, 1921–1924), 1: 20–23.

108 The anecdote about Dürer: Matthias Quad, *Teutscher Nation Herligkeit: Ein außführliche Beschreibung des gegenwärtigen Standts Germaniae* (Cologne: 1609), 429; Albrecht Dürer, *Schriftlicher Nachlass*, Hans Rupprich, ed., 3 vols. (Berlin: Deutscher Verein für Kunstwissenschaft, 1956–69), 1: 188n317. In the Netherlands Dürer is shown a work by an old master who died, according to the locals, in a poorhouse; the artist, thinking that his hosts are mocking the old painter, reproaches them for not making him famous.

109 Van Mander on Bouts, *Lives*, Miedema, ed., 206v.

109 Van Mander on the compositions of the old painters: in his didactic poem, *Grondt der edel vry Schilderconst* (Foundation of the noble and free art of painting), the first part of his *Schilder-Boeck*. *Das Lehrgedicht des Karel van Mander*, Rudolf Hoecker, ed. and transl., with commentary (The Hague: Nijhoff, 1916), V, 44, pp. 112–13.

109 Michelangelo's views on the art of painting as reported by Francisco de Holanda: *On Antique Painting*, Alice Sedgwick Wohl, transl. (University Park: Pennsylvania State University Press, 2013), see for example 180–81.

109 On the topos of wondering what Dürer would have been if he had known the works of antiquity: Jan Białostocki, *Dürer and His Critics, 1500–1971* (Baden-Baden: Koerner, 1986), 53.

109–10 Quad von Kinckelbach on Dürer's works as relics: quoted in Henry Ley, "Dürer in the Seventeenth Century," in Michael Levey, ed., *Essays on Dürer* (Manchester, UK: Manchester University Press, 1973), 105, without reference.

110 Hollar's etchings after Schongauer's drawings: *The New Hollstein: German Engravings, Etchings and Woodcuts, 1400–1700, Wenceslaus Hollar*, Part 3, Simon Turner, ed. (Ouderkerk: Sound + Vision, 2010), 880–81; Franz Winzinger, *Die Zeichnungen Martin Schongauers* (Berlin: Deutscher Verein für Kunstwissenschaft, 1962), no. 56.

110 For the list of English writers who mentioned Dürer, see Lucy Gent, *Picture and Poetry, 1560–1620: Relations between Literature and the Visual Arts in the English Renaissance* (Leamington Spa: Hall, 1981), 74n.

110 On the editions of Dürer: Białostocki, *Dürer and His Critics*, 71.

110 On the Cranach-like *Venus and Cupid* by Heinrich Bollandt, see Werner Schade, "Bollandt als Nachbildner Cranachs," in *Cranach und die Kunst der Renaissance unter den Hohenzollern*, exhibition catalogue, Berlin, Schloss Charlottenburg (Berlin: Stiftung Preussische Schlösser und Gärten, 2009), 80–85. The painting is in the Alte Pinakothek, Munich, A.P. 5465.

110–11 On the collection of Charles I, see Oliver Millar, *The Queen's Pictures* (London: Macmillan, 1977), 29–63.

111 On the hypothesis that the painting mentioned by Mazzoleni was La Perla, see Giovanni Agosti, *Disegni del Rinascimento in Valpadana* (Florence, 2001), 474.

111 Thomas Browne, *Pseudodoxia epidemica*, Book V, chap. 6, Robin Robbins, ed., 2 vols. (Oxford: Clarendon Press, 1981), 1: 386.

111–12 Federico Borromeo, *De pictura sacra*, Pamela M. Jones, ed., Kenneth S. Rothwell, Jr., transl. (I Tatti Renaissance Library) (Cambridge, MA: Harvard University Press, 2010), on images of sphinxes: I.5.2; on Charon's boat by Michelangelo: I.5.1; portraits of Christ made "not by human hands": II.2.7; on Christ as a shepherd and as Orpheus: II.2.3–4; on Crucifixions with three or four nails: II.3; on Hercules and the lion: I.3.1. On the Triclinium mosaic, see Pamela M. Jones, *Federico Borromeo and the Ambrosiana: Art Patronage and Reform in Seventeenth-Century Milan* (Cambridge, UK: Cambridge University Press, 1993), 195–99.

112 Sebastiano Vannini's emendation of Vasari: Giovanni Previtali, *La fortuna dei primitivi dal Vasari ai neoclassici* (Turin: Einaudi, 1964), 48. Giulio Mancini, *Considerazioni sulla pittura*, Adriana Marucchi, ed., 2 vols. (Rome: Accademia Nazionale dei Lincei, 1956), 1: 48–49, 45–46, 59, 61, 104.

113 *Paper Museum of Cassiano dal Pozzo*, Series A, *Antiquities and Architecture*, Part 2, *Early Christian and Medieval Antiquities*, vol. 1, *Mosaics and Wall Paintings in Roman Churches*, John Osborne and Amanda Claridge, eds. (London: Harvey Miller, 1996).

113 On Philibert de l'Orme's opinion of Gothic: Paul Frankl, *The Gothic: Literary Sources and Interpretations through Eight Centuries* (Princeton, NJ: Princeton University Press, 1960), 860, or Ludger J. Sutthoff, *Gotik in Barock* (Munich: LIT, 1990), 278.

114–16 On the fresco at Grottaferrata, see Richard E. Spear, *Domenichino*, 2 vols. (New Haven, CT: Yale University Press, 1982), 159–71, and Giuseppe Zander, "La chiesa medioevale della Badia e la sua trasformazione del 1754, in un manuscritto criptense inedito del Padre Filippo Vitale," *Palladio*, n.s. 3 (1953): 120–31.

117 Ferrante Carli on anachronism: quoted in Silvia Tomasi Velli, *Le immagini e il tempo: narrazione visiva, storia e allegoria tra Cinque e Seicento* (Pisa: Edizioni della Normale, 2007), 143. Mancini, *Considerazioni sulla pittura*, 1: 134.

117 Franciscus Junius on originals and copies: *The Painting of the Ancients: in three bookes: declaring by historicall observations and examples,*

the beginning, progresse, and consummation of that most noble art (London, 1638), Book 3, chap. 7, 10, 348. The modern edition is Franciscus Junius, *The Literature of Classical Art*, 2 vols., Keith Aldrich, Philipp Fehl, and Raina Fehl, ed. (Berkeley: University of California Press, 1991), vol. 1, *The Painting of the Ancients*, here p. 306.

119 Dong Qichang quoting Wang Wei on "clouds, peaks, and cliffs": Osvald Sirén, *The Chinese on the Art of Painting: Texts by the Painter Critics, from the Han through the Ch'ing Dynasties* (Beijing: Vetch, 1936), 132.

119 On Dong Qichang's imitation of Dong Yuan: *The Century of Tung Ch'i-ch'ang, 1555–1636*, Wai-kam Ho, ed., exhibition catalogue, 2 vols. (Kansas City, MO: Nelson-Atkins Museum of Art, 1992), vol. 1, plate 57, and the essay by James Cahill, 72–76; vol. 2, no. 57, pp. 72–73.

119 Gentlemen are not artists: Pliny, *Natural History*, vol. 9, Loeb Classical Library (Cambridge, MA: Harvard University Press, 1952), H. Rackham, transl., 35.vii.19–21. "After Pacuvius [tragic poet and amateur painter of the 2nd century BC], painting was not esteemed as handiwork for persons of station.… Titedius Labeo, a man of praetorian rank who had actually held the office of Proconsul of the Province of Narbonne, and who died lately in extreme old age, used to be proud of his miniatures (*parvis tabellis*), but this was laughed at and actually damaged his reputation."

119 On amateur drawing in premodern Europe, see Wolfgang Kemp, *Einen wahrhaft bildenden Zeichenunterricht überall einzuführen: Zeichnen u. Zeichenunterricht der Laien 1500–1870* (Frankfurt: Syndikat, 1979), and Ann Bermingham, *Learning to Draw: Studies in the Cultural History of a Polite and Useful Art* (New Haven, CT: Yale University Press, 2000).

119–22 Dong Qichang on imitating trees of old masters: Sirén, *Chinese on the Art of Painting*, 143; on the danger of imitating them too closely, 148; quoting Mo Shih-lung on taking old masters as models, 141; comparing real to painted landscapes, 138; quoting Mo Shih-lung on imitation of style of the calligrapher Wang Xizhi, 140; on the impossibility of creating new forms, 143; on the priority of Wang Hsia, 146–47.

122 Comments of Hsie Chao-chih: Sirén, *Chinese on the Art of Painting*, 166, and Lin Yutang, *The Chinese Theory of Art* (New York: Putnam, 1967), 131–32.

122 Dong Qichang on the survival of pre-Song painting: Sirén, *Chinese on the Art of Painting*, 144.

123–24 Franciscus Junius, *The Painting of the Ancients*, Aldrich, Fehl, and Fehl, eds.: on ancient image cults: Book 2, ch. 7; on EK: Book 3, chap. 5, 10, p. 280; on Philostratus: Book 3, chap. 6, 3, p. 288; on the rules of art, and on the decadence of late antique art: Book 3, chap. 6, 6, p. 293.

124–25 Francis Bacon, *The New Organon* (Cambridge, UK: Cambridge University Press, 2000), on the Greeks: I, lxxi, p. 58; on the quantity of worthless books: I, lxxxv, p. 70; on his own new way: Preface, p. 29; on "anticipations of nature": I, xxvi, p. 38; on scientific method: I, lxi, p. 50.

125–26 Bacon on philosophy as the Idols of the Theater: I, xliv, p. 42; on the mechanical arts: I, lxxiv, p. 61; on the history of the mechanical arts: "Outline of a natural and experimental history," in *New Organon*, pp. 227, 233–38; on truth not dwelling in the felicity of a particular time: *New Organon* I, lvi, p. 47.

126 John Dewey and the question of art as knowledge: *Art as Experience*, 288–89.

126 Bacon on Dürer and Apelles: *Essays, or Counsels Civil and Moral* (1625), Samuel Harvey Reynolds, ed. (Oxford, 1890), 304–5, quoted by Białostocki, *Dürer and his Critics*, 59.

126 Bacon on "outstanding works of art": *New Organon* II, xxxi, p. 150.

1650–1700

128–29 On the market for old painters in Florence: Richard A. Goldthwaite, "Economic Parameters of the Italian Art Market," in Marcello Fantoni, Louisa C. Matthew, and Sara F. Matthews-Grieco, eds., *The Art Market in Italy: 15th–17th Centuries* (Modena: Panini, 2003), 433.

129 On Rubens as the owner of a Perugino (the only pre-1500 picture he owned): Jeffrey Muller, *Rubens: The Artist as Collector* (Princeton, NJ: Princeton University Press, 1989), 12.

129 On the prices of paintings, see Pierre Gérin-Jean, "Prices of Works of Art and Hierarchy of

Artistic Value on the Italian Market (1400–1700)," in Fantoni et al., *The Art Market in Italy*, 181–94.

129 On the concierge of the Palazzo Barberini and Pietro Rossini: Friedrich Polleross, *Die Kunst der Diplomatie: Auf den Spuren des kaiserlichen Botschafters Leopold Joseph Graf von Lamberg (1653–1706)* (Petersberg: Imhof, 2010), 26, 96–99, 24.

130 John Aubrey on glass painting: *Remaines of Gentilisme and Judaisme*, in Aubrey, *Three Prose Works*, John Buchanan-Brown, ed. (Carbondale: Southern Illinois University Press, 1972), 158. In fact, the art of stained glass was well established in Britain a century before King John.

130 Olof Rudbeck on Uppsala: Kelsey Jackson Williams, *The Antiquary: John Aubrey's Historical Scholarship* (Oxford, UK: Oxford University Press, 2016), 38–39.

130 Bacon on method: *New Organon* I, lxi, p. 50.

131 On Athanasius Kircher's collections, see *Athanasius Kircher: Il museo del mondo*, Eugenio Lo Sardo, ed. (Rome: De Luca, 2001).

131 Filippo Buonarroti on Egyptian art: *Osservazioni istoriche sopra alcuni medaglioni antichi* (1698), cited by Haskell, *History and Its Images*, 125, without page reference.

132 On the African fetish, see William Pietz, "The Problem of the Fetish," parts 1 and 2, *Res: Anthropology and Aesthetics* 9 (1985): 5–17, and 13 (1987): 23–45.

133–34 On the gallery pictures of David Teniers, see Zirka Zaremba Filipczak, *Picturing Art in Antwerp, 1550–1700* (Princeton, NJ: Princeton University Press, 1987), 125–39.

134, 136–37 Carlo Cesare Malvasia, *Felsina pittrice = Lives of the Bolognese painters*, Elizabeth Cropper and Lorenzo Pericolo, eds., vol. 1, *Early Bolognese Painting* (Washington, DC: CASVA, and London: Harvey Miller, 2012), on the early Bolognese frescoes, 205; on Bologna and the Indies, 209, 211; on the fourteenth-century Bolognese and on Tubalcaine, 215; on Caterina Vigri, 260–61; on the fifteenth-century painters, 243.

137 Filippo Baldinucci, *Notizie dei professori del disegno da Cimabue in qua*, 7 vols. (Florence: S.P.E.S., 1974–75) (a reprint of the Florentine edition of 1845–47).

137–38 André Félibien on the Crucifix by Pietro Cavallini in S. Paolo fuori le mura: *Entretiens sur les vies et les ouvrages des plus excellents peintres anciens et modernes (1666–1688)*, 2nd ed. (Paris, 1690), 97. The Crucifix was also mentioned by Malvasia (*Early Bolognese Painting*, 312–13) and Ridolfi as well as Vasari (Milanesi 1: 541, Bettarini-Barocchi 2: 188).

138 Joachim von Sandrart, *Academie der Bau-, Bild- und Mahlerey-Künste von 1675, Leben der berühmten Maler, Bildhauer und Baumeister*, A. R. Peltzer, ed. (Munich: Hirth, 1925). See the online edition, http://ta.sandrart.net/de/.

138–39 Sandrart on Chinese painters: *Academie*, Peltzer, ed., 297; on the drawings by Grünewald, 81–82; on the priority of Israhel van Meckenem, 317; on the prices paid for drawings, 322, 64.

139 On Sandrart's purchase of Dürer's tomb: Białostocki, *Dürer and his Critics*, 71–72.

139 Van Mander's list of Dürer's paintings: *Lives*, Miedema, ed.: 209r–209v.

139 Malvasia's catalogue of the Bolognese prints has been edited by Lorenzo Pericolo and translated by Naoko Takahatake, as *Felsina pittrice = Lives of the Bolognese Painters*, vol. 2, part 2, 1, *Life of Marcantonio Raimondi and Critical Catalogue of Prints by or after Bolognese Masters* (London: Harvey Miller, 2017).

140 Quotations from Shitao, from Sirén, *Chinese on the Art of Painting*. Shitao on the non-method of the ancients, 184–85; on the superior man borrowing from the old masters, 187; on the artist who is "always himself," 188; on forming a school of one's own, 190.

1700–1750

142 Montfaucon on the lost Merovingian and Carolingian monuments and on the glass painting depicting the meeting of Charlemagne and Constantine V: *Monumens de la monarchie françoise*, 5 vols. (Paris, 1729–1733), 1: ii, and 1: 277, plate XXIV.

144 Montfaucon on the Bayeux Tapestry: *Monumens de la monarchie françoise*, 1: 371–75; 2: 1–3.

144 Filippo Buonarroti on early Christian art: *Osservazioni sopra alcuni frammenti di vasi* *antichi di vetro ornati* (Florence, 1716), 84–85; quoted by Previtali, *La fortuna dei primitivi*, 30–31. I have used the translation of Haskell, *History and Its Images*, 126.

145 On Scipione Maffei, see Previtali, *La fortuna dei primitivi*, 76–81.

145 Antonio Francesco Gori on Restoro d'Arezzo: *Storia antiquaria etrusca* (Florence, 1749), ccvii–ccviii.

145 The life of Cranach by Johann Friedrich Christ was published in *Fränckische acta erudita et curiosa* (Nuremberg, 1726), 1: 341–47, reprinted in Christian Vöhringer, ed., *Kunstliteratur der Neuzeit: eine kommentierte Anthologie* (Darmstadt: Wissenschaftliche Buchgesellschaft, 2010), 191–94.

145 On the absence of negative comments on Gothic architecture by northern European writers, see Hermann Hipp, *Studien zur "Nachgotik" des 16. und 17. Jahrhunderts in Deutschland, Böhmen, Österreich und der Schweiz* (PhD diss., University of Tübingen, 1979), 594.

146 For the quotes from Christopher Wren, see Eduard Sekler, *Wren and His Place in European Architecture* (London: Faber and Faber, 1956), 74–75, and Lydia M. Soo, ed., *Wren's "Tracts" on Architecture and Other Writings* (Cambridge, UK: Cambridge University Press, 1998), 43–44.

146–47 On Aichel, see Heinrich Gerhard Franz, "Gotik und Barock im Werk des Johann Santini Aichel," in *Wiener Jahrbuch für Kunstgeschichte* 14 (1950): 65–130.

147 Jacques-Germain Soufflot's admiration for Gothic: the text is reprinted in Michael Peztet, *Soufflots Sainte-Geneviève und der französische Kirchenbau des 18. Jahrhunderts* (Berlin: de Gruyter, 1961), here 137–39.

147 On the Deutschordenskirche in Vienna, see Ludger J. Sutthoff, *Gotik in Barock* (Munich: LIT, 1990), 241–60.

147 Johann Fischer von Erlach, *Entwurff einer historischen Architectur* (Vienna, 1721), 4–5.

148 Alexander Pope's parody of Chaucer (1715), first published, anonymously, in 1727 as "A Tale of Chaucer, lately found in an old manuscript."

148–49 Sontag, "Notes on 'Camp'" (1964), in Sontag, *Essays of the 1960s and 70s*, David Rieff, ed.

(New York: Library of America, 2013), 263.

149 Roger de Piles, *Conversations sur la connoissance de la peinture et sur le jugement qu'on doit faire des tableaux* (Paris, 1677); on what appears and doesn't appear in the painting, 69–70.

149 Roger de Piles, *Cours de peinture par principes* (1708) (Paris: Gallimard, 1989), "balance des peintres," 236–41.

150 Bacon quoting Heraclitus: *New Organon*, Book 1, xlii, p. 41. Another translation of the fragment is: "Although the law (logos) is universal, the majority live as if they had understanding peculiar to themselves." See Kathleen Freeman, *Ancilla to the Pre-Socratic Philosophers: A Complete Translation of the Fragments in Diels'* Fragmente der Vorsokratiker (Oxford, UK: Blackwell, 1948), no. 2, pp. 24–25.

150 Jean-Baptiste Dubos, *Réflexions critiques sur la poésie et la peinture* (1719), quoted in *La querelle des anciens et des modernes: XVIIe—XVIIIe siècles*, Anne-Marie Lecoq, ed. (Paris: Gallimard, 2001), 673–74.

151 Dubos on connoisseurship: *Réflexions critiques*, quoted in Julius S. Held, "The Early Appreciation of Drawings," *Studies in Western Art, Acts of the 20th International Congress of the History of Art* (Princeton, NJ: Princeton University Press, 1963), vol. 3, p. 94. Antoine Joseph Dézallier d'Argenville, *Abrégé de la vie des plus fameux peintres*, vol. 1 (Paris, 1745), xix, quoted Dubos's opinion in order to refute it.

151 On the early framing of drawings under glass and on the first auction catalogue to describe drawings, see Held, "Early Appreciation of Drawings," 80, 73n5.

151 On the transformations in collecting practices, see Krzysztof Pomian, *Collectors and Curiosities: Paris and Venice 1500–1800* (Cambridge, MA: Polity, 1990).

151–52 P.-J. Mariette, *Description sommaire des desseins du cabinet de feu M. Crozat* (Paris, 1741).

152 Mariette on Watteau: *Abecedario de P. J. Mariette et autres notes inédites de cet amateur sur les arts et les artists*, Anatole de Montaiglon and Philippe de Chennevières, eds. 6 vols. (Paris, 1851–1860), 6: 112.

1750–1770

153–54 Johann Joachim Winckelmann, *Gedanken über die Nachahmung der griechischen Werke in der Malerei und Bildhauerkunst* (1755) (Stuttgart: Reclam, 1969). On gilding, 38; "noble simplicity and quiet greatness," 20.

154 Winckelmann on the "epidemic" of bad taste in the seventeenth century: *Geschichte der Kunst des Altertums* (1764) (Vienna: Phaidon, 1934), 335; *History of the Art of Antiquity*, Harry Francis Mallgrave, transl. (Los Angeles: Getty Research Institute, 2006), 319: "In the last century, a noxious epidemic became rife in Italy…. Bernini and Borromini forsook nature and antiquity in painting, sculpture, and architecture just as Marino and others did in poetry."

154 Winckelmann on the "only way to become great": *Gedanken über die Nachahmung*, 4.

154 James Adam on the collection of Cassiano dal Pozzo: quoted by Francis Haskell in his introduction to *Mosaics and Wall Paintings in Roman Churches*, John Osborne and Amanda Claridge, eds. (London: Harvey Miller, 1996), 17.

154–55 Winckelmann on the "essence of art" and the "cause of beauty": *Geschichte der Kunst des Altertums*, 9–10; *History of the Art of Antiquity*, 71.

155–56 Winckelmann on the body types in Raphael's compositions: *Erläuterung der Gedanken von der Nachahmung der griechischen Werke* (1756), published in *Gedanken über die Nachahmung*, 88; on absence of smallpox: *Gedanken über die Nachahmung*, 7.

156 Winckelmann on art and freedom: *Geschichte der Kunst des Altertums*, 133; again I cite the recent English translation, *History of the Art of Antiquity*, Part 1, chap. 4, 234; on *Unbezeichnung*: *Geschichte der Kunst des Altertums*, 150; *History of the Art of Antiquity*, Part 1, chap. 4, 196; on Greeks conscious of their own grandeur: *Geschichte der Kunst des Altertums*, 133; *History of the Art of Antiquity*, Part 1, chap. 4, 242.

156 Winckelmann on the Correggios in Sweden: *Gedanken über die Nachahmung*, 3.

156–57 Winckelmann on the lover on the seashore: *Geschichte der Kunst des Altertums*, 393; *History of the Art of Antiquity*, 351.

157 Diderot's doubts about Winckelmann and the imitation of antiquity: *Salon de 1765*, Else Marie Bukdahl and Annette Lorenceau, eds. (Paris: Hermann, 1984), 277–79; *Diderot on Art*, vol. 1, *Salon of 1765 and Notes on Painting*, John Goodman, transl. (New Haven, CT: Yale University Press, 1995), 157.

158 Diderot on art under republic and monarchy: "Notes on Painting," in *Salon of 1765 and Notes on Painting*, 229. The "Notes on Painting" were an appendix to the *Salon* of 1765.

158 Diderot on Boucher: *Salons de 1759–1761–1763*, Jean Seznec, ed. (Paris: Flammarion, 1967), 38, 40.

158 Diderot on sculpture and nudity: *Salon de 1765*, 283; *Salon of 1765*, 160.

158 On the study of landscape at the French Academy: Nikolaus Pevsner, *Academies of Art, Past and Present* (Cambridge, UK: Cambridge University Press, 1940), 177.

159 On Greuze's *Accordée du Village* represented by the commedia dell'arte: J. A. Jullien [= Desboulmiers], *Histoire anecdotique et raisonnée du Théâtre Italien* (1769), VII, 15–16.

160 Plato, *Timaeus*, 21a–26a, Benjamin Jowett, transl., in *Collected Dialogues*, Edith Hamilton and Huntington Cairns, eds. (Princeton, NJ: Princeton University Press, 1961), 1157–58.

160 Francis Bacon quoting the *Timaeus*: *New Organon*, I, lxxi, p. 59.

160 *Description of the Villa of Mr. Horace Walpole*, 2nd ed. (Strawberry Hill, 1784).

161 The Halfpennys on Chinese and Gothic architecture: quoted in Sutthoff, *Gotik im Barock*, 297.

161 Walpole on *sharawadgi*: Walpole, *Letters*, vol. 2 (Oxford: Clarendon Press, 1903), 433, no. 308.

161 Walpole on Gothic as bad Latin: *Anecdotes of Painting in England*, 3 vols. (London, 1849), 1: 116n1, quoted by Georg Germann, *Gothic Revival in Europe and Britain: Sources, Influences, and Ideas* (Cambridge, MA: MIT, 1972), 41; see also 54–55 on Strawberry Hill.

162 On Mariette and Walpole, see the introduction by Roseline Bacou to *Le cabinet d'un grand amateur: Pierre-Jean Mariette*, exhibition catalogue (Paris: Musée du Louvre, 1967).

163 Giovanni Battista Piranesi on Palladio, quoted by John Wilton-Ely in his introduction to Piranesi, *Observations on the Letter of Monsieur Mariette: with Opinions on Architecture, and a Preface to a New Treatise on the Introduction and Progress of the Fine Arts in Europe in Ancient Times* (1765) (Los Angeles, CA: Getty Research Institute, 2002), 3.

163 Piranesi's image of the Temple of Vespasian was published in *Vedute di Roma* (1756): see Henri Focillon, *Giovanni-Battista Piranesi, 1720–1778* (Paris: Laurens, 1918), no. 819.

165 Piranesi on disfigured and deformed Greek art: Piranesi, *Observations on the Letter of Monsieur Mariette*, 116.

165 Luigi Vanvitelli on Piranesi's qualifications as an architect: quoted in Wilton-Ely, introduction to Piranesi, *Observations on the Letter of Monsieur Mariette*, 37. Wilton-Ely quotes another similar jibe by Vanvitelli in *Piranesi as Architect and Designer* (New Haven: Yale University Press, 1993), 85n27.

1770–1790

167 J. W. von Goethe, "Von deutscher Baukunst," *Sämtliche Werke* (Munich: Hanser, 1985–1998) (cited henceforth as MA, for "Münchener Ausgabe"), 1.2: 415–23. On the "thousand ready hands," 415; on the "great and whole impression," 418–19.

168 On the 1744 description of the cathedral where Goethe found the text of the inscription about Erwin von Steinbach: MA 1.2: 841–42.

168 Goethe on the "quiet intimations" and the "vast and grounded building": "Von deutscher Baukunst," 419–20.

169 J. G. Herder on Ossian: "Auszug aus einem Briefwechsel über Ossian und die Lieder alter Völker," in Herder et al., *Von deutscher Art und Kunst* (1773), Hans Dietrich Irmscher, ed. (Stuttgart: Reclam, 1999), 57.

169 Goethe's reading of Laugier was somewhat inattentive. He names the Parisian church that combined German and Greek forms as the Madeleine, whereas Laugier discussed St. Gervais, and moreover did not say what Goethe says he said. See Laugier, *Essai sur l'architecture* (Paris, 1753), 18–19 and 42, and on Gothic, 5–6.

169 Goethe on the "painters of painted dolls": "Von deutscher Baukunst," 422.

170 Friedrich Gottlieb Klopstock on the ancients and on imitation, see Eduard Beaucamp, "Klopstock contra Winckelmann: aus der Frühzeit deutscher Kunstkritik," in Herbert Beck et al., eds., *Ideal und Wirklichkeit der bildenden Künste im späten 18. Jh.* (Berlin: Mann, 1984), 257.

170 Goethe on the soft modern doctrine: "Von deutscher Baukunst," 420–21; "approach, and acknowledge," 421–22.

170 John Carter on Gothic: Sutthoff, *Gotik in Barock*, 293–94.

171–73 Goethe on art that is "plastic, shaping, long before it is beautiful," and "characteristic art the only true art": "Von deutscher Baukunst," 421; the feeble aesthetes (*schwache Geschmäckler*) "dizzied" by Erwin's Colossus, 415.

173 Wilhelm Heinse on cathedrals and temples: Sutthoff, *Gotik in Barock*, 293–94.

173 On the topic of the rediscovery of the late medieval Italian painters, see Lionello Venturi, *Il gusto dei primitivi* (Bologna: Zanichelli, 1926); Giovanni Previtali, *La fortuna dei primitivi dal Vasari ai neoclassici* (Torino: Einaudi, 1964); *La fortuna dei primitivi*, Angelo Tartuferi and Gianluca Tormen, eds., exhibition catalogue (Florence: Galleria dell' Accademia, 2014).

173 On Abbé Rive and the Rohan Hours, see Michaela Braesel, *Buchmalerei in der Kunstgeschichte: Zur Rezeption in England, Frankreich und Italien* (Cologne: Böhlau, 2009), ill. 28, and Anna Delle Foglie and Francesca Manzari, *Riscoperta e riproduzione della miniatura in Francia nel Settecento: L'abbé Rive e l'Essai sur l'art de vérifier l'âge des miniatures des manuscrits* (Rome: Gangemi, 2016), 177–78.

175 Justus Möser, "Deutsche Geschichte," in Herder et al., *Von deutscher Art und Kunst*, 136.

1790–1810

176 On the early history of the Louvre, see Andrew McClellan, *Inventing the Louvre: Art, Politics, and the Origins of the Modern Museum in Eighteenth-Century Paris* (Berkeley: University of California Press, 1999).

179 Friedrich Schlegel only likes old painting: "Nachricht von den Gemälden in Paris" (1802, publ.

1803), in *Ansichten und Ideen von der christlichen Kunst* (this is the title Schlegel himself chose for the writings on art gathered in his collected works [1823]), in Hans Eichner, ed., *Kritische Friedrich-Schlegel-Ausgabe*, vol. 4 (Paderborn: Schöningh, 1959), 13–14.

180 Giovanni Lami, *Dissertazione* (1757), published in Leonardo da Vinci, *Trattato della pittura* (Florence, 1792), liii–lxii, quotes drawn from lviii–lix and lxii–lxiv.

181 [Alexis-François Artaud de Montor], *Considérations sur l'état de la peinture en Italie, dans les quatre siècles qui ont précédé celui de Raphael* (Paris, 1808); here quoted from the second edition of 1811, pp. 4–5.

182 Friedrich Schiller on poets being or seeking nature: "Über naïve und sentimentalische Dichtung" (1795), Julius A. Elias, transl., *Naïve and Sentimental Poetry and On the Sublime* (New York: Frederick Ungar, 1966), 106.

182 Wilhelm Heinrich Wackenroder, *Herzensergiessungen eines kunstliebenden Klosterbruders* (1796), in Wackenroder, *Sämtliche Werke und Briefe*, vol. 1, *Werke*, Silvio Vietta, ed. (Heidelberg: Winter, 1991), 51–145.

182 Wackenroder reading Quad: Waetzoldt, *Deutsche Kunsthistoriker*, 21.

183 Wackenroder on the shortcomings of the art theorists: *Herzensergiessungen*, 55; on Raphael and Bramante, 56–57.

183 Schlegel on the best kind of art criticism: *Kritische Fragmente* (= "Lyceum" fragments) (1797), no. 57; in Schlegel, *Kritische Schriften und Fragmente*, Ernst Behler and Hans Eichner, eds., 6 vols. (Paderborn: Schöningh, 1988), 1: 243.

183–84 Ludwig Tieck, *Franz Sternbalds Wanderungen: eine altdeutsche Geschichte* (1798), Marianne Thalmann, ed. (Munich: Winkler, 1964), chap. 8, pp. 55–56.

184 William Beckford, *Biographical Memoirs of Extraordinary Painters* (London, 1780), 15–17, 38–44.

184 Wackenroder on the laconic chroniclers: *Herzensergiessungen*, 82.

184–85 Schlegel on poetry and art: "Nachtrag italienischer Gemälde" (1803), in *Ansichten und Ideen*, 76; on the lack of deep feeling in the present day:

"Dritter Nachtrag alter Gemälde" (1804, publ. 1805), in *Ansichten und Ideen*, 147.

185 J. G. Herder, "Conclusions Drawn from the Comparison of the Poetry of Diverse Peoples of Ancient and Modern Times" (1796), translated by Marcia Bunge in Herder, *Against Pure Reason: Writings on Religion, Language, and History* (Eugene, OR: Wipf & Stock, 1993), 143.

185 Schlegel on spirits: *Kritische Fragmente* (1797), no. 44; in *Kritische Schriften und Fragmente*, 1: 242.

186 Schlegel on the thirteenth-century glass painting in the Musée des Monuments français: "Zweiter Nachtrag alter Gemälde" (1804, publ. 1805), in *Ansichten und Ideen* 105–6.

186 On Alexandre Lenoir, see *Un musée révolutionnaire: le musée des Monuments français d'Alexandre Lenoir*, Geneviève Bresc-Bautier et al., eds., exhibition catalogue, Musée du Louvre (Paris: Hazan, 2016).

186–87 Schlegel on the master of the altarpiece in Cologne: "Dritter Nachtrag alter Gemälde," in *Ansichten und Ideen*, 142.

187–89 Wackenroder on tolerance for unfamiliar art: *Herzensergiessungen*, 87–88.

187 Herder on poetry in different times and places, and on considering poems and flowers in context: "Conclusions Drawn from the Comparison of the Poetry of Diverse Peoples of Ancient and Modern Times" 141, 144.

189 On Pierre Sonnerat, William Hodges, the Society of Antiquaries, and Edward Moor, see Partha Mitter, *Much Maligned Monsters: History of European Reactions to Indian Art* (Oxford: Oxford University Press, 1977), 115–16, 123–24, 141, 178–80.

190 Schlegel's address to Novalis: *Ideen* (1800), no. 156, in Schlegel, *Kritische Schriften und Fragmente*, Behler and Eichner, eds., 2: 234.

190 On the *Oriental Scenery* of the Daniells, see Mitter, *Much Maligned Monsters*, 126–29.

192 Johann Heinrich Meyer, "Einleitung: Sechzehntes und siebzehntes Jahrhundert," in Goethe, ed., *Winkelmann und sein Jahrhundert* (Tübingen, 1805), MA 6.2: 229.

192 Goethe, "Skizzen zu einer Schilderung Winkelmanns," in *Winkelmann und sein Jahrhundert*, MA 6.2: 352.

193 Schlegel on Winckelmann: *Athenaeum-Fragmente* (1798), no. 149, in *Kritische Schriften und Fragmente*, 2:118.

194 Friedrich Schelling: I quote from *System of Transcendental Idealism* (1800), Part 6, § 1, Peter Heath, transl. (Charlottesville: University Press of Virgina, 1978), 221–22.

194 Goethe on the *Altertumsforscher* as the only ones who were able to ignore the Kantian revolution: "Skizzen zu einer Schilderung Winkelmanns," in *Winkelmann und sein Jahrhundert*, MA 6.2:372.

194–95 G. W. F. Hegel, *Phänomenologie des Geistes* (Frankfurt: Suhrkamp, 1970), VII, C, pp. 547–48; I have quoted from the translation by A. V. Miller, *Phenomenology of Spirit* (Oxford, UK: Oxford University Press, 1977), 455–56.

1810–1830

196 Julius von Schlosser on Ph. O. Runge: *Die Kunstliteratur*, 609–10; *La letteratura artistica*, 705–6.

196 Philipp Otto Runge on art and the "eternally marvellous": letter to Carl Schildener, February 19, 1805, in Runge, *Briefwechsel: eine Auswahl*, Peter Betthausen, ed. (Leipzig: Seemann, 2010), 193.

197 Runge on the "permanent rhythm," and on the inner connection of the work with nature: quoted by Otto Böttcher, *Philipp Otto Runge: sein Leben, Wirken, und Schaffen* (Hamburg: Friederichsen, de Gruyter, 1937), 73, 75.

198 Plutarch, *The Oracles at Delphi No Longer Given in Verse*, 12, 400a, Frank Cole Babbitt, ed. and transl., in Plutarch, *Moralia* (Loeb Classical Library) (Cambridge, MA: Harvard University Press, 1936), 5:290–91.

198 On Overbeck's *Finding of Moses*, see Cordula Grewe, *The Nazarenes: Romantic Avant-Garde and the Art of the Concept* (University Park: Pennsylvania State University Press, 2015), 113–15.

200 Raffaelle Stern and Giuseppe Valadier's restoration of the Arch of Titus: Alessandro Conti, *Storia del restauro e della conservazione delle opere d'arte* (Milan: Electa, 2002), 235.

201 Stendhal, *Promenades*, 846, quoted in Alba della Fazia Amoia and Enrico Bruschini, eds., *Stendhal's Rome: Then and Now* (Rome: Edizioni di storia e letteratura, 1997), 24.

201 Schlegel on "hieroglyphs": "Dritter Nachtrag alter Gemälde" (1804, publ. 1805), in *Ansichten und Ideen*, 151; the footnote on Runge added in 1823 is p. 151, n. 1.

201 Schlegel on "the best theory of art": "Aussichten für die Kunst in dem Österreichischen Kaiserstaat" (1812), *Ansichten und Ideen*, 229–30.

202 Jacques-Nicolas Paillot de Montabert, *Dissertation sur les peintures du moyen âge, et sur celles qu'on a appellées gothiques* (1812) (Paris: Allia, 2002).

202 On the history and principles of the art historical monograph, see Gabriele Guercio, *Art as Existence: The Artist's Monograph and Its Project* (Cambridge, MA: MIT, 2006).

202 Sydney Owenson on her subject's preeminence: *Life and Times of Salvator Rosa*, 2 vols. (London, 1824), 1:19–20.

204–5 Carl Friedrich Rumohr, *Italienische Forschungen: Zur Theorie und Geschichte neuerer Kunstbestrebungen*, 3 vols. (Berlin, 1827–1831). On Duccio, 2:32; on Giotto, 2:73–74; on guilds, 2:400–1.

205–6 On Blake's ideas about art, ancient and modern, see Anthony Blunt, *The Art of William Blake* (New York: Columbia University Press, 1959), and David Bindman, *Blake as an Artist* (Oxford: Phaidon, 1977).

206 Blake on Dürer: Joshua Reynolds, *Discourses on Art*, Robert R. Wark, ed. (San Marino, CA: Huntington Library, 1959), 51, 299.

206 André Félibien on Dürer: *Entretiens*, ed. 1705, II, 236–37; see the German translation of this passage in Heinz Lüdeke and Susanne Heiland, eds., *Dürer und die Nachwelt* (Berlin: Rütten & Loening, 1955), 109–10, citing the 1672 ed. of the *Entretiens*, 324–25.

206 Roger de Piles on Dürer: Jan Białostocki, *Dürer and His Critics, 1500–1971* (Baden-Baden: Koerner, 1986), 53.

206 Winckelmann on Dürer and Holbein: *Geschichte der Kunst des Altertums*, 44; *History of the Art of Antiquity*, Part 1, chap. 1, 122–23.

207 On Jean-Baptiste Seroux d'Agincourt, see Ingrid R. Vermeulen, *Picturing Art History: The Rise of the Illustrated History of Art in the*

Eighteenth Century (Amsterdam: Amsterdam University Press, 2010), chap. 3, and Ilaria Miarelli Mariani and Simona Moretti, eds., *Seroux d'Agincourt e la documentazione grafica del Medioevo* (Vatican City: Biblioteca Apostolica Vaticana, 2017).

207 Goethe on "rhetoric and versifying": this is from a piece he published in the *Morgenblatt für gebildete Stände* in 1816 advertising his own forthcoming tract, *Kunst und Altertum am Rhein und Mayn*, quoted below; MA 11.2: 315.

207 William Young Ottley, *A Series of Plates Engraved after the Paintings and Sculptures of the Most Eminent Masters of the Early Florentine School* (London, 1826), 1–2.

208 Arthur Schopenhauer, *Die Welt als Wille und Vorstellung* (1818/1844), Third Book, The World as Representation, Second Aspect, § 45, in *Sämtliche Werke* (Frankfurt: Suhrkamp, 1986), 1: 313. I quote from the translation by E. F. J. Payne, *The World as Will and Representation* (New York: Dover, 1969), 222.

209 G. W. F. Hegel, *Vorlesungen über die Ästhetik*, 3 vols. (Frankfurt: Suhrkamp, 1970); *Aesthetics: Lectures on Fine Art*, T. M. Knox, transl., 2 vols. (Oxford, UK: Clarendon Press, 1975). On Indian art: Part 1, I, 1, B, *Ästhetik*, 1: 432; *Aesthetics*, 1: 334–35. Here and throughout I have used Knox's translation.

209–10 Sulpiz Boisserée's discovery of the tomb of Erwin von Steinbach: Goethe, MA 1.2: 841.

210–11 Goethe on early German and Netherlandish art: this and the following passages are quoted from the section "Heidelberg" in the treatise *Kunst und Altertum am Rhein und Mayn* (1816), the first number of his own journal, which would run for another sixteen years, *Kunst und Altertum* (later *Über Kunst und Altertum*); MA 11.2: 9–89. On the man enclosed by customs and traditions, and on the original artist: MA 11.2: 81–82; on the painting by the Master of Veronica: MA 11.2: 68, 71; on local patriotism: MA 11.2: 82.

211 Leopoldo Cicognara, "Del Bello" (1808), in Paola Barocchi, ed., *Testimonianze e polemiche figurative in Italia: l'Ottocento dal Bello ideale al Preraffaellismo* (Messina: D'Anna, 1972), 1: 9–11; quoted by Ferdinando Bologna, *La coscienza storica dell'arte d'Italia* (Torino: UTET, 1982), 167.

212 Lionello Venturi on historicism and realism: *Painting and Painters* (New York: Scribner's, 1945), 117.

213–14 Heinrich Heine on Peter Cornelius: Heine, *Werke* (Frankfurt: Insel, 1968), 2: 303.

214 On Saint-Simon's influence on Karl Marx, see Margaret A. Rose, *Marx's Lost Aesthetic: Karl Marx and the Visual Arts* (Cambridge, UK: Cambridge University Press, 1984).

214 Charles Fourier, *Le nouveau monde amoureux* (Paris: Anthropos, 1967), 329–32.

1830–1850

215 On Hegel and the Boisserées, see Terry Pinkard, *Hegel: A Biography* (Cambridge, UK: Cambridge University Press, 2000), 374.

216–21 Hegel on the "content of Romantic art": Part 2, III, Introduction, 3, *Ästhetik*, 2: 138–39; *Aesthetics*, 1: 526; on art vs. history, on Greek and Christian art, and on art's highest vocation: Introduction, *Ästhetik*, 1: 23–24; *Aesthetics*, 1: 9–11; on the historical study of art, and the "art-doctors" (*Ärzte der Kunst*): Introduction, *Ästhetik*, 1: 30–31; *Aesthetics*, 1: 14–15.

221 The uncut pages in Wilhelm Meister's library: *Wilhelm Meisters Lehrjahre*, Book 1, 10; MA 5: 35.

222 Erich Auerbach, "Vico and Aesthetic Historism" (1949), in Auerbach, *Scenes from the Drama of European Literature* (1959) (Minneapolis: University of Minnesota Press, 1984), 183.

222 On Kugler's dissertation, see Jörg Trempler, "Kunst und Wissenschaft: Franz Kuglers Promotion und Habilitation oder die Zeichnung als Prüfungsgegenstand," in Horst Bredekamp and Adam S. Labuda, eds., *In der Mitte Berlins: 200 Jahre Kunstgeschichte an der Humboldt-Universität* (Berlin: Gebr. Mann, 2010), 55–65.

222 For Rám Ráz, *Essay on the Architecture of the Hindus*, see Partha Mitter, *Much Maligned Monsters: History of European Reactions to Indian Art* (Oxford, UK: Oxford University Press, 1977), 180–86.

223 On H. G. Hotho on van Eyck, and on Schnaase, see Lionello Venturi, *History of Art Criticism*, 209–10, and Michael Podro, *The Critical Historians of Art* (New Haven, CT: Yale University Press, 1982), 31–43.

223–24 Schopenhauer, *Die Welt als Wille und Vorstellung* (1818/1844), Third Book, The World as Representation, Second Aspect, § 36, in *Sämtliche Werke* (Frankfurt: Suhrkamp, 1986), 1: 264–66. I quote from the translation by E. F. J. Payne, *The World as Will and Representation* (New York: Dover, 1969), 184–85.

225 Vincenzo Camuccini's restoration at Santa Costanza: Alessandro Conti, *Storia del restauro*, 229.

225 On the "Old German" festivals or pageants of 1828 and 1840, see Matthias Mende, *Dürer-Bibliographie* (Wiesbaden: Harrassowitz, 1971), nos. 10000–10006, and Białostocki, *Dürer and His Critics*, 129–31.

225 Gérard de Nerval, *Sylvie*, Bertrand Marchal, ed. (Paris: Gallimard, 2005), 21.

226 On the origins of archeology in the fifteenth century: Brunelleschi's biographer Antonio Manetti reported that Brunelleschi and Donatello studied the ruins of Rome together, taking measurements, estimating heights, making drawings. Vasari relayed this account (Milanesi 2: 337–39; Bettarini-Barocchi 3: 147–49). The joint junket may never have happened. Alberti undertook his own proto-archeological researches in Rome. See Anthony Grafton, *Leon Battista Alberti: Master Builder of the Italian Renaissance* (New York: Hill & Wang, 2000), 54–55.

226 Letter of Delacroix to Auguste Jal, from Tangiers, June 4, 1832: *Correspondance générale de Eugène Delacroix*, André Joubin, ed. (Paris: Plon, 1935), 1: 330.

227 The literature on historicist architecture in the nineteenth century is vast; as a sample I mention only two studies on the Byzantine revival that I find illuminating: J. B. Bullen, *Byzantium Rediscovered* (London: Phaidon, 2003), and Robert S. Nelson, *Hagia Sophia, 1850–1950: Holy Wisdom, Modern Monument* (Chicago: University of Chicago Press, 2004).

227 A. Welby Pugin, *Contrasts* (London, 1836), plate 12, "New Church—Open Competition. The Practice of Architecture in the Nineteenth Century Satirised." See Pevsner, *Academies of Art*, 246.

227–28 Joseph von Hormayr on the purpose of the art museum: *Die geschichtlichen Fresken in den Arkaden des Hofgartens in München* (Munich, 1830), 10; quoted by Sabine Fastert, *Die Entdeckung des Mit-*

telalters: Geschichtsrezeption in der nazarenischen Malerei des frühen 19. Jahrhunderts (Munich: Deutscher Kunstverlag, 2000), 278.

228 On the report of the Committee on Arts, 1836, see Kenneth Clark, *The Gothic Revival* (1928) (London: Constable, 1950), 147.

229 Karl Schnaase on Schnorr von Carolsfeld: "Der Kreuzzug Kaiser Franz I" (1840); Kugler on the Nazarenes: *Kunstblatt* 1843, no. 58 (July 20), 247; Springer on the Nazarenes: all three quoted by Fastert, *Die Entdeckung des Mittelalters*, 316–17.

229 Anna Jameson, *Visits and Sketches at Home and Abroad*, 4 vols. (London, 1834), 1: 259–63; 2: 137.

229 Hegel against anachronism: Part 2, III, 3, 3, *Ästhetik*, 2: 238–39; *Aesthetics*, 1: 608.

230 Hegel on the "prose of the world": *Ästhetik*, 1: 197–99; *Aesthetics*, 1: 148–50.

230 Vischer on the Nazarenes: *Jahrbuch der Gegenwart*, 1844, pp. 46ff. On Vischer, see also James J. Sheehan, *Museums in the German Art World: From the End of the Old Regime to the Rise of Modernism* (Oxford, UK: Oxford University Press, 2000), 96.

230 Heinrich Heine on the *Kunstperiode*: his review of Wolfgang Menzel, *Die deutsche Literatur* (1828), in Heine, *Sämtliche Schriften* (Munich: Hanser, 1968), 1: 455. See the discussion in Georg Lukács, *German Realists in the Nineteenth Century* (1951), Jeremy Gaines and Paul Keast, transl. (Cambridge, MA: MIT, 1993), 132–33, quoting Heine's *Französische Maler* (1831).

230–31 Georg Büchner, *Lenz* (Stuttgart: Reclam, 1969), 18–19.

1850–1870

232 Leopold von Ranke on relativism: *Über die Epochen der neueren Geschichte. Vorträge dem Könige Maximilian II. von Bayern im Herbst 1854 zu Berchtesgaden gehalten. Vortrag vom 25. September 1854*. Ranke, *Über die Epochen der neueren Geschichte: Historisch-kritische Ausgabe*, Theodor Schieder and Helmut Berding, eds. (Munich: Oldenbourg 1971), 60. Passage quoted in Hermann Glaser, ed., *The German Mind of the 19th Century: A Literary and Historical Anthology* (New York: Continuum, 1981), 149–51.

233 Leon Battista Alberti on the accumulation of medical knowledge: *On the Art of Building in Ten Books*, Book 6, § 2, Joseph Rykwert, transl., with Neil Leach and Robert Tavernor (Cambridge, MA: MIT, 1988), 157.

234 On the Germanisches Nationalmuseum, see Peter N. Miller, *History and Its Objects: Antiquarianism and Material Culture since 1500* (Ithaca, NY: Cornell University Press, 2017), 173–99.

234 On Murray and Baedeker: James Buzard, *The Beaten Track: European Tourism, Literature, and the Ways to Culture* (Oxford: Oxford University Press, 1993), ch. 1.

235 The restorations by Bianchi and Molteni: Conti, *Storia del restauro*, 271, 251. The frescoes by Giotto in the Bardi Chapel were covered with whitewash in the eighteenth century. They were exposed again only in 1852. Bianchi's *St. Louis* was removed in 1958–1961.

235 Ruskin on the painters of the fifteenth and seventeenth centuries: *Modern Painters*, vol. 1 (1843), in *Works*, vol. 3 (London: George Allen, 1903), 84–85.

235–36 Ruskin on Italian Gothic architecture: *Stones of Venice*, 3 vols. (1852), in *Works*, vols. 9–11 (London: George Allen, 1903). On noble ornamentation: I, ii, 70; on ignoble ornamentation: I, xx, 253; on the function of modern architecture: I, xxx, 411; on the lovable "mystery and unity" of the weave-motifs in Byzantine capitals: *Works*, vol. 10 (London: George Allen, 1904), II, v, 163, and the "strange disquietude" of the Gothic spirit: II, vi, 214; on Gothic balancing facts and design: II, vi, 231.

236 The old stories about Titian's painting technique: Mary P. Merrifield, *Original Treatises on the Arts of Painting*, 2 vols. (London, 1849), 1: cxxiii.

237–38 Gottfried Semper, "Science, Industry, and Art" (1852), in Semper, *The Four Elements of Architecture and Other Writings*, Harry Francis Mallgrave and Wolfgang Herrmann, transl. (New York: Cambridge University Press, 1989), quotes drawn from 132–38.

238 Semper, *Der Stil in den technischen und tektonischen Künsten oder praktische Ästhetik: ein Handbuch für Techniker, Künstler und Kunst-freunde*, 2 vols. (Frankfurt, 1860); *Style in the Technical and Tectonic Arts, or, Practical Aesthetics*, Harry Francis Mallgrave and Michael Robinson, transl. (Los Angeles, CA: Getty Research Institute, 2004). On style theory vs. art history: *Style*, 277.

239–40 Eugène Viollet-le-Duc, *Entretiens sur l'architecture*, 2 vols. (Paris, 1863–1872), on the "current anarchy" in art: *Entretiens* V, 1: 145; on the nineteenth century lacking an architecture of its own: X, 1: 450; on modern education in the arts, and on Le Brun: V, 1: 149; on the submission to tradition in ancient and eastern architecture: XV, 2: 183.

240 On the modern architecture of "reminiscences": *Entretiens* VIII, 1: 323–4; difficulty of learning and forgetting: III, 1: 99; impossible to invent a new architecture: VI, 1: 175.

240 Viollet-le-Duc on medieval architecture as "progress" over the ancients: *Dictionnaire raisonné de l'architecture française du XIe au XVIe siècle*, 10 vols. (Paris, 1854–1868), art. "Style," 8: 496.

240 Viollet-le-Duc as relativist: *Entretiens* I, 1: 16. On the imagination of the civilized and the primitive: VI, 1: 178–79.

240 Ruskin on the cathedral front: *Stones of Venice*, II, vi, 178.

241 Viollet-le-Duc on his own century sharing this problem: *Entretiens* III, 1: 96; not revival of past forms but knowledge of the principles: I, 1: 32; architecture must become scientific: VI, 1: 174; on the superiority of the critical spirit to tradition in the thirteenth century: VI 1: 240; on Gothic form corresponding to structure: VII, 1: 284.

242 Burckhardt's belief that philosophy subordinates, while history coordinates: see Lionel Gossman, *Basel in the Age of Burckhardt: A Study in Unseasonable Ideas* (Chicago: University of Chicago Press, 2000), 216–22, 241–42.

242 Filarete, "reborn": *Traktat über die Baukunst*, W. von Oettingen, ed. (Vienna, 1890), 428; *Treatise on Architecture*, John R. Spencer, ed. (New Haven, CT: Yale University Press, 1965), 175–76.

243 Jules Michelet, *Histoire de France*, vol. 7, *Renaissance* (Paris: Éditions des Équateurs, 2008), 11–12, 15.

243 Michelet, *Le Peuple* (1846) (Paris: Flammarion, 1974), 246.

243–44 For more quotations of French authors about the Renaissance, before Michelet, see Stephen Bann, "Inventing the Renaissance in Nineteenth-century France," in Lina Bolzoni and Alina Payne, eds., *The Italian Renaissance in the Nineteenth Century: Revision, Revival, and Return* (Cambridge, MA: Harvard University Press, 2018), 7–24.

244 On the role of Burckhardt's title in the reassignment of the Italian word *rinascimento* to designate the period, see the *Grande dizionario della lingua italiana* (Torino: Unione Tipografico-Editrice, 1992), 16: 492: "il termine, diffusosi con il rifiorire degli studi sul Cinquecento italiano ed europeo e consacrato nell'uso dall' opera di J. Burckhardt." Adolfo Bartoli, *I precursori del Rinascimento* (Florence, 1876), 9, 37n2.

244 Hippolyte Taine, "The Philosophy of Art," in *Lectures on Art* (New York: Holt, 1875), 36–38.

245 Henri Focillon's praise for Taine: *Vie des formes*, 87; *Life of Forms*, 141.

245–46 Gottfried Keller, *Der Grüne Heinrich* (first version): Keller, *Sämtliche Werke*, Thomas Böning and Gerhard Kaiser, eds., vol. 2 (Frankfurt: Deutscher Klassiker Verlag, 1985), on the festival in Munich: book 3, chap. 5, 565; on the strangeness of the cult of the past: book 3, chap. 6, p. 577.

246–47 Jacob Burckhardt, *Weltgeschichtliche Betrachtungen* (1905), Rudolf Max, ed. (Stuttgart: Kröner, 1969); translated as *Force and Freedom: Reflections on History* (New York: Pantheon, 1943). On culture and spontaneity: *Weltgeschichtliche Betrachtungen*, 57; *Force and Freedom*, 140; on culture in modern life: *Weltgeschichtliche Betrachtungen*, 68–69; *Force and Freedom*, 152.

247 Henry Adams, *The Education of Henry Adams* (New York: Modern Library, 1996), chap. 6, "Rome," p. 88.

248 Henry James, *A Small Boy and Others* (1913), quoted in F. O. Matthiessen, *The James Family* (New York: Knopf, 1961), 86.

248–49 Baudelaire, "L'art philosophique" (1868), in *Oeuvres complètes* (Bibliothèque de la Pléiade), Claude Pichois, ed. (Paris: Gallimard, 1976), 2: 598–605, here 598. Translation my own, but see "Philosophic Art," in Baudelaire, *The Painter of Modern Life and Other Essays*, Jonathan Mayne, transl. (London, 1964), 204–12, here 204.

250 Edmond and Jules de Goncourt, *French Eighteenth-Century Painters: Watteau, Boucher, Chardin, La Tour, Greuze, Fragonard*, Robin Ironside, transl. (London: Phaidon, 1948), 55, 3.

251 Walter Pater on antiquarianism: Pater, "Notes on Leonardo da Vinci," *Fortnightly Review* 12 (1869): 494; reprinted in Pater, *Studies in the History of the Renaissance* (1873). *Studies in the History of the Renaissance*, Matthew Beaumont, ed. (Oxford: Oxford University Press, 1986), 57 (this is the text of the first edition of 1873).

251 Erich Auerbach, *Literary Language and Its Public* (1958) (Princeton, NJ: Princeton University Press, 1965), 328.

1870–1890

252 Nietzsche, "Vom Nutzen und Nachtheil der Historie für das Leben," in *Unzeitgemässe Betrachtungen* (1874), *Sämtliche Werke*, Giorgio Colli and Mazzino Montinari, eds., 15 vols. (Berlin: de Gruyter, 1967–1977), 1: 245–334. I will use the translation by Richard T. Gray, "On the Utility and Liability of History for Life," in *Unfashionable Observations, The Complete Works of Nietzsche* (Stanford, CA: Stanford University Press, 1995), 2: 85–167.

252 On Europe's "historical fever": "Vom Nutzen und Nachtheil der Historie," 246, "On the Utility and Liability of History," 86.

252 Statistics on students and professors in Germany: Charles E. McClelland, *State, Society, and University in Germany, 1700–1914* (Cambridge, UK: Cambridge University Press, 1980), 165, 240–44.

252 On the teaching of art history in German universities: Franz Xaver Kraus, *Über das Studium der Kunstwissenschaft an den deutschen Hochschulen* (Strasbourg, 1874), 8–9.

253 On art history in Vienna: *Geschichte der Wiener Universität von 1848 bis 1898* (Vienna, 1898), 333–35, and Julius von Schlosser, "Die Wiener Schule der Kunstgeschichte," *Mitteilungen des Österreichischen Instituts für Geschichtsforschung*, Ergänzungs-Band (supp.) 13, Heft (no.) 2 (1934).

253–54 On Hans Makart's lunettes: Beatrix Kriller and Georg Kugler, *Das Kunsthistorische Museum: Die Architektur und Ausstattung* (Vienna: Brandstätter, 1991), 211–45.

254 On Makart's "Historical Procession": *Makart: Ein Künstler regiert die Stadt*, exhibition catalogue, Vienna, Wien Museum (Munich: Prestel, 2011).

254 Nietzsche on festivals: *Die fröhliche Wissenschaft* (1882), § 89, *Sämtliche Werke* 3: 446; translated by Walter Kaufmann as *The Gay Science* (New York: Vintage, 1974), 144.

255 Nietzsche on artistic historicism as a "world's fair": "Vom Nutzen und Nachtheil der Historie für das Leben," 279; "On the Utility and Liability of History for Life," 116.

255 Nietzsche on the monumental history that believes greatness will be possible again, on the occupation with the classical and rare, and on causes and effects: "Vom Nutzen und Nachtheil der Historie für das Leben," 260–62; "On the Utility and Liability of History for Life," 98–99.

255 Nietzsche on the "connoisseurs of greatness": "Vom Nutzen und Nachtheil der Historie für das Leben," 265; "On the Utility and Liability of History for Life," 102.

256–57 Nietzsche on the study of history serving the present: "Vom Nutzen und Nachtheil der Historie für das Leben," 251; "On the Utility and Liability of History for Life," 89; on the connoisseurs of art: "Vom Nutzen und Nachtheil," 264; "Utility and Liability," 101; on the habits of the antiquarian: "Vom Nutzen und Nachtheil," 268; "Utility and Liability," 105; on the critical history that judges and condemns: "Vom Nutzen und Nachtheil," 264; "Utility and Liability," 102; on the suspension of forgetfulness, and on the dangers and limits of critical history: "Vom Nutzen und Nachtheil," 269–70; "Utility and Liability," 107; on the tolerance of even the Greeks for the hieratic style: "Vom Nutzen und Nachtheil," 267–68; "Utility and Liability," 105; on the surfeit of history: "Vom Nutzen und Nachtheil," 279; "Utility and Liability," 115.

257 Anselm Feuerbach's dream: James J. Sheehan, *Museums in the German Art World from the End of the Old Regime to the Rise of Modernism* (New York: Oxford University Press, 2000), 95, citing Hans Schröter, *Das Verhältnis der Maler zu den öffentlichen Galerien Deutschlands im 19. Jh.* (PhD diss., Berlin, 1954), 114.

258 Eugène Fromentin, *Les maîtres d'autrefois* (1876), in Fromentin, *Oeuvres complètes*, Bibliothèque de la Pléiade (Paris: Gallimard, 1984), 567–809. On his non-method: 568; on Dutch artists, 675. The book was translated into English already in 1913.

258 The original articles by Giovanni Morelli were published in the *Zeitschrift für bildende Kunst*, vols. 9, 10, and 11 (1874–76). They later appeared as books: *Die Werke italienischer Meister in den Galerien von München, Dresden, und Berlin* (Leipzig, 1880), and *Kunstkritische Studien über italienische Malerei*, vol. 1, *Die Galerien Borghese und Doria Pamfili in Rom* (Leipzig, 1890). Here I quote from the English edition of 1900: Morelli, *Italian Painters: Critical Studies of Their Works, The Borghese and Doria-Pamfili Galleries in Rome* (London, 1900).

259–63 Morelli on *literati* and archeologists, 6; on blindness of art-lover trained in lecture hall, 7; on the "deeper qualities of the mind," preface, 45; on Botticelli's *Calumny of Apelles*, 35; on the Fornarina and the Madonna del Cardellino, 46; on why we study the fifteenth-century painters, 8; on the Donna Velata, 54; on connoisseurs and art historians, 14–15; on the tourists and their guidebooks, 2, 4; on the ignorance of the public, 34; more on the study of the fifteenth-century painters, 34–35; on the "trained and cultivated eye" of the connoisseur, 11.

263–64 Walter Pater, *Studies in the History of the Renaissance*, Matthew Beaumont, ed. (Oxford, UK: Oxford University Press, 1986). On the "concrete works of art" of the Renaissance, 6; on tracing the outbreak of the human spirit into the Middle Ages, 5; on the "care for physical beauty" in *Aucassin et Nicolette*, 11; on the worship of the body challenging the limits of the religious system of the middle age, 5; on the assertion of liberty, 16; on Pico della Mirandola and the charm of pagan story, 18; on the *Birth of Venus* and the Greeks, 33.

264 Pater on the Renaissance as realism, 62; on Leonardo da Vinci and the love of toys, 58; on the lack of historical sense in the fifteenth century, 20; on Winckelmann, 6; on the one who is wise only too late, *ophimatheis*, 92.

264 Burckhardt on the "pure history of styles and forms": *Briefe*, Max Burckhardt, ed., 11 vols.

(Basel: Schwabe, 1949–1986), 6: 34, letter of April 20, 1875, no. 675.

264–65 Konrad Fiedler, "Bemerkungen über Wesen und Geschichte der Baukunst" (1878), in Fiedler, *Schriften über Kunst* (Munich: Piper, 1914), 2: 431–79; "Observations on the Nature and History of Architecture," in *Empathy, Form, and Space: Problems in German Aesthetics, 1873–1893*, Harry Francis Mallgrave and Eleftherios Ikonomou, eds. and transl. (Santa Monica, CA: 1994), 125–46. I quote from this translation. On scholarship explaining everything about a work of art except what makes it a work of art: "Bemerkungen," 437; "Observations," 128; on Asiatic, Egyptian, and Greek building: "Bemerkungen," 447, 451; "Observations," 132, 134; on the awareness of Romanesque architecture of unformed matter: "Bemerkungen," 469; "Observations," 142.

266 Fiedler on the origins of reality in the mind: "Moderner Naturalismus und künstlerische Wahrheit" (Modern Naturalism and Artistic Truth) (1881), in Fiedler, *Schriften über Kunst* (Cologne: DuMont, 1977), 124.

266 Robert Vischer on the "unconscious": "On the Optical Sense of Form: A Contribution to Aesthetics" (1873), in *Empathy, Form, and Space*, 92.

266 On the discovery of Paleolithic painting: Ulrich Pfisterer, "Altamira—oder: Die Anfänge von Kunst und Kunstwissenschaft," *Vorträge aus dem Warburg-Haus* 10 (2007), 15–79.

1890–1900

268 Alois Riegl contrasting ancient vegetal ornament to Arts and Crafts: *Stilfragen: Grundlegungen zu einer Geschichte der Ornamentik* (Berlin, 1893), 232; *Problems of Style: Foundations for a History of Ornament*, Evelyn Kain, transl. (Princeton, NJ: Princeton University Press, 1992), 207.

269 Konrad Fiedler on the artist restaging the construction of reality: "Moderner Naturalismus und künstlerische Wahrheit" (Modern Naturalism and Artistic Truth) (1881), in *Schriften über Kunst* (1977), 125.

269–71 Adolf von Hildebrand, *Das Problem der Form in der bildenden Kunst* (1893); I quote from the translation by Harry Francis Mallgrave and Eleftherios Ikonomou, "The Problem of Form in the Fine Arts," in *Empathy, Form, and Space*, 227–79. On Greek relief sculpture as the ideal art form, 252; on the perception of landscape, 238–40; on seeing in relief as stabilizing, 252.

271 Konrad Fiedler on form-creation as a kind of thinking, on architecture as the liberation of form from material, quoting Semper, and on form tending toward autonomy: "Bemerkungen über Wesen und Geschichte der Baukunst" (1878), in Fiedler, *Schriften über Kunst* (Munich: Piper, 1914), 2: 439–41; "Observations on the Nature and History of Architecture," in *Empathy, Form, and Space*, 129–30.

272–73 Oscar Wilde, "The Critic as Artist" (originally published in 1890 as "The True Function and Value of Criticism"; reprinted in Wilde, *Intentions* (London, 1891), and in *The Artist as Critic: Critical Writings of Oscar Wilde*, Richard Ellman, ed. (New York: Random House, 1968), 340–408, here 348–49, 354, 365, 389.

273 The quantity of art history books: in 1950 there were still only 29,184 books in the library of the Kunsthistorisches Institut in Florence. By 1996 the tally had increased to 207,824 books; see Hans W. Hubert, *Das Kunsthistorische Institut in Florenz von der Gründung bis zum hundertjährigen Jubiläum* (1897–1997) (Florence: Il Ventilabro, 1997). According to the current librarian Jan Simane there were 306,238 books on the shelves in 2017. In other words, the library between 1950 and 1996 acquired an average of 3,000 new books per year, amounting to expansion over the entire period of 700%. Since 1996 the library has grown at the rate of 4,500 books per year.

274 Wilhelm Vöge, *Die Anfänge des monumentalischen Stils im Mittelalter: eine Untersuchung über die erste Blütezeit französischer Plastik* (Strasbourg: Heitz, 1894), xx–xxi: "eigenartig, ab- oder ausgeartet."

275 On art history at the United States, see Priscilla Hiss and Roberta Fansler, *Research in the Fine Arts in the Colleges and Universities of the United States* (New York: Carnegie Corporation, 1934).

275–79 Bernard Berenson, *Lorenzo Lotto: An Essay in Constructive Art Criticism* (New York, 1895). On "deducting" the habits, xvii; on the "bitterness" in the Family Portrait, 322; on the Recanati

Annunciation, 221–22; on Lotto's "Japanese" sense for decoration, 200; on the "perfect criticism," 308; on "vicarious experience," v.

280–81 Vernon Lee on art and imagination: *Renaissance Fancies and Studies* (New York, 1896), 69; on "rudimentary" art, 94; on Annunciations, 87, 85.

1900–1910

282 Berenson on tactile values: *The Florentine Painters of the Renaissance* (New York: Putnam, 1896), 4. He says that "tactile values" is a better term than "form" because form is the significance of an object already extracted and presented to us by the artist; pre-processed, as it were, whereas tactile values we realize for ourselves, within ourselves.

283 On the figure of St. Louis by Bianchi, see Conti, *Storia del restauro*, 270–71, mentioning Crowe and Cavalcaselle as well as Ruskin. Ruskin's paean to this figure is in *Mornings in Florence* (1875–1877) (New York: Caldwell, 1890), 7–18. Cf. Raimond van Marle, *The Development of the Italian Schools of Painting*, (The Hague: Nijhoff, 1924), 3: 136–38, and fig. 82.

283 Henry Adams on the dynamos: *The Education of Henry Adams* (1907), chap. 25, "The Dynamo and the Virgin" (1900) (New York: Modern Library, 1996), 380–82.

283 Henri Bergson, "The Life and Work of Ravaisson" (1904), in Bergson, *The Creative Mind* (New York: Philosophical Library, 1946), 220–52.

284 Warburg on the religious ritual as "primal mint" (*Urprägewerk*): Gombrich, *Aby Warburg: An Intellectual Biography* (London: Warburg Institute, 1970), 244; a passage Gombrich found in the then-unpublished notebooks.

284 Proust on Swann in the "archives": *À la recherche du temps perdu*, Bibliothèque de la Pléiade (Paris: Gallimard, 1954), 1: 313.

285 Warburg, "Sandro Botticelli's 'Geburt der Venus' und 'Frühling'" (1893), in Warburg, *Die Erneuerung der heidnischen Antike, Gesammelte Schriften*, 2 vols. (Leipzig: Teubner, 1932), 1: 1–59; "Sandro Botticelli's 'Birth of Venus' and 'Primavera,'" in Warburg, *The Renewal of Pagan Antiquity* (Los Angeles, CA: Getty Research Institute, 1999), 89–156.

286 Warburg on Quattrocento painting as an "art of life" and an "occasional art": "Bildniskunst und florentinisches Bürgertum" (1902), in Warburg, *Die Erneuerung der heidnischen Antike*, 1: 89–126, here 113; "The Art of Portraiture and the Florentine Bourgeoisie," *The Renewal of Pagan Antiquity*, 185–221, here 202; Warburg compares the painted portraits to wax votive effigies: "Bildniskunst und florentinisches Bürgertum," 1: 100; "Art of Portraiture and the Florentine Bourgeoisie," 190; my translation.

287 Warburg on Vignoli and phobic reflexes: Gombrich, *Aby Warburg*, 217.

287 Warburg on pictorial symbols as concretizations of "emotionally heightened gestures," and his first use of the term *Pathosformel*: "Dürer und die italienische Antike" (1905), in *Die Erneuerung der heidnischen Antike*, 1: 443–49, here 445–46; "Dürer and Italian Antiquity," in *Renewal of Pagan Antiquity*, 553–58, here 553, 555.

287 Warburg, "Italienische Kunst und internationale Astrologie im Palazzo Schifanoia zu Ferrara" (1912), in *Die Erneuerung der heidnischen Antike*, 2: 459–81; "Italian Art and International Astrology in the Palazzo Schifanoia, Ferrara," *Renewal of Pagan Antiquity*, 563–91.

288 Warburg on contemporary theater and Botticelli: "Sandro Botticelli's 'Geburt der Venus' und 'Frühling'", 1: 37; "Sandro Botticelli's 'Birth of Venus' and 'Primavera,'" 125.

289 Warburg on America: Warburg's lecture of 1923 is based on his study trip to the American Southwest of 1895: *Images from the Region of the Pueblo Indians of North America*, Michael P. Steinberg, transl. (Ithaca, NY: Cornell University Press, 1995), 54.

289 Alois Riegl, *Die spätrömische Kunst-Industrie, nach den Funden in Österreich-Ungarn*, vol. 1 (Vienna: K. K. Hof- und Staatsdruckerei, 1901). The work was reprinted in a smaller format by the Österreichische Staatsdruckerei in 1927; that edition has since been reprinted (Berlin: Mann, 2000). The English translation is *Late Roman Art Industry*, Rolf Winkes, transl. (Rome: G. Bretschneider, 1985).

290 Vasari's praise for Ravenna: *Lives* (1568), in the text after the Proemio, "Pittura," chap. 29, *Le vite de' più eccellenti pittori, scultori ed architettori,*

Rosanna Bettarini and Paola Barocchi, eds., 6 vols. (Florence: Sansoni, 1966–1987), 1:148.

291 Riegl on the *Kunstwollen*: *Spätrömische Kunstindustrie* (1927), 401. The conclusion to this book, from which this passage is drawn, was translated by Christopher S. Wood in Wood, ed., *The Vienna School Reader* (New York: Zone Books, 2000), 95.

292 Riegl on the self-exclusion of Byzantine art from history: *Spätrömische Kunstindustrie*, 231.

294 Riegl, "Das holländische Gruppenporträt," *Jahrbuch des allerhöchsten Kaiserhauses* 22 (1902): 71–278, reprinted in 1931 in two volumes by the Österreichische Staatsdruckerei (1931). Translated by Evelyn M. Kain and David Britt as *The Group Portraiture of Holland* (Los Angeles, CA: Getty Research Institute, 1999).

297 Alois Riegl on the primacy of creative thought even in prehistoric art: *Problems of Style*, 33.

298 Worringer and Theodor Lipps on art as "objectified self-delight," in the appendix on "Transcendence and Immanence in Art," *Abstraktion und Einfühlung: ein Beitrag zur Stilpsychologie* (Munich: Piper, 1976), 179; *Abstraction and Empathy: A Contribution to the Psychology of Style* (New York: International Universities Press, 1953), 132.

298–99 Worringer on naturalism: *Abstraktion und Einfühlung*, 62–63, 68; *Abstraction and Empathy*, 27–28, 33 (translations my own).

1910–1920

302 Sigmund Freud, *Totem and Taboo: Some Points of Agreement between the Mental Lives of Savages and Neurotics*, James Strachey, transl. (Standard Edition) (New York: W. W. Norton, 1989), 113.

303 Wassily Kandinsky on necessity: "Über die Formfrage," in *Der Blaue Reiter*, Kandinsky and Franz Marc, eds. (Munich: Piper, 1912), 74; in *Der Blaue Reiter: Dokumentarische Neuausgabe*, Klaus Lankheit, ed. (Munich: Piper, 1965), 132; and in "On the Question of Form," in *The Blue Rider Almanac*, Lankheit, ed. (New York: Viking, 1974), 147.

303 Franz Marc on Meier-Graefe's rediscovery of El Greco: *Der Blaue Reiter* (1912), 1; *Der Blaue Reiter* (1965), 21; *The Blue Rider Almanac* (1974), 55.

303–4 Marc's review of the show at Heinrich Thannhauser's gallery in Munich: Andreas Hüneke, ed., *Der Blaue Reiter: Dokumente* (Stuttgart: Reclam, 1991), 31.

303 On the exhibition "Meisterwerke muhammedanischer Kunst," see Eva-Maria Troelenberg, "Framing the Artwork: Munich 1910 and the Image of Islamic Art," in Andrea Lermer and Avinoam Shalem, *After One Hundred Years: The 1910 Exhibition "Meisterwerke muhammedanischer Kunst"* (Leiden: Brill, 2010), 60.

304 Marc on Worringer: Hünecke, ed., *Der Blaue Reiter*, 445.

304 Marc on the nineteenth century: "Zwei Bilder" (Two Pictures), in *Der Blaue Reiter* (1912), 8–10; *Der Blaue Reiter* (1965), 33–35; *The Blue Rider Almanac* (1974), 65–66.

304–5 Marcel Janco's reminiscences of Tzara: "Creative Dada," in Willy Verkauf, *Dada: Monograph of a Movement* (Teufen: Arthur Niggli, 1957), 32, 44; or in the edition of 1975 (London: Academy), 20, 28.

305–6 Kandinsky on theorists, and on the relativity of form: *Der Blaue Reiter* (1912), 89–90, 75; *Der Blaue Reiter* (1965), 164–66, 137; *The Blue Rider Almanac* (1974), 169–70, 149.

306 Worringer's contribution to *Im Kampf um die Kunst* (Munich: Piper, 1911), reprinted in Hünecke, *Der Blaue Reiter*, 429–32.

306 Hans Tietze on the Blaue Reiter: Hünecke, ed., *Der Blaue Reiter*, 156.

306 Sigmund Freud on trench warfare: Verkauf, *Dada*, 76, without reference.

307 Erica Tietze-Conrat on "Die Kunst der Frau": *Zeitschrift für bildende Kunst*, N.F. 22 (1911): 146–48, reprinted in Tietze-Conrat, *Die Frau in der Kunstwissenschaft: Texte 1906–1958*, Almut Krapf-Weiler, ed. (Vienna: Schlebrügge Editor, 2007), 60–66.

307 Heinrich Wölfflin, *Kunstgeschichtliche Grundbegriffe: Das Problem der Stilentwicklung in der neueren Kunst* (Munich: Brückmann, 1915). The familiar English translation is *Principles of Art History: The Problem of the Development of Style in Later Art*, M. D. Hottinger, transl. (London: Holt, 1932). *Principles of Art History: The Problem of the Development of Style in Early Modern Art,*

Jonathan Blower, transl. (Los Angeles, CA: Getty Research Institute, 2015), is sometimes more but also sometimes less accurate than Marie Hottinger's version. Translations here are my own.

307 Wölfflin on artists and art historians: *Grundbegriffe*, 11; *Principles* (1932), 10–11; *Principles* (2015), 92.

308 Wölfflin, "Prolegomena to a History of Architecture" (1886), *Empathy, Form, and Space: Problems in German Aesthetics, 1873–1893*, Harry Francis Mallgrave and Eleftherios Ikonomou, eds. and transl. (Santa Monica, CA: 1994), 149–90.

308 Wölfflin on the most general forms of representation: *Grundbegriffe*, 14; *Principles* (1932), 13; *Principles* (2015), 95.

309–10 Wölfflin on naturalism: *Grundbegriffe*, 13–14; *Principles* (1932), 13; *Principles* (2015), 94–95; on the effect of picture on picture: *Grundbegriffe*, 242; *Principles* (1932), 230; *Principles* (2015), 309; on "visual possibilities": *Grundbegriffe*, 11; *Principles* (1932), 11; *Principles* (2015); on the individual component that "loses its privileges" in Baroque art: *Grundbegriffe*, 165; *Principles* (1932), 157; *Principles* (2015), 236; on "all our previous categories": *Grundbegriffe*, 167; *Principles* (1932), 159; *Principles* (2015), 238.

310 Wölfflin on Dürer's and Rembrandt's *Death of the Virgin*: *Grundbegriffe*, 167–68; *Principles* (1932), 161; *Principles* (2015), 238.

310–11 Wölfflin on the leisurely classic art and the bound Baroque figure: *Grundbegriffe*, 178; *Principles* (1932), 169; *Principles* (2015), 248.

311 Wölfflin's book reviews (including two of publications by Aby Warburg): see the bibliography in Wölfflin, *Kleine Schriften*, Joseph Gantner, ed. (Basel: Schwabe, 1946), although this is incomplete.

311 Wölfflin on Susanna and Delilah: *Grundbegriffe*, 188; *Principles* (1932), 175; *Principles* (2015), 253.

311–14 Wölfflin on the object of analysis as "the schema and the visual and formal possibilities": *Grundbegriffe*, 237; *Principles* (1932), 220; *Principles* (2015), 305; on vision itself having a history: *Grundbegriffe*, 19; *Principles* (1932), 17; *Principles* (2015), 99; on people seeing what they want to see: *Grundbegriffe*, 11; *Principles* (1932), 11; *Principles* (2015), 93.

314–15 Wölfflin on the art of 1800: *Grundbegriffe*, 246–47; *Principles* (1932), 233–34; *Principles* (2015), 313.

316 Wölfflin on the tectonic style: *Grundbegriffe*, 156; *Principles* (1932), 149; *Principles* (2015), 228.

316–17 Roman Jakobson on perception as the subject matter of painting: "Futurism" (1919), in Jakobson, *Language in Literature* (Cambridge, MA: Harvard University Press, 1987), 33.

1920–1930

320 The fabricated letter by Velazquez: Carl Justi, *Velazquez und sein Jahrhundert*, 2 vols. (Bonn, 1888), 1: 284–90.

320 For the frequency of use of the term *Kunstwissenschaft*, see the lists and graphs at the website DWDS (Digitales Wörterbuch der deutschen Sprache) as well as Google Books Ngram Viewer.

321 Julius von Schlosser, *Die Kunstliteratur: ein Handbuch zur Quellenkunde der neueren Kunstgeschichte* (Vienna: Schroll, 1924); reprinted by Schroll without alterations in 1985. Often cited is the convenient third Italian edition, with updated bibliography by Otto Kurz: *La letteratura artistica: manuale delle fonti della storia dell'arte moderna* (Florence: La nuova Italia, 1964). A French translation, *La littérature artistique: manuel des sources de l'histoire de l'art moderne* (Paris: Flammarion, 1984), went quickly out of print. There is no English translation, although see the translation by Karl Johns of Schlosser's chapter on Vasari, *Journal of Art Historiography* 2 (2010).

321–22 Schlosser on Alberti: *Die Kunstliteratur*, 107; *La letteratura artistica*, 122; on Vasari: *Die Kunstliteratur*, 265–84; *La letteratura artistica*, 303–22; on Lomazzo: *Die Kunstliteratur*, 373, 394; *La letteratura artistica*, 429, 454; on Ghiberti: *Die Kunstliteratur*, 87–90; *La letteratura artistica*, 101–4.

322 Erwin Panofsky, *Die Gestaltungsprinzipien Michelangelos, besonders in ihrem Verhältnis zu denen Raffaels* (Berlin: de Gruyter, 2014).

323 Panofsky, "Die Perspektive als 'symbolische Form,'" in *Vorträge der Bibliothek Warburg 1924–1925* (Leipzig: Teubner, 1927): 258–330. Reprinted in

Panofsky, *Aufsätze zu Grundfragen der Kunstwissenschaft* (Berlin: Hessling, 1964), 99–168. Translated by Christopher S. Wood as *Perspective as Symbolic Form* (New York: Zone Books, 1991).

324 Panofsky on Renaissance painting as a metaphor of the "intellectual distance between the present and the past": *Studies in Iconology* (Oxford, UK: Oxford University Press, 1939), 28. In an article of 1930, a ne plus ultra of reflective historical scholarship, Panofsky explained Vasari's concept of a Gothic "period style," an early achievement of distanced or disinterested art history. His starting point was the Gothic frame Vasari drew around the drawing he owned and attributed to Cimabue (see p. 90). "The First Page of Giorgio Vasari's 'Libro': A Study on the Gothic Style in the Judgment of the Italian Renaissance" (1930) in Panofsky, *Meaning in the Visual Arts* (Garden City, NY: Doubleday, 1955), 169–235.

324 Carl Einstein, *Negerplastik* (Leipzig: Verlag der Weissen Bücher, 1915), translated by Sebastian Zeidler as "Negro Sculpture," *October* 107 (2004): 122–38. On form vs. content: *Negerplastik*, viii; "Negro Sculpture," 126.

325 Einstein on cult objects not mingling with life: *Negerplastik*, xiii, "Negro Sculpture," 129; on the African work absorbing time and rendering space with form: *Negerplastik*, xvi–xvii, "Negro Sculpture," 131; on "pictorial surrogates for form: *Negerplastik*, ix, "Negro Sculpture," 126–27.

326 Einstein on the artist of today not a partisan of pure form: *Negerplastik*, xii, "Negro Sculpture," 129.

326 Einstein on the "grip of mechanized reality": "Aphorismes methodiques," *Documents* 1, no. 1 (1929): 32–34, translated by Charles W. Haxthausen as "Methodological Aphorisms," *October* 107 (2004): 146–50, here 147.

326 Einstein on the dream, the miracle, and modern art: *Kunst des 20. Jahrhunderts (Propyläen Kunstgeschichte)* (1926), in Einstein, *Werke*, 5 vols. (Berlin: Medusa, 1980), 5: 263–65 (this is the text of the third edition of 1931); quoted by Zeidler, *Form as Revolt: Carl Einstein and the Ground of Modern Art* (Ithaca, NY: Cornell University Press, 2015), 209. Generally my reading of Einstein's texts has been guided by Zeidler's book.

326 Einstein on the "free, autistic figurations"

of painterly form: "Methodological Aphorisms," 149.

326 Einstein on metamorphosis beyond the imposed world picture: from a manuscript on Braque, in Einstein, *Werke* 3: 322, quoted by Zeidler, *Form as Revolt*, 212.

327 Einstein's letter to Kahnweiler discussing miracles: *Werke* 4: 156; both these passages were quoted by Zeidler, *Form as Revolt*, 216–17.

327 Wilhelm Pinder on the "cast of the dice": I am indebted to the discussion of Pinder's essay and book of 1926, "Kunstgeschichte nach Generationen" and *Das Problem der Generation*, in Frederic J. Schwartz, *Blind Spots: Critical Theory and the History of Art in Twentieth-Century Germany* (New Haven, CT: Yale University Press, 2005), 108–18.

328 Panofsky, "Zum Problem der historischen Zeit," appendix to an article of 1927 on the sculptures at Reims, reprinted independently in Panofsky, *Aufsätze zu Grundfragen der Kunstwissenschaft*, 77–83, here 77.

328 Karl Barth, "Biblical questions, insights, and vistas" (1920), in Barth, *Word of God and Word of Man* (1925) (Boston: Pilgrim Press, 1928), 55, 68.

1930–1940

329 Fritz Saxl's letter to Erwin Panofsky of January 5, 1932, about the possible relocation of the Warburg Library: Panofsky, *Korrespondenz 1910 bis 1968: eine kommentierte Auswahl*, 5 vols., Dieter Wuttke, ed. (Wiesbaden: Harrassowitz, 2001–2011), vol. 1, no. 296, pp. 458–60. On the telegram of April 1933 informing Panofsky of his dismissal from his professorship "but sealed with a strip of green paper which bore the inscription: 'Cordial Easter Greetings, Western Union,'" see Panofsky, "Three Decades of Art History in the United States: Impressions of a Transplanted European," in *Meaning in the Visual Arts* (Garden City, NY: Doubleday, 1955), 321.

329 On the exiled German art historians, see Ulrike Wendland, *Biographisches Handbuch deutschsprachiger Kunsthistoriker im Exil*, 2 vols. (Munich: Saur, 1998), and Karen Michels, *Transplantierte Kunstwissenschaft: deutschsprachige*

Kunstgeschichte im amerikanischen Exil (Berlin: Akademie, 1999).

330 On the reassignment of university posts in Germany: *Magister und Scholaren, Professoren und Studenten: Geschichte deutscher Universitäten und Hochschulen im Überblick* (Leipzig: Urania, 1981), 179.

330 Pinder, *Vom Wesen und Werden deutscher Formen: Geschichtliche Betrachtungen*, vol. 3, *Deutsche Kunst der Dürerzeit* (Leipzig: Seemann, 1940), 393.

331 On the lecture series in the museum in Philadelphia: Panofsky, *Korrespondenz*, 1: 730–31, no. 463, letter from Fiske Kimball.

332 On classicism in modernity: Panofsky and Fritz Saxl, "Classical Mythology in Medieval Art," *Metropolitan Museum Studies* 4 (1932–1933): 228–80.

332 Panofsky on El Lissitzky: *Perspective as Symbolic Form*, 153–54, n. 73.

332 Erich Auerbach on Friedrich Meinecke and historicism: *Mimesis: The Representation of Reality in Western Literature* (1946) (Princeton, NJ: Princeton University Press, 1953), 443–44.

333 On the exchange between Einstein and Saxl, see Spyros Papapetros, "Microcosme et macrocosme entre l'académie et l'avant-garde: Notes sur la correspondence de Carl Einstein (*Documents*) et Fritz Saxl (Bibliothèque Warburg)," *Gradhiva*, n.s. 14 (2011): 121–40.

333 On Panofsky's "cool" reception of Benjamin's book, see Howard Eiland and Michael W. Jennings, *Walter Benjamin: A Critical Life* (Cambridge, MA: Harvard University Press, 2014), 295.

333 The exchange between Einstein and Panofsky: Panofsky, *Korrespondenz*, 1: 557–58, nos. 346–47, January 4/6, 1933.

333 Walter Benjamin's review of Sedlmayr et al. was translated by Thomas Y. Levin as "Rigorous Study of Art: On the First Volume of Kunstwissenschaftliche Forschungen," *October* 47 (1988): 84–90; reprinted in Christopher S. Wood, ed., *The Vienna School Reader: Politics and Art Historical Method in the 1930s* (New York: Zone Books, 2000), 439–51. This is an interpolation of two versions of "Strenge Kunstwissenschaft. Zum ersten Bande der Kunstwissenschaftliche Forschungen," first version

1931, second version published in *Literaturblatt der Frankfurter Zeitung*, July 30, 1933 (vol. 66, no. 31), both in Benjamin, *Gesammelte Schriften*, vol. 3, Hella Tiedemann-Bartels, ed. (Frankfurt: Suhrkamp, 1972), 363–74.

334 On Sedlmayr, Benjamin, and Schapiro: Evonne Levy, *Baroque and the Political Language of Formalism (1845–1945): Burckhardt, Wölfflin, Gurlitt, Brinckmann, Sedlmayr* (Basel: Schwabe, 2015), 344; and Levy, "Sedlmayr and Schapiro Correspond, 1930–1935," *Wiener Jahrbuch für Kunstgeschichte* 59 (2010): 235–64.

334 Martin Heidegger, *Der Ursprung des Kunstwerkes* (1950) (Stuttgart: Reclam, 1960): 79–80; I have quoted the translation by Albert Hofstadter, "The Origin of the Work of Art," in Heidegger, *Poetry, Language, Thought* (New York: Harper & Row, 1971), 15–87, here 77–78.

335 Heidegger, *Besinnung* (1938/39, published 1997). The quotations are drawn from the translation by Parvis Emad and Thomas Kalary, *Mindfulness* (London: Continuum, 2006), 26–28.

338 Walter Benjamin on the origin: *Der Ursprung des deutschen Trauerspiels* (1928) *Gesammelte Schriften*, vol. 1.1 (Frankfurt: Suhrkamp, 1991), 226. My translation, but see *The Origin of German Tragic Drama*, John Osborne, transl. (London: Verso, 1977), 45.

339–40 Focillon, *Vie des formes* (Paris: PUF, 1934); I quote from the translation by Charles B. Hogan and George Kubler (1942), *The Life of Forms in Art* (New York: Zone Books, 1989). On artistic time and social time: *Vie des formes*, 98; *Life of Forms*, 152, 154; on Taine: *Vie des formes*, 87; *Life of Forms*, 141; on architecture: *Vie des formes*, 93–94; *Life of Forms*, 148–49; on form and content, form and world: *Vie des formes*, 6; *Life of Forms*, 38; on miracles: *Vie des formes*, 2; *Life of Forms*, 32; on the cathedrals: *Vie des formes*, 34; *Life of Forms*, 75.

340–41 Emil Kaufmann, *Von Ledoux bis Le Corbusier: Ursprung und Entwicklung der autonomen Architektur* (Vienna: Passer, 1933); on nineteenth-century historicism, 61. Translated by Guy Ballangé as *De Ledoux à Le Corbusier: origine et développement de l'architecture autonome* (Paris: Éditions de la Villette, 2002).

341 Lionello Venturi, *Cézanne: son art, son oeuvre* (Paris: Rosenberg, 1936), 13, 65.

342 John Pope-Hennessy, *Giovanni di Paolo, 1403–1483* (London: Chatto & Windus, 1937), on "forcible expression" in the Trecento, 43; on Giovanni di Paolo's "visual pecularities" and "emotional stress" and the "candescent personality," 146–49.

342 Focillon on art and artistic activity: *Vie des formes*, 3; *Life of Forms*, 33.

344 Roberto Longhi on the Brancacci Chapel: "Fatti di Masolino e di Masaccio," *Critica d'arte* 5 (1940): 145–91; transl. by David Tabbat as "Masolino and Masaccio," in Longhi, *Three Studies* (Riverdale-on-Hudson, NY: Stanley Moss–Sheep Meadow Press, 1996), here 21–22 (I have used this translation).

345 Paul Valéry on biography and art history: "Degas Danse Dessin" (1936), in Valéry, *Oeuvres* (Bibliothèque de la Pléiade) (Paris: Gallimard, 1960), 2: 1169.

345 Venturi on Cézanne's "way of feeling": *Cézanne*, 13.

1940–1950

347–48 Stella Kramrisch, *The Hindu Temple*, 2 vols. (Calcutta: University of Calcutta, 1946). All references are to vol. 1. On the Hindu temple as sum total of rites, vii; on the structure and the rites, 165; on the origin in sacrifice, 146; on the fire-altar, 140; on the pyramidal superstructure, 179–187.

348–49 Kramrisch on the materials: *Hindu Temple*, 108, 125; on the memory of the building, 154; "Oh, how was it that I built it?" 8; on the origins of architecture in Brahma, 360; on the monument in space, 103; on the sight of knowledge (*darsana*), 8.

350 Hans Sedlmayr, *wieder-geholt* ("re-collected"): *Die Entstehung der Kathedrale* (Graz: Akademische Druck- u. Verlagsanstalt, 1988), 507.

351 Kramrisch on the angels, in Kramrisch, *Exploring India's Sacred Art: Selected Writings*, Barbara Stoler Miller, ed. with biographical essay (Philadelphia: University of Pennsylvania Press, 1983), 3.

351 Gombrich on the Baroque ceiling paintings: "Icones symbolicae: Philosophies of Symbolism and Their Bearing on Art" (1948, though the quoted passage does not appear in the original publication), in Gombrich, *Symbolic Images* (*Studies in the Art of the Renaissance*, 2) (London: Phaidon, 1972), 123.

352 Rudolf Wittkower speaks of the "hierarchy of values" on the first page of his *Architectural Principles in the Age of Humanism* (London: Warburg Institute, 1949).

354 On the paleolithic caves and art history, see Whitney Davis, "Beginning the History of Art," in Davis, *Replications: Archaeology, Art History, Psychoanalysis* (University Park: Pennsylvania State University Press, 1996), 131–70.

354 Georges Bataille, "L'art primitif," *Documents* 7 (1930): 389–97, transl. by Michelle Kendall and Stuart Kendall as "Primitive Art," in Bataille, *The Cradle of Humanity: Prehistoric Art and Culture* (New York: Zone Books, 2005), 35–44.

355 Maxim Gorky quoted by F. D. Klingender, *Marxism and Modern Art: An Approach to Social Realism* (London: Lawrence & Wishart, 1943), 37.

356 Klingender on the "sub-conscious" and the "pre-social": *Marxism and Modern Art*, 7; on "sterile" avant-garde art, 11.

356 Nikolaus Pevsner, *Academies of Art, Past and Present* (Cambridge, UK: Cambridge University Press, 1940), vii–viii.

358 Edmund Wilson, *Memoirs of Hecate County* (1946) (New York: L. C. Page, 1959), 137, 145.

358–59 Clement Greenberg, "Avant-Garde and Kitsch," *Partisan Review* 6 (1939): 34–49; reprinted in Greenberg, *Art and Culture* (Boston: Beacon, 1961), 3–21. Greenberg on the "motionless" academicism of "formal cultures" and their "superior consciousness of history," 4, 9; on avant-garde artists rejecting relativities, 5; on art as content of avant-garde art, 3.

359 Greenberg, "Towards a Newer Laocoon," *Partisan Review* 7 (1940): 296–310.

359 Schapiro, "On the Aesthetic Attitude in Romanesque Art," in K. Bharatha Iyer, *Art and Thought*, Festschrift Ananda Coomaraswamy (London: Luzac, 1947); passages are quoted from the reprint in Schapiro, *Romanesque Art* (New York: Braziller, 1977), 10, 23, 1.

360 Berliner, "The Freedom of Medieval Art," *Gazette des Beaux-Arts* 6. pér., 28 (1945): 263–88; reprinted in Berliner, *"The Freedom of Medieval Art" und andere Studien zum christlichen Bild*, Robert Suckale, ed. (Berlin: Lukas, 2003).

1950–1960

361–62 André Malraux on abstraction, see Leo Steinberg, "The Eye is a Part of the Mind" (1953), in Steinberg, *Other Criteria: Confrontations with Twentieth-Century Art* (New York: Oxford University Press, 1972), 290, quoting Malraux's *Psychology of Art* (1949) but without page references.

362 Étienne Gilson, *Painting and Reality* (New York: Pantheon, 1957), 259, 265n25.

362 Leo Steinberg on Constable: *Other Criteria*, 292.

362 *Ars sacra: Kunst des frühen Mittelalters*, exhibition catalogue (Munich: Bayerische Staatsbibliothek, 1950).

362 On Angelico Surchamp, see Janet T. Marquardt, *Zodiaque: Making Medieval Modern, 1951–2001* (University Park: Pennsylvania State University Press, 2015).

363 Rudolf Wittkower on the completion of the Duomo in Florence: *Gothic vs. Classic: Architectural Projects in Seventeenth-Century Italy* (New York: Braziller, 1974), 78–81.

364 Hans-Georg Gadamer on art and art history: *Wahrheit und Methode* (Tübingen: Mohr, 1960), 77, xxviii; my translation, but see *Truth and Method* (New York: Crossroad, 1975), 73, xii–xiii.

365 Theodor W. Adorno, "Valéry Proust Museum," in Adorno, *Prisms*, Samuel Weber and Shierry Weber, transl. (London: Spearman, 1967), 175–85, esp. 184–85.

366–67 Heinrich Böll, *Billard um halb zehn* (1959) (Munich: Deutscher Taschenbuch Verlag, 1974), 137, 126, 135; all quotes drawn from sections 5 and 6 of the novel.

368 Erwin Panofsky, *Gothic Architecture and Scholasticism* (Latrobe, PA: Archabbey Press, 1951), 21, 36, 49.

368 Pierre Bourdieu, "Postface" to Panofsky, *Architecture gothique et pensée scolastique* (Paris: Les Éditions de Minuit, 1967), 133–67.

369 Lionello Venturi, *Painting and Painters: How to Look at a Picture, from Giotto to Chagall* (New York: Scribner's, 1945), 147–48.

369–70 Schapiro on the "elementary aesthetic components": "Style," in *Anthropology Today*, A. L. Kroeber, ed. (Chicago, 1953), 287–311, here 291; reprinted in Schapiro, *Theory and Philosophy of Art: Style, Artist, and Society* (New York: Braziller, 1994), 51–101, here 57.

370 Riegl, *Spätrömische Kunstindustrie* (Vienna: Österreichische Staatsdruckerei, 1927), 151n1. My translation, but see *Late Roman Art Industry*, Rolf Winkes, transl. (Rome: Bretschneider, 1985).

370 Robert Goldwater on Riegl: Goldwater, *Primitivism in Modern Art* (New York: Harper, 1938), 26–27, 33.

370 Schapiro on Riegl: "Style," 301–2 and 78–80 in the 1953 and 1994 versions.

370 Schapiro on art as evidence of the unity of mankind, and "no privileged content or mode of representation," and relativism: "Style," 291 and 57–58.

372 Panofsky on the "underlying principles which reveal the basic attitude of a nation": *Studies in Iconology*, 7.

372 On Panofsky and the avant-garde: Gerda Panofsky, *Erwin Panofsky von Zehn bis Dreissig und seine jüdischen Wurzeln* (Passau: Dietmar Klinger, 2017), 120–21, writes of Pan's excited response to an exhibition of Italian Futurists in Berlin in 1912 and his later admission that at that point he was unaware of the *Demoiselles d'Avignon*.

373 Ernst Fischer, *Von der Notwendigkeit der Kunst* (Dresden: Verlag der Kunst, 1959); translated as *The Necessity of Art: A Marxist Approach*, Anna Bostock, transl. (Harmondsworth: Penguin, 1963), 41, 40.

374 Arnold Hauser, *The Philosophy of Art History* (New York: Knopf, 1958), 3.

374 José Ortega y Gasset, "On Point of View in the Arts," *Partisan Review* 16 (1948), reprinted in *Dehumanization*, 107.

374–75 Alfred Neumeyer, "Art History: Victory without Trumpet," in Lynn White, Jr., ed., *Frontiers* *of Knowledge in the Study of Man* (New York: Harper & Row, 1957), 178–93.

376 H. W. Janson on Moissac: *History of Art: A Survey of the Major Visual Arts from the Dawn of History to the Present Day* (New York: Abrams, 1969), 221–22, 224.

376 Ernst H. Gombrich on St.-Trophime in Arles: *The Story of Art*, 4th ed. (London: Phaidon, 1952), 125.

377 Gombrich on Neo-Platonism and conceptualism: *Art and Illusion*, 155–56.

CONCLUSIONS: NOVISSIMA

378 The shift toward the modern: because university faculties still represent the traditional fields, the change in distribution of dissertation topics is not as dramatic as one might think. According to the list of the 141 dissertations completed in American doctoral programs in 1982, compiled by the College Art Association and published in the *Art Bulletin* 65 (1983): 354–60, only 5% dealt with art produced in the previous generation, i.e., 1945–1980, and 8% dealt with art produced in the next generation back, 1910–1945. Eighty-seven percent, then, were about art made before 1910. According to the list of the 218 dissertations completed in 2017, exactly one generation or thirty-five years later, now posted online (http://caareviews.org/dissertations/year/2017/completed), 18% dealt with art produced in the previous generation, i.e., 1980–2015, and 15% with art produced between 1945 and 1980. (Some theses spanned more than one period, of course; in such cases I have tried to locate them in the period where they belong in spirit.) In other words, the share of dissertations focusing on art of the immediately preceding generation has increased by a factor of 3.6, while the share focusing on art of the preceding two generations combined has increased by a factor of 2.5. The number of dissertations dealing with art of the preceding two generations, however, is still only 33% of the total, a minority. And in fact the majority of dissertations, 57%, are even today about art made before 1910. It is worth noting that the total number of American dissertations in art history has increased since 1982 only by a factor of 1.5.

378 On the reform of the Advanced Placement World History exam: *New York Times*, June 22, 2018, p. A17.

380 Sianne Ngai, *Our Aesthetic Categories: Zany, Cute, Interesting* (Cambridge, MA: Harvard University Press, 2012).

381 Renato Poggioli on the historicity of the avant-garde: Poggioli, *Theory of the Avant-Garde* (1962) (Cambridge, MA: Harvard University Press, 1968).

381 Niklas Luhmann on the "double framing" achieved by the art of theater as developed in the sixteenth and seventeenth centuries and by perspectival painting: *Art as a Social System* (Stanford, CA: Stanford University Press, 2000), 110, 257–58.

382 Wassily Kandinsky on the question of form: *Der Blaue Reiter* (1912), 88; *Der Blaue Reiter* (1965), 162; *The Blue Rider*, 168.

382 Robert Klein, "Notes sur la fin de l'image," in Klein, *La forme et l'intelligible* (Paris: Gallimard, 1970), 377–78; "Notes on the End of the Image," in Klein, *Form and Meaning* (New York: Viking, 1979), 172.

383–84 Umberto Eco, *A Theory of Semiotics* (Bloomington: Indiana University Press, 19), 272.

384–85 Siegfried Kracauer, *History: The Last Things Before the Last* (New York: Oxford University Press, 1969): on Herder, and the idea of something *being* rather than *having* a clock, a phrase Kracauer found in an essay on Herder by W. von Leyden, 146; on the conviction of homogenous time, 139; on Focillon and Kubler, 143–45.

385 Fredric Jameson on Wölfflin: *Marxism and Form* (Princeton, NJ: Princeton University Press, 1971), 322–23.

386 Gombrich, "Norm and Form: The Stylistic Categories of Art History and their Origins in Renaissance Ideals" (1963), in Gombrich, *Norm and Form*, Studies in the Art of the Renaissance I (London: Phaidon, 1966), 1: 93–94.

388 Adorno on the truth-content of modern art: *Ästhetische Theorie*, 168; *Aesthetic Theory*, 110.

389 Emil Kaufmann on relativism as a product of aesthetic autonomy: *Von Ledoux bis Le Corbusier: Ursprung und Entwicklung der autonomen Architektur* (Vienna: Passer, 1933), 60.

390 Nietzsche on late-born artists: *Die fröhliche Wissenschaft*, V, 354, in *Sämtliche Werke*, 3: 591; I use the translation by Walter Kaufmann as *The Gay Science* (New York: Random House, 1974), 298.

391 The limits of Nietzsche's relativism: this is the analysis of Malcolm Bull, *Anti-Nietzsche* (London: Verso, 2011).

392 Michel Foucault on *parrhesia*: Foucault, *Fearless Speech* (Los Angeles, CA: Semiotext(e), 2001).

393 Gombrich, "Meditations on a Hobby Horse" (1951), in Gombrich, *Meditations on a Hobby Horse: And Other Essays on the Theory of Art* (London: Phaidon, 1963), 1–11.

394 Gombrich, *Art and Illusion: A Study in the Psychology of Pictorial Representation* (New York: Bollingen Foundation, 1960). On the artist facing a limited array of choices, 376; on cultures determining what is possible, 86; on pictures as "relational models" of reality, 253. An unexpected defense of Gombrich's model is Wolfgang Iser, *The Fictive and the Imaginary: Charting Literary Anthropology* (Baltimore, MD: Johns Hopkins University Press, 1993), 284–89, and *How to Do Theory* (Oxford, UK: Oxford University Press, 2006), 52–55.

394 Nelson Goodman on Gombrich: Goodman, *Languages of Art: An Approach to a Theory of Symbols* (Indianapolis, IN: Hackett, 1976), 7, 10, 33.

396–97 George Kubler, *The Shape of Time: Remarks on the History of Things* (New Haven, CT: Yale University Press, 1962). On the "history of things" versus the "bristling ugliness of the phrase 'material culture,'" 9; on invention succeeded by reproductions and copies, 39; on the "inverted colonial action," on Frank Lloyd Wright and Henry Moore, the Renaissance, and the "mortmain action," 108; on "the replication that fills history," 71; on the "mute existential declaration of things," 24; on the "mosaic of pieces in different developmental stages" and the "cultural bundles" that make up a period juxtaposed by chance, 28, 122 (Kracauer thought Kubler was exaggerating here, *History*, 152); on "existence without meaning," 25.

398 *Painting for Kubler* (1966–68), acrylic on canvas, 68 × 56 ½ inches. Private collection. The phrases are tracked back to their sources and partial sources in Kubler by John C. Welchman, "Spaces Between, or Debt to the Prior: John Baldessari's Quotidian Dialectics," in *John Baldessari: Paintings, 1966–68* (New York: Craig Starr Gallery, 2017), n.p. The painting is also discussed by Pamela Lee, "Ultramoderne, or How George Kubler Stole the Time in Sixties Art," *Grey Room* 2 (2001): 60–63, and in her book *Chronophobia: On Time in Art of the 1960s* (Cambridge, MA: MIT, 2004), 240–41.

398 Kubler on the impossibility of grasping the moment of actuality: *Shape of Time*, 18.

398 On Focillon and Kubler's concepts of "actuality," see Molly Nesbit, *The Pragmatism in the History of Art* (Pittsburgh, PA: Periscope, 2013), 55–66.

398 For Gombrich's unrealized study of visual culture, see E. H. Gombrich and Didier Eribon, *Looking for Answers: Conversations on Art and Science* (New York: Abrams, 1993), 105.

401 John Berger, *Ways of Seeing* (Harmondsworth: Penguin, 1972). On the illusion that art "justified most other forms of authority," *Ways of Seeing*, 29; on the art of the past as "mystified," 11; on visual art as advertising, 139.

404 "We believe our ancestors were like us": Karl Ove Knausgård, *A Time for Everything* (Brooklyn, NY: Archipelago, 2009), 7.

404 Carl Einstein's presentism: *Negerplastik* (Leipzig: Verlag der Weissen Bücher, 1915), vi; "Negro Sculpture," *October* 107 (2004): 125.

404–5 Foucault, "Nietzsche Genealogy History" (1971), in *The Essential Foucault*, Paul Rabinow and Nikolas Rose, eds., Donald F. Brouchard and Sherry Simon, transl. (New York: New Press, 2003), 351–69, esp. 364–68.

406 Michael Baxandall echoing Cézanne, in Hans-Ulrich Obrist, *Interviews* (Milan: Charta, 2010), 2: 328–29; here he dismisses the remark as a joke.

406 See *The New Art History*, A. L. Rees and Frances Borzello, eds. (London: Camden Press, 1986).

407 "Art has no face": Kazimir Malevich, *The World as Objectlessness* (Basel: Hatje Cantz, 2014), 191.

408 On Jacob Burckhardt's withholding of the truth: Friedrich Nietzsche to Carl von Gersdorff, November 7, 1870, Nietzsche, *Briefwechsel*, Giorgio Colli and Mazzino Montinari, ed., 2. Abt, Bd. 1 (Berlin: de Gruyter, 1977), 155.

INDEX

miracles, artworks as, 18–21, 33, 70, 94, 327–28, 340

Mo Shih-lung, 121

modernity: academic focus on modern art, 378; in architecture, 351–52; Baudelaire on modern art, 238–49; Burckhardt on modernity's lack of culture, 247; as contestation of harmony by dissonance, 6, 128, 213, 308, 309, 314, 316, 359, 362, 381, 382; Fiedler on, 265, 266, 268–69; first public museum of modern art, 228; form, modern art's disengagement from, 380–86; Gadamer on, 364–65; Gombrich versus Janson on, 377; Hegel on, 217–20, 222, 229–30; paleolithic cave paintings and, 355; past, modernist breach with, 378–81, 388–89, 404, 442n; postwar reconciliation between art and, 361–62; prosaic or realist art and, 229–31; purely optical constitution of modern work of art, 292; relativism in art history and, 389–92; religion, art's separation from, 273; Ruskin on, 235; as secularization, 390–91; Sedlmayr on, 357; Semper on, 237–38; social history of art and, 360; standing outside, modern sense of, 328; tension between study of art of past and criticism of art of, 331–34; Wölfflin on art of, 309–10, 317; Worringer on, 300, 301. *See also* "old" versus "modern" art; *specific modernist movements*

moderno style, 79–80, 85

Moissac, portal sculpture at, 376

Molteni, Giuseppe, 235

Monaco, Lorenzo, 65

Mondrian, Piet, 202, 309

Monet, Claude, 265, 309

monogrammists, 145, 233

monographs, 202–5, 228, 250, 341–42

Monserrate, Antonio, 100–101, 102

Montaigne, Michel de, 77–78, 102

Montfaucon, Bernard de, 141–44, *143*, 146, 177, 180, 190

monumental history, Nietzsche on, 255–56, 260, 405

monuments, origins of art history in, 22–23

Moor, Edward, 189–90, *191*, 197, 209

Moore, Henry, 396

Morelli, Giovanni, 258–63, 267, 278, 280

Morris, Robert, 398

Morris, William, 236

Mortimer, John Hamilton, 205

Möser, Justus, 173–75

Mosler, Karl Joseph Ignaz, 206, 209

Mostaert, Jan, 108

Muffel, Jakob, 59

Mummius, 62

Munch, Edvard, 309

Munkácsy, Mihály, 253

Muratori, Ludovico Antonio, 185

Murillo, Bartolomé Esteban, 248

Murray's guides, 234, 282–83

museums: Adorno's "Valéry Proust Museum" on, 365; annalistic art history promoted by, 257–58; art historians talking about works in, 258–62; connoisseurship versus ethos of, 279; debunking of cult of art and, 401–2; first public displays of royal collections, 178; formalism and modern encyclopedic art museum, 271; Fourier on exhibiting live nudes, 214, 254; *Kunstkammer* and *Wunderkammer*, 131–32, 133, 134, 379; new public museums of nineteenth century, 227–28; of ornamental and applied arts, 234; Riegl on, 294. *See also* collection of art objects, drawings, and prints; *specific museums*

Mussolini, Benito, 330

N

Nagler, G. K., 233

National Gallery, London, 228, 235, 237, 401

naturalism, 268, 269, 273, 293, 296, 298–99, 301, 306, 309, 328, 354, 373

nature: art viewed as direct cognition of, 196–97, 201, 208, 231, 362; formalism and, 271, 272

Nazarenes, 45, 198–205, 212–14, 217, 222, 226, 229, 230, 235, 315

Nazis/National Socialism, 329–30, 351, 357, 361, 366

neoclassicism and neoclassicists, 146, 154, 166, 228, 314, 352

Neoplatonism, 166, 377

Nerval, Gérard de, *Sylvie*, 225

Neue Pinakothek, Munich, 228

Neumann, Franz Ignaz, 36, 37

Neumeyer, Alfred, 374–75

"new art history" of late 1970s and 1980s, 405–8

Nicholas V (pope), 58, 83

Nietzsche, Friedrich, 44, 160, 233, 244, 252, 254, 255–57, 259, 260, 269, 273, 335, 390, 391, 404–5

non-European art: African, 132–33, 306, 324, 325–26, 327, 338, 381; Buddhist, 118, 122, 306, 339, 347; Chinese, 12, 40, 54–55, 60, 65, 99, 117, 118–23, *120*, 138, 139–40, 161, 207, 222, 239; drive for inclusion of, in art history, 375; European/Christian reactions to, 71–75, *72*, 99–102, 132–33, 209, 306; Hegel on, 222; Indian/South Asian, 99–102, 189–92, *191*, 197, 209, 222–23, 226, 239, 331, 346, 347–52; intellectual obstacles to European capacity to articulate art-quality of, 339; Islamic world, 10, 85–86, 100, 102, 303–4; Japanese, 207, 278, 305, 339; medieval art treated similarly to, 212–13; Precolumbian, 21, 54, 55, 73, 100, 226, 385, 396; Arthur Schopenhauer on, 306; Semper on, 239; Warburg on, 289; Wölfflin excluding, 316

northern/Netherlandish art versus Italian art, 103–5, 107–11, 118

Norton, Charles Eliot, 252, 275, 375

Notre-Dame cathedral, Paris, 142, 147, 239

PHOTO CREDITS